Medieval and
Early Modern Times

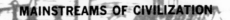

MAINSTREAMS OF CIVILIZATION

VOLUME I: ANCIENT CIVILIZATIONS:
PREHISTORY TO THE FALL OF ROME
Carlton J. H. Hayes and James Hanscom

VOLUME II: MEDIEVAL AND EARLY MODERN TIMES:
THE AGE OF JUSTINIAN TO THE EIGHTEENTH CENTURY
Carlton J. H. Hayes and Frederick F. Clark

VOLUME III: MODERN TIMES:
THE FRENCH REVOLUTION TO THE PRESENT
Carlton J. H. Hayes and Margareta Faissler

THE AGE OF JUSTINIAN TO THE EIGHTEENTH CENTURY

Medieval and Early Modern Times

CARLTON J. H. HAYES
FREDERICK F. CLARK

THE MACMILLAN COMPANY, NEW YORK
COLLIER-MACMILLAN LIMITED, LONDON

THE AUTHORS

Carlton J. H. Hayes

Late Seth Low Professor Emeritus of History in Columbia University

Frederick F. Clark

Headmaster, The Cate School, Carpinteria, California

Maps: Christie McFall

Charts: Leonard Hyams

ILLUSTRATION SOURCES

ALINARI—ART REFERENCE BUREAU: 253, 265, 273 top. *Courtesy of THE AMERICAN MUSEUM OF NATURAL HISTORY:* 340. *AUSTRIAN FEDERAL PRESS AND INFORMATION SERVICE:* 479. *BIBLIOTHÈQUE NATIONALE, PARIS:* 113. *BRITISH INFORMATION SERVICES:* 392. *Courtesy of THE BROOKLYN MUSEUM:* 232. *BROWN BROTHERS:* 201, 349. *CASA DE PORTUGAL:* 332. *COLLIER'S ENCYCLOPEDIA:* 357, 378. *CULVER PICTURES, INC.:* 455. *EMBASSY OF SPAIN, WASHINGTON:* 310. *EWING GALLOWAY, N. Y.:* 240. *FRENCH EMBASSY PRESS AND INFORMATION DIVISION:* 106, 141 right, 374, 381, 472. *THE FRICK COLLECTION:* 280, 367, 481. *GRAMSTORFF BROS., INC.:* 273 bottom. *THE GRANGER COLLECTION:* 12, 93, 127, 178, 281, 339, 363, 397, 439. *HISTORISCHES BILDARCHIV:* 147, 151, 190, 227, 248, 251, 423, 428. *ITALIAN CULTURAL INSTITUTE:* 41. *ITALIAN STATE TOURIST OFFICE:* 29 left, 262. *KUNSTHISTORISCHES MUSEUM, VIENNA:* 314, 426. *THE LIBRARY OF CONGRESS:* 463. *MARBURG—ART REFERENCE BUREAU:* 141 left. *THE METROPOLITAN MUSEUM OF ART:* 64 (Bequest of Cora Timken Burnett, 1957); 98 (Gift of John Pierpont Morgan, 1917); 119 (Gift of John Pierpont Morgan, 1907); 284 (Fletcher Fund, 1919); 294 (Gift of Robert Lehman, 1955); 328 (Rogers Fund, 1918); 362 (Bequest of Annie C. Kane, 1926); 434 (Dick Fund, 1917). *MINISTERIO DE INFORMACIÓN Y TURISMO, MADRID:* 65, 237. *MINISTRY OF TOURISM AND INFORMATION, TURKEY:* 29 right. *THE NEW YORK PUBLIC LIBRARY:* 37, 255, 297, 469, 485; 97 (Spencer Collection). *THE PIERPONT MORGAN LIBRARY:* 3, 22, 89, 122, 134, 164, 173, 185. *ROYAL CONSULATE GENERAL OF GREECE:* 53. *SOVFOTO:* 411. *From ART THROUGH THE AGES by Helen Gardner, copyright © 1926, 1936, 1948, 1954, 1959, 1964 by Harcourt, Brace & World, Inc., and reproduced with their permission:* 40. *From MEDIEVAL GARDENS by Sir Frank Crisp,* © *1924 by Coward-McCann, Inc.:* 113. *From THE BAYEUX TAPESTRY, edited by Sir Frank Stenton, published by Phaidon Press, London; distributed in the U.S.A. by New York Graphic Society:* 170. *From HERE I STAND by Roland H. Bainton, Copyright 1950 Pierce and Smith (Abingdon Press):* 304.

COVER ILLUSTRATIONS

FRENCH EMBASSY PRESS AND INFORMATION DIVISION, top right; *ALINARI—ART REFERENCE BUREAU,* bottom right.

4-J

The Macmillan Company, New York

Collier-Macmillan Canada, Ltd., Toronto, Ontario

Printed in the United States of America

Contents

PROLOGUE   *1*

PART ONE: THE EARLY MIDDLE AGES   *3*

1 THE ROMAN WORLD IN THE FIFTH CENTURY   *5*

The Decline of the Roman Empire   The Early Christian Church

2 THE GERMANIC KINGDOMS AND THE EMPIRE OF JUSTINIAN   *17*

The Germanic Kingdoms of Western Europe   The Eastern Roman Empire under Justinian

3 THE BEGINNINGS OF MEDIEVAL CIVILIZATION   *32*

European Life in the Sixth Century   The Patristic Writers   Art and Architecture

4 THE BYZANTINE EMPIRE   *45*

The Invaders of Byzantium   Byzantine Government   The Break between the Roman and Byzantine Churches   The Byzantine Way of Life

5 THE RISE OF ISLAM   *57*

The Arab Background   The Growth of Islam   Islamic Life   The Decline of the Islamic Empire

6 THE AGE OF CHARLEMAGNE AND THE END OF THE EARLY MIDDLE AGES   *69*

The Growth of the Frankish Empire   Europe in the Age of Charlemagne   The Collapse of Charlemagne's Empire   The Second Wave of Invasions   Local Government and the Church in the Tenth Century

PART TWO: THE HIGH MIDDLE AGES   *89*

7 FEUDALISM AND CHIVALRY   *91*

Feudalism: Government by Personal Loyalties   Chivalry: The Knightly Code of Behavior

8 THE MANOR AND THE TOWN   *103*

The Manorial System   The Growth of Commerce   Medieval Towns

9 THE MEDIEVAL CHURCH   *116*

The Sources of Religious Influence   The Monastic Reformers   Heretics and the Inquisition   The Rise and Decline of Papal Authority

10 MEDIEVAL LEARNING AND ART   132

Medieval Education   &   Medieval Philosophy   &   Romanesque and Gothic Architecture

11 THE MEDIEVAL HOLY ROMAN EMPIRE   144

Germany and Italy in the Early Tenth Century   &   The Establishment of the Empire   &   The Empire at Its Peak   &   Frederick Barbarossa   &   The Decline of the Empire

12 THE MEDIEVAL FRENCH MONARCHY   158

France under the Early Capetians   &   The Great Capetian Monarchs

13 THE MEDIEVAL ENGLISH MONARCHY   169

The Norman Conquest   &   Henry II and the Common Law   &   King John and Magna Carta   &   The Development of Parliament   &   English Civilization

14 THE CRUSADES   182

The Background of the Crusades   &   The First Three Crusades   &   The Decline of the Crusades   &   The Crusades in the West   &   The Effects of the Crusades

15 THREE EMPIRES OF THE EAST   196

Mongols   &   Ottoman Turks   &   Russia, the "Third Rome"

16 THE DECLINE OF MEDIEVAL CIVILIZATION   211

The Decline of Papal Power   &   The Decline of Feudalism   &   The Hundred Years War

PART THREE: AN ERA OF TRANSITION   227

17 STRENGTHENING THE NATIONAL MONARCHIES   229

The National Monarchy in England   &   France: The Supremacy of Louis XI   &   The Rise and Decline of Portugal   &   The Unification of Spain   &   The Triumph of Localism in the Holy Roman Empire   &   Dynastic Rivalries in the Sixteenth Century

18 THE TRANSITION TO A MODERN ECONOMY   245

Commerce and Banking   &   The Continuing Growth of Cities   &   The Merchant and Banking Middle Class   &   Changes in Government and Society

19 THE ITALIAN RENAISSANCE   261

The Renaissance Man   &   Renaissance Humanism   &   Renaissance Art

20 THE NORTHERN RENAISSANCE   277

The Invention of Printing   ☙   Christian Humanism   ☙   The Fine Arts in the North   ☙   The Growth of National Literatures ☙   Science during the Renaissance

21 THE PROTESTANT REFORMATION   290

The Background of the Reformation   ☙   Martin Luther and Lutheranism   ☙   Zwingli and the Swiss Reformation   ☙   John Calvin and Calvinism   ☙   The Church of England   ☙   Other Protestant Sects   ☙   Protestant and Catholic Similarities and Differences

22 THE CATHOLIC REFORMATION AND THE WARS OF RELIGION   309

The Catholic Reformation   ☙   The Early Religious Wars   ☙ The Thirty Years War

23 EUROPE AND THE FAR EAST   323

The Background of Exploration   ☙   Portuguese Voyages and Discoveries   ☙   Asia on the Eve of the Western Invasion   ☙ The Europeans in the Far East

24 EUROPE AND THE NEW WORLD   338

The Discoveries and Colonies of Spain   ☙   The Portuguese in Brazil   ☙   The Caribbean   ☙   Exploration in North America ☙   The French in North America   ☙   The English in North America

PART FOUR: THE AGE OF ABSOLUTISM   357

25 THE GOLDEN AGE OF SPAIN   359

Spain in the Early Sixteenth Century   ☙   The Golden Age   ☙ The Golden Age of Spanish Literature and Art   ☙   Spain after the Golden Age

26 ABSOLUTISM TRIUMPHANT: FRANCE IN THE SEVENTEENTH CENTURY   372

The First Bourbons   ☙   The Age of Louis XIV: The Early Decades   ☙   The Age of Louis XIV: The Later Decades

27 ENGLAND UNDER ELIZABETH AND THE STUARTS   387

The Elizabethan Age   ☙   The Stuarts and the English Revolution

28 TWO GIANTS OF EASTERN EUROPE: THE OTTOMAN EMPIRE AND RUSSIA   404

The Expansion and Decline of the Ottoman Empire   ☙   Russia Becomes a Great Power

29 PRUSSIA, AUSTRIA, AND THE STRUGGLE FOR GERMANY 418

Germany after the Treaties of Westphalia   The Rise of
Brandenburg-Prussia   Habsburg Austria   Prussia vs.
Austria

30 BRITAIN AND FRANCE IN THE EIGHTEENTH CENTURY 432

Britain under the First Three Georges   The Old Regime of
France   The Economic Revolutions

31 COMMERCIAL AND DYNASTIC WARS 450

The Background of the Wars   The War of the League of
Augsburg   The War of the Spanish Succession   The
War of the Polish Succession   The War of the Austrian
Succession   The Seven Years War   The European
Powers in 1763

32 SCIENTIFIC THOUGHT AND THE AGE OF ENLIGHTENMENT 466

Reaction against the Age of Reformation   The Beginnings
of Modern Science   Science and the Enlightenment
Political Philosophy of the Enlightenment   The Liberal
Reformers   The Fine Arts

GLOSSARY 492

MAPS:

EUROPE	6	EUROPEAN COMMERCE, 1450	246
THE GERMANIC KINGDOMS	20	ITALY, 1494	252
ENGLAND IN THE TIME OF ALFRED THE GREAT	21	CATHOLIC, PROTESTANT, AND ORTHODOX REGIONS OF EUROPE, 1570	300
THE EASTERN ROMAN EMPIRE, 565	26	EUROPE AFTER THE TREATIES OF WESTPHALIA, 1648	320
THE BYZANTINE EMPIRE	47	EUROPEANS IN ASIA AND AFRICA, 1700	334
ISLAM, 632-750	62	THE NEW WORLD, 1700	347
THE GROWTH OF THE FRANKISH EMPIRE	72	SPANISH LANDS IN EUROPE	364
DIVISION OF THE FRANKISH EMPIRE BY THE TREATY OF VERDUN, 843	77	THE EXPANSION OF FRANCE UNDER LOUIS XIV	382
THE SPREAD OF CHRISTIANITY IN EUROPE	82	THE EXPANSION OF THE OTTOMAN EMPIRE, 1481-1683	405
CENTRAL AND WESTERN EUROPE IN 1190	152	THE EXPANSION OF RUSSIA IN EUROPE, 1533-1796	413
THE CRUSADER STATES	187	THE PARTITIONS OF POLAND	414-415
THE MONGOL DOMINIONS	198	THE EXPANSION OF PRUSSIA	429
THE RISE OF THE OTTOMAN EMPIRE, 1326-1481	200	INDIA, 1700-1763	460
THE GROWTH OF MUSCOVY	207	BRITISH EXPANSION IN NORTH AMERICA	461
FRANCE DURING THE HUNDRED YEARS WAR	219	EUROPE, 1763	462
EUROPE IN THE SIXTEENTH CENTURY	242		

Prologue

This book summarizes almost 1,400 years of human experience, from the collapse of the Western Roman Empire in the fifth century to the eve of the French Revolution in the eighteenth. After the first of these two great turning points, Europe slowly developed a new way of life, which reached its height in the civilization of the High Middle Ages of the twelfth and thirteenth centuries. But in the fourteenth and fifteenth centuries this civilization collapsed. Its collapse led to an era of great and sometimes violent change, marked by such developments as the Renaissance, the Reformation, and the discovery and colonization by Europeans of the four corners of the earth. And this, in turn, was followed by the seventeenth- and eighteenth-century age of absolutism and "enlightenment," when many ideas about government, society, and the world we live in began to take their modern forms. These developments centered in Europe. But that continent was never completely isolated from the rest of the world: the Islamic and Byzantine empires of the Middle East affected and were affected by European affairs, as were the ancient civilizations of Asia.

History is the record of all human experience. Even in a short textbook like this, which can only touch upon the high points of history, you will find that there is a great deal to be learned and understood. Developing certain habits of thought will make learning and understanding easier and more meaningful.

First, remember that there are continuing themes of history. These themes reappear in the histories of many different ages and countries, and they are still important in our world of today. A knowledge of how they developed in the past will help you better to understand the present and the future. Among the most significant themes of this book are these: (1) *The struggle for political power* between different groups of people: kings, landowners, merchants and townsmen, peasants and farmers. Each country in every age has had to decide which people—and how many of them—will take part in the government. (2) *The role of religion and religious institutions in government and daily life.* What should be the relationship between religious leaders

1

and government? To what degree can and should religious ideas and religious leaders affect people's everyday activities? (3) *The rise of national states.* Beginning in the Middle Ages and continuing into modern times, men gradually transferred their political loyalties from their local communities and lords to their kings and countries. (4) *The slow beginning of the change from an agricultural to an urban society.* For most of history, the great majority of men have lived and worked on the land; but after the early Middle Ages, ever-increasing percentages of the people lived in towns and devoted themselves to manufacturing and commerce. (5) *The growing impact of Europe on the rest of the world, and of the world on Europe.* After Columbus's time, it is impossible to separate the history of Europe from that of the rest of the world. (6) *Continuing changes in the ways men think of themselves and their world,* as reflected by developments in the arts, literature, science, and philosophy.

Second, as you trace these themes through history, remember the major categories into which historians divide their huge subject. Among the most important of these are (1) *political* history, about governments and the men who control them; (2) *economic* history, about how men produce, distribute, and consume goods; (3) *social* history, about men's everyday relationships with each other, both as individuals and as members of groups; and (4) *cultural* history, about how men express their ideas and ideals in literature, the arts, science, and philosophy. Each of these categories is a major subject in itself.

Third, to fix in your mind the significance of important eras, seek out the "evocative details." These are the details that evoke—bring to mind—the principal characteristics of each era and help shed light on its significance. An evocative detail may be a person who stands as a symbol of his time—Charlemagne, or Innocent III, or Louis XIV. Or it may be an event—the destruction of the Spanish Armada, or the discovery of America. Or it may be a date—1066, or 1453, or 1763. Before you have completed your study of this book, each of these evocative details should bring to mind a significant historical development.

If you are interested in people and in the world around you, you should find history fascinating, even though it may require hard work at times. You should also find it enlightening; for, just as you know old friends best, you will know your own world better if you know how it came to be as it is.

PART 1

THE EARLY MIDDLE AGES

In European history, the period from the fifth to the fifteenth centuries —from the collapse of the Western Roman Empire to the rise of the modern world—is called the "Middle Ages." The medieval period ("medieval" means "of the Middle Ages") has three major divisions: the Early Middle Ages, the High Middle Ages, and the Late Middle Ages.

The Early Middle Ages, from the fifth to the tenth centuries, are sometimes also called the "Dark Ages." After Rome collapsed and its civilization decayed, the darkness of poverty, ignorance, and despair spread across much of Europe. The political unity that Rome had imposed ended in the fifth century. In western Europe, little Germanic kingdoms rose and fell as their warrior leaders won short-lived control of limited areas. In eastern Europe and North Africa the Eastern Roman Empire survived, and for a brief moment in the sixth century it seemed likely to restore unity to the Mediterranean basin. But after the death of the great Emperor Justinian in 565, the power of the Eastern Roman Empire also declined.

Eventually three great empires arose where once there had been only Rome. The Eastern Roman Empire, now called the Byzantine Empire, regained strength and unified southeastern Europe under powerful emperors and the Greek Orthodox Church. In western Asia, North Africa, and Spain, Islam, the religion and state founded by Muhammad, developed a potent civilization of its own. In western Europe the Frankish Empire combined Germanic, Catholic, and Roman customs and around the year 800 flowered under Charlemagne. But Charlemagne's empire did not last. After its collapse, western Europe returned to relative darkness for more than a century.

The five centuries of the Early Middle Ages were a period of poverty and confusion. But they were also a time of gradual change, when men found new ways of life and thought to meet the new and difficult problems created by the collapse of Roman government and economic life.

The Roman World in the fifth Century

In 410, when barbarians captured Rome and occupied it for a few days, Jerome wrote, "The lamp of the world is extinguished, and it is the whole world that has perished in the ruins of this one city." Rome had been mistress of all the civilized western world for centuries; but before the year 500 not only the power of Rome, but to all appearances most of its civilization as well, was in ruins.

THE DECLINE OF THE ROMAN EMPIRE

In the second century the Roman Empire included the entire Mediterranean basin and extended north in Europe to Britain and the Rhine and Danube rivers; west to the shores of the Atlantic; south in Africa to the Sahara; and east in Asia to the valley of the Tigris and Euphrates rivers. This vast area was knit together by the Roman government, whose officials enforced the Roman law throughout the empire. Latin was everywhere the language of government; in the western part of the empire, it was also the language of commerce and of the growing Christian Church. (In the eastern part, the main language was Greek.) *Pax Romana*, the "Peace of Rome" that resulted from so large an area being under one rule, made it

possible for merchants to sail the seas and travel the magnificent Roman roads in safety.

The Romans were a practical people who imported many of their artistic and philosophical ideas from Greece. Their own major contributions were engineering triumphs such as roads, aqueducts, bridges, and buildings, which were so solidly constructed that some are still used today. Most of the empire was agricultural, but in the large and prosperous cities craftsmen produced goods that were marketed throughout the empire.

In the late second century A.D., it was generally taken for granted that this huge and peaceful state would last forever.

FACTORS CONTRIBUTING TO DECLINE

There is no entirely satisfactory explanation for Rome's slow decline and ultimate collapse. One historian blames Christianity, which, he maintains, demanded the people's loyalty at a time when the state needed it more. Another maintains that Rome, like a man, just grew old and died. A third says that it collapsed from neglect and corruption. Probably there is some truth in each of these explanations and in many of the others that have been suggested.

There is no question that the government slowly became less and less effective. After the first century B.C., when Julius Caesar set the example, generals were increasingly likely to seize power. Many of them did not know how to use power effectively, and so were deposed by other generals. Military rule made people cynical and officials corrupt, so that all gradually lost their sense of loyalty to the government and its emperors.

The very size of the government made it costly, and taxes increased rapidly. These fell most heavily on businessmen and on the poor, so that business in the cities declined, and workers fled to the countryside. The widespread commerce, which once had knit the empire together, fell off; and the unity of the Roman Empire declined with it.

THE BARBARIAN TRIBES

In northern and eastern Europe, beyond the boundaries of the empire, lived the uncivilized tribes that the Romans called "barbarians." Nearest the Atlantic were the Celts, or Gauls; to their east and north were the Germanic tribes; and in eastern Europe were the Slavs. Behind them, moving restlessly across the Asiatic plains, were other peoples, among them the Huns, the Bulgars, the Magyars, and the Mongols.

The Germanic peoples were the most important of the barbarians. There were three principal Germanic groups: the Scandinavians, who lived in the north (present-day Sweden and Norway); the West Germans—Sueves, Alamanni, Franks, Saxons, and others—who lived between the Rhine and the Elbe rivers (present-day Germany); and the East Germans, who had migrated from Scandinavia to southeastern Europe in the second century. The most numerous of the East Germans were the Goths, who were divided into Visigoths (West Goths), living in the lower valley of the Danube River (present-day Romania), and the Ostrogoths (East Goths), occupying the north shore of the Black Sea in what is now the Soviet Union.

The life of most of the Germanic tribes was only a step beyond that of nomadic hunters. Each tribe followed a war leader, called a *princeps* by the Romans. His band of warrior-followers was called a *comitatus* in Latin or a "witan" in the Germanic languages. The Germans had many gods— among them Freya, the goddess of love and fertility; Thor, the god of war; and Woden, the "allfather" whose mantle was the starry sky—and for the most part they opposed Christianity. Most of the tribes had not been influenced by Roman civilization. But a few, most notably the Goths, had adopted some Roman customs, and some had become Christians.

A battle between a Roman legion (those with helmets) and Germanic warriors (those with long hair and beards): from a sculpture on the triumphal arch of the Emperor Marcus Aurelius in Rome. Built in the second century A.D., when the power of Rome was still at its height, the column celebrates the emperor's victories in a campaign against the Germanic tribes of the upper Danube valley (present-day Austria and southern Germany).

Beginning in the fourth century, Huns and other Asiatic tribes began pushing westward across the plains north of the Caspian Sea. No one knows why. Perhaps they needed food; perhaps they had lost battles with other nomadic tribes; perhaps there had been a long drought. Whatever the reason, as they moved westward they drove the Germanic tribes ahead of them, across the frontiers of the faltering Roman Empire.

THE FALL OF ROME

At the same time, important changes were taking place within the Roman Empire. In 330 the Emperor Constantine moved the capital east to Constantinople, in the more heavily populated, Greek-speaking eastern part of the empire. In 395 Rome once again became a capital, but only of the western, Latin-speaking half of the empire; Constantinople remained capital of the East, and there was an emperor in each city. Meanwhile the empire had been weakened by the number of Germanic tribes who had been allowed to settle peacefully within its borders. These Germans made up an ever-increasing percentage of the army. They were a dangerous kind of ally for Roman emperors to have to depend on for defense against their Germanic kinsmen who lived outside the empire.

In 376 the Visigoths, fleeing the advancing Huns, asked and received permission to cross the Danube and settle within the empire. They soon quarreled with the Emperor Valens. In 378 they killed Valens and defeated his army in a battle at Adrianople, near Constantinople. Later, still seeking a place to settle, the Visigoths moved toward Rome, which they captured and sacked in 410—the event that so distressed Jerome. (Above, page 5.) They then moved on to the Iberian peninsula (modern Spain), where they established their own kingdom.

In order to meet the threat of the Visigoths, the Western Roman emperor ordered troops moved from the Rhine River, the northern frontier of the empire, into northern Italy. This left the province of Gaul (modern France) unprotected from the Germanic tribes to the east of the Rhine. In 406 a tribe called the Vandals crossed the Rhine. Over a period of years the Vandals moved through Gaul and Spain to North Africa, where in the 430's they established a kingdom of their own. Other Germanic tribes— the Burgundians, the Sueves, the Franks—soon established themselves in parts of Gaul and Spain. Then came an invasion of the Asiatic Huns under their leader Attila. Although he did not capture the city of Rome, Attila destroyed much of Gaul and northern Italy before his death in 453. In 455

Rome was captured and plundered by Vandal pirates operating out of their kingdom in North Africa. Finally Italy was overrun by a series of Germanic chieftains. One of these chieftains, Odovacar (or Odoacer) by name, deposed and killed the last of the Western Roman emperors in 476. Odovacar became the ruler of Italy, acknowledging the Eastern Roman emperor in Constantinople as his overlord.

Thus after 476 the Western Roman Empire no longer existed, even in name. Its lands were now divided among a number of small, disorganized Germanic kingdoms. Such unity as remained in western Europe came largely from the growing power of the Christian Church.

THE EARLY CHRISTIAN CHURCH

When Jesus was born, most Romans worshiped gods similar to those of the Greeks. This religion was administered by priests who were more government officials than anything else. Few people took it seriously, although most went through the motions of the ceremonies as a civic duty. More important were several Oriental religions that had ardent supporters among the Romans.

THE GROWTH OF THE CHURCH

At first most Romans thought that Christianity was just another of these Oriental faiths. But they soon discovered that it had appeal that the others lacked. Jesus had actually lived. His parables and personal tenderness helped bring his message home to his followers. His doctrines were simple but meaningful. His insistence upon a single, all-powerful God inspired deep faith. His assurance of life after death attracted many who were repelled by the dull afterlife that was all the official religion could promise.

The Romans neither tolerated Christianity nor seriously attempted to erase it completely. As the emperors lost followers, Christianity gained. Finally in 313 the Emperor Constantine granted religious toleration to all religions, and several years later he himself became a Christian.

In 381 the Emperor Theodosius made Christianity the official religion of the Roman Empire. Thereafter the church, now being called "Catholic" (universal), proceded to enforce its doctrines everywhere. Now Christian and not pagan priests were supported by the state; now non-Christians were persecuted, prevented from holding public office, and threatened with fines, banishment, or even death; and now priests were given many special privileges, including the right to their own courts for trying heretics.

THE ARIAN HERESY AND THE COUNCIL OF NICAEA

Some of the increasing number of Christians became "heretics"; that is, they adopted "heresies," beliefs that differed from those held by the main body of the church. The most important of these heretics was Arius (died 336). Arius did not accept the usual Christian belief that Jesus had been both God and man at one and the same time. He believed, rather, that God was separate from every created being, and that Jesus had been a created being—even though he was God on earth. He therefore concluded that Jesus was a sort of secondary God—divine, but not so divine as God himself. Arius's teachings won many followers, called "Arians." Arianism created such a controversy that in 325 the Emperor Constantine called a church council at Nicaea in Asia Minor to settle the problem. There the assembled churchmen decided that the Arians were heretics, and they formally defined the doctrine of the Trinity (that there are three Persons in one God) in the "Nicene Creed."

THE ORGANIZATION OF THE CHURCH

Although it was huge, spreading from Jerusalem all the way to the British Isles, the church was admirably organized to govern its affairs. There was a hierarchy (a system of officials arranged in graded orders) of "secular" clergy, who administered the worldly affairs of the church and worked with the laymen (church members who were not priests). Each local parish had a priest, who conducted services and ministered to the people. Parish churches were grouped into "dioceses," each administered by a bishop. The bishop usually lived in the largest town of the diocese and had a church of his own, called a "cathedral" because it contained his throne (*cathedra*). According to the doctrine of "apostolic succession," bishops were the successors of Christ's apostles and had special authority to ordain new priests and to confirm new members in the church. As the authority of Roman officials declined, bishops often assumed considerable political power; in many parts of Europe they were to all intents and purposes the real rulers. Gradually the more important bishops assumed authority over the less important, so that it became customary to accept one cathedral city in each region as the "metropolis," or mother city. The bishops of these cities were called "metropolitans" or "archbishops," and presided over the other bishops in the archdiocese.

The burial of Jesus: an ivory carving of about 400 A.D. On either side of the tomb are the two Roman soldiers assigned to guard it; behind them are two mourners. The directness and simplicity of this carving are typical of the early Christians and their art.

Throughout the early history of the church, the bishop of Rome held a special place in the hearts of the faithful. He was the head of the church in the city that for so long had been the center of the civilized world. He was also, according to the doctrine of the "Petrine succession," the successor of Saint Peter, to whom Christ had said, "Thou art Peter, and upon this rock I will build my church, and the gates of hell shall not prevail against it. And I will give thee the keys of the kingdom of heaven." The bishop of Rome came to be called "pope" (Latin *papa*, father), and by the middle of the fifth century his supremacy over all other archbishops and bishops was generally accepted.

THE FIRST MONASTERIES

The secular clergy remained "in the world" and worked among laymen; the "regular" clergy (so called because they followed a *regula*, or rule) withdrew to isolated places where they could lead simple lives and devote themselves to work, prayer, and contemplation. The first of these "monks" (from the Greek *monachos*, one who lives alone) was Saint Anthony, who retired to the Egyptian desert in the third century.

Eventually monks began to live together in organizations called "monasteries," which first appeared in the fourth century. The most important of the early founders of monasteries was Benedict (d. 543). Originally a hermit, he attracted so many followers that he founded a monastery (which still exists) on Monte Cassino in Italy. To govern this monastery, he wrote the so-called "Benedictine rule," which is followed by many monks today. Benedictine monks swore to uphold the three vows of poverty, chastity, and obedience and accepted the leadership of the "abbot" (elected head of the monastery). Their daily routine included five hours of prayer, five hours of physical labor, and a variety of special assignments for the benefit of the monastery or the people of the surrounding countryside.

Benedictine monasteries were established all over Europe. They served as hospitals, hotels, model farms, and, most important, as refuges for men of learning, who filled their libraries with books that preserved the learning of Greece and Rome as well as of Christianity. By going out from their communities to convert the heathen and advise the Germanic rulers, they helped to civilize the barbarians and to restore order in an age of chaos. It is difficult to overestimate the importance of the quiet and humble followers of Saint Benedict in the years that followed the fall of Rome.

THE CONVERSION OF THE BARBARIANS

Christianity was the religion of Rome before the barbarian invasions, and there was good reason to fear that when the Roman Empire was destroyed its church would disappear as well. But the missionary spirit that had begun with the apostles of Jesus lived on; and, although the barbarians at first seemed poor prospects for conversion, they soon adopted Christianity.

The Visigoths, who had been converted by Ulfila, the "apostle of the Goths," were already Christians when they entered the empire and defeated Valens in 378. Ulfila's followers successfully converted most of the other Germanic tribes as well; but these missionaries were Arians, who spread the Arian heresy among the Germanic tribes at about the same time that Catholic bishops were stamping it out among the people who inhabited the remnants of the Roman state. As a result, the religious differences between the Arian Christian invaders and the Catholic Christians whom they conquered heightened the hatred of the two groups for each other.

Meanwhile, influenced by Saint Patrick and his followers, the Celtic people of Ireland became Christians; but they retained some local customs that set them apart from both the Catholics and the Arians. In the fifth and sixth centuries the Catholics sent missionaries to work among the Franks, who were in the former Roman province of Gaul, and among the Anglo-Saxons, who had conquered most of Britain. These missionaries, many of whom were Benedictines, not only converted pagans to Christianity but also encouraged Arian and Celtic Christians to accept Catholic doctrines. They met with such success that by the seventh century the dissident groups had, for the most part, accepted the leadership of the pope in Rome and the doctrine of the Trinity as expressed by the Council of Nicaea.

Christendom now included most of the former Roman Empire. In the next century Saint Boniface and other Benedictines converted the Germanic peoples east of the Rhine River, in what is now central Germany. Christianity thus began to move into areas that the Romans had never conquered.

⚓ ⚓ ⚓

By the time the last of the Roman emperors was deposed in 476, western Europe seemed to be in a state of almost complete political disarray. But there were more remains of Roman grandeur than at first met the eye. Most obvious was the Catholic Church, which conquered its conquerors by converting them to Christianity and encompassing an ever larger share of the European continent within its realm. Less obvious were other Roman remains: the Latin language; some aspects of Rome's system of government, reflected in the admirable government of the church; the Christian Church itself; the memory of a time when all the civilized world was one state; and many Roman customs and laws which, as we shall see, the Germanic chieftains attempted to adopt.

A German horseman: from the column of Marcus Aurelius.

🌿 **A NOTE TO THE STUDENT:** The five parts of the questions and activities that you will find at the end of each chapter are designed to aid you not only in reviewing the material in the chapter but also in understanding the importance of that material and relating it to our own times.

The first part, *People, Places, and Terms*, is designed to help you fix in your mind the factual knowledge of the chapter. You should be able to explain fully who the person was, where the place was, or what the term means. You should also be able to explain how and why the person, place, or term was important to the times.

Getting Organized says just what it means. A clear and factual answer to each of these questions will enable you to grasp the main ideas and events of the chapter. Every attempt should be made to use the names and terms listed in the first section.

Understanding the Big Picture will help you tie the chapter together so that you can see the relationships between the many men, events, and ideas that it contains.

Mastering the Map will make the places and events of the chapter more real to you and, hopefully, will increase your awareness of the importance of geography to history.

Finally, *For the Thoughtful* will help you to judge and interpret men and events and to relate them to our own time.

People, Places, and Terms

Constantine	Ulfila	*comitatus*
Theodosius	Patrick	Catholic
Celts	Boniface	Arian
Germanic peoples		Council of Nicaea
Slavs	Mediterranean Sea	secular clergy
Huns	Britain	layman
Scandinavians	Rhine River	bishop
West Germans	Danube River	diocese
Franks	Rome	cathedral
Saxons	Constantinople	apostolic succession
East Germans	Gaul	archbishop
Visigoths	Italy	pope
Ostrogoths	Monte Cassino	regular clergy
Vandals	Ireland	*regula*
Attila		monk
Odovacar	*Pax Romana*	monastery
Arius	*princeps*	Benedictine rule
Benedict	witan	abbot

Getting Organized

1. How extensive was the Roman Empire in A.D. 200? What are some of the possible reasons that its government gradually weakened after the second century?
2. Who were the "barbarians"? Which were the most important groups, and where did each live? Describe the political customs of the Germanic tribes. What are possible reasons for the Germanic tribes' seeking new homelands?
3. What important changes took place in the Roman Empire in the fourth century? Which Germanic tribes invaded the empire? When? Where did each settle? How did these invasions affect the Roman state?
4. Why did Christianity appeal to the peoples of the Roman Empire? Which emperor granted toleration to Christianity? When? When did Christianity become the official Roman religion? What effect did this have?
5. What was the Arian heresy? What action did the Council of Nicaea take?
6. Describe the organization of the church. How did the leaders of the secular clergy come to acquire political power? How did the office of archbishop come into being? How and why did the bishop of Rome come to be regarded as pope?
7. How and where did the regular clergy live? What rules did they follow? What influence did they have on the world outside the monasteries?
8. How did it happen that some of the Germanic peoples became Arian Christians? Did they remain Arians? What parts of Europe had adopted Christianity by the eighth century?
9. What were Rome's principal legacies to Europe?

Understanding the Big Picture

1. Why did Rome collapse before the invading Germanic peoples? What customs did the Germanic peoples bring to the areas that they took over?
2. Why was Christianity able to survive the collapse of the Western Roman Empire? How did its organization help it to survive and grow?

For the Thoughtful

1. Why were the relatively disorganized and uncivilized Germanic peoples able to take over much of the Roman Empire? Can you think of other examples in history in which a less civilized people has conquered a wealthier and more civilized state? How can this happen?
2. What explains the great popularity and widespread growth of Catholic Christianity during the period of Roman decline? Do any of these same reasons help explain the size and influence of the Catholic Church today?

the Germanic kingdoms and the Empire of Justinian

By the end of the fifth century the Germanic barbarian tribes had shivered the Western Roman Empire to pieces. The one-time Roman province of Britain was a nest of tiny Anglo-Saxon kingdoms. Gaul and Spain were divided among Franks, Visigoths, and other tribes. The Ostrogoths, cousins of the Visigoths, governed northern Italy and the Adriatic coast. There was a Vandal kingdom in Africa. The only remnant of the Roman Empire was in the eastern Mediterranean where, from their luxurious capital at Constantinople, the Eastern Roman emperors attempted to maintain unbroken the traditions of the ancient world.

THE GERMANIC KINGDOMS OF WESTERN EUROPE

After the collapse of the Western Roman Empire in the fifth century, the Germanic kingdoms of western Europe began to develop new forms of government and ways of life. It was from these beginnings that modern Europe eventually developed.

17

FEATURES OF THE GERMANIC KINGDOMS

The Germanic kingdoms were all rather similar. Their kings, chosen for their prowess in battle, were barbarian warriors (although they usually adopted some of the trappings of their Roman predecessors by taking such titles as "consul" or "Augustus" and claiming to have inherited the authority of the ancient Roman emperors). These kings quickly gave up their pagan beliefs and allied themselves with the Christian bishops—sometimes for religious reasons, sometimes because the church, the most powerful organization that remained after the collapse of Rome, was a valuable ally. Sometimes a Germanic king would pose as a patron of the arts, but usually he was happiest when he was fighting his many enemies.

Each king was surrounded by a court of warriors called a "witan" in the Germanic languages or a *comitatus* in Latin. His supporters swore to support him, and in return he often called for their advice and approval before starting any new campaign. Usually a king would give his best warriors estates so that they could afford to pay the costs of war themselves, and as a result a class of landowning soldiers called "eorls" came into being. These warriors with large estates were the ancestors of the later noble class of the Middle Ages.

The Germanic invaders often were only small minorities in the countries they ruled; the common people (the Germanic name for them was "ceorl") were usually the descendants of the inhabitants of Roman days. Most were *coloni,* who could not be deprived of the land they tilled, but were not allowed to leave it either. They were the ancestors of the medieval serfs. Less lucky were the slaves, who had been captured in war or in raids on nearby territories; they had no rights at all. Most of the common people were Catholic Christians, and often they spoke a language different from that of their rulers. As time went on, the Germanic invaders and their subjects intermarried; the Ostrogoths in Italy, for example, eventually ceased to exist as a separate people and were completely absorbed into the native population.

Usually the Germanic kings tried to establish systems of law. Their laws, called "edicts" or "dooms," combined Roman and Germanic customs. The countries in southern Europe, where Roman traditions were more deeply ingrained, retained many Roman laws; but everywhere Germanic customs were introduced by barbarian chieftains who had no real understanding of Roman ways.

THREE PRINCIPAL GERMANIC KINGDOMS

Three typical Germanic kingdoms illustrate the essential similarities and differences among them all and show how new ideas about government, law, and the ownership of land developed out of a haphazard combination of Roman and Germanic customs.

Theodoric and the Ostrogothic Kingdom in Italy. In 476 Odovacar deposed the last Western Roman emperor and set up his own kingdom in Italy. (See page 10.) He soon made an enemy of the Eastern Roman emperor, who was supposedly his overlord but who could exercise no control from far-off Constantinople. The emperor therefore asked Theodoric, chief of the Ostrogoths (then living in the Balkan Peninsula), to put down the rebellious Odovacar. Theodoric (ruled 474-526), glad to have an excuse to invade Italy, in 489 began a five-year war that ended when he killed Odovacar with his own hand, made himself king of Italy, and established his Ostrogoths as a new ruling class.

Theodoric retained many Roman customs in his kingdom, acknowledged the authority of the Eastern Roman emperor, gave his officials Roman titles, and preserved much of the Roman law in a series of published "edicts," or decrees. In the Roman tradition, he tolerated many religious beliefs; but he kept military power, which was the only power that counted in those days, in the hands of his Ostrogoths. He tried to make his capital city of Ravenna the Constantinople of the west, filling it with handsome public buildings (a few of which still stand) and attracting to his court Boethius, a philosopher, and Cassiodorus, a historian, who were two of the most learned men of the time.

Theodoric ruled wisely and won the loyalty of both the Italians and the Ostrogoths, so that Italy enjoyed three decades of peace and prosperity. But his successors allowed his state to break up into little, independent principalities whose rulers warred among themselves and ignored or forgot the Roman heritage that Theodoric had tried to preserve.

Clovis and the Frankish Kingdom in Gaul. While Theodoric was establishing his Ostrogothic kingdom, another chieftain named Clovis (ruled 481-511) was creating an even larger Frankish kingdom in what we now call France. North of the Alps and far from Rome, the Frankish people were less influenced by Roman ways than were the Ostrogoths.

Originally the head only of a little tribe called the Salic Franks (or "salty" Franks, so-called because they lived near the sea), Clovis set out at the age

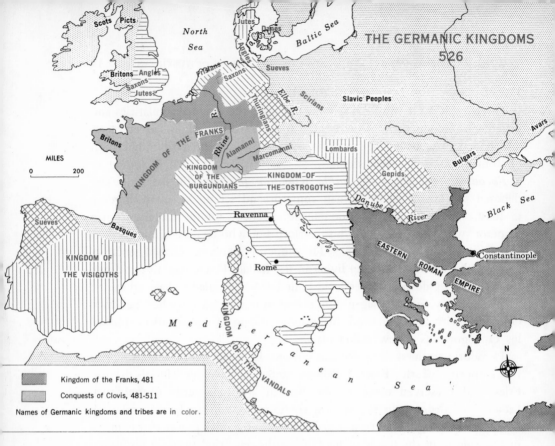

Scots Picts

*North
Sea*

Jutes

Danes *Baltic Sea*

Britons Angles
Saxons
Jutes

Frisians

Angles Saxons

Sueves

Elbe R.

Scirians

Slavic Peoples

Avars

Britons

Thuringians

KINGDOM OF THE FRANKS

Rhine

Alamanni

Marcomanni

Lombards

Bulgars

MILES
0   200

KINGDOM
OF THE
BURGUNDIANS

KINGDOM OF
THE OSTROGOTHS

Gepids

Danube River

Black Sea

Sueves

Basques

Ravenna

EASTERN
ROMAN
EMPIRE

Constantinople

KINGDOM OF
THE VISIGOTHS

Rome

M e d i t e r r a n e a n   S e a

KINGDOM OF THE

VANDALS

N

Kingdom of the Franks, 481

Conquests of Clovis, 481–511

Names of Germanic kingdoms and tribes are in color.

of fifteen to conquer as many neighboring tribes as he could. A master of intrigue, treachery, and deceit, he dominated northern France by the time he was twenty-three. Before he died he had conquered an empire that stretched from the North Sea almost to the Mediterranean and from the Pyrenees to central Europe. (See map above.)

In 493 Clovis married a Christian princess and, tradition has it, was converted to Catholic Christianity after a great victory over the rival tribe of the Alamanni in 496. Posing as the champion of his new faith, and with the support of the bishops, he conquered pagan tribes east of the Rhine and Christian heretics in the south of France. Clovis was largely responsible for the triumph of Catholicism in western Europe.

Clovis was fascinated by Roman customs. He titled himself "Augustus" in the Roman tradition; tried hard to make his unruly warriors behave like Roman courtiers; and gave their leaders huge grants of land, which he hoped they would develop into peaceful and prosperous estates like the old Roman villas. But the Franks acted like the Germanic warriors they were and resisted the temptation to become country gentlemen. Clovis probably did not understand Roman customs very well himself: he tried to write a law code for his people in the Roman manner, but his "Salic Law" was really only a list of Germanic customs.

One of Clovis's greatest achievements was to stop the continuing press of Germanic invasions from the east. He did this by advancing across the Rhine and introducing relatively stable government, written laws, and the Catholic Church into central Europe. Would-be attackers from the east could make no headway against the Frankish state, and western Europe became somewhat more peaceful than it had been. Although Clovis's successors, like those of Theodoric, quarreled among themselves and lost much of their influence over their followers, Clovis's Frankish state did not die; for it blended Roman and Germanic traditions more effectively than did its neighbors, and its bishops and warriors banded together to repel invaders when they had to.

Alfred and the Anglo-Saxon Kingdom in Britain. After the Romans withdrew from Britain in the fifth century, Germanic tribes—Angles, Saxons, and Jutes—invaded the island and drove the original Celtic inhabitants back into the mountain fastnesses of the northern and western parts of the island.

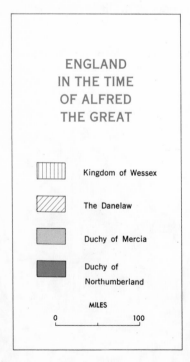

ENGLAND
IN THE TIME
OF ALFRED
THE GREAT

Kingdom of Wessex

The Danelaw

Duchy of Mercia

Duchy of
Northumberland

MILES

0   100

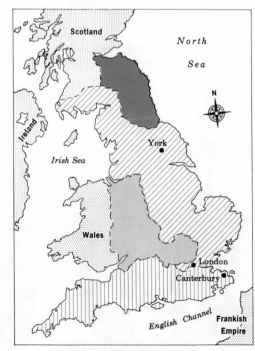

British life at this time was so chaotic that Christianity was not introduced there until the seventh century, and no stable kingdoms appeared until the eighth century—at the very time when the Danes (Vikings) were starting still another wave of invasions. (Chapter 6.)

Against this background, the achievement of Alfred the Great (king 871-899), ruler of the Anglo-Saxon kingdom of Wessex, is particularly significant. After a series of defeats, he rallied his armies to drive the Danes into northeastern England and forced them to accept Christianity. Then he turned to developing his own kingdom of Wessex into the first prosperous English state since Roman times.

Like other Germanic kings, Alfred was strong because he could command the loyalty of his principal followers—high nobles called "ealdormen" (eorls) and lesser lords called "thegns," who were the mounted soldiers in his army—and because he allied with the church and made bishops and priests into his trusted assistants. He put ealdormen in charge of large regions called "shires" (counties), and he divided these into smaller areas called "hundreds," which were governed by thegns. The "ceorls" (common people) were mostly peasant farmers who shared their produce with their lords and in wartime trooped out to fight as members of the "fyrd" (militia). For protection, Alfred dotted the countryside with little forts called

The Angles, Saxons, and Jutes on their way to invade Britain: from the "Miracles of St. Edmund," an English manuscript of the time of Alfred the Great.

"burghs," which often became centers for towns, as the names of such modern cities as Canterbury and Scarborough testify.

Alfred recorded the Anglo-Saxon law, which was more concerned with the prevention of feuds than with abstract principles of justice. Each man had his "wergild," or cash value, which was determined by his rank in society. Anyone who wronged him was expected to pay a fine based upon his wergild and the amount of the wrong. A murderer, for example, had to pay the slain man's entire wergild to the family of the victim. Then the murder could be forgotten.

Courts in Alfred's time consisted of a thegn and a group of ceorls called "doomsmen." An accused person could prove his innocence by "compurgation," or getting others to swear that he was not guilty. Or he might be subjected to "trial by ordeal," in which he would, for example, pick a stone out of boiling water. If his hand healed soon enough to satisfy the doomsmen, he was considered innocent. These primitive customs have greatly influenced modern law: the thegn has become a judge; the dooms-men, the jury; the wergild, a money fine; and compurgation, the present custom of having character witnesses.

Alfred did all he could to encourage learning, of which there was little in those days. He persuaded a Welsh scholar named Asser to join his court and one year gave him two monasteries as a Christmas present. He had others translate Latin works into Anglo-Saxon; apparently encouraged the writing of the *Anglo-Saxon Chronicle*, the principal source of knowledge of this period; and may even have been the translator into Anglo-Saxon of the *Church History of the English Nation*, a work in Latin by a monk called "the Venerable Bede." All in all, he did the best he could to make a backward and primitive country peaceful, prosperous, and civilized.

OTHER GERMANIC KINGDOMS

Other Germanic kingdoms were as important in their day as those of the Ostrogoths, Franks, and Anglo-Saxons. North and west of the Alps was a Burgundian state that was absorbed by the Franks in the sixth century. The Visigothic kingdom in Spain lasted 300 years before it was finally overrun by Muslims in the eighth century. The Vandal kingdom in North Africa had a brief moment of glory as one of the major powers in the Mediterranean in the fifth century. All of these kingdoms had much in common with those that we have discussed, but none exerted as much influence on the later history of Europe.

⚜ ⚜ ⚜

In the centuries that followed the downfall of the Western Roman Empire, these Germanic kingdoms destroyed the unity that Rome had imposed upon western Europe. Yet despite the confusion of the time, the seeds of a new political and social order were planted. Nor was the Roman tradition entirely destroyed. The church preserved Roman traditions of thought, law, and government, and it treasured other traditions of its own that dated all the way back to the time of Jesus. Theodoric, Clovis, Alfred, and lesser kings and lords helped create a Germanic legal tradition, and in Italy Roman law was still preserved and occasionally even enforced. Germanic warriors were establishing a whole set of customs of their own that would culminate in the feudal system of the twelfth century.

Meanwhile Roman traditions were preserved almost intact in eastern Europe, where the Eastern Roman Empire remained dominant. There, in the sixth century, a great emperor came to power and devoted much of his life to an attempt to re-establish Roman political unity throughout the Mediterranean basin.

❧ THE EASTERN ROMAN EMPIRE UNDER JUSTINIAN

During the fifth century the Eastern Roman Empire was plagued by a series of weak and vicious rulers, palace revolutions, oppressive taxes, and government scandals. Even so, it escaped the great wave of Germanic invasions that overran the West; it was able to protect its boundaries, preserve its prosperity, and retain most of its ancient Roman traditions. Many of the Germanic kings continued to pay lip service to the Eastern Roman Emperors in Constantinople. The Eastern Empire was an island of comparative stability in an age of turbulent change.

During the sixth century the Emperor Justinian brought the Eastern Empire to a new peak of power and almost succeeded in bringing all the lands bordering the Mediterranean under his jurisdiction.

JUSTINIAN AND THEODORA

Justinian (emperor 527-565) came from a family of Balkan peasants. He might never have become prominent at all had not his uncle, an illiterate politician, gone to Constantinople and managed to usurp the imperial throne. Justinian served his uncle brilliantly, first in the army and later as his aide and the real ruler of the empire. At the age of forty-five he assumed the crown himself.

Justinian was no lover of warfare. Physically weak, he preferred the library to the battlefield; ate, slept, and drank little; and worked at the business of being an emperor from early morning until late at night. He was imaginative and loved to make great plans; but he was practical, too, and was willing to spend long hours on the details of carrying out his plans. At the same time he was an effective politician, a good friend—and a merciless enemy. One contemporary who had felt the sting of his wrath called him "crafty, hypocritical . . . double-dealing, clever . . . a fickle friend, a trustless enemy, and an ardent devotee of assassination and robbery." But this writer was prejudiced; the record seems to show that Justinian was as trustworthy as any of the Eastern emperors.

For companionship and advice Justinian relied upon his wife, the beautiful and controversial Theodora. She was the daughter of a bear trainer in a circus, and reportedly she was none too virtuous. Certainly Justinian married her over the protests of his courtiers. Whatever her background, Theodora won both support and affection from the people. She had the strength of character to lead her husband's bodyguards in a successful effort to suppress a revolution. Justinian showered her with money, jewelry, and political authority that almost equalled his own. For her part, Theodora protected heretics, religious refugees, and outcasts whom her husband would have persecuted, and so helped keep the imperial peace.

THE ATTEMPT TO CONQUER WESTERN EUROPE

Justinian's greatest hope was to restore the power of the Roman Empire in western Europe. Assigning small forces to protect his eastern and northern boundaries, he turned his largest armies and his finest general, Belisarius, against the declining Vandal kingdom in North Africa. By 533 Belisarius had overwhelmed the Vandals and destroyed their state. The Vandals disappeared from history.

Three years later Belisarius led one of Justinian's armies against the Ostrogothic kingdom in Italy, and in 540 he was able to send the keys of Ravenna, the capital, to the emperor as a token that he had conquered the Ostrogothic state. But just when the authority of the Eastern Empire seemed to have been established in Italy, a great national leader named Totila appeared to lead an Ostrogothic revolt, called the "Gothic War," that for eighteen years raged up and down the Italian peninsula. Totila was a worthy

KINGDOM OF
THE FRANKS

KINGDOM OF
THE VISIGOTHS

Ravenna

Danube River

Black Sea

Corsica

Italy

Balkan
Peninsula

Constantinople · Chalcedon

Asia Minor

SASSANID EMPIRE

Rome

Sardinia

Cartagena

M e d i t e r r a n e a n   S e a

Sicily

Carthage
Numidia

Athens

Crete

Cyprus

Antioch

Damascus

Jerusalem

A r a b i a

Alexandria

Libya

Egypt

Red Sea

N

MILES

0   400

rival of Belisarius and his successor; Justinian's armies had to capture Rome
five different times, and the city underwent three sieges before it was
finally subdued. Its population had once been almost 1,000,000; by the end
of the war there were only 40,000 left, half of whom were paupers living
on the charity of the pope. All the inhabitants of Milan were killed or
driven off, and other cities were almost as badly hit by the war. Many
monuments of the great days of the Roman Empire were destroyed, and
the entire country was impoverished. Only decaying buildings and broken
statues remained to remind men of the grandeur that once was Rome.
The Roman Senate ceased to exist. But Justinian's armies controlled Italy
—what was left of it.

Justinian sent other armies to seize the islands of the western Mediterranean and the coastal lands of the Visigothic kingdom in Spain. He succeeded in dominating the fringes of the Mediterranean; but his troops never
were able to march far inland, and the great land mass of northern Europe,
which had been so important a part of the Roman Empire, remained in the
hands of the Germanic kingdoms. In the later years of Justinian's reign,
so many of his troops were needed to protect the eastern and northern
boundaries of the empire that he had to abandon his attacks in the west.
Justinian's armies had never been large, even by the standards of the sixth
century. They depended for their success upon heavily armed cavalrymen

called *cataphracti*, who rode larger horses than did their Germanic enemies. These forces could win battles, but they could not occupy rebellious states successfully. Justinian's dream of conquering all Europe was only a forlorn hope.

THE CORPUS JURIS CIVILIS

Justinian's most significant achievement was the *Corpus Juris Civilis*, or "Body of Civil Law," in which his judges and lawyers summarized the system of Roman law that had gradually built up over a period of more than a thousand years. The Roman law insured justice for the individual and safety for the state. In the centuries just before Justinian, it had been improved by philosophers who introduced the concept of "fundamental law," the principles of which were believed to be found in nature and to apply to all men and all nations at all times. The Christians had further modified the law by lessening the penalties for minor crimes and increasing the punishments for certain offenses that the Romans often had tolerated. Most of these changes were for the good. But their introduction resulted in confusion, and sometimes the changes made the laws contradictory. To remedy the resulting legal chaos, Justinian appointed a committee of jurists who worked for years to organize the legal system into a single code. The result was the *Corpus Juris Civilis*, published in 533.

The *Corpus Juris Civilis* was divided into three parts. The first, called the *Codex*, was a summary of all the legislation of earlier times organized according to its subject matter. The second, the *Digest*, summarized the opinions of judges and lawyers about this legislation. The third, the *Institutes*, was a little textbook that stated clearly and simply the principles on which these laws and opinions were based. Later these three parts of the *Corpus* were supplemented by *Novellae*, or "New Laws," which listed legislation made after the original summaries had been issued.

These documents are a complete record of Roman legal customs. They outline the rights granted to each individual—to a fair and speedy trial, for example—and they show that although moral offenses were severely punished, there was still an allowance made for normal human frailty. The *Corpus Juris Civilis* was a harsh code by modern standards, decreeing death for many crimes now considered minor. But the sixth century was a harsh and cruel time, and the *Corpus* was a moderate code for its day. It has influenced lawyers ever since, for it reflected the finest legal traditions of the ancient world as modified by the best influence of Christianity.

JUSTINIAN AND THE CHRISTIAN CHURCH

For most of his life Justinian was a practicing Catholic who supported the authority of the popes in Rome against a number of heretical sects. But as he grew older, he adopted the heresy that Christ could not suffer bodily pain, and he fought bitterly with the Catholics, who disagreed with him.

One of Justinian's most memorable accomplishments is the church of Hagia Sophia ("Holy Wisdom"; also frequently called "Sancta Sophia") in Constantinople. He himself supervised its construction, which required the labor of 10,000 men for seven years. Hagia Sophia is magnificent. On the outside it shows only massive walls crowned by enormous domes, but inside its pillars and rooms of colored marble glow in the light that pours through great, high windows. Everywhere are mosaics portraying Christ and his saints in brilliant colors with imaginative symbolism; they are among the finest achievements of early Christian art. Hagia Sophia, like the *Corpus Juris Civilis*, blends the best of the classical and Christian worlds; for fourteen hundred years its size, beauty, and awesomeness have dazzled all who see it.

THE TRAGEDY OF JUSTINIAN

Justinian deserves to be called "the last of the Roman emperors." His accomplishments—the conquest of Italy, the *Corpus Juris Civilis*, Hagia Sophia—were the crowning achievements of the sixth century. Yet Justinian is just as important for what he failed to accomplish. He was never able to reunite western Europe with the Eastern Roman Empire. In fact, the expenses of his armies and wars, of his brilliant court, and of his huge buildings were so great that he undermined the finances of his empire and left his successors unable to continue his programs. In the west—particularly in Italy, where the Gothic War left the country in ruins—he completed the destruction of Roman political power and prevented any further efforts to unite the peninsula under Roman or Italian leadership. This was Justinian's tragedy: by attempting to restore the ancient Roman Empire, he only hastened its demise. Despite his good intentions, Justinian had speeded the separation of the eastern and the western worlds, and there was no longer hope of re-establishing unity of any kind to all the lands of the ancient Roman Empire.

            ♛ ♛ ♛

In the Eastern Roman Empire, ancient legal and political traditions were carefully preserved by the emperors who succeeded Justinian. Constanti-

Left, the Emperor Justinian: a mosaic in the Basilica of San Vitale, Ravenna, Italy. Right, the interior of Hagia Sophia in Constantinople (now called Istanbul), Turkey. After Constantinople was conquered by the Turks in 1453, Hagia Sophia became a Muslim mosque, and its mosaics were covered with Turkish inscriptions; but recently most of these have been removed, and some of the mosaics have been restored to their original condition.

nople remained far richer and more prosperous than any other city in the Mediterranean. In the west, little Germanic kingdoms squabbled for the remnants of power and glory that remained, imposing their own semi-barbaric laws and military traditions on what they remembered of ancient Roman ways of government. The only institution that could unify the two worlds was the Christian Church, but this was still too weak to enforce order and discipline on unruly German kinglets, on Byzantine emperors, or even on its own heretical sects.

Yet, amid all the confusion, poverty, and ignorance in western Europe, as early as the sixth century the law codes, the witans, and the immature Germanic governments were planting the seeds of new ways of life that would come to full maturity later.

People, Places, and Terms

Theodoric
Boethius
Cassiodorus
Clovis
Salic Franks
Angles
Saxons
Jutes
Celts
Alfred
Asser
Bede
Burgundians
Justinian
Theodora
Belisarius

Britain

Gaul
Spain
Italy
Rome
Eastern Roman
 Empire
Constantinople
Ravenna
North Sea
Pyrenees Mountains
Rhine River

witan
comitatus
eorl
ceorl
coloni
edict

doom
Salic Law
ealdorman
shire
hundred
thegn
fyrd
burgh
wergild
doomsman
compurgation
trial by ordeal
trial by battle
Gothic War
Cataphracti
Corpus Juris Civilis
Hagia Sophia

Getting Organized

1. What were the chief common characteristics of the Germanic kings? What was the role of the witan? the eorls? the ceorls? What kind of laws did the Germanic kings establish?
2. What circumstances led to Theodoric's invasion of Italy? What Roman customs and traditions did Theodoric try to preserve in his Ostrogothic kingdom?
3. What territories did Clovis conquer? Under what circumstances did he become a Christian? Did his conversion help him in any way? How did he attempt to retain Roman customs and traditions? What were the results of this attempt? Why are his military conquests significant?
4. What were the conditions in England when Alfred the Great came to power? How did he organize his kingdom?
5. Describe the system of law under Alfred. In what ways has this system influenced modern law? How did Alfred promote learning in his country?
6. What kind of ruler was Justinian? How did Theodora help him rule? What was Justinian's great aim? How successful was he?
7. Why did Justinian issue the *Corpus Juris Civilis?* What does it consist of? Why is it important?
8. Why was Justinian's reign both important and tragic? What happened to his empire after his death?

Understanding the Big Picture

1. What did the Ostrogothic, Frankish, and Anglo-Saxon kingdoms have in common? Did they deal with their common problems in similar ways? How was each of these kingdoms unique?
2. Which of the three Germanic kings, Theodoric, Clovis, or Alfred, was the most successful in uniting his kingdom?
3. Compare each of the three kings with Justinian. In what ways was each like him? Unlike him?
4. How did the Germanic kingdoms both preserve and destroy Roman customs and traditions? How did Roman customs and traditions affect the Germanic kingdoms?
5. Make a chronological chart showing, in parallel columns, the principal events in the reigns of Theodoric, Clovis, Alfred, and Justinian.

Mastering the Map

1. Study the map of the Germanic kingdoms in 526 on page 20. Note the boundaries of the Ostrogothic and Frankish states. What was the relation of these kingdoms to the Eastern Roman Empire?
2. Study the map of England in the age of Alfred the Great on page 21. What were the boundaries of the various parts of England? Which part did Alfred rule? Why didn't he rule the whole island?
3. Study the map of Justinian's Eastern Roman Empire on page 26. What lands did he control? What was the relation of his empire to the Ostrogothic and Frankish kingdoms?

For the Thoughtful

1. In your opinion, why did Britain's early "golden age," the reign of Alfred, come 300 years after that of the other kingdoms discussed in this chapter?
2. Would you say that the Germanic kingdoms deliberately destroyed Roman civilization? Give reasons for your opinions.
3. What specific elements of the Germanic civilizations are still present today in America? Mention in particular political, legal, and religious traditions that have modern American counterparts.
4. From your knowledge of earlier history, explain why the Eastern and Western Roman Empires drifted apart. What was Justinian's role in the final break? Do you think that the history of the sixth and seventh centuries contributed to the present split between eastern and western Europe?

3

the Beginnings of Medieval Civilization

Like men of all times, the people living in the fifth to tenth centuries were far more aware of conditions in their own time than they were of changes from the past or of the beginnings of what might become a new civilization. Yet, as we have seen, new kinds of government were being developed in these centuries. (See pages 18-24.) At the same time there were also new developments in the relationships among classes of people, in religion and philosophy, and in architecture and the other arts. For example, the so-called "patristic" writers created a new literature in the fourth, fifth, and sixth centuries, while other Christians built churches decorated with magnificent testimonies to their skill and faith. These earliest stages of what later would become a flowing civilization give this period its importance.

🌸 EUROPEAN LIFE IN THE SIXTH CENTURY

By the end of the sixth century, a new kind of society had come into being in western Europe. A new way of life was developed to meet the special problems of the times.

When the political power of the Roman Empire declined, other aspects of life also suffered. Cities shrank as their once prosperous merchants grew poor; commerce and manufacturing fell off; and standards of living declined. A few persons, however, profited from the depression and political confusion. Germanic kings resisted the feeble efforts of Roman rulers to tax them, as did the new class of landed aristocrats who lived on great rural estates called "villas." As time went on, the latter expanded their villas by taking over smaller estates and abandoned farms; eventually they fortified their houses and lived like independent rulers. Roman rulers feared and resented these landlords, but they were too weak to do anything about them.

Small landholders were less lucky. Too poor to resist Roman tax collectors, their richer neighbors, or the Germanic invaders, many a farmer in desperation traded his land and freedom for safety by becoming a *colonus*, or tenant farmer. Giving his land to a villa owner, he received it back as a *precarium*, a loan that was his and his descendants as long as the villa owner was faithfully served. In return, the villa owner agreed to protect his tenants from the attacks of their enemies.

As the years passed, the decline of commerce forced the villas to become less and less dependent on the outside world. Commerce fell off as the faltering Roman government ceased to coin money and barter (the direct exchange of one product for another) became the usual method of trade. It declined further as Vandal pirates on the Mediterranean attacked shipping and as bandits infested the once magnificent but now decaying Roman roads. The little commerce that remained was heavily taxed and often unprofitable. So the workers in the cities lost their jobs and fled to the countryside, seeking not only work but also protection from invading Germanic armies. They were glad to exchange freedom for the security of the *colonus*. The cities, their market places and workshops all but abandoned, their temples, public baths, theaters, aqueducts, and public buildings in decay, survived mainly as centers of the church.

Germanic tribesmen who overran western Europe often took over the villas from their Roman owners. They had no desire to destroy the lands they had conquered and so kept the landed estates largely intact. Many adopted customs of their subject peoples and began speaking Latin; and some even learned to read. They became Christians, as had Clovis; attempted to preserve Roman law, as had Theodoric; and settled down to enjoy the benefits of the life of Roman landowners. But they did not really understand Roman ways and could not really practice them.

THE PATRISTIC WRITERS

The great days of Roman art, literature, and philosophy had passed even before the death of the Roman Empire. Some sensitive men, repelled by the barbarity of the invasions, consoled themselves by writing pale imitations of the poetry of earlier Romans. Others, more thoughtful and original, turned to Christianity for inspiration, and in the fourth, fifth, and sixth centuries they created a whole new body of literature that has profoundly influenced all subsequent Christian thinkers. Called the "patristic" writers because they were "fathers" of the church (from the Latin *pater*, "father"), these men were keenly aware of the classical tradition of Greece and Rome. They were well read in Greek and Roman literature, familiar with Roman customs, and dedicated to many Roman traditions; but though they wrote in Greek and Latin and even copied the style of Roman authors, they were influenced most by their Christian faith. They combined in their writings much of the best of both classical and Christian thought. In so doing, they created a new philosophy that was uniquely their own.

THE FOUR DOCTORS

In the age of the barbarian invasions and the decline of the empire, Latin Christendom produced some of its greatest philosophers. Four of these, the so-called "Four Doctors"—Ambrose, Jerome, Augustine, and Gregory—laid the foundations of later Christian thought.

Ambrose. Ambrose (340?-397) was the son of a Roman official. Tradition has it that he one day attempted to control a riotous crowd that had gathered in his home city of Milan to elect a new bishop. In the midst of the confusion a child shouted, "Ambrose for bishop!" Suddenly—to his surprise, for he was not even a Christian—Ambrose found himself elected. So he was baptized and made a deacon, a priest, and finally a bishop—all in one week. The new cleric became the greatest statesman of the fourth-century church. He lived a good and simple life, and he made his diocese a peaceful haven in the midst of the turmoil of the last days of the empire. Ambrose gave his land to the church and his money to the poor, wrote hymns that are still sung today (he was probably the man who introduced hymn singing into Christian ritual), and wrote sermons and religious tracts in which he successfully blended classical and Christian ideas.

Jerome. Jerome (340?-420) was a fourth-century contemporary of Ambrose. A classically-educated monk, he was secretary to the pope, who commissioned him to translate the Bible from its original Greek and Hebrew into Latin. Jerome's version, called the "Vulgate" because it was written in the everyday or "vulgar" Latin of the fourth century (as distinguished from the "classical" Latin of the first century), was both a superb piece of scholarship and a magnificent work of art. It was used throughout Europe for centuries and is still the official version of the Catholic Church.

Augustine. The third and greatest of the Four Doctors was Augustine (354-430), a younger contemporary of Ambrose and Jerome. Son of a pagan official and his Christian wife, Augustine (like Ambrose) was at first a pagan himself. He taught rhetoric and studied law in Milan, where he kept a mistress and flirted with a form of heresy that he hoped would give him a complete understanding of the world in which he lived. This proved unsatisfactory, and Augustine was tormented by uncertainty and guilt until he came under the influence of Ambrose and turned to Christianity in his search for the deep religious faith he knew he needed.

In his *Confessions,* one of the most moving religious autobiographies ever written, Augustine recounted his conversion to Christianity. Overwhelmed by the sense of his own inadequacy, he pleaded with his God for faith: "How long, how long? Tomorrow and tomorrow? Why not now? Why not this very hour make an end to my uncleanness?" Then he heard a voice telling him to open his Bible, and, he continued, "I snatched [the Bible] up, opened it, and in silence read the paragraph on which my eyes first fell: 'Not in rioting and drunkenness, not in chambering and wantonness, not in strife and envying, but put on the Lord Jesus Christ and make no provision for the flesh . . .' "

Thus Augustine found the faith he sought, and ever since he has been the symbol of deep devotion to God. He left his friends in Milan and went to North Africa, where he founded the Augustinian order of monks, the oldest monastic brotherhood in the west. Later he reluctantly left his monastery to become bishop of Hippo, a little town in North Africa, from which his influence spread all over Europe. He was an able administrator of his diocese, but his real life was the life of the mind. In a stream of letters and books, he poured out his criticism of beliefs he considered heretical and emphasized the necessity of a personal relationship between man and God.

Augustine developed his philosophy in three of the most important books ever written on Christianity: the *Confessions, De Trinitate* ("Concerning the Trinity"), and *De Civitate Dei* ("On the City of God"). *De Trinitate* was the first successful attempt to explain the difficult doctrine of the

Trinity in terms that ordinary people could understand. The *Confessions* was an account of his search for faith and the religious life, written in the form of a personal confession to God. On one level it is simple autobiography; on another it is religious philosophy at its most profound.

Augustine's third great book, *De Civitate Dei*, was inspired by the sack of Rome by the Visigoths in 410. As a young man, Augustine, like everyone else, had assumed that Rome would last forever—and suddenly the "Eternal City" had collapsed before a disorganized barbarian horde! In *De Civitate Dei*, Augustine attempted to explain this incredible event in religious terms. In a long introduction he discussed at length the decline of religion and morality, implying that the Romans no longer deserved to rule the world. Augustine maintained that the "city of man," by which he meant Rome and all other human institutions, can be no better than the people who create it, and therefore it is doomed to be imperfect and cannot last. In the second half of his book he offered in contrast his vision of the "city of God" in all its splendor. Here he described God and his angels, Satan and his devils, the creation of the world and the fall of man from grace, and he told of the coming, crucifixion, and resurrection of Christ, of the growth of the church, of the end of the world, of the Last Judgment, and of the final triumph of the city of God over the city of man. In his hymn to the promise and glory of a world in which God and not man will rule, Augustine offered Christians a disorganized, emotional, personal, and yet magnificent picture of the Christian faith. In broad strokes he disposed of much of the glamor of the memory of the classical world and called for an age of faith, of which he was both prophet and promoter. No other book so influenced the minds of medieval men.

Gregory the Great. The fourth of the "Four Doctors," Pope Gregory I (540?-604; pope 590-604) made the church an organization strong enough to effectively spread Augustine's teachings. Born more than a century after Augustine's death, Gregory witnessed the Gothic War and the last years of Justinian's reign. (See page 25.) As a young man he devoted himself to politics in Rome, eventually becoming prefect (roughly the same office as mayor) of his declining city. Suddenly, about 574, he gave up all his wealth and honors, became a monk, and converted his home into a monastery. Soon he was called back to the outside world to become papal ambassador to Constantinople, where he assumed the delicate task of safeguarding the interests of Catholic Christians against the attacks of Arians and of Byzantine politicians. His stay in the east convinced him that if

Pope Gregory I, the Great: an ivory carving from the time of Charlemagne. (Chapter 6.) The pope, at work in his study, is being inspired by the Holy Spirit in the form of a dove. The three scribes below Gregory probably are making copies of his manuscript.

Catholicism was to survive, it must cast off the influence of the Byzantine emperors and assume independent policies of its own in Italy. Returning to Rome, he reluctantly assumed the papacy. In the fourteen years he was pope, he attained his goal: by a rare combination of worldly wisdom and religious idealism, he made the papacy a world power.

Pope Gregory lived as austerely as any monk, wearing coarse robes, eating simple food, and surrounding himself with equally austere advisers. Calling himself *servus servorum Dei*, "servant of the servants of God," he used his income to help the impoverished people of Rome rather than to pay for displays of papal pomp. Yet he was a practical man. He made peace with the Lombards, the most recent Germanic conquerors of Italy, on terms that protected the right of Catholics to worship as they wished. He made troublesome bishops in North Africa and Gaul obey his orders, and he worked hard to convert Visigoths in Spain and Anglo-Saxons in Britain to his faith. He made the papal estates in Italy, called the Patrimony of Saint Peter, a source of power and profit, which he used for the good of his

church and the strength of his office. Before he died he was the most significant figure in Europe.

And still Gregory found time to think and write about Christian faith.
Less influenced by the Roman tradition than were Ambrose and Jerome,
Gregory both reflected and shaped medieval attitudes in his distrust of the
world and his fear of sin. He had little faith in the power of human reason,
for he believed that man, if left to himself, would only sink deeper and
deeper into sin. But he had infinite faith in the power of God and in His
grace, in the blessings made possible by Christ's sacrifice, in the good
influence of the saints, and in the ability of the Christian sacraments to save
the repentant sinner. After Gregory, Christians paid less and less attention
to science and the classics and more and more attention to the mysteries of
Christianity and the joys and terrors of life after death.

LESSER CHRISTIAN LEADERS

Although the four major fathers of the church—Ambrose, the adminis-
trator-priest; Jerome, the scholar-priest; Augustine, the convert-bishop with
his glowing faith; and Gregory, the idealistic yet practical pope—were the
men who most shaped the emerging Christian church, others were also
influential. As early as the fourth century two eastern bishops completed
works that influenced later popes and prelates. Eusebius (260?-?340), the
scholarly bishop of Caesarea, wrote in Greek a *Church History* in which he
established a Christian tradition of historical writing; and John Chrysostom
(355?-407), whose last name means "golden-mouthed," was an archbishop
of Constantinople whose eloquent sermons were carefully preserved and
often imitated.

In the fifth and sixth centuries Christian leaders in the Germanic kingdoms of western Europe established new, distinctively Christian patterns
of thought. Cassiodorus (490?-?583), the scholar who served Theodoric the
Ostrogoth, wrote textbooks of the arts and sciences for future priests.
Cassiodorus's texts often treated major subjects in a few pages filled with
what today would be considered silly and misleading comments, but they
were used all during the later Middle Ages. Also in Theodoric's court was
the more capable scholar Boethius (480?-?524), who compiled summaries
of pagan classics and essays on the Christian faith. He became active in the
affairs of the Ostrogoths, eventually becoming prime minister. But Theodoric later accused him of treason and sentenced him to death for plotting
a revolution. To pass the hours in prison while he was awaiting his fate,

Boethius wrote his last and greatest book, *The Consolation of Philosophy*, in which, surprisingly, he never mentioned his Christian faith. Stoically, he reminded himself that he had had a good life and that, since it was bound to end anyway, he might as well accept the approach of death calmly. Even though Boethius's book might well have been written by an ancient pagan, it became widely popular with Christian scholars in the Middle Ages.

In the sixth century a Frankish bishop, Gregory of Tours (538?-593), wrote *The History of the Franks*, which opened with the creation of the world and carried the story up to the year 591. Gregory, as he himself admitted, was only a "stolid ox" in his command of Latin; and his book paints a sometimes unwittingly vivid picture of the decline of Roman learning in the kingdom that Clovis had founded. In Visigothic Spain, Isidore of Seville (560?-636) summarized the learning of the seventh century in his *Etymologies*. As the name of his book suggests, Isidore believed that the Latin name of an object revealed its real significance—a good idea, but one that sometimes led him astray. His method led him, for example, to this conclusion: "the liver [*iecur*] has its name because there is resident the fire [*ignis*] which flies up into the brain. Thence it is spread into the eyes and other heated members, and by that heat it changes into blood, the liquid it has drawn from food, and this blood it supplies to the several members [limbs] to feed and nourish them . . ." Yet despite such misinformation, Isidore's book was a useful summary of the learning of the time. It was the student's guide to general knowledge for the next 500 years.

ART AND ARCHITECTURE

The decline of Rome affected art and architecture much as it did literature and religious thought. The Christians had little use for Roman temples and other public buildings. They allowed the barbarians to strip the gold and silver ornaments from what was left of the decaying cities, and they hardly protested when the invaders tore the Colosseum in Rome stone from stone to get at its metal dowels, which could be hammered into spear points. New construction, what there was of it, was limited almost entirely to churches. The Christians adopted two Roman types of construction, the basilica and the dome, for their churches; but they ignored the Roman traditions of realistic painting and sculpture, preferring instead symbolic works that were more suitable to portraying Christian ideas.

BASILICA CHURCHES

Many churches were modeled on the old Roman law courts, and like the law courts they were called "basilicas." The basilica churches were rectangular buildings with a high central section called a "nave." (The church was thought of as a ship that carried the faithful safely through the stormy seas of life—hence "nave," from the Latin *navis*, "ship.") At one end of the nave there was usually a semicircular section called the "apse," which enclosed the altar. Many of these basilica churches survive, especially in Italy and southern France.

The Basilica of Sant' Apollinare in Classe, built in the sixth century in Theodoric's old capital of Ravenna, is typical of these buildings. It is not impressive on the outside, offering only unadorned walls and blank windows to the outer world. But the interior is far different: it seems to glow in light that seeps through translucent marble panels and streams through perforated marble windows. The nave of Sant' Apollinare, two stories high, is separated from the aisles to left and right by rows of columns that march down the sides toward the apse. Within the apse is the altar, impressively raised on a small, stage-like platform.

The basilica is filled with carvings and mosaics (designs made by fitting together small pieces of stone or glass). These not only display the skill but also testify to the faith of the church's builders; for this was the house of

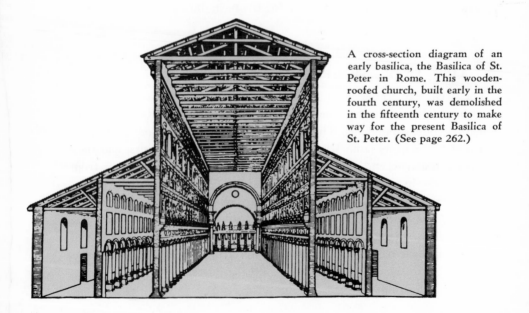

A cross-section diagram of an early basilica, the Basilica of St. Peter in Rome. This wooden-roofed church, built early in the fourth century, was demolished in the fifteenth century to make way for the present Basilica of St. Peter. (See page 262.)

The Basilica of Sant' Apollinare in Classe, Ravenna. The mosaic of the Transfiguration dates from the sixth century, when the basilica was built, as do the mosaics of the bishops between the windows of the apse. The mosaic above the arch was added in the seventh century. The portraits on the wall of the nave were added many centuries later. There were originally mosaics on the floor and the walls, but these have disappeared.

God, adorned to prove that he was the greatest of kings. The semi-dome over the altar is covered by a mosaic picturing the Transfiguration of Christ. It is dominated by a figure of Saint Apollonaris, the patron saint of the church; he stands in a green field, surrounded by birds, animals, and trees. Across the foreground march twelve sheep, representing the apostles; in the background are three more sheep, symbolizing the three disciples who were with Christ at the time of his Transfiguration. Overhead, emerging from the clouds, are figures of Moses and Elias. In the center of the sky is a giant medallion with a cross, the symbol of Christ, and above the cross is the hand of God.

CHRISTIAN SYMBOLIC ART

The mosaics in Sant' Apollinare make no attempt at realism as we know it, but instead are designed to symbolize religious stories and ideas for men who cannot read and write. In the words of Gregory the Great, pictures "can do for the illiterate what writing does for those who can read." The uneducated but pious sixth-century worshiper could see this mosaic every time he looked up above the altar, and in one glance he was reminded of the Old Testament and the New, of the nature of the Trinity, of the existence of Christ and the story of the Transfiguration, and of the protection of his patron saint.

Like the mosaics in Sant' Apollinare, most Christian art in the centuries after the fall of Rome was highly symbolic. Saints' heads were ringed with gold to indicate their holiness. Boats symbolized the church. Fish were especially popular as a symbol of Christ, as the word "fish" in Greek is an acrostic of Christ's name. Christ was often pictured as a shepherd and his followers as sheep, as in the mosaic in Sant' Apollinare. Sometimes even pagan symbols were used—the peacock, for example, which stood for eternal life. All these symbols were familiar to the sixth-century worshiper.

Stone carving was also used to decorate churches, at first only in the interiors but later on the exteriors as well. The *cathedras* (bishops' thrones) and tombs were elaborately carved, and enamelers, goldsmiths, weavers, and illustrators were kept busy ornamenting articles for use in the churches.

CENTRAL CHURCHES

As the Christians slowly became more prosperous and more expert in building their churches, the simple basilica style gave way to more elaborate structures. Wooden roofs were replaced by roofs of tile. As time went on the increasing use of stone led to the construction of domes (a Roman invention) and eventually to a style of church with the floor plan of the Greek cross—four relatively small wings attached to a large domed central section. The "central" style was much used in northern Italy, but the most famous example is the great church of Hagia Sophia in Constantinople. (See page 28.)

⚓ ⚓ ⚓

Thus during the early "Dark Ages" a new way of life began to take shape. Although the cities were in decay and the masses of people lived in grinding poverty on isolated rural estates, the seeds of a new civilization were being planted by writers, priests, and artisans. The Four Doctors and lesser Christian preachers and scholars created a new literature and philosophy based more on Christian faith than on pagan tradition. Artists and artisans whose names we will never know built churches that were magnificent testimonies to their skill and to their belief in God. Eventually these seeds would grow and blossom into the unique achievements of the twelfth and thirteenth centuries.

But that was still in the future. At the same time that new Germanic and Christian ways were developing in western Europe, another Christian way of life was flourishing in eastern Europe. There, in the Byzantine Empire, Roman traditions were more carefully preserved, although they were greatly modified by the men who lived in what was at that time the richest and most powerful country in Europe.

People, Places, and Terms

Ambrose	villa	*The Consolation of*
Jerome	*colonus*	*Philosophy*
Augustine	*precarium*	*History of the Franks*
Gregory the Great	barter	*Etymologies*
Cassidorus	patristic writers	basilica
Boethius	Four Doctors	nave
Gregory of Tours	Vulgate	apse
Isidore of Seville	*Confessions*	mosaic
	De Trinitate	*cathedra*
Milan	*De Civitate Dei*	central style
Hippo	*servus servorum Dei*	

Getting Organized

1. What group of people profited from the decline of the political power of the Roman Empire? What group suffered? How did the second group become subjected to the first?
2. Why did commerce decline? What effect did this decline have on the cities and their inhabitants?
3. What was the attitude of the Germanic tribesmen toward the ways of life that they found in the Roman Empire?
4. What were the reactions of literary men to the decline of Rome? To what extent were the patristic writers affected by classical literature?
5. Who were the Four Doctors and why were they important? Answer the following questions about each of the four men: Where did he live? What did he hope to accomplish? How influential was he during his lifetime? What was his most important achievement?

6. How was Augustine converted to Christianity? How did he explain the collapse of Rome? What conclusions did he draw from it? What was his attitude toward the future of the world and of man? How did he conceive of the relationship of man and God?

7. In what ways did each of the following men reflect the change to learning based on new ideas and Christianity: Cassiodorus, Boethius, Gregory of Tours, Isidore of Seville?

8. What was the Christian attitude toward the temples and other buildings of the Roman Empire? What did a basilica look like? How was the interior of Sant' Apollinare in Classe decorated? Why was it decorated in this manner? What is symbolic art? Give examples of Christian symbolism.

10. Explain the differences between the basilica and central styles of church. What major elements of the central style was borrowed from the Romans? What was specifically Christian?

Understanding the Big Picture

1. What were the general effects of the economic decline of the late Roman era? Why did this decline lead to a largely rural society rather than to an urban one?

2. How were the patristic writers typical of the times in which they lived? How did they combine ideas from the old Roman civilization and from the new emerging civilization?

3. How did the architects of this new civilization react to the legacy of the Roman world? In what ways was their art Roman? In what ways Christian?

For the Thoughtful

1. Do you think that the fall of Rome has been good for Europe in the long run, or do you think that Europe would be generally better off if it had continued under a single government, as in the heyday of the Roman Empire? Support your opinion with specific evidence.

2. How and to what extent do you think economic changes affect political history? Explain your conclusion in terms of the period discussed in this chapter.

3. Undoubtedly the average thoughtful Roman citizen knew much that the average sixth-century European did not know. In your opinion, whose knowledge was the more important and worthwhile? Whose knowledge would be more likely to be valued today?

4. In what ways does art in all its forms reflect economic, political, social, intellectual, and religious thought? Answer this question by drawing on your knowledge of sixth- and twentieth-century art forms.

4

the Byzantine Empire

After Justinian died, the Eastern Roman Empire was no longer able to play a significant role in the history of western Europe. After the sixth century, historians refer to it as the "Byzantine Empire" (after Byzantium, the little Greek town that had originally occupied the site of Constantinople). The new name is significant: it indicates that the tradition of ancient Rome had declined and that the empire that governed the eastern Mediterranean had become more Greek than Roman. With unique characteristics of its own, clearly different from those of ancient Rome and the contemporary Germanic kingdoms, the Byzantine Empire was no longer Roman nor capable of claiming universal leadership.

It is important to remember, however, that Byzantium was never overrun by alien invaders, as the Western Roman Empire had been, and that therefore many Roman traditions were followed without interruption. The Germanic kingdoms were new and short-lived; the Byzantine Empire was old and continuous. To the men of the east, whether Greek, Slav, or Muslim, the Byzantine Empire was *the* Roman Empire.

THE INVADERS OF BYZANTIUM

For centuries after Justinian's death, the Byzantine Empire was attacked by one invader after another. Some of these aggressors managed to seize valuable provinces, but they were never able to take Constantinople or to destroy the empire. Throughout the Middle Ages Byzantium served the weak and disunited little countries of western Europe as a buffer state, protecting them from would-be conquerors from Asia and the Near East.

SLAVS, AVARS, AND BULGARS

Three different alien peoples crossed the Danube River, Byzantium's European boundary, in the sixth and seventh centuries. First came thousands of Slavs, who fled south into the Balkan Peninsula trying to escape the Avars, an Asiatic tribe of professional raiders. The Avars caught up with the Slavs, overran them, and moved on, reaching the gates of Constantinople in 591 before they were finally defeated and thrown back north of the Danube. There they established an empire of their own, which lasted for two centuries. The Slavs remained behind in Byzantine territory, where they retained their own language and customs and so were a constant problem for their Byzantine rulers.

In the seventh century the Bulgars came out of Asia, established their own kingdom south of the Danube, and intermarried with the Slavs who were already there. In the ninth century they conquered much of the Balkan Peninsula and made repeated attacks on Constantinople. But the Byzantines successfully fought off each attack, eventually began to reconquer what they had lost, and finally in the eleventh century brought the Bulgars completely under Byzantine control.

SASSANID PERSIANS AND ARABS

Meanwhile a more dangerous foe, the Sassanid Empire, was attacking the eastern and southern borders of the empire. The Sassanids governed a revival of the ancient Persian Empire that stretched from the Caspian Sea to the desert sands of Arabia. Fanatical Zoroastrians in religion, in the sixth century they began a holy war against Christianity that even Justinian could hardly contain. Early in the seventh century, they invaded Byzantine possessions in the eastern Mediterranean, seized Egypt and Jerusalem, and marched north to take Chalcedon, just across the Bosporus from Constantinople. It took the Byzantine Emperor Heraclius (emperor 610-

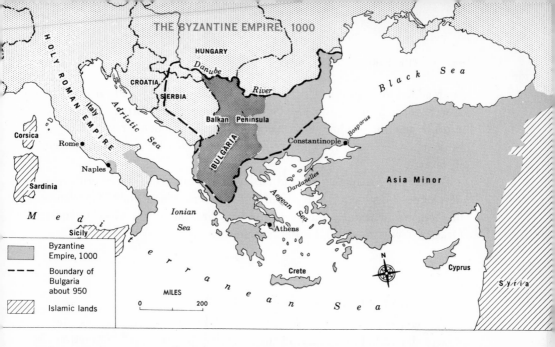

HOLY ROMAN EMPIRE

HUNGARY

Danube

CROATIA

SERBIA

River

Balkan Peninsula

BULGARIA

Black Sea

Bosporus

Constantinople

Adriatic Sea

Corsica

Rome

Naples

Sardinia

M e d

Sicily

Ionian
Sea

Dardanelles

Aegean Sea

Athens

Asia Minor

Cyprus

Syria

Byzantine
Empire, 1000

Boundary of
Bulgaria
about 950

Islamic lands

MILES

0   200

Crete

i   t   e   r   r   a   n   e   a   n   S   e   a

N

641) ten years to marshal an army to counterattack, but in 627 he drove the
Sassanids back to their homeland in the Tigris and Euphrates valley and
destroyed their military power completely.

No sooner had the Byzantines defeated the Sassanids than a new and even
greater threat, the Arab Muslims, galloped out of the Arabian Peninsula.
These successors of Muhammad, founder of the religion and state of Islam
(Chapter 5), conquered Egypt in 642. Before the end of the seventh
century they had overrun all the other Byzantine possessions in North
Africa and the Middle East and gained control of the Mediterranean Sea.
In 717 they even besieged Constantinople, but without success. After an
Islamic revolution in 750 the Byzantines were able to reconquer some of
their lost territories; but they were never able to drive the Muslims from
any of the lands east and south of Asia Minor.

THE RESULTS OF THE INVASIONS

The invasions greatly reduced the size of the Byzantine Empire; but by
so doing they made it more compact and therefore more easily governed.
In the year 1000 the emperor at Constantinople ruled only Asia Minor,
part of the Balkan Peninsula, three provinces in Italy, and some islands in
the eastern Mediterranean. (See map above.) Yet his empire remained a
commercial center with large and prosperous cities strategically located on
the trade routes between Europe and the East. Fertile, highly cultivated

lands added to its prosperity. It also had a well-organized and fairly efficient government. It was probably better off without its former provinces in Europe and the Middle East, which brought it much prestige but little trade and which cost far more to govern and defend than they contributed in taxes.

Byzantium remained rich and strong, a crossroads of the world. It also developed a distinctive way of life of its own, which combined elements of Roman civilization, the Hellenistic civilization of the Greeks, and the Oriental civilizations of the Persians and Muslims.

BYZANTINE GOVERNMENT

The emperor was the absolute ruler of Byzantium—at least as long as he was able to hold his office. In the early days he was usually elected by the senate, the people, or the army, or all three; later it became the custom to allow the son of an emperor to succeed to the throne and then to depose him if he proved to be weak or incompetent. A reigning emperor was considered sacred and appointed by God, and he was revered by his people in much the same way that their pre-Christian ancestors had worshiped the god-kings of ancient days. He lived in an elaborate palace, was surrounded by a lavish court, and took part in one complicated ceremonial after another. In civil government the emperor was supreme, for he both made the laws and enforced them. His power over the church was almost as great; he appointed the patriarch of Constantinople, who acted as head of the church in the east; he called church councils and published their decrees; and in general he directed the activities of the priests.

After Justinian there were half a dozen great Byzantine emperors, and occasionally a dynasty of powerful rulers would reign for a considerable time. But all too often the problem of the succession to the throne was settled by violence and "palace revolutions," in which one faction of the ruling clique would oust the reigning emperor and replace him with another of its own choice. Between 395 and 1453 there were 107 Byzantine emperors, or approximately one every ten years. Of these, only thirty-four died natural deaths while they were still in office; eight were killed in battle or in accidents; all the others were either assassinated or forced to abdicate (surrender their offices) as the result of some sixty-five revolutions. Women often played an important role in these intrigues. One of them, the Empress

Irene, became regent after her husband died, then blinded and imprisoned her son when he tried to take the throne from her. She ruled for five years before she, too, was ousted.

Usually the government's lesser workers were more admirable than the people who headed it. In Constantinople there was a well-organized bureaucracy (organization of lesser officials and clerks) who handled the daily activities of the government. The empire was divided into provinces called "themes," each of which was governed by a military ruler called a "strategos" (general). Despite the power of the emperor, there was considerable self-government in the themes, where the palace intrigues that disrupted the capital seemed far away and unimportant. The loyalty of the people to their government, which seemed fair and stable, was more or less assured. This stability more than made up for the revolutions in the palace and in the army.

🕮 THE BREAK BETWEEN THE ROMAN AND BYZANTINE CHURCHES

As western Europe and the Byzantine Empire became more and more isolated from each other, differences between the Christian religious practices of Rome and Constantinople increased. Romans said their religious services in Latin; the Byzantines used Greek. Roman priests were clean-shaven and were expected not to marry; Byzantine priests were bearded and often married. Roman bishops were supposedly free from secular (political) control; Byzantine patriarchs were considered state officials, and the head of the church in Byzantium, the patriarch of Constantinople, was appointed by the emperor himself. Byzantine emperors bitterly resented the alliances of the popes with Frankish rulers (Chapter 6), whom they considered their inferiors in rank, power, and culture. They also resented, and strongly resisted, the attempts of the popes in distant Rome to regulate a church that in Byzantium was looked upon as a part of the government.

THE ICONOCLASTIC CONTROVERSY, 726-843

During the reign of the Byzantine Emperor Leo III (emperor 714-741), a dispute over theology drove the popes and patriarchs further apart. Leo, a devout but practical man, was worried by two developments in the church: the growing wealth of the monasteries, whose monks, landholders as they were, opposed his efforts to reform the system of landowning; and the increasing veneration of icons (sacred paintings or statues), which he feared would lead to paganism. His efforts to reduce the power of the monks and to rid the church of icons led to a major struggle between the church and state called the "Iconoclastic Controversy."

In 726 Leo ordered the destruction of all icons in the churches and monasteries, and his followers enthusiastically rushed around smashing statues and earning the name "Iconoclasts" (image-breakers). Many monks and priests, eager to defend both their beloved icons and their property rights, opposed the Iconoclasts. The pope, who favored icons, excommunicated Leo, denied him the right to take part in religious services, and declared him and his followers to be heretics.

The struggle over icons that Leo had begun continued for more than a century after his death. It was not until 843 that the Emperor Michael III (emperor 842-867) admitted defeat and allowed the icons to be restored to Byzantine churches. The controversy left the eastern and western Christians more divided than they had been, for most western Europeans had supported the popes, while many Byzantines had supported their emperors.

THE SEPARATION OF THE ORTHODOX
AND CATHOLIC CHURCHES, 1054

During the two centuries after the end of the Iconoclastic Controversy, the Byzantine Empire enjoyed its greatest power and cultural achievement, and its church leaders shared the power and self-confidence of the emperors. At the same time western Europe was divided among weak, poverty-stricken, and often short-lived kingdoms, and church leaders there were frequently occupied in resolving disputes among themselves over matters of faith and church government. Not surprisingly, differences between eastern and western Christians became ever greater.

In 1054 the pope sent a legate (representative) to Constantinople. Largely as a result of political and cultural differences (although supposedly because of a dispute over the nature of the Trinity), the papal legate and the patriarch of Constantinople excommunicated each other. After this event the Roman and Byzantine churches drifted so far apart that their separation was generally taken for granted; and, although it was not so regarded at the time, 1054 later came to be accepted as the definite date of the schism.

After the schism, the church of the Byzantines called itself the Orthodox Church. Reflecting the Greek Byzantine tradition in its language and forms of worship, it was tied closely to the Byzantine government and was headed by the patriarch of Constantinople. The Roman Catholic Church, using the Latin language of ancient Rome and headed by the Roman pope, continued to dominate the religious life of western Europe. Each church considered itself to be the true heir of the pure Christian tradition, catholic in the sense that it included all true Christians and orthodox in the sense that its beliefs truly reflected Christ's teachings. Whatever the merits of the claims of each church, one fact was certain: the Christian Church, like the old Roman Empire, had divided into two different and often hostile parts.

🐚 THE BYZANTINE WAY OF LIFE

The rulers of Byzantium were far more concerned with the prosperity of their people than were the primitive lords of western Europe. They encouraged the immigration of Slavic peasants, so that by the tenth century the provinces around Constantinople, in both Europe and Asia Minor, were heavily populated and covered with prosperous farms. Small, independent farmers were protected by law from the owners of large estates who sought to increase their holdings. The cities were larger and more numerous than those of western Europe and had many more skilled craftsmen. Most crafts were regulated by the government and developed little with the passage of time; but they were stable and prosperous, for Byzantine goods were of such high quality that they were in great demand not only throughout the empire but also in western and Muslim lands. Constantinople became one of the great commercial cities of the world, where foreigners gathered to buy local products and to exchange the goods of much of Europe and Asia.

THE CITY OF CONSTANTINOPLE

Lying in the center of the empire, at the crossroads of two continents, was the city Constantine had built "in obedience to the command of God" beside the harbor of the ancient Greek town of Byzantium. For ten centuries Constantinople was the most beautiful, the most civilized, and the richest city in the world. In the tenth century it was at its height. It had a million inhabitants and was probably the largest city in the world, surpassing ancient Rome and the contemporary Muslim capital at Bagdad in wealth, trade, art, and luxury. It was a cosmopolitan city; most of its inhabitants were Greek or Slavic, but there were substantial numbers of Scandinavians, Russians, Italians, Jews, and Asian and African Muslims. It was a center of trade, religion, and government, with "as many churches as there are days in the year," shops, factories and storehouses, tenements and palaces, built in many styles of east and west and covering the hills that rose behind the harbor.

Constantinople's location was one of its greatest assets. Lying across the trade routes of two continents, it controlled the only practical land route from the Middle East to Europe; and it also controlled the Bosporus, one of the two straits that separate Europe from Asia Minor and control the outlet of the Black Sea. For a harbor it had the Golden Horn, a narrow inlet on the European shore that offers ships a deep, safe, and spacious anchorage. Like Rome, Constantinople was built on seven hills; unlike Rome, it was protected by water on three sides and on the fourth by fortifications that made successful assaults all but impossible.

Justinian's church of Hagia Sophia was only one of many fine churches built on the central plan (see page 42), which the Byzantines followed as long as their empire lasted. They displayed their riches in their buildings; Basil I built his "New Church" in the ninth century, "all adorned," according to a contemporary account, "with fine pearls, gold, shining silver, mosaics, silks and marble in a thousand varieties." Basil's imperial palace, of which the New Church was a part, was filled with masterpieces of art and ingenuity. In his throne room he had a golden tree filled with golden birds, near which were golden griffins and lions. When the ambassador of a foreign state was ushered in, the birds in the tree sang, the griffins stood up, and the lions roared and swished their tails. Bedazzled by this display, several ambassadors reported to their princes that such an emperor was so rich and powerful that it would be foolish to attack him.

In Constantinople, according to a celebrated historian, "For God there was the grand Church of Hagia Sophia, for the Emperor the Sacred Palace, and for the people the Hippodrome." The political power of the common people of Constantinople was greater than even their numbers or prosperity would indicate. The people often formed mobs that overthrew emperors, so the wise ruler saw to it that they were kept satisfied. Many did little work, and none was taxed. All were amused by great shows and athletic contests staged at government expense in the great arena called the Hippodrome. The people joined organizations called the "Greens" and the "Blues" according to the colors worn by the athletes who represented them; riots between the two groups were common and occasionally had political overtones.

Like any great city, Constantinople had a bewildering variety of people; sometimes their only common attribute seemed to be their love of fantastic dress. Rich merchants displayed their wealth on their bodies, adorning themselves with embroidered silken robes, gold, silver, and jewels. Wherever they went, armies of slaves and retainers accompanied them. Some built magnificent houses that rivaled the palaces of the ruling class. No wonder that one medieval visitor wrote that Constantinople contained "two thirds of the world's wealth."

BYZANTINE LEARNING AND ART

The Byzantines, severely restricted by a government that tolerated no political or religious dissent, added little that was new to European ways of life and thought. Yet they made an important contribution to the later development of European civilization; for by carefully preserving the heritage of the past, they made it available for later generations in western

Christ's Entry into Jerusalem: a Byzantine mosaic of the eleventh century, in the monastery of Dafni, Greece. Byzantine mosaics were made by fitting together small pieces (called "tesserae") of jewel-like colored glass or polished stone. In order to catch and reflect light from every direction, the tesserae were fixed on the wall at slightly varying angles, and their edges were purposely left rough. Backgrounds were usually of shimmering gold, and as many as fifty other colors or shades of color might be used in a single mosaic.

Europe to build upon. One of the emperors put together a great library of ancient learning. The university at Constantinople gave scholarships to able students, who studied philosophy, science, mathematics, and theology. Its professors compiled *The Greek Anthology* and wrote histories and books on medicine that combined Oriental and western knowledge and ideas.

The Byzantine civilization was most original in its art. The Iconoclastic Controversy forced artists to turn from religious to secular subjects. Many of them portrayed people in a way that emphasized their physical strength and beauty, much in the tradition of the ancient Greeks. After the end of the controversy, a thriving school of religious art was re-established, which portrayed Christ and his disciples in awesome dignity. Byzantine artists later carried these traditions to western Europe. Byzantine mosaics, which depended for their effect almost entirely upon bright and beautiful colors and in which the figures were symbolic and not realistic at all, were superb. The curved surfaces of the arches and domes of Byzantine buildings "gave depth to rich, dark, gleaming compositions in mosaics, irresistibly potent in their assault upon the senses."

The Byzantines were also outstanding for their lesser arts and handicrafts. They mastered the art of enameling (a method for applying a brilliant finish to metal or earthenware) and were especially skilled at manuscript illumination. (Chapter 6.) Byzantine luxury fabrics—silk, linen, cotton, and wool—were world famous. The government encouraged goldsmiths, gem cutters, and artisans of many other kinds, who flourished in Constantinople and the other cities of the empire.

♢ ♢ ♢

In the five centuries between the fall of Rome and the year 1000, the Byzantine Empire shrank in size but remained one of the strongest states of the Mediterranean region. Its scholars added little to man's knowledge, but they carefully preserved much of the heritage of ancient Greece and Rome. The influence of its artists and architects can be seen in buildings and paintings throughout Europe and North Africa.

Byzantine influence reached far beyond the boundaries of the empire. Russians and other Slavic peoples adopted Orthodox Christianity, an alphabet based on Greek, and Byzantine ideas of government and law. Constantinople was filled with men from all parts of Europe who had come to trade in this great city, which in its heyday was the only important place where the east and the west mingled.

At the same time, Byzantium stood as an impassable barrier between the Sassanid Persians, Asiatic nomads, and Arab imperialists on the one hand and the weak and divided little states of western Europe on the other. Byzantine soldiers bought the time that Europe needed to regain its strength and work out a new way of life of its own.

Even so, western Europeans tended to consider the Byzantines as dangerous enemies who hoped to impose an alien emperor on Germanic kings and the Orthodox religion on the Catholic popes. Far more dangerous enemies to the westerners, however, were the Arab Muslims, who combined political ambition, warlike ferocity, and religious fervor to build—in less than a century—an empire that stretched from Portgual to India.

People, Places, and Terms

Avars	Danube River	icon
Slavs	Balkan Peninsula	excommunication
Bulgars	Asia Minor	schism
Sassanid Persians	Black Sea	Orthodox Church
Muslims	Bosporus	palace revolution
Heraclius	Dardanelles	abdicate
Leo III	Golden Horn	bureaucracy
Michael III		theme
Ignatius	patriarch	strategos
Basil I	Iconoclastic	Hippodrome
	Controversy	

Getting Organized

1. How was the Byzantine Empire endangered by the Avars? The Slavs? The Bulgars? The Sassanid Persians? The Muslims? What happened to each of these groups?
2. How did the invasions affect Byzantine government? Byzantine territorial possessions? Byzantine commerce?
3. How much power did the Byzantine emperors have over the empire? Over the church? How were the emperors chosen and what were the weaknesses of that system? In what ways did local government differ from the central government of the emperors?
4. What differences were there between the Roman Church and the Byzantine Church? What was the Iconoclastic Controversy? When is the schism considered to have taken place? What happened at that time?

5. How did the Byzantine government attempt to foster prosperity? How successful was it?
6. Describe Constantinople in the tenth century. To what extent did its location make it prosperous? How and to what extent did the common people of Constantinople influence their government?
7. What was the principal contribution of Byzantine civilization to later European civilization? In what was Byzantium most original?

Understanding the Big Picture

1. What effect did the invasions have on the development of the Byzantine Empire? Did these invasions help or hinder its development?
2. What long-term developments led to the schism in the Christian Church?
3. How much control did the Byzantine government have over its empire? In what ways was it a good government? What were its weaknesses?

Mastering the Map

Compare the map of the Byzantine Empire in 1000 (page 47) with the map of the Justinian's empire in 565 (page 26). What lands did the Byzantine Empire lose? To whom were they lost? Explain how and from whom the Byzantine Empire protected western Europe. Why could it be said that Constantinople controlled the "crossroads of the world"?

For the Thoughtful

1. What kept the Eastern Roman (Byzantine) Empire from crumbling into little pieces as the Western Roman Empire had?
2. To what extent was the schism in the Christian Church brought about by the earlier political separation of Rome and Constantinople? To what extent did the schism increase differences that already existed? What conclusions might be drawn regarding the influence of political events on religion? Of religion on political events?
3. Byzantine traditions were later to be an important influence in the development of Russia. What evidence of this influence can you find in the Soviet Union of today? What grounds are there for the idea that the origins of the Cold War may be traced as far back as the time of Justinian? Be specific in your answers.
4. Do you consider the legacy of the Byzantine Empire to be as important to the modern world as that of the Western Roman Empire? Explain fully your answer.

⟨⟨⟨ 5
the Rise of
Islam

Three of the world's great religions originated in the arid lands near the eastern shores of the Mediterranean. The oldest, Judaism, was for centuries largely confined to this region. Christianity, the area's second great religion, spread slowly north and west across Europe over the course of several centuries. By contrast, Islam, the youngest of the three, spread west to the Atlantic and east to India in less than a hundred years. Founded early in the seventh century by Muhammad, Islam in the eighth and ninth centuries was not only a religion but also a state—probably the strongest and most aggressive state in the world. At a time when Europe was still trying to dig out from under the wreckage of the Roman Empire and when Byzantium was struggling to protect its endangered boundaries, Islam was dotted with prosperous cities, crisscrossed by busy caravan routes, and led by mighty rulers.

In the tenth century the Islamic empire broke up, and its power rapidly declined; but its scientists, doctors, architects, writers, and craftsmen had created a way of life that Muslims still follow; and, during the brief era when its star was ascendant, it seemed likely to engulf Christendom and dominate the entire western world.

✿ THE ARAB BACKGROUND

By A.D. 600, the Arabs had been inhabiting the arid Arabian Peninsula for centuries, and for uncounted ages their life had remained unchanged. Most were "Bedouins" (desert dwellers), true nomads who followed their herds of horses and camels from place to place in an unending search for water and pasturage, occasionally varying their daily routine by attacking unwary caravans or isolated outposts of the Roman Empire. The Bedouins moved around too much to form permanent governments, instead living in patriarchal (family) groups that were loosely organized into tribes, each of which maintained an uncertain supremacy over the strip of desert through which it wandered. These Bedouins were fiercely independent, handsome, hardy, strong, and warlike. They were famous for their bravery in hit-and-run warfare and proud that they never had been subdued by Roman legions. Their hospitality was lavish, and they had a code of right and wrong that it was death to violate.

A minority of the Arabs, called the "house dwellers," lived in trading towns and seaports in the Hejaz, an area along the Red Sea coast. There were two principal inland towns: Mecca, a center of commerce and religion, and Yathrib, a smaller town 210 miles north of Mecca. Mecca was the site of a small, rudely built, square building called the "Kaaba" (cube), which housed a sacred black stone that the Arabs believed the Angel Gabriel had given to Abraham. Here, as in other cities along the main trade routes from Africa to the Orient, there were considerable numbers of Jews and Judaized Arabs.

In the early Christian era most Arabs practiced a form of star worship that lacked any organized clergy or theology. They believed in one supreme God, called *Allah* in Arabic. Many of the Arabs were familiar with the Hebrew Old Testament and the teachings of Jesus.

By the start of the seventh century, the apparently unchanging course of Arab history was deflected by two unforeseen developments: the climate of the Arabian peninsula became even drier than it had been, and the population rapidly increased. Suddenly the Arabs found they had to seek more land on which to graze their herds. An aggressive Ethiopian state in Africa blocked expansion to the south; but to the north lay the Byzantine and Sassanid empires, both of which were weakened by their centuries of war with each other. (See page 46.) If the Arabs could only unite, they could easily seize all the rich lands that looped from the shores of the eastern Mediterranean around into the valleys of the Tigris and Euphrates.

🐚 THE GROWTH OF ISLAM

The religion Muhammad founded gave the Arabs the unity they needed. Islam forged an empire by combining religion and government in a way that attracted the unquestioning loyalty of a vigorous and warlike people.

Muhammad (570-632) seemed an unlikely person to found a great religion. Born in Mecca, he spent years traveling with caravans but probably never learned to read and write. Eventually he married his employer, a wealthy widow; and, having money and leisure, he was able to devote himself to thinking seriously about religion. He became convinced that the Angel Gabriel had appeared to him in a vision to tell him that he was divinely appointed to become the prophet of God.

Muhammad called himself "the Prophet." He named his religion "Islam" (submission to God) and his followers "Muslims" (people who submit). He accepted many Jewish and Christian teachings, including much of the Old Testament. He believed that Jesus was a great prophet, but not God or the Son of God. Although he made no claim to being himself divine, Muhammad promised eternal bliss to his followers, and he called on them to wage a holy war to spread Islam and establish a Muslim Arab state.

Few people accepted Muhammad's teachings at first, and in 622 his enemies forced him to flee for his life from Mecca to Yathrib. (This flight, which is called the "Hegira," is the event from which Muslims date their calendar.) In Yathrib, Muhammad was more successful: so many of the people accepted his teachings that he renamed the city Medina, "the city of the Prophet," and organized a government and a fanatical army. By 630 Muhammad's army had conquered so much of the Arabian peninsula that he was able to return in triumph to Mecca and force his opponents there to adopt Islam.

Muhammad died two years later. He left the Arabs with a religion that they could fervently support, and he had assembled a group of disciples who were able to successfully carry his work forward.

THE ISLAMIC RELIGION

Muhammad's followers adopted the Islamic confession of faith: "There is no God but Allah, and Muhammad is his Prophet." Muslims do not accept the many gods of the pagans or even the three-in-one God of the Christians, but worship only the one-God, Allah, whom they believe to be all wise, all powerful, and all merciful. They believe Allah to be the God of the Christians and the Jews as well as of the Muslims, and they revere the Biblical prophets and Jesus; but they insist that the last and greatest prophet of all was Muhammad.

During the Prophet's lifetime his disciples copied down his sayings in Arabic free verse and later assembled them into the *Koran*, the Islamic holy book. The *Koran* is filled with poems which testify eloquently to the faith of Islam:

> Praise be to God, Lord of the worlds!
> The compassionate, the merciful!
> King on the day of reckoning!
> Thee *only* do we worship, and to Thee do we cry for help.
> Guide Thou us on the straight path,
> The path of those to whom Thou hast been gracious . . .*

Like Christianity, Islam stresses the immortality of the soul and the certainty of a life after death. The *Koran* refers constantly to the Last Judgment, when the earth will end and the dead will rise to be judged by God. The damned will fall into a fiery furnace, but the saved will rise to the Muslim heaven, a lovely garden watered by gushing springs and shaded by thornless trees under which the faithful can loll to eat the plentiful food and drink the divine liquor of God.

Like Christianity, Islam emphasizes kindness and forgiveness. The *Koran* says:

> The Lord hath not forsaken thee, neither hath He been displeased.
> And surely the future shall be better for thee than the past.
> And in the end shall thy Lord be bounteous to thee
>   and thou be satisfied.
> Did He not find thee an orphan and gave thee a home?
> And found thee erring and guided thee,
> And found thee needy and enriched thee?
> As to the orphan therefore wrong him not;
> As to him that asketh of thee, chide him not away;
> And as for the favors of thy Lord, tell them abroad.*

Islam also includes many Arabian customs. Muhammad allowed polygamy and condoned slavery—even encouraged it, if the slaves were "unbelievers." He forbade drinking wine and eating certain foods. And he required all Muslims who could to make a pilgrimage to Mecca to kiss the sacred black stone in the Kaaba.

* From *The Koran*, translated by J. M. Rodwell (Everyman's Library, New York: Dutton, and London: Dent, 1937).

A group of mounted standard-bearers, trumpeters, and drummers of an Islamic army: a miniature from an Arabic manuscript of the Middle Ages.

Islam is less formal than most of Christianity. It has no organized clergy, no statues or other images, and no elaborate ritual. Instead, Muslims pray by themselves five times each day and publicly on Fridays, the Islamic sabbath. They also fast from sunrise to sunset during one month of each year (called "Ramadan"), and they are expected to give alms regularly.

The Muslims of the seventh century were far more fatalistic and warlike than were the Christians. Muhammad told his followers:

> The sword is the key of heaven and of hell; A drop of blood shed in the cause of God, a night spent in arms, is of more avail than two months of fasting and prayer; whoever falls in battle, his sins are forgiven; at the Day of Judgment his wounds shall be as resplendent as vermilion, and odorous as musk; and the loss of his limbs shall be supplied by the wings of angels and cherubim.

No wonder the Muslims were brave warriors who carried their faith into regions of which Muhammad had not even known.

THE EXPANSION OF ISLAM

Muhammad's disciples created the office of "caliph," or successor of the Prophet, for their leader. The early caliphs set out on a holy war against their neighbors. In little more than a decade after Muhammad's death, Muslim armies had taken Egypt, Palestine, and Syria from the Byzantines, and they had conquered the remnants of the Sassanid Empire. The skilled

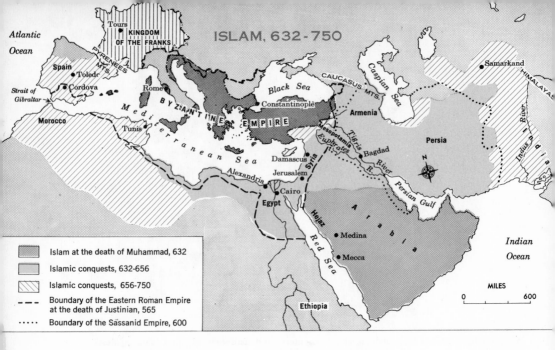

Arabian cavalrymen, fighting with furious religious fervor, were more than a match for the Byzantine and Persian armies, which had exhausted themselves warring against each other. (See page 46.) The native peoples often welcomed the Muslim conquerors warmly, for the Arabs did not murder or loot, they respected the customs of the countryside, and they offered everyone the opportunity to become a Muslim.

In the middle of the seventh century, the so-called "Ommiad" caliphs established a sort of hereditary monarchy, which ruled Islam for almost a century (661-750). From their capital at Damascus in Syria, the Ommiads set out to expand Islam in all directions. In North Africa their armies marched westward from Egypt, capturing Byzantine provinces as they went, and in 711 crossed the Strait of Gibraltar into Spain. By 721 they had conquered the Visigothic kingdom in Spain and were at the Pyrenees, on the boundaries of the Frankish monarchy. They crossed the mountains and marched across the Frankish kingdom, where they were finally defeated by the Frankish leader Charles Martel at the battle of Tours in 733. Only this setback, complicated by a revolt in North Africa, prevented further Muslim expansion into Europe. The later history of Europe might have been quite different if the Franks had lost that battle.

Meanwhile other Islamic forces moved east from Persia, conquering with astonishing ease lands occupied by Turks, Chinese, Tibetans, and Indians. By the eighth century, Islam stretched from the Pyrenees to the Himalayas.

The Ommiad caliphs grew corrupt and extravagant, and in 750 Islam was shaken by a great revolution. The leaders of the revolution, called "Abbassids" because they claimed descent from an uncle of Muhammad named Abbas, massacred all but one of the Ommiads. The surviving Ommiad fled to Spain, where he established himself as caliph. The Abbassid dynasty ruled the rest of Islam for five centuries (750-1258) from their new capital at Bagdad on the Tigris River, far to the east of the original center of Islamic power. The Islamic world was now oriented toward the Middle East; and the Arab threat to Europe, though by no means ended, was much decreased.

Some of the early Abbassids were fabulous monarchs. One of them, Harun al-Rashid (caliph 786-809), was particularly famed for his support of science and art—and as the caliph in the tales of the *Thousand and One Nights*. But powerful as they were, the Abbassids could not effectively govern all of their huge empire, which broke up into a number of semi-independent caliphates and provinces late in the eighth century. By the end of the ninth century the Abbassids, although still rulers of all Islam in theory, actually controlled only the region around their capital at Bagdad. They withdrew behind a facade of pomp and ceremony, protected by hired Turkish soldiers and known to few outside their royal household.

ISLAMIC LIFE

Islam's way of life, like that of Byzantium, was partly the original creation of its thinkers and artists and partly adapted from the traditions of other countries and earlier civilizations. The Arabs borrowed readily from the customs of such conquered countries as Egypt and Persia; and they adopted many Greek traditions that had been preserved by their arch-enemy, the Byzantine Empire. At its best, Arabic civilization was cosmopolitan, with major centers in Spain, North Africa, and the Middle East as well as in the capital city of Bagdad. Each center had its own distinctive flavor, although all were united by common bonds, not only of religion but also of the Arabic language, which was the language of learning, government, and commerce throughout Islam.

ISLAMIC LITERATURE, LEARNING, AND SCIENCE

Literature flourished. *A Thousand and One Nights* is only one of many great Arabic literary achievements. There were many historians, one of whom, al-Masudi (d. 956) wrote a comprehensive history of the world in thirty volumes. Arabic theologians created a large body of religious literature based upon the *Sunnah,* stories about the Prophet told by his early followers.

The Hellenistic learning of ancient Greece was introduced to Islam during the Abbassid dynasty. Some of the principal Greek schools, such as the one at Alexandria, were taken over by Arab conquerors. Whole regiments of scholars at Bagdad devoted their lives to translating the classical Greek writers into Arabic. There were huge libraries in which Islamic savants collected books in Greek, Arabic, and the languages of India and China; the one at Alexandria was the largest in the world. The scholar al-Kindi wrote an estimated 265 volumes in an attempt to unite Greek and Arab philosophy and learning into a single body of knowledge.

The Arabs were far ahead of contemporary Christian scholars in practical science and mathematics. Arab pharmacists had to take a prescribed course of study, and Arab doctors wrote medical encyclopedias. Arab astronomers developed the astrolabe, a forerunner of the modern sextant, which made it possible to navigate ships accurately out of sight of land. The mathematician al-Khwarizmi (780-?850) wrote the first known textbook on arithmetic and gave algebra its name. Omar Khayyám (d. 1123), a Persian best known as the poet who wrote the *Rubáiyát,* was also a mathematician; he introduced an accurate calendar and developed a system of algebra that was the forerunner of modern analytical geometry.

Preparing medicine from honey: an illustration from a thirteenth-century Arabic translation of a Greek treatise on medicines. Arab physicians not only preserved the medical knowledge of the ancient Greeks but also made important additions to it. Some of their writings on medicine became standard reference works throughout Europe and Asia.

The Court of the Lions in the Alhambra, a palace in Granada, Spain, built by the Moors (the Muslim conquerors of Spain) in the thirteenth and fourteenth centuries. The Alhambra is extremely plain on the outside, but its interior is lavishly decorated. Arched doorways such as this lead from the courtyards, of which there are several, into rooms whose walls are covered with colored tile, ornamental plasterwork, and Arabic poetic inscriptions. Most of the rooms and courtyards have fountains, from which the water flows in open channels.

ISLAMIC ARCHITECTURE

Arabic mosques, which were centers of worship, government, and trade, made use of ideas from a wide variety of sources in a distinctively Arabic way. They were laid out on a floor plan derived from the central style used in such Christian churches as the Hagia Sophia. (See page 42.) Distinctively Arabic touches were the minarets, tall, slender towers with balconies from which the people were called to worship; the onion-like shape of the domes; and the arcades of gracefully curved horseshoe-shaped arches. Some of these elements were used in the lavish palaces that caliphs and merchant princes built in the principal cities of Islam. Among the many early Islamic buildings that still survive are the huge mosque of Omar in Jerusalem and the magnificent Alhambra palace in Spain. Today the influence of Islamic architecture can be seen in almost every tropical city, for Arabic buildings were efficiently ventilated and admirably adapted to hot climates.

ARAB COMMERCE

The Germanic peoples all but wiped out the trade of the regions of Europe that they conquered. In contrast, the Arabs preserved, and at first increased, the commerce of the vast territories that they absorbed into Islam. Since there was no more trade with Europe, they opened new routes to the Far East. Their ships dominated the Mediterranean. The Muslims were the most advanced navigators of their time, using the astrolabe and the compass, which they imported from China, to make the first long voyages out of sight of land. They developed the triangular "lateen" sails, which enabled them to tack ships into the wind. After they had defeated the Byzantine fleet in 655, the Mediterranean became a Muslim lake, and the trade of Islam rapidly increased.

Arabic products became the standard of excellence for the world. Their textiles were especially fine, as our modern vocabulary attests. Damask is patterned after a luxurious cloth first made in Damascus. Our words *cotton*, *satin*, and *muslin* are all derived from Arabic, as are *scarlet*, *lilac*, *crimson*, and *saffron*, which take their names from Arabic dyes. The world's finest leather was tanned in Morocco, the best steel was forged in Damascus and Toledo, and the richest rugs and tapestries came from Persia.

THE DECLINE OF THE ISLAMIC EMPIRE

As Islam became rich and powerful, the religious fervor that had been the source of its strength gradually declined, and a variety of discords developed among the Muslims. By the end of the tenth century Islam had broken up into three caliphates, and political unity was never regained. In the principal capital of Bagdad were the Abbassids, supreme in theory but actually controlling only the nearby provinces in the Middle East. The Fatimid caliphs, who were descended from Muhammad's daughter Fatima, ruled most of North Africa from their capital in Cairo. The Abbassids were never recognized in Spain, where the only branch of the Ommiad dynasty to survive the revolution of 750 made its capital at Cordova. Even these three caliphates could not hold together. Each soon broke up into smaller states; the caliphs gradually lost their political authority, retaining only spiritual influence.

The religion of Muhammad survived the political decline of the Islamic empire, remaining as the only bond that held together the many racial and cultural groups of Islam. The Muslims rarely tried to force their faith on their conquered peoples, nor did they persecute those who disagreed with them. However, most of the people under Arabic domination willingly adopted Islam, for Muslims had political and financial rights that were denied to unbelievers.

Although the Arabs were prosperous for a time, their commerce did not expand over the years, and gradually it became stagnant. Much of the territory of Islam was not only arid but also lacked both rich soil for farming and raw materials for industry. Once the political power of the empire declined, it was difficult to expand, or even to continue, the once productive caravan routes to the Far East. The distrust of Christians and Muslims for each other made trade with Europe all but impossible. Consequently, Arabic commerce and industry stopped growing.

♣ ♣ ♣

The Muslims made many important contributions to history. They deserve to be remembered not only for their huge empire but also for their advanced science and learning. But their most lasting contribution was the religion of Islam, which alone among their institutions prospered during the decline of the Arab state and today claims some 430,000,000 adherents.

People, Places, and Terms

Muhammad	Morocco	Kaaba
Charles Martel	Strait of Gibraltar	Allah
al-Masudi	Pyrenees	Muslim
al-Kindi	Tours	Hegira
al-Khwarizmi	Himalayas	*Koran*
Harun al-Rashid	Bagdad	Last Judgment
Omar Khayyám	Alexandria	polygamy
	Cairo	caliph
Arabia	Cordova	Ommiad caliphate
Hejaz		Abbassid caliphate
Red Sea	Bedouin	*A Thousand and*
Mecca	Islam	*One Nights*
Medina	house dwellers	*Sunnah*
Damascus		

Getting Organized

1. Who were the Bedouins? Where did they live? How did they make a living? What was their religion? What two developments changed the course of Arabian history? Why?
2. Who was Muhammad? How and why did he become the prophet of a new religious faith? How did his new religion view Judaism and Christianity?

3. Did the Arabs accept Muhammad's faith quickly? How did Muhammad spread his new faith?
4. What do Muslims believe to be the nature of God? What is the *Koran?* What is the Islamic view of life after death? Of everyday morality? What was the administration of the Islamic religion? What is the Islamic view of warfare?
5. How did Islam spread after Muhammad's death? Why were the Muslims able to conquer their neighbors? How far did the Ommiad caliphate extend the Islamic empire? What was the importance of Charles Martel's victory?
6. Who were the Abbassids? When and how did they come to power? What characterized the Abbassid caliphate?
7. In what ways was the Arabic civilization cosmopolitan? What elements united their civilization? How original and advanced was their literature? Their science and mathematics? Their architecture?
8. Why was the wide use of the Arabic language important? In what ways did Arabic products influence the rest of the world?
9. In the tenth century what was the state of Arabic political, religious, and commercial developments? Which of these aspects of the Arab civilization was the longest lasting?

Understanding the Big Picture

1. What were the conditions of the Arab world prior to Muhammad's rise? In what ways did Islam help the Arabs to create an important civilization? Why did Islam spread so quickly?
2. Compare Muhammad's role in the rise of Islam to Jesus's role in the rise of Christianity. What are the major differences between Islam and Christianity? Did Islam borrow anything from Judaism?

Mastering the Map

Study the map of Islam on page 62. When did this empire grow the most? How could it spread so quickly? What were the chief geographical obstacles to its growth? What was the geographical relationship of this empire to western Europe and the Byzantine Empire?

For the Thoughtful

1. Why did the Islamic religion spread so much faster than Christianity? Would you say that Islam is a less spiritual religion than Christianity, that it emphasizes "earthly" things more than Christianity? Why?
2. Did Muhammad change Arabian history by himself, or would the Arabs have spread just as far and fast without him? What conclusions might one draw regarding the importance of great men to history?

6

the Age of Charlemagne
and the End of the
Early Middle Ages

By the end of the ninth century, the Early Middle Age was coming to an end. Its last and best-known part is called the Age of Charlemagne. Early in the ninth century Charlemagne united most of western Europe under Frankish rule, cementing his state together by combining Germanic customs, the remnants of the western Roman tradition, and the Christian church. But because Charlemagne's empire was largely held together by his wisdom and strength of character, his state did not long outlive him. By the middle of the ninth century the Frankish Empire had been destroyed by a series of poor rulers, just as a wave of new invasions by Viking, Hungarian, and Muslim warriors beset disturbed Europe. But Charlemagne lived on as a legend that inspired almost every ambitious monarch of the Middle Ages, to whom the myth of Charlemagne and his empire was as important as the reality.

THE GROWTH OF THE FRANKISH EMPIRE

Charlemagne's Frankish Empire descended from the kingdom that Clovis had built in the fifth century. (See pages 19-21.) Although after the time of Clovis the Frankish state was poor and weak, it was nonetheless stronger than its neighbors. It remained more or less intact for three centuries, eventually gained strength, and finally came to dominate western Europe.

THE MEROVINGIAN KINGS

Descendants of Clovis, called "Merovingians" because Clovis was descended from a warrior named Merowech, ruled France until 751. They ignored the Roman traditions so dear to Clovis's heart and were little more than barbarian chieftains, surrounding themselves with a Frankish version of the *comitatus* (see page 18) and devoting themselves to petty struggles for land and power. After a few generations they became so unimportant that they are justly called the *Rois Fainéants*, the "do-nothing kings."

The Frankish state grew poorer and poorer. Roads went unrepaired, and towns were mere clusters of hovels surrounding the court of a noble or the cathedral of a bishop. What had once been prosperous Roman Gaul became a region of isolated and poverty-stricken estates, ruled by bishops or lords and populated by peasants who scratched a bare living from the soil.

But the church grew rich from gifts by the pious and by those who were too weak to protect their own lands (and therefore turned them over to the church for safekeeping, remaining as tenants). Thus the bishops became great landlords. In the wealthy monasteries the monks often ignored their traditional rules, forgot their learning, and made little effort to improve themselves or their country. There were few schools, and many of the clergy never learned to read and write.

THE MAYORS OF THE PALACE

The Frankish kingdom became divided into three large, partially self-governing duchies. When the Merovingian kings ceased to rule in the seventh century, the real power of the royal government fell into the hands of a sort of prime minister called the *major domus*, "mayor of the palace," who was often duke of one of the duchies as well. Late in the century Duke Pepin II seized two of the duchies, became mayor of the palace, and enlarged his title to *dux et princeps Frankorum*, "leader and prince of the Franks." He was now more than just an official of the king, he was a hereditary ruler himself.

Pepin's son, Charles Martel ("the Hammer"), who was *major domus* from 714 to 741, laid the groundwork on which his descendants built the great Frankish Empire. He created an army of mounted warriors like Justinian's *cataphracti* (see page 27) called *vassi dominici,* "vassals of the lord," to whom he granted large estates in return for their promise of faithful service. These powerful cavalrymen defeated the Muslims at the battle of Tours in 733 (see page 62) and extended Charles's authority in Germany and south-western France.

Charles's son, Pepin III (*major domus* 741-768) called Pepin "the Short," continued the expansion of the Frankish kingdom by conquering the Frisians on the shores of the North Sea and driving the last of the Muslims back across the Pyrenees. Even more important, he established a partnership with the popes. The popes were quarreling with the Byzantine emperors and were endangered by a Germanic tribe called the Lombards, who had marched south and besieged Rome. In 751 the pope gave Pepin permission to depose the last of the do-nothing kings and to take the title of king for himself. In return, Pepin and his *vassi dominici* marched into Italy, conquered the Lombards, and presented the keys of the Lombards' cities to the pope. This gift, called the "Donation of Pepin," was the basis upon which the popes for centuries claimed temporal (political) control of central Italy.

THE REIGN OF CHARLEMAGNE

Pepin's son was Charlemagne (ruled 768-814), whose name means "Charles the Great." He looked every inch an emperor. He was a general who preferred peace. He was a harsh enemy but a good and kind friend. He was a great ruler who found time to be a good father to his children. And he so dominated Europe that his era is called the "Age of Charlemagne."

Charlemagne's Conquests. Charlemagne conducted fifty-three separate campaigns in pursuit of his chief goal, which was to unite all the Germanic tribes into a single Christian state. He conquered the Lombards and thus brought all of northern Italy into his empire. He subdued the tribes between the Rhine and the Elbe and gave them the choice between Christianity and death—and one afternoon executed 4,500 people. Moving eastward, his armies captured Bavaria and drove the Avars (see page 46) from the upper Danube valley. In Spain he cheerfully fought both the Muslim Arabs and the Christian Basques and carved out a province for himself called the "Spanish March." Before he died, he controlled western Europe from the Pyrenees to the Carpathians and from the Baltic Sea to the Mediterranean.

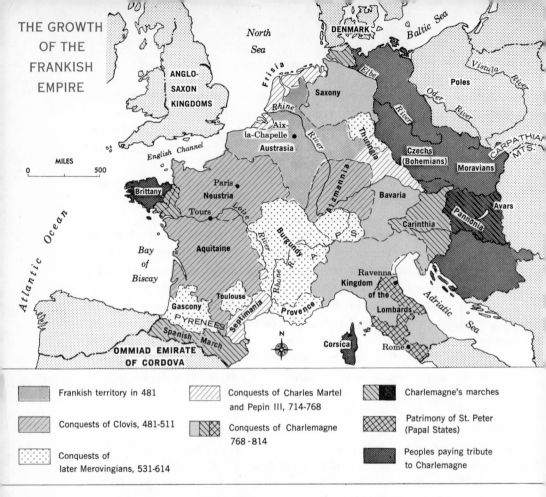

THE GROWTH
OF THE
FRANKISH
EMPIRE

North
Sea

DENMARK

Baltic Sea

ANGLO-
SAXON
KINGDOMS

Frisia

Rhine
River

Elbe

Vistula River

Poles

Saxony

Oder River

Aix-
la-Chapelle

Rhine

Thuringia

Czechs
(Bohemians)

Moravians

CARPATHIAN MTS.

Austrasia

Paris

Neustria

Tours

Alamannia

Bavaria

Avars

Carinthia

Pannonia

MILES
0   500

English Channel

Brittany

Atlantic Ocean

Bay
of
Biscay

Aquitaine

Loire River

Burgundy

Saône R.

Rhone R.

Provence

Ravenna

Kingdom
of the
Lombards

Adriatic Sea

Gascony

Toulouse

Septimania

PYRENEES

Spanish March

OMMIAD EMIRATE
OF CORDOVA

N

Corsica

Rome

Patrimony of St. Peter

Legend:

- Frankish territory in 481
- Conquests of Clovis, 481-511
- Conquests of later Merovingians, 531-614
- Conquests of Charles Martel and Pepin III, 714-768
- Conquests of Charlemagne 768-814
- Charlemagne's marches
- Patrimony of St. Peter (Papal States)
- Peoples paying tribute to Charlemagne

Charlemagne's Government. By establishing a hierarchy of landholders
from whom he required strict obedience and military service, Charlemagne
established a highly organized and effective government that rivaled the
power of Byzantium. He left local government to the *vassi dominici*, but
grouped their little territories into units called "counties," each of which
was jointly governed by a bishop or archbishop and a "count" (Latin
comes, companion of the king). The counties near the frontier, called
"marches," had special military rulers called "margraves" (counts of the
marches). From his capital at Aix-la-Chapelle (modern Aachen, in western
Germany), Charlemagne sent out messengers called *missi dominici* to
supervise the counts and margraves and to punish those who misbehaved.

Everyone was expected to obey Charlemagne's "capitularies," or laws.
These laws restated the old Germanic customs of the wergild and trial

by ordeal. (See page 23.) But they also illustrated the increasing influence of Christianity; for, as one of them said, "every man should seek to the best of his strength and ability to serve God and walk in the way of His precepts."

Charlemagne and the Church. Charlemagne was a pious man and a generous patron of the church, to which he bequeathed two thirds of his personal possessions. He put great pressure on the clergy to reform their morals, improve their educations, and better serve the people. He allowed bishops to try cases involving religious issues in their own courts, and he appointed some of them to high government offices. On the other hand, he

Charlemagne, as he probably appeared about the time of his coronation by the pope in 800. This small bronze statue is believed to be an authentic likeness of the emperor. The ball in his left hand is the imperial orb, a symbol of his power as emperor.

did not hesitate to use the church for his own purposes, expecting the bishops to contribute toward the cost of his military campaigns and to support his attempts to increase the power of the central government.

Like Pepin, Charlemagne allied himself closely with the popes. When Leo III was driven from his papal throne in Rome by a mob in 799, Charlemagne marched into the Eternal City and restored the pope to office. On Christmas Day, 800, while Charlemagne was worshiping in Saint Peter's Basilica, the great church of Rome, Leo displayed his gratitude by setting a jeweled crown on Charlemagne's head as the crowd chanted the ancient Roman ritual, "Hail to Charles the Augustus, crowned the great and peace-bringing Emperor of the Romans." The Frankish king was now a Roman emperor with all the power of the church behind him.

In theory Charlemagne's coronation made him the first Germanic ruler to attain equal status with the Byzantine emperor in Constantinople. In fact, it was a further step in the break between the East and the West, for no Byzantine emperor would recognize a Frankish king as his equal. The supremacy of the Frankish state also speeded the Germanization of western Europe, thereby increasing the cultural differences between Europe and Byzantium and hastening the separation of the church into Greek and Latin branches. (See pages 49-51.)

In other ways Charlemagne's coronation by the pope affected the history of Europe for a thousand years. The fact that Charlemagne was crowned by the pope gave him and his successors a claim to spiritual authority; the fact that the pope crowned the emperor gave the papacy a claim to temporal power. The overlapping claims of popes and emperors were to lead to centuries of struggle between church and state.

Charlemagne's coronation was the climax of his forty-six-year reign. Under him the church and state worked hand in hand to weld Europe into a single spiritual and secular empire that would be a worthy rival to the Byzantine Empire and to Islam.

☙ EUROPE IN THE AGE OF CHARLEMAGNE

The political unity that Charlemagne imposed on western Europe did not make Europe notably more prosperous. The emperor was, however, somewhat more successful in his efforts to encourage a revival of learning and art.

THE ECONOMY OF NINTH-CENTURY EUROPE

Charlemagne ordered the roads and bridges of Europe repaired, but very few people passed over them. The Muslims had cut off most trade with the east, and they controlled the Mediterranean to the extent that, as one Muslim boasted, "The Christians could no longer float a plank upon the sea." There was so little demand for money that Charlemagne's government coined only silver pennies. The cities, ruled by bishops who thought only of the church or nobles who thought only of war, grew smaller than ever. What little trade there was between different provinces was mostly conducted by merchants from the Mediterranean basin.

Charlemagne unwittingly changed the nature of landholding. When Clovis had distributed estates among his followers, he had hoped that the new owners would spend their time cultivating their lands. Charlemagne, on the other hand, required his landowners to serve as warriors, and they therefore thought of their estates primarily as a source of income to pay military expenses. This kind of thinking, which led the lords to ignore the management of their estates, hindered the improvement of agriculture and doomed the masses of peasants to centuries of poverty.

THE CAROLINGIAN RENAISSANCE

Charlemagne used much of his income to establish centers of learning. The result of his efforts is called the "Carolingian Renaissance" (*Carolingian* is derived from Charlemagne's name in Latin, *Carolus Magnus; renaissance* is French for "rebirth.") Charlemagne attracted the most famous scholars of his day to his court, and he employed the greatest of them all, the Englishman Alcuin of York (735-804), to establish a palace school, where the middle-aged emperor and his family studied Latin, astronomy, and rhetoric.

Alcuin became abbot (head of a monastery) at Tours in 796. There he established a "scriptorium," a sort of medieval publishing house in which the monks copied by hand Jerome's Vulgate Bible and the works of the classical authors and the Fathers of the Church. These ninth-century monks not only made many of the most accurate surviving copies of ancient texts but also introduced two new developments in bookmaking. The first, the technique of "illuminating," was the first European book illustration; artists beautified the pages of their manuscripts by elaborately decorating the first letters of paragraphs and by filling the margins with intricate designs and tiny illustrations based on the text. The second, the "Carolingian minuscule," was probably the first form of handwriting to use both capitals and small letters.

In 787 Charlemagne issued a capitulary accusing the clergy of "uncouth language" and "unlettered tongues" and asking monasteries and cathedrals to establish schools for priests and laymen. One bishop set up a school in every parish of his diocese, and the major monasteries welcomed students who wanted to study grammar, music, and arithmetic as well as theology and the classics. Many regions still lacked schools, and many of the ones established in the first flush of enthusiasm soon died; but others survived, and some are the origins of Europe's major universities.

The Frankish buildings of Charlemagne's time display the influence of Italian and Byzantine architecture. Charlemagne's church at Aix-la-Chapelle, for example, was built on a central plan like the Hagia Sophia in Constantinople, had walls that were decorated with mosaics by Byzantine artists, and contained columns imported from Rome and Ravenna.

The Carolingian Renaissance produced little good literature except a famous biography of Charlemagne written by his secretary, a monk named Einhard. Certainly Charlemagne's renaissance pales by comparison to the Italian Renaissance of the fifteenth century. (Chapter 19.) Yet it did make important contributions of its own by helping preserve the traditions of ancient learning and by establishing schools that maintained this tradition until later generations could build more solidly upon it.

🐾 THE COLLAPSE
OF CHARLEMAGNE'S EMPIRE

Charlemagne's empire began to disintegrate immediately after he died, and a generation later it was only a memory. Its success had been based upon the forcefulness and wisdom of its ruler, and his successors simply could not control the vast area—or each other.

Charlemagne had made military chieftains of the ruling lords, and they were only too eager to use their power for themselves rather than for a distant king. After Charlemagne was dead, the different parts of Europe had little to bind them together. There was no trade to speak of; language varied from province to province; and the church, the only institution to which all men pledged loyalty, was not politically strong enough to improve matters much.

The names by which we identify Charlemagne's descendants suggest that they inherited little of his genius. Men called Louis the Pious, Louis the

ANGLO-
SAXON
KINGDOMS

DENMARK

Saxony

Elbe River

Frisia

Rhine River

Aix-la-
Chapelle

Thurin-
gia

Bohemia

Moravia

Lotharingia

Franconia

Verdun

Paris

Francia

Danube

Austria

River

Brittany

Alsace

Swabia

Bavaria

Loire

Fontenoy

R.

N

Burgundy

Carinthia

Aquitaine

R.

Lombardy

Croatia

Rhone

Septimania

Gascony

Provence

Tuscany

OMMIAD EMIRATE
OF CORDOVA

MILES

0   150

Corsica

Rome

Stammerer, Charles the Bald, Charles the Fat, and Charles the Simple had
not the ability to win the loyalties of men. Charlemagne's only son, Louis
the Pious (emperor 814-840) was modest and gentle to a fault, and he
could not govern his own children. Following a Frankish custom, Louis
divided his empire during his lifetime among his four sons. These youths
quarreled with their father and among themselves, actually defeating poor
Louis in battle and imprisoning him for a time in a monastery. After his
death, the three who survived him immediately went to war with each
other and met at the great battle of Fontenoy in 841. None of the sons was
the winner, and the unity of the Frankish Empire was utterly destroyed.
Two years later, in 843, the three brothers signed the Treaty of Verdun,
which formally partitioned Charlemagne's empire into three kingdoms. The
western kingdom, the ancestor of modern France, went to Charles the Bald.
The eastern kingdom, ancestor of modern Germany, was assigned to Louis
the German. The now empty title of emperor, the Italian possessions, and a
long, string-bean-shaped strip of territory stretching along the west bank of
the Rhine from the Alps to the North Sea went to the eldest son, Lothaire.
The strip of land has been known successively as Lotharii Regnum, Lotharingia, and Lorraine, and the French and Germans have fought over it for
more than a thousand years.

Any sense of unity that Charlemagne had created was only a memory by the middle of the ninth century. To add to the growing confusion, Europe was at this time subjected to a second wave of invasions, which threatened to be as destructive as the first.

✥ THE SECOND WAVE OF INVASIONS

Just as the first wave of barbarian invasions had hastened the fall of the Western Roman Empire, a second wave of invasions speeded the final collapse of the Frankish state.

THE VIKINGS

Nearly all of our information about the Vikings comes from their "sagas" —long, heroic narrative poems that are half fact and half fancy—so we do not know for certain why they suddenly ventured forth from their homes in the Scandinavian peninsula to raid, pillage, and plunder the countryside of Europe. Perhaps the population had suddenly increased; perhaps a drought had affected their crops. Whatever the reason, piracy and plundering became their principal source of livelihood. From the ninth to the eleventh century they sallied out of their fiords in small war parties led by their *jarls* (similar to the Anglo-Saxon eorls). They sailed into the harbors of Europe, waded ashore to raid castles and villages, destroyed for the love of it, looted until they could carry no more, and finally retired to their ships to go home again, to feast and boast of their deeds.

Europeans gave them many names—Northmen, Norsemen, Normans, Norwegians, Danes—but they were all Vikings. One group of Vikings sailed east across the Baltic Sea and, following the rivers, worked its way south to the Black Sea. They settled in the east Slavic region around Novgorod, conquered the inhabitants, and established a kingdom with a capital at Kiev. From there they assailed the Byzantine Empire. Reaching the walls of Constantinople in 865 and again in 907, they demanded and received tribute. This group of Vikings came to be called "Rhos" or "Rus"; the Slavic peoples with whom they intermarried became the Russians.

Other groups went westward. Some sailed north of the British Isles, through the Shetland Islands to Iceland, where they established a kingdom about 850. Some adventurers went on to Greenland; and one, named Leif Ericson, sailed on to North America, which he called "Vinland." The remains of a Norse settlement, possibly Leif Ericson's Vinland, were recently discovered in Newfoundland.

Other Vikings went toward western Europe. Around 850 a Norse kingdom was established in Ireland, and soon afterward Vikings from Denmark subdued some of the Anglo-Saxon kingdoms in England and established a province called the "Danelaw." Only Alfred the Great (see page 22) was able to hold out against them. No part of the Atlantic coast of Europe was spared from Viking attacks. By 859 they had rounded Gibraltar and sailed on into the Mediterranean. The remains of the Carolingian empire suffered particularly. The first raids had been made during the reign of Charlemagne, but it was not until after the death of Louis the Pious in 840 that they grew into expeditions of thousands of warriors in hundreds of tiny ships. We know of forty-seven separate expeditions against France in the ninth and tenth centuries alone. Paris was pillaged in 856, pillaged again in 861, and burned in 865. Twenty years later it survived a thirteen-month seige, which was lifted only when the king of the moment, Charles the Fat, bought off the attackers with 700 pounds of silver and permission to pillage Burgundy. Not a major center in France was spared. In 909 a church meeting reported:

> The cities are depopulated, the monasteries ruined and burned, the country reduced to solitude . . . As the first men lived without law . . . so now every man does what seems good in his own eyes, despising laws human and divine . . . the strong oppress the weak; the world is full of violence against the poor, and of the plunder of ecclesiastical goods . . . men devour one another like fish in the sea.

That same year, in an effort to divert the attackers, the Frankish king Charles the Simple conceded to a Norman chieftain named Rollo the lands along the northern shore of France, an area ever since called Normandy. Like other Vikings everywhere, the Normans quickly adopted the culture of their conquered territories and became Christians, and they even paid at least lip service to the idea of a Frankish monarchy. Later one of the Norman dukes, William the Conquerer by name, carried many Frankish customs with him to England. (Chapter 13.)

THE SARACENS AND THE MAGYARS

Throughout the ninth century the Saracens, as the Europeans called the Muslims, attacked Italy and the islands of the Mediterranean from their

North African base at Tunis. For many years it seemed entirely possible that Italy would become another Muslim state; in 846 Saracen pirates actually looted and burned the Basilica of Saint Peter, just outside Rome, and later they destroyed Saint Benedict's monastery at Monte Cassino. Muslims swept the Byzantine fleet from the sea, captured Crete, and subdued Sicily. Christian commerce in the Mediterranean practically disappeared. Christians did not regain control of the Mediterranean until the eleventh century.

In eastern Europe a horde of Asiatic nomads left their native haunts east of the Caspian, circled north of the Black Sea, and about the year 900 descended on Europe. They called themselves Magyars; but the Europeans, reminded of the Asiatic Huns who had devastated Europe in the fifth century, called them Hungarians. Certainly they inherited all the savagery and destructiveness of their Asiatic predecessors. They drove the Slavs from the broad plains north of the Danube and occupied the territory that ever since has been called Hungary. Then they struck northward to Poland, westward to northern Italy and Bavaria, and from there north toward Saxony and the Rhine valley. By 942 they had also gone far enough south and east to force Constantinople to pay them tribute. They were not brought under control until the first of the Holy Roman emperors, Otto the Great of Saxony, defeated them at the battle of the Lechfeld in 955.

Surprisingly, the Magyars were subdued by this defeat. They settled down to an agricultural life in Hungary, where they learned Christianity from the Slavic natives. By 1001 they were fully converted, and the pope anointed their leader, Stephen (king 997-1038), as a Christian king. The modern Hungarian language is of Asiatic origin, a heritage from these early conquerors.

LOCAL GOVERNMENT AND THE CHURCH IN THE TENTH CENTURY

The collapse of the Frankish Empire and the devastation brought by the later invasions brought renewed chaos to Europe. Yet there were two important developments that, although they emerged only gradually, were by the end of the tenth century promising better times for the future. Local governments assumed much of the authority that Charlemagne had once commanded; and missionaries in northern and eastern Europe carried Roman and Byzantine ideas of religion and government to peoples who had previously known little except barbarism.

GOVERNMENT BY LOCAL LORDS

Whenever strong central governments become weak, local leaders usually eagerly seize power for themselves. Charlemagne had made each man choose a master, the lesser lords serving the greater, and had made only the principal bishops, dukes, counts, and margraves pay allegiance directly to him. When his successors proved to be weak, these principal lords became independent in all but name; yet they continued to require their own subordinates (called "vassals") to serve them as before. Consequently, although the kings and emperors still wore their crowns, the real units of government were the local duchies and counties controlled by warlike and energetic dukes and counts.

THE SPREAD OF CHRISTENDOM

As the political control of Europe passed from the kings to the lords in tenth-century Europe, so the control of the church passed from the popes to the bishops. A series of weak popes could not enforce their authority over the bishops who, far from Rome, could govern their dioceses much as they pleased. The bishops were aided by "canons" (cathedral clergy), who developed over the years an elaborate system of church or "canon" law. Other priests went out into the countryside to establish parishes in the little villages, whose inhabitants previously had had to travel to the cathedral towns to worship or to wait for traveling priests to visit their homes.

Meanwhile missionaries introduced Catholicism to vast areas of northern and eastern Europe. They converted the kings of Denmark, Sweden, and Norway in the tenth century, and the Scandinavian peoples soon forgot their old Norse gods and became Catholics. The ruler of Bohemia, Boleslav II (duke 967-999) also became a Catholic in the tenth century and encouraged missionaries to establish a bishopric at Prague, the Bohemian capital. (An earlier Bohemian convert had been the martyred "good King Wenceslas" of Christmas carol fame.) From Prague, other missionaries went out to convert the Slavic peoples in Poland. Hungary also joined the Catholic fold as the century ended. (Above, page 80.)

Greek Christian missionaries from Byzantium competed vigorously with the Catholics in eastern Europe. In the ninth century Cyril, the "Apostle of the Slavs," and his brother Methodius, both of whom had been educated in Constantinople, won many followers in eastern and central Europe. They translated the Bible and the hymns and ceremonies of the Greek Church into the Slavic languages, using a new alphabet that,

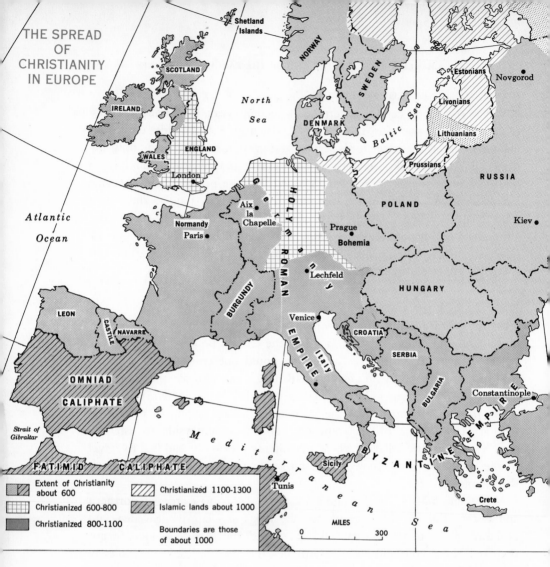

North
Sea

Atlantic
Ocean

Baltic Sea

Shetland
Islands

NORWAY

SWEDEN

DENMARK

SCOTLAND

IRELAND

ENGLAND

WALES

London

Estonians

Novgorod

Livonians

Lithuanians

Prussians

RUSSIA

POLAND

Kiev

Aix
la
Chapelle

Normandy

Paris

Prague

Bohemia

Lechfeld

HUNGARY

BURGUNDY

LEON

CASTILE

NAVARRE

Venice

CROATIA

SERBIA

OMNIAD

CALIPHATE

Strait of
Gibraltar

Mediterranean Sea

BULGARIA

Constantinople

BYZANTINE EMPIRE

FATIMID   CALIPHATE

Tunis

Sicily

Crete

MILES

0   300

Extent of Christianity
about 600

Christianized 600-800

Christianized 800-1100

Christianized 1100-1300

Islamic lands about 1000

Boundaries are those
of about 1000

according to tradition, was invented by Cyril. (It is still called the "Cyrillic" alphabet and is still used in writing several Slavic languages, most notably Russian.) Toward the end of the tenth century the principal Russian monarch, Vladimir of Kiev (reigned 980-1015), married the daughter of a Byzantine emperor and encouraged Byzantine missionaries to convert his Slavic subjects, who soon became Orthodox Christians and accepted the leadership of the patriarchs of Constantinople.

As a result of missionary activity, eastern Europe became divided into Catholic and Orthodox regions. The Catholic Poles, Bohemians, and Hungarians accepted the leadership of the popes in Rome, tended to adopt western European ideas of government, and traded with the west. Orthodox

Christians in Byzantine territories and Russia accepted the leadership of the patriarchs of Constantinople, adopted Byzantine ideas of government, and traded with Byzantium. In this way the Slavic peoples became divided by more than geography. Much of the history of eastern Europe is the story of the struggle between Roman and Byzantine civilizations—a struggle that continues even today.

🐝 🐝 🐝

Charlemagne almost—but not quite—managed to unify Europe into a single state. Although he failed, he succeeded in another sense: for the Carolingian Renaissance that he stimulated preserved something of the heritage of ancient Rome, and the legend he created reminded men that Europe had once been unified. Meanwhile, in the confusion that followed his death, ninth and tenth century local lords preserved and developed a unique system of local government, and missionaries nearly doubled the size of Christendom.

People, Places, and Terms

Merovingians	Elbe River	*Roi Fainéant*
Pepin II	Bavaria	*major domus*
Charles Martel	Spanish March	*dux et princeps*
Pepin the Short	Aix-la-Chapelle	*Frankorum*
Lombards	Fontenoy	*vassi dominici*
Charlemagne	North Sea	Donation of Pepin
Einhard	Scandinavia	temporal
Alcuin	Novgorod	county
Leo III	Kiev	count
Louis the Pious	Iceland	march
Vikings	Greenland	margrave
Rus	Newfoundland	*missi dominici*
Leif Ericson	Ireland	capitulary
Rollo	Denmark	Carolingian
Saracens	Paris	Carolingian
Magyars	Normandy	Renaissance
Cyril	Tunis	abbot
Methodius	Hungary	scriptorium
Vladimir of Kiev	Sweden	minuscule
	Norway	illumination
Baltic Sea	Bohemia	Treaty of Verdun
Carpathian Mts.	Prague	canon law
Rhine River	Poland	Cyrillic alphabet

Getting Organized

1. What happened to the Frankish state after the death of Clovis? Why were the later Merovingians called *Rois Fainéants?* Describe the poverty of Merovingian France. What was happening to the church during this period?

2. What was a *major domus?* How did Charles Martel build up a strong army? What did this army accomplish? How did Pepin the Short extend the power of France? What historic agreement did he make with the pope?

3. What was Charlemagne's chief object? How successful was he in this aim?

4. How did Charlemagne rule his empire? What was the role of the *missi dominici?*

5. What was Charlemagne's attitudes toward the church? How much control did he have over it? What happened on Christmas Day, 800? How did this event come about? What were its long-term results?

6. Describe the economy of the Carolingian empire. How did Charlemagne's policies affect the development of agriculture?

7. What is meant by the term "Carolingian Renaissance"? What were the achievements of this renaissance?

8. Why did Charlemagne's empire collapse after he died? In what way were the battle of Fontenoy and the Treaty of Verdun important steps in the decline of the Frankish Empire?

9. Where did the Vikings come from? What are possible reasons for their raids? How did they attack a territory? What areas did they reach? Where did they establish their own rule?

10. How did the Saracens attack Europe? What areas did they threaten or conquer? What areas did the Magyars raid? Where did they settle?

11. What kind of government gradually emerged during the tenth century? Why? What were its advantages?

12. What development in the church paralleled the political development in the tenth century? What new areas of Europe were converted to Roman Catholicism? To Orthodox Christianity? What was the long-range effect of the competition among missionaries?

Understanding the Big Picture

1. Why did the government of the Merovingians fail? How were the mayors of the palace able to gain control of the kingdom?

2. How did Charlemagne deal with the power and military strength of the Frankish nobles? How complete was Charlemagne's authority over his empire? Over the church? Did his power increase after 800? How?

Mastering the Map

1. Study carefully the map of the Frankish Empire on page 72. Which ruler added the most territory? How large was it at its height?
2. Study the boundaries of the three parts of the empire after the Treaty of Verdun (map, page 77). How do they correspond to modern political boundaries? What conclusion might one reach regarding the long-range importance of the treaty?
3. Study carefully the map of the spread of Christendom on page 82. During what period did Christendom expand the most? How and why did it expand so greatly? Where were the chief obstacles to its growth?

For the Thoughtful

1. Compare the decline of the Merovingian kingdom to the decline of the Frankish Empire, citing parallels and differences.
2. How important to European history was Charlemagne? Was he as influential to history as Muhammad? Explain fully.

Summing up the Early Middle Ages

The three civilizations that arose out of the ashes of the Roman Empire were, by the year 1000, quite different from one another.

In eastern Europe and Asia Minor, Byzantium stood fast against its attackers and jealously guarded its Roman heritage, its powerful monarchy, its great capital at Constantinople, and its Orthodox Christian religion.

The Islamic empire, stretching from the Atlantic coasts of Spain and Africa all the way to the Indian Ocean, was divided into three major caliphates; but it retained its distinctive form of government, religion, and art.

In western Europe Charlemagne's Frankish Empire had collapsed, but Europe still was united by the Roman Catholic religion and by the memory of Charlemagne, and it had a vigorously growing system of local governments.

The man of the year 1000 would probably have thought that of the three different civilizations, that of western Europe was the least promising. But at the end of the tenth century, the customs of Europe were stronger

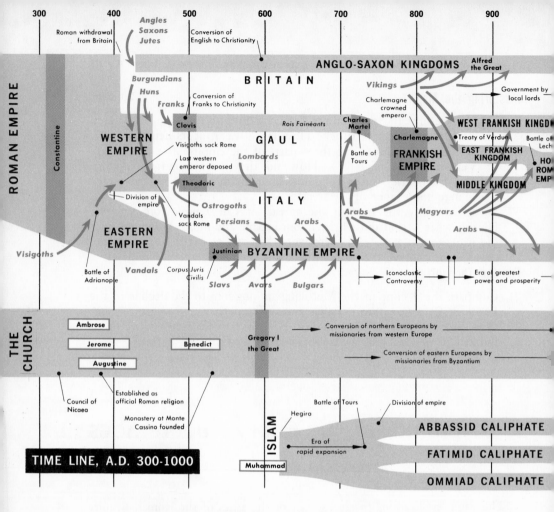

TIME LINE, A.D. 300-1000

than they might have seemed to the casual observer. In the years to come they would blossom into one of history's greatest achievements, the civilization of the high Middle Ages.

Some Questions to Answer

1. What survived the fall of Rome? In answering, consider such questions as: Did the Roman Empire fall completely, or did any of its ideas and institutions remain to influence early medieval developments?
2. How does the period from 500 to 1000 compare in its cultural achievement to the classical period of Greece and Rome? What influences affected early medieval culture?
3. What factors explain the rise of the Byzantine, Islamic, and Frankish empires? Why did each decline? Why, in general, do empires rise and decline? What was the effect of the Roman Empire on each of these three empires?

4. Defend the theory that the period from 500 to 1000 should be called the "Dark Ages." Demonstrate clearly that this was a period barren of any significant hope, achievement, or progress. Be as specific as you can.

5. Now, attack the theory that says that the above period should be called the "Dark Ages." Demonstrate clearly that many important institutions and ideas were either growing rapidly or were just under the surface. Show that this was a period of progress. Support your answers with specific evidence.

Further Reading for Part One

GENERAL ACCOUNTS

BURY, J. B. *A History of the Later Roman Empire.* 2 vols. New York: Dover, 1957 (paper). A standard book on Byzantine history, particularly the early period.

CANTOR, NORMAN F. *Medieval History.* New York: Macmillan, 1963. A good survey that stresses intellectual developments.

DAWSON, CHRISTOPHER. *The Making of Europe.* New York: Sheed & Ward, 1946; Cleveland: World (paper).

GIBB, H. A. R. *Mohammedanism: An Historical Survey.* 2nd ed. New York: Oxford University Press, 1953 (paper). A difficult but excellent essay on Islam by an expert on the subject.

HUSSEY, JOAN M. *The Byzantine World.* New York: Harper, 1961 (paper). A very helpful short account.

LOT, FERDINAND. *The End of the Ancient World and the Beginnings of the Middle Ages.* New York: Harper, 1961 (paper). An excellent account that demonstrates the unique characteristics of medieval civilization.

MOSS, HENRY ST. L. B. *The Birth of the Middle Ages.* New York: Oxford University Press (paper).

PAINTER, SIDNEY. *A History of the Middle Ages.* New York: Knopf, 1953. An excellent survey by an expert on the period.

PIRENNE, HENRI. *A History of Europe.* 2 vols. Garden City, N. Y.: Doubleday, 1958 (paper). An interpretation of European history by a distinguished Belgian historian.

SOUTHERN, R. W. *The Making of the Middle Ages.* New Haven: Yale University Press, 1953 (paper). A highly readable introduction.

STRAYER, JOSEPH R. *Western Europe in the Middle Ages: A Short History.* New York: Appleton-Century-Crofts, 1955 (paper). An interesting interpretation for those who have already acquired some knowledge of the period.

WALLACE-HADRILL, JOHN M. *The Barbarian West,* A.D. *400-1000.* New York: Harper, 1962 (paper). A good survey that emphasizes the history of Italy and of the Franks.

BOOKS ON SPECIFIC SUBJECTS

DANIEL-ROPS, H. *The Church in the Dark Ages*. New York: Dutton, 1959; Garden City, N. Y.: Doubleday (paper). A readable account.

DUCKETT, ELEANOR S. *Alfred the Great, the King and His England*. Chicago: The University of Chicago Press, 1956; 1958 (paper).

———. *Gateway to the Middle Ages*. Vol. I, *Italy*. Vol. II, *France and Britain*. Ann Arbor: University of Michigan Press, 1961. Two useful and readable introductory histories.

LEWIS, BERNARD. *The Arabs in History*. New York: Harper, 1960 (paper). A good, short account that stresses the medieval period.

McEVEDY, COLIN. *Atlas of Medieval History*. Baltimore: Penguin (paper). An invaluable aid; accurate and thorough.

PIRENNE, HENRI. *Mohammed and Charlemagne*. New York: Barnes & Noble, 1955; Cleveland: World (paper). Advances the thesis that the Arab invasion of the Mediterranean area was more harmful to Europe than were the Germanic invasions.

RAND, EDWARD K. *Founders of the Middle Ages*. New York: Dover (paper). A useful little book with brief sketches of a number of persons, including most of the patristic writers.

STEPHENSON, CARL. *Medieval Feudalism*. Ithaca, N. Y.: Cornell University Press, 1956 (paper). A good short handbook.

WHITELOCK, DOROTHY. *The Beginnings of English Society*. Baltimore: Penguin (paper). A fine treatment of Anglo-Saxon England.

WINSTON, RICHARD. *Charlemagne: From the Hammer to the Cross*. New York: Knopf, 1956 (paper). A first-rate biography.

SOURCE MATERIALS

AUGUSTINE. *The City of God*. The major work of the greatest of early Christian theologians; difficult but readable. (Available in several editions.)

———. *Confessions*. Also difficult, but readable and fascinating. (Available in several editions.)

BEDE. *History of the English Church and People*. Translated by J. SHERLEY-PRICE. Baltimore: Penguin (paper). An account by an eighth-century scholar.

BETTENSON, HENRY (ed.). *Documents of the Christian Church*. New York: Oxford University Press, 1947. A useful handbook of documents, with notes and comments on them.

EINHARD. *Life of Charlemagne*. Ann Arbor: University of Michigan Press, 1960 (paper). Written by Charlemagne's secretary; an excellent example of hero-worship.

ROSS, JAMES BRUCE, and McLAUGHLIN, MARY MARTIN (eds.). *The Portable Medieval Reader*. New York: Viking, 1946 (paper). A useful collection of all kinds of medieval writing.

the high middle ages

In the broadest sense, the terms "Middle Ages" and "medieval" (which means "of the Middle Ages") refer to a span of about ten centuries, from the collapse of the ancient world to the rise of the modern world—roughly from the fifth to the fifteenth centuries. Informally, however, these terms are frequently applied to the "high" Middle Ages, the way of life that flourished in western Europe after the tenth century and reached its peak in the twelfth and thirteenth centuries.

"Middle Ages" is a misleading term, for it seems to say that the way of life of the tenth to fifteenth centuries was nothing more than a connecting link between the ancient and modern worlds. This was far from the case. The civilization that began to take shape in the tenth century developed many unique characteristics, unlike anything that had gone before. Among these were feudalism, a system of government based on personal loyalties; chivalry, an elaborate code of behavior for the ruling classes; the manorial system, the base of the medieval economy, which determined the way of life of the great majority of the people; and the guilds, associations of master craftsmen, which controlled the expanding trade and had great influence on the lives of the important and growing minority of the people who lived in the towns. The most important institution of all was the Catholic Church, which deeply influenced everyone in medieval Europe and whose leaders, wielding great political as well as spiritual power, attempted to bring all Europe together into a unified Commonwealth of Christendom.

A culminating event of the Middle Ages was the crusades of the twelfth century, when thousands of the greatest knights of Europe marched east to restore the Holy Land to Christendom. In their prime the crusades, the feudal system, and the political power of the church combined to create a powerful and unique civilization whose heritage, including as it does such monumental achievements as scholastic philosophy and the Gothic cathedrals, can easily stand comparison with that of any age before or since.

7
feudalism and Chivalry

Feudal lords and knights dominated the political and military life of Europe during the Middle Ages. From the tenth century to the fourteenth, they ruled through a system of government called "feudalism" and modeled their personal behavior on a picturesque but significant set of beliefs called "chivalry."

FEUDALISM:
GOVERNMENT BY PERSONAL LOYALTIES

When there were no strong governments, only a lord who was also a warrior could hope to retain his lands. As time went by, lords came to make alliances with each other, which they hoped would assure some safety to their landholdings. A lesser lord would become a "vassal" of a greater lord, placing himself under the protection of the greater lord and agreeing to perform certain services, mostly military in nature. In return, the greater lord agreed to protect the lands of his vassal.

Such agreements were the basis of a form of government called "feudalism" (from the Latin *feudum*, a grant of land). By the end of the tenth century, feudalism was developing a formal hierarchy (pyramid of power). (See page 81.) The king, at the peak, claimed to own the entire kingdom. One step below him were "tenants-in-chief," vassals who held their lands directly from the king. These lords in turn divided their possessions among tenants of their own by a process called "subinfeudation." These vassals had vassals of their own, who were likely to have vassals of *their* own—and so on until, at the bottom of the hierarchy, were the individual knights, or "castellans" (castle-holders), who had only an estate or two and no vassals. This hierarchy constantly changed as stronger lords seized territories from weaker lords in the constant struggle for land and power.

Feudalism began in France, spread to England and the rest of western Europe during the eleventh century, and by the twelfth century had been adopted in many parts of central Europe as well. Feudalism reached its highest development in France, where the rights and duties of lords and their vassals were most clearly defined. English and German knights modeled themselves on the French, although of course there were a number of national variations.

THE FEUDAL CONTRACT

Feudalism was based on the holding of land and on a personal relationship between lord and vassal. Because the terms of each feudal relationship were settled in each case by the lord and the vassal, feudalism cannot properly be called a "system." Yet certain practices and certain rights—rights of both lord and vassal—eventually came to be hallowed by custom.

The feudal contract was based on a ceremony called "investiture," in which the vassal knelt in the presence of the lord and his court to swear that he would serve his master. The vassal received in turn a written charter, a staff, or even a blade of grass or clod of dirt as a symbol of the estate, or *feudum*, that was being turned over to him. In the investiture the lord usually promised to provide the *feudum* (or "fief," as it was also called) and agreed to protect it from his vassal's enemies. He also promised to "do justice" to his vassal; that is, to hear his complaints in open court in the presence of his other vassals, and to see that members of his vassal's family received justice as well. If the lord denied justice, the vassal had the right to declare the feudal contract invalid—if he dared, for to do so usually meant war.

A knight paying homage: an illumination from a thirteenth-century English manuscript. The knight is wearing "chain mail"—flexible armor made of joined metal links—which was the usual kind of armor throughout most of the Middle Ages. The crosses on the knight's tunic indicate that he is a crusader. (Chapter 14.)

In return, the vassal promised to do "homage" and "fealty." Homage, (from the French *homme*, "man") was the vassal's acknowledgment that he was the lord's "man," or servant; fealty was his pledge to obey his lord's commands. The vassal also agreed to provide services for his lord. The most important of these was the obligation to serve in his army for at least forty days a year (an obligation that he could sometimes buy his way out of by paying a "scutage," or "shield tax"). He also promised to spend a certain amount of time each year at his lord's court, partly to help guard it, and partly to give counsel (which the lord occasionally was obligated to accept). Some vassals also took charge of various aspects of their lord's government and spent all their time as members of his court. In addition, the vassal agreed to make certain payments to his lord. He paid a "relief," usually the equivalent of a year's income from his fief, when he received his investiture. He also was responsible for the three traditional feudal "dues," ransom, dowry, and knighting. These were special contributions made to ransom the lord if he were captured in battle, to help provide a dowry for the lord's eldest daughter when she married, and to contribute toward the costs of the ceremony when his eldest son was knighted. In addition to all these, the lord could require his vassal to make special gifts to help pay for building a new castle, going on a crusade, or undertaking an especially ambitious war. Finally, when the lord made his regular tour of his vassal's estates, he had the right to be entertained properly, partly as a sign of respect and partly because such hospitality was a sizable portion of his income.

INHERITANCE

Many rulers broke up their states by dividing them among their sons, as Louis the Pious had divided the Frankish Empire. (See page 77.) As time went on, however, it became customary to require that an estate be passed intact from generation to generation, a practice called "entail." "Primogeniture," the inheritance of the estate by the eldest son, also became customary. Entail and primogeniture led to the establishment of numerous hereditary ruling families whose heads spent much of their time trying to add to the family estates that they would leave to their descendants. Such activity led to innumerable feudal wars as one family tried to seize the properties of its neighbors by force.

At the same time, vassals often tried to win independence from their lords, and every new feudal ruler could expect a series of minor rebellions that he would have to put down if he hoped to keep his state intact. Feudal vassals had little loyalty to government as such; only a strong lord could win and keep the personal loyalty of his sometimes reluctant followers.

FEUDALISM AND THE CHURCH

The church was linked inseparably with the feudal system. The church not only exerted great influence over men's minds but also ruled vast estates, so the feudal lords were eager to see that bishops and abbots—and even popes—were friendly allies. They often tried to influence the election of church officials. Since many of the prelates were younger sons or brothers of feudal rulers, there was a close connection between the upper clergy and the feudal classes.

At the same time, the church tried to influence the feudal lords. As early as the eleventh century, it attempted to limit the constant feudal struggles by the "Peace of God" and the "Truce of God." The Peace of God declared that feudal warfare could not take place on church property, and it promised sanctuary in churches and abbeys to fugitives from combat. The Truce of God forbade fighting from Wednesday evening until Monday morning, on holidays, and during the religious seasons of Christmas and Lent, providing a sort of medieval long weekend for the knights and limiting the effectiveness of their campaigns. Unfortunately, both the Peace of God and the Truce of God were usually ignored, even though those who broke them were threatened with excommunication (being cut off from communion with the church).

THE EFFECTS OF FEUDALISM

Feudalism was necessary and valuable during the Middle Ages, for it provided the only form of government that could protect the people against invasions, raids, and ordinary thieves. Before there were strong monarchies, feudalism provided a system of strong local and regional governments.

Feudalism also revived the idea of law and order, emphasizing men's obligations to other men. Based on the idea of a contract between the lord and his vassal, it set limits to the power and ambition of even the greatest of rulers. For example, Edward I, one of the great medieval kings of England, once ordered his vassal Roger Bigod to go on a campaign in France. Bigod pointed out that this was not required by his feudal contract. Edward retorted, "By God, earl, you will either go or hang." Nothing daunted, the earl replied, "By the same oath, O king, I will neither go nor hang." He neither went nor was hanged, for the contract was there for all to see— and even a king had to obey the law.

Feudalism also had its disadvantages. It preserved the division of Europe into hundreds of tiny states ruled by almost independent lords, making it difficult to form larger, better organized nations. It also exalted the aristocrats and set them apart from the rest of the people. Feudal lords were supposed to have a sense of *noblesse oblige* (obligation of the nobility), but few felt any responsibility for the welfare of their peasants. The close ties between the church and the feudal rulers also led to ferocious struggles between church and state in the later Middle Ages. Finally, and most important, feudal rulers devoted too much of their time to "private war"— the endless series of little wars and blood feuds that characterized the Middle Ages. A lord might want to increase his state, a vassal to win independence or enlarge his fief, a town to become free, or a lord to seize a town. Relatives might war over the family possessions, or rivals war over some real or imaginary insult. Feudal wars, however, were not like the total wars of the twentieth century. They were usually short (vassals could seldom be made to fight more than forty days a year); they were usually fought by tiny armies of knights, while the peasants stayed in the fields; and the knights were rarely killed or even seriously hurt, because they wore heavy armor.

All in all, the disadvantages of feudalism were probably fewer than the advantages. The only alternative was anarchy (no government at all). And, as time went on, the feudal lords became more civilized and less warlike.

⚜ CHIVALRY:
THE KNIGHTLY CODE OF BEHAVIOR

Chivalry was the standard of values and behavior that grew out of the needs of the medieval knightly class. Its development therefore lagged a century or so behind that of feudalism, reaching its height in France in the late twelfth and thirteenth centuries. There were three aspects of the code of chivalry: the feudal chivalry of the knights themselves, religious chivalry, and the tradition of courtly love.

FEUDAL CHIVALRY

Feudal chivalry was essentially the military code of the warrior on horseback. The very word "chivalry" derives from the French words *cheval* (horse) and *chevalier* (mounted warrior). Only a relatively few men could afford to be chevaliers. A war horse was a rare beast, costing as much as four oxen or twenty-four sheep—at a time when most peasants did not have one ox or three sheep to their names. Armor was very expensive, and the costs of campaigning were high. Most knights therefore required substantial fiefs to provide the income necessary to ply their warlike trade.

The knight was a skilled professional who had gone through a long period of on-the-job training. As a boy of seven or eight he had probably been sent by his father to serve as a "page" or "varlet" (little vassal) in the court of a neighboring lord, where he learned manners and took care of the arms and armor of the knights. At fourteen or fifteen he became a "squire" (from the French *ecuyer*, "shield-bearer") and began to drill in the use of sword and shield and to take part in sham battles with the other squires. If his master went to war, the squire tagged along to learn about bravery and the art of campaigning in the field.

A squire being dubbed by the Holy Roman emperor: an illustration from a German manuscript of the fifteenth century. The pope (right) looks on.

The young man was usually considered ready for the honor of being dubbed a knight when he was nineteen or twenty. After a night of prayer, he ceremonially dressed in full armor and received the "accolade" (a slap across the neck with the flat of the sword) from his father or from the knight he had served. A knight at last, the young man concluded the ceremony by giving a public exhibition of his skill and daring. He then took his place among the members of the chivalric class.

The knight who delivered the accolade usually admonished the young man with the words "*Soix preux*." "*Soix preux*" can be roughly translated "Conduct yourself as a true knight." Roland, the hero of the greatest of medieval epics, *The Song of Roland*, is an example of proper knightly conduct. He was loyal and respectful to his lord Charlemagne, brave to the point of foolhardiness, a mighty warrior, a natural leader of men, impervious to hardship, a true friend to his companions, and an honorable lover to his chosen lady. He chose to die rather than to retreat or surrender —or even to call for help. Roland was *preux*.

A knight was also expected to be courteous, to treat his prisoners well, not to try to escape if captured, and to fight by the honorable rules of battle. He was expected to be generous, to entertain visitors lavishly, and to give lavish gifts to his friends and lords. In other words, he was expected to be a gentleman. But the word "gentleman" meant something different in those days from what it means today. The word "gentle" derives from the Latin *gens*, meaning "family"; the medieval gentleman was a man of aristocratic birth who was, as a member of the knightly class, *preux*, courteous, and generous. He therefore thought of the ill-mannered peasants as a race apart, rarely bothering to treat them kindly or thoughtfully. He would be gentle with his bitterest knightly rivals, who were members of his own class; but he thought nothing of destroying peasant homes, taking peasant property, and insulting peasant girls.

RELIGIOUS CHIVALRY

The church attempted to influence the code of chivalry just as it tried to influence the feudal system. As the churchman John of Salisbury wrote:

> But what is the office of the duly ordained soldiery? To defend the Church, to assail infidelity, to venerate the priesthood, to protect the poor from injuries, to pacify the province, to pour out their blood for their brothers . . . and, if need be, to lay down their lives . . . For soldiers that do these things are saints.

Churchmen helped invest knights and lords, crowned kings, and gave advice and occasionally even military support to the feudal aristocrats. For

A jousting scene: a French ivory carving of the fourteenth century. Jousts and tournaments were a favorite form of chivalric entertainment. In jousts, two mounted knights rode full tilt at each other, as here. The object was to unseat one's opponent by striking his shield with great force with one's lance. In tournaments, two teams of knights fought each other in mock battles. Elaborate sets of rules were developed for these events.

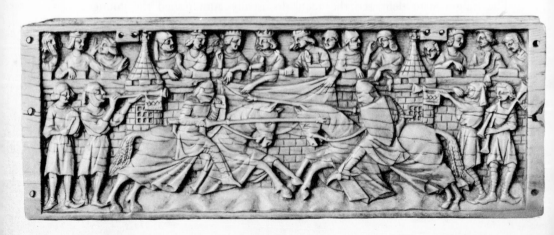

example, in the eleventh century Bishop Odo of Bayeux rode into battle beside his brother, William the Conqueror of England, swinging an iron ball on the end of a chain. As a cleric he had sworn not to draw blood, but he hoped he could fight and still remain true to his oath by bloodlessly crushing his enemies.

The medieval church sponsored the crusades, those attacks by the flower of medieval knighthood on the infidel Muslims in the Holy Land (Chapter 14), and it established three orders of warrior priests to take part in them. Nine French knights who had taken vows as canons of the church organized the "Knights Templars" in 1129 and persuaded the famous monk Bernard of Clairvaux to draw up monastic laws for them to follow. Later two other similar groups were founded, the "Teutonic Knights" and the "Knights of Saint John in Jerusalem" (usually called the "Hospitalers" because they were attached to the Hospital of Saint John). All three made brilliant military records and attracted many members and much wealth. But riches brought ruin; the orders grew corrupt, became involved in politics, and were finally dissolved in the fourteenth century.

Among the most famous medieval poems are the tales of knights who went on religious quests. There was Sir Galahad of King Arthur's legendary Round Table, who devoted his life to seeking the Holy Grail, the cup from which Christ drank at the Last Supper. After many trials he finally found it. Miraculously he became a priest and was assumed up into heaven, with the Grail shining like a brilliant star above his head. Like Roland, Galahad was the model for hundreds of pious knights who saw themselves as defenders of the faith.

COURTLY LOVE

Until the eleventh century knights were likely to feel that women, like peasants, were a necessary evil. They expected their wives to run the household, bear children, and stay out of the way. But as the traditions of courtly love developed, the knights' attitudes gradually changed.

The idea of courtly love was popularized by "troubadours" in southern France. These poet-entertainers went from castle to castle singing of ancient kings and legendary heroes who, they insisted, had been inspired by their ladies to be better men in every way. Smitten by love, they accomplished great deeds, withstood hunger, hardship, and grievous wounds without complaint, and treated friend and foe with honor and compassion. The ladies liked this, and even the knights began to write troubadour poems. By the thirteenth century Pope Innocent III was writing troubadour poems dedicated to the Virgin Mary.

In the middle of the twelfth century Eleanor of Aquitaine, who was wife of the king of France and later of the king of England, helped spread the tradition of courtly love across western Europe. Eleanor's daughter, Marie of Champagne, held "courts" in her castle in which matters of love were formally debated and the rules of love carefully recorded. Her chaplain wrote that

> Love is a certain inborn suffering derived from the sight of and excessive meditation upon the beauty of the opposite sex, which causes one to wish above all things the embraces of the other.

Among the rules of love he listed were these:
> I. Marriage is no real excuse for not loving.
> II. He who is not jealous cannot love.
> VI. No one should be deprived of love without the very best of reasons.

THE LITERATURE OF CHIVALRY

Proud of their heritage, knights and their ladies encouraged troubadours to create a whole literature of *chansons de geste*, or "songs of great deeds." These were long narrative poems that told of heroic knights, beautiful ladies, honor and treachery, love and war, and defeat and victory, and extolled the accomplishments of legendary figures. In the late twelfth century Chrétien de Troyes recounted the tales of King Arthur and the knights of the Round Table. He wrote of Arthur and Lancelot and Queen Guinevere and had finished the first 9,000 lines of a 32,000 line *chanson* about Percival when he died in 1183. Later the German troubadour Gottfried von Strassburg wrote of the tragic love of Tristan and Isolde. The French chanson *The Song of Roland* was sung in a dozen versions.

Other medieval literature was less ennobling. There were *fabliaux*, little poems about animals, which sometimes bitterly satirized human greed, lust, and avarice. One of these "human" animals, Reynard the Fox, has reappeared in the literature of every century since the fall of Rome.

There were also love poems. This is taken from the collection called the *Roman de la Rose*, "The Romance of the Rose":

> Woman should gather roses ere
> Time's ceaseless foot oertaketh her,

For if too long she make delay,
Her chance of love may pass away,
And well it is she seek it while
Health, strength and youth around her smile,
To pluck the fruits of love in youth,
Is each wise woman's rule, forsooth.

In a gentler mood is this poem in which the hero Aucassin sings of his lovely lady Nicolette:

Nicolette, white lily flower,
Sweetest lady found in bower,
Sweet and grape that brimmeth up
Lily flower, so white, so sweet,
Fair the flowering of thy feet,
Fair thy laughter, fair thy speech,
Fair our playing, each with each.

🐚 🐚 🐚

When there were no large, strong states, the feudal system provided a system of government on a smaller scale that protected the vassals and placed some restrictions on the lords. It preserved some sense of law and worked in the best interests of both master and man. In chivalry these feudal aristocrats created a system of personal values that emphasized honor, bravery, justice, and faith.

But feudalism and chivalry directly affected only a small portion of the people of medieval Europe. Most men were peasants living on the manors, and a few inhabited the small but growing towns.

People, Places, and Terms

Roland	justice	varlet (page)
John of Salisbury	homage	squire
Eleanor of Aquitaine	fealty	accolade
Chrétien de Troyes	scutage	*Sois preux*
	relief	gentleman
lord	dues	Knights Templars
vassal	entail	Teutonic Knights
hierarchy	primogeniture	Hospitalers
tenants-in-chief	Peace of God	courtly love
subinfeudation	Truce of God	troubadours
castellan	*noblesse oblige*	*chansons de geste*
investiture	anarchy	*fabliaux*
fief	chivalry	*Roman de la Rose*

Getting Organized

1. Explain the basic idea of the feudal hierarchy. Where did it develop? To what places did it spread?
2. In what ways was the feudal contract both a personal and a legal relationship? According to this contract, what did the lord promise to provide the vassal? What did the vassal promise the lord?
3. How did medieval men pass their possessions from one generation to the next? How were the feudal laws enforced? How did the church contribute to the feudal system?
4. What were the advantages of the feudal system? What were the disadvantages?
5. Why did chivalry apply only to the warrior class of knights? How did a future knight gain his training? What were the qualities and characteristics expected of a good knight? How did the knights treat the peasants?
6. How did the church affect chivalry? Did the knights respect the church? Would they die for it?
7. What was courtly love? How did it arise? How was it supposed to affect chivalry?
8. With what subjects did the literature of the twelfth and thirteenth centuries deal? What were the most important works?

Understanding the Big Picture

1. In what ways was the feudal contract an economic relationship? A military relationship? A political relationship? A legal relationship? A personal relationship? Which of these was the most important?
2. In what ways was the church involved in the feudal system? Did this system apply to all of medieval society? Explain.
3. How did the church and women affect the morality of the knights? What would the knights have done without these restraining influences?
4. Do you think that the literature of the troubadours reflected accurately the spirit of the medieval period? Explain.

For the Thoughtful

1. Was the feudal system a good system to meet the needs of the medieval period? Support your answer with specific evidence.
2. As a standard of values and behavior, how did chivalry differ from modern standards of morality? What possible explanations are there for these differences?
3. How rigid was the class structure of the medieval period? Compare it to the class structure of twentieth-century America. Give specific similarities and examples of differences.

The Manor and the Town

8

Most of recorded history recounts the activities of the rich and powerful, who during the Middle Ages were the members of the feudal nobility and the leaders of the church. But the vast majority of the people, probably 90 per cent, were commoners who lived on the great rural estates called "manors." There was also a small but important minority in the towns, which slowly grew in numbers and size as commerce and manufacturing slowly increased.

THE MANORIAL SYSTEM

In the areas of western Europe where feudalism was most highly developed—roughly modern England, France, Germany, and the Low Countries (Belgium and the Netherlands)—the manor was the smallest unit of feudal government throughout the Middle Ages. Basically it was a fortified farm that a lord could conveniently govern and from which he could collect the income he needed. A fief (see page 92) might consist of one or a hundred manors, depending on the size of the lord's estate. Each manor usually had one or two tiny villages nestled near its castle, to which the peasants could flee for safety in case of attack. Surrounding the villages were cultivated fields and, beyond them, the forests and untilled lands that separated the manor from others in the neighborhood.

The roots of the "manorial system" can be traced back to the Roman villa system. (See page 33.) It was fully developed by the twelfth century, and some aspects of it long outlived the Middle Ages. Traces of it can still be found in many parts of Europe.

THE CASTLE AND ITS PEOPLE

Medieval Europe was dotted with castles—by the twelfth century there were as many as 10,000 in Germany alone—which towered above the tiny hovels that peasants built nearby. Before the year 1000 these castles were primitive, consisting of little more than wooden towers surrounded by an open field and a palisade (a wooden fence designed to delay a surprise attack). If the lord were unusually prosperous, there might be a stone tower (called a "keep" or "donjon") built on a hill, on an island in a river, or where the bend of a stream provided a natural moat for protection.

A traveler in the twelfth century would be more likely to see a castle of the type we know today: a large and elaborate structure that could house many people in safety from attack. Coming out of the forests and passing the plowed fields, the traveler would first cross an open area used by the knights as an exercise ground. Passing through a gate in an outer palisade, he would cross the "lists," an enclosed area in which tournaments and military drills were held. Then he would enter the castle proper by crossing the drawbridge over the moat and entering the outer gates, which were protected by a "portcullis," a heavy iron grille which could be dropped quickly in case of attack.

The high outer wall of the castle was strengthened at intervals by towers with narrow windows from which archers could shoot at attackers. It surrounded the castle's outer ward, or "bailey." In this large yard the traveler would find the stables, the smithy, the bakehouse, the mews (where the lord's falcons were kept), and a little chapel. The bailey was the bustling center of the daily life of the lord's many retainers.

If he had business with the lord, the traveler might be allowed to pass across still another moat and through the gate of an even higher wall into the inner ward, which was the heart of the castle's defense. The inner wall had truly formidable towers, to which the defenders could retreat to pour

The castle of Coucy, France, as it probably appeared in the late Middle Ages. The large round tower is the donjon; the smaller round towers with conical roofs are at the corners of the inner wall. Behind the donjon are the palais and the inner ward; in front of it, the inner moat (here shown almost empty of water) and drawbridge. In the foreground, parts of the chapel, the outer wall, and the bailey can be seen.

boiling oil and a steady barrage of rocks and arrows on any attackers who had penetrated to the bailey. Within the inner wall was the "palais," where the lord himself lived. Built in the eleventh or twelfth century, the palais would be of the graceful "Gothic" design, with the ceilings of the rooms ribbed and vaulted like those of the Gothic churches. (Chapter 9.) Here, where comfort was more important than defense, were "arrases," huge embroidered tapestries (named for the town of Arras in Flanders, where many of them were made) hanging near the walls to prevent drafts. The floors were covered with rushes, for rugs had not yet come into vogue. The furniture was scanty but beautifully carved. The traveler would find the palais, like the bailey, full of people, for it was the capitol as well as the home of the lord. Probably he would be ushered into the lord's bedroom for his interview; for even the medieval lord had little privacy, and his bedroom seemed a logical place to keep his treasury and to greet his visitors.

A large castle had many officials to direct its operation. In addition to the knights who protected it and the squires who were knights in training, there were the "seneschal," who was second in command and the lord's principal lieutenant in battle; the "marshal," who was in charge of the stable; and the "chamberlain," who ran the housekeeping of the castle. If the lord was a very great man, these assistants might well be of noble birth and knights as well, serving also on the field of battle.

The lord lived as elaborately as he could, for his rank and power were judged in large part by the magnificence of his way of life. Dozens of people ate their meals at his table, and feast days were excuses for eating and drinking bouts. He entertained his retainers, his neighbors, and his own overlord regularly, and he often traveled about the countryside to enjoy the hospitality of his friends and vassals, whose duties in this regard were often outlined in their feudal contracts.

THE PEASANT VILLAGE

The differences between the castle and the manor reflected the differences in the status of the lord and his peasants. Near the castle was an agricultural village of some 200 to 500 souls, who lived in cottages made of wattle (mud-plastered branches) and roofed with thatch. Some of these cottages had chimneys, but most had only a hole in the roof through which the smoke of the family fire could escape; disastrous fires were commonplace. The average peasant owned only a few stools for furnishings and, if he were

Peasants cutting and raking hay: a miniature from a Flemish manuscript of the fifteenth century. In the background, protected by the River Seine and by its notched wall, is part of the city of Paris, dominated by its Gothic royal chapel (right). The field in which the peasants are working is on the river's left bank, today a crowded part of France's capital city.

wealthy, a bedstead. The household utensils were made of wood, although a well-to-do peasant might have an iron pot and a few knives.

The farmlands that surrounded the village and the castle were usually divided into three great fields, which were planted successively to wheat in one year and rye the next, and then allowed to lie fallow for a year—a sort of crude system of crop rotation that slowed, if it did not prevent, the slow deterioration of the soil. Few peasants owned land outright, for almost all land was held by the lords; but each family usually had the use several long, narrow strips scattered among the three fields.

This "three-field system" of agriculture was usually carried out by peasant men, women, and children, who worked together at planting and harvesting time and cultivated their strips of land independently the rest of the time. Because no one peasant could afford a complete set of tools, the ownership of heavy implements, such as plows and wagons, was shared by the community. The three-field system encouraged the people to co-operate with each other; but it discouraged ambitious peasants from planting new crops or trying new methods, so farming methods changed little from one century to the next.

Most peasants, like small farmers today, were jacks of all trades, but there were some who specialized in specific occupations. A "bailiff" superintended the villagers' work, assisted by a "provost." There were also wagoners, cowherds, shepherds, and dairymaids who worked on the land, and the village or castle usually also contained workshops for smiths, wrights, carpenters, tanners, and bakers.

There were three classes of peasants: the slaves, who could be bought and sold like cattle; the serfs, who could neither leave the manor nor be forced to go; and the freemen, who usually owned small pieces of land and could come and go as they chose. With the passing of the years, the number of slaves tended to decline; but the proportion of freemen, which was never very large, did not increase significantly, and most peasants were serfs. Although the peasant led a degraded life in many ways, he had a double defense against ill usage. First, the lord knew that a sullen and lazy peasantry meant less grain in his own storehouse and that a runaway serf was hard to replace. Second, medieval people were bound by the customs of their forebears, and the "custom of the manor" protected the peasants from many a harsh and unjust lord. Justice had to be enforced in open court in which even the serfs could participate. A peasant could not refuse to work, but neither could his lord evict him; and thus lords and peasants had to respect each other's rights.

For every right the peasant had, there were obligations owed to his lord. The lord usually kept the "demesne lands," about one third of the manor, for himself. The peasants had to work on the demesne an average of three days a week, sowing and harvesting the lord's grain and caring for his animals. In addition to this work (called the *corvée*), the peasant had to give the lord a share of his crops and an occasional special gift, such as a pig from every new litter or one of a string of fish caught in the lord's moat. The lord also profited from his monopolies. All grain had to be ground in his mill, bread baked in his oven, and beer brewed in his vats. In each instance some of the product went to the lord. Payments were arranged to fall most heavily on the serfs; the freemen were relatively lightly taxed.

Each village had a parish priest and a chapel. The chapel was the center of village life, serving not only as a religious but also as a social center. The villagers were expected to pay tithes equal to one tenth of their income for the support of the church. Some of this money went for the relief of the poor; the rest was divided among the priest, the officials of the church, and the lord. Usually the lord had more influence than the bishop over the local church, for he appointed the priest, built the chapel, and often collected the tithes himself.

THE GROWTH OF COMMERCE

The castle and the manor were all the average peasant knew. They must have seemed the same from one generation to the next, promising some small measure of order and safety in a confused and violent age. But change was in the air. In the ninth century the prolonged decline of commerce that had begun when Rome fell leveled off, and an almost imperceptible growth of population and an increase in wealth began. At the time of William the Conqueror (1066), England had only about 1,500,000 people; three centuries later it had nearly 4,000,000. Everywhere in northern Europe men were cutting down the forests to bring new land under the plow, and their herds of cattle and sheep were increasing in size and quality. The homes of lords and even of peasants were becoming larger and more comfortable, and the standard of living was slowly rising.

As a consequence towns grew to house craftsmen who made goods the manors could not produce and became centers in which these goods and others from distant places could be traded.

THE TOWNS OF ITALY AND FLANDERS

The earliest medieval towns began to prosper in the eleventh century. Trade between Italy and Constantinople had never entirely ceased; and when the Muslims' control of the Mediterranean weakened early in the century, a number of Italian cities were quick to open new sea lanes. Venice, at the head of the Adriatic, expanded its trade with the east; and from the western coast of Italy, Genoa and Pisa sent ships to the ports of southern France. These last two cities were strong enough to drive the Muslims from Sardinia in 1016, and by the end of the century, with the help of the Norman conquerors of Sicily, they had swept the Muslims from all the western Mediterranean. In the twelfth century, crusaders from western Europe established Christian kingdoms in the Holy Land (Chapter 14), which carried on a flourishing trade with the Italian cities.

At about the same time, another group of towns in the province of Flanders, along the North Sea, grew rapidly. The region had been famous since Roman days for its woolen cloth. As more and more people demanded their product, the number of weavers in such Flemish towns as Bruges, Ghent, and Arras multiplied, and merchants went from them to such distant places as Germany, Wales, and northern England to buy raw wool. By the end of the eleventh century Scandinavian merchants were sailing south to Flemish markets to exchange their northern products, furs and hunting hawks, for Flemish cloth, and Englishmen came to sell tin from their mines.

TRADE ROUTES

Each of these two regions thus developed its own trade routes. At first the Italian and Flemish traders had little contact with each other, for ships were still too primitive to brave the storms of the Atlantic, and robbers and barons subjected overland caravans to attack and heavy tolls. In the twelfth century, however, the counts of Champagne, in central France, established fairs where Flemish and Italian merchants met; and the nobles, realizing that they, too, profited from growing trade, began to leave the merchants alone.

By the twelfth century, with the blessing of the nobles, merchants were crisscrossing Europe along a network of trade routes. The principal route began in the Levant (the eastern shore of the Mediterranean), where Italian ships took on cargoes of luxury goods from the east and carried them to the ports of Venice, Pisa, and Genoa. Here these products were sold to merchants who shipped them either by sea to the harbors of southern France and then by caravan up the valley of the Rhone or overland through Lombardy to Champagne, the Rhineland, and Flanders. In the other direction, the merchants carried the products of northern Europe to the Mediterranean and the Levant. By 1300 lesser routes branched off into Spain, England, and the more remote parts of France and Germany, and a water route extended all the way from Italy, along the coastline of Spain and France, to Flanders and ports on the Baltic. On the Baltic and North Sea coasts, a group of German towns established a commercial league called the "Hanse." (Chapter 18.)

☙ MEDIEVAL TOWNS

Along these routes, at the mouths or headwaters of rivers or at other important locations, dozens of little towns grew up to profit from commerce and from manufacturing (by hand) their own regional products. Partly the result of the increasing commerce and at the same time an important cause of it, these towns were tiny at first; and even in the thirteenth century, most were no larger than modern villages. Probably fewer than five per cent of the population of Europe lived in them, and most peasants and many knights had never visited one. As late as 1400 only a few, such as Venice and Milan, could boast a population of as much as 100,000. Paris was the metropolis of the north with 80,000 souls, and England had only one large town, London, which was half that size.

LIFE IN THE TOWNS

Medieval towns were colorful but hardly sanitary. Originally they were little more than clusters of merchants' houses built near the walls of a protecting castle or monastery and surrounded by outer walls of their own. Space in these little walled commercial areas was at a premium, because the walls were expensive to build; so streets were no wider than foot paths, and houses were built narrow and high with overhanging upper stories that shut out the sun from the streets. When no more land was available within the walls, another section would be built and walled, and soon it would be just as cramped and ill-designed as the old.

Most of the houses in the towns were built by tradesmen, who set up their shops on the first floor and lived with their families in an apartment

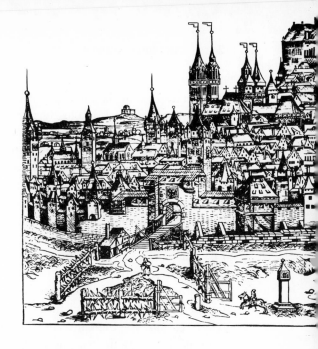

A part of the city of Nuremberg, in southern Germany, as it appeared at the end of the Middle Ages. Nuremberg preserved its medieval aspect until the Second World War, when much of the medieval heart of the city was destroyed.

above. Wood was the most popular building material. Disastrous fires were frequent until, as the forests were cut away and the "burghers" (as the town-dwellers were called) grew more prosperous, wood was replaced by brick, stone, and half-timbering combined with plaster (a method of building that we associate with "Tudor" architecture today).

There were no public utilities. The cities were filthy, because housewives threw their garbage into the streets to be eaten by roaming cattle and swine. Open wells (often polluted) or the nearby river provided water. No city had a professional police force, although some had a night watch of burghers who took turns making the rounds. When not on duty, the prudent burgher stayed home.

The towns resounded with the ringing of church bells, which praised the saints, announced services, or warned that there was danger in the streets. As the castle dominated the manor, so the cathedral towered over the town. There were also many lesser churches, each honoring its patron saint and dedicated to the glory of God: in 1200, little London, with no more than 40,000 people, had 120 churches in addition to huge Saint Paul's Cathedral. The pious went to church every day, leaving behind generous gifts that were used to build still more and larger churches or to pay for statues, for stained-glass windows, or for the services that marked the passage of the religious year. Less imposing, but still impressive, were the castles and palaces of the kings and nobles, some of whom chose to live in the towns, and the mansions of a new and rising class of merchant princes.

THE GUILDS

Free enterprise in the modern sense was unknown to medieval men, who chose to live and work in closely regulated societies. The craftsmen of the towns organized themselves into "guilds," which regulated economic life and also played an important role in their social and political activities.

Guilds Merchant. The earlier form of the guild was the "guild merchant," whose function was to assure that all of the trade of a town would be in the hands of its residents. Outsiders could compete with the guild members only by paying a heavy fee and agreeing to trade only in a certain limited area and only at certain times of the year. All guild members had to be inhabitants of the town, and only they could elect the town officials. Guild members enjoyed other benefits, for the guild functioned in some ways rather like an insurance company, providing financial aid and protection for needy members and their families.

Craft Guilds. By the thirteenth century, as handmade products became increasingly important in commerce, the guilds merchant were frequently replaced by "craft" guilds. Membership in a craft guild was restricted to workers in a specific trade. These guilds became so specialized that by 1292 there were 130 regulated professions in Paris, ranging from the guild of firewood cutters to the guild of sculptors.

The organization of the craft guilds reflected the manufacturing methods of the time. Everything was made by hand. Almost always the entire process took place in small shops, where a "master" of the craft, with a few assistants, fashioned raw materials into finished goods, and where he also sold his output. The work often required much skill, and craftsmen developed great pride in the quality of their products.

Each shop was owned by the master, who was required to be a member of the guild and to follow its elaborate regulations. He was limited in the type and quality of the raw materials he could use, in the methods by which he could make his product, and even in the hours he could work. (For example, night work was often forbidden because poor light made for bad quality and eyestrain.) Prices were usually fixed; for nearly everyone accepted the medieval concept of the "just price," guaranteeing the worker a fair wage for his skill and labor and the purchaser a fair price for his product. Modern business competition was unknown.

The craft guilds also regulated the ways in which young men were trained to become masters. At the age of seven or eight a boy would become an "apprentice," signing an agreement that he would work for a master craftsman for seven years for room, board, clothing, and a set of tools. In return, the master agreed to teach him the elements of the trade, so that at the end of his apprenticeship the boy could produce a "masterpiece" that would make him eligible to become a free laborer, or "journeyman." These young men were employed by the masters for a daily wage as skilled assistants in his shop. After a number of years the ambitious journeyman might become eligible to join the guild, become a master, and start a shop of his own. This apprenticeship system provided the basic education of young workers until about a century ago, when the factory system made many crafts unnecessary; but it is still followed today in some places by such skilled tradesmen as carpenters, plumbers, and bricklayers.

THE GOVERNMENT OF THE TOWNS

Before 1100 few towns had any self-government; but as they became stronger during the twelfth century, many were able to demand charters from the lords. No two of these charters were exactly alike, but they usually included three important provisions: (1) all citizens of the cities were freemen who could come and go as they pleased; (2) the citizens were freed of the labor services that were required of peasants on the manors, but instead paid a money tax for land and protection; and (3) no lord could seize their property.

Gradually various forms of town government developed. In a few communities the burghers won the right to elect an official who could conduct commercial courts. In Italy, the first country where towns became strong,

A medieval street scene: a miniature from a medieval French manuscript. Several craftsmen can be seen at work in their shops: tailors at the left, an apothecary (druggist) at the right, and weavers and a barber in the background. Narrow, winding streets such as this, typical of medieval towns, can still be found in the older parts of many European cities.

a few towns were able to throw off the yoke of feudal or ecclesiastical rulers in the late eleventh century. These towns established "communes," or associations of townsmen, who administered their own local governments virtually free from outside control. Not warriors themselves, but still active participants in the wars and political struggles of their time, the Italian townsmen often hired professional soldiers called *condottieri* to fight their battles for them. Unfortunately, the townsmen usually became embroiled in so many quarrels with each other that their attempts at self-government failed, and the Italian towns fell into the hands either of groups of great noble or merchant families, of political bosses called "despots," or of the *condottieri* they had employed to protect them.

The medieval manors existed in western Europe wherever there was feudalism, and the peasants who labored on them produced the wealth that enabled their feudal lords to hunt, fight, and build their enormous stone castles. The towns only began to grow large as the Middle Ages drew to a close in the thirteenth and fourteenth centuries, and their inhabitants, though few in numbers, were the only people who did not properly fit into the feudal and manorial scheme of life. But lords, peasants, and townsmen all had one thing in common: their absolute reliance on the Catholic Church as their sole guide along the stormy voyage to heaven. The church was the most significant single institution of the age.

People, Places, and Terms

Venice	bailey	tithe
Genoa	palais	Hanse
Pisa	arras	burgher
Sardinia	seneschal	guild
Sicily	marshal	guild merchant
Flanders	chamberlain	craft guild
Champagne	three-field system	master
Rhone River	bailiff	apprentice
Levant	provost	journeyman
	slave	just price
manor	serf	commune
keep (donjon)	freeman	*condottieri*
lists	demesne	despot
portcullis	*corvée*	

Getting Organized

1. Describe a typical medieval castle and the activities that went on within its walls.
2. Who were the most important of the manor officials and what were their functions? Did the lord of the manor live richly or simply? Why?
3. Describe a typical peasant village. What was the three-field system and why was it necessary?
4. What were the three classes of peasant and how did they differ? What rights did the peasants have from the lord? What obligations did the peasant owe the lord? How were these obligations enforced?
5. In Europe where were the major trade centers and trade routes? What function did the fairs of Champagne serve?
6. Describe a typical medieval town. Would you like to have lived in one? Why? What was the position of the cathedral in the town?
7. In the towns, what functions did the guilds merchant serve? What functions did the craft guilds serve? By what process did a young boy become a master in a guild?
8. How were medieval towns governed? What rights did the citizens of the towns have?

Understanding the Big Picture

1. Describe the life of a typical medieval peasant. How much control over his life did the lord of the manor have?
2. In the eleventh and twelfth centuries what was the state of Europe's commercial development?
3. What was the difference between the guilds merchant and the craft guilds? Why did the craft guilds supplant the guilds merchant?

For the Thoughtful

1. Compare the life of the peasant with the life of the typical person in modern society. Why do you think the medieval peasant accepted his rather dismal way of life?
2. Compare the training of a future master to the training of a future knight. Does the average young man of our own society get as much training as his medieval counterpart? Explain.
3. How similar were the guilds to our own modern trade unions? To chambers of commerce? Do you think our unions evolved from these guilds?
4. Why can it be said that the growing towns were the natural enemies of the feudal system?

9

the Medieval Church

During the Middle Ages the Catholic Church was more powerful than any of the feudal states of western Europe. At its height, early in the thirteenth century, the church seemed about to create a "Commonwealth of Christendom," incorporating all of Catholic Europe into a single, unified state dedicated to establishing the ideals and practices of medieval Christianity. All during the Middle Ages the busy clergy of the Catholic Church were everywhere, and even the lowliest monks or priests had an influence over the minds and souls of men that the mightiest king could not command. Never before or since in the history of western Europe has organized religion so potently influenced every aspect of men's lives.

THE SOURCES OF RELIGIOUS INFLUENCE

Modern men can hardly conceive of the importance of the Roman Catholic Church in the lives of all the people of central and western Europe during the Middle Ages. On the manors the parish church was the center of religious and social life. In the towns cathedrals towered over shops and palaces. Bishops were feudal lords, monks and priests were advisers to kings and princes. The clergy baptized the newborn children, taught the young, married the adults and guided them through their lives, and buried the dead. They cared for the poor and counseled the rich. Inspired by the clergy, kings and commoners united to build the churches and cathedrals that are still the pride of Europe and to crusade against the heretic at home and the infidel abroad, firm in their faith that only the church could lead them through the stormy world to a safe port in heaven.

THE SACRAMENTS

To Catholics then, as now, the sacraments of the church were the "outward signs instituted by Christ to give grace," without which salvation was almost impossible. There were seven sacraments. Four marked the principal events of man's life: (1) baptism, administered to the tiny child, cleansed him from original sin and made him a Christian, the child of God and the heir of heaven; (2) confirmation, administered to the youth, and symbolized by the laying on of hands and anointing with oil, gave him the "gifts" of the Holy Ghost and made him a strong and perfect Christian and a soldier of Jesus Christ; (3) matrimony united man and woman in lawful and holy marriage, which no human could dissolve; and (4) extreme unction, administered to those near death, gave health and strength to the soul and, perhaps, to the body as well.

Regularly throughout his life the Catholic took part in two other sacraments, penance and the Holy Eucharist. In the sacrament of penance, the repentant Christian, after confessing his sins to a priest and resolving not to repeat them, was absolved from them and made amends by performing an assigned penalty or penance, such as saying prayers, denying himself worldly pleasures, or doing "good works" which were especially pleasing to God. The Holy Eucharist, the sacrament of the Lord's Supper, involved changing bread and wine by a priest (according to the doctrine of "transubstantiation") into the substance of the body and blood of Christ, which was then partaken by the faithful. The elaborate ritual of the Mass developed around this sacrament, and the churches and cathedrals were designed to house this ceremony.

The seventh sacrament was reserved for the clergy; this was "holy orders," which consisted of the laying on of hands by a bishop to candidates for the clergy. This gave them the power, authority, and grace to perform their sacred duties as the ministry of the church and successors of Christ's apostles.

Generally, only priests could administer the sacraments, and only a bishop could administer confirmation and holy orders. The men of the

Middle Ages were therefore convinced that the clergy were indispensable. Life without the continual presence of the priesthood was unimaginable to them, for they believed that the world was a constant struggle between the forces of God and the devil, and the priests were the leaders of the struggle for God who must direct every little skirmish.

PRAYER AND RITUAL

The church slowly evolved an elaborate set of prayers and rituals reflecting the dignity and importance of its role in the salvation of souls. Early Christians had recited the Lord's Prayer and a *Credo* (creed) together, and gradually other prayers were added and elaborate rites formulated, especially for the celebration of the Mass. Saint Ambrose (see page 34) composed the famous hymn *Gloria in Excelsis Deo* late in the fourth century, and in the Middle Ages other clerics contributed such magnificent hymns as the *Stabat Mater* and the *Dies Irae,* celebrating the Virgin Mary and the day of judgment.

Medieval life was punctuated by religious festivals, for which men and women of all classes dressed in their best, went to church, and took a holiday. Some of these festivals marked the passage of the Christian year through its various "seasons," such as Christmas, Lent, and Easter. Others celebrated patron saints: some 25,000 saints had been canonized by the tenth century, and every town and village, church and cathedral, guild and country had its patron saint, whose "day" was an occasion for worship and rejoicing, parading in the streets, and ringing of bells.

Religious relics and statues were everywhere. There were saints' statues in little niches by the roadside, and the churches and cathedrals were covered with them. Churches treasured relics of their patron saints. The grave of Saint Peter was venerated in the basilica in Rome that bore his name; other churches had bits of the True Cross, the blood of a martyr, or the hair, bones, or possessions of saints, preserved in richly decorated little containers called "reliquaries" made by the most skillful of medieval craftsmen.

In the twelfth century the most venerated of all religious figures, next to Christ, was the Virgin Mary. Thousands of churches and cathedrals were dedicated to *Notre Dame,* "Our Lady," and adorned with a statue of her, often holding the Christ Child in her arms. What the courts of love were to chivalry, the "Cult of Mary" was to religion and to daily life— a softening and civilizing influence.

The sacrament of baptism: a section of "The Seven Sacraments," a tapestry woven in Flanders in the fifteenth century. The priest who is administering the sacrament is holding the infant above the baptismal font (bowl). Behind him are two assisting priests, and at the right are the child's father and mother. The man at the left is probably the godfather (sponsor in the Christian faith) of the child.

CANON LAW

Another great source of strength to the church was its system of canon law, which dated well back before the fall of Rome and has been added to continually ever since. By the twelfth century, church courts tried most cases in which clergymen or church property were involved. They also decided disputes over matters affected by religious belief, such as marriage, inheritance, faith, and morals. In the eleventh century the canon law was confused and often contradictory and outdated, but in the twelfth and thirteenth centuries it was revised to become the most effective legal system of the time. The most important of the legal reformers was a Benedictine monk named Gratian who, in the middle of the twelfth century, wrote a book called the *Decretum* in which he listed the canon laws in an orderly way and then stated the principles on which they were based. He taught at the university of Bologna, in Italy, which soon became a center for legal studies. In the next century universities at Paris in France and Oxford in England also trained legal scholars who spread the revised canon law throughout Europe.

Canon law was widely used by laymen, who found it fairer and more lenient than the laws of their secular lords. Clergymen discovered that it freed them from reliance on the civil courts and allowed them to success-fully defy the attempts of kings and counts to dominate the church.

THE MONASTIC REFORMERS

"In religion," a wit once said, "nothing fails like success." All during the Middle Ages the great mass of the people were firmly and enthusiastically Catholic. So were most of the clergy. But this does not mean that the his-tory of the medieval church was not stormy or that the church itself was above reproach. Pious people gladly paid their tithes and showered the clergy with gifts; church estates grew larger and larger and the men who administered them richer and richer. And riches sometimes brought cor-ruption. Some clergymen grew fat and lazy, others neglected their vows, and a few devoted themselves to feudal politics.

As a result, devout Christians from the tenth to the thirteenth centuries were constantly working for reform in an attempt to wipe out corruption. Monks formed new orders that followed the strictest of rules, hoping by their example to influence the other, older orders to do the same. Some of the canon clergy (those who administered the cathedrals) followed the monks' example. And new groups of "mendicant" (begging) friars refused to have anything at all to do with property, instead going among the people to teach and preach and obtaining what they needed on a day-to-day basis. Some of these reformers were among the most significant leaders of the Middle Ages.

CLUNIAC, CARTHUSIAN, AND CISTERCIAN MONKS

Distressed by corruption in the monasteries, Duke William I of Aquitaine in 910 founded a monastery at Cluny. The "Cluniac" monks refused to accept gifts of land that would require them to serve lay lords, and they followed a far stricter rule than was customary in the older orders. Eventu-ally there were 300 Cluniac monasteries, all governed by the abbot at Cluny, who was responsible directly to the pope.

Late in the eleventh century a wave of religious enthusiasm swept across Europe, sending hermits to live alone in the hills and forests and filling the roads with pilgrims and crusaders. This enthusiasm led some to join the monasteries of a new order called the "Carthusians," whose monks rarely left their cells, fasted three days each week, and never ate meat.

This same religious revival led other monks to found another new order, a branch of the Benedictines called the "Cistercians." In an effort to revive the original piety of the Benedictine order, the Cistercians followed Saint Benedict's rule (see page 13) to the letter, labored in fields and monastic workshops, and refused to accept most kinds of gifts. In the early twelfth century the leader of the Cistercians was Bernard of Clairvaux (1091-1153), the "uncrowned king of Christendom." Bernard was influenced by the gentle "Cult of Mary" to sympathize with the human frailties of his followers, but he enforced the strictest of religious discipline just the same. He became so famous for his preaching and holiness that when he reluctantly left his monastery, he was able to influence the election of popes, persuade kings to go on crusade, and help found the Knights Templars. During Bernard's life, the number of Cistercian monasteries increased from five to 350. Almost single-handedly, he brought Europe to a peak of religious enthusiasm.

CANON PRIESTS: AUGUSTINIANS AND PRAEMONSTRATENSIANS

Canon priests (the cathedral clergy) worked among the people, but they lived together in obedience to a rule originally drawn up in the fifth century by Saint Augustine (see page 35) for his priests in Hippo. These "Augustinians" had become lax by the twelfth century, however, and in an effort to reform them (much as the Cistercians reformed the Benedictines) a friend of Bernard's named Norbert of Xanten in 1119 founded a new order called the "Praemonstratensians," who rigidly followed Augustine's rule and often retired to desolate places to renew their dedication to their vows.

THE FRIARS: FRANCISCANS AND DOMINICANS

As the thirteenth century began, groups of laymen in Italy and southern France became disgusted with worldly churchmen and began to take up heretical beliefs. To prevent this, two remarkable young men, Francis of Assisi (1182-1226) and Dominic (1170-1221), organized orders of "friars"

St. Francis of Assisi: from a French-Flemish manuscript of about 1265. The early popularity of the Franciscan order was due in part to the remarkable personality of its founder. Francis was noted for his enthusiasm, gaiety, and, above all, love. His love extended to all mankind and, indeed, to all created things. On the occasion depicted here, Francis turned from the group he was addressing to preach a sermon to a flock of birds, exhorting them to praise their Creator.

(from the Latin *frater*, "brother"). The friars, instead of living in monasteries, went out into the world as missionaries.

Francis, the son of a well-to-do Italian merchant, had retired to the hills to live in the midst of unspoiled nature and to preach. Soon he attracted a group of followers, whom he organized in 1210 as the "Order of Friars Minor." Members of the order, called "Franciscans," were forbidden to own property or to marry. The Franciscans wandered from place to place, much like modern revivalists, warning against the materialism of their times and calling for a return to the religious enthusiasm that Bernard had kindled a century earlier.

Dominic was a Spanish priest who, shocked at finding thousands of heretics in southern France, won permission from the pope in 1216 to establish the "Order of Preachers," whose members devoted themselves to teaching and preaching against heresy. These friars, usually called the "Dominicans," founded some of the best schools and universities in Europe and were among the most illustrious teachers of the next two centuries.

The Franciscans sought to arouse the religious emotions of medieval men and women; the Dominicans contributed to the strength and coherence of Catholic doctrine.

🐚 HERETICS AND THE INQUISITION

The monastic reformers all worked within the framework of the church. Neither the reformers nor most laymen questioned any of its doctrines or thought of disputing Catholic teachings. But off and on during the Middle Ages, groups of heretics adopted creeds different from those of the Catholic Church and challenged the authority of its priests.

Most medieval men detested heresy as treason against God and had no sympathy for the idea of religious liberty. To medieval men, heresy was a dangerous and contagious disease like smallpox, whose victims must be isolated from society and cured by any means available. The faithful assumed that heretics had lost their souls and that they might lead others to lose their souls as well. Therefore the church did all it could to stamp out heresy wherever it appeared and either to restore heretics to the Catholic fold or to punish them.

The church attempted to wipe out heresy by many methods. Cistercians, Cluniacs, and other monastic groups sought to strengthen the papacy in the hope that the pope could wipe out corruption that might lead to criticism of the church and eventually to heresy. Franciscans and Dominicans went among the heretics to preach the Catholic faith. When all else failed, the church resorted to fire and sword with crusades and the Inquisition.

THE ALBIGENSIAN CRUSADE

Toward the end of the twelfth century southern France became a hotbed of heresy. Followers of Peter Waldo (called the "Waldensians") went among the people to preach their own interpretation of the Bible, in open violation of the orders of their archbishop. An even more dangerous group was the "Albigensians," who maintained that the God of the Old Testament was really the devil and that therefore the Catholic Church was worshiping an evil being. By 1208 there were so many Albigensians that

Pope Innocent III called for an "Albigensian Crusade" to exterminate them. An army marched into southern France, besieged an Albigensian stronghold, scaled its walls, and began to massacre its inhabitants. A soldier told a papal official who was present that many good Catholics as well as heretics were being executed. "Kill all, kill all," the official replied. "God will know his own." The crusade accomplished its goal; but the fighting went on for nearly twenty years, and the population and prosperity of one of the richest regions of France was destroyed.

THE INQUISITION

During the Albigensian Crusade the church established the "Inquisition," a special court charged with finding and putting down heresy and punishing heretics. "Inquisitors"—usually Dominicans, because the shock of the Albigensian heresy was what had prompted Dominic to found the order—soon appeared throughout Christendom. The inquisitors encouraged informers to furnish names of suspects, who were often seized and tried in secret without being allowed to challenge their accusers face to face. Torture was often used to encourage witnesses to give evidence and to force suspects to confess. Some suspects were acquitted of the charges against them; but more were convicted, stripped of their property, and jailed. Unrepentant heretics were "turned over to the secular arm," which in most cases meant that they were to be executed (by laymen, for the clergy were forbidden to draw blood). Most convicted heretics were burned alive. On one occasion in 1212, eighty heretics were burned in one town in a single day.

Such excesses led men to doubt the wisdom of the Inquisition, and by the middle of the thirteenth century calmer heads prevailed. The Inquisition continued on a limited scale, however, and was later revived in the Catholic struggle against Protestantism in the sixteenth century. (Chapter 22.)

❧ THE RISE AND DECLINE OF PAPAL AUTHORITY

The Cluniacs had attempted to insure a high level of piety by concentrating control of their order in a single abbot. In the same spirit, other reformers hoped to purify the entire church by increasing the authority of the popes. Medieval men made little distinction between religious and worldly authority, believing as they did in the Commonwealth of Christendom in which the powers of church and state were inseparably entwined. It was, therefore, easy to argue that the popes, as the successors of Saint Peter, should have control over clergy and laymen alike. The great medieval popes therefore tried not only to centralize the government of the church but also to require that emperors obey their religious commands—even though these might conflict with powers the rulers felt were theirs alone.

THE AUTHORITY AND REVENUES OF THE PAPACY

In the eleventh and twelfth centuries, reformers successfully increased the influence and power of the popes. One of the most important reforms concerned the method of choosing the pope. Originally the pope, as bishop of Rome, had been elected (like all other bishops) by the clergy of his diocese. But as the political importance of the papacy increased after the collapse of the Roman Empire, political leaders increasingly sought to control the elections. All too often they were successful: Byzantine emperors, Holy Roman emperors, or unscrupulous Italian nobles either finagled the papal election or, openly defying tradition, simply placed their own candidate on the papal throne. Such practices offended the reformers. In 1049 Pope Leo IX, who had been selected by the Holy Roman Emperor Henry III, refused to be crowned until his "nomination" had been confirmed by the Roman clergy. The next pope, Nicholas II, influenced by the monk Hildebrand (later Pope Gregory VII), decreed in 1059 that· henceforth popes would be chosen by an "electoral college" composed of certain specified leaders (called "cardinal clergy" or "cardinals") of the Roman clergy. Another reform enabled the pope to veto the election of archbishops, thus assuring the eventual choice of a man of whom he approved. And finally, the reformers began to send papal representatives called "legates" to the important centers of Europe, where they supervised and protected the interests of the church.

The real key to assuring papal control of the church was the right of the popes to appoint trustworthy bishops. Many kings and lords claimed the right to choose their own local prelates (a practice called "lay investiture"), because the prelates were often temporal rulers as well as spiritual leaders. The popes claimed that the interests of the church came first and that they alone should appoint the bishops. As a result, "investiture controversies" were fought out in every major country of Europe and were never completely settled during the Middle Ages.

The papal *curia* (court) grew as the popes became more powerful; and the traditional sources of papal income, the Papal States around Rome and religious fees and taxes, became inadequate. The popes therefore increased their demands on their vassals and the charges for the use of church courts, drawing ever-larger sums of money from foreign countries. A bishop was expected to pay "first fruits," a sum roughly equal to a year's income from his diocese, when he took office, and to give "subsidies" when the pope demanded them. Priests contributed "tithes" equal to one tenth of their income, and laymen contributed generously for the services of the church. In some regions a tax of a penny on each hearth, called "Peter's Pence," was collected each year and sent to Rome.

It was one thing to levy taxes and quite another to collect them. At first the bishops collected the papal taxes, then the Knights Templars, and in the fifteenth century they were collected for a fee by Italian merchants. No matter who collected them, they were unpopular and caused a good deal of criticism of the papacy.

THREE GREAT MEDIEVAL POPES

The rise, height, and decline of the medieval papacy are symbolized by three outstanding popes of the eleventh, twelfth, and thirteenth centuries. All three were pious, confident, well-trained, and ambitious for themselves and for the church. Each used every weapon he had to attain his goal, the establishment of a Commonwealth of Christendom.

Gregory VII. As the monk Hildebrand, the future Pope Gregory VII (pope 1073-1085) served as a cardinal under five different popes before he himself became pope. Always the reformer, he was largely responsible for the creation of the College of Cardinals and was the first to use papal legates, and he was a determined opponent of clerical marriage and of simony (the selling of church offices).

Pope Gregory was convinced that the Commonwealth of Christendom was possible only if the church could control the princes of Europe and the pope could control the church by appointing its bishops. This belief brought him head on into an investiture controversy with the Holy Roman Emperor Henry IV, the most powerful ruler in Europe. Henry governed lands extending from the North Sea to central Italy, and he believed that his authority came from God just as surely as did the pope's. Because Henry could not trust his nobles to obey him, he needed the support of bishops whom he could trust. He had no intention of surrendering the selection of bishops to any Roman pope.

Almost immediately after he was crowned pope, Gregory ordered Henry to stop appointing bishops. The emperor called his bishops to a council at the German city of Worms in 1076, got them to declare that Gregory should be deposed, and wrote a letter urging the pope to "come down, come down from thy throne to be accursed of all generations."

In reply, Gregory excommunicated Henry. The German nobles of the Holy Roman Empire invited the pope to come north across the Alps to Germany to help them choose a new emperor. Desperate, Henry hurried south to Italy in mid-winter of 1077 and appeared, dressed as a humble pilgrim, to plead for mercy before the pope at Canossa. Gregory kept Henry standing for three days in snow before readmitting him to the church. Gregory's victory seemed complete—and ever since, the phrase "going to Canossa" has meant the submission of secular to religious authority.

But the papal victory made some German nobles and bishops fear that the papacy might be becoming too powerful. The nobles therefore switched their support to Henry, who with their aid captured Rome in 1083 and set up an "antipope" of his own. Two years later Gregory VII died in exile,

Henry IV at Canossa: an illumination from a manuscript of the time. Henry, kneeling, is asking the abbot of Cluny (left) and Countess Matilda of Tuscany to make a plea in his behalf with Pope Gregory VII.

worn out by his struggle to establish papal supremacy and crying, "I have loved justice and hated iniquity, therefore I die an exile."

True enough—but his struggle with Henry IV weakened the Holy Roman Empire (Chapter 11) and set a precedent that made possible the triumphs of Innocent III a century later.

Innocent III. The twelfth century, which began fifteen years after Gregory's death, was a time of triumph for the medieval church. This was the age of Bernard of Clairvaux, of the Praemonstratensians, of the first crusades to the Holy Land (Chapter 13), and of the establishment of the Knights Templars. It seemed entirely possible that the popes might become the temporal rulers of all Europe. No man brought this dream closer to reality than Innocent III (pope 1198-1216), who devoted his life to extending papal power.

Innocent was the pope who helped Francis and Dominic establish their orders of friars and who preached the Albigensian Crusade against heresy. He was also feudal overlord of Naples and Sicily, Sardinia, the Christian states in Spain, five Slavic states in eastern Europe, and a Christian kingdom founded by crusaders in Palestine.

He also dominated the greatest kings of his age. He rejected one Holy Roman emperor, forced another to surrender much of his control over the German church, and procured the election of a third. He made the king of France take back an unwanted wife. He imposed an interdict (which forbade the holding of church services) on England in a dispute with its king, causing the panic-stricken monarch to cede his country to the papacy and receive it back as a fief.

Innocent's greatest achievement was the Fourth Lateran Council, which met in Rome in 1215. Among the 1500 notables who assembled to approve Innocent's decrees were 400 bishops, 800 abbots and priors, and representatives of every major European monarch. The council declared that the church was one and universal, defined a number of controversial doctrines, and increased support for education. It reformed the clergy by forbidding priests to marry, worship relics, or get drunk. It required non-Christians to wear a distinctive badge. The Fourth Lateran Council was the climax of Innocent's reign and the peak of papal power.

During his pontificate (papal reign) of eighteen years, Innocent III brought the church power and prestige that his predecessors had only dreamed of. No other man came so close to fulfilling the medieval ideal of creating a commonwealth in which church and state would work together to establish everywhere the ideals and practices of medieval Christendom.

Boniface VIII. An energetic and ambitious old man, Boniface VIII (pope 1294-1303) hoped to make the papacy even more influential than it had been during Innocent's time almost a century earlier. The thirteenth-century church seemed more powerful than ever, but there were signs of trouble to come. Monarchs in England and France were winning the loyalty of their people, to some extent at the expense of the church. Europe was increasingly prosperous and men became more interested in material things than they had been—and less devoted to their religion. The Inquisition had to put down little groups of heretics in many parts of Europe.

But Boniface paid no attention to these developments. Kings opposed him because he insisted his authority was greater than theirs. Churchmen opposed him because he used some of his papal income to enrich his family. And when he issued two papal bulls (official statements signed with his personal *bulla*, or seal) that contained extreme doctrines of papal authority, he became involved in a major struggle with King Philip IV of France. The first of these, the bull *Clericis laicos* of 1296, forbade the clergy to pay taxes to the kings, and it threatened the excommunication of any monarch who tried to tax the church. The second, the bull *Unam sanctam* of 1302, stated that there is only one church and that of "this one and only church there is one body and one head"—the pope. The papal power, he continued, is "ordained of God: and whoever resists it resists the ordinance of God, for the power of kings and captains comes only from the church" and can be exercised only "at the will and by permission of the priest," because "it is altogether necessary for every human creature to be subject to the Roman pontiff."

Philip IV of France (king 1285-1314) had resisted the first bull, and the second was too much for him to accept. Calling an assembly of French nobles and churchmen, he won their support for his struggle against the pope. Then he sent an agent to Italy where, with the connivance of some Italian nobles, he penetrated the papal palace at Anagni and threatened the pope with death while his men plundered the palace. Boniface, an old man of 75, died soon after from the shock.

In 1305 Philip, determined that no other pope would ever defy him, obtained the election of a French archbishop as Pope Clement V. The new pontiff never even went to Italy, but was crowned north of the Alps and remained there. For most of the rest of the fourteenth century, the popes lived in a magnificent palace at Avignon on the Rhone River, on the border of the kingdom of France. (See map, page 152.)

Boniface's tragedy was that he failed to realize that men had developed loyalties to their political rulers that no pope could hope to overcome. By claiming domination he could not enforce, he brought to an abrupt end the medieval concept of the papacy that Gregory VII and Innocent III had worked to build. After Boniface VIII, men could no longer hope to establish a Commonwealth of Christendom.

⚜ ⚜ ⚜

The medieval church was a unique combination of the human and the divine. Composed of human beings who had all the weaknesses and faults of their kind, it was still something more than just a group of individuals. Throughout the Middle Ages it not only reminded men that they could be better than they were, but it inspired dozens of outstanding leaders and millions of nameless ordinary people to work to establish a Commonwealth of Christendom in which each man had his own individual but secure role to play.

Before this dream was shattered early in the fourteenth century, the medieval church also inspired two of the greatest achievements of European history: scholastic philosophy and Gothic art and architecture.

People, Places, and Terms

Gratian	sacraments	Augustinians
Bernard of Clairvaux	baptism	Franciscans
Norbert of Xanten	confirmation	Dominicans
Francis of Assisi	matrimony	heresy
Dominic	extreme unction	Waldensians
Hildebrand	penance	Albigensians
(Gregory VII)	Holy Eucharist	Albigensian Crusade
Henry IV	transubstantiation	Inquisition
Innocent III	holy orders	inquisitor
Boniface VIII	Cult of Mary	College of Cardinals
Philip IV	canon law	legate
Clement V	canon clergy	lay investiture
	Decretum	first fruits
Bologna	Cluniac monasteries	subsidy
Oxford	Carthusians	tithe
Canossa	Cistercians	Peter's Pence
Avignon	Praemonstratensians	simony

antipope	Fourth Lateran	*Clericis laicos*
interdict	Council	*Unam sanctam*
pontificate	bull	

Getting Organized

1. What were the seven sacraments and what function did each serve? What importance did they give to the clergy?
2. What was the importance to medieval men of the ritual of the church? Religious festivals? Relics? Patron saints? The Virgin Mary?
3. What was canon law? Over what areas did it have jurisdiction?
4. What was the aim of the reforming monks? What new monastic orders were founded? What old orders were reformed?
5. What is heresy? What were the different ways used by the church to wipe it out?
6. What were the three ways in which the power of the popes was increased by medieval reformers? How successful were the popes in their reforms? How did they gain their money?
7. What was the contribution to the development of the power of the papacy and of the church of Gregory VII? Innocent III? Boniface VIII?

Understanding the Big Picture

1. How and to what extent did the church influence the everyday life of a medieval man?
2. How was the problem of corruption within the church dealt with by the popes and monks? What was the extent of this corruption?
3. With what great problems did the medieval popes have to deal? How did they attempt to deal with these problems? Which pope was the most successful?

For the Thoughtful

1. From your knowledge of the medieval popes, compare their power and influence to that of the pope today. What great changes have affected the differences between the two?
2. In your opinion, what should be the relationship between church and state? Why was there a conflict over this issue in the Middle Ages? Is there any such conflict in modern society? If so, how does it differ from the medieval conflict? How is it similar?
3. Compare Innocent's power over Europe to Charlemagne's power over Europe. Who had more power? Explain fully.

10

mediEval
LearninG and ARt

In much the same spirit that some monks, friars, and priests went out to preach among the people or to reform the church, others founded schools and universities and developed a religious philosophy called "scholasticism," which attempted to combine classical, Christian, and worldly knowledge into a single system of belief.

At the same time still others, most of them laymen whose names we will never know, were expressing their faith in God in art and architecture. Until the twelfth century they built churches and cathedrals in the simple but handsome Romanesque style. In the twelfth century this was replaced by the Gothic style, which dominated European architecture and art until the fifteenth century.

Although the medieval concept of the papacy did not survive the fourteenth century, scholasticism and the Romanesque and Gothic styles are still influential. They are the most enduring monuments of the Middle Ages.

MEDIEVAL EDUCATION

All medieval learning was connected with the church. During the first six centuries after the fall of Rome, monasteries and cathedrals were the only islands of learning in a sea of ignorance. Even in the twelfth and thirteenth centuries, the church made little effort to educate any who were not planning to join the clergy. It discouraged laymen from studying, for it feared that they might become heretics or rabble rousers. As late as the sixteenth century there were only 26,000 schoolboys in England's population of 5,000,000 (although, of course, sons of nobles were educated as pages and squires, and future craftsmen were apprentices; but none of these boys went to school to study academic subjects).

GRAMMAR SCHOOLS

Most medieval boys received their education in "grammar schools" taught by priests. These were literally "grammar" schools: after learning to read and write a little of their native language, the students, often still only seven years old, began to study Latin grammar, so that the language of the church and of all learning would be as familiar to them as their native tongue. Then they went on to study the "seven liberal arts," which were divided into two groups: the *trivium,* or elementary arts of grammar, rhetoric, and logic, and the *quadrivium,* or more advanced studies of arithmetic, geometry, music, and astronomy. The *quadrivium* was often required only of boys planning to attend the universities.

Grammar school life was hard. Classes lasted ten or twelve hours a day. Lazy or unruly boys were flogged regularly. Even so, discipline sometimes broke down; and one schoolmaster, a well-known philosopher named John the Scot, was stabbed to death with their pens by his irate pupils.

THE UNIVERSITIES

The first universities in Europe became prominent in the twelfth century. The word *universitas* in Latin means "all," and was often used to denote a corporation or guild. The universities were really guilds (see page 112), either of masters or of students. The University of Paris, for example, was a guild of "masters of arts" who expected their students to study for seven years. After the students had completed part of their curriculum, they took examinations and were made "bachelors of arts." Then, at the end of seven years, they presented "masterpieces" in the form of a sample lesson or of a "thesis," an academic proposition that they had to defend in public against all comers. If they succeeded in this, they were allowed to join the guild and become masters of arts themselves. Academic robes symbolized their new status. In many universities the style of these robes has remained unchanged to the present day; they are the origin of the cap and gown worn by college graduates in the United States today.

A master lecturing to his students: an Italian woodcut of the fifteenth century. Both master and students are wearing academic gowns. Note the small size of the room and its lack of furniture.

Oxford University in England was founded by students called home from Paris during one of the twelfth century wars between the kings of England and France. After a riot in Oxford in 1209, a group of students and their masters moved to Cambridge, where they set up a rival university. In such ways were the medieval universities founded.

University life then was far different from what it is now. Each master taught his own students, from whom he collected tuition if he could. The students at first lived in rented rooms in town, but later tended to band together to live in private dormitories called "colleges" (from *collegia*, another Latin word for "guild"). University officials found it hard to keep order, although Oxford students were required to attend daily Mass, forbidden to take bows and arrows to class, and punished if they "sinned with sleep." Most were studying for the priesthood, but some were "gentlemen scholars" who paid tuition but were not expected to study; they merely stayed around to enjoy the atmosphere.

Books were rare and expensive before the days of printing, so most of the masters taught by reading slowly while their students took the copious notes that were their only textbooks. The undergraduate subjects were still the seven liberal arts; but as time went on, more specialized subjects grew popular, and many students went to take graduate work at Paris in theology, or to Italy to study law at Bologna or medicine at Salerno.

🐚 MEDIEVAL PHILOSOPHY

As time went on, the teachers in the universities were no longer content merely to teach subjects handed down from earlier times, and many of them went on to make important contributions to learning. In the Middle Ages theology, the study of God and of religious doctrines, was the "queen of the sciences," and a number of monks and priests created a religious philosophy, called "scholasticism," that is perhaps the greatest single achievement of the era.

BERNARD OF CLAIRVAUX

Bernard of Clairvaux (1091-1153), the leader of the Cistercians (see page 121) never taught in a university, but he profoundly affected those who did. Bernard believed that the world was a snare and a delusion and that man was a piteous creature who could not rise above its temptations. He insisted that man should therefore turn his back on the world to study and contemplate God, who had graciously revealed himself to man through the Scriptures and the inspired writings of the fathers of the church. By having faith and unquestioningly accepting God's word and love, sinful man could rise above himself to communicate directly with his Maker. This doctrine, called "mysticism," was the most widely held philosophy of the twelfth century.

ABELARD AND HIS FOLLOWERS

Peter Abelard (1079-1142), a contemporary of Bernard, was a completely different kind of person. He was a wandering scholar who went from university to university searching for knowledge, a popular teacher who thrived on the adulation of his students, and partner in one of the great love affairs of medieval times—with the beautiful and brilliant Héloïse— even though he supposedly was preparing to become a priest.

Abelard's greatest work was *Sic et non*, ("Yes and No"), in which he listed 158 questions concerning faith and reason and quoted apparently conflicting answers from the Bible, the church fathers, and decrees of church councils. What he probably was trying to do was to point out that the sources on which Bernard relied were in basic disagreement and that reason and not faith must be man's guide to knowledge.

This was more than Bernard could accept. Although Abelard never denied the importance of faith, some of his followers challenged the doctrine of transubstantiation (see page 117), and others disputed the right of the clergy to have temporal authority. Therefore, at Bernard's urging, a church council in 1141 specifically condemned sixteen of Abelard's teachings. When the pope ordered him to be silent and teach no more, Abelard retired to the monastery at Cluny.

But although Abelard had lost his battle with Bernard, others quickly took up the cause of reason and logic. Only seven years after the council that condemned Abelard, an Italian monk named Gratian used his principles to write a monumental *Concordance of Discordant Canons* in an effort to bring order to the often confused canon law. Gratian's book, called the *Decretum* for short, was immediately accepted and widely used. (See page 119.) John of Salisbury (d. 1180) wrote an orderly summary of traditional learning in his *Book of the Seven Arts* later in the twelfth century. Interest in reason led to renewed study of classical authors, and even Ovid, the first-century Roman author of *The Art of Love*, became popular.

ALBERTUS MAGNUS

In the thirteenth century Albertus Magnus (1193-1280) continued the new emphasis on reason. A German who taught at Cologne and, for a time, in Paris, he read widely in Greek and Roman authors. He was particularly influenced by the thinking of Aristotle, who had carefully noted down his observations of the world around him and attempted to organize them in a reasonable way. Albertus Magnus summarized his philosophy when he wrote, "The sublimest wisdom of which the world could boast flourished in Greece. Even as the Jews knew God by the Scriptures, so the pagan philosophers knew Him by the natural wisdom of reason, and were debtors to Him for it by their homage."

THOMAS AQUINAS

Thomas Aquinas (1225-1274), a student of Albertus Magnus, attempted to combine Bernard's reliance on faith and Abelard's and Albertus's emphasis on reason into a single philosophy. In doing so, he established himself as the greatest of medieval philosophers and of Catholic theologians.

St. Thomas Aquinas: an Italian painting, believed to be the work of Bartolommeo degli Erri (1430-1479?). The figures at the left represent St. Thomas at his studies. At the right he is shown at his desk writing, aided by Sts. Peter and Paul.

Aquinas attempted to reconcile Bernard and Abelard by making a distinction between the "passive" and the "active" intellects. The passive intellect, he believed, was that part of the mind that records, camera-like, impressions of the world; the active intellect is that part of the mind that analyzes these impressions and, using both reason and faith, goes beyond them to determine universal truths. To Aquinas, reason without faith was meaningless—but so was faith without reason.

In his greatest book, the *Summa theologia* ("The Sum Total of Theology"), Thomas Aquinas attempted to unify all knowledge of the world and to describe the nature and destiny of Christian man. He believed that God had in His mind a notion of the perfect man, which Aquinas called man's "essence." At the same time, each individual has his own personal qualities, which Aquinas called his "being." To Aquinas, the object of each Christian human being should be to attain his essence, or to be as much like God's idea of the perfect man as possible.

The question Aquinas then asked was: How can a human being under-stand his essence so he can work to attain it? Since the fall of Adam from grace, the theologian believed, no man could understand his essence un-aided; only faith could lead him to God and an understanding of the essence of man. But once faith was attained, understanding naturally fol-lowed, and then at last man could use his reason to help him do the good works by which he would fulfill his essence. Here again, Aquinas combined Bernard and Abelard; faith was the first requirement, but reason then became the tool by which man accomplished the tasks that God had set for him.

Aquinas added little to the knowledge of his times, but he combined in a single philosophy the conflicting beliefs of his contemporaries. His *Summa* has been compared to the medieval cathedrals, those magnificent buildings that testify to the faith and love of God of their builders. Aquinas has come to be considered *the* philosopher of the Commonwealth of Christendom, because he taught that man and nature, faith and reason, church and state, were all parts of God's single great plan and that each with its own being and essence was a part of the larger whole.

MEDIEVAL ARCHITECTURE

Medieval builders attempted to express in stone what Aquinas had ex-pressed in books—their love for God and their faith in the church. On the façades of a number of medieval churches is the motto *Domus Dei et Porta Coeli*, "This is the House of God and the Gate to Heaven." No wonder that pious medieval men lavished their wealth, talent, and time on their churches and cathedrals, which dominated (and still do) the landscape of Europe to an even greater extent than office buildings and shopping centers dominate America.

THE ROMANESQUE STYLE

Until the end of the twelfth century, most European churches were built in the "Romanesque" style. The Romanesque borrowed heavily from early Christian architecture. (See pages 39-41.) Before the eleventh century most Romanesque churches had wooden roofs, and most eventually burned down or were torn down. Then builders learned to make stone "barrel vaults" (essentially, one arch placed behind another, making a rounded look), and the great age of Romanesque building began. The trouble with barrel vaulting was that it was very heavy, so that the supporting walls had to be thick and could only be pierced by small windows. As a result, the interiors of Romanesque churches were low, dark, and gloomy. But the architects made up for this by lavish use of exterior sculptures and by decorating interior columns with carvings.

Romanesque architecture varied from place to place. In Italy, where Roman influence was strongest, the basilica plan (see page 40) was extensively used. In northern Europe, many Romanesque structures were covered with weird carvings of animals and plants from Germanic mythology. In England, where Romanesque style is usually called "Norman," buildings were unusually massive and often severely plain and simple.

In the eleventh and early twelfth centuries, the monastic orders, with their huge estates, were likely to be wealthier than the bishops in the towns, so much Romanesque building was done by the monasteries. The largest and most impressive Romanesque church of all was built for the monks at Cluny; those who saw it (before it was destroyed in 1810-1811) said that it was so beautiful that it could not have been designed by a mere human being.

THE GOTHIC STYLE

In the late twelfth century, Romanesque architecture rapidly gave way to what is now called the "Gothic" style, which predominated in Europe until the fifteenth century. Gothic churches have been compared to many things: to praying hands pointed upward toward God; to Aquinas's philosophy that summarized medieval man's religious faith and worldly knowledge; to modern skyscrapers that symbolize the wealth, pride, and ambition of their builders.

The differences between the Gothic and Romanesque are immediately obvious. In the Gothic, the pointed arch replaced the round Roman arch of the Romanesque; a soaring upward quality replaced the heavy quality of the Romanesque; and light, window-filled walls replaced the heavy blank walls of the Romanesque. Two simple developments made these differences possible. One was the discovery that a vaulted ceiling need not be the same strength everywhere, but that light stone sheathing could be supported by heavier but graceful ribs that carry the weight down to piers placed between the nave and the aisle. The second was the discovery that the outward thrust of the weight of the vault could be absorbed by masonry arches called "flying buttresses," which were connected to heavy piers set into the outward walls of the aisle. It thus became possible to build churches and cathedrals higher than ever before and to fill their walls with huge stained-glass windows, which filtered glorious colored light into the interiors.

Most Gothic churches and cathedrals were built in the towns. By the middle of the twelfth century, the bishops and the townsmen had grown rich enough to be able to afford gigantic buildings that would testify to their faith and display their wealth. In France, where the style originated and was most fully developed, the first Gothic cathedral was started at Sens in 1130. In a little more than a century, others, each larger and more elaborate than the ones that had gone before, were begun in such towns as Laon, Paris, Chartres, Rouen, Reims, Amiens, and Beauvais. In a single century eighty cathedrals and 500 churches of comparable size were started. Some were so large that it took three centuries to complete them; others are not finished even today. The Cathedral of Notre Dame de Paris (many cathedrals were dedicated to *Notre Dame,* "Our Lady") is by no means the largest, but its vaulted ceiling rises almost 110 feet, its main section stretches almost 400 feet east and west, and it can comfortably hold 9,000 people.

The interiors of the cathedrals were dominated by a haunting sense of unworldliness created by the flooding colored light, the tall columns, and the delicate tracery of the ribs that support the vaulted ceiling. The façade, which faced west toward the setting sun, was covered with sculpture which was incorporated into the design of the building. The doors, usually three, were framed by recessed portals filled with statues; above them was usually another row of statues; and above them was a great circular "rose window," through which the afternoon sunlight streamed into the nave. Above towered the spires, which in Notre Dame de Paris rise 207 feet, the height of a modern twenty-story building. The sculpture depicted everything that medieval men knew or dreamed of: kings, knights and ladies, saints and sinners, virtues and vices, angels and demons, plants and animals, stories from the scriptures and scenes from everyday life. This sculpture, subordinate to the master plan of the cathedral or church though it was, is often powerful, vigorously depicting beauty and brutality in terms that even the most uneducated peasant could understand.

As time went on, Gothic architecture was constantly refined, and most of the structures that were built over a period of time contain examples of several styles. Early Gothic tended to be simple and plain; in the thirteenth century it grew increasingly elaborate and complex. There was "decorated Gothic," so called because it was so elaborate; "perpendicular Gothic," which emphasized to an even greater degree than usual the upward sweep of the lines of the building; and "flamboyant Gothic," named for the flame-

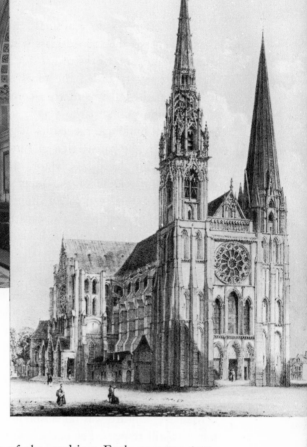

Above, the Gothic cathedral at Amiens: a view of the nave, facing the main entrance and the rose window. Right, the cathedral at Chartres. The flying buttresses can be seen at the side of the church along the part of the wall that is in the shade.

like effect of the designs of the ribs of the vaulting. Each country developed its individual variations of the Gothic style. English cathedrals usually had one main spire at the center of the building; Italian Gothic retained more of the Roman classical influence; Spanish Gothic incorporated Islamic arches and ornaments; German Gothic was so highly ornamented that the outlines of the buildings are all but lost in the mass of detail. Although the style was originally designed for churches, it was adapted for other buildings as well, notably the Palais de Justice in Rouen, the Doge's Palace in Venice, and the house of the merchant prince Jacques Coeur (Chapter 18) in Bourges.

But even the cathedrals were not used solely for worship. The sanctuary was reserved for the priests, but the nave was for the people. On feast days, of which there were as many as thirty a year, everyone took the day off from work to assemble there for processions and entertainments. Men met in the aisles to conduct business, attend guild meetings, or simply to talk. Guilds donated the stained-glass windows along the aisles and saw to it that these magnificent works of art not only celebrated God and the saints but also that they recorded the faces and achievements of their donors. The medieval cathedral was often a combination of church, town hall, place of business, and public park.

Cathedral building reached its height about 1200, significantly at about the same time as the papal reign of Innocent III. (See page 128.) It continued, although with decreasing vigor, throughout the thirteenth century, and ended in the middle of the fourteenth century, with the waning of the Middle Ages. But even today thousands of Gothic churches and cathedrals still survive, reminding Europeans today of the time when the Commonwealth of Christendom almost became a reality.

Medieval schools and universities taught few students, but they taught them well. If they added little in the way of technical knowledge of the world, the scholastic philosophy their teachers expounded was one of man's most successful attempts to understand his world, his God, and himself. The Romanesque and Gothic styles of art and architecture were schools in themselves, expressing the religion of their builders so well that they continue to be used for many church and educational buildings today.

Medieval culture was far different from the culture of the modern world, but it is still respected as one of mankind's noblest achievements.

People, Places, and Terms

Peter Abelard	*trivium*	*Book of the Seven*
John of Salisbury	*quadrivium*	*Arts*
Albertus Magnus	*universitas*	passive intellect
Thomas Aquinas	master of arts	active intellect
	bachelor of arts	*Summa theologia*
Oxford	thesis	essence
Cambridge	college	being
Salerno	theology	Romanesque
Cologne	scholasticism	barrel vault
Sens	mysticism	Gothic
	Sic et non	flying buttress
grammar school	*Concordance of*	rose window
seven liberal arts	*Discordant Canons*	

Getting Organized

1. What was the purpose of the medieval grammar school? Of what did its curriculum consist?
2. What were the stages of progress through a medieval university? In what ways did university life differ from that of today?
3. Summarize the ideas of Bernard of Clairvaux. How influential were they?
4. What kind of man was Abelard? What were the methods and probable purpose of *Sic et non?* What were its immediate effects? Its long-term influence?
5. What was the basis of the thinking of Albertus Magnus?
6. Summarize the philosophy of Thomas Aquinas. What was the importance of his work?
7. What were the basic features of Romanesque architecture? Who built most of the Romanesque churches?
8. What two discoveries made possible the development of Gothic architecture? Describe the interior and exterior of a Gothic cathedral.
9. What variations developed in Gothic architecture over the years? What purposes other than religious did the cathedrals serve? When did cathedral building reach its height? How long did it last?

Understanding the Big Picture

1. Compare and contrast the thought of Bernard, Abelard, and Aquinas. What were their differences? In what ways were they similar?
2. Compare Romanesque and Gothic architecture. Which style seems to you to be better suited to the purposes of medieval men? Why?

For the Thoughtful

1. Compare the medieval system of education to that of today. What are the advantages of each system? Which aspects of medieval education have survived to the present, and which have disappeared? Why, in each case? Would you favor a revival of any of the abandoned features of medieval education? Which? Why?
2. Which of the great medieval philosophers best reflects your own thought? In what ways? Which best reflects the thinking and attitudes of modern society in general?
3. Compare the influence of religion today with its influence in the Middle Ages in the fields of education, philosophy, and architecture. How much influence has religion maintained? How much lost? Do you approve? Why?

11

the Medieval holy Roman Empire

By the eleventh century there began to emerge in western Europe states that proved stronger than any other governments in that area since Roman times. Three of these were the early phases of nations still important in today's world. Of these, the so-called "Holy Roman Empire" was the first, the most interesting, and the most influential.

The idea of a Christian empire had deep roots both in Roman and in Germanic tradition, and it was dear to the hearts of the rulers of the church. Few of the Germanic conquerors of the Roman Empire were able to forget the greatness of the state they had destroyed; both Clovis and Charlemagne, for example, had assumed Roman titles and had sought to revive Roman forms of government. The Catholic Church had converted Rome's conquerors to a belief in the unity of all true believers and had promoted the concept of a Commonwealth of Christendom. The Holy Roman Empire attempted to combine these Roman and Christian traditions; it was a political expression of the medieval dream of unity that was exemplified in religion during the papal reign of Innocent III. (See page 128.) For three centuries it was also the strongest and most influential state in Europe.

GERMANY AND ITALY
IN THE EARLY TENTH CENTURY

The Holy Roman Empire developed from the East Frankish kingdom of Louis the German, which had been carved out of the Carolingian empire by the Treaty of Verdun in 843. (See map, page 77.) This area, roughly the same as modern West Germany, was inhabited by various Germanic tribes who, although they had been conquered by Charlemagne, had never been subjected to Roman customs nor even to Frankish customs for any length of time. They were therefore far more Germanic in their language, customs, and outlook than were the people of the other parts of what had been Charlemagne's empire.

In the East Frankish kingdom the Carolingian kings, the descendants of Charlemagne and of Louis the German, were ineffective rulers. By the time the last of them, Louis the Child, died in 911, what royal government there was had vanished. Germany, as the country was beginning to be called, was divided into great tribal or "stem" duchies, whose dukes were descendants of the earlier Germanic tribal chieftains. The countryside was dotted with the fortresses (in the tenth century one could hardly call them castles) of the petty nobles, many of whom, the "robber barons," lived by preying on their neighbors and on any passing merchants. Proud and warlike, the petty nobles thrived on political confusion and resisted any attempts to control them. Feudalism was not so highly developed here as in France, so there was less subinfeudation (see page 92), whose complicated but definite pattern of loyalties might have kept the nobles somewhat in check. Nor was primogeniture (the inheritance of an entire estate by the eldest son) well established. The German crown was not hereditary at all; instead, the dukes elected a king from among their own number.

Most of the German people were peasants living on the scattered and primitive manors. Because the manorial system was not yet highly developed, most of the peasants were free men rather than serfs. They were, however, subject to military service, which was made especially necessary by the raids of the formidable Magyars (Hungarians) on the eastern frontier. There were only a few small trading towns, but some were already self-governing, and all were always resentful of any attempts to infringe on their local liberties.

In tenth-century Germany, the only powerful and effective organization was the church. It had established itself in Germany even before the area had been conquered by Charlemagne, and indeed had played a large part in helping him establish effective control over much of the area. After the power of Charlemagne's successors waned, the church maintained its position of importance. Its leaders, the bishops and the abbots of the great monasteries, not only led the only organization in Germany whose members could read and write, but also were rulers of vast estates in many parts of the country. Especially powerful were the archbishops of Mainz, Trier, and Cologne.

To the south, across the Alps in Italy, all semblance of central government had disappeared. The tenth-century popes, often controlled by the Roman aristocracy, could scarcely control the Papal States around Rome. Sicily had fallen to the Arabs. In the northern part of the peninsula, sordid chieftains squabbled for the lands that had once been the heart of the Roman Empire and more recently had been part of Lothair's middle kingdom. (See page 77.) Powerless popes who attempted to interfere were usually put to rout. In the tumult, however, several cities—among them Venice, Genoa, and Pisa, and later Florence and Milan—shook off their lords, formed their own government, and gradually became wealthy and powerful by monopolizing the growing trade between Europe and the Levant. (See page 109.)

🐝 THE ESTABLISHMENT OF THE EMPIRE

After the death in 911 of the last Carolingian, and again in 919, the German dukes chose a king from among their own number. Neither of these kings was able to influence the other dukes in any significant way; but the second of them, Henry the Fowler, duke of Saxony (king 919-936), was able before he died to insure that the crown would pass to his son Otto. Henry thus established a dynasty, called the "Saxon," that ruled Germany for more than a century and, more important, created the Holy Roman Empire.

OTTO THE GREAT

The predominance of the Saxon dynasty was established by Otto I "the Great" (king 936-973). Otto devoted his long reign to bringing all of Germany under his control, and was remarkably successful.

The basis of Otto's control of Germany was his alliance with and control of the powerful German church. To make an ally of the church, he gave

The Emperor Otto I, the Great, and his wife Editha: from statues, believed to have been completed shortly after the emperor's death, in the cathedral at Magdeburg. The emperor is holding the scepter (part of which has since broken off) and the orb, symbols of royal power. The nineteen balls within the orb represent nineteen tons of gold that, according to tradition, Otto gave for the construction of the cathedral. The book in Editha's hand is a Gospel (the first four books of the New Testament).

it vast estates, in return expecting—and receiving—large contributions to his treasury and many soldiers, drawn from the church's estates, for his army. He also appointed many of the higher clergy to positions of importance in his government. In order to assure the continuing support of the church, he reserved for himself the right to appoint its bishops and abbots. This "lay investiture" was thus one of the principal sources of his strength.

With the support of the church, Otto was able to subdue the stem duchies and install his relatives as their rulers. Those nobles who were foolhardy enough to rebel against him soon found that their estates were forfeited to the church and turned over to royal officials called "advocates," who administered them in Otto's interest.

Once in command of Germany, Otto turned on the Magyars and in 955 defeated them so soundly at the battle of the Lechfeld (see page 80) that he ended forever the threat of their invasions. Not content with defense, he led his armies eastward, enlarging his kingdom and opening the way for large numbers of German settlers in lands until that time dominated by the Slavs. This conquering of territories to the east is one of the first examples of the *Drang nach Osten* ("drive to the east"), a policy that German rulers followed throughout the Middle Ages and off and on ever since.

Otto, who regarded himself as the successor to Charlemagne, in 951 turned his attention for the first time to the Italian part of what had been Charlemagne's empire, where an Italian queen had been imprisoned by a rival for her throne. Otto defeated the queen's enemies, rescued her from prison, married her—and took her crown for himself. Some years later he returned to Italy, this time because the pope asked for protection against the uncontrollable Roman people. In 962 the grateful pope crowned him emperor, in the tradition of Charlemagne, and the Holy Roman Empire was formally launched (although it did not yet have that name, which came later). To his temporal power as German king, Otto now had added the spiritual power of the church. Crowned by the pope, he saw himself as *rex et sacerdos*, "king and priest," and a revolt against him was thus also a revolt against the anointed of the church. Wearing the imperial crown, Otto was a symbol of the union of church and state, and he governed an empire that stretched from the North and Baltic Seas to the Mediterranean and from the Meuse River in France to the Oder River in eastern Germany.

THE LATER SAXON EMPERORS

Otto the Great apparently had himself crowned by the pope in order to increase his control over the German church; he did not think of himself as a particularly "Roman" emperor. Not so his successors. Otto II (emperor 973-983) neglected Germany in order to strengthen his hold on Italy, where he was killed fighting the Arabs. His son Otto III (emperor 983-1002) actually settled in Rome and, guided by his tutor, Pope Sylvester II (pope 999-1003), began what he hoped would be a renewal of the Roman Empire. Both Otto III and Sylvester died before their plans could bear fruit; and the next emperor, Henry II (emperor 1002-1024) devoted his reign to re-establishing imperial control in Germany, which had declined because the preceding emperors had paid too much attention to Italy. But the idea of a renewed Roman Empire embracing all of Catholic Christendom survived to haunt future emperors.

THE EMPIRE AT ITS PEAK

When Henry II, the last of Otto's direct descendants, died in 1024, the German lords elected Conrad of Franconia as emperor. The Franconian dynasty ruled for a century, during which Conrad (emperor 1024-1039) and his son Henry III (emperor 1039-1056) brought the empire to a new peak of power and influence. Inheriting Otto's distrust of the hereditary nobles, they replaced as many of them as possible with *ministeriales* (from the Latin *minister*, or servant), knights whose only authority came directly from the emperors and whose children could not inherit their offices. Realizing that a strong monarch needed a large and guaranteed income, Conrad and Henry revived long-forgotten taxes, made the nobles pay their feudal dues, and opened silver mines that provided them with a steady flow of precious metal. The dukes and nobles rebelled as usual; but, also as usual, they were soundly put down. With a loyal and efficient group of royal officials, adequate money, and firm control of the empire, the future of the Franconians seemed assured. But then they became involved with the popes.

THE INVESTITURE CONTROVERSY

Oddly enough, Henry III's desire for reform weakened the empire at the moment of its greatest strength. He was as eager to reform the church as he was the state. When three men claimed to be pope, he ousted them all and installed the idealistic Leo IX (pope 1049-1054). It seemed only natural and proper that an emperor who was *rex et sacerdos* should concern himself with reform of the church; but Henry's son soon found that a great and ambitious pope could be his most effective rival.

Henry III died before any open power struggle broke out and was succeeded by his six-year-old son, Henry IV (emperor 1056-1106). During the boy's childhood the German nobles shook off the controls that Henry III had imposed. At the same time the religious reformers consolidated their control of the papacy and allied themselves with the Norman rulers who had recently conquered Sicily and southern Italy. When young Henry IV came of age, filled with the ambition and vitality of youth, he found the reforming Pope Gregory VII (see page 126) opposing his effort to regain his father's control of the church. The immediate issue between the two was lay investiture of bishops (above, page 147), which Henry felt was his God-given privilege—and which was necessary if he were to dominate the empire. Gregory was equally determined that no layman should interfere with the papal control of the Catholic Church. The conflict between Henry and Gregory led, as we have seen (see page 127), to Canossa in 1077 and to Gregory's being driven from Rome and his death in exile in 1085.

THE WEAKENED EMPIRE

Gregory's initial victory was followed by apparent defeat; but he won in the long run, because from that time forward no emperor could dominate the church. After decades of turmoil and conflict, the empire and the papacy finally arrived at a compromise in the "Concordat of Worms" (so called because it was signed in the German town of that name) of 1122. The Emperor Henry V surrendered his claim to invest the bishops with the symbols of their religious office, and the popes gave up their demand to govern the religious estates. The canon clergy were to elect the bishops in the presence of the emperor, so that while the church could choose its own leaders, the emperor could influence their choice.

The struggle weakened the Holy Roman Empire in both its German and Italian lands. In the future, an extraordinary emperor might be able to dominate the empire by sheer ability or military strength, but lesser men would find their power fading away. For three quarters of a century (1076-1152), the feudal lords in Germany defied their emperors with increasing bravado and re-established their independence from all royal controls. In Italy some cities allied with the popes against the emperors, and others sided with the emperors against the popes. All used the conflict between the two to increase their independence from any central control.

⚜ FREDERICK BARBAROSSA

In 1125 the Franconian family died out, and the almost meaningless title of emperor became a prize sought by two of the most powerful noble dynasties, the Welfs and the Hohenstaufens. Each petty lord and warring faction took sides. In 1138 the German nobles chose a Hohenstaufen prince as Emperor Conrad III (1138-1152) over a Welf rival, who then refused to pay him homage. Conrad punished him by seizing Welf lands, and Germany was laid waste by the war between the rival families. What had begun as a struggle between church and state ended as feudal chaos.

In the middle of the twelfth century, just when the Holy Roman Empire seemed about to die, the nobles chose Frederick of Hohenstaufen

The Emperor Frederick I, Barbarossa, as a crusader: from a manuscript of 1188, when Frederick was about to depart on the crusade that cost him his life.

as its emperor. A compromise candidate (his mother had been a Welf), Frederick I—called "Barbarossa" because of his red beard—turned out to be "the noblest of medieval kings, the most imposing, the most heroic, the most brilliant of a long line of German Emperors." By intelligence and force of will Barbarossa was able to make the empire the leading state in Europe once again.

Frederick Barbarossa (emperor 1152-1190) refused to learn the lesson of Canossa and the Concordat of Worms. Convinced that as emperor he was *rex et sacerdos*, he reasserted his authority over the popes and brought the church lands in Italy under his personal domination. He extended the boundaries of the empire and forced its reluctant nobles to admit that he was their lord. He reunited Germany and Italy. Only a Barbarossa, convinced he was ordained by God to restore the empire to its former glory, could have accomplished these things.

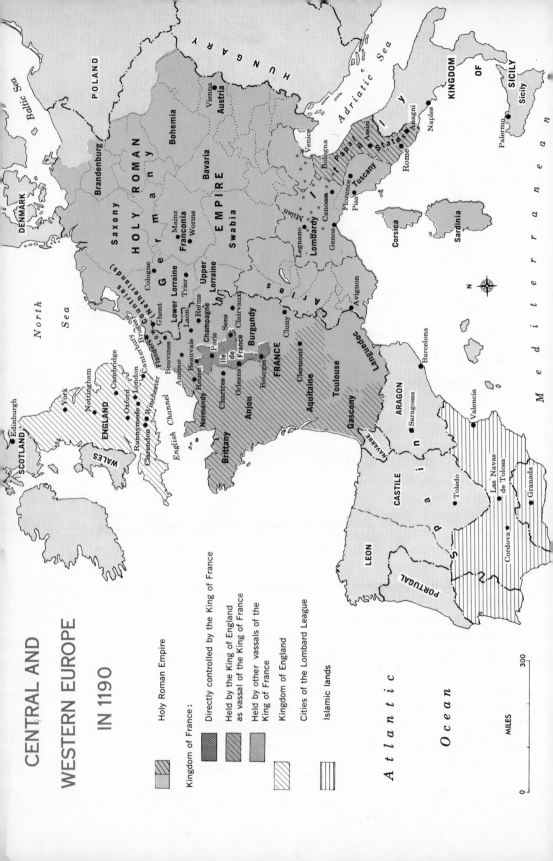

CENTRAL AND
WESTERN EUROPE
IN 1190

Holy Roman Empire

Kingdom of France:

Directly controlled by the King of France

Held by the King of England
as vassal of the King of France

Held by other vassals of the
King of France

Kingdom of England

Cities of the Lombard League

Islamic lands

0   300
MILES

N

SCOTLAND
Edinburgh

WALES
ENGLAND
York
Nottingham
Cambridge
Oxford
London
Winchester
Runnymede
Canterbury
Clarendon

North
Sea

Baltic Sea

DENMARK

POLAND

Brandenburg

Saxony

HOLY ROMAN

Germany

EMPIRE

Bohemia

Vienna
Austria

HUNGARY

Bavaria

Swabia

Franconia
Mainz
Worms

Cologne
Lower Lorraine
Trier
Upper
Lorraine

Low Countries (Netherlands)
Flanders
Ghent
Bruges

English Channel

Bouvines
Amiens
Beauvais
Laon
Reims
Champagne
Paris
Ile
de France
Chartres
Rouen
Normandy
Orleans
Bourges
Sens
Clairvaux
Burgundy

Arles

Cluny

Legnano
Milan
Lombardy
Genoa

Venice

Bologna
Florence
Pisa
Tuscany

Adriatic Sea

Canossa

Assisi
Papal
States
Rome
Anagni

Naples

KINGDOM
OF
SICILY

Palermo

Sicily

Mediterranean

Corsica

Sardinia

FRANCE
Clermont
Anjou
Aquitaine
Toulouse
Gascony
Languedoc
Avignon

Brittany

Atlantic
Ocean

NAVARRE

ARAGON
Barcelona
Saragossa
Valencia

Spain

LEON
PORTUGAL
CASTILE
Toledo
Cordova

Las Navas
de Tolosa
Granada

Frederick started his reforms at home, in his own duchy of Swabia, where he established a system of regular taxes and appointed better government officials. Once this was done, he was able to force the other dukes to recognize his supremacy and to put down a revolt by his Welf cousin, Henry the Lion, with a minimum of bloodshed. Then he was strong enough to march north into Denmark and east into Poland and Hungary, continuing the *Drang nach Osten* that Otto had begun two centuries before.

As soon as Germany was under control, Frederick turned to Italy, the site not only of Rome, but also of the prosperous and independent Lombard city-states. At first the pope encouraged Frederick's interest in Italy, for he hoped Frederick would restore some order to the turbulent country. But the towns opposed him from the first, forming an alliance called the "Lombard League" to resist the emperor and the hated military governors, called *podestàs*, that he sent to rule over them. Later Pope Alexander III, realizing that Frederick meant to govern Rome as well as the Italian towns, excommunicated Frederick and joined the Lombard League. Together the papal and Italian forces defeated a German army at the Battle of Legnano in 1176 and forced Frederick to run for his life. Nothing daunted, Frederick recouped his fortunes by brilliant diplomacy, won his way back into the good graces of the pope, and in 1183 persuaded the towns to pay him taxes in return for the right to govern themselves within their city walls. The pope also retained his local independence; but Frederick had restored northern Italy to the Holy Roman Empire. He strengthened his position by marrying his son to the daughter of the Norman king of Sicily, thus trapping the pope and the Italian towns between his imperial possessions in Germany and his in-law's possessions in the south.

Frederick was about to renew his attack on papal power in 1187 when news came that Saladin the Turk had captured Jerusalem from the Christian crusaders. So the great emperor moved eastward, in company with King Richard the Lion-Hearted of England and King Philip Augustus of France, on the Third Crusade; and in 1190 he drowned while fording a river in Asia Minor. For centuries his countrymen believed that he was not really dead but merely asleep in a hidden cave and that he would awaken and reappear to save his country in time of need. Frederick became a German folk hero. Like King Arthur in England and Charlemagne in France, he was as much a legend as a historical person, and his people would never forget him.

✿ THE DECLINE OF THE EMPIRE

Barbarossa's reforms and driving ambition made the Holy Roman Empire great again. But his success could not outlive him, for it was due almost entirely to his own overwhelming personality. His son was a weakling, and his grandson lost all that he had created.

FREDERICK II

Barbarossa's grandson, Frederick II (emperor 1220-1250) was called, with good reason, *Stupor Mundi*, "the wonder of the world." He was a remarkable man who devoted as much energy to intellectual and artistic pursuits as his grandfather had to war and politics. He lived in Sicily, where he made his court the cultural center of Europe, crowded with poets and scholars and the ladies of his international harem. He wrote poetry and a book that still is the last word on falconry (the art of hunting with falcons). He also presided over the collapse of the Holy Roman Empire.

Frederick II lived so far away that he could not control the distant German nobles, and the local lords and bishops won independence in all but name. He was more interested in Italian affairs; but the cities of northern Italy were rebellious and too strong for him to control, and the popes who succeeded Innocent III were determined to keep the church and the Papal States free of any temporal control. When Frederick meddled in church affairs, the popes tried to depose him, and when he failed to go on crusade, they excommunicated him. Frederick fought back against his enemies, but he lost more battles than he won, his power withered, and the empire began to break up.

THE LATER EMPIRE AND THE HABSBURGS

For two centuries after Frederick II died in 1250, the Holy Roman Empire existed mostly in name. For a quarter-century there was no emperor at all. When Rudolph of Habsburg was finally elected in 1278, he could accomplish little more than to take over the important duchy of Austria, which, with its capital of Vienna, remained in his family until 1918. Occasionally an emperor tried to reunite Germany and Italy; but even though one of them was hailed by the poet Dante (chapter 19) as the unifier of Italy, none of them was successful. Few of them dreamed the glorious dreams that had haunted Barbarossa, and none had even a share of his ability. Most were content to govern what they could of Germany and to co-operate with the popes, who occasionally found them useful allies.

The Golden Bull of 1356. The German princes systematized the election of the Holy Roman Emperors in the "Golden Bull" of 1356, which granted seven "electors" sovereign authority within their own territories and the right to choose the emperor. Three of the electors, the archbishops of Mainz, Trier, and Cologne, were churchmen, and four were laymen: the king of Bohemia, the margrave of Brandenburg, the duke of Saxony, and the count palatine of the Rhine. By forcing candidates for the imperial throne to make concessions in return for their votes, the electors were able to increase their own autonomy and to prevent the re-establishment of any strong government in Germany.

The German lords developed the habit of meeting occasionally in a "Diet," or parliament. In this body each of the three ruling groups was represented; there was a College of Electors, a College of Spiritual and Temporal Princes, and a College of Representatives of the Free Cities. The emperors could call meetings of the Diet, but each state was so jealous of its own interests ("particularism," the Germans called it) that they could never agree on anything important for very long. Germany was doomed to centuries of feudal localism.

The Aftermath of Failure. The failure of the Holy Roman Empire had several lasting political results. (1) A powerful and aggressive empire might have prevented independent governments from being established in Poland, Hungary, and the Scandinavian countries, and it could possibly even have interfered in the affairs of England and France. But a weak imperial government made it possible for national monarchies to develop elsewhere in Europe. (2) A weak central government allowed the establishment of powerful princely families in Germany. The Wittelsbachs, who held Bavaria after 1180, and the Habsburgs, who held Austria after 1278, were dislodged only after the First World War in 1918. The Hohenzollerns, originally robber barons, obtained Brandenburg in 1415 and used it as the basis on which to build Prussia and the modern state of Germany; they, too, survived until 1918. (3) Switzerland was founded by hardy German peasants who hid in the valleys of the Alps and defied their feudal overlords. (4) Finally, the towns of both Germany and Italy were able to maintain their independence and create the city-states that were to play a significant role in the growth of commerce and culture.

After 1438 the nobles always chose the emperor from among the members of the Habsburg family, who were grateful for the honor and occasionally were able to use their imperial title for their own advantage. But the Habsburgs, although possessing some influence, never really could dominate Germany, and they rarely tried.

⚜ ⚜ ⚜

The Holy Roman Empire was a magnificent dream and a sad failure. Western Europe was not ready for a reborn Roman Empire, and the authority of church and state could not be successfully combined—even in the Middle Ages. The methods of a Germanic feudal monarchy were inadequate and could not effectively control so large an area for long.

Some historians have judged Otto and his successors harshly. When most rulers had their hands full trying to govern their own home territories, the Holy Roman emperors overextended themselves by trying to unite Germany and Italy and, at the same time, to challenge the claims of the church to temporal authority. Their soaring ambition led to their downfall; but they labored mightily in their lost cause, and they almost made their dream come true.

If, like the feudal kings of France and England, they had limited themselves to lesser but more realistic goals, they might have succeeded.

People, Places, and Terms

Otto the Great	Meuse River	*Drang nach Osten*
Henry III	Oder River	*ministeriales*
Henry IV	Worms	Concordat of Worms
Saxons	Austria	Lombard League
Franconians	Vienna	*podestà*
Welfs		Golden Bull
Hohenstaufens	stem duchies	electors
Frederick Barbarossa	advocates	Diet
Frederick II	Battle of the Lechfeld	particularism
Habsburgs		

Getting Organized

1. How did the people live in Germany in the tenth century? What was the relationship of these people to the government? What was their attitude toward it? What was the position of the church? In what condition was Italy?

2. How much control over his empire did Otto the Great enjoy? What was his relationship with the church? With the German nobles? What new areas did he add to the empire?

3. What important reforms to restrict the power of the nobles did the early Franconians introduce? What was their relationship with the church? What effect did the investiture controversy have on the empire?

4. What were Frederick Barbarossa's great accomplishments? Did he extend the empire? What was his relationship with the church? With the nobles? Was he a successful emperor?

5. What damage did Frederick II do to the empire? Why did imperial power decline during his reign?

6. After 1250 how much power did the emperors have? How were they chosen? How much power did the nobles have?

7. What were the political results of the failure of the Holy Roman Empire?

Understanding the Big Picture

1. Who was the greater emperor, Otto the Great or Frederick Barbarossa? Who had more control over his empire? Over the church?

2. In what ways was the establishment of a strong imperial government obstructed by the nobles? By the papacy?

3. Why did the Holy Roman Empire decline?

4. Make a chronological chart showing the rise and decline of the Holy Roman Empire.

Mastering the Map

Study carefully the Holy Roman Empire on the map on page 152. Which were the major duchies? Did the emperor control all of the major duchies and cities? What geographical factors contributed to the decline of the empire?

For the Thoughtful

1. Did the Holy Roman Empire decline because of mistakes by the men who ruled it, or because of the insoluble problems that they faced? Support your conclusion with specific evidence.

2. How were the problems faced by Otto and Barbarossa similar to those faced by Charlemagne? How different? Who was the most successful in dealing with these problems?

3. Compare and contrast the decline of the Holy Roman Empire to the decline of the Roman Empire and of the Arab empire.

4. Was the Holy Roman Empire as powerful an empire as the other empires that you have studied? Support your answer fully.

৵৩ 12
the Medieval
french Monarchy

For more than a century after the division of Charlemagne's empire by the treaty of Verdun in 843 (see map, page 77), the history of the West Frankish (French) kingdom of Charles the Bald was much like that of the East Frankish (German) kingdom. Descendants of Charlemagne usually occupied the throne, although on occasion they were replaced by members of a rival family. But the king, of whatever family he might be, exercised little power; he was ruler of France in name only. The real power was divided among a number of counts and dukes, who ignored their feudal obligations to the king and ruled their counties and duchies as independent states. The king actually controlled only a small area in central France, and frequently he had difficulty controlling even that.

In 987 the nobles elected Hugh Capet king of France. Although Hugh could do little to control the unruly nobles, he was able to pass the crown on to his son; and his son, in turn, did likewise. Thus was launched the "Capetian" dynasty, which ruled France until 1328, when the Middle Ages were drawing to a close. The early Capetian kings counted for little. But there were forces that tended to increase the royal power, and several of the kings were quick to take advantage of them. As a result, three of the later Capetian kings—Philip II "Augustus" (1180-1223), Louis IX, "Saint

Louis," (1226-1270) and Philip IV "the Fair" (1285-1314)—were able to bring peace and prosperity to their country by making it the most highly centralized monarchy of the Middle Ages. When they reigned, France replaced the Holy Roman Empire as the leading feudal monarchy in Europe. Theirs was the age of troubadours, of Gothic cathedrals and budding universities, and of victories over the English and the popes. Nowhere in Europe were the ideals of chivalry and the concept of the feudal monarchy more highly developed. The bright sun of the medieval high noon shone most brightly on France.

FRANCE UNDER THE EARLY CAPETIANS

In the eleventh century the Capetian monarchs had all they could do to maintain control over their own lands and to prevent the feudal lords from usurping the few royal privileges that the kings possessed. Slowly, however, without much fanfare, they improved their system of government and made an effective alliance with French religious leaders. These achievements, together with economic changes (of which the most notable was the growth of towns; see pages 109-110) enabled them to prepare the way for the mighty monarchs who succeeded them.

THE FEUDAL DUCHIES AND COUNTIES

Until the early twelfth century, several of the rulers of the principal French provinces were as strong as the monarchs to whom they paid lip service. These provinces loom large in French history. To the northwest were Brittany, a Celtic stronghold, and Normandy, ruled by descendants of the Viking Duke Rollo. (See page 79.) After 1066 the duke of Normandy was also the king of England. (Chapter 13.) In northeastern France were Flanders and Champagne. The old Roman camps where the people of Flanders huddled to escape from the Viking invaders became the sites of such flourishing commercial cities as Ghent and Bruges (see page 109), while Champagne grew rich from the profits of the early medieval fairs. (See page 109.) To the east was the duchy of Burgundy, whose duke also ruled the "Free County of Burgundy" or "Franche Comté," a part of the Holy Roman Empire. In southern France was the huge and powerful duchy variously called Aquitaine or Guienne, and on its borders was the other major southern province, Toulouse. (See map, page 152.)

In the center of these duchies were the crown lands (the lands governed directly by the king), called the "Île de France" and including the two important cities of Paris and Orleans. Although smaller than the other provinces, the Île de France was significant because of its advantageous central location and its support of the Capetian monarchs. The early kings sensibly worked hard to govern this territory effectively and well, and they used it as a base in bringing under their control the stronger but less orderly neighboring duchies.

STRENGTHENING THE ROYAL GOVERNMENT

In the Île de France the Capetians slowly built up the best organized government in France. At the local level of government, they replaced hereditary officials, who felt safe in their jobs and so often ignored the king's commands, with officials called "provosts," whom they could trust; and they made the king's court an effective tool by ousting their hereditary advisers and replacing them with more trustworthy lesser lords, churchmen, and townsmen, whom they could hire and fire at will.

The royal income was small at first, derived largely from the Île de France. But the kings increased it slowly as they learned to collect their feudal dues more efficiently, and they added new sources of revenue by chartering and then taxing newly founded towns.

Gradually the royal influence spread across France. The successors of Charlemagne's *missi dominici* (see page 72) still traveled around the countryside reminding people that they did have a king after all; and when the local lords failed to provide the justice that they promised, more and more people appealed to the kings to resolve their grievances. But the increase in the kings' authority was not steady: there were long periods when it actually declined. The nobles vigorously resisted the passing of the crown from father to son. If the kings had not successfully allied themselves with the church and the growing towns, they might never have become powerful at all.

The Alliance with the Church. Charlemagne had become *rex et sacerdos* when the pope crowned him Roman emperor, and his successors as kings of France clung as stubbornly to their claims to sacred authority as did their contemporaries, the German Holy Roman emperors. Louis VI "the Fat" (1108-1137) cemented the alliance of church and state when he made his boyhood adviser, Abbot Suger (1081?-1151) of the monastery of Saint-Denis, his unofficial prime minister. Saint-Denis, named for the patron saint of France, whose relics it treasured, was near the royal palace in Paris. The burial place of the French kings, it was a center of learning whose monks taught that the king was cloaked with religious authority. Suger, who was such a saintly man that even his adversary Bernard of Clairvaux never questioned his motives, made no distinction between treason and heresy when he excommunicated Louis's enemies. Louis in return helped Suger to enforce the Cluniac reform of the church. (See page 120.) The alliance strengthened both men, increasing the power of the church and helping Louis force his reluctant vassals to submit to his will. When the next king, Louis VII (king 1137-1180), went on crusade, Sugar continued as chief minister and continued to improve the organization of the government. Kings had learned that clergymen could be their most effective officials; Louis and Suger merely cemented an alliance that had begun long before.

The Alliance with the Towns. The Capetian kings also took advantage of the slow but steady increase in population and in trade. (See pages 108-110.) As the population rose, men cut down forests and drained swamps to construct new manors, most of which became the property of the kings. Merchants who profited from the growing trade in France and who governed the growing towns were quick to support a king who promised them the peace they craved. Towns chartered by the king paid taxes, which the king could spend as he pleased, and they provided him with many of his ablest and most trusted counselors.

The economic changes that the towns fostered worked also to the king's advantage. The most important of these was the change from barter (the direct exchange of goods) to the use of money. The early Capetians had been hard put to it to keep their rebellious subjects in their place when their vassals had refused to pay their feudal dues or had gone home as soon as the forty days service a year they owed their king (see page 93) had ended. But when feudal dues and services were "commuted" to money payments, the increased income made it possible for the kings to pay the salaries of trustworthy mercenary (hired) soldiers and loyal government officials.

✣ THE GREAT CAPETIAN MONARCHS

In the course of a century and a half, from 1180 to 1314, France was fortunate to have three of the outstanding kings of medieval Europe. During their reigns the loyalty of Frenchmen gradually shifted from the church and local lords to the king and the French nation. But the kings did not have an easy time of it. When Philip Augustus took office in 1180, the popes were at the height of their influence, and much of France was in the hands of English kings—who believed that they had as rightful a claim to their French possessions as did any Capetian monarch.

PHILIP II "AUGUSTUS"

No one would call Philip II (king 1180-1223), like his older contemporary Frederick Barbarossa, the "noblest of medieval kings"; for Philip was a careful, calculating ruler who never dreamed of imperial glory. But in his canny way he was more successful than Barbarossa, in spite of a variety of difficult obstacles.

Philip's most dangerous enemies were the English kings. In 1066 William the Conqueror, who as duke of Normandy was a vassal of the king of France, had seized the English throne. (Chapter 13.) He and his successors were as interested in expanding their French possessions as they were in governing England. By the beginning of Philip's reign, Henry II of England controlled Normandy in northern France, Anjou in the west, and the huge southern domain of Aquitaine, thus surrounding Philip's royal domain on three sides. (See map, page 152.) Henry and his sons sought to gain control of the rest of France; but Philip outsmarted them. He tricked Henry's sons into fighting their father and each other instead of the French. After Henry's death in 1189, his sons were less of a threat. Richard the Lion-Hearted spent much of his ten-year reign on a fruitless Crusade. Richard's brother and successor, John, stayed closer to home, but had the disadvantage of being the worst king in English history. Philip took advantage of the absence of one English king and the mistakes of the next to win the loyalty of the nobles in parts of France controlled by England. By 1204 he had driven the English from Normandy and Anjou, leaving them only Aquitaine, far from their island kingdom.

John was resourceful, however, and made an alliance with the Holy Roman emperor Otto IV (who was trying to prevent Frederick II from inheriting the empire, and was temporarily successful). John and Otto planned to invade France from two directions and squeeze Philip from Paris. But John unwisely delayed his attack and allowed Philip to throw all his armies against Otto in the battle of Bouvines (1214). Otto's armies were crushed, and John's plans went for nought. On the field of Bouvines, in one of the most significant medieval battles, Philip saved France from English and German domination, hastened the decline of the Holy

The Louvre, Paris, as it appeared about 1220, in the time of Philip Augustus. The Louvre was then a fortress of the French kings. Later, in the reign of Philip the Fair (see pages 165-166), it became their capital. Most of it was torn down in the sixteenth century to make way for a much larger and more beautiful palace, now France's principal art museum.

Roman Empire, and forced the panic-stricken John to surrender many of his royal privileges to his nobles in return for peace at home.

Philip continued the close association of the kings and the church that earlier kings had established. He was apparently not a pious person, but he contributed generously to religious causes and gladly agreed to Innocent III's request to send an army against the Albigensian heretics in southern France. (See page 123.) He gave the conquered territories to the leader of the army, whose son returned them to the monarchy, so that for the first time the kings had a personal stronghold in southern France.

Philip continued to improve the royal administration in Paris. He extended his influence in the provinces by appointing paid officials called *baillis* to administer the feudal principalities. The *baillis* collected taxes for the royal treasury, supervised the royal estates, and represented the king with the nobles. To the south, where the nobles refused to accept the *baillis* because they were not knights, he sent hired men from the feudal aristocracy called "seneschals."

LOUIS IX, "SAINT LOUIS"

Louis IX (king 1226-1270), the grandson of Philip II, was twelve when he became king, and the feudal nobles might have successfully rebelled against the rising royal power had not his strong-willed and pious mother, Blanche of Castile, served as an effective regent. His mother trained the young king well. Early in his career Louis determined to be the best monarch of his age—and he succeeded.

Louis IX was feared because he was just. He was just even to his enemies. When he defeated the English in battle, he made a peace that allowed them to keep the few possessions they had left. When he was captured by the Saracens on crusade, he insisted that his full ransom should be paid, even though the Saracens had mistakenly accepted a much smaller sum than had been agreed upon. Fairness to Saracens was totally unheard of. By the middle of his reign his reputation had spread across Europe, and many monarchs turned to him to arbitrate (judge and settle) their disputes.

His justice brought him an increase of his power in France as well. Louis sat, day after day, under a great oak at the royal residence of Vincennes, hearing all cases that were brought before him. He allowed serfs to appeal

King Louis IX of France as a young man: an illustration from a French Bible of about 1250.

to his courts over the heads of nobles. He heard the cases of towns against feudal lords. He appointed better officials than any of his predecessors and encouraged them to restrict feudal warfare. He made France so peaceful and himself so popular with the people that the kingship was revered for a century after his death—even more than the papacy, as Boniface VIII was to discover, to his sorrow, a generation later.

Louis IX showed great practical wisdom in improving the government of France. He established a uniform coinage and a standard system of law that was based more upon Roman than German models. Equally important, he developed the *Parlement* of Paris, a high court of trained lawyers, nobles, and clergymen, which became the supreme court of the realm. He guaranteed safety to those who laid their troubles and complaints before him, and he decreed that royal agents must enforce his decisions within forty days. To pay the costs of administering his reforms, he introduced a new money tax, called the *taille*, on income and property. His legislation as well as his character added to the strength of the monarchy.

A pious and holy man, a friend of the church and a model of upright living, Louis willingly accepted the calls of the popes to go on crusade. In 1248 he went on a six-year struggle in Egypt and Palestine, and in 1270 he led an attack on Arab Tunis, during which he died of the plague. Less than thirty years later a grateful church canonized him (formally declared him a saint). He was the classic ideal of a medieval Christian king.

Ironically, Saint Louis weakened the church he loved so much. He taught his subjects to look to the king instead of to the pope for moral leadership, while churchmen grew corrupt from the wealth and power that he lavished upon it. The fact that Frenchmen were more loyal to their king than to their church had a decisive impact upon the struggle that developed between two determined leaders, Louis's grandson King Philip IV of France and Pope Boniface VIII.

PHILIP IV "THE FAIR," 1285-1314

Philip IV "The Fair," grandson of Saint Louis, earned his nickname from his complexion, not his policies, for he was a clever and unscrupulous king who took advantage of his ancestors' reforms to make himself supreme in France. The nobles having been brought under control, Philip realized that the only force that could challenge his authority was the church—so he determined to dominate it. The issue was the familiar one of the Middle Ages, the right of a king to appoint the bishops and to tax the clergy. Philip was determined to control the church in France, and Pope Boniface

VIII was equally determined to exercise all the papal powers that he claimed in his bulls *Clericis laicos* and *Unam sanctam.* (See page 129.)

In 1302 Philip called the first meeting of the "Estates-General" in an effort to strengthen his hand against the pope. This assembly of the three "estates" of France—the clergy, the nobility, and the commoners from the towns—was necessary because Philip needed money and he was not yet strong enough to dispute the feudal tradition that a king must have the consent of his people before he could make them pay taxes over and above the usual feudal dues. The Estates-General was an effective device for bringing Frenchmen together and winning their support. Philip got his money, and France held the first parliament in its history.

Then Philip's men went to Anagni and captured the pope. (See page 129.) Even though they quickly released him, the indignity drove the old man to his grave. In 1305 a subservient College of Cardinals elected a Frenchman, who, as Pope Clement V, transferred the papacy from Rome to Avignon. There it remained in "Babylonian Captivity" (named after that of the Jews in Babylon) until 1377. For most of the fourteenth century French-born popes lived under the watchful eyes of the French kings. This was the first triumph of a medieval state over the church, and one of the most significant signs of change in the Middle Ages.

Philip IV made his government obey his royal wishes. He laid new taxes that increased his revenues to ten times those of Louis IX. He established a *Chambre des Comptes* (treasury department) to collect the taxes and to keep accurate records of his income and expenses. He used his new wealth to maintain a standing army, which was ready for battle whenever he needed it. Freed from dependence on the nobles and the church, Philip and his successors were the strongest monarchs in Europe.

Before he died Philip personally governed most of central France, and his vassals who ruled the rest did exactly as he told them. His highly organized government, administered by his hand-picked officials, enabled him to extend his influence even more. The towns looked to him for leadership and grew and prospered as a result of the royal peace. The largest of them, Paris, was his capital and the site of the principal royal palace, called the "Louvre." Before the century was over men in all parts of France thought of Paris as the center of their nation.

Other and more subtle changes marked the emergence of national feeling. Gradually the language of the Île de France supplemented the many local dialects in other parts of France and made it possible for Frenchmen everywhere to talk to each other in a common tongue. Then a vernacular literature, symbolized by the *fabliaux*, those ironic little songs about animals, and *chansons de geste*, such as "The Song of Roland," became popular, giving all Frenchmen a common literary heritage. France in the early fourteenth century was more unified in politics, language, and tradition than any other country in western Europe.

♔ ♔ ♔

France succeeded where the Holy Roman Empire had failed. It established a stable monarchy and unified its country and people to a greater extent than had been seen before in western Europe. In one sense the English kings were less successful, for they never managed to win unchallenged control over their government. But in the process, they unwittingly contributed to the creation of a peculiarly English kind of monarchy, which contained the seeds of modern ideas of representative democracy.

People, Places, and Terms

Hugh Capet	Flanders	Capetians
Louis VI	Champagne	Battle of Bouvines
Suger	Burgundy	*bailli*
Philip Augustus	Aquitaine	*Parlément* of Paris
Louis IX	Toulouse	*taille*
Philip IV	Île de France	Estates-General
	Saint-Denis	Babylonian Captivity
Brittany	Paris	*Chambre des Comptes*
Normandy		

Getting Organized

1. Under the early Capetians, how much authority did the monarch have over his kingdom? What were the chief obstacles to the authority of the monarch?
2. What were the chief duchies and counties of France? How much power did their rulers have? How did the early Capetians extend their authority into these duchies?
3. How did Louis VI's alliance with Abbot Suger aid royal authority? How did this alliance help the church?
4. How did the early Capetians' alliance with the towns increase royal authority? How did this alliance help the towns and their inhabitants?
5. What were Philip Augustus's principal accomplishments? Why were the English kings his most important enemies? How did Philip overcome their threat? What was the importance of his victory at Bouvines to the three major countries of West Europe?

6. Explain Philip's association with the church. How did it help both parties? How did he improve royal administration?
7. Why was Saint Louis honored throughout Europe? What was the result of his sense of justice? How did he improve the government of France? How did he indirectly weaken the church?
8. Why is the thirteenth century called "the summer of medieval France"? What were its intellectual and artistic achievements?
9. Describe the principal events and results of Philip IV's struggle with the church. What important institution grew out of this struggle and why is it important? How did Philip improve his government? At his death how much power did Philip IV have? Describe the emergence of national feeling in thirteenth-century France and explain how this feeling helped the power of the king.

Understanding the Big Picture

1. Make a chronological chart showing the major events and achievements of the great medieval French kings. Emphasize in this chart the ways in which the French monarchy was growing in authority.
2. What were the major obstacles to the absolute (unlimited) power of the French monarchs? How did the Capetian kings deal with these obstacles? What important alliances did the kings make?
3. What was the relationship of the Capetians to the church? Did this relationship help or hinder royal authority?

Mastering the Map

Study carefully the map of France on page 152. What areas were controlled by the French kings, by the English kings, or were ruled by semi-independent vassals? How, geographically speaking, were the French kings able to unite their country while the Holy Roman Emperors could not? How do geographical factors help to explain this difference?

For the Thoughtful

1. Compare the political developments of France and of the Holy Roman Empire. Why did the power of the French monarchs increase while that of the emperors declined? In answering this question, discuss the roles of the nobles, the church, and the towns in each country.
2. How important was feudalism to the political developments in France and the Holy Roman Empire? Was feudalism dying out in both of these countries? Support your conclusion with specific evidence.
3. From your knowledge of the medieval French monarchy, can you predict what would be the future course of the French monarchy? What role would the nobles, the church, and the towns be likely to play in this future development? Support your answer with specific evidence.

๙๏ 13
The Medieval
English Monarchy

William the Conqueror and his Norman knights jolted England from its island isolation in 1066, and for centuries thereafter English history was deeply affected by its close relationship with France. After the Norman Conquest the English kings were also lords of vast estates in France, while most English nobles were of French ancestry, spoke French, and involved England in their wars and quarrels in France. Strangely enough, the involvement with France helped lead to the development of peculiarly English customs of law and government. While their kings were absorbed with their French possessions, Englishmen managed to limit the power of the monarchy, to establish Parliament, and to foster the growth of the system of common law, which has been the heritage of English-speaking peoples ever since.

๙ THE NORMAN CONQUEST

In the middle of the eleventh century, most of England was ruled by a Saxon monarchy whose king, the saintly Edward "the Confessor" (king 1042-1066), left his government to his earls while he devoted himself to the church and to building Westminster Abbey near London. When he died, his crown was claimed by his nephew, Duke William of Normandy, and by a Saxon earl named Harold. The English lords elected Harold; so William crossed the English Channel at the head of 5,000 Norman warriors and, at the battle of Hastings (1066), defeated the Saxon army. Harold was shot through the eye with an arrow, and the Saxons reluctantly accepted William as their king.

WILLIAM I "THE CONQUEROR"

William I (king 1066-1087) promptly set out to establish firm control over his English kingdom. He turned half the lands of England over to his trustworthy Norman followers and took one fifth of them for himself. He reorganized the government by making the old Saxon witan (see page 18) into a "Great Council," which included the great lords of the realm and met regularly under William's direction, and by establishing a *Curia Regis*, a permanent council of royal advisers. He had a Norman monk made archbishop of Canterbury and primate (highest-ranking church official) of England.

In 1086 William made every feudal lord take the "Salisbury Oath," which recognized him as the only supreme ruler of the country. This made every

The battle of Hastings, October 14, 1066: a section of the Bayeux Tapestry. The tapestry, twenty inches wide and 230 feet long, was embroidered in Normandy after the Norman conquest of England. It depicts the conquest and the events that led up to it in some seventy-two scenes. Here Norman knights are shown attacking a ridge held by the English.

lord directly responsible to the king, so that conspiring against him became illegal and, more important, difficult. And in the same year, to make sure that everyone paid his full share of taxes, he had his officials compile the "Domesday Book," which listed all taxable property in England down to the last hog and sheep. That William could have such a list made is evidence of his complete domination of England—its Saxon people, its Norman lords, its Catholic churchmen. To this day the Domesday Book is the best source of information about English life in the eleventh century.

HENRY I "BEAUCLERC"

The conqueror's son William II (king 1087-1100) ruled England badly for thirteen years before he was finally shot with an arrow and succeeded by his younger brother Henry I (king 1100-1135). Henry, called "Beauclerc" ("Good Clerk") because he could read and write, carried forward the strengthening of the monarchy begun by William the Conqueror. Immediately after he mounted the throne, Henry won the support of the barons (the higher-ranking members of the nobility) by signing a "Charter of Liberties," which listed and guaranteed their rights—the first link in a chain of guarantees of individual liberties that stretches to the American Constitution. Then he compromised an investiture controversy with the pope, winning the support of the churchmen. Finally, he married a Saxon princess who was a direct descendant of King Alfred (see page 22), thereby gaining the loyalty of the Saxon peasants.

Once he had the support of his people, Henry set out to dominate his government. He streamlined the *Curia Regis* by reducing its size and replacing hereditary members with lesser barons whom he could control. Then he gave these new officials specific duties for which he held them responsible. One was "justiciar," a viceroy (vice-king) who ruled when the king was away on the continent. Another was the "chancellor," or head legal officer. A third became the "treasurer," who collected the taxes and supervised government expenses. Henry also clarified the duties of the *Curia* by assigning it specific tasks. Sitting as the "exchecquer," it made financial policy; as a court of appeals, it decided cases at law; and as an advisory council, its members followed the king wherever he went in England.

Henry appointed "shire-reeves" (later called "sheriffs") to share the government of the shires (counties) with hereditary lords, and he selected officials called "coroners," who had among their many duties the responsibility to investigate sudden or violent deaths. He sent itinerant (traveling) judges to go from place to place, competing with the older feudal law courts controlled by nobles. Together these royal officials made sure that decisions made by Henry and his *Curia* were enforced throughout England.

🌿 HENRY II AND THE COMMON LAW

After a period of civil war over the succession to Beauclerc's throne, his grandson became King Henry II (king 1154-1189). This second Henry was a sort of medieval high-pressure businessman who rushed around exhausting everybody but himself. He governed one of the largest territories of any medieval monarch, for he was already duke of Normandy and count of Anjou in France when he assumed the English throne; and by marrying Eleanor of Aquitaine (see page 100), the divorced wife of Louis VII of France, he acquired Aquitaine—most of southern France—as well. He spent most of his reign fighting in France (see page 162); but he occasionally swept across England issuing orders that greatly influenced the growth of English law.

The English barons could still try law cases in their own courts until 1166, when Henry's "Assize of Clarendon" brought the system of justice under royal control. This edict ordered twelve men from each hundred and four from each manor to report crimes to the royal sheriff of their county. These groups were the originals of modern grand juries, which investigate crime and "indict" (formally accuse) criminals. (In the next century it became customary to try cases before a "petit" or trial jury under the supervision of a royal judge. The trial jury decided whether the accused was guilty or innocent; the judge saw to it that legal forms were followed and pronounced sentence on the guilty. This system of grand and petit juries is still functioning after eight centuries.)

Henry also brought the barons under the royal law in his "Grand Assize," which stated that all cases involving property (and the barons were property-holders, of course) should be subject to jury trial.

Henry's assizes made the English law a "common law" for all Englishmen. When local judges found that their decisions could be appealed to higher courts, and even to the *Curia Regis*, they began to base their decisions on "precedents," or similar decisions that had been upheld in the past. The royal judges, and Henry, too, were willing to abide by these precedents, which formed a relatively stable base upon which a whole system of law was built up over the centuries. This common law, which consists of these precedents as altered by "statutes" (laws passed by the Great Council and by its successor, Parliament) serves as the basis for the legal systems of most English-speaking countries, including our own.

Like Frederick Barbarossa, that other vigorous twelfth-century monarch who reigned at almost exactly the same time (see pages 150-153), Henry II found that the church and its own system of canon law (see page 119) threatened his personal control of his kingdom. So he managed to get his friend Thomas à Becket elected archbishop of Canterbury. Becket had never been a particularly pious sort of priest, and he had served Henry loyally as chancellor for eight years; he seemed likely to be a good puppet who would bring the church under royal influence. But Becket changed when he became archbishop. When Henry attempted to bring churchmen under the English common law, Becket fled to France and from exile defied his king. After five years the two men were reconciled, and Becket returned to England; but he continued to insist that the church should be free of temporal control until 1170, when in Canterbury cathedral, four of Henry's knights assassinated him on the steps of his altar.

Whether Henry was responsible for the murder in the cathedral is still debated; but at the time his people blamed him for it. The king, dressed as a humble pilgrim, went to pray at the altar and renounced his plan to

The murder of Thomas à Becket, as depicted in an English manuscript of the twelfth century.

bring the clergy under the common law. Until the fifteenth century the English clergy were free from royal control, and England had a dual system of law, common and canon. In France Philip the Fair brought the church under royal domination. (See page 166.) Not so in England, where the church remained free and independent. Becket was the symbol of this independence, and a cult of Saint Thomas the Martyr grew up to honor him. He was the "holy, blissful martyr" that the poet Geoffrey Chaucer's Canterbury pilgrims went to seek, and the word "canter" came into the language to describe the gait at which men rode to Canterbury to worship at his shrine.

Henry's later years were saddened by unsuccessful wars against Philip Augustus of France (see page 162) and by rebellions inspired by his wife and his sons. In 1189 he died, cursing his enemies and crying "Shame, shame on a conquered king"; for he had suffered many defeats, and he felt he had been a failure. Yet Henry II had given his people—even his barons—a respect for the monarchy and for the common law, so that thereafter, instead of trying to overthrow the monarchy, Englishmen merely tried to establish their own rights within its framework.

Henry was succeeded by his son, Richard I "the Lion-Hearted," (king 1189-1199), who spent most of his reign on crusade (Chapter 14), in a German prison, or fighting the French. He was a brave warrior who became a medieval folk hero, but he was a poor king. Always short of money, he "commuted" feudal dues (see page 93) for cash payments. By paying a "scutage" (or "shield tax"), knights could stay at home, and Richard was able to hire professional soldiers. Everyone was happier, and England was one step further removed from feudalism.

☙ KING JOHN AND MAGNA CARTA

The great achievement of English political development in the twelfth century was the common law. In the thirteenth century it was Parliament, and the establishment of individual freedoms, for the barons at least. But before these could be accomplished, England had to suffer the reign of probably the worst king in its history.

When Innocent III ruled the Catholic Church and Philip Augustus ruled France, England had John (king 1199-1216), sometimes called "Lackland" and later known as "Softsword." He quarreled with his nobles, fought with the French, and disputed with the church—all unsuccessfully. He was so bad a king that no later English monarch has taken his name. Yet in the long run his defeats were good for England.

John fought bitterly with Philip Augustus of France, who encouraged John's French vassals to revolt and succeeded in driving the English out of Normandy in 1204. (See page 162.) A decade later John attempted to organize a two-pronged attack on Philip with the aid of the Holy Roman Emperor Otto; this led only to another disaster at Bouvines in 1214. (See page 162.) Thus John lost the principal English possessions in France. His successors concentrated on their English possessions and hastened the development of English government and law. But not John, for he had other problems of his own.

John became involved in an investiture controversy with Innocent III over the selection of an archbishop of Canterbury. In 1207 Innocent appointed the able and learned Stephen Langton. John rejected Langton and tried to impose his own puppet as archbishop of Canterbury, so that he could keep most of the income of the office for himself. With the support of the bishops, Innocent placed England under an "interdict," which forbade any religious services. While John hesitated, unable to make up his mind what to do next, Innocent moved to the attack by threatening to excommunicate him and urging Philip Augustus to invade England. As French armies were massing in 1213, John suddenly surrendered completely. He agreed to Innocent's terms, made Langton the archbishop, and, most startling of all, surrendered England as a fief to the pope, whose vassal he now became. His royal prestige was gone beyond recall.

In 1215 John found himself in even deeper trouble. The English barons, who had been strong supporters of the earlier kings, had been angered by the taxes John made them pay, the promises he had failed to keep, and the damage he had done to England's prestige. A year earlier, led by Langton, they had drawn up a charter of liberties based on the one granted more than a century earlier by Henry I. (Above, page 171.) Now, after John had returned from his latest whipping by the French, the barons met him in a meadow called Runnymede and forced him to sign the basic English constitutional document, "Magna Carta" ("Great Charter").

In Magna Carta, John was forced to make concessions to almost everyone who had a complaint against him. He swore that "the English Church shall be free and hold its rights entire and its liberties uninjured." He promised to respect the specific rights and privileges of the nobles. He guaranteed that "the city of London shall have all its ancient liberties and free customs." In terms that would appear again and again in constitutional documents, he accepted the fundamental principle of the rule of law, that "no freeman shall be taken or imprisoned . . . except by the legal judgment of his peers [equals] or by the law of the land," and he guaranteed the right to a trial within a reasonable time. He agreed that "no scutage or aid [that is, taxes] shall be imposed in our kingdom except by the common council of our kingdom"—a provision that future Parliaments were to find most useful in controlling the kings. Finally, a committee of nobles was established to watch over the king and punish him if he violated the charter.

Thus the English nobles forced John to accept the principle that the power of the law was greater than the power of the king, and that a king who failed to serve the best interests of the people forfeited his right to rule. As one historian says, "A king had been brought to order . . . a tyrant had been subjected to the laws. . . . A process had been begun that was to end in putting the power of the crown in the hands of the community at large."*

🏵 THE DEVELOPMENT OF PARLIAMENT

When John died the year after Runnymede, two of the three basic elements of English government had been established: the common law and the idea that the law was greater than the king. Before the end of the thirteenth century the third element, Parliament, appeared.

HENRY III AND THE FIRST PARLIAMENT

John's son Henry III (king 1216-1272) was a pious but weak king who allowed much power to fall into the hands of the officials of the church, many of whom were foreigners. This created much anticlericalism (feeling against the clergy). The greater barons demanded more authority until in 1258 they forced Henry to allow a commission of twenty-four barons to rule England. The lesser barons and townsmen, resenting the power of the great barons, supported the king against the commission. The quarrel was finally submitted to the saintly King Louis IX of France, who decided in favor of the king.

* G. M. Trevelyan, *History of England* (New York, Doubleday, 1956), Vol. 1.

This quarrel led to the calling of the first parliament. The greater barons rose up against Henry, defeated him in 1264, and attempted to establish a new governing council. To win the support of the people, the barons' leader, Simon de Montfort, called an assembly in 1265. To it were invited not only the great barons and clergy, who had made up the earlier councils, but also representatives of the knights of the shires (the lesser nobility) and from the towns. Thus two new groups were for the first time recognized as important elements of the English kingdom. Although this assembly soon disbanded without having done anything, it is generally considered to have been the first Parliament.

EDWARD I AND THE MODEL PARLIAMENT

Henry III was succeeded by Edward I (king 1272-1307), one of England's most vigorous, intelligent, and ambitious kings. Edward conquered Wales and Scotland, so that all of Great Britain was for the first time under English control. Scotland regained its independence a few years after Edward's death, but Wales remained a part of the English kingdom from Edward's time forward. At home Edward won the nickname "the English Justinian," because in a series of statutes he made the common law better organized and more reasonable. One of his statutes made the lords give up certain special privileges; another made all purchasers of land direct vassals of the king; a third placed limits on gifts of land to the church. All increased the power of the monarchy.

In 1295, when Edward was involved in a war with France, he called an assembly of the four most powerful groups of his realm in order to win the support of the people. Called the "Model Parliament" because it served as a model for later Parliaments, it consisted of the bishops; the barons; two representatives of the knights of each shire (county); and two representatives from each important town. The first two groups attended because of their high rank; members of the other two groups were elected by their peers (equals) in the countryside and the towns. At first all four groups met together. Eventually, however, their differing interests led them to separate into the House of Lords, which included the bishops and the barons, and the House of Commons.

Edward probably thought of Parliament as little more than a discussion group (the word *parliament* derives from the French *parler*, "to talk"); but he soon found that its members had demands to make. Before they would give him money for his war in France, they made him promise to give up

A meeting of Parliament early in the reign of Edward I. The king is on the raised throne. At his sides are King Alexander III of Scotland, Prince Llewelyn of Wales, and the archbishops of Canterbury and York. On the benches at the right are the barons. Dignitaries of the church occupy the benches at the lower left and one bench at the bottom. In the center are judges, and below them the representatives from the towns and the shires. This picture, from a manuscript of the time, is probably the oldest depiction of Parliament.

all right to tax "except by the common consent of the realm"—that is, with the consent of Parliament. In this way Parliament won the "power of the purse": by refusing to agree to new taxes, it could force the kings to do as it wished. As Parliament became more influential it won other rights, such as the power to impeach and try royal officials for misbehavior, and to be the sole judge of the qualifications of its members.

By the end of Edward's reign the peculiarly English concept of government, in which a strong king with powerful royal officials is still limited by the common law and by Parliament, was complete.

🏵 ENGLISH CIVILIZATION

For three centuries after the Norman Conquest the ruling classes of England proudly retained their Norman French customs and language. In England itself, Anglo-Saxon peasants spoke their Germanic dialects and resisted the Norman lords in every way they could. But gradually Normans adopted Saxon words, and French words entered the Saxon dialect. The two races intermarried until no one was sure who was Norman and who was Saxon. The two languages merged into one, until

> Learned, unlearned, old and young
> All understood the English tongue.

The English developed their own variations of Gothic architecture, which retained Romanesque features long after they had been abandoned in France. The thirteenth century was a great age for cathedral building; Henry III rebuilt Westminster Abbey at a cost of $90,000,000 in modern money, and Winchester Cathedral was rebuilt 556 feet long—the longest in Europe. The universities at Oxford and Cambridge flourished, although they had somewhat lower standards than the universities on the continent. In London lawyers settled in buildings abandoned by the outlawed Knights Templars and formed their "Inns of the Court," where they gave their apprentices unequaled training to prepare them to practice the common law for which England was already famous.

Most of England was still rural, and most of the 100 towns of the thirteenth century would today be considered villages. Only London was of any considerable size or importance in 1300: it had 40,000 inhabitants, four times as many as any other English town but far smaller than Paris, Constantinople, Venice, or Rome. Probably 90 per cent of the population lived on manors and tilled the soil much as they had in the days of William the Conqueror.

The thirteenth century, when there were fewer wars in France, was a time of relative peace and prosperity when the English united into a proud and unique people.

⚜ ⚜ ⚜

At the end of the thirteenth century Englishmen could be proud of their strong and relatively stable government. They were not doomed to localism as were the people of the Holy Roman Empire, and their kings were more bound to obey the people's wishes than were the kings of France. But for all that, England was a smaller country than either of the other great medieval monarchies, and its great influence on European history would come much later.

People, Places, and Terms

William the Conqueror	Hastings	exchecquer
Harold	Canterbury	shire-reeve
Normans	Runnymede	Assize of Clarendon
Henry I	Thames River	grand and petit juries
Angevins	Wales	common law
Plantagenets	Scotland	precedent
Henry II	Westminster Abbey	statute
Thomas à Becket	Oxford	Constitutions of Clarendon
Eleanor of Aquitaine	Cambridge	scutage
Richard the Lion-Hearted	London	Magna Carta
John	*Curia Regis*	peer
Stephen Langton	Salisbury Oath	Parliament
Henry III	Domesday Book	anticlericalism
Simon de Montfort	Charter of Liberties	Model Parliament
Edward I	justiciar	House of Lords
	chancellor	House of Commons
	treasurer	power of the purse

Getting Organized

1. How did William the Conqueror come to be king of England? How did he gain control over his new kingdom? What measures did he employ? How did he gain his income?
2. How did Henry I win the support of the nobles, the church, and the people? How did he strengthen his government?
3. What kind of man was Henry II? What territories did he rule?
4. What were Henry II's three great assizes and what did each establish? How was the common law enforced? What was the role of precedents in Henry's legal system?
5. What brought Henry II into conflict with the church? Why did Thomas à Becket oppose him? With what result? What was the effect of the struggle between the two men on church-state relations in England?
6. Why were Henry II's last years unhappy ones? What had he accomplished? What did his son Richard accomplish?
7. What was John's problem with France? How was it resolved? What was his problem with the church? How was it resolved? Why did the barons revolt in 1215? What are the important provisions of Magna Carta? What was its long-term significance?
8. What problems did Henry III face? How successful was he in dealing with them? What precedent was set during his reign?

9. What were Edward I's great accomplishments? Describe the member-ship and structure of the Model Parliament. How much authority did it have over the king? Why was Parliament a more potent enemy or a stronger ally to the king than the former feudal barons?
10. What evidence of national feeling was there in England in the thir-teenth century? How did the English people make a living in the thirteenth century?

Understanding the Big Picture

1. Make a chronological chart of the rise of the English monarchy. Stress those institutions that weakened the absolute power of the kings and those that strengthened the central government.
2. Which of the English kings discussed in this chapter do you consider the most successful in dealing with his problems? Support your opinion with specific evidence.
3. What role was played in the development of the English monarchy by the church? The feudal barons? The rising middle class? The develop-ment of common law?
4. Do you think that it was a good thing for *both* countries that England was thrown out of France? Explain your answer fully.
5. Why was the Magna Carta so important? Why is it still revered by freedom-loving people today?

Mastering the Map

Study carefully the map of England on page 152. How did geography contribute to England's loss of its French possessions? Why was that loss a good thing for England?

For the Thoughtful

1. What was the overall development of the English monarchy? How similar was the monarchy of Edward I to the English monarchy today?
2. Compare the reigns of Frederick II of the Holy Roman Empire, Philip IV of France, and Edward I of England. How does each of the three reigns illustrate the differing trends of the three countries?
3. Compare the government of medieval England to the government of the United States today. Compare also the two systems of law. What American institutions can be directly traced to medieval England? Which cannot?
4. Which of the three medieval monarchies that you've studied most strongly reflected Roman influences? Which most reflected feudal customs?

14

the Crusades

The crusades were a culminating event of the Middle Ages. These great expeditions against the Muslims in the Holy Land and elsewhere displayed on a grand scale the peculiar medieval blend of the ideals of the Christian Church and the professional warrior. At their best the crusaders were idealistic soldiers of the Cross fighting a holy war against the infidel. At their worst they were a greedy rabble scrambling for plunder and glory.

The idea of a holy war to spread Christianity was as old as the Middle Ages. Clovis in the fifth century had conquered pagan Gaul in the name of the church. Three hundred years later Charlemagne had done the same to the Saxons. A struggle between French Christians and the Moors (the Muslim rulers of Spain) began in the eighth century and continued off and on throughout the Middle Ages.

In the eastern Mediterranean, however, there had been relative peace, for the Byzantine Empire stood between the European Christians and the center of Muslim power. But in the late eleventh century the Byzantine power declined at the same time that the aggressive Seljuk Turks became dominant in Islam. Meanwhile, the growing towns of northern Italy had become eager to expand their trade with the Near East, and a series of vigorous popes hoped to enlarge Christendom and to bring the Orthodox Christians of the Byzantine Empire under Roman Catholic influence.

When the Turks began to interfere with Christian pilgrims to the Holy Land, the Byzantine emperor appealed for aid from the west. Pope Urban II called a council of the church at Clermont, in southern France, and on a cold November day in 1095 appealed for a crusade to restore the Holy Land to Christian rule:

> Let hatred [he cried] depart from among you; let your quarrels end. Enter upon the road to the Holy Sepulchre; wrest that land from a wicked race and subject it to yourselves. Undertake this journey eagerly for the remission of your sins, and be assured of the reward of imperishable glory in the Kingdom of Heaven.

The crowd responded, "God wills it!" The era of the crusades had begun.

⚜ THE BACKGROUND OF THE CRUSADES

The crusades did not just happen. They were the outcome of a century or more of change in all three major regions that bordered on the Mediterranean Sea: Islam, the Orthodox Christian Byzantine Empire, and Catholic Christian western Europe. Finally these changes combined to produce the Council of Clermont, which led in turn to two centuries of warfare that profoundly affected all three regions.

THE RISE OF THE SELJUK TURKS

In the eleventh century Islam, already in a period of decline (see page 66), was invaded from the east. The Seljuk Turks, a tribe of nomads, came out of the deserts of Turkestan in Central Asia and moved southward into Persia, where in 1040 they established a state of their own. In 1055 they moved west, conquering Bagdad and bringing Mesopotamia under their control. Then they moved against the Byzantine Empire. Invading Asia Minor and Syria, they overwhelmed the Byzantine armies in the battle of Manzikert (1071) and established their own sultanate in Asia Minor. Thirteen years later they captured Antioch in Syria and thus almost completely destroyed Christian rule in Asia. At the same time they warred successfully against the Arab Fatimite caliphs in Syria and Egypt. Everywhere they went they made themselves political and military masters.

Like the nomadic invaders of Europe, the Seljuk Turks soon settled down. They adopted Islam and many of the customs of the people they conquered, and their domain broke up into a number of squabbling little states.

Soon there were Turkish "sultanates" in Asia Minor, Persia, Mesopotamia, and Syria. Each of these little states was torn by internal discord and foreign wars; but they were all orthodox Muslims, stricter than the earlier Arab states in their religious beliefs, less tolerant, and, when the need arose, more likely to unite to pursue a common aim. The Turkish invasions strengthened Islamic power at a time when the Byzantine Empire was in decay.

THE BYZANTINE EMPIRE IN PERIL

In the ninth and tenth centuries Byzantium had been the strongest Christian state (see pages 47-48); but in the eleventh century it grew steadily weaker. The central government was torn by violence and intrigue. Great landowners established private armies and defied their emperors, and government officials fought them in an attempt to restore unity to the empire. Magyars from Hungary invaded the Balkan Peninsula, and the Seljuk Turks seized Asia Minor.

Alexius I (emperor 1081-1118) tried to save the Byzantine Empire by playing a game of devious oriental politics. When this failed, in despair he sent messengers to Pope Urban II, regretting the differences between the eastern and western Christian churches and pleading for help to save the empire and to preserve Christianity in the east.

CHRISTIAN INTEREST IN THE HOLY LAND

Christians had made pilgrimages to the Holy Land from the earliest times, and these pilgrimages continued after the area had come under the control of the Arabs. But the rise of the Seljuk Turks created new, unsettled conditions that interfered with travel to the Holy Land. Pope Gregory VII (pope 1073-1085) would have sent crusaders to protect the pilgrims had he not been distracted by his bitter struggle with the Holy Roman emperor. (See pages 126-127.)

Growing trade also influenced European attitudes toward the Middle East: Europeans, especially merchants in northern Italy, were afraid that the Seljuk Turks would cut off their profitable commerce with the Byzantines.

Consequently, Pope Urban II was eager to respond to the Byzantine plea for aid against the Muslims. Convinced of the need for reuniting the Roman and Orthodox churches, he hoped to extend his authority over all Christendom, enlarge its boundaries, and make Rome once again the capital of the world.

A medieval battle. This scene, from a French illustrated Bible of about 1250, is typical of the battles of the crusades. The mounted knights engage in hand-to-hand combat, while an archer shoots at them from a tower. At the left a man is lifted from the ground as he clings to the sling of a giant catapult so that the stone may be hurled with greater force.

THE FIRST THREE CRUSADES

Thus Urban called for a crusade. He demanded revenge against the "infidel" (literally "unfaithful") Turks, "an accursed race, wholly alienated from God," who had invaded Christian lands and "depopulated them by pillage and fire." He appealed to the vanity of the feudal nobles, telling them that upon them, "above all others, God has conferred remarkable glory in arms, great bravery, and strength to humble the heads of those that resist." He told them that Europe was poor, but that "Jerusalem is a land fruitful above all others, a paradise of delights." Most important of all, he promised that they could be "assured of the reward of imperishable glory in the kingdom of heaven."

THE FIRST CRUSADE

Few medieval men could resist an appeal like this. "God wills it!" the throngs shouted, and thousands sewed the cross of the crusader on their tunics. To encourage them further, the pope and his council declared a three-year truce in private war, so that warriors could take time out to fight the infidel; he granted crusaders remission of their sins; and he promised to protect their families and their property while they were away. Priests and monks preached the crusade all over Europe. Forty thousand people responded.

The first to leave were some 10,000 ignorant and untrained peasants who left their huts to follow leaders with names like Walter the Penniless and Peter the Hermit eastward to Jerusalem. They lived off the countryside as they marched. Emperor Alexius hurried these unwelcome allies through his empire and into Asia Minor, where they quarreled among themselves and destroyed Christian property. Most were soon massacred by the Turks.

The main body of the First Crusade consisted of 20,000 or 25,000 knights and men at arms, most of them French, led by a number of great lords. In 1097 they marched against the Turkish sultanate in Asia Minor. For two years they moved slowly south and east, invading Syria and taking Antioch before moving on Jerusalem. On July 15, 1099, they captured Jerusalem.

THE CRUSADER STATES

Both the Byzantines and the crusaders were pleased by the military outcome of the First Crusade. Alexius regained control of Asia Minor, the heartland of his empire, and the conquering Europeans won a strip of land that extended all the way from the upper Tigris River valley along the eastern shore of the Mediterranean to the boundary of Egypt. For half a century the crusaders held unchallenged sway over the Holy Land.

Godfrey of Bouillon was chosen head of the "Latin Kingdom of Jerusalem" with the title of "Defender of the Holy Sepulchre" (instead of king, because he refused to wear a royal crown where Christ had worn the crown of thorns). His brother Baldwin of Lorraine ruled the northernmost crusader state as count of Edessa. Between their two states were the lesser states of Antioch and Tripoli. In theory the other rulers were vassals of the defender of the Holy Sepulchre; in fact, ambitious lords made themselves as independent as possible, in the feudal tradition, and fought each other for the spoils of conquest.

The crusader states resembled the feudal states of Europe in other ways. The rulers surrounded themselves with feudal courts. Italian merchants set up trading posts in their ports. A steady stream of pilgrims, soldiers, settlers, and merchants flowed back and forth between the Middle East and western Europe. The Holy Land became an outpost of Catholic Christianity. But there were significant differences between the crusader states and western Europe. Catholicism was the official religion; but the government was tolerant, and most of the native people remained Orthodox

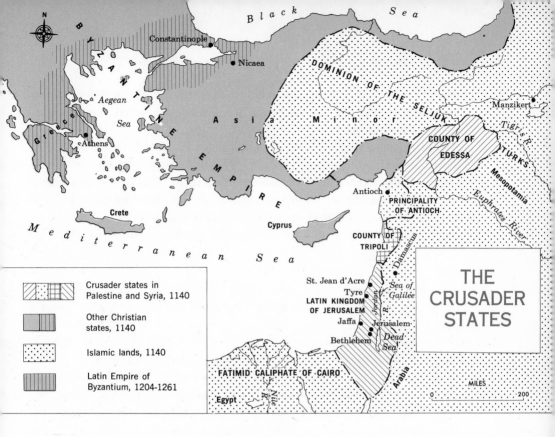

THE CRUSADER STATES

Crusader states in
Palestine and Syria, 1140

Other Christian
states, 1140

Islamic lands, 1140

Latin Empire of
Byzantium, 1204-1261

Christians, Jews, or Muslims. Even the Europeans adopted many of the customs of the land they had conquered: they wore turbans and flowing Arab robes, went to Arab doctors, taught the Koran in their Christian schools, and intermarried with Syrian women.

Early in the twelfth century crusaders formed the military-religious orders of the Templars and Hospitalers. (See page 99.) But religious enthusiasm soon waned, and these warrior-monks joined in the feudal squabbles of the secular rulers. As the Christians became more divided among themselves, the Muslims learned to play one group off against another. Finally, in 1144, Edessa, the outpost of Christian power in Syria, fell to the Turks, and the three remaining Christian states found themselves threatened by a new infidel invasion.

THE SECOND CRUSADE

When Bernard of Clairvaux (see page 121) heard of the fall of Edessa, he left his monastery to preach a Second Crusade. This time kings as well as nobles took up the cross. Louis VII of France (see page 161) and the Holy Roman Emperor Conrad III led so many warriors eastward that, Bernard reported to the pope, "Cities and castles are emptied; there is not left one man to seven women, and everywhere there are widows to still living husbands." Few of those husbands were still alive when the ill-starred Second Crusade ended.

Distrusting each other, French and Germans traveled separately, and both looted Byzantine cities on their way. The Byzantines retaliated by mixing chalk with the crusaders' flour and rushing them, still divided and unprepared, into Asia Minor, where the Turks made short work of them. Encouraged by success, the Turks moved on to attack the Holy Land. The Second Crusade accomplished only the snuffing out of thousands of lives.

THE THIRD CRUSADE

A quarter century later the Turks found in Saladin a leader who effectively united them against the Christians. Saladin (1138-1193) was a political and military genius. Born in Armenia and educated in Damascus, he became a general for the Turkish sultan of Syria. After bringing Syria under his own control, he conquered Egypt and became sultan of a state that stretched from Egypt to Mesopotamia and surrounded the crusader states on three sides. He refrained from attacking the crusader states, however, until a petty Christian lord attacked a caravan in which his sister was traveling. Then, in 1187, he destroyed a Christian army and seized Jerusalem. By 1189 he had overrun all of the Latin Kingdom except the city of Tyre.

Three of medieval Europe's greatest kings led the Third Crusade to recapture the Holy Land for Christianity. Frederick Barbarossa, the aged Holy Roman Emperor, marched his army overland and was drowned in 1190 while trying to ford a little river in Asia Minor. Richard the Lion-Hearted of England and Philip Augustus of France traveled by water, with Richard stopping on the way to fight Christians in Sicily and Cyprus. Together, they managed to conquer the city of Acre in 1191, after a siege of a year and a half. Then Philip, pleading illness, returned to France, leaving Richard to face the Muslims alone.

For two years Richard and Saladin, champions of their faiths, carried on a war that became part of medieval legend. Richard's little army twice fought to within twelve miles of Jerusalem, but it could not capture the city. In 1192 the two heroes signed a truce that gave the crusaders a few coastal towns and the right to travel to Jerusalem, which remained in Turkish hands. Thus the Third Crusade left the crusaders with a foothold in the Middle East, but little else.

🪷 THE DECLINE OF THE CRUSADES

Greedy for glory and loot though they were, the crusaders of the eleventh and twelfth centuries fought the Muslims to protect Byzantium and regain the Holy Land for Christendom. Few thirteenth-century crusaders were better than ordinary thieves.

THE FOURTH CRUSADE

During the twelfth century the Byzantine Empire grew weaker as nobles fought private wars, the cities ignored the central government, and tax gatherers collected huge sums—and kept them for themselves. Bands of monks wandered around robbing and looting. European crusaders demanded food and military supplies, the Turks again attacked in the east, and the country grew steadily poorer. Byzantium was nearly defenseless and ripe for conquest.

Soon after Innocent III (see pages 128-129) mounted the papal throne in 1198, he called the Fourth Crusade to re-establish the former glory of the Latin Kingdom of Jerusalem. The crusaders assembled in Venice to make the trip to the Holy Land; but they lacked the money to pay for their journey. The merchants of Venice persuaded the crusaders to attack Zara, Venice's rival merchant city on the Adriatic Sea, in part payment for their journey to Jerusalem. Later the Venetians talked the crusaders into joining in an attack on Constantinople in the hope of converting the Orthodox Christians there to Catholic Christianity and of looting that weakened but still rich city. The goal of the Venetians was control of the eastern Mediterranean, which would be theirs if Constantinople fell.

The crusaders gave in to temptation: in 1203 they captured Constantinople and set up a puppet emperor on the throne. The next year the Byzantines threw out their unwanted ruler, but the crusaders recaptured the city. In Easter week of 1204 they tore the altar of Hagia Sophia apart for its gold and jewels, ransacked the libraries, and seized many of the greatest Byzantine art treasures, which are still the pride of Venice. Pope Innocent was appalled. "These defenders of Christ," he lamented, "who should have turned their swords only against the infidels, have bathed themselves in Christian blood. They have respected neither religion, nor age, nor sex."

Venetians and crusaders divided the Byzantine Empire. Venice seized Crete, parts of Greece, and islands in the Aegean Sea. The crusaders established a "Latin Empire of Byzantium," which lasted half a century. In 1261 the native Byzantines recaptured Constantinople and restored local rule and Orthodox Christianity to what remained of the Byzantine Empire.

The Fourth Crusade discredited the crusading movement and so intensified the hatred of Catholic and Orthodox Christians for each other that the two groups never joined to fight the Muslims again. The weakened Byzantine Empire eventually fell to Muslim Turks, who went on to seize much of eastern Europe. Only the north-Italian cities gained from the Fourth Crusade. The Venetians dominated trade on the eastern Mediterranean. Genoa won some commercial concessions from the Byzantine emperors. Northern Italy grew rich from the profits of this control of the eastern trade routes.

THE LAST CRUSADES IN THE MIDDLE EAST

There were other crusades during the thirteenth century, but they were pathetic efforts. There was a "Children's Crusade" whose only noteworthy

Knights preparing to embark on a crusade: a miniature from an Italian manuscript of the fourteenth century. The banners show the coats of arms of the pope (the crossed keys of St. Peter), the Holy Roman emperor, France, England, and others.

result was that many of the little crusaders were sold into slavery. The Holy Roman Emperor Frederick II (see page 154) went on crusade to get the pope to lift a ban of excommunication which had been placed on him. The saintly King Louis IX of France (see pages 164-165) led two crusades; he was captured on the first, and he died during the second, in 1270. After him, no one made any further attempts to save the Holy Land.

🐚 THE CRUSADES IN THE WEST

Although the principal crusades were directed against the infidels in the Holy Land, similar military expeditions marched against Muslims in the Iberian peninsula (modern Spain and Portugal) and against those men who opposed the papal power in western Europe proper. To pious medieval Christians it seemed only natural to use force wherever necessary to extend and preserve the power and influence of the church.

THE CONQUEST OF THE IBERIAN PENINSULA

Most of the Iberian peninsula had been a part of Islam since the eighth century. By 1034, however, the old caliphate of Cordova had broken up into more than twenty quarreling kingdoms, and for the first time the Christians were able to attempt the conquest of Spain. From their tiny kingdoms in the northern part of the peninsula—Leon, Castile, Navarre, and Barcelona—Christian knights began a series of successful crusades against the Moors (the Muslims of the Iberian peninsula). By 1055 they had occupied Toledo and central Spain, and the Moorish power seemed doomed. But Berber warriors from North Africa came to the aid of their fellow Muslims, and for the rest of the eleventh century Spain was the scene of bitter battles. During this struggle one of the great heroes of Spanish history, Rodrigo Diaz, called the "Cid" ("master"), fought first for his native Castile, then for the Moors, and finally for himself as ruler of Valencia on the Mediterranean coast. Cruel, self-seeking, and haughty, but fearless and daring, the Cid became a legend in Spain and a model for later Spanish noblemen.

The church encouraged a number of Spanish crusades, and French warriors and Cluniac monks rushed to aid the Spanish Christians. Throughout the twelfth and thirteenth centuries the effort to oust the Moors from the Iberian peninsula continued. Gradually it was successful; Saragossa, the key to eastern Spain, fell in 1118; the king of Portugal conquered Lisbon in 1147. In 1212 the combined armies of the growing Christian states won a decisive victory at the battle of Las Navas de Tolosa, which drove the Moors from all but the southern coast and the city of Granada. The rest of the peninsula was divided among the Christian kingdoms of Portugal, Castile, and Aragon. (See map, page 152.)

CRUSADES IN EUROPE

There were a number of crusades conducted in various parts of Europe. The largest of these was the Albigensian Crusade (see pages 123-124) against heretics in southern France. Another was directed against the Slavs to the east of the Holy Roman Empire. In the thirteenth century several popes called for crusades against their enemies the Holy Roman emperors; but Christians were reluctant to fight a "holy war" against fellow Christians, and this attempt to make a political weapon out of the crusading spirit backfired. The idea died hard, however, and as late as the sixteenth century popes were calling for new crusades against their enemies.

🕮 THE EFFECTS OF THE CRUSADES

The crusades failed to achieve their main purpose, which was to restore the Holy Land to Christendom and destroy Islam. The crusader states soon disappeared, after having helped arouse Islam to a "holy war" of its own that ultimately led to the conquest of Constantinople and much of eastern Europe by Muslims. (Chapter 15.) The Byzantine Empire was weakened, and its collapse became almost inevitable. On the other hand, crusaders in the west did drive the Moors from most of the Iberian peninsula and the islands of the Mediterranean, thus assuring that the western Mediterranean would be free for Europe's growing commerce.

But the most significant effects of the crusades were on the civilization of Europe itself. Historians disagree on the precise importance of the crusades in relation to later events in Europe; perhaps what happened would have happened anyway, even if there had been no crusades. But it is generally agreed that, at the very least, the crusades hastened certain developments.

THE CRUSADES AND PAPAL POWER

In the short run the crusades undoubtedly increased the power and influence of the popes. But the tragedy of the Fourth Crusade and the crusades that followed led to criticism of the popes who had called them. Papal taxes imposed to pay for crusades were later misused and came to be much resented, even by the clergy. In the long run, therefore, the crusades may well have hastened the decline of papal power that came in the fifteenth and sixteenth centuries.

THE RISE OF ROYAL AUTHORITY

The crusades probably helped the kings extend their authority over the great nobles, thus weakening the feudal system. Many powerful lords died on crusade, and others spent their fortunes to pay the costs of crusading. At the same time, the kings used the crusades as an excuse to impose new taxes, which gave them the income they needed to war on their rebellious vassals. The crusades also led to an increased cost of living, which hurt most those nobles who obtained their limited cash income from their feudal manors. Many nobles sold their traditional feudal rights to their peasants and to the towns in order to defray the expenses of their trip to the east. They never regained these rights, and the appetite of the people for even greater freedom was whetted.

INFLUENCE ON THE ARTS AND SCIENCE

The crusades revolutionized warfare. Europeans developed heavier armor and learned how to use new weapons like the crossbow. Merchants and townsmen copied Muslim weavers, goldsmiths and silversmiths, architects and scholars. Returning crusaders introduced to western Europe knowledge of Arabic numerals, algebra, Greek philosophy, and Arab medicine.

THE GROWTH OF COMMERCE

Growing trade between the east and west had started before the crusades, and indeed was one of the causes of the First Crusade. The crusades speeded this growth. The Fourth Crusade assured the Italian cities control of trade in the eastern Mediterranean. The silks, spices, and sugar brought back by the early crusaders were at first luxuries, but upper-class Europeans soon came to look on them as necessities. Trade in these and other products led to new trade routes and new commercial towns all over Europe. The greatness of Venice can be traced directly to the crusades, and the wealth that made possible the Italian Renaissance in the fifteenth century (Chapter 19) grew out of commerce stimulated by the crusades.

THE CRUSADES AND ASIA

The crusades helped Europeans to rediscover Asia. Of the thousands who went to the Holy Land, a few went farther eastward to Persia and, in the thirteenth century, all the way to China. Returning travelers drew maps and wrote guidebooks that helped others to follow their footsteps. Enterprising "Frankish" merchants (Orientals referred to all Europeans as "Franks") established settlements in Syria, the first overseas colonies set up by Europeans. The journals of Marco Polo, a traveler to China, and the fictional adventures of Sir John de Mandeville were widely read, stimulating great interest in travel and geography. When the Portuguese first sailed down the western coast of Africa on the voyages that would eventually take them all the way to India, they hoped they were starting a crusade to attack the western flank of Islam.

🜲 🜲 🜲

Perhaps Europe would have developed as it did even if no crusade had ever marched out of western Europe. But for whatever reason, Europe was a far different place after the crusades had ended from what it had been when they began. The date of the fall of the last crusader stronghold, at Acre in 1291, is as good a date as any for the end of the High Middle Ages.

People, Places, and Terms

Seljuk Turks	Clermont	Edessa
Urban II	Turkestan	Acre
Alexius I	Bagdad	Venice
Conrad III	Antioch	Zara
Saladin	Mesopotamia	Latin Empire
Baldwin of Flanders	Manzikert	of Byzantium
Moors	Jerusalem	
Berbers	Latin Kingdom	sultanate
The Cid	of Jerusalem	infidel

Getting Organized

1. Who were the Seljuk Turks? Where did they come from? Where did they go? What threat did they pose to the Byzantine Empire? to Christianity?
2. Why did Pope Urban II accept the plea of Alexius for help? Who went on the First Crusade? Why did they go?

3. How successful was the First Crusade? What arrangements were made at its conclusion? Name and describe the crusader states. How successful was the Second Crusade?
4. How did the Third Crusade start? Who were the major figures in this conflict? What was its eventual outcome?
5. What happened to the Fourth Crusade? How were the crusaders distracted from their original purpose? What cities did they conquer? With what results?
6. What did the later crusades accomplish? How did the crusades end?
7. What was the crusade in the west? How much of the Iberian peninsula did the Moors control in the early eleventh century? How much did they control after the middle of the thirteenth century?
8. What was the effect of the crusades on Islamic power? On the Byzantine Empire? On the unity of Christendom? On the Iberian peninsula? On papal power? On royal authority? On feudalism? On arts and sciences? On commerce?

Understanding the Big Picture

1. Make a chronological chart showing the principal events of the crusades.
2. Why did the crusades start? Why did so many people accept the call to drive back the infidel?
3. Which of the different crusades do you consider to have been the most important? Why? Which was the most successful? Which the least successful? Why?
4. What was the overall effect of the crusades on the power of the church? Of the kings?

Mastering the Map

1. Study carefully the map of the crusader states on page 187. How extensive were the crusader states? What geographical factors helped or hindered their fight for survival? Explain your answer fully.
2. Study Spain on the map on page 152. How much territory did the Moors once control? By 1212 how much did they control?

For the Thoughtful

1. In what ways were the crusades a good example of the power of the medieval church at its height? Explain fully.
2. Would you be surprised if religious feeling similar to that of the twelfth and thirteenth centuries swept twentieth-century Europe or America? Do religious issues today influence men as they did in the time of the crusades? Do any kinds of moral issues stir men as they did the crusaders?

15

three Empires
of the East

After the crusades lost their vigor and the Byzantine Empire began to wither away, three new empires arose to the east of Europe. The first, created by the barbaric Mongols, flowered briefly and soon died. The other two lasted far longer: the Ottoman Empire, which conquered Byzantium, survived until the twentieth century; and Russia began a slow rise to power that eventually made it one of the two "superpowers" of the present day. All three of these eastern empires developed in ways far different from the more civilized contemporary states of western Europe.

THE MONGOLS

In the thirteenth century, at the same time that the Christians were weakened by the fiasco of the Fourth Crusade and the Latin Empire of Byzantium (see pages 189-190), their Muslim enemies were divided and nearly overwhelmed by attacks from the Mongols. Foes of Christianity, of Islam, and of civilization itself, the Mongols swarmed out of eastern Asia to invade the Middle East. Like the Huns, Magyars, and Seljuk Turks

196

before them, the Mongols had previously been occupied herding horses and sheep, wandering from place to place, and amusing themselves with banditry and war.

GENGHIS KHAN

The Mongols were subjects of the emperors of China until, for some unknown reason, in the middle of the twelfth century they left their ancestral home in Mongolia, repudiated Chinese rule, and began to migrate. One of their chieftains, Genghis Khan (1162-1227; also referred to as Jenghiz Khan and Chingis Khan) united a number of Mongol clans and went on the warpath. After reducing parts of northern China, he turned on Turkestan, destroying the cities of Bokhara and Samarkand so thoroughly that they were still in ruins a century later.

Genghis has been compared to Attila the Hun, but he was a better warrior and a political genius who called himself "God in Heaven . . . the power of God on Earth, the Emperor of Mankind." He founded effective governments in the lands he conquered, surrounded himself with poets and scholars and 500 wives, and made his court at Karakorum a center of art and learning in which were blended the cultures of India, Islam, Orthodox Christianity, and China.

THE MONGOL EMPIRE

Genghis's sons and successors continued his conquests, in the Far East adding China, Korea, and Burma to the Mongol Empire; in the Near East overrunning Persia and the Abbassid Caliphate; and moving southward until they were finally stopped by an Egyptian army near Acre in 1260. Another group of Mongols, called the "Tatars" or the "Golden Horde," moved into Russia, destroying Moscow and Kiev and entering central Europe before withdrawing to establish a capital at Sarai on the Volga. Thus the Mongol Empire at its greatest extent reached from Kiev to the Pacific and from the Arctic wastes to the Arabian Sea—the largest state in history.

The Mongol threat slowed the struggle between Christendom and Islam. Popes, Holy Roman emperors, and the Seljuk Turks turned from fighting each other to defending themselves from the common Mongol enemy. But the Mongol Empire soon fell apart. Its leaders quarreled with

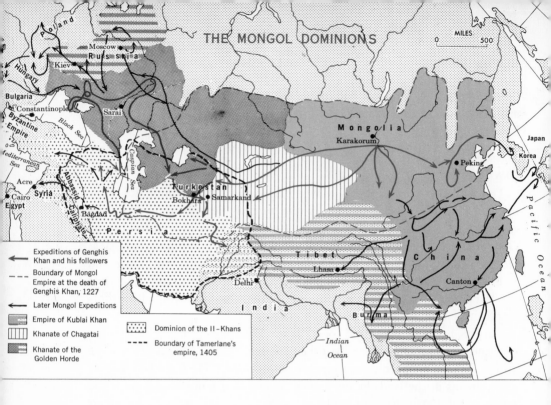

Poland
Moscow
Kiev
Russia
Hungary
Bulgaria
Constantinople
Byzantine
Empire
Sarai
Black Sea
Mediterranean
Sea
Acre
Cairo
Egypt
Syria
Abbassid
Bagdad
Caliphate
Caspian Sea
Persia
Turkestan
Bokhara
Samarkand
Mongolia
Karakorum
Peking
Japan
Korea
Pacific Ocean
China
Canton
Tibet
Lhasa
Delhi
India
Burma
Indian Ocean

MILES
0   500

Expeditions of Genghis Khan and his followers
Boundary of Mongol Empire at the death of Genghis Khan, 1227
Later Mongol Expeditions
Empire of Kublai Khan
Khanate of Chagatai
Khanate of the Golden Horde
Dominion of the Il–Khans
Boundary of Tamerlane's empire, 1405

each other while their people were settling down and absorbing the customs of their subject nations. In the Far East the Mongols who conquered China were absorbed by the Chinese, although a Mongol dynasty founded by Kublai Khan (emperor 1280-1294) ruled China for almost a century and was made famous throughout Europe in the writings of the Italian traveler Marco Polo. (See page 194.) In the Middle East the Mongols adopted Islam, and in Europe the Tatars either retreated from Poland and Hungary or turned Christian and intermarried with the local population. For over two centuries, however, from their capital just north of the Caspian Sea, the Mongol "Golden Horde" dominated Russia.

The Mongols brought about many changes wherever they went. In Islamic lands (Persia, Mesopotamia, and Syria) they ended the previous governments and pushed the center of Islamic civilization back from Bagdad in the valley of the Tigris to Cairo in the valley of the Nile. After the power of the Seljuk Turks was destroyed, only disorganized tribes remained to war among the ruins; Arabs, Persians, Kurds, Turks, and Mongols vied with each other for temporary supremacy. Not until the fourteenth century did one nationality, the Ottoman Turks, become dominant.

TAMERLANE

Late in the fourteenth century a second leader arose who, like Genghis, united Mongols and other tribes in Central Asia and led them in a series of conquests. Starting as chieftain of a tribe near Samarkand, Tamerlane (Timur the Lame, 1336?-1405), whom his enemies called the "Prince of Destruction," subdued west-central Asia, Persia, and Mesopotamia. In 1398 he invaded India, where he won a great victory near Delhi. His empire fell apart after his death, but his followers who remained in India founded a state called the Mughal (or Mogul) Empire, which survived four and a half centuries until it finally surrendered to the British in 1857.

& THE OTTOMAN TURKS

In the middle of the thirteenth century the Mongols destroyed the power of the first important Turkish tribe, the Seljuk Turks, who had led the militant Muslims against the crusaders in the eleventh and twelfth centuries. (See pages 183-184.) In the fourteenth century the Ottoman Turks, members of a clan supposed to have been founded by a leader named Osman (1259-1326), took advantage of the confusion caused by the breakup of the Mongol Empire and the weakening of the Byzantine Empire to begin 300 years of conquest.

Osman and his tribesmen were originally border guards serving the Byzantines in Asia Minor, not far from Constantinople. They gradually absorbed other Turkish tribes and expanded the area under their control. Although they were Muslims, they won the support of Christians by tolerating their religion and offering to grant special tax exemptions to any who would adopt Islam—an offer many Christians were willing to accept. Their subject peoples learned to speak Turkish and intermarried with their Ottoman neighbors; the Turks in turn learned to become farmers and adopted Byzantine forms of government. Gradually they became strong enough to become the champions of Islam and to renew the struggle with Christendom that the Mongol invasions had interrupted.

EXPANSION OF THE OTTOMAN TURKS

During the first half of the fourteenth century the Ottoman Turks, with the aid of other Muslims, won most of Asia Minor. In 1354 they crossed the Dardanelles into the European part of Byzantium, moving into Thrace

and establishing their capital in the European city of Adrianople. Constantinople was now surrounded by its enemies; it survived only because the Turks chose to move into the Balkan Peninsula where, in 1389, they defeated the Yugoslavs in the bitter battle of Kossovo. Next the Ottomans moved on to overwhelm the Bulgarians, while their navies ravaged the Aegean Sea and attacked Venetian colonies.

The pope called a crusade, led by the king of Hungary and including knights from England, France, and Germany, which marched confidently down the Danube valley, only to be destroyed by a better-organized Turkish army. But the Ottoman invasion of Europe nevertheless came to a temporary halt, for the Turks were forced to turn east to defend themselves from Tamerlane (above, page 199), whose forces invaded Asia Minor. At the same time there was a dispute over the Ottoman crown, so that it took fifty years for the Turks to restore unity and regain the lands that they had held in 1400. Then, in 1451, the able young Sultan Mehmed II (or Mohammed II; sultan 1451-1481) decided that the time had come to take Constantinople.

THE FALL OF CONSTANTINOPLE

Constantinople, which had been the capital of the Eastern Roman Empire and could therefore claim to be the "second Rome," now faced the fate of the first Rome—conquest by an alien enemy. The desperate emperors, who controlled little more than the city itself, turned to the popes for aid. In 1439 the Emperor John VIII traveled to Italy to attend the Catholic council of Florence, where he promised to unify the Catholic and Orthodox Churches under the pope in return for an alliance against the Turks. His effort failed. A crusade called by the pope was crushed in 1444; and the Orthodox clergy, fearing the power of the pope, opposed the emperor's policies and thus further weakened Byzantium in the face of the Ottoman aggressor.

Mehmed II mustered an army of 150,000 men, built forts to control the naval approaches to Constantinople, and in 1453 laid siege to the city. The Byzantine Emperor Constantine XI made the best defense he could. To prevent an attack from the sea, he stretched an iron chain across the mouth of the harbor and manned the walls with his army of only 10,000 defenders. Most were Greek Byzantines, of whom many were monks and priests.

The siege of Constantinople, 1453. The Ottoman Turks, after having gained entrance to the harbor by sliding their boats down a hill, are storming the walls of the city.

There were also soldiers sent by the pope, and others were sent by Venice and Genoa, which had realized too late that Constantinople was the key to their prosperous trade with the east. At first the walls held back the attackers, although Mehmed battered them with the largest cannon he could find. Then the Ottomans hauled some seventy light boats up a hill and slid them down into the waters of the harbor. The defenders divided their forces to meet this new attack, and finally, after a siege of months, the Ottomans were able to successfully storm the walls. On May 29, 1453, they broke into the city, killing the scattered bands of Christian soldiers who remained to fight to the death. In one of these bands was Constantine XI, the last of the Caesars, the last emperor of the city founded eleven centuries earlier by the first Constantine. When he died, the last historical link with ancient Rome was broken, the last major Christian citadel in the eastern Mediterranean was gone, and the triumph of the Ottomans was complete.

Mehmed and his successors, who felt almost as strongly about Constantinople as had the Christians, made it their capital and principal city. They converted the Orthodox church of Hagia Sophia (see page 28) into a Muslim mosque—Mehmed himself destroyed its Christian altar—and built new mosques and palaces of their own. But, true to the Ottoman tradition, they did not persecute the Christians, instead allowing them to worship in the smaller churches and encouraging them to become Muslims. Many Christians did. Hagia Sophia was used as a mosque until the twentieth century, when it became a museum. Constantinople is still the seat of the patriarch who is nominal head of the Orthodox Church, and it is also the most important city of the Turkish Muslims.

Constantinople conquered, the Turks moved on to new triumphs. In the next century they conquered many of the islands of the Aegean, almost all the rest of the Balkan Peninsula, and the lower Danube basin. By 1560 they had seized most of Hungary and were threatening Vienna.

Meanwhile, far to the north, their future rivals, the Russians, were emerging from barbarism in the vast plains of eastern Europe and northern Asia.

🏵 RUSSIA, THE "THIRD ROME"

From the Carpathian Mountains of Hungary all the way to the Pacific shores of Asia, lie low, rolling plains that cover one sixth of the land surface of the earth. They are broken only by the low range of Ural Mountains, which only in theory separates Europe from Asia, and by rivers that flow north into the Arctic Ocean or Baltic Sea or south to the Caspian and Black Seas. This immense area divides naturally into four distinct regions. On the north there is frozen tundra, cold and dreary and until recent times inhabited mostly by reindeer. Just to the south of this is a strip of forests of pine, fir, and birch. This merges gradually into a third region of open steppes, prairie-like country with the thick, black soil for which Russia is famous. The southernmost region is hot, dry, and salty; it was the route across which Asiatic tribes hurried on their way to more desirable lands to the north and west.

THE PEOPLES OF THE RUSSIAN PLAINS

From prehistory onward, this area was the scene of one invasion after another. In the later fifth century A.D. began the slow but massive migrations of Slavs, who fanned out from the region north and east of the Carpathians. Some, the Serbs, Croats, and Slovenes, were the South Slavs (Yugoslavs), who settled in the Balkan Peninsula. (See page 46.) Others, the West Slavs—Poles, Czechs (Bohemians), and Slovaks—settled in central Europe. The largest group, the East Slavs, occupied the eastern plains and eventually became the Russians (or "Great Russians"), Ukrainians ("Little Russians"), and Byelorussians ("White Russians"). The East Slavs were conquered many times by other peoples, with whom they intermarried, beginning the mixture of races that has characterized Russia ever since.

Russia began to emerge as a political unit in the ninth century, when Vikings sailed up the rivers from the Baltic Sea, raiding and trading. (See page 78.) According to tradition, the Slavs sent them a message: "Our land is great and rich, but there is no order in it. Come and rule over it." So in 862 foreign princes established the first great Russian state.

THE RUSSIAN VIKING STATE OF KIEV

Rurik, the Viking leader who answered the Slavs' plea, set up a capital at Novgorod in the north. Later the capital was moved to Kiev on the Dnieper. His followers were called "Varangians" or "Rus," and eventually all his Slavic subjects came to call themselves "Russians." The rivers were a natural roadway to the Black Sea and Constantinople; every year the Viking Russians sent a fleet of river boats laden with products of the north

—furs, wax, tar, honey, and, most important of all, slaves—for the markets of Constantinople. They returned with money and with Byzantine ideas of religion and government. About 990 the Kievan prince Vladimir I "the Great" (reigned 980-1015) was converted to Byzantine Christianity. Byzantine priests and monks moved into Russia, introducing the Byzantine idea that the prince was not only a political but also a religious leader. Since the head of the Russian church was appointed by the patriarch of Constantinople and was usually a Byzantine, the civilization of Kiev was modeled in many ways on that of Constantinople.

There were important differences, however, between the Byzantine and Russian churches. The Russian Orthodox Church did not adopt the Greek language, but retained the native Slavonic tongue. Therefore the priests rarely learned to read Greek and Latin and were never exposed to such pagan authors as Plato and Aristotle or to such western church fathers as Ambrose and Augustine. Moreover, only the higher clergy had much of any education at all; the parish priests knew little more than their ignorant peasant parishioners. Cut off from western European civilization, the rulers of Kiev were little affected by the ideas that guided the thoughts of other European princes, and their people remained even less civilized than the peasants of Germany and France.

For a time the state of Kiev, with its trade with Constantinople, prospered and became one of the most powerful of all European principalities. Yaroslav "the Wise" (reigned 1019-1054) brought large areas under his control, codified the laws, and built the magnificent Cathedral of Saint Sophia in Kiev. He married his daughters to the kings of France, Hungary, and Norway, his sister to the king of Poland, and his son into the ruling family of Byzantium. But he divided his state among his five sons who, quarreling, could not stave off an invasion of a bloodthirsty tribe called the Cumans, who in the late eleventh century settled in the south and blocked the river route to Byzantium. Trade fell off, and Kiev declined. To escape the invaders, the people of Kiev fled north in a second Slavic migration.

This second Slavic migration led to the growth of new cities and further intermixture of the Russians with other peoples. North of Kiev, Novgorod prospered and developed a form of republican government. Northeast of Kiev, tiny Moscow welcomed refugees; and another city, Vladimir, became capital of a powerful duchy. The Kiev region was left to the Cumans and the few Russians who remained.

THE GOLDEN HORDE

In 1223 a reconnaissance party of Genghis Khan's Mongols galloped out of the east, defeated the prince of Kiev, crushed him between the boards on which they spread their victory feast, and disappeared. The Russians were frightened and bewildered; a chronicler noted that "No one knows for certain who they are, or from where they come, or what is their language, or race or faith, but they are called Tatars." Fifteen years later they reappeared under Baku, a grandson of Genghis. After sacking Moscow, Vladimir, and Kiev, the Tatars established a state called the "khanate of the Golden Horde," which, from its capital at Sarai, lorded it over the Russian princes for two centuries. (Above, page 198.)

The Tatars looked upon Russia primarily as a source of tribute (money payments) and, so long as the tribute was paid, they allowed the Russian princes and Orthodox priests to rule much as they had before the Mongol conquest. Gradually a sort of Russian feudal system came into being. Russian princes traveled to Sarai, the Tatar capital on the Volga, and sometimes all the way to the grand khan in Asia to pay homage to the Tatars and to win the privilege of collecting the Tatar tribute. Under the princes was a noble class of "boyars," who ran the local governments. The peasants lived in tiny villages called "mirs," paid heavy taxes, and were prevented from fleeing to freer territories to the north and west. The Tatars, like other pagans, were tolerant of Christianity, welcomed the prayers and assistance of the Orthodox priests, and allowed the church to keep its estates as long as it paid tribute like the secular rulers. Eventually the Tatars even gave the priests some relief from taxation.

The Tatars encouraged the idea that the princes were the absolute rulers of their estates and that the nobles and peasants were the servants, not the masters, of their government. They taught that force was the only way by which the huge country could be governed effectively, and they made the priests the agents of the princes. Cut off from trade with the outside world, Russian cities grew smaller than ever, and their people moved to the mirs and became peasants. The Russians and their rulers, not understanding the civilization of western Europe, became suspicious of it and of all outsiders. The Tatars, even less civilized than their Russian subjects, delayed the development of Russian civilization, so that it remained semi-barbarous at a time when the rest of Europe was experiencing the Renaissance. (Chapters 19 and 20.)

THE RISE OF MUSCOVY

During the fourteenth century Muscovy, the territory around Moscow, became the most important of the Russian states. It had many natural advantages. Located near the headwaters of rivers that flow to the north and south, it also lay on the trade route to the east. Near the southern edge of the tree belt of the plains, it had the necessary raw materials for forest industries, but was also near the rich black soil of the steppes. Its people, many of whom had fled from the invaders of Kiev, supported a strong government, and they were blessed with a number of able and ambitious princes. One of them, Ivan I "Kalita" ("Moneybag"), persuaded the Tatars to appoint him to collect all their tribute from the other Russian rulers and assumed the title "sovereign prince of Russia." Then he persuaded the head of the Russian Orthodox Church to move from Vladimir to Moscow. In this way, by allying himself with the church and the Tatars, Ivan was able to extend his authority over other Russian princes and to lay the foundations of the modern Russian state.

The Muscovites still had to contend with two foreign powers. The Tatars, worried by the growing strength of Muscovy, marched to conquer it; but in 1380 they were thrown back. Thereafter, though the Golden Horde remained supreme in theory, its actual power declined. The other rival was more dangerous; in the Baltic Sea region Lithuania, the last pagan state of Europe, adopted Catholic Christianity and allied itself with Catholic Poland to attack Orthodox Russia.

To face these foreign threats, the Muscovites under Ivan the Great created an autocratic state that succeeded in driving back its enemies.

RUSSIAN AUTOCRACY: IVAN THE GREAT
AND THE "THIRD ROME"

Ivan III "the Great" (reigned 1462-1505) had three goals: to absorb as many Russians as he could into Muscovy; to end the rule of the Golden Horde; and to make himself the unchallenged ruler of his country.

Ivan attacked any other Russian state that defied him. When some citizens of Novgorod proposed an alliance between their city and the Polish-Lithuanians, Ivan attacked and conquered their city, bringing its huge territories under Muscovite control. Next he turned eastward, conquering non-Russians as well as Russians. Then he defied the Tatars and declared his independence of the Golden Horde. Finally he drove the Polish-Lithuanians from part of the Ukraine. He had accomplished his first two goals.

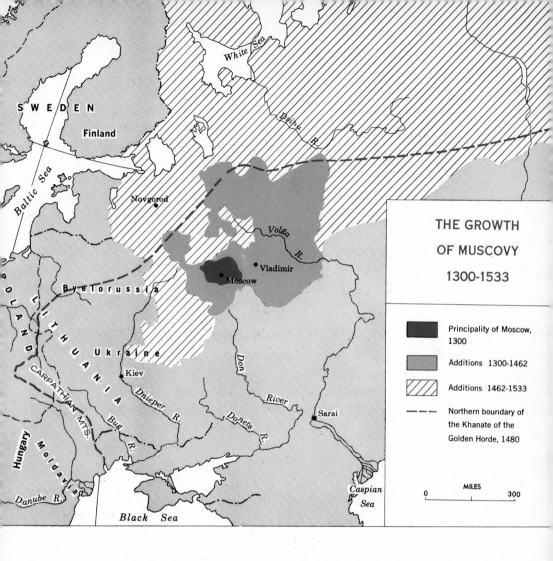

He succeeded in his third goal by making himself the absolute monarch
of Muscovy. The pope arranged Ivan's marriage with a Catholic niece of
the last emperor of Byzantium in the hope that she would lead Orthodox
Russia into the Catholic fold. Instead, she carried to Moscow not Catholicism but Byzantine ideas about autocracy. She encouraged Ivan to use the
Byzantine title of "autocrat" and the Roman title of "Caesar," which became
"tsar" in Russian. She employed Italian architects to rebuild Moscow's
Kremlin, a fortified area at the center of the city. Within its walls Ivan
ruled in Byzantine splendor, isolated behind a façade of ceremony from
the princes and boyars (nobles) who had surrounded the earlier rulers.

Then he set about making all Russians the servants of the state. The princes and boyars who did not do as he wished lost their estates; those who remained held land on condition that they serve the tsar. In return, they were given increased authority over their peasants, who fell further from freedom as they were forbidden to leave their land unless they were free from debt. Since this was rarely the case, they were little better than serfs of their landlords. In this way the Russian people became the servants of the lords, and the lords the servants of the Russian state. Serfdom, which died out in most of Europe in the late Middle Ages, remained in Russia until 1861.

Another idea that Ivan imported from Byzantium was that Moscow had become the "third Rome." "Two Romes have fallen," a Russian monk wrote, "a third stands, and a fourth shall not be." The idea was that when the original Rome fell to barbarian invaders (because of its Catholic "heresy"), the capital of Christendom had moved to Orthodox Constantinople, the "second Rome." Now that Constantinople had been captured by the infidel Turks (the Russians maintained), the center of Christianity had moved to Moscow, the "Third Rome." The tsars were therefore the heirs of both the Roman and Byzantine emperors and had no limit to their authority. When the Russian Orthodox Church accepted this belief, the churchmen, like the nobles, became the dutiful servants of the state. There was no institution or class to challenge the tsars.

THE RUSSIAN AUTOCRATIC STATE

Thus the pattern of Russian government and society had been clearly established by the end of the fifteenth century. The tsar who headed the state was limited by neither law nor custom; his claims to authority, deriving both from the Tatar experience and from the doctrine of the "third Rome," were unlimited. The boyars still existed, but their power depended on the good will of the tsar and their ability to serve him. The peasants were almost without rights, and, like the boyars, existed to serve their master.

The Russian Orthodox Church was also the servant of the tsar, to whom it gave the trappings of religious authority. Separated from the Catholic Church by differences in belief, and even from the Greek Orthodox Church by a different language, it claimed that the center of Christendom had passed from Rome and Constantinople to Moscow, the "third Rome." But it developed no original thinkers, and its priests had little or nothing to teach their ignorant parishioners.

The isolation of Russia from Europe was made complete by Polish, Lithuanian, and Scandinavian enemies to the west and the Ottoman Empire to the south. Since carrying on foreign trade was extremely difficult, and the peasant mirs offered no market for domestic manufacturing, cities remained small and poor. The peasant people continued to live like medieval serfs in their tiny communities scattered across the forests and the steppes.

& & &

Huge in size, but poor and isolated, Russia continued to follow its primitive ways until, during the seventeenth and eighteenth centuries, more enlightened tsars attempted to bring it within the sphere of European civilization—with limited success.

People, Places, and Terms

Mongols	Ivan Kalita	Volga River
Tatars	Ivan the Great	Dnieper River
Genghis Khan		Novgorod
Kublai Khan	Turkestan	Lithuania
Tamerlane	Bokhara	
Ottoman Turks	Samarkand	Russian Orthodox
Osman	Moscow	Church
John VIII	Kiev	boyars
Mehmed II	Sarai	mir
Constantine XI	Delhi	autocrat
Slavs	Mughal Empire	tsar
East Slavs	Adrianople	Kremlin
Rurik	Carpathian Mountains	"third Rome"
Yaroslav the Wise	Ural Mountains	

Getting Organized

1. Who were the Mongols? Who was Genghis Khan and what did he accomplish? How large was the Mongol Empire at its height? Who was Tamerlane and what areas did he conquer? What happened to the Mongols?
2. When and under whom did the Ottoman Turks first become important? How did they treat the Christians and the other people that they conquered? What areas of Asia Minor and Europe did they conquer? How did Europe react to this new menace?
3. Why did Mehmed II decide to conquer Constantinople? How did Constantinople try to get help from its European neighbors? How did Mehmed II finally conquer the great city? How did he change it?

4. Describe Russian geography. When and where did Slavic civilization begin? Who were Russia's original inhabitants? Why did they call to the Vikings for help?
5. Describe Kievan Russia. What ideas did it adopt from other civilizations? How did Russia differ from Constantinople and western Europe? What were the results of the second Slavic migrations?
6. When did the Mongols come to Russia? How did they rule Russia? How tolerant were they? What impact did the Tatars (Mongols) have on Russian civilization?
7. How did the state of Muscovy arise? What steps did Ivan Kalita take to increase Moscow's strength? What rivals did he face and how did he deal with them?
8. What were Ivan the Great's aims? How successful was he in achieving them? How did he rule? Why was Moscow called the "third Rome"?

Understanding the Big Picture

1. Why did the three great eastern empires arise as they did? What effect did they have on each other? On the people that they conquered? On the Byzantine Empire? On western Europe?
2. What was the importance of the fall of Constantinople?
3. Describe Russian autocracy. How much power did the Russian tsars have? How did they use their power? In what ways was Russia different from western Europe? From Byzantium?

Mastering the Map

1. Study carefully the map of the Mongol dominions on page 198. How large an empire was it?
2. Study the map of the rise of the Ottoman Turkish Empire on page 200. What peoples did they conquer or threaten? How large was their empire by 1481?
3. Study carefully the map of the growth of the Russian state on page 207. During what period in its early history did Russia expand the most? What obstacles did it encounter? What was the effect of geography on early Russian history?

For the Thoughtful

1. To what extent and in what ways did the three eastern empires affect western Europe?
2. How does the early history of Russia contribute to a better understanding of twentieth-century Russia and the Cold War?
3. Why were the Mongols and Turks generally successful against their Christian opponents? Why did Mongol power and influence finally fade?

16

the decline of medieval civilization

As the fourteenth century began, the medieval way of life entered a period of rapid decline. The institutions that had dominated the Middle Ages—the Catholic Church, the feudal system, and the French and English monarchies—lost much of their power and influence. Unable to adjust to changing conditions, churchmen, nobles, and kings fought, without success, to preserve the old order of things. But their efforts only helped to destroy that which they were trying hard to preserve. Gradually, toward the end of the fifteenth century, the monarchies regained their strength, new ideas and institutions began to emerge, and the modern era began; but Europe had first to undergo a century and a half of turmoil as the Middle Ages violently died.

THE DECLINE OF PAPAL POWER

When Pope Boniface VIII was unable to enforce his claims against Philip IV of France (see pages 129-130, 165-166), the papacy could no longer hope to become dominant in European political life. In 1305 Philip forced the papacy to move to Avignon (see pages 130, 166), and there it remained, in "Babylonian Captivity," for most of the fourteenth century.

THE BABYLONIAN CAPTIVITY OF THE PAPACY

The apparent subservience of the popes to the kings of France earned the papacy the distrust of every country that opposed the growing power of France. The English Parliament forbade the popes to appoint foreigners to church offices in England, forbade appeals from English to papal courts, and stated that papal decrees would not be effective in England unless approved by Parliament. In 1366 it refused to continue the annual payments to the pope promised by King John a century and a half earlier. The Germans in the Holy Roman Empire openly opposed any increase there of the power of the popes and forbade them to interfere in the election of the emperors, whom the popes had traditionally crowned. The Golden Bull of 1356, which established the method of the emperors' election (see page 155), made no mention of any papal rights or claims.

The Italians, particularly distressed by the loss of the papacy, attempted to bring it back. In 1347 one Cola di Rienzi seized Rome and demanded that the pope return, but Rienzi was excommunicated and driven away. More effective was the saintly Catherine of Siena, who wrote the pope innumerable eloquent, earnest letters imploring him to return to Rome and lead a moral reform of Europe. Finally Pope Gregory XI returned to Rome in 1377, and the next year he died there. A newly elected pope agreed to remain in Rome, and the Babylonian Captivity was finally ended.

THE GREAT SCHISM

The Babylonian Captivity was followed by an even greater disaster, the "Great Schism." The Italian successor to Gregory XI had been elected by French cardinals under pressure from a Roman mob. As soon as the cardinals could slip away from Rome, they met again and, declaring their earlier election invalid, selected another Frenchman. The Italian refused to resign, and there were then two popes. Each of them attempted to depose the other, appointed his own bishops and cardinals, and claimed that he alone was rightful head of the church. In general, the friends of France rallied around the Frenchman and his successors; the enemies of France supported the Italian. For nearly forty years the "Great Schism" continued, to the profit of the politicians and the injury of the church.

As a result thoughtful men began to question the whole theory of papal power. Marsilius of Padua (1290?-?1343), in a book called *Defender of the Peace*, theorized that all rulers derive their authority from the people, whom they are duty bound to serve. In the political state the princes therefore should be guided by their subjects' wishes as expressed in parliaments. Similarly the popes should be guided by church councils. As the princes have no right to interfere in religious matters, so the popes have no right to interfere in politics. Another writer, William of Ockham (1300?-?1349), wrote eloquently in support of the separation of church and state and the supremacy of a general church council over the pope.

As it happened, the Great Schism was finally ended by a series of general councils of the church, which drew representatives from all Catholic Christendom. The first attempt to end the Great Schism was made by the Council of Pisa, which in 1409 chose a new pope to replace the other two; but the other popes refused to resign, and then there were three. Soon thereafter the Holy Roman emperor persuaded one of the three popes to call another council, which met at Constance in southern Germany from 1415 to 1417. The Council of Constance forced the Pisan pope to resign, accepted the voluntary resignation of the Roman pope, and deposed the French pope. In 1417 it elected a new pope, and the Great Schism was ended.

THE CONCILIAR MOVEMENT

Since a council had been able to depose and elect popes, some people now came to believe that councils had rightful authority over the popes. The Council of Basel (1431-1449) attempted to limit the pope's power and even tried to depose him and elect another in his place. Many leaders supported this "conciliar movement" and its doctrine that the councils were supreme over the popes. But the conciliar movement was too revolutionary. Later popes condemned it, and eventually all Catholic Christians repudiated the supremacy of the councils.

But the popes never regained all their former powers. At the time of the Council of Basel, bishops and kings in both France and the Holy Roman Empire adopted "pragmatic sanctions" (decrees) that restricted the right of the popes to tax and to hear appeals from local church courts. Kings assumed many of the governing functions that had once belonged to the church. There were great popes during the later fifteenth century, but they were obliged to abide by "concordats" (treaties between the papacy and a government) that conceded to monarchs, notably the kings of France and Spain, the right to nominate bishops and abbots and to restrict the issuance of papal decrees within their countries.

John Huss being led to the stake to be burned. On his head is a paper hat with a caricature of the devil, identifying Huss as a heretic. The execution of Huss did not put an end to the movement that he had led. After his death, Bohemian reformers broke with the Catholic Church and established the Unity of Brethren, more commonly called the Moravian Church. This was really the first Protestant church; but its impact was little felt outside Bohemia until the beginning of the more widespread Protestant Reformation of the sixteenth century (Chapter 21), of which it was a forerunner.

THE RISE OF HERESY

Another problem facing the church in the fourteenth and fifteenth centuries was the rise of heresy (beliefs opposed to those of the church).

Many of the heretics were mystics. Mysticism—the idea that each person can have a direct and personal relationship with God—was not by itself a heresy. Indeed, it had been taught by such great medieval churchmen as Bernard of Clairvaux. (See page 135.) But later mystics went further, preaching that individuals did not need the church to serve as an intermediary. The largest of the German mystical sects was the "Brethren of the Free Spirit," who believed that the world was God in physical form (a doctrine called "pantheism") and that since all living beings revert to God when they die, there can be no hell or purgatory. The Brethren often wandered from place to place like mendicant friars, begging what they needed and seeking converts to their beliefs. Others sought to promote mystical ideas within the framework of the Catholic Church. Most notable were the German Dominicans Johannes Eckhart (1260?-?1327; usually called Meister ["Master"] Eckhart) and his disciple Johannes Tauler (1300?-1361), who accepted the mystical doctrine of the unity of man and God, but insisted that only the church and its sacraments could guide man to God.

In the late fourteenth century two heretical leaders, John Wycliffe (1320?-1384) in England and John Huss (1369?-1415) in Bohemia founded heretical movements that were to have a significant influence in later centuries. Wycliffe, a priest and teacher at Oxford, believed in "predestination," that is, that God has determined everything that will ever happen and that man is therefore only an agent who carries out God's will. In the mystical tradition, he taught that the best way to attain knowledge of God was directly from His word, that is, the Bible, which he translated into English so that more people could read it. Wycliffe concluded that the clergy were mere conveniences and that the pope had no temporal authority. Many Englishmen welcomed his doctrines, and possibly one fourth of them became "Lollards," as his followers were called. Huss adopted most of Wycliffe's theories and gained a number of followers in Bohemia. He was seized and burned at the stake as a heretic by the churchmen of the Council of Constance, but his followers in Bohemia kept his ideas alive.

⚜ THE DECLINE OF THE FEUDAL SYSTEM

At the same time that the power of the church was being attacked from many sides, a number of developments gradually undermined the feudal system.

One such development was the slow spread throughout Europe of the ideas of Roman law (see page 27), which had always been accepted in southern Europe and eventually became the basis of the legal systems of most European countries. Roman law held that the power of the king was unlimited, and so the feudal idea that nobles had rights that kings could not violate gradually withered away. At the same time, many Europeans began to feel loyalty to their countries that rivaled their loyalty to their feudal lords and to the church. Intelligent kings sensed this shift in loyalty and strove to become the symbols of their countries in the minds of their people.

The military basis of feudalism was destroyed by a revolution in the methods of warfare, which made the medieval knights out of date. Returning crusaders brought home the crossbow, and English peasants mastered the art of shooting the longbow; both these long-range weapons shot arrows that could pierce a knight's chain mail or kill his horse. Knights began wearing heavier plate armor, but it was so clumsy and heavy that they were less effective in battle than they had been and often were quite helpless if they were knocked off their horses. Another import from the east, gunpowder, made it possible to build cannon that could knock down stone walls, and so medieval castles also became out of date. Now that the kings' mercenaries (hired soldiers) could fight the nobles on more even terms, feudalism's days were numbered.

Growing commerce also weakened men's loyalty to feudal institutions. Commercial towns won charters from the kings and strongly supported any central government that could protect their trade from the raids of robber barons. The growing middle class of merchants and tradesmen, which had no place in feudalism, resented the haughty feudal aristocrats and supported the monarchs against them. Most of the lawyers and government officials who were replacing churchmen as the trusted servants of the monarchs were from the towns. Townsmen also tended to support kings in their struggles with bishops and popes, because the church, which taught that lending of money for interest was a sin and which looked with distaste on trade, did not strike merchants as much of an ally.

In the middle of the fourteenth century (1348-1349) a plague called the "Black Death" swept across Europe, killing between 20 and 40 per cent of its population. Some peasants felt that the Black Death was a judgment of God and went around beating each other with sticks as punishment for their sins. But others took advantage of the labor shortage it created to demand special privileges and higher wages from their feudal lords.

All of these developments weakened the feudal nobility. But, unaware that their cause was doomed, they fought for two centuries to retain their power. From 1300 almost to 1500 they struggled so violently that for a time Europe seemed on the brink of a new dark age of anarchy and chaos. Six of the nine kings who ruled England between 1307 and 1485 were murdered or deposed. France was almost conquered by foreigners and almost divided once again into little feudal states. Time and again ambitious feudal lords, seeking personal power and prestige, would almost overthrow the monarchy; but they always fell to fighting among themselves, and so failed to complete the destruction of the monarchies. But not until the end of the fifteenth century were the kings strong enough to put down the feudal nobility altogether. When they finally succeeded, feudalism's day was over.

⚜ THE HUNDRED YEARS WAR

During much of the fourteenth and fifteenth centuries, the histories of England and France were inseparably linked by what has come to be called the "Hundred Years War." The war hastened the downfall of feudalism and the decline of the church's influence in both countries. It also temporarily weakened the monarchy in each country. But the monarchies later recovered, in part because the war helped each country to feel, more than ever before, a sense of national unity.

THE BACKGROUND TO THE WAR

In the 1320's a new generation of monarchs appeared in the persons of Edward III (king 1327-1377) of England and Philip VI (king 1328-1350) of France. Both enjoyed war, and both were rather stupid. These two men led their countries into the war that dragged on, with intermissions, for 116 years, from 1337 to 1453.

The Hundred Years War began in Flanders, where English and French interests came into conflict. The prosperous townsmen of Flanders (see page 109) were weavers who depended on England both for raw wool and as a market for their finished cloth. The count of Flanders was a vassal of the king of France, on whose support he depended in order to stay in power. The weavers, resenting attempts of their counts to limit their trade with England, on several occasions rose up (with English aid) against the count and his French ally. In one such uprising in the 1330's a merchant named Jacob van Artevelde succeeded in ousting the count and establishing his own government. Artevelde promptly made an alliance with the English.

Relations between the French and English were also aggravated by English possession of Aquitaine in southern France and by English ambitions to regain Normandy, which King John had lost more than a century earlier. (See pages 162, 175.)

When the war started, the announced cause was a dispute between Edward III and Philip VI over the French throne. Edward, a grandson of Philip the Fair, claimed that he was the rightful king of France. In 1337, therefore, he dispatched troops to aid van Artevelde and to assert his claim to the French throne. Once his soldiers set foot in France, the conflict that lasted more than a century had begun.

THE COURSE OF THE WAR

The Hundred Years War fell into four distinct periods. In the first (1337-1360) Edward III and his brilliant warrior son Edward the "Black Prince" had things much their own way. After defeating the French fleet at the naval battle of Sluys in 1340, they invaded France and won a great victory at Crécy in 1346. They used artillery for the first time in a successful siege of Calais the following year. After an interruption caused by the Black Death, the Black Prince devastated southern France and in the battle of Poitiers (1356) captured the king of France and many of France's most important knights. In 1360 the French recognized Edward III as the outright ruler of Aquitaine, and Edward did not press his claim to the French throne.

In the second phase of the war (1369-1395) the French recovered most of what they had lost. They won few major battles, but let the English march around the countryside while they chipped away at their flanks and cut off their supplies. This wore down the English, who were also weakened by troubles at home, so that they withdrew to a series of coastal fortresses and left the French in control of the interior of the country.

As the fourteenth century began, both England and France were on the verge of anarchy. Charles VI of France (king 1380-1422) suffered from periods of insanity, and his followers bickered furiously among themselves. In England the Lollards opposed the authority of the church (above, page 215), the Scots threatened to invade, and the Welsh rose in rebellion. Then a great military leader, Henry V (king 1413-1422), ascended the English throne and led his armies to new victories in the third phase of the war (1415-1420). His archers defeated the French chivalry at Agincourt in 1415; in the next four years he conquered Normandy and marched to the gates of Paris. In 1420 Charles VI sued for peace. He recognized Henry as ruler of the French lands that the English had conquered; gave his daughter to Henry as his wife; and, most important, made Henry heir to the throne of France, disinheriting his weakling son, the Dauphin (eldest son) Charles. Henry seemed about to unite England and France into a single monarchy. But two years later both he and Charles VI died, and a nine-month-old baby, Henry VI of England, inherited their thrones.

Both England and France were now in confusion. The Dauphin Charles, although he claimed to be king of France, did not fight vigorously for his throne and failed to rally the French to his cause. In England, the nobles saw an opportunity to defy the monarchy, and the government became so weak that robber bands freely roamed the countryside. Even so, English armies campaigned successfully in France until, in 1429, only the southern part of France acknowledged Charles as king. Total victory for the English seemed likely.

The final phase of the war (1429-1453) began with a miracle. In the village of Domremy in northeastern France, a French peasant girl named Joan of Arc heard mysterious "voices" directing her to lead an army to free

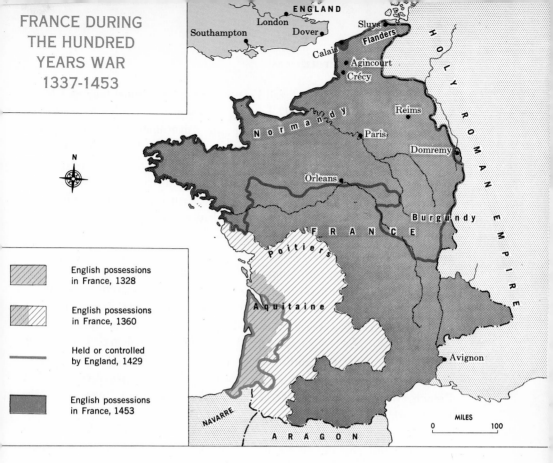

ENGLAND
London
Southampton   Dover
Sluys
Flanders
Calais
Agincourt
Crécy

Reims
N o r m a n d y
Paris
Domremy

Orleans
B u r g u n d y

F R A N C E
P o i t i e r s

A q u i t a i n e

Avignon

NAVARRE
A R A G O N

H O L Y   R O M A N   E M P I R E

N

English possessions
in France, 1328

English possessions
in France, 1360

Held or controlled
by England, 1429

English possessions
in France, 1453

MILES
0   100

France from the English. Although she had never learned to read and
had known nothing but village life, she was able to convince the Dauphin
Charles and his officers of her divine mission. In 1429, riding at the head of
an army of four or five thousand soldiers, she set out to save the city of
Orleans, which was under English attack. The young girl, wearing armor
and carrying a sword said to have been used by Charles Martel at the battle
of Tours (see page 62), convinced the soldiers that she was a crusader
and a saint.

Joan was as remarkable in performance as in promise. Her troops defeated
an English army; raised the siege of Orleans; drove the English from north-
central France; and regained Reims, the traditional coronation place of the
French monarchs. Then she returned to get Charles and stood beside him
in Reims cathedral while he was solemnly crowned King Charles VII of
France. It was her supreme achievement. In 1430 she fell into the hands of
the English. The ungrateful Charles made no attempt to rescue her, and
in 1431 the English had her burned as a witch.

Joan's achievement crystallized France's growing national feeling. Charles VII, called the "Well-Served" because of his excellent advisers, reformed the army and the administration of the government finances, crushed the opposition of rebellious French nobles, and in 1450-1451 finally drove the English from almost all of France. The disheartened and disorganized English saw they had no hope of regaining their French possessions, and in 1453 they finally went home, leaving only a small garrison to defend the city of Calais. The Hundred Years War had ended.

THE RESULTS OF THE WAR

While the kings were off fighting their battles, their restless nobles and peasants fought to end the restrictions imposed by monarchs and churchmen. The English Parliament used the war as an excuse to require kings to get Parliamentary permission to lay new taxes and to appoint royal officials. The French Estates-General won similar privileges. The English Parliament limited the authority of the pope to appoint foreigners to church positions in England, and it restricted appeals to papal courts. The French established a national "Gallican" church of their own within the framework of Catholicism.

The Black Death (above, page 216) and the war combined to create a labor shortage, and peasants agitated for higher pay and greater freedom. In 1358 a peasant revolt called the *Jacquerie* almost overthrew the French government before the nobles could put it down. In 1381 English peasants under the leadership of Wat Tyler marched on London and were pacified only when the king rode out to meet them and promised that he would improve their lot. (He didn't keep his promise.)

In both countries the nobles also were rebellious and nearly succeeded in regaining the liberties they had had in the ninth and tenth centuries. They assassinated rivals and seized property of weaker neighbors. In many parts of both countries, law and order almost broke down completely, and peaceful people were in constant danger of losing their property to brigands. The most spectacular examples of rebellious nobles were the dukes of Burgundy, who built a state that stretched from Flanders to the Alps, allied themselves first with one side and then with the other in the Hundred Years War, and fought to take over the throne of France. But with the end of the Hundred Years War the French kings were able to turn more of their resources against Burgundy, and the Burgundian power was soon destroyed.

Once the Hundred Years War was over, it became clear that its effect had been to strengthen the kings at the expense of the nobles and the church. In 1453 the government of Charles VII was supported by a standing army, an effectively organized civil service, and the loyalty of the middle class in the towns. War with the English and the example of Joan of Arc made the French more loyal to their country than ever before. The English still had to undergo one last violent feudal conflict, but in 1485 a new dynasty, the Tudors, would find their people eager to unite behind a strong monarchy.

In both countries the right of the popes to appoint bishops and abbots and to hear appeals from local courts had been successfully challenged. The popes had returned to Rome, but they could no longer command the power and prestige of earlier popes.

Tired of quarreling nobles and churchmen, many Europeans toward the end of the fifteenth century were willing and eager to look to the monarchs of the emerging national states and to secular artists and thinkers for leadership. When that happened, the Middle Ages had ended.

People, Places, and Terms

Cola di Rienzi	Charles VII	Council of Pisa
Catherine of Siena	Wat Tyler	Council of Constance
Gregory XI		conciliar movement
Marsilius of Padua	Flanders	Council of Basel
William of Ockham	Sluys	pragmatic sanction
Meister Eckhart	Crécy	concordat
Johannes Tauler	Calais	mysticism
John Wycliffe	Poitiers	Brethren of the
John Huss	Agincourt	Free Spirit
Edward III	Domremy	predestination
Philip VI	Orleans	crossbow
Jacob van Artevelde	Reims	longbow
Edward the Black	Burgundy	gunpowder
Prince		Black Death
Charles VI	Babylonian Captivity	Hundred Years War
Henry V	Great Schism	Gallican
Joan of Arc	*Defender of the Peace*	*Jacquerie*

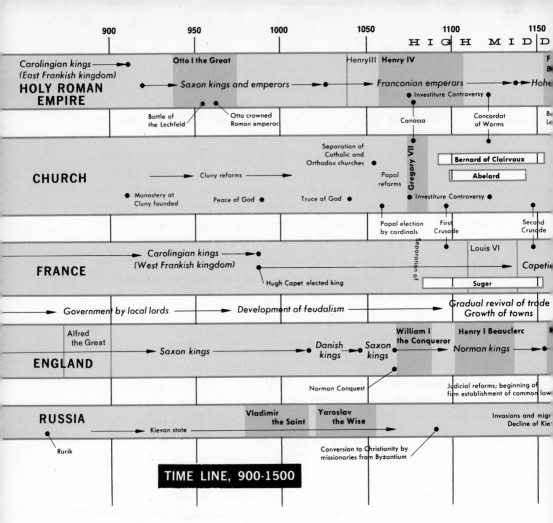

TIME LINE, 900-1500

Getting Organized

1. What was the Babylonian Captivity? How did it hurt the influence of the church? What was the Great Schism? What was its effect? How was the Great Schism ended?

2. What was the conciliar movement? What was its effect? Who were the most important of the men and women who were trying to change the church in the fourteenth and fifteenth centuries? What did each believe?

3. How did each of the following factors weaken the power of the nobles: Roman law, the crusades, national loyalty, economic changes, the Black Death, and military changes? How was the church affected by these developments?

4. What brought on the Hundred Years War?

5. Trace the four major phases of the Hundred Years War. What was the turning point of the final phase of the war?

222

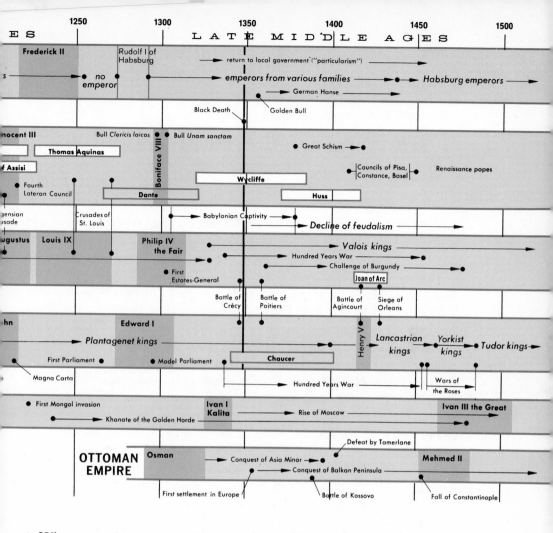

The timeline chart shows:

Top axis: 1250 | 1300 | 1350 | 1400 | 1450 | 1500

ES — LATE MIDDLE AGES

Frederick II — Rudolf I of Habsburg — no emperor — return to local government ("particularism") — emperors from various families — Habsburg emperors

German Hanse

Black Death — Golden Bull

nocent III — Bull *Clericis laicos* — Bull *Unam sanctam* — Boniface VIII — Great Schism

f Assisi — Councils of Pisa, Constance, Basel — Renaissance popes — Wycliffe

Thomas Aquinas

Fourth Lateran Council — Dante — Huss

gensian usade — Crusades of St. Louis — Babylonian Captivity — Decline of feudalism

ugustus — Louis IX — Philip IV the Fair — Valois kings

Hundred Years War — Challenge of Burgundy — Joan of Arc

First Estates-General — Battle of Crécy — Battle of Poitiers — Battle of Agincourt — Siege of Orleans

hn — Edward I — Plantagenet kings — Henry V — Lancastrian kings — Yorkist kings — Tudor kings

First Parliament — Model Parliament — Chaucer

Magna Carta — Hundred Years War — Wars of the Roses

First Mongol invasion — Ivan I Kalita — Rise of Moscow — Ivan III the Great

Khanate of the Golden Horde

OTTOMAN EMPIRE — Osman — Defeat by Tamerlane — Conquest of Asia Minor — Mehmed II

Conquest of Balkan Peninsula

First settlement in Europe — Battle of Kossovo — Fall of Constantinople

6. What were the results of the war, both in France and in England, on the power of the king? Of the nobles? Of the peasants? Of the church?

Understanding the Big Picture

1. Why did the power of the church decline in the later Middle Ages? Give as many examples of this decline as possible.
2. Why did the power of the nobles decline in the later Middle Ages? How did they react to their decline in power?

For the Thoughtful

1. Contrast the power of the nobles in the fourteenth and fifteenth centuries to the power that they held in the ninth and tenth centuries. Why was their power different in the two eras?
2. Contrast the influence of the church in the fourteenth and fifteenth centuries to its influence under Innocent III. Why had it declined?

223

Summing up the high middle ages

In the eleventh century the political, economic, and religious institutions of the Middle Ages—feudalism, chivalry, the manor, the guilds, the town, and the medieval church—took shape and grew and developed vigorously.

The late twelfth century was the heyday of the Middle Ages, when such feudal monarchs as Barbarossa in the Holy Roman Empire, Philip Augustus in France, and Henry II in England dominated their countries, and when Innocent III brought the church to its peak of power.

The church and the feudal monarchies were still strong in the thirteenth century, but there were already signs of change as the crusades became corrupted, the Holy Roman Empire came apart, and kings, nobles, and churchmen struggled for power everywhere. Even so, this was the century of Thomas Aquinas and the Gothic cathedrals, of Saint Louis in France and of Edward I, the English Justinian.

The decay of the Middle Ages was evident in the fourteenth and fifteenth centuries. The popes were forced to live in Babylonian Captivity, the Hundred Years War weakened both France and England, and the Holy Roman Empire became little more than a name.

By the end of the fifteenth century, the Middle Ages were over. But they left behind them a marvelous heritage—of chivalry, and religious faith, and Gothic art. Out of feudal traditions grew the system of English common law and of representation in Parliaments; the medieval church created a great philosophy and the high hope that all men could live together in a world dominated by moral principle and faith in God; and Gothic cathedrals still exist to remind us of the dedication and skill and talent of the thousands of nameless men of the Middle Ages who built these testaments to their faith and their civilization.

Some Questions to Answer

1. Describe society in the Middle Ages. How did men make a living? How equal were men in the Middle Ages? Could all men live together peacefully and constructively? What tensions were there between the classes?

2. What forces and influences affected the thoughts of most medieval men? What effect did the church have on man's everyday behavior and thought? What effect did chivalry have? What did medieval man think of himself and of his place on earth?

3. Compare and contrast the development of the monarchies in the Holy Roman Empire, France, and England. How were developments in each country affected by the nobles? By the development of feudalism? By relations with the church? By geography? By the personalities of the monarchs? By ties with the old Roman Empire?

4. Describe feudalism. How and why was it effective? How did it meet the needs of the day? Why did it finally decline? What factors influenced this eventual decline?

5. Describe the medieval church at its height. How influential was it? Why did its influence decline? What factors influenced this decline?

6. It has been said that the crusades and the Hundred Years War were the dying gasps of the Middle Ages. Do you agree? Why, or why not?

7. Discuss the legacy of the Middle Ages to the modern world, mentioning as many aspects of the modern world as you can think of that first appeared or were influenced by the Middle Ages.

Some Books to Read

GENERAL ACCOUNTS

DAWSON, CHRISTOPHER. *The Making of Europe*. New York: Sheed & Ward, 1946; Cleveland: World (paper). An interesting and challenging survey.

HUIZINGA, JOHAN. *The Waning of the Middle Ages*. New York: St. Martin's; New York: Doubleday, 1954 (paper). Stresses developments in France and the Netherlands; a must for anyone interested in the Middle Ages.

PAINTER, SIDNEY. *A History of the Middle Ages*. New York: Knopf, 1953. An excellent survey by an expert on the period.

PIRENNE, HENRI. *A History of Europe*. 2 vols. New York: Doubleday, 1958 (paper). By a distinguished Belgian historian; emphasizes historical interpretation.

BOOKS ON SPECIFIC SUBJECTS

ADAMS, HENRY. *Mont-Saint-Michel and Chartres*. New York: Doubleday, 1959 (paper). A fascinating analysis of medieval ways of thought as demonstrated in medieval architecture and literature.

BALDWIN, MARSHALL W. *The Medieval Church*. Ithaca, N.Y.: Cornell University Press, 1953 (paper). A good introduction for the beginning student.

BARRACLOUGH, GEOFFREY. *The Origins of Modern Germany*. New York: Macmillan, 1946; New York: Putnam, 1963 (paper). A fine account of medieval Germany.

BENNETT, HENRY S. *Six Medieval Men and Women*. New York: Cambridge University Press. Informative sketches of typical medieval people.

CAM, HELEN M. *England Before Elizabeth*. New York: Humanities Press, 1950. An excellent, lively introduction.

COULTON, GEORGE G. *The Medieval Scene*. New York: Cambridge University Press, 1959 (paper). A good description of the way people lived.

FAWTIER, ROBERT. *The Capetian Kings of France*. Trans. by LIONEL BUTLER and R. H. ADAMS. New York: St. Martin's, 1960 (hard covers and paper). A fine discussion of the French monarchy from 987 to 1328.

KELLY, AMY. *Eleanor of Aquitaine and the Four Kings*. Cambridge, Mass.: Harvard University Press, 1950; New York: Knopf, 1957 (paper). A fascinating woman, Eleanor was wife of two kings and mother of two others.

McEVEDY, COLIN. *The Penguin Atlas of Medieval History*. Baltimore: Penguin (paper). Compact but quite complete.

PAINTER, SIDNEY. *French Chivalry: Chivalric Ideas and Practices in Medieval France*. Baltimore: Johns Hopkins University Press, 1940; Ithaca, N. Y.: Cornell University Press, 1957 (paper). A good discussion of medieval ideas and behavior.

PAINTER, SIDNEY. *Medieval Society*. Ithaca, N. Y.: Cornell University Press, 1951 (paper). Excellent introduction to medieval ways of life.

PAINTER, SIDNEY. *The Rise of the Feudal Monarchies*. Ithaca, N. Y.: Cornell University Press, 1951 (paper). A useful survey of the Holy Roman Empire, France, and England.

POWER, EILEEN. *Medieval People*. Rev. ed. New York: Barnes & Noble (hard covers and paper). Fascinating biographies of typical medieval people.

STEPHENSON, CARL. *Medieval Feudalism*. Ithaca, N. Y.: Cornell University Press, 1956 (paper). A good short handbook.

SOURCE MATERIALS

CHAUCER, GEOFFREY. *The Canterbury Tales*. Trans. into modern English by NEVILL COGHILL. Baltimore: Penguin (paper). A medieval masterpiece that provides remarkable insights into late medieval society.

DOWNS, NORTON. *Basic Documents in Medieval History*. Princeton, N. J.: Van Nostrand, 1954 (paper). A valuable collection.

FROISSART, JEAN. *The Chronicles of England, France, and Spain*. New York: Dutton, 1961 (paper). Written about 1400 and still quite readable.

HANSCOM, JAMES H., HELLERMAN, LEON, and POSNER, RONALD. *Voices of the Past: Readings in Medieval and Early Modern History*. New York: Macmillan, 1966 (paper). A collection of the writings of the times.

JOINVILLE, JEAN DE, and VILLEHARDOUIN, GEOFFREY DE. *Memoirs of the Crusades*. New York: Dutton (paper). Observations by two crusaders.

ROSS, JAMES BRUCE, and McLAUGHLIN, MARY MARTIN, eds. *The Portable Medieval Reader*. New York: Viking, 1946 (paper). A useful collection of all types of medieval literature.

part 3

an Era of transition

The transition from the medieval to the modern world took place during the fifteenth, sixteenth and seventeenth centuries. This was a time of rapid and violent change as the institutions of the Middle Ages first were challenged and then were either modified or replaced altogether.

In the fifteenth century the feudal monarchies of the Middle Ages began to grow into states whose people soon developed strong national loyalties. Economic developments modified the manorial system and contributed to a rapid growth in the size and influence of towns and cities, and to the rise of a middle class of merchants and manufacturers.

At the same time, men were becoming more interested in the world around them. This important change in men's attitudes, called the "Renaissance," was encouraged by a revival of interest in the art and philosophy of ancient Greece and Rome. The Renaissance began in Italy and later spread to northern Europe.

When the Renaissance was in full bloom, the "Protestant Reformation" began in northern Europe. This religious revolution brought about the rise of Protestant faiths, which challenged the supremacy of the Catholic Church in Europe. Later there was a parallel "Catholic Reformation" as the Catholic Church clarified its doctrine and strengthened its organization. The two "Reformations" clashed head on in a series of bloody wars that left Europe divided into Catholic and Protestant regions.

In the fifteenth century the first Portuguese and Spanish explorers opened new trade routes to the Far East and discovered a "New World" in America. They were followed by merchants and colonists who carried European ideas to the four corners of the world—and returned with strange new products and ideas from distant places. European history thus became an integral part of the history of the world.

By 1700 European life had been transformed, and the modern age had begun.

17

Strengthening the National Monarchies

In the last half of the fifteenth century, after the influence of the church and of feudalism had waned, the rulers of the states along the Atlantic coast of Europe—England, France, Portugal, and Spain—hastened to strengthen their personal control over their governments. Led by able kings who made the most of their growing opportunities, these countries took long steps in the direction of autocracy (government by an unlimited ruler) and nationalism (a sense of particular loyalty to the nation over and above other loyalties). In general, three developments marked the period. First there was a violent period of feudal unrest. This in turn strengthened the alliance between the monarch and the middle-class townsmen. And finally, this alliance in turn made possible the formation of stable institutions of government led by the king and his middle-class officials.

THE NATIONAL MONARCHY IN ENGLAND

In England the weakness of the royal government, the loss of the Hundred Years War (see page 220), and economic distress led to thirty years of civil war. The country was divided between two political factions, which fought bitterly for control of the monarchy. Each faction was led by descendants of younger sons of Edward III. (See page 217.) Henry VI (king 1422-1461; 1470-1471) was a great-grandson of a duke of Lancaster, and therefore his followers were called "Lancastrians." His opponent was Richard, duke of York; his followers were called "Yorkists." The symbol of the Lancastrians was a red rose; that of the Yorkists was a white rose. Their on-again, off-again conflicts were therefore called the "Wars of the Roses."

THE WARS OF THE ROSES

Henry VI was an ineffective king who suffered frequent periods of insanity. In 1455 Richard, duke of York, openly revolted against Henry and his strong-willed queen. Richard was killed in 1460; but the next year his nineteen-year-old son Edward was able to defeat the queen and proclaim himself king. The Lancastrians continued the struggle for the throne, and even won it back briefly. But Edward IV (king 1461-1470; 1471-1483) was an able soldier and a dynamic leader who was finally able, in 1471, to defeat the Lancastrian army at the battle of Tewkesbury and murder the hapless Henry VI. Edward managed to avoid trouble with Parliament by living within his royal income (which he increased by "benevolences"—gifts forced from his subjects). He gave England a decade of relative peace before he died at the age of forty-one, a victim of too much good living.

Edward was succeeded by his brother, Richard III (king 1483-1485). Richard proved fatal to the Yorkist cause. He was a capable man and a fine soldier, but he lost the support of the people by murdering his enemies and by trying to marry his niece, the daughter of Edward IV. He is also believed by many to have murdered Edward's two young sons in order to assure himself the throne (but these murders have never been proved, and are still a matter of debate among historians). In 1485 a new Lancastrian claimant to the throne, a Welshman named Henry Tudor, raised anew the standard of the red rose, killed Richard and defeated his troops at the battle of Bosworth, and mounted the throne as Henry VII.

The Wars of the Roses were over. The Tudor dynasty, the most illustrious in English history, began to restore peace and order to England.

THE REIGN OF HENRY VII

Henry VII (king 1485-1509) promptly began to heal the wounds left by the Wars of the Roses by marrying Elizabeth of York, so that future kings of England would have the blood of both factions in their veins. England was ready to receive him warmly. Constant warfare had thoroughly discredited the nobles of both parties. The new monarch was a master of public relations, his manner contrasting strongly with the unpleasant ways of Richard III. Henry made the interests of England his own, and he reigned with the support of the great majority of Englishmen.

Henry limited the power of the barons. He had Parliament pass acts forbidding private armies and enabling him to punish his enemies for treason. He created a "Court of Star Chamber" (so named because stars were painted on the courtroom ceiling) made up of judges he knew would enforce his new laws strictly. They imposed such heavy fines that Henry did not need to levy heavy taxes on his people (and ever since, the term "Star Chamber proceedings" has been used to describe harsh and unfair methods of trial). The Yorkists continued to back rival claimants for Henry's throne. Henry executed one of these rivals; another was put to work in the royal kitchen.

Henry won the loyalty of the merchants by signing a commercial treaty that guaranteed trade with Flanders. He strengthened his foreign relations by arranging marriages of a daughter to the king of Scotland and of a son to Catherine of Aragon, daughter of the king of Spain. By spending as little money as possible, he tightened his control of the English government, because he did not have to call Parliament into session very often to ask for money. This policy pleased the middle classes, who did not like to pay taxes. Henry received what money he needed from his estates, from the fines imposed by the Court of Star Chamber, or by benevolences that those he did not like were forced to pay.

Henry did not set up a large government organization. To control the countryside, he created new lords to replace those who had been killed or exiled. More important, he encouraged the growth of the system of "justices of the peace." These men were country gentlemen who devoted themselves to the welfare of their neighborhoods. They administered justice and carried on such few functions of local government as were necessary. They were not paid, but rather served just for the honor of the office. For three centuries the local government of England was in the hands of such unique officials. Henry had fewer checks on his powers than did any of the monarchs who had preceded him. During the last twenty years of his reign, Parliament met only once. What few major government officials there were owed their position to him and did his bidding. Hardly any rebellious barons challenged his authority. Henry was, as a contemporary said, "a wonder for wise men."

When Henry VII died in 1509, his country was at peace, its merchants were prospering, its influence was growing, and its people were willing to support the monarchy almost without question. The royal treasury was the richest in Europe, Parliament was a rubber stamp, and the barons had been permanently weakened. Only the church stood as a possible opponent to the growth of autocracy, and Henry's son would soon take care of that. (Chapter 21.) The Tudor dynasty that Henry had founded ruled to the end of the sixteenth century, presiding over one of England's greatest periods of intellectual and cultural achievement. (Chapter 27.)

⚜ FRANCE: THE SUPREMACY OF LOUIS XI

The Valois dynasty ruled France during the fourteenth and fifteenth centuries. Although during this time France was weakened by the disasters of the Hundred Years War and by fighting among the provincial rulers, the central government continued to rest on the foundation laid by Philip IV. (See page 165.) The later Valois kings built on this foundation, so that by the end of the reign of Louis XI, the greatest of the Valois monarchs, autocracy was firmly established in France.

King Louis XI of France: portrait by Jean Fouquet (1416?-1480). Louis's personality was as unattractive as his appearance, and many of the French people came to hate him for his harsh and grasping ways. Yet he was an extremely intelligent man, masterful at achieving his goals, and he left his country stable, militarily strong, and prosperous.

THE VALOIS GOVERNMENT

From Philip IV the Valois kings inherited the *chambre des comptes,* which controlled the royal finances, and the powerful regional courts called *parlements.* The French bureaucracy was much larger than the English; the *Parlement* of Paris alone had 167 members (compared to only 12 royal judges in all England); and the *baillis* and seneschals, who represented the king in the provinces (see page 163), were a numerous and unusually loyal group of royal officials. There were provincial assemblies called "estates," which could be called upon for financial assistance. The king personally controlled the income from several taxes, most notably the *gabelle,* a tax on salt, and the *taille,* a property tax.

Certain policies of Charles V (king 1364-1380) and Charles VII (king 1422-1461) helped to increase the royal authority by assuring the kings an effective and well-financed government. The kings established a standing army of professional soldiers, commanded by trained and loyal captains; an organized system of government agencies, headed by middle-class officials; and an improved system of controlling the royal finances, initiated by the merchant prince Jacques Coeur. (Chapter 18.) At the end of the Hundred Years War, however, kings still had to contend with a number of powerful lords and with a people that had less of a sense of nationality than had the English. It remained for one of the least attractive figures in French history, the deformed and unpleasant Louis XI, to enforce the will of the central government over his rebellious nobles.

THE REIGN OF LOUIS XI

As a young man Louis XI (king 1461-1483) spent much of his time organizing a series of rebellions against his father, Charles VII. After his father's death he returned from exile to ascend the throne. No man could have looked less like a king. His body was ungainly and his face ugly, and he dressed like a common citizen. He preferred taverns to palaces and the company of retired criminals to that of nobles. Once, when he saw some people smiling at him as he hurried to Paris, he imposed a heavy fine on their entire town. But despite his notable lack of charm, Louis XI was one of the most effective monarchs in French history.

In his struggle against the great nobles who were his most dangerous opponents, Louis sought the support of churchmen and merchants. Although he continued to limit papal authority in France, he pleased the churchmen by revoking the document that had established a national "Gallican" church.

He taxed the merchants heavily, but he won the support of many by appointing them to high office. Priests and burghers helped Louis subdue all but one of France's semi-independent duchies, even though a "League of Public Weal" was organized against him. His greatest achievement was to destroy forever the threat of Burgundy to the French monarchy. (See page 221.)

He subdued other neighboring principalities by force, bribery, or promises. Finally by arranging the marriage of his son to the heiress of Brittany, the way was paved for the absorption of the last important French duchy into the national monarchy.

Like Henry VII of England, Louis left his country with an increased sense of national unity and with a strong and well-organized central government. The remaining noble houses of importance were allied by marriage to the royal family. Even though Louis was succeeded by two weak kings from whom the dukes attempted to regain their independence, the central government had become so strong that it survived their attacks.

♠ THE RISE AND DECLINE OF PORTUGAL

Portugal, on the western coast of the Iberian peninsula, for a brief period became one of the great powers of Europe. Conquered by the Moors in the eighth century, it remained in their hands until it was recovered for Christendom by Spanish crusaders and their French allies in the late eleventh century. For three centuries there was the usual medieval struggle among kings, nobles, and clergy, complicated by invasions by Spaniards and Moors. Then, during the fifteenth century, Portugal was united, its sailors established an immense empire, and the little country became one of the principal European monarchies.

Fear of the Spanish and the Moors led the Portuguese to make alliances with distant countries. In 1294 they signed a commercial treaty with England, beginning an alliance that has continued to the present. The long coastline, dotted with harbors at the river mouths, attracted Italian sailors who taught the Portuguese new methods of sailing and told them of the profitable but dangerous trade with the East. Cut off from safe land routes with the rest of Europe, Portugal inevitably became a seafaring country.

The Aviz dynasty of strong kings led Portugal to economic prosperity and political unification. John I (king 1385-1433), who founded the dynasty, strengthened the parliament called the *Cortes*, which elected him king.

With English aid, he drove the Spanish and the Arabs from his boundaries. He reformed the government and encouraged agriculture and commerce; but he made such huge grants of land to the nobles that they were able to withstand his attempts to control them. John founded the Portuguese empire by seizing Arab territory in Morocco, and he encouraged his youngest son, Prince Henry "the Navigator" (Chapter 23), to sponsor a series of voyages of exploration along the African coastline, which eventually led to the discovery of the first sea route to India.

The Portuguese empire reached its height during the reigns of John II (king 1481-1495) and Emanuel I (king 1495-1521). John "the Perfect" crushed the opposition of the great lords. He forcibly converted to Christianity those Jews whom he did not execute or drive from his country. He made the richest commercial enterprises into royal monopolies, which he rented out to the men who would pay the highest fees. His navy destroyed an Egyptian fleet that challenged Portuguese shipping and foiled a Turkish attempt to control the trade with the East. Emanuel "the Fortunate" directed an extension of the empire which eventually included lands on both the west and east coasts of Africa; Brazil; islands in the Atlantic and Indian oceans; and possessions in the Persian Gulf, India, the East Indies, China, and Japan. (Chapter 23.) By the middle of the sixteenth century, Portugal was one of the richest and most powerful countries in Europe.

Emanuel was succeeded by a series of well-intentioned kings who were dominated by their advisers. The government gradually weakened, and in 1580 it was easily conquered by the Spaniards. Although Portugal regained its independence sixty years later, it had by then lost most of its empire. Portugal never again played an important role in European history.

🔱 **THE UNIFICATION OF SPAIN**

Centuries of crusading against the Moors (see pages 191-192) failed to unite the Iberian peninsula into a single Christian state. Portugal, as we have seen, remained independent for all but sixty years of its history. During the middle of the fifteenth century the rest of the peninsula was divided among Castile, Aragon, and the Moorish state of Granada. It seemed unlikely that these three would soon be combined into an autocratic monarchy like those of England and France.

The Christian kingdoms of Aragon and Castile were plagued by the usual contending political groups—kings, lords, clergy, and townsmen. The kings attempted to win the support of the towns by granting them unusually liberal charters and representation in local parliaments called *cortes*, and the Moorish and Jewish artisans and merchants who formed the backbone of the Spanish prosperity were allowed to worship as they pleased. But the lay and clerical nobles on their huge estates were able to defy the royal authority, to win exemption from taxes and some laws, and to remain semi-independent rulers.

In 1469 Ferdinand, heir to the crown of Aragon, married Isabella, heiress to the crown of Castile. This marriage associated the two kingdoms and paved the way for the creation of a single Spanish monarchy. Both Ferdinand (king 1479-1516) and Isabella (queen 1474-1504) were strong monarchs. Devoutly Catholic, they made the church an ally. For example, they persuaded the pope to agree to a concordat that gave them the authority to appoint bishops and abbots, and they introduced to Spain the Inquisition (see page 124), which they used against their enemies much as Henry VII of England used his Court of Star Chamber. They reorganized the central government, codified the laws, and sent royal officials into every part of the country to perform the governmental functions once performed by the nobles. Winning the support of the middle classes, Ferdinand and Isabella reduced the power of the nobles; but they retained the support of the great lords by giving them flattering if unimportant positions at the court.

United, the Spaniards were finally able to drive the last of the Moors from the country. Granada fell in 1492. Later the Spanish attacked the Moors in North Africa, conquering the cities of Oran and Tripoli. Immediately the religious toleration that had marked earlier Spanish history ceased. The Jews were driven from the country in 1492. A decade later the Moors were exiled from Castile. Spain became infamous for its intolerance toward dissenters of any kind.

After winning absolute control of Spain, Ferdinand and Isabella turned their attention elsewhere. In 1492 they sponsored Columbus's voyage to the New World, and later they encouraged the formation of the Spanish empire in South and Central America. (Chapter 24.) Ferdinand was also king of Sicily, which involved him in a complicated struggle for domination of Italy and in a league with the Holy Roman emperor and the pope against France. He and Isabella had no son to succeed them, but their daughters all made important marriages. The eldest, Joanna, married Philip of Habsburg, whose father was the Holy Roman Emperor Maximilian I; her son Charles V was to inherit much of Europe. Another daughter, Isabella, married a king of

Queen Isabella I of Spain: portrait by Juan de Flandes. Energetic, efficient, and patriotic, Isabella skillfully blended old ways and new in her policies. It was Isabella who championed Christopher Columbus and convinced her husband and co-ruler, Ferdinand, that Spain should support Columbus's voyages. Because of the sincerity of her faith, the pope awarded Isabella the title *La Católica,* "the Catholic."

Portugal. The third, Catherine of Aragon, married first one and then the other of the sons of Henry VII of England. The desire of Henry VIII of England to divorce her was an important factor in the English Reformation. (Chapter 21.)

Ferdinand and Isabella led Spain into the mainstream of European history and made it one of the richest and most important monarchies.

⚜ THE TRIUMPH OF LOCALISM · IN THE HOLY ROMAN EMPIRE

In Germany the disorder created by the weakening of the authority of the Holy Roman emperor led to political confusion. The Golden Bull of 1356 (see page 155) placed the election of the emperor in the hands of the lords who least wanted a strong central government. Anyone who hoped to be elected emperor had to promise the electors not to interfere in their local governments; thus the formation of a strong central government was almost impossible. After 1438 the head of the Habsburg family, who was also the hereditary archduke of Austria, was always elected emperor.

In Austria he was as much an autocrat as the contemporary kings of the national states to the west, and as time went on he made increasing attempts to extend his control over the lesser rulers in the empire. Although the emperor was sometimes able to influence events because of his great prestige, there were, in effect, more than 300 independent governments in Germany. The heads of the little German states won autocratic powers within their own boundaries, and some of them established effective government at the local level similar to that achieved by Louis XI in France and Henry VII in England at a national level.

National feeling led some Germans to desire a restoration of central government. Although Swiss nationalism led to the separation of Switzerland from the empire in all but name, Germans elsewhere sought the restoration of the power of the emperor. The most important of the early Habsburg emperors was Maximilian I (emperor 1493-1519), handsome, affable, a poet and a scholar. Called the "last of the knights," he dreamed of restoring the glory of the empire by dominating the German states, driving back the French in the west and the Turks in the east, and regaining the old imperial possessions in Italy. But Maximilian was far more successful at bringing lands outside the empire under Habsburg control than he was within the empire itself. By marrying the heiress of the duke of Burgundy, he brought the Netherlands and the Franche Comté (a part of Burgundy) into the Habsburg domains. By arranging the marriage of his son to Joanna, the eldest daughter of Ferdinand and Isabella of Spain, he paved the way for a Habsburg empire that was soon to dominate much of Europe. But Maximilian was not able to reduce the independence of the German principalities.

Italy, too, was divided among a number of governments. In the north, towns became independent and prosperous, even though they were torn within themselves by disputes between the wealthy and the workers and between adherents of the emperors and of the popes. Towns fought bitterly with each other, hiring soldiers whose leaders, called *condottieri*, often seized power and became despots. During the fifteenth century, the larger cities began to dominate the smaller, and three, Venice, Milan, and Florence, came to control much of northern Italy. After 1450 some of the popes, as interested in ruling the Papal States as they were in governing the church, became deeply involved in Italian wars and politics. In the south, the kingdoms of Naples and Sicily (sometimes united as the "kingdom of the Two Sicilies") passed into the hands of the kings of Aragon and thus to Spain.

🐝 DYNASTIC RIVALRIES IN THE SIXTEENTH CENTURY

The kings who established autocratic rule devoted most of their time to reorganizing their governments or to controlling the rebellious vassals inside their boundaries. The next generation of monarchs, their own lands firmly under control, looked about for new lands to conquer. As a result, during the sixteenth century they subjected Europe to a series of violent wars. The object of each monarch was to extend the territories of his dynasty (ruling family), for the prestige and glory of the monarch and the good of his country came to be looked upon as being the same thing. The monarchs also developed the attitude that they were not bound by the same rules of law and morality that applied to everyone else. The attitude was summed up in a little book called *The Prince*.

MACHIAVELLI AND "THE PRINCE"

The author of *The Prince* was a Florentine named Niccolò Machiavelli (1469-1527), whose experiences in Italy brought him to two conclusions: that men were wicked, and that chaotic Italy had to be united under one prince. He wrote *The Prince* to guide this ruler who would unify his homeland. Machiavelli's philosophy was simple. He believed that because men are evil, they must be controlled by the ruler for the good of the country. Observing the methods of the most successful monarchs of his day, he concluded that the ruler must make his own interests and those of the state identical. To accomplish his ends, the prince is justified in doing whatever he thinks is necessary: he may assassinate, lie, cheat, steal, or wage war. However, the prince must remain popular, and he therefore must give the impression that he is kind and thoughtful. He must bring the church under his control, as religion teaches men to be humble and to obey authority. In short, since the end justifies the means, the monarch's actions are above the laws of religion and morality.

HABSBURG VS. VALOIS

The sixty-five-year struggle between the reigning Valois kings of France and the Habsburgs of Germany and Spain illustrates clearly how the contemporary autocratic monarchs applied the principles of Machiavelli to advance their dynastic ambitions. Their rivalry led to a series of wars that involved much of Europe during the first half of the sixteenth century.

The Emperor Charles V: portrait by Titian (1477-1576; Chapter 20). By the time he was twenty, Charles had inherited lands vaster than the empire of Charlemagne. During his long reign he traveled constantly, seeking to expand his holdings, to defend them from the advancing Ottoman Turks, and to check the spread of Protestantism. His efforts were for the most part unsuccessful. After almost forty years, discouraged and completely worn out, he abdicated and retired to a monastery.

The conflict began in 1494 with a struggle for the spoils of rich but divided Italy. Charles VIII of France (1483-1498) coveted the kingdom of Naples and marched at the head of his armies through Italy to take possession of it. Pope Alexander VI, alarmed by the threat of having a powerful neighbor to the south of the Papal States, formed a "Holy League" with Spain, Venice, Milan, and England, which forced Charles to retreat. But Charles's successor, Louis XII (king 1498-1515), renewed the struggle for control of Italy by conquering Milan. Louis then formed an alliance with France's former enemies Pope Julius II, King Ferdinand of Spain, and the Holy Roman Emperor Maximilian I. The purpose of the alliance was to seize and divide the rich Po valley, which belonged to prosperous but militarily weak Venice. Like most such alliances, this one did not last long. Ferdinand quit as soon as he had won his share of the spoils. The pope, whose fear of France revived, formed a second "Holy League" against France, this time with Venice and England as allies. The English then invaded France and defeated the French in the "Battle of the Spurs" (1513), so-called because of the haste with which the French cavalry retreated. The defeated French were again forced out of Italy. But they returned two years later and, after a great victory at Marignano, once again added Milan to their possessions.

After only a few years of peace, the Habsburg Emperor Charles V renewed the struggle. Charles (emperor 1519-1556) was elected Holy Roman emperor when he was only nineteen. At that time he was told, "God has set you on the path to a world monarchy." It seemed so. From his grandparents Ferdinand and Isabella he had in 1516 inherited Spain, its rapidly growing possessions in the New World, and the Italian kingdoms of Naples, Sicily, and Sardinia. From his Habsburg grandfather, Maximilian I, he inherited Austria and other lands in southern Germany. From his grandmother, Maximilian's wife Mary of Burgundy, he inherited the Netherlands and Franche Comté. In 1526 both Bohemia and Hungary became parts of the Habsburg domains (although most of Hungary was soon conquered by the Ottoman Turks; see page 202). Charles, who had been brought up in the Netherlands and spoke neither Spanish nor German when he assumed office, was unsympathetic to the national interests of these countries. He was primarily concerned with increasing his dynastic possessions.

Opposing Charles V was Francis I (king 1515-1547) of France, a king who was in turns energetic and lazy. His kingdom was almost surrounded by the Spanish and German possessions of Charles V.

Charles attacked in 1521. Four years later he captured Francis at Pavia, in northern Italy. To regain his freedom, Francis agreed to cede Milan, other Italian lands, and the French part of Burgundy to Charles; but as soon as he was free, he withdrew his promise. Charles's victory was his undoing, for it aroused other monarchs to fear his growing power. Henry VIII of England, who had been his ally against France, turned against him; and Pope Leo X, more fearful of Habsburg power in Naples than of French power in northern Italy, aligned himself with Francis. Charles's troops retaliated by capturing and sacking Rome in 1527, an act that horrified all Catholic Europe. Meanwhile, Charles had also to wage war in Germany, where the Protestant followers of Martin Luther rebelled (Chapter 21), and in Hungary, where the Turks were attacking. Thus, after eight years of war, Charles was forced to sign the Treaty of Cambrai (1529), which restored Burgundy to France and Europe to about the same condition it had before the conflict had begun.

The peace did not last long. Francis, although Catholic, allied himself with German Protestants in order to add to Charles's troubles in the Holy Roman Empire. He also made a treaty with the Muslim Turks against the emperor. Two brief and indecisive wars followed, followed by still another between Charles's and Francis's successors. Finally, in 1559, with the Treaty of Cateau-Cambrésis, France and the Habsburgs made their peace. The

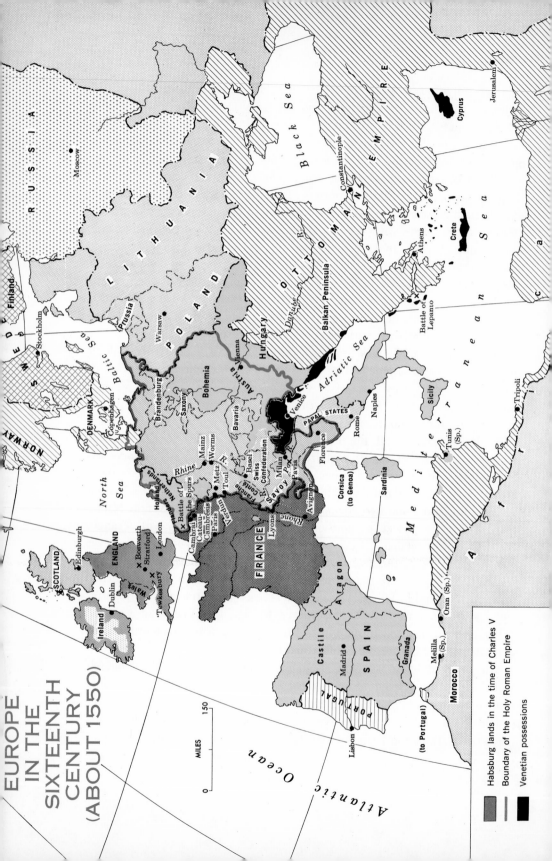

EUROPE
IN THE
SIXTEENTH
CENTURY
(ABOUT 1550)

MILES

0   150

RUSSIA

Moscow

Finland

SWEDEN

Stockholm

NORWAY

DENMARK

Copenhagen

Baltic Sea

LITHUANIA

Prussia

Warsaw

POLAND

Black Sea

Constantinople

OTTOMAN EMPIRE

Cyprus

Jerusalem

Crete

Athens

Balkan Peninsula

Danube

Hungary

Vienna

Austria

Bohemia

Brandenburg

Saxony

Bavaria

Adriatic Sea

Battle of
Lepanto

Venice

PAPAL STATES

Rome

Naples

Sicily

Tripoli

Tunis (Sp.)

Sardinia

Corsica
(to Genoa)

Mediterranean Sea

Africa

Florence

Mainz

Worms

Metz

Toul

Verdun

Basel

Swiss
Confederation

Milan

Savoy

Pavia

Franche Comté

Avignon

Rhine

Holland

Battle of
the Spurs

Cambrai

Cateau-
Cambrésis

Paris

Lyons

Rhone

FRANCE

Aragon

SPAIN

Castile

Madrid

Granada

Melilla
(Sp.)

Oran (Sp.)

Morocco

Lisbon

PORTUGAL
(to Portugal)

Atlantic Ocean

North Sea

Edinburgh

SCOTLAND

ENGLAND

London

Bosworth

Stratford

WALES

Tewkesbury

Dublin

Ireland

Flanders

Netherlands

Legend

Habsburg lands in the time of Charles V

Boundary of the Holy Roman Empire

Venetian possessions

Habsburgs gained nothing of importance; France gained the three bishop-rics of Metz, Toul, and Verdun, which previously had been German.

The wars were marked by broken treaties and shifting alliances. The English discovered a policy that they followed thereafter for centuries: they supported the weaker side in European quarrels, to prevent the stronger from dominating the continent. Both sides used religion as a weapon. At the time a bitter struggle was taking place between Catholics and the newly formed Protestant churches (Chapter 22); but the Catholic mon-archs, preoccupied by their struggles with each other, failed to put down the rising Protestant sects in Germany and France, and even allied with the Protestants when it might advance their personal ambitions. These wars set a pattern that was constantly repeated in the next two centuries.

By the end of the fifteenth century, kings in most parts of western Europe were in firm control of their governments, and the governments were much stronger than those of the medieval monarchies. The kings of the major states along the Atlantic seacoast had subdued their nobles. They had either reduced the political power of the churchmen or made the churchmen close allies of their governments. In most places the growth of autocratic monarchy was accompanied by increasing national feeling, which led the people to unite behind their monarchs to a degree previously unknown. But the monarchs all too often used their growing strength to advance their own dynastic interests.

People, Places, and Terms

Henry VI	Charles V	autocracy
Richard of York	Francis I	nationalism
Edward IV		Wars of the Roses
Richard III	Portugal	Lancastrians
Henry VII	Morocco	Yorkists
Louis XI	Castile	Court of
John I	Aragon	Star Chamber
Henry the Navigator	Naples	Justice of the Peace
John II	Milan	Cortes
Emanuel II	Metz	The Prince
Ferdinand	Toul	Battle of Pavia
Isabella	Verdun	Treaty of Cambrai
Maximilian I	Kingdom of the	Treaty of
Niccolò Machiavelli	Two Sicilies	Cateau-Cambrésis

Getting Organized

1. How was England divided in the fifteenth century? Who were the principal figures in the Wars of the Roses? How did these wars end?
2. How did Henry VII establish royal control in England? What steps did he take to retain the obedience and loyalty of his subjects?
3. How effective was Valois government? How had the earlier Valois monarchs strengthened their control of France?
4. How did Louis XI strengthen the French monarchy? What groups opposed his rule? What accounts for his success?
5. How did Portugal rise in power in the fifteenth and sixteenth centuries? At its height how powerful was this small nation? Why did it decline?
6. Describe the political divisions and disunity of Spain before the marriage of Ferdinand and Isabella. What measures did these two monarchs take to unite and strengthen their country?
7. What factors worked against the establishment of a strong central government in the Holy Roman Empire? What were the principal bases of the emperor's strength? What were the accomplishments of Maximilian I?
8. Why did the new autocratic kings act as they did? How did Machiavelli's principles affect the growth of autocracy?
9. What were the reasons for the conflict between the Valois kings of France and the Habsburgs of Germany? Where were the battlegrounds for this conflict? Who were the principal figures in this struggle? What was the outcome of this struggle?

Understanding the Big Picture

1. What were the major obstacles to the establishment of stronger monarchies? Which were common to all countries? Which were more local in character?
2. Compare and contrast the methods of Henry VII of England and Louis XI of France.
3. Why did Portugal and Spain become so important in European affairs in the fifteenth and sixteenth centuries?
4. Summarize the reasons why Italy and Germany remained disunited at a time when all of the other European nations were becoming united.

For the Thoughtful

1. What were the most important causes of the new strength of the various European monarchies?
2. Are any of the methods and innovations of the new monarchs similar to those used by rulers today? What evidence that Machiavellian principles have (or have not) died out is offered by current events?

18

the transition to a modern economy

By 1500 Europe was humming with commerce and manufacturing. New trade routes had been established and old ones enlarged to link the various parts of the continent together. Along these routes cities and towns prospered, often in what previously had been poverty-stricken agricultural regions. Expanding trade made whole areas of Europe important for the first time.

In the growing towns and cities, merchants and craftsmen restlessly experimented with new concepts of trade and manufacturing. Increasing use of money created new opportunities for bankers and investors. As the townsmen became more numerous and more self-confident, they demanded and won recognition from even the most powerful kings and parliaments. Some cities became independent states; some joined together in leagues to promote and protect their growing commerce. A few of the richest townsmen became powerful enough to influence governments even more than did the nobles and the bishops.

Changes in the countryside were less dramatic but equally important. Some peasants rebelled successfully against medieval restrictions of life on the manors. Others were employed by urban merchants to perform elementary manufacturing processes in their rural homes. Still others left

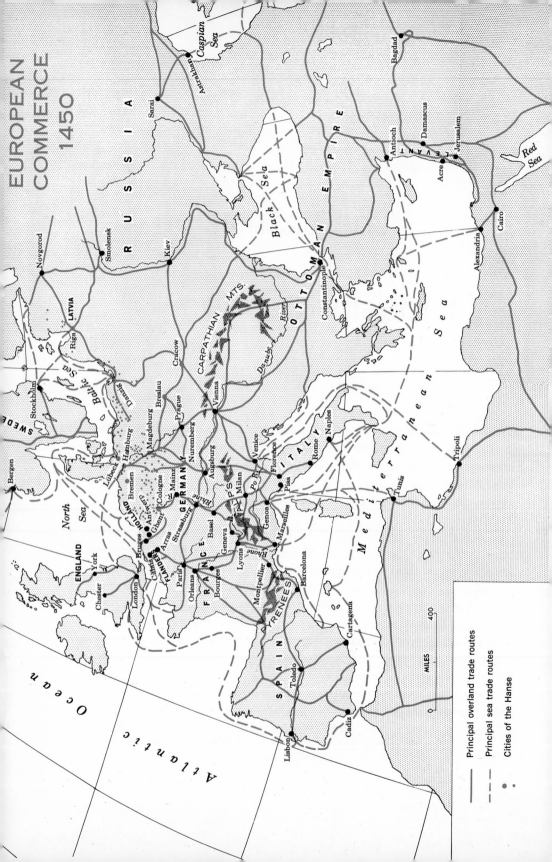

EUROPEAN
COMMERCE
1450

RUSSIA

Caspian Sea

Astrakhan

Sarai

Novgorod

Smolensk

Kiev

LATVIA

Riga

Black Sea

CARPATHIAN MTS.

Danube River

OTTOMAN EMPIRE

Constantinople

Bagdad

Damascus

Antioch

Jerusalem

LEVANT

Acre

Red Sea

Cairo

Alexandria

Baltic Sea

SWEDEN

Stockholm

Bergen

Cracow

Breslau

Vienna

Magdeburg

Prague

Nuremberg

Augsburg

Lübeck

Hamburg

Bremen

GERMANY

Cologne

Mainz

Rhine

Milan

Po R.

Venice

Florence

ALPS

ITALY

Rome

Naples

Tripoli

Tunis

Mediterranean Sea

North Sea

HOLLAND

Antwerp

Ghent

Bruges

FLANDERS

Arras

Calais

Strasburg

Basel

FRANCE

Geneva

Lyons

Rhone

Pisa

Genoa

Marseilles

Montpellier

Barcelona

PYRENEES

Cartagena

ENGLAND

York

Chester

London

Paris

Orleans

Bourges

SPAIN

Toledo

Cadiz

Lisbon

Atlantic Ocean

MILES

0   400

Principal overland trade routes

Principal sea trade routes

Cities of the Hanse

the manors altogether and moved to the towns to work in the shops and little factories.

Thus as the sixteenth century began, Europe was undergoing a transformation from medieval to modern ways of economic life and thought, a process that paralleled the political transformation from feudal to autocratic monarchies.

COMMERCE AND BANKING

By 1500 merchants finally had become more familiar figures on the roads than armed knights. They still dealt mostly in European goods, such as salt made by evaporating the water of the Mediterranean Sea; wool and lead from England; wines from France and Germany; or cloth, leather, and metal goods from Italy. But an increasing percentage of their merchandise was made up of luxury products of the East, which they had imported by sea from the Levant to Italy and then carried overland to the farthest corners of Europe.

EXPANDING TRADE ROUTES

The old medieval trade routes (see page 109) still continued, supplemented by a network of new routes that bound all Europe in a web of commerce.

There were three main groups of these routes. The first centered on northern Italy, from whose ports ships sailed east to the Levant to trade European products for Oriental luxuries. Other ships sailed west along the coast to southern France and Spain, carrying Sicilian grain and Italian-made merchandise to exchange for French wines and Spanish wool.

A second group of routes connected the cities of northern France, Germany, and the Low Countries (Flanders, Holland, etc.) with the agricultural regions of England and the Baltic coast. Most of the trade along these routes was in agricultural produce and timber, pitch, and other shipbuilding products, although an increasing proportion consisted of textiles woven in the cities of the Low Countries.

In the long run the most important group of routes was the third, which connected the Italian cities with northern Europe. Some routes were roads through the Alpine passes; others were sea lanes that followed the coastline around Spain. Northward flowed Oriental luxuries and the manufactures of Italy; south returned the textiles and raw materials of the north.

A trading ship of the fifteenth century. Such ships, although small by present-day standards, could carry cargoes large enough to show handsome profits.

Most of the early commerce was conducted on overland routes, but this was slow and expensive. No roads were paved, so that wagons or carts often bogged down in mud or broke their axles in ruts. Pack animals could carry only light and compact products. Thus more and more traffic came to be carried in ships, which were much improved during the late Middle Ages. Early in the fourteenth century the first of the "Flanders Fleets" made the 2,500 mile voyage from their home port of Venice around southern Italy and the coast of Spain to the Atlantic ports of northern Europe, carrying cargoes of sugar, wines, spices, and armor to exchange for wool, cloth, leather, and hides in England, and cutlery, brass, and bowstrings in Flanders. In these fleets were vessels called "great galleys," sometimes as much as 150 feet long and manned by crews of 200 sailors and oarsmen, which could transport bulky goods relatively inexpensively. In the interior of Europe, rivers came to be the main highways of commerce.

Cities fortunate enough to be on these major routes prospered. Seaports like Venice, Cadiz, Lisbon, Calais, London, Bruges, Antwerp, and Hamburg offered safe harbors to merchant vessels. Cities on the major rivers, such as Basel, Mainz, and Cologne on the Rhine or Lyon on the Rhone, were centers for the distribution of goods. Other cities, most notably such textile centers of the Low Countries as Arras and Ghent, prospered more from manufacturing than from trade.

In major cities, to which local tradesmen flocked to buy and sell, merchants from distant parts of Europe often established trading posts called "factories." Often the merchants of these factories won special political and economic privileges from rulers eager to encourage commerce.

THE EARLY GROWTH OF CAPITALISM

Growing trade and new methods of manufacturing fostered the development of the economic system called "capitalism," which was based on the use of privately owned property to create profits. Increased markets encouraged energetic and ambitious men to invest capital (goods or money devoted to making additional goods or money) in all sorts of enterprises.

The capitalists developed two new systems of manufacturing. In one system, a capitalist employed a large number of journeymen and apprentices in his workshop for money wages. Under the old guild system, each of these men would have carried out all stages of manufacturing, from raw materials to finished product. In the new and larger workshops, the work was divided: each worker specialized in one stage of manufacturing, passing the partly finished product on to another worker who completed the next stage. The capitalist supplied the tools and materials, paid the workers a set wage, and kept the profits from the sale of the finished product.

The other new system was the "putting-out" system, which avoided workshops altogether. A capitalist simply distributed ("put out") raw materials among peasants who lived near his town. The peasants worked on them in their own cottages and were paid fixed fees for their work. Here again, each peasant usually completed only one phase of manufacturing, and the capitalist would pass the goods from one to another until the product was completed. In both systems, the capitalist supplied all the money, materials, and tools, and he kept all the profits. By manufacturing on a large scale, he could become very wealthy indeed.

THE DEVELOPMENT OF BANKING

The growth of commerce made it almost impossible to continue the barter system (the direct exchange of one product for another), which had characterized much of medieval trade. Little money had been coined in the Middle Ages, for there had been a shortage of gold and silver. But during the fourteenth century the older gold and silver mines were exploited as fully as possible, and new mines were opened. Their output was minted into coins for use in commerce. The wide use of such Italian coins as the Florentine "florin" and the Venetian "ducat" led kings everywhere to establish their own systems of coinage, which provided their people with money of a guaranteed value. Soon coinage was used, not only by merchants, but by workers who received their pay in silver and by peasants who preferred paying money rents instead of labor services to their lords.

The use of money created a need for banks. The first bankers were moneychangers, whose business was to exchange a coin of one region for that of another. Later, as townsmen began to accumulate money to invest, they began to make loans for interest—despite the disapproval of the church, which considered this a sin, called "usury." Jews were exempt from the Christian prohibition of usury, and many became bankers; but many Christians also made large loans to monarchs, avoiding the accusation of usury by accepting commercial or other privileges in place of direct interest payments. Loans were often highly risky, and interest rates ran as high as 200 per cent per year.

☸ THE CONTINUING GROWTH OF CITIES

All during the Middle Ages, and even more so in the fifteenth and sixteenth centuries, new towns were established and old ones grew. By 1500 there were probably 400 towns in France, 150 in England, and similar numbers in the Holy Roman Empire and in Italy. Most were very small: Wittenberg in Germany was typical with 2,000 souls; Geneva was considered large with 16,000; and there were only half a dozen, such as Paris, Venice, and Florence, with 100,000 people. London increased from 75,000 in 1500 to 200,000 in 1600.

Many medieval towns had been primarily centers of the church or of government; but all became increasingly dominated by their merchants and craftsmen. Most of the smaller market towns were only centers of local trade. The larger and more prosperous, however, attracted a wide variety of people as merchants from far places came to trade or, if they happened to be capital cities as well, government officials came to report to the king in his court. Most had much more political freedom than rural regions, and those that had their charters directly from the king escaped the clutches of feudalism altogether.

THE CITIES OF NORTHERN EUROPE

Most of the cities of northern Europe in the late Middle Ages were situated along the coastline, on major rivers, or in the manufacturing regions of the Low Countries. As they shook off the control of feudal nobles, they banded together in groups to stimulate their trade, played an often decisive role in the political controversies of their regions, and rapidly developed their growing industries.

A port of the Hanse in the fifteenth century. The men in the foreground are merchants. Behind them, a ship is being unloaded at the dock, and in the distance another puts out to sea.

The German Hanse. For more than two centuries a league of German cities dominated trade along the northern coasts of Europe. Called the "Hanse," it had been founded in the fourteenth century by Lübeck and Hamburg and by 1450 numbered more than 100 cities. It had its own government, navy, system of weights and measures, and even its own mariner's charts of the coast of Europe from Latvia to Lisbon. After 1500, however, the member cities quarreled, and in the Baltic Sea region they were unable to resist the rising power of Sweden. New trade routes replaced those of the Hanseatic sailors, and the confederation withered away.

Manufacturing Cities in Flanders. The cloth trade of northern Europe was long centered in the cities of Flanders, where the North Sea meets the English Channel. Near wool-growing regions in England and Germany, and on the sea lanes, merchants in such cities as Arras, Ghent, and Bruges developed the "putting-out" system in which raw wool was "put out" to workers who made it into cloth in their own cottages for set fees. Although the Flemish were a largely independent people, they were torn by struggles among themselves, which led to foreign intervention. These struggles, which were a cause of the Hundred Years War (see page 217), helped bring about the eventual decline of Flanders as a textile center during the fifteenth century.

HOLY ROMAN EMPIRE
Switzerland
A L P S
Milan
VENICE
Padua
Venice
MANTUA
Po R.
HUNGARY
FERRARA
GENOA
MODENA
SAVOY
Genoa
Pisa
Florence
Arno R.
FLORENCE
OTTOMAN
EMPIRE
SIENA
Adriatic Sea
(to Venice)
Corsica
(to Genoa)
PAPAL STATES
Rome
Sardinia
(to Spain)
Naples
KINGDOM
N
OF THE
MILES
0   100
TWO SICILIES
(to Spain)

In 1494, the city-states of northern Italy were at the height of their power and prosperity, which had been steadily increasing for centuries. Florence was the intellectual and cultural capital not only of Italy but of all Europe. (Chapter 19.) But Italy was soon to be thrown into chaos by the first of the French invasions (see pages 240-241), from which only Venice emerged unharmed.

THE CITIES OF ITALY

A few Italian cities dominated both the sea lanes of the Mediterranean and the overland routes to northern Europe. Although plagued by internal revolts, they grew rich from their textile, banking, and industrial activities.

Milan. On the upper valley of the Po River, not far from the Alps, Milan became a center of the silk, wool, and armor industries in the fourteenth century. Led by ambitious dukes, the Milanese seized the port of Genoa and dominated northern Italy.

Venice. The author Petrarch was especially impressed by Venice, built on islands at the head of the Adriatic Sea. "I see," he wrote,

> . . . vessels as big as my mansion, their masts taller than its towers. They are as mountains floating on the waters. They go to face incalculable dangers in every portion of the globe. They bear wine to England, honey to Russia, saffron, oil and linen to Assyria, Armenia, Persia and Araby, wool to Egypt and Greece. They return heavily laden with products of all kinds, which are sent hence to every part of the world.

After the Fourth Crusade (see page 189), Venice controlled a large empire and most of the trade in the eastern Mediterranean. It was governed by a few of its richest and most aristocratic families, who elected a "doge" (duke) and a senate, which made and strictly enforced the laws and rigidly regulated the city's commerce. The profits were enormous, and although the people sometimes complained, they did not dare rebel. Venice remained independent and stable until Napoleon finally conquered it in 1797.

Florence. After Venice, Florence, "the city of flowers," was the richest city in Italy. It ruled a number of smaller cities in northwestern Italy, including the port of Pisa, from which its merchants sailed to all parts of the world. It employed 30,000 workers in 200 large workshops and was the home of some eighty banking houses. Florence was governed by the *popolo grasso*, the "fat people" or rich merchants, but the *popolo minuto* or "thin people," as the workers were called, rebelled frequently and made the city's politics very lively indeed.

Many other cities in northern Italy were only slightly smaller and less influential than Milan, Venice, and Florence, and had similar customs and economic interests. In central Italy, Rome, the home of the popes, was predominant, and in the south was Naples, capital of the twin kingdoms of Naples and Sicily (the "Two Sicilies"). Only Naples was governed by foreign princes, first French and then Spanish. Otherwise, the history of Italy in the fifteenth and sixteenth centuries is the history of its city-states.

"Procession in St. Mark's Square [Venice]": a painting by Gentile Bellini (Chapter 19). Such processions, in which a group of citizens honored their patron saint—and at the same time displayed their wealth with great pomp and ceremony—were frequent in prosperous Venice. St. Mark's Church, in the background, was lavishly decorated, for every returning Venetian voyage was required to bring something new to add to it.

CITIES AND POLITICS

Every major European government had already in earlier centuries been influenced by the growth of towns. Townsmen had won representation in the English Parliament, the French Estates-General, the Spanish Cortes, and the Diet of the Holy Roman Empire. Towns had secured important rights of self-government and economic freedom and had encouraged the kings to limit the power of the nobles. By serving as officials in the royal government, townsmen had helped bring order and peace to the countryside. As the towns continued to grow, so did their political importance.

Many cities in Germany and northern Italy were "communes." These self-governing cities of the type of Venice and Florence were often republics in which a clique of rich merchants controlled the government and used it for their own purposes. Occasionally the workers in a commune would seize power and establish a democracy of sorts, but these rarely lasted long, and the wealthy class usually quickly regained control. As a rule of thumb, the smaller the city, the more likely it was to be ruled by the wealthier citizens through some sort of elected council.

The cities often banded together for self-protection, developing the "balance-of-power" system to a fine art. The purpose of this system was to prevent larger states from gobbling up smaller ones. The little states would agree to consider an attack against one of them an attack against them all. Thus their combined armies could hope to equal, or "balance," the armies of the aggressor. These balance-of-power leagues often rose and fell with bewildering rapidity as the rulers of each state, seeking the best possible alliance, threw aside their former friends and joined their recent enemies. The balance-of-power system made history confusing, but it enabled the little cities of Italy to preserve their independence against the attacks of kings and emperors.

🐚 THE MERCHANT AND BANKING MIDDLE CLASS

Only one twenty-fifth of the estimated 60,000,000 inhabitants of Europe in 1500 lived in cities or towns, and few of these had any influence on the policies of kings and dukes. Europe was still predominantly rural and governed by an aristocracy of rural landholders and their monarchs. Yet by the sixteenth century a new social class, the "middle class" of merchants and bankers, was occupying a new place of importance in European life.

A moneychanger of fifteenth-century Flanders: detail of a painting by Quentin Massys (1466?-1530). The money-changer, a forerunner of the modern banker (see page 250), is weighing the coins submitted to him for exchange—a process necessary to detect counterfeit coins, which were then quite common. His sober, businesslike attitude is typical of the rising middle class of the time.

THE MIDDLE CLASS

Most of the middle class members were "petty burghers," keepers of small shops or master craftsmen who lived in much the same way as their ancestors in earlier medieval times. (See pages 110-111.) They belonged to their guilds and worked side by side in their shops with their journeymen and apprentices, and they often bitterly resisted the new methods introduced by the capitalists. In a city like Florence they were respected but not influential citizens.

Increasingly the cities were controlled by an upper middle class of capitalist merchants and bankers. These rich men were commoners, but they often associated on almost equal terms with the aristocratic nobles; and their children often married nobles, who were glad to get some of the money of the wealthy families. In some ways the merchants imitated the nobles by patronizing the arts, building huge mansions and filling them with costly furniture, and adopting aristocratic mannerisms. But in other ways they were a far different breed of men. They worked hard, were proud of the ways in which they made their money, and openly sought profits—despite the disapproval of the church and of the aristocrats, who pretended to be above such worldly goals. They were less attached to feudal and medieval traditions, and more willing to experiment with new ideas about economics, government, and even religion.

THE MERCHANT PRINCES

In the fifteenth century, for the first time, merchant princes began to exert significant influence on the world in which they lived.

Jacques Coeur. Jacques Coeur (1395?-1456), born the son of a craftsman, rose to become an adviser to king Charles VII of France. He used profits made by trading with the infidels in the East to set up a shop in the city of Montpellier, where he sold "every class of merchandise, especially that required by the king, the dauphin, and the nobles." Soon he had dozens of warehouses all over France staffed with 500 agents. By 1450 he had equipped a military expedition at his own expense and was lending money lavishly to the king. But Coeur rose too far, too fast. Jealous nobles had him arrested for murder; he was banished from France, and his property was confiscated. But he left many monuments behind, including a house at Bourges that is a monument of late Gothic architecture.

Jacob Fugger "the Rich." The Fugger family made their home city of Augsburg one of Europe's banking centers. They started in the textile trade, then expanded into banking, and finally ended up meddling in politics. Jacob Fugger "the Rich" (1459-1525) studied to be a monk, but became a banker instead, lending vast sums to the Holy Roman Emperor Maximilian I and providing the funds that enabled Maximilian's grandson, Charles V, to bribe the electors who chose him Holy Roman Emperor in 1519. Fugger never failed to remind his emperor that he owed his election to a banker, and was amply rewarded with money, jewelry, and the right to exploit copper, gold, and silver mines in Hungary. Like other merchants of this time, Fugger was far from humble; he wrote this epitaph for his tomb in Augsburg:

> To the best, greatest God! Jacob Fugger of Augsburg, the ornament of his class and his people, imperial councillor under Maximilian I and Charles V, who was behind no one in the attainment of extraordinary wealth, in generosity, purity of morals, and greatness of soul, is, as he was not comparable with anyone else in his lifetime, even after death not to be counted among the mortals.

His successors were even wealthier than he—until a sixteeth-century king of Spain defaulted on his debts and drove them into bankruptcy.

The Medici. The Medici of Florence claimed that they were descended from Perseus, a hero of Greek mythology; but their known wealth and prominence dates from the leader of a wool carders' revolt in Florence during the late fourteenth century named Salvestro dei Medici. His descendants were textile merchants who branched out into cloth manufacturing and established warehouses all over Europe. Next they added banking to their activities, taking favors from princes and popes in lieu of interest. By siding with the *popolo minuto* in Florence against the rich merchants, the Medici became as successful in politics as they were in banking. In 1434 Cosimo de Medici seized the government, and for the next three centuries the stories of the Medici and of Florence are inseparable. Medici became kings and queens, dukes and princes, popes and cardinals, and patrons of Renaissance art and learning. Some of the greatest aristocrats of early modern times were descendants of the late medieval wool carder Salvestro dei Medici.

CHANGES IN GOVERNMENT AND SOCIETY

The growth of towns, of capitalism, and of the middle class influenced every aspect of European life in the fifteenth and sixteenth centuries. No other development contributed so much to the decline of medieval customs.

CHANGES IN GOVERNMENT

Townsmen increasingly served as officials in the royal governments, supporting their kings against the disorderly nobles. Like Coeur and the Fuggers, they lent money to their monarchs; or, in such communes as Florence, merchant bankers like the Medici actually controlled their governments. The communes often banded together into commercial leagues like the Hanse, or to preserve the balance of power in the face of attacks by larger states. By these actions they hastened the downfall of feudalism; in Italy they even prevented the formation of any central government at all.

CHANGES IN SOCIETY

The growth of capitalism separated the merchant and banking middle class from the workers they employed. This change led to unrest, strikes, and even revolutions, and seriously weakened the old medieval guild system.

Increasing use of money led to a "price revolution," a prolonged inflation of prices that increased the cost of living by some 300 per cent during the sixteenth century. The medieval shortage of money was more than satisfied by exploiting European mines and importing gold and silver from Spanish colonies in the New World. (Chapter 23.) Prices increased faster than wages, so the chief sufferers from this "price revolution" were the wage earners in the towns and cottages and the landholders who depended on the rental income of their estates. The development of business led to cycles of prosperity and depression as businessmen expanded their trade too much and then, when their warehouses began to fill, cut back on production. When this occurred, the workers in the towns and the peasants who could not pay their rents often rose up in revolt.

The rising middle class usually sided with the king in politics, but it often made close alliances with the nobles as well. Some burghers married into noble families. Nobles who were tired of the discomfort and isolation of their ancient castles moved to the cities, where they could enjoy a more varied life. Even nobles who remained in the country adopted capitalistic methods. In England especially they enclosed their manors' fields with hedges, ousted the peasants, and raised sheep whose wool they could sell for cash. This "enclosure movement" was the nobles' answer to peasant revolts.

The rise of the middle class tended to weaken the traditional class distinctions. Burghers did not fit into the customary class groupings, for they based their social position more on wealth than family background. On a lower level, the peasants won freedom from serfdom and often left the manors to join the working class in the towns. On the other hand, economic changes tended to separate the higher clergy (bishops and archbishops) from the parish priests. In the Middle Ages it had not been unusual for a peasant's son to become pope. This rarely happened after the fifteenth century, when impoverished nobles encouraged their younger sons to enter the church because they could not support them. These well-born bishops sought an ever larger share of the church income for themselves, so that they could live in the style of great noblemen. Satisfying the bishops' demands led, in turn, to impoverishment of parish priests. As fewer able men were attracted to the priesthood, many people became increasingly dissatisfied with the church and openly critical of it.

⚜ ⚜ ⚜

No aspect of European life was untouched by the economic changes of the fifteenth and sixteenth centuries. Church and manor, village and town were all shaking off their feudal traditions and groping uncertainly for a new set of standards and customs that would suit the new circumstances. Out of the confusion caused by political and economic change there appeared, first in Italy and later in northern Europe, a "new learning" and a "new art" that commonly go by the name "Renaissance."

People, Places, and Terms

Jacques Coeur	Lübeck	capital
Jacob Fugger	Milan	putting-out system
Salvestro dei Medici	Genoa	barter
Cosimo de Medici	Venice	usury
	Florence	commune
Cadiz	Pisa	Hanse
Lisbon	Naples	doge
Calais	Augsburg	*popolo grasso*
Bruges		*popolo minuto*
Antwerp	Flanders Fleet	balance of power
Hamburg	great galley	price revolution
Lyon	factory	enclosure
Ghent	capitalism	

Getting Organized

1. With what types of merchandise did the European merchants deal? Which were the three most important groups of European trade routes? How was merchandise transported from one place to another? What were the major trade cities?
2. Describe the economic system called capitalism. What new systems of manufacturing developed under it?
3. What was the effect of coinage on the European economy and on the old feudal system? How did the use of coins create a need for banks? Describe how the early bankers operated.
4. How large were the medieval cities? Which were the biggest? Describe a typical medieval city.
5. Describe the chief characteristics of the following cities or groups of cities: the Hanse, the cities of Flanders, Milan, Venice, Florence, Rome, and Naples.

6. How were the various European governments influenced by the growth of towns? How did the communes work? Who dominated the city governments? Describe the balance of power and its chief effects.
7. Who belonged to the new middle class? Were all its members equal in income and social status? What was the relationship of the middle class to the nobility?
8. Describe the principal achievements and importance of Jacques Coeur, Jacob Fugger, and the Medici.
9. How did the growth of towns, of capitalism, and of the middle class bring about political changes? Economic changes? Social and cultural changes?

Understanding the Big Picture

1. What were the different ways by which a member of the middle class would make a living in the fifteenth century? Describe each of these occupations.
2. How did the economic changes of the fifteenth and sixteenth centuries affect the political and economic power of the old feudal lords? How were they affected by such developments as the increased use of coins and capitalism?
3. What role did the cities play in late medieval life? To what extent did they change the old medieval social and political structure?
4. Summarize the ways in which economic changes significantly altered medieval ways of life.

Mastering the Map

Study the map of European commerce in 1450 on page 246. Trace the major trade routes. What effect did commerce have on the cities that were along these routes? In what ways did the geography affect the location of these routes?

For the Thoughtful

1. Using your knowledge of the role of economics in the fall of the Roman Empire, compare the influence of economic changes on the decline of Rome and on the decline of medieval institutions. Be specific.
2. How important are economic changes and influences to history? How much do they affect such things as politics, morality, and social structure? (Base your answers on material in this chapter and on your knowledge of other periods of history).
3. Compare the class structure of Europe in 1500 to that of the United States in our own times. How different are the two structures? What different influences determine the two developments?

19

The Italian
Renaissance

During the years 1350-1600, first in Italy and later in northern Europe, there was a change in man's attitude toward himself and toward the world, a change that parallels the economic and political changes of the time. Because an important aspect of this change of attitude was a rebirth of interest in the classical culture of the ancient Greeks and Romans, the entire period is called the "Renaissance," or "rebirth." But this rebirth was only one aspect of a vast movement. In the larger sense the period that we call the Renaissance was based upon a growing appreciation of life in this world, of art for its own sake, and of learning for the understanding it could give man about himself and his world.

One has only to compare the Gothic cathedral at Chartres (see page 141) with the Renaissance Basilica of Saint Peter at Rome to see the revolution in attitudes that the Renaissance created. Chartres is dominated by its tall forests of columns and arches, its upward-thrusting spires, and its flying buttresses. Its sculpture fits into the larger pattern of the building. Its glorious stained glass windows flood the interior with mellow colors that enhance the mood of worship and contemplation. The cathedral is the culmination of generations of patient advance from the simple stone churches of the early Middle Ages. It is the finest expression of the medieval dream of heaven.

The interior of the dome of the Basilica of St. Peter, Rome. Designed by Michelangelo, the dome is 138 feet across and rises more than 400 feet above the floor of the church.

Saint Peter's illustrates the curious Renaissance combination of religious piety and classical tradition. It is fronted by rows of classical pillars, and it is dominated by a huge dome modeled on the domes of ancient Rome. It is filled with sculptures that stand alone and with realistic paintings done with materials that were unknown when Chartres was built. It is brilliantly lit, so that these works of art are easy to see and appreciate. Saint Peter's luxury displays the power and wealth of the Renaissance popes who ordered it built and the creativity of the great artists whose best work it houses.

Chartres was the gift to God of the anonymous men of the Middle Ages. Saint Peter's was equally a gift to God, but it was the gift of individualistic men of the Renaissance who expressed at one and the same time their love of this world and their hope for the next.

🐚 THE RENAISSANCE MAN

During the twelfth and thirteenth centuries the men of the towns and cities of northern Italy had been freer than the burghers of northern Europe. One reason was that the Italian cities were not likely to be under the confining influence of nobles or kings. A second was that their control of trade between Europe and the East had not only made them prosperous but also had brought them into contact with the Byzantine Empire and Islam. A third reason was that they lived in what had been the heart of the old Roman Empire, and the classical traditions of the ancient world were stronger there than in other parts of Europe. Finally, because many of the Italian cities were communes, their people had more liberties and self-government than those in the north.

In this atmosphere, individualism—living one's life in one's own way—grew and finally blossomed in the "Renaissance man," who had many abilities and did his best to make good use of them all. One Renaissance man expressed the faith of most when he wrote:

> This is the culminating gift of God, this is the supreme and marvelous felicity of man . . . that he can be what he wishes to be. Animals, from the moment of their birth, carry with them from their mother's bodies all that they are destined to have or to be; the highest spirits [angels] are from the beginning what they will be forever. But God the Father endowed every man from birth with the seeds of every possibility and every life.

The history of the Renaissance is filled with examples of individuals who typify different aspects of Renaissance thought. One, Baldassare Castiglione (1478-1529), wrote *The Book of the Courtier,* the Renaissance gentleman's guide to proper behavior. "The gentlest gentleman of the Renaissance," Castiglione carried the virtues of chivalry over into the days of the Renaissance; his advice is good even today when he writes:

> . . . in all that he does or says, I would have our courtier follow certain general rules which, in my opinion, briefly comprise all I have to say. And the first and foremost among these is that he should avoid affectation above all else . . . Next, let him consider well what he does or says, the place where he does it, in whose presence, its timeliness, the reason for doing it, his own age, his profession, the end at which he aims, and the means by which he can reach it. . . .

Another Renaissance type was Giovanni Pico della Mirandola (1463-1494). Pico was a scholar who studied and admired the ancient Greeks,

Christ, Moses, and Muhammad and who attempted to reconcile the teachings of the three religions of the west, Christianity, Judaism, and Islam. He once challenged one and all to come to Rome to debate any of 900 different ideas, but called off the affair when some of the ideas were declared heretical by the pope. Pico was a noble, rich and brilliant, and a man of action, "tall and finely molded, with something of divinity in his face." He was only thirty-one when he died; had he lived longer, he might have become one of Italy's foremost philosophers.

A third Renaissance type was the "tyrant," the ruler of one of the Italian cities. The most famous of these was Lorenzo "the Magnificent" (1449-1492), a member of the Medici banking family (see page 257), who ruled Florence with the aid of an army of spies and a rubber-stamp council of devoted followers. Lorenzo was a cruel man who once ordered some enemies hanged from his palace windows. He lived a scandalous private life and occasionally flew into violent rages. But he was also a writer of elegant prose and graceful poetry, and he sponsored a school in which some of Italy's finest artists, writers, and churchmen studied the Greek classics. Although excommunicated by one pope, he persuaded another to make his fourteen-year-old son a cardinal. (The boy later became Pope Leo X.) As a contemporary remarked, "If Florence was to have a tyrant, she could never have a better or more pleasant one."

Castiglione, Pico, and Lorenzo the Magnificent were all men of many talents and achievements, but none compared with Leonardo da Vinci (1452-1519), sculptor, painter, engineer, and architect. Early in his career he had "taken all knowledge as his sphere," and no task seemed too difficult for him to attempt. As an engineer he built a canal in northern Italy and designed the fortifications of Milan. He was fascinated by the anatomy of the human body and drew diagrams to illustrate its proportions and muscular system. Some magnificent sculpture is attributed to him. Above all, he is remembered for his paintings, of which two, "The Last Supper" and "Mona Lisa," are considered to be among the supreme achievements of mankind.

Like so many Renaissance men, Leonardo was fascinated by the world he lived in. He studied geometry and applied its principles in his art as well as his engineering. He compiled notebooks of drawings showing in perfect detail everything that interested him. He designed a flying machine and a tank, and he once built the king of France a clockwork lion that roared and reared on its haunches to display the arms of France painted on its

Leonardo da Vinci: a self-portrait. Leonardo's attitude toward himself is revealed by this pencil sketch, which shows a proud man conscious of his own intelligence and power.

chest. He saw and studied and was influenced by everything in the world around him.

Courtier, philosopher, despot, artist—the "Renaissance man" was all of these. The common denominator was interest in the world in which he lived, personal ambition, a desire to attain perfection, and, above all, an individualistic desire to express himself in everything he did.

RENAISSANCE HUMANISM

The most important single influence on the Renaissance was the revived study of the classical writers of Greece and Rome, which is called "humanism."

HUMANIST ATTITUDES AND INTERESTS

First in Florence, and later everywhere in Italy and most of western Europe, eager scholars ransacked cathedral and monastery libraries in search of forgotten manuscripts. They imported others from Constantinople and the Levant and distributed copies to churchmen, princes, and wealthy merchants. One duke of a small Italian city employed almost forty copyists to transcribe hundreds of books by ancient authors.

The name "humanism" implies a new attitude toward man and his world. The classical authors were considered particularly "human," because they were more concerned with man's problems and possibilities on this earth than with the more remote issues of God and the nature of reality that had interested medieval philosophers. The humanists of the Renaissance devoted their lives to studying the "humanities which are to be found in Greek and Latin literature"; and they glorified the ancient world at the expense of the Middle Ages, which they looked upon as backward.

Consequently, students in Renaissance schools and universities read the ancient secular authors. Poets and writers wrote in the classical style and used classical Latin (as opposed to church or "vulgar" Latin). Architects turned from the medieval Gothic (their name for barbaric) style to design buildings in the manner of the Parthenon of ancient Athens and the Pantheon of ancient Rome. Artists painted the gods and heroes of classical myth.

Humanists dominated the Renaissance. Machiavelli (see page 239) wrote about sixteenth-century Italian problems—using classical forms and upholding the classical law of ancient Rome. The Medici in Florence founded a "Platonic Academy" to draw humanists to Florence. Churchmen filled Rome with churches and palaces in the classical style.

At the same time humanism contradicted many of the ideals of medieval theology, replacing the doctrines of self-denial and mysticism that had inspired Bernard of Clairvaux (see page 135) with a worldliness and self-indulgence. Humanists belittled medieval theology and assailed monasticism, raising doubts in the minds of many men about these two pillars of the medieval church. Some humanists even doubted the truth of Christianity itself; but most, for all their belief in the classics, continued to be devout Christians.

DANTE, PETRARCH, AND BOCCACCIO

The works of three great Italian authors of the thirteenth and fourteenth centuries illustrate the way in which humanistic ideas gradually replaced medieval traditions. Dante (Dante Alighieri, 1265-1321), a Florentine author and poet, wrote *The Divine Comedy*, a long poem that is an encyclopedia of late medieval ideas. Dante filled it with medieval symbolism, medieval people, and a typically medieval concern with the problems of the Trinity and of predestination. But he also discussed Homer, Hector, Plato, Socrates, and other classical figures. Written in beautiful Italian, the *Divine Comedy* helped set a standard of good language usage for later writers, and was copied by dozens of imitators. Critics agree that it is a unique master-piece and one of the great poems of all time.

Petrarch (Francesco Petrarca, 1304-1374) was perhaps the first "Renaissance man," for he loved life and was eagerly interested in everything around him. Petrarch was both a lyric poet and a humanist scholar. He wrote songs and poems in Italian dedicated to his distant idol, the beauteous Laura, and in so doing he perfected the verse form that bears his name ("Petrarchan sonnet"). He also burrowed deep into dusty libraries to uncover ancient manuscripts, and in Latin he wrote an epic poem on a Roman general and shorter biographies of other ancient worthies. He made a successful career as a courtier to princes and prelates; but his proudest moment was on Easter Sunday in 1341, when, dressed in royal robes, he was crowned poet laureate of Italy by the Senate of Rome.

His friend Giovanni Boccaccio (1313-1375) took the world as he found it. He, too, was an accomplished courtier and a writer of love poems (to a girl he called Fiammetta, "the little flame") and of treatises in Latin on mythology. But he is best remembered as the author of the *Decameron*, a series of stories based on old medieval *fabliaux* (see page 100), in which he criticizes many practices of the church and its clergy and wholeheartedly favors the pleasures of earthly love. He brought the *fabliaux* up to date and spiced them with classical learning. Boccaccio's stories embody Renaissance worldliness—with just a touch of Christian morality, which is equally typical of the Renaissance.

Dante, the humanist poet and medieval philosopher; Petrarch, the lover of life and classicist; and Boccaccio, the worldly moralist, were the three greatest writers of the Italian Renaissance. Their successors uncovered almost all the ancient works we know today and revived the knowledge of the Greeks, but they added few new ideas of their own.

🐌 RENAISSANCE ART

The fine arts of painting, sculpture, and architecture were the highest achievements of the Italian Renaissance. Like the humanists, Renaissance artists were inspired by classical examples and often chose their subjects from Greek and Roman myth and legend. They copied the ancient style and showed the same regard for accurate observation as the ancient Greek sculptors whose works they treasured.

Although the artists were interested in the world around them, their approach to it was artistic rather than scientific. That universal genius Leonardo tinkered with inventions ranging from a flying machine to a water pump, and he recorded in detail all manner of the physical characteristics of human beings. But unlike modern scientists, he rarely bothered to ask *why* things looked and acted as they did; if his observations seemed to contradict the classical theories of Aristotle, he assumed that he had made a mistake. Italian artists were interested in natural beauty, but they cared relatively little for scientific facts.

In the prosperous Italian towns, artists found wealthy patrons who supported their experiments with new subjects and (especially in painting) with new techniques. Most medieval painting had been done on wooden panels or as "frescoes" (pictures painted in watercolors on wet plaster walls.) By the sixteenth century, artists had mastered the art of "easel painting"—making detached pictures on canvas, wood, or similar material—and were using oil paints, which could be mixed into a wider variety of brighter colors than could water paints. They also developed the technique of shading from light to dark, called "chiaroscuro," which made it possible to create the appearance of depth in a painting (an effect that medieval artists had been unable to attain).

Nearly every city in northern Italy developed its own school of artists, who usually painted in distinctive styles that distinguished them from the schools of other cities. The greatest artists tended to congregate in three cities which were, in succession, the centers of the Italian Renaissance: Florence under the Medici during most of the fifteenth century; Rome under the "Renaissance Popes" late in the fifteenth and early in the sixteenth centuries; and rich, mercantile Venice in the middle of the sixteenth century.

THE FLORENTINE RENAISSANCE

Florence was the first center of Renaissance humanism and art. Dante, Petrarch, and Boccaccio were all Florentines by birth or adoption. So, too, was the painter Giotto (Giotto di Bondone, 1275?-1337), who, like his contemporary Dante, added the first touches of the Renaissance outlook to the ideas of the Middle Ages. As his Renaissance biographer noted, Giotto "freed himself from the rude manner of the Greeks [Byzantines], and brought back to life the true art of painting, introducing the drawing from nature of living things." He was as much concerned with his subjects as living human beings as he was with medieval symbolism. In his most famous work, a series of frescoes done for the Arena Chapel in Padua depicting scenes from the life of Jesus and Mary, he did not arrange his paintings in the formal patterns of the medieval style, but instead gave them real human (and occasionally even awkward) positions and emotions. He perfected a style that was so realistic that he once was able to paint a fly on the nose of a portrait done by another painter—who tried unsuccessfully to brush it off.

Early fifteenth-century Florentine artists continued the work that Giotto had begun. Two monks of the early fifteenth century painted brilliant religious works. Fra Angelico (1387-1455) painted unearthly and delicate angels that gave him his name, which means "Brother Angel"; and Fra Filippo Lippi (1406?-1469) was famed for his madonnas (depictions of the Virgin Mary) and nativities (paintings of the birth of Jesus). During his brief career, Masaccio (1401-1429) improved the technique of chiaroscuro and used it to picture the details of human anatomy accurately.

In 1434 Cosimo de Medici, father of Lorenzo the Magnificent, became the real ruler of Florence. Under him and his famous son, the arts of Florence prospered as never before. Cosimo made his personal library and the library of a local monastery into two of the finest collections of classical writings in the world. He founded the Platonic Academy, which introduced ancient Greek language and literature into Italy, and he attracted the best artists and writers of the age to Florence. Lorenzo continued his father's work. During the administrations of these two men (1434-1492), Florence enjoyed six decades of unparalleled cultural activity.

Unquestionably Leonardo da Vinci (above, page 264) was the greatest Florentine artist of the Medici era, but others approached his mastery of painting. Sandro Botticelli (1444-1510) was the finest of the "neo-paganists" or "neo-classicists," painters who looked to ancient Greece and Rome for their inspiration. Botticelli drew to a large extent from Greek myth for the subjects of his paintings. He bathed his pictures in a glow of delicate light which he imagined had been typical of Greece's "Golden Age" of antiquity. His "Birth of Venus," for example, shows the goddess of love rising on a shell from the sea, surrounded by other figures from Greek mythology. But for all his concern with mythology, Botticelli was a close observer of nature. In the "Birth of Venus," for example, the delicate flowers in the background are drawn so accurately that botanists can immediately identify their species.

The neo-classicism that affected Botticelli also influenced Florentine sculptors and architects. Florence's sculptors rivaled its painters. Lorenzo Ghiberti (1378-1455) spent twenty-two years working on two sculptured bronze doors for the baptistry of Florence's cathedral. These were so popular that he was commissioned to spend twenty-two more years finishing a matching pair. The twenty panels of the four doors are devoted to religious themes; but their realistic style is inherited from ancient Rome, and in their excellent use of perspective they are typical of the Renaissance. Donatello (1386?-1466) was even more realistic than Ghiberti: some of his statues are almost exact imitations of their subjects (a style called "naturalism"). Like Roman sculptors, Donatello depicted every anatomical feature of his subjects. Art critics today are likely to attack this carefully accurate depiction of reality, but few sculptors have ever rivaled the popularity of Ghiberti and Donatello.

Florentine architects derided medieval buildings and attempted to bring about a return to Greek and Roman styles. But without realizing their debt, they had learned about lightness of line and grace of proportion from medieval architects, with the result that "neo-classic" buildings of the Renaissance are not so heavy and stolid as the ancient buildings that they were modeled on. Giotto designed a tower for Florence's Gothic cathedral, and the architect Filippo Brunelleschi (1377?-1446) added a dome without destroying the harmony of the original building. In other buildings Brunelleschi used such Roman features as columns and round arches more gracefully than had the Romans. Florence is filled with buildings done in the Renaissance neo-classical style that Brunelleschi inspired.

The Florentine Renaissance ended soon after the death of Lorenzo the Magnificent in 1492. The people quarreled among themselves, and Florence's subject cities revolted. In desperation the Florentines turned to a leader of a new kind, a Dominican monk named Girolamo Savonarola. Savonarola asserted that Florence's troubles were caused by its Renaissance worldliness and called for a return to the somber piety of medieval times. He convinced the Florentines to burn their "luxuries" in huge bonfires and to attempt to wipe out sin with fire and sword.

But the Florentines would not stand such a leader for long. When Savonarola supported a French invasion of Italy and his government failed to pay its debts, they supported rival churchmen against him. Savonarola was imprisoned, tortured, and finally burned at the stake as a heretic. He had not been the first to object to Renaissance worldliness, nor would he be the last. He failed in his attempt to erase it in Florence—but he did drive away many of the finest artists and humanist scholars. Leadership of the Renaissance passed to Rome.

THE ROMAN RENAISSANCE

The Renaissance came late to Rome. Until about 1450 the popes' attention was taken up with the problems of the Babylonian Captivity and the Great Schism (see pages 212-213); and, for the most part, they were distrustful of humanism and of neo-classicism in art. But from about 1450 to 1527, a series of "Renaissance popes" enthusiastically adopted Renaissance ideas and did their best to restore Rome's ancient glories.

Renaissance neo-classical architecture was most fully developed in Rome, where the popes ordered medieval buildings razed to provide sites for magnificent new structures. Medieval cities had no parks or plazas, and their streets were narrow and crooked. But, inspired by a desire to attain a classical harmony in their buildings and cities, Renaissance Romans (and men in other cities too) built wide avenues and straight streets and opened large parks and plazas to display their new buildings. Their interest was not confined to churches and cathedrals; some of Rome's public buildings and palaces are among the best examples of Renaissance architecture.

Nicholas V (pope 1447-1455) was the first of the Renaissance popes. A humanist, he founded the Vatican Library to house his growing collection of classical manuscripts. He also drew up the first plans for a new Saint Peter's Basilica in Renaissance neo-classical style. His successors ordered additional buildings, including the Sistine Chapel, a private chapel that takes its name from the pope who ordered it built, Sixtus IV (pope 1471-1484).

From 1492 to 1521 three Renaissance popes brought the Roman Renaissance to its peak. The three popes were Alexander VI (pope 1492-1503), father of Cesare Borgia, the model for Machiavelli's *Prince;* Julius II (pope 1503-1513); and Leo X (pope 1513-1521), son of Lorenzo the Magnificent. They increased the papal income; they played important roles in Italian politics; and by supporting the finest artists of the time, they brought the center of artistic activity from Florence to Rome.

By far the greatest figure of the Roman Renaissance was Michelangelo Buonarotti (1475-1564). Michelangelo had as wide a variety of interests as did his fellow Florentine, Leonardo da Vinci. He was a painter, sculptor, engineer, poet, and student of physiology and anatomy. He served the

Medici in Florence before Julius II brought him in 1505 to Rome, where his first major task was to paint the ceiling of the Sistine Chapel. It took Michelangelo four years to cover the vaulted ceiling, nearly an acre in size, with frescoes depicting the creation of the world, the fall of man, the expulsion from Eden, and the flood. The series of huge paintings are surrounded by figures of the prophets of the Old Testament, figures from classical myth, cherubs, and angels. The ceiling of the Sistine Chapel is almost as much an encyclopedia of Renaissance culture as the Chartres Cathedral is of the culture of the Middle Ages. It combines classical and Christian elements, new techniques and old subjects, simplicity of form and strength of line to create an overpowering effect. Michelangelo was not merely a painter: his sculptures, such as the "Pieta" in Saint Peter's and figures made for the tomb of Julius II, are realistic yet dignified; he engineered the defense of Florence against an attack in 1529; and as an architect he designed the dome of Saint Peter's. (See page 262.)

The "divine" Raphael (Raffaello Santi, 1483-1520) was a painter and architect in the service of Julius II and Leo X best known for his harmoniously beautiful paintings. Like Michelangelo, Raphael combined classical and Christian elements in his art. For example, his "School of Athens," a fresco on one wall of an apartment he decorated for Julius II, shows Plato and Aristotle surrounded by numerous other figures of classical antiquity. On the opposite wall a similar fresco summarizes Christian theology. Raphael is most famous for his madonnas, sentimental paintings of the Virgin and Child against almost empty backgrounds.

The Roman Renaissance was on a larger scale than the Florentine. Roman buildings were grander and more elaborate, Roman paintings more colorful, and Roman statues more grandiose. But for all its spectacular achievements, the Roman Renaissance did not last long. The fall of the Medici in Florence weakened the balance-of-power system (see page 254), which had enabled the Italian cities to defend themselves against attacks from across the Alps. At the same time, the ambitions of the popes brought Rome into European power politics. The rulers of France, Spain, and the Holy Roman Empire cast envious eyes on wealthy Italy: it became a prize for which they competed, and a battleground for their armies. (See pages 240-241.) In 1527 soldiers of the Holy Roman Emperor Charles V seized Rome, looted its libraries, churches, and palaces, and stole or destroyed treasures worth an estimated $125,000,000. Rome never recovered. The center of the Renaissance in Italy passed to Venice.

Above, "God Creating Man": a detail of Michelangelo's Sistine Chapel frescoes. Right, the "Alba Madonna": a painting by Raphael. The gentle and serene quality of Raphael's work is in striking contrast to the majesty and vigor of Michelangelo.

THE VENETIAN RENAISSANCE

Venice's golden age reached its height after Rome's decline set in. A peaceful region in the midst of war-torn Italy, rich from the profits of its trade with the eastern Mediterranean and uniquely beautiful in its watery setting, Venice developed a school of art that flourished throughout the sixteenth century. Venetian artists learned the techniques of earlier Renaissance painters; but because of their city's trade with the east, they also came to know Byzantine art and were influenced by it. To a greater extent than other Italian painters, they used bright colors, chose exotic subjects, and emphasized the formal organization of their paintings.

Venetian painting originated with the brothers Gentile Bellini (1429?-1507) and Giovanni Bellini (1430?-1516). Gentile, who was briefly court painter to the Ottoman sultan in Constantinople, introduced oriental ideas into his paintings, which display the richness and pomp of Venetian life. Giovanni is best known as the teacher of two of the city's greatest artists, Giorgione and Titian. Giorgione (1478-1511) painted allegories with rural settings, using rich colors. Titian (1477-1576) was the most respected painter of his day. Among his hundreds of paintings are dramatic portraits of such patrons as the Holy Roman Emperor Charles V (see page 240); but he was at his best in magnificent allegorical paintings and in the religious paintings he did as an old man. No painter has ever surpassed his effective use of color.

Two later painters continued the Venetian tradition. Tintoretto (1518-1594), whose ideal in painting was to combine "the drawing of Michelangelo with the coloring of Titian," painted both religious and mythological subjects. Paolo Veronese (1525-1588) was a master of design and color, but he lacked the emotional depth of the other Venetian painters. His paintings are often cluttered with elaborate but trivial details. After Veronese, Venetian painting declined, offering little besides photographic realism or elaborate and stagy display pieces. It continued to be richly decorative and very popular, but it was no longer original or first rate.

        ⚜ ⚜ ⚜

Except in Venice, the Italian Renaissance did not long survive the sack of Rome by the soldiers of Charles V in 1527. Most of Italy fell into a period of decline that lasted three centuries. But the ideas of the Renaissance did not die; they were carried across the Alps, where men of other nationalities created what is called the "Northern Renaissance." Although it was in some ways different from the Italian Renaissance, the Northern Renaissance was an outgrowth of the accomplishments of the artists and humanist scholars of Renaissance Italy.

People, Places, and Terms

Baldassare Castiglione
Giovanni Pico della
  Mirandola
Lorenzo the Magni-
  ficent
Leonardo da Vinci
Dante
Petrarch
Giovanni Boccaccio
Giotto
Fra Angelico
Filippo Lippi
Masaccio
Sandro Botticelli
Lorenzo Ghiberti
Filippo Brunelleschi
Girolamo Savonarola
Nicholas V

Sixtus IV
Alexander VI
Cesare Borgia
Julius II
Leo X
Michelangelo
Raphael
Gentile Bellini
Giovanni Bellini
Giorgione
Titian
Tintoretto
Paolo Veronese

Renaissance
St. Peter's
individualism
Renaissance man

*The Book of the
  Courtier*
"The Last Supper"
"Mona Lisa"
humanism
Platonic Academy
The Divine Comedy
Petrarchan sonnet
The Decameron
easel painting
fresco
chiaroscuro
neo-paganism
neo-classicism
"The Birth of Venus"
Renaissance popes
Sistine Chapel
"The School of
  Athens"

Getting Organized

1. What was the Renaissance? What does its name mean? Is the name a good one? Why, or why not? What does a comparison of Chartres cathedral with the basilica of Saint Peter's tell us about the Renaissance?
2. Why were the Italian townsmen in the Middle Ages freer than their northern counterparts? What is meant by individualism? What role did it play in the Renaissance?
3. What was the ideal of the Renaissance man? How was each of the following a good representative of that type: Castiglione, Pico della Mirandola, Lorenzo the Magnificent, and Leonardo da Vinci?
4. What was humanism? How and why was it new? How were each of the following men humanists: Dante, Petrarch, and Boccaccio?
5. How and why did Italian painting, sculpture, and architecture enjoy such a golden age in the fifteenth and sixteenth centuries? Describe the characteristics of this new art.
6. Describe the Florentine Renaissance. Who were the principal artists of this city? What did each contribute to the Italian Renaissance? How and why did the Florentine Renaissance end?

7. Why did Rome lead the cultural Renaissance of early sixteenth-century Italy? What was the role of the popes in the Roman Renaissance? Who were the principal artists of Rome? What did each contribute to the Italian Renaissance?
8. How and why did the Venetian Renaissance differ from that of Rome and Florence? Who were its principal artists? What did each contribute to the Italian Renaissance? What happened to this aspect of the Renaissance?

Understanding the Big Picture

1. Why did the cultural aspect of the period called the Renaissance start in Italy rather than in the northern part of Europe? What conditions existed that helped this cultural boom to occur?
2. Define humanism. Show clearly how its interests differed from those of the medieval period, citing specific examples.
3. What were the usual subjects of the art works of the various painters, sculptors, and architects of the Italian Renaissance? How did they depict these subjects?
4. Which of the three great Italian cities enjoyed the greatest "Renaissance"? Compare and contrast the achievements of all three cities.

For the Thoughtful

1. What conditions seem to be necessary for a city or nation to enjoy a golden age of art and literature? To answer this question draw on your knowledge not only of Renaissance Italy but also of other "golden ages" and of twentieth-century America.
2. Compare the writings of the Italian humanists to the writings of the medieval writers that you have studied, such as Augustine, Abelard, and Aquinas. How do they differ? Why do they differ?
3. Do you think that art and literature reflect the atmosphere, opinions, politics, and economics of the times? Answer this question using examples from both Renaissance Italy and twentieth-century America.

Mastering the Map

Study the map of Italy in the Renaissance on page 252. Locate all of the major city-states of Italy. How did the strength of one of these city-states (for example, Florence) affect the prosperity and cultural achievement of another (for example, Rome)? What was the importance of the balance of power to the cultural achievements of the Renaissance? Demonstrate your point on the map.

20

the northern Renaissance

The ideas of the Italian Renaissance did not begin to take root north of the Alps until about 1500. In northern Europe, the Renaissance took a form different from what it had had in Italy. Northern humanists, more influenced by the heritage of the medieval church than were the Italians, were more inclined to adapt Renaissance modes of thought to Catholic teachings. Northern painters, too, were more influenced by medieval traditions and less by Greek and Roman examples. And in the northern Renaissance the most brilliant achievements were those of writers rather than, as in Italy, those of painters and sculptors.

THE INVENTION OF PRINTING

The Italian Renaissance had been the achievement of a tiny percentage of the people. In the north, by contrast, a far greater percentage of the people were affected by the new modes of thought. The main cause was the development of printing, which brought the price of books within the reach of the middle classes.

MOVABLE TYPE AND PAPER

The technique of printing from a carved wooden block had been known in Europe before the fifteenth century. But carving many pages of words onto wooden blocks would have required so much time and effort that no one thought of making books in this way; printing was used mostly to reproduce illustrations. The rapid development of printing, which began about 1450, was based on the invention of movable type. It is not certain just where or when the idea of using small individual blocks for individual letters originated; but this "movable type" was being used in the Netherlands and in the Rhine valley of Germany by 1450. Credit for its invention is often given to Johann Gutenberg (1400?-?1468), a printer of the city of Mainz, who used it in an edition of the Bible published in 1456. He may or may not have been the first to use the invention. In any case, the idea spread rapidly; by 1500 there were some 200 presses in operation in Europe.

The development of printing was closely related to an increase in the use of paper. During the Middle Ages, all writing had been done on either papyrus or parchment, both of which were expensive. Paper, as we know it, was first made in China in the second century. The Muslims learned how to make it in the eighth century, and they were exporting it to England and France before 1300. The demand for it was slight until fifteenth-century printers discovered that it served their purposes as well as parchment and was far less expensive. Techniques of manufacturing paper were then introduced to Europe, and its use spread rapidly, making it possible to print books at comparatively low cost.

EARLY PRINTERS AND THEIR BOOKS

Although those wealthy enough to own handwritten books looked on printed books with scorn, they were rapidly accepted by scholars, churchmen, and members of the middle class. Johann Froben of Basel set up a press on which he printed an edition of the New Testament in Greek and the works of his friend Erasmus, the most famous of northern humanists. In Italy the greatest of all the presses was established by the scholar Aldus Manutius in Venice. His "Aldine Press" manufactured thousands of copies of the Greek and Latin classics with accurate texts, beautiful use of type, and fine bindings. They were sold throughout Europe for the equivalent of two or three dollars in modern money.

The printers developed a number of new type "faces" (designs). At first most printers used heavy letters based on medieval styles of handwriting. Later a Frenchman named Nicolas Jenson developed the first of the "roman" type faces, so called because it was copied from the letters carved on ancient Roman monuments. Still later Aldus Manutius introduced the first of the even lighter type faces called "italic."

The influence of printing is hard to overestimate. A medieval copyist could produce only two books a year; Froben, by contrast, printed an edition of 24,000 copies of a book by Erasmus. Books were available for the first time to a large audience of scholars, priests, and merchants, and the demand for them rose apace. Printed books had fewer errors than those that were hand copied, and they were more easily read, so that scholarship improved. Finally, political pamphlets stimulated interest in government, and printed Bibles led some men to read and interpret the Scriptures in their own ways. Widespread knowledge about politics and religion led to unrest and cries for reform. Modern history would be far different if there were no printing.

🕮 CHRISTIAN HUMANISM

Like the Italian humanists, the northern European humanists of the sixteenth century had immense faith in the potential worth of the human being. They established schools, taught in universities, and attempted to spread knowledge in every other way they could. Like the Italians, they agreed that the ideas of the classical writers, the fathers of the church, and the Bible did not necessarily conflict with each other. But the northern humanists differed from the Italians in important ways. The northerners were not so carried away with the glories of antiquity, and they were less likely to separate classical from Christian teaching. The northern humanists were first of all concerned with applying the ideas of the Renaissance to the study of religion and the modernization of Catholic doctrine and practices. Because religion was as important to them as the classics, these northern philosophers are called "Christian humanists."

ERASMUS OF ROTTERDAM

The greatest of the Christian humanists was Desiderius Erasmus (1466?-1536). An international figure, he lived at various times in his native Netherlands and in France, Germany, Italy, England, and Switzerland. He corresponded with Pope Leo X and the Protestant leader Martin Luther, the Holy Roman emperor and the kings of France and England. Froben of

Sir Thomas More: portrait by Hans Holbein, the Younger. More, the greatest of the English humanist writers, was also a brilliant and versatile lawyer and, for a time, a leading English statesman. A man of powerful and complex personality, he was noted in his day for his great warmth and charm. A contemporary described him as "a man of an angel's wit and singular learning; and as time requireth, a man of marvelous mirth and pastimes, and sometime of as sad gravity, as men say, a man for all seasons."

Basel published his books and Aldus of Venice asked his advice. No scholar was ever more famous in his lifetime, and yet Erasmus died despised by many of the men he had influenced most strongly because he continued to abide by his humanistic principles.

Erasmus studied at the University of Paris, where he developed a strong dislike of the attitudes and methods of his professors. It seemed to him that they emphasized less important aspects of the Christian faith at the expense of the truly important ones. In his words:

> . . . You worship the saints, you like to touch their relics; do you want to earn Peter and Paul? Then copy the faith of the one and the charity of the other and you will have done more than if you had walked to Rome ten times.

In the humanist tradition, Erasmus believed that the best way to challenge this kind of thinking was to make the Bible and the best of the classical writings available to as many people as possible. In 1516 he published his own edition of the New Testament, writing in the preface "I wish that all women might read the Gospel and the Epistles of Paul. I wish that they might be translated into all tongues of all people, so that not only the Scots and the Irish, but also the Turk and the Saracen might read and understand."

Desiderius Erasmus of Rotterdam: portrait by Hans Holbein, the Younger. Erasmus dedicated his life to Christian scholarship. In his words, "It was not for empty fame or childish pleasure that in my youth I grasped at the polite literature of the ancients, and by late hours gained some slight mastery of Greek and Latin. It has long been my cherished wish to cleanse the Lord's temples of barbarous ignorance, and to adorn it with treasures brought from afar, such as may kindle in generous hearts a warm love for the Scriptures."

Erasmus published the book for which he is best known, *In Praise of Folly*, in 1511. It is a gentle, humorous attack that points out the major problems of the Catholic Church at that time—too much formality, too much quibbling about minor theological points, too much luxury and pomposity, and too much corruption in high places and low.

Unfortunately the opening decades of the sixteenth century marked the end of the time when such gentle criticism of the church was effective. In 1517 Martin Luther began open criticism of the church in Germany, which led to a struggle that divided Europe into bitterly opposing religious parties. (Chapter 21.) Erasmus, the advocate of calm reason and compromise, refused to accept either the belief of some men that the Catholic Church must be overthrown or the belief of others that it must be maintained without change. Both extremist groups attacked this moderate humanist reformer. Saddened and distressed, he wrote,

> My reason tells me to take my way along a quieter and less dangerous road. I cannot help it if I hate discord and division, while loving peace and mutual understanding, for I have long realized how dark and complicated are human affairs . . . My one wish is that all of us should unite to bring about the victory of the Christian cause and the triumph of the peace which is spoken of

281

in the Gospels, to bring this about without violence and by means of truth and reasonableness, so that in the end we should understand one another perfectly, both as to priestly dignity and the freedom of the people whom our Lord Jesus Christ desired to set free.

But the times were not ripe for truth and reasonableness. Extremists won control of both sides in the struggle over religion, and humanism had no attraction for them.

THE LESSER HUMANISTS

Christian humanism was an international movement. In Spain, Francisco Cardinal Jiménez (1437-1517) established a university at Alcala where future bishops studied Greek, Latin, and Hebrew as well as the traditional medieval subjects. In France, Jacques Lefèvre d'Étaples (1450?-?1537) taught his students at the University of Paris directly from the Bible rather than from medieval commentaries, saying "We must affirm nothing of God but what the Scriptures tell us about Him."

England was a center of humanistic thought. There John Colet (1467?-1519) taught Oxford students directly from the Bible and later, as dean of St. Paul's Cathedral in London, founded a school to teach boys humanistic learning and personal piety. Among his followers was Sir Thomas More (1478-1535), an adviser to King Henry VIII and friend of Erasmus, who outlined a humanistic idea of the ideal society in a book he entitled *Utopia*. Like Erasmus, he gently but wittily criticized the evils of his age, proposing a state in which all inequalities were abolished, towns kept clean, manual labor restricted to six hours a day, and education made available to everyone. When Henry VIII separated the Church of England from the papacy (Chapter 21), More remained a faithful Catholic and was executed, a martyr to his faith.

In Germany, humanists led a movement to reform the Catholic Church. Johann Reuchlin (1455-1522), who had been criticized for teaching directly from the Bible like Lefèvre and Colet, defended himself by publishing statements of support from prominent humanists under the title *Letters of Eminent Men*. In 1515 another volume appeared, apparently in opposition to the first, entitled *Letters of Obscure Men*. Opponents of Reuchlin at first assumed that the second book was a statement of the case against the humanists. To their dismay, they soon learned that it had been written by a group of humanists and was a merciless parody of their opponents' arguments. Thousands read it, guffawed, and never took the opponents of the humanists seriously again.

Most of the Christian humanists of northern Europe were priests who devoted their lives to their church. They criticized it lovingly, and merely attempted to modernize and reform it according to humanistic principles. But their books and pamphlets were widely distributed, and they focused attention on the weaknesses of their church more than they emphasized its strengths. As a result, they unintentionally contributed to the growth of the Protestant Reformation that Martin Luther touched off in 1517. Most of the humanists opposed Luther; but there is much truth to the quip that "Erasmus laid the egg that Luther hatched."

✿ THE FINE ARTS IN THE NORTH

Northern art, like northern humanism, differed from that of Italy. Northern artists were more influenced by the traditions of medieval art than were the Italians; but they adopted the Italian interest in depicting the world realistically and accurately. Some of them used techniques that the Italians looked down on—engraving, for example, which they used in book illustrations that won them a wide audience of people who rarely saw oil paintings.

FLEMISH PAINTING

There was an era of unique artistic achievement in Flanders before the Northern Renaissance began. In the prosperous cities such as Antwerp and Bruges, artists developed a style that, while basically medieval in some ways, placed new emphasis on realistic figures, minute details, and bright colors. A famous example of this school of art is the Ghent Altarpiece, completed early in the fifteenth century by the brothers Hubert and Jan Van Eyck (1366?-1426 and 1370?-1440). Closed, the altarpiece shows pictures of the donors and a monochrome (one-color painting) of the Annunciation. Opened, there is a picture, brilliant, colorful, symbolic, of the redemption of man. It is filled with tiny people, angels, animals, and flowers, all painted with the closest attention to detail and finished to enamel-like gloss and smoothness.

Later Flemish artists were somewhat influenced by the Italians. Hieronymus Bosch (1450?-1516) used Italian techniques to paint a series of

"St. Jerome in His Study": an engraving by Albrecht Dürer. The great scholar is shown in a quiet, sun-filled sixteenth-century room—the kind of surroundings dear to the scholarly Christian humanists. The lion is a symbol traditionally associated with St. Jerome.

medieval fantasies, presenting unreal horrors in realistic detail. In the sixteenth century Pieter Brueghel the Elder (1528?-1569) displayed a preference for everyday subjects, painting figure-filled scenes of Flemish villages and peasant feasts and dances.

GERMAN PAINTING

For a brief half-century, from about 1500 to 1550, German painting reached a peak of originality and creativity.

Three German artists towered above the others and created the finest art of the northern Renaissance. The eldest of these was Albrecht Dürer (1471-1528), a friend of Erasmus and a follower of Martin Luther, sometimes called the "Leonardo of Germany." He filled his sketchbooks with drawings of people, animals, plants, and designs, and in his later years he worked at establishing laws of perspective and human proportion. He was popular and successful as a painter, but he is now best remembered as an engraver and wood cutter. Many of his engravings, such as "Saint

Jerome in his Study," are filled with peace and quiet. His woodcuts, on the other hand, often depict scenes of violent activity, which he suggests by means of bold lines and sharp angles.

Lucas Cranach (1472-1553), a contemporary of Dürer, worked in a far different style. Cranach, like the Italians, took delight in portraying nudes and classical scenes. But, unlike the Italians, he preferred to paint small and realistic canvases that are most notable for their delicate charm.

The youngest of the three Germans, Hans Holbein the Younger (1497?-1543), whose father of the same name was also a well-known painter, was forced to leave Germany because of difficulties in his native Augsburg during the Reformation. With a letter of introduction from Erasmus, he went to England, where Sir Thomas More helped him win an appointment as court painter to King Henry VIII. He painted dozens of brilliant portraits of members of the English court, bringing out their personalities by his ability to select effective poses and to use a minimum of distracting background. His famous portraits of More and Erasmus (see pages 280-281) express the personalities of the two great humanists better than any words or photographs possibly could.

🐚 THE GROWTH OF NATIONAL LITERATURES

In northern Europe, Renaissance enthusiasm for life was best expressed in literature. What Michelangelo was to Italy, Shakespeare was to England.

Most of the Christian humanists wrote in Latin, the language of learning and the church. But other writers used the vernacular (everyday) languages, with the result that new literary styles developed in several countries and their languages developed into their modern forms. Hundreds of books of poetry and on such subjects as religion, history, and politics were written in the vernacular languages, printed on the new presses, and widely read by men who were more at home in their native tongues than in Latin. In France the speech of the region near Paris came to be accepted as the standard language; in Germany, the High Middle German of the medieval troubadours; and in England, the speech of London that was used by the poet Chaucer. Generations of writers shaped and polished these tongues and created national literary traditions.

The two greatest writers of sixteenth-century France were François Rabelais and Michel de Montaigne. Rabelais (1494?-1553), a one-time monk, recounted the story of two giants in mock-heroic terms in two books called *Pantagruel* and *Gargantua*. In the process he made fun of almost everything that the men of his time held most dear. His writing was earthy at times, and as a result the adjective "Rabelaisian" has come to mean coarse humor and satire. By contrast, the style of Montaigne (1533-1592) was highly polished. His essays, masterpieces of French prose style, range widely over many subjects but usually emphasize the importance of the individual.

The Renaissance had a greater impact on literature in England than anywhere else. As early as the fourteenth century, Geoffrey Chaucer (1340?-1400), an official of King Richard II, traveled on royal service to Italy in the time of Petrarch and Boccaccio and became familiar with Italian literature. Returning home, he wrote *The Canterbury Tales* in English, combining medieval *fabliaux* with a Renaissance individualism and sense of style.

English literature bloomed in the sixteenth century. Humanists like Sir Thomas More wrote in English as well as Latin. Thomas Cranmer's *Book of Common Prayer*, prepared for the Church of England in 1549, enabled Englishmen to worship in their native tongue. Toward the end of the century one of England's greatest poets, Edmund Spenser (1552?-1599) wrote his *Faerie Queene*, an allegory glorifying Queen Elizabeth I.

In the last years of the century England bloomed with playwrights and poets, notably Thomas Kyd (1557?-?1595), Christopher Marlowe (1564-1593), and Ben Jonson (1573?-1637). But one stands out above them all. William Shakespeare (1564-1616) left his little town of Stratford-on-Avon to go to London, where he wrote the plays, songs, and sonnets that, among other things, captured the spirit of England in the reign of Queen Elizabeth I. Some plays were based on classical subjects, some on medieval history, some on mythology. Some were tragedies, some were comedies. All were filled with unforgettable characters into whose mouths Shakespeare put some of the finest poetry ever written. Shakespeare drew upon his knowledge of all the world, but as much as anything else he was an Englishman who was proud of his country and devoted to his queen. Has there ever been a more effective appeal to love of country than these lines describing England from *Richard II?*

> This royal throne of kings, this sceptered isle,
> This earth of majesty, this seat of Mars,
> This other Eden, demi-paradise,
> This fortune built by nature for herself

> Against infection and the hand of war,
> This happy breed of men, this little world,
> This precious stone set in a silver sea . . .
> This blessed plot, this earth, this realm, this England.

No Italian, Frenchman, German—artist, writer, humanist, scholar, poet, prince, or prelate—better expressed the full range of the Renaissance than Shakespeare. He combined a love of the world and of nature, a joy in beauty, an affection for the classics, a pleasure of new discovery, a deep religious feeling, a joy in human life, and a faith in mankind that have never been equaled.

⚜ SCIENCE DURING THE RENAISSANCE

The origins of modern science can be traced to the Middle Ages. Medieval philosophers established traditions of careful scholarship, and such men as Roger Bacon (1214?-1294) advocated "experimental" science. The half-science of alchemy (which attempted to turn base metals into gold) and Arab ideas in mathematics also contributed to a growing knowledge of the world.

During the Renaissance, such new inventions as the compass, gunpowder, and printing were eagerly adopted. But the attitude of the humanists was basically not at all scientific. While they believed in carefully studying the world around them, they also revered the classical authors and accepted as final truth the ancients' ideas about the nature of the world. Leonardo da Vinci's attitude was typical of the Renaissance: he studied the human body carefully, but he was more interested in its beauty than in its actual workings.

Most medieval and Renaissance astronomers were really astrologers who were paid to cast horoscopes predicting the future. Astronomy thus fortified superstition, and astronomers made no serious effort to determine the real nature of the universe by studying the skies. Instead, they accepted the belief of Ptolemy, an Egyptian astronomer of the second century A.D., that the universe was geocentric (earth-centered). According to his belief, the earth stood still while the rest of the universe—sun, moon, stars, planets— revolved around it. This explanation seemed to agree with the account of the creation in the Bible and with the Renaissance desire for balanced and orderly explanations of everything.

Nicolaus Copernicus (1473-1543), a Polish priest who had studied. in Italy, was the first to seriously challenge Ptolemy's beliefs. His book *On the Revolution of Heavenly Bodies* was published shortly before his death in 1543. In it, Copernicus maintained that the universe is heliocentric (sun-centered), not geocentric. According to his theory, the earth is just another planet; and, like the other planets, it revolves around the sun. This idea directly contradicted the Biblical account of the Creation. It also hurt the pride of Renaissance humanists, for Copernicus's system made the earth seem less important than it had been in Ptolemy's. Moreover, it seemed to contradict common sense, for to the humanists it seemed obvious that they remained in one place while the sun, moon, stars, and planets circled around them. Copernicus's theory therefore won few adherents for a century and a half.

♢ ♢ ♢

Copernicus's theory was one of many sixteenth-century attacks on a system of beliefs that had gone unchallenged for centuries. At the same time another attack, one that had far greater immediate effect, was being led by religious reformers. The resulting "Protestant Reformation," which was at once a result of the Renaissance and a cause of its decline, plunged Europe into a series of bitter religious wars that lasted more than a century.

People, Places, and Terms

Johann Gutenberg	Lucas Cranach	Christian humanism
Johann Froben	Hans Holbein	*In Praise of Folly*
Nicolas Jenson	François Rabelais	*Utopia*
Desiderius Erasmus	Michel de Montaigne	*Letters of*
Francisco Jiménez	Geoffrey Chaucer	*Eminent Men*
Jacques Lefèvre	Thomas Cranmer	*Letters of*
d'Étaples	Edmund Spenser	*Obscure Men*
John Colet	Thomas Kyd	Ghent Altarpiece
Sir Thomas More	Christopher Marlowe	vernacular
Johann Reuchlin	Ben Jonson	*Gargantua*
Hubert and	William Shakespeare	*On the Revolution*
Jan van Eyck	Nicolaus Copernicus	*of Heavenly*
Hieronymus Bosch		*Bodies*
Pieter Brueghel	movable type	geocentric
Albrecht Dürer	Aldine Press	heliocentric

Getting Organized

1. In what general ways did the Northern Renaissance differ from the Italian?
2. Who were the most important figures in the development of printing? What did each contribute? What was the importance of printing?
3. What is a Christian humanist? In what ways were they similar to the Italian humanists? In what ways different? What were the aims and accomplishments of Erasmus? Name the other important Christian humanists and the achievements of each.
4. How and why did northern art differ from Italian art? Who were the principal Flemish painters? With what subjects did each deal? Who were the principal German painters? With what subjects did each deal?
5. What is vernacular language? Who were two important French writers of the sixteenth century? Who were the most important of the sixteenth-century English writers? What did Shakespeare write? Why is he unique?
6. What was the attitude of the humanists toward science? What revolutionary theory did Copernicus put forward? What effect did it have at the time? Why?

Understanding the Big Picture

1. Citing specific examples, show how Christian humanism differed from the approaches and outlook of the Middle Ages.
2. What were the usual subjects of the paintings of the northern artists? How did northern art differ from Italian art? Why?
3. Compare and contrast the achievements and contributions of Erasmus and Shakespeare. In what way are they both part of the same intellectual movement?

For the Thoughtful

1. Compare the northern and Italian Renaissances in the following areas: the reasons for the start of the two movements, their literary accomplishments, their art works, their attitudes toward religion, their concern for science and for scientific detail, and the duration of the two movements.
2. What do the works of the sixteenth-century northern artists and writers reveal about the politics, society, and religion of northern Europe in the sixteenth century? Be specific.
3. How do the accomplishments of the northern Renaissance compare with those of other eras? Compare its achievements in particular to those of the Italian Renaissance.

21
The Protestant
Reformation

The history of the Middle Ages and the Renaissance, hopefully, is interesting and valuable because it provides meaningful insights into the past and because it helps explain why men act as they do. Events of the sixteenth century, however, strike even closer to home: this was the time when the Catholic and Protestant churches separated. Most Americans today are members of one of the churches and are deeply concerned about the relationships of one church with another and of all with the government. For this reason, it is especially difficult to study the sixteenth century coolly and objectively.

It is even difficult to arrive at a name for the era. Protestants call it the "Age of the Reformation," because it was a time when the church was "reformed" to be more like that of the early Christians. Catholics call it the "Age of the Protestant Revolt," because some men revolted against much of the great body of doctrine and tradition that had been built up over centuries.

It is also difficult to try to determine just why the leaders of that time acted as they did. For example, did Henry VIII of England break with the papacy because he had fallen in love with the beautiful Anne Boleyn? Because he sincerely disagreed with Catholic doctrine about the powers of the pope? Because he wanted a son to succeed him and the pope refused to annul his marriage to a woman who could not give him one? Or for a combination of these reasons? And were the Jesuits, who headed the Catholic "Counter-Reformation," bloodthirsty and power hungry zealots, as some believed? Or were they idealists attempting to preserve their ancient faith by the best means they knew?

In this chapter we will use the terms "Protestant Reformation" and "Age of the Reformation" simply because they are the ones used by most American historians—at the same time recognizing the fact that a desire for reform led to revolt. We will also assume, probably correctly, that both Catholic and Protestant leaders were honest men doing the best they could. Some may have been mistaken, or even foolish; but, for the most part, their motives were above reproach.

The Age of the Reformation had two phases. In the first, roughly the first half of the sixteenth century, men such as Luther, Zwingli, and Calvin attracted many followers to their newly organized churches, while the Catholics reformed and reorganized their church under such men as Loyola and Pope Paul III. In the second phase, the middle of the sixteenth to the middle of the seventeenth centuries, there were bitter struggles among the religious groups to dominate Europe. This chapter will survey the origins and first phase of the Protestant Reformation; the next will outline the Catholic Reformation and the century of religious wars that constitutes the Reformation's second phase.

⚜ THE BACKGROUND OF THE REFORMATION

People grew dissatisfied with the teachings and practices of the Catholic Church in the fifteenth century for many reasons. Some were religious, some were political, and others grew out of social and economic unrest.

CAUSES OF RELIGIOUS UNREST

After the Conciliar Movement (see page 213) had ended, a series of strong Renaissance popes reasserted the supremacy of the papacy over churchmen in all parts of Europe. Early in the sixteenth century the assembled Catholic prelates in the Fifth Lateran Council formally reaffirmed the bull *Unam sanctam* of 1302 (see page 129), which declared the pope supreme in church and state.

But at the same time the personal policies of the Renaissance popes were creating much dissatisfaction. Some had been grossly immoral, and most resorted to long-forgotten taxes and to the "sale" of indulgences to pay the costs of the Roman Renaissance. Indulgences were a remission (forgiveness) by the church of punishment for sin. Originally they had been granted to men who went on crusade. Later they were extended to those who helped pay for the crusades, and later still to those who contributed to other religious causes. Early in the sixteenth century Pope Leo X was granting indulgences to those who made contributions for the building of the Basilica of St. Peter in Rome. (See page 271.) Many devout Catholics opposed the granting of indulgences in this way. They felt that such a policy, by encouraging people to believe they could purchase forgiveness of their sins (and of the sins of dead relatives), was leading to a decline in moral standards and a separation of faith and morals.

Other clergymen also aroused resentment. Bishops and abbots often acted more like noblemen than like servants of God, and uneducated or lazy priests and monks often did not fulfill their religious duties.

Popular religious movements, too, led to criticism of Catholic practices and teachings. Wycliffe in England, Huss in Bohemia, and Eckhart in Germany (see pages 214-215) taught thousands that the road to salvation lay, not in formal worship, reading, and study, but in personal, humble obedience to God. In an age when men were filled with fear—of the Turks advancing from the east, plagues and famines, wars and disease—religious groups promising salvation to their followers sprang up all across Europe. Humanists like Erasmus also criticized the church in books like *In Praise of Folly* and taught men to believe in the importance of personal reading and interpretation of the Scriptures. (See pages 280-281.)

CAUSES OF POLITICAL AND ECONOMIC UNREST

Monarchs of the growing national states also were often opposed to the popes. To them, the pope often appeared to be an Italian ruler who was trying to tax their subjects and to influence not only their religious but also their political practices. In a series of concordats, kings forced popes to surrender some of their authority over the bishops, and they frequently schemed to seize property of the church. Townsmen supported the kings and opposed any alliance between the bishops and the hated nobles. In Germany even the lesser nobility, the "knightly class," opposed alliances between the church and the greater princes.

Kings and townsmen were unhappy with the church's efforts to enforce medieval restrictions on business, such as the ban on usury (see page 250), when the churchmen were often worldly themselves. They envied the profits of church estates; and, as shrewd businessmen, they did not feel that they were getting their money's worth for their contributions when so much of the money was being used to pay for the Roman Renaissance.

Therefore, early in the sixteenth century large numbers of people demanded religious reform. When this had happened before, the church had responded in time to prevent open revolt on a large scale and to maintain the unity of the Commonwealth of Christendom. This time the church reformed too late; for when the reforming monk Martin Luther nailed his "Ninety-five Theses" on the door of a church in Wittenberg on October 31, 1517, he unintentionally signed the death warrant of the Commonwealth of Christendom and unwittingly created a new "Protestant" church. That day the Age of the Reformation began.

⚜ MARTIN LUTHER AND LUTHERANISM

At first Martin Luther (1486-1546) seemed to be just one of a long line of German religious reformers. But he was such a strong personality, and his beliefs won so many followers, that Germany soon became divided into two bitterly opposing religious camps. Lutheranism was the first of the major Protestant faiths, and one of the strongest.

MARTIN LUTHER AND THE NINETY-FIVE THESES

Many portraits of Martin Luther survive. They show a man with heavy features and a stubborn expression. But beneath the slanting forehead and the beetling brows are a pair of small but piercing eyes—the eyes of a man driven by great ideas and willing to fight for them, whatever the consequences may be.

Luther was a native of central Germany. He attended a university whose professors, unaffected by the Italian humanists, taught that only God could save a man or condemn him, but that each individual had the *possibility* of preparing the way for his own salvation. Made aware of the power of God when he was almost killed by a lightning bolt, young Luther became an Augustinian monk, hoping that this would assure him entry into heaven. But he was distressed by other monks' lack of faith and

Martin Luther, the inaugurator of the Protestant Reformation, as he appeared about 1530: portrait by Lucas Cranach, the Elder. (See page 285.) Although there had been many reform movements, sects, and heresies before Luther, it was he who made the first real break in the unity of Catholic Christendom. Luther also is an important figure in the histories of music and of German literature. This is one of several portraits of him by Cranach, who was his supporter, banker, and close friend.

by the worldliness of the papal court in Rome, which he visited briefly. He became a professor at the University of Wittenberg, where he was popular and successful; but he was secretly gnawed by doubts of his worth as a person, and he feared that he was a miserable sinner who was unable to do anything that would please his God. In 1515 he was lecturing on Saint Paul and pondering the apparent conflict between God's mercy and His wrath when, one day, he found the answer he sought:

> Night and day [Luther later wrote], I pondered until I saw the connection between the justice of God and the statement, "The righteous shall live by his faith." Then I grasped that the justice of God is that righteousness by which through grace and sheer mercy God justifies us through faith. Thereupon I felt myself to have been reborn and to have gone through the open doors into Paradise.

In these words Luther declared that having faith in God was the only road to salvation. And man can only hope to attain faith in God, he believed, by reading the Scriptures and by trying to live a humble, reverent, and moral life as best he can.

This doctrine struck at the heart of the Catholic concept that *both* faith and good works are roads to heaven. It also was at odds with the idea of indulgences. By 1515 indulgences had become a controversial issue. The archbishop of Mainz, who had promised 24,000 ducats to Pope Leo X to be used for the building of Saint Peter's, had been authorized by the pope to issue indulgences to raise the money. Monks traveled from town to town collecting contributions for indulgences. Luther's ruler, Duke Frederick III "the Wise" of Saxony, forbade the sale of indulgences in his territory. But Luther's students often traveled to nearby Magdeburg to get them from a monk named Johann Tetzel, who promised that "so soon as coin in coffer rings, the soul from purgatory springs."

Convinced that indulgences were a poor substitute for faith, Luther on that fateful October 31, 1517, posted on the Wittenberg church door his "Ninety-five Theses" (propositions to be publicly argued), which included these controversial beliefs:

1. Our Lord and Master Jesus Christ . . . meant the whole life of the faithful to be an act of penitence.
6. The pope has no power to remit any guilt, except by declaring and confirming that it has been remitted by God.
21. Therefore those preachers of indulgences are in error who allege that through the indulgences of the pope a man can be freed from every penalty.
37. Every true Christian, living or dead, partakes of all the benefits of Christ and the Church, which are the gift of God, even without letters of pardon . . .
95. And so trust to enter heaven rather through many tribulations than through the false confidence of peace.

"He has touched the crown of the pope and the stomachs of the monks," Erasmus quipped, sending a copy of the Theses to friends in England. The response was tremendous; sales of indulgences fell off, and monks appealed to Pope Leo to keep Luther quiet. Leo, thinking the affair to be just another dispute among monks, did nothing. The Theses were printed and distributed all over western Europe. After two years, Luther was called to account. In 1519 he was forced by a papal representative to publicly question the authority of the pope and of church councils and to admit that he agreed with some of the heretical beliefs of Huss and Wycliffe. In the course of his efforts to defend himself, Luther came to the unshakeable conclusion that salvation was by faith alone and that it could not be won by the "works" (including sacraments) required by the Catholic Church. He finally declared that every man can interpret the Bible for himself.

The reformer had become a heretic, and in 1520 he was excommunicated. Luther publicly burned the document that announced his excommunication;

he was no longer a Catholic but a Lutheran. In the next years he spelled out his beliefs in detail. He insisted that there were only two meaningful sacraments, baptism and the Lord's Supper (a simplified form of the Mass), because only these two could be directly traced to the Bible. He held that rulers had religious as well as political responsibilities. And he re-emphasized his doctrine of salvation by faith alone, telling his followers to live as much like Christ as possible.

Pope Leo, suddenly aware of the seriousness of Luther's challenge, instructed the young Holy Roman Emperor Charles V to do something about Luther. Luther accordingly was brought to trial before the Diet of the Holy Roman Empire, which met at Worms in 1521. At the Diet of Worms, Luther's accusers asked him to recant his beliefs. He replied:

> Unless I am convicted by Scripture and plain reason—I do not accept the authority of popes and councils, for they have contradicted each other—my conscience is captive to the Word of God. I cannot and I will not recant anything, for to go against conscience is neither right nor safe. Here I stand. I cannot do otherwise. God help me. Amen.

The Diet responded by declaring Luther an outlaw and forbidding him to publish his writings or publicly defend his principles. The issue was clearly drawn.

THE SPREAD OF LUTHERANISM

Luther was soon the most famous man in Germany. Many churchmen were impressed by his theological insistence on faith, and many laymen were horrified by his descriptions of the decadence of the clergy. As Germans, they responded to his argument that the Catholic Church was dominated by Italians who sought to control and tax the German people. Rulers approved Luther's belief that they had religious authority, and some of them supported Lutheranism because they believed it would enable them to seize church property. Peasants were eager to cease paying tithes.

Led by the Holy Roman Emperor Charles V, Luther's opponents closed ranks. Charles saw Lutheranism as a threat to his control of his German possessions, which were the heart of a Habsburg empire that stretched from Hungary to Spain. (See map, page 242.) He allied with the pope, the Catholic prelates, and a number of loyal German princes. But because of his commitments in other parts of his far-flung empire, and particularly because of his wars with France (see pages 240-241), Charles failed to concentrate his armies against the Lutherans.

Declared an outlaw by the Diet of Worms, Luther spent a year (1521-1522) secluded at the castle of the Wartburg writing sermons and tracts and translating the Bible into German. Leadership of his movement passed into the hands of religious radicals. In the name of freedom the German knights (the lesser nobility) rebelled against the princes. They were defeated and their leader was forced to flee. Meanwhile in Wittenberg one of Luther's fellow professors was demanding the abolition of the Mass and of all religious art. Luther had to leave his quiet castle to restore order.

During the 1520's most of the rulers in northern Germany adopted Lutheranism. So, too, did the major cities of western Germany, such as Augsburg, Nuremberg, and Hamburg. From the cities, like ripples in a pond, Lutheranism rolled across the countryside, where many peasants came to believe that it would solve all their problems. In 1525 they revolted and, in a series of bloody uprisings, attempted to establish the new religion and

The title page of Martin Luther's translation of the Bible. Besides being important in the history of Lutheranism, Luther's translation is generally recognized as one of the great masterpieces of German literature. The page reads: "God's Word endures forever. The Bible: that is, the entire Holy Scripture [in] German. Martin Luther, Wittenberg. Favored with the approval of the Elector of Saxony. Printed by Hans Lufft. 1534."

at the same time to end the feudal system. But they were no match for the well-armed and organized princes, who put them down mercilessly.

When Luther saw that the peasants' rebellion could lead only to chaos, he turned on them bitterly. For the rest of his life he was suspicious of all efforts at political reform. This attitude cost him the support of many peasants and led to the establishment of splinter movements, which divided Lutheranism just as it seemed on the verge of victory. Encouraged, the Catholics regrouped and, with the support of many princes, fought successfully during the 1530's to stem the tide of change.

In 1530 Lutheran leaders wrote a definitive statement of their beliefs. Called the "Augsburg Confession," it repeated Luther's doctrines on salvation by faith, the authority of the Bible, and the "priesthood of all believers" (meaning that a Christian who had faith could serve God as well as could an ordained priest). Asserting that they were restoring the church to its original purity, the Lutherans gladly took the name "Protestants" as an indication of their protest against what they considered the errors of Catholicism. Later other religious leaders also called themselves Protestants, even though their ideas differed in important respects from Lutheran doctrines.

THE PEACE OF AUGSBURG OF 1555

The Lutherans continued missionary work, winning over the kingdoms of Denmark, Norway, and Sweden as well as most of northern Germany. The Catholics retained most of southern Germany by making concessions to the rulers there, and Germany was thus divided. The plans of Charles V to attack Lutheran rulers continued to be delayed by his wars with the French. Charles finally attacked in 1546, the year of Luther's death. His armies won the first battles, but the Protestants allied with his French enemies and forced a truce. In 1555 the Peace of Augsburg was signed, ending a decade of religious war.

The Peace of Augsburg ended all pretense of religious unity in Germany. Its basis was the principle that each man must follow the religion of his ruler. In effect, this principle allowed each German prince to choose between the Lutheran and Catholic faiths, and his subjects had either to accept his choice or move. For nearly a century central Europe was governed by this principle, which assured the continuation of Protestant Lutheranism and strengthened the princes as the real rulers of the Holy Roman Empire. From this time on, religion as well as politics divided Germany and hindered its unification into a single state like France or England.

🐚 ZWINGLI AND THE SWISS REFORMATION

After the Swiss priest Huldreich Zwingli (1484-1531) heard Luther preach, he remarked that their thoughts were so similar that all Luther had taught him was the courage to speak what he already believed. In 1519 Zwingli began to teach the new faith in Zurich. He flooded Switzerland with Luther's pamphlets and became the leader of the Protestants there. But the two men had their differences. Zwingli was more of a humanist than Luther, more nationalistic, and more desirous of stamping out all traces of Catholicism. He encouraged Zurich to outlaw veneration of saints and fasting during Lent and to allow priests to marry. Later the city's council abolished the Mass and even destroyed the organs in the churches, on the theory that God should be worshiped only with the spirit.

Zwingli established a theocracy (government by religious leaders) in Zurich that influenced other northen Swiss cities. Aggressive Zurich rulers sent missionaries into Catholic parts of Switzerland and so provoked a war. Luther, who at the time still hoped that a compromise with the Catholics in Germany was possible, hoped to avoid conflict and so refused to help Zwingli. In 1531 the Swiss reformer, fighting as a common soldier, was killed in a battle, and his army was routed. But his church survived, and many Swiss remained Protestants. These Swiss Protestants later became closely associated with Calvinism.

🐚 JOHN CALVIN AND CALVINISM

Two decades after Luther posted his Ninety-five Theses, the Frenchman John Calvin (1509-1564) founded a religious movement that spread from its capital in Geneva to make converts in all parts of Europe.

Calvin received a humanistic education in France before he became dissatisfied with Catholicism. He outlined his beliefs in a book entitled *The Institutes of the Christian Religion*. Calvin was pessimistic about man but optimistic about God. Man, he insisted, was corrupt and helpless, incapable of doing anything good by himself. But, Calvin believed, although man is helpless, he is not without hope; for "If God is with us, who can be against us?" In His infinite mercy, God has chosen some men, called by Calvin the "elect," to be saved from damnation. Once chosen, the elect are unshakeable, because their election "cannot be altered by any of the storms of the world." Luther had sought salvation by faith. Calvin did not seek salvation: he was sure that as one of the elect he had already been granted it.

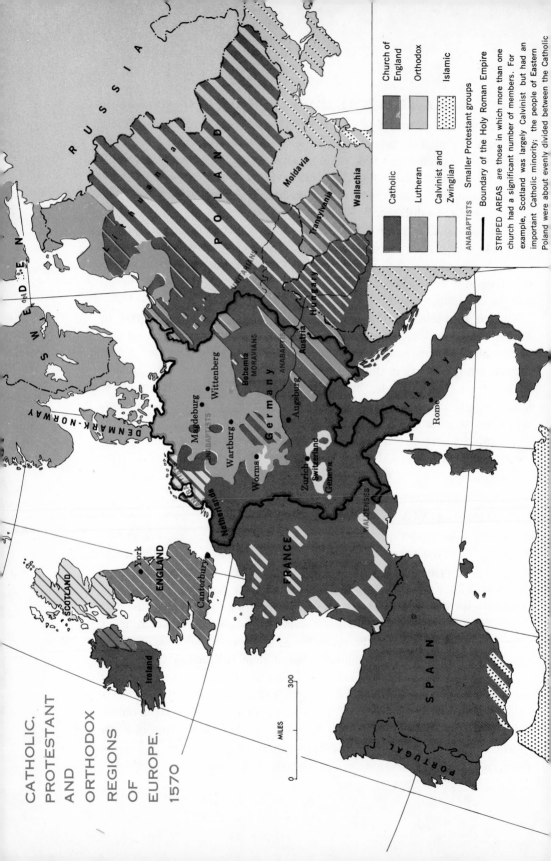

CATHOLIC, PROTESTANT AND ORTHODOX REGIONS OF EUROPE, 1570

MILES
0   300

Catholic
Lutheran
Calvinist and Zwinglian

Church of England
Orthodox
Islamic

ANABAPTISTS   Smaller Protestant groups

—— Boundary of the Holy Roman Empire

STRIPED AREAS are those in which more than one church had a significant number of members. For example, Scotland was largely Calvinist but had an important Catholic minority; the people of Eastern Poland were about evenly divided between the Catholic

RUSSIA

SWEDEN

DENMARK-NORWAY

Lithuania

POLAND

Moldavia

Wallachia

Transylvania

Hungary

Austria

Bohemia

MORAVIANS

ANABAPTISTS

Germany

Wittenberg

Magdeburg

Wartburg

Worms

Augsburg

Zurich

Switzerland

Geneva

Netherlands

WALDENSES

Italy

Rome

FRANCE

SPAIN

PORTUGAL

SCOTLAND

York

ENGLAND

Canterbury

Ireland

John Calvin: from an engraving after a portrait by Hans Holbein, the Younger. Unlike Luther, Calvin was not primarly an original thinker; rather, his great contribution was the logic and organization that he brought to Protestant thought.

To him the duty of those God had elected to save was not to seek salvation, but to honor God by establishing His Holy Commonwealth on earth.

Calvinism became a political religion when Calvin and the elect who followed him went out to enforce God's decrees as they understood them. Calvin himself established a model theocracy in the Swiss city of Geneva and ruled it with an iron hand. He forbade dancing, gambling, drama, jewelry, and even colorful clothing, as well as all Catholic customs. He burned some Protestant fugitives from Catholicism because they were not Calvinists, and all others who disagreed with him were expelled from Geneva. Calvin trained his followers from other countries to return to their homes as Calvinist missionaries; these men spread Calvinism rapidly across Europe, winning adherents from Hungary to Scotland.

Although it seemed likely to some that Calvinists and Lutherans might unite against Catholicism, differences between them proved to be too great. Lutherans tended to be nationalistic Germans and were willing to work with established governments; Calvinists looked beyond national boundaries and favored establishing theocracies of their own. More important were religious differences. Lutherans, for example, were willing to use Catholic forms of worship that did not contradict their own interpretation of the Bible; Calvinists insisted that only those forms of worship that they considered to be expressly authorized by the Bible should be retained. Calvinism was thus a more revolutionary type of Protestantism than was Lutheranism.

THE CHURCH OF ENGLAND

The English adopted a religion midway between Catholicism and Calvinism, called "Anglicanism" or, officially, the "Church of England." The Reformation on the European continent was often conducted in the face of bitter opposition by the kings, and the reformers often rejected all or most Catholic forms of worship. In England, by contrast, the Reformation was led by the king, and the Anglicans retained most of Catholicism's traditional customs.

THE BACKGROUND OF THE ENGLISH REFORMATION

The English of Luther's time were pious but anticlerical—that is, they opposed many policies of the clergy. Some were distressed by corruption in the monasteries, but there was no large group demanding thorough religious reform. Henry VIII (king 1509-1547), long regarded as a loyal Catholic, opposed Lutheranism in England. He had even written a book defending all seven Catholic sacraments, for which Pope Leo X rewarded him in 1523 with the title "Defender of the Faith."

Marital difficulty parted the king from the papacy. Henry's queen, Catherine of Aragon, a daughter of Spanish rulers Ferdinand and Isabella, had borne him six children, but only the Princess Mary had survived infancy. Henry needed a male heir to assure the continuation of his dynasty. His desire to have a new wife was stimulated by his love for Anne Boleyn, a young woman of his court.

Hoping that Anne would give him a son, Henry sought the pope's approval of an annulment of his marriage with Catherine. Pope Clement VII (pope 1523-1534) was in a difficult position; in a time of religious turmoil he was eager to please Henry; but if he approved the annulment, he would antagonize Catherine's nephew, the Emperor Charles V, who was his principal supporter in the struggle with Protestantism on the continent. He therefore postponed a decision as long as he could.

Henry grew impatient. Determined to remarry whether the pope liked it or not, he turned to the archbishop of Canterbury, Thomas Cranmer, for advice. Cranmer suggested that Henry seek approval by the universities of his annulment. A few in the universities approved it, the annulment was proclaimed, and Henry married Anne Boleyn. The pope then excommunicated Henry, and the break between king and pope was complete.

Henry's marital troubles were by no means over. Anne, too, failed to bear him a son (although she did present him with a daughter, the future

Queen Elizabeth I), and for alleged affairs with youthful courtiers her out-raged husband ordered her beheaded. Then a third wife bore him a son but died in childbirth. Three more wives followed in quick succession: one was divorced, another was put to death, and the third managed to out-live him.

THE DEVELOPMENT OF THE ANGLICAN CHURCH

Meanwhile Henry reorganized the church in England. He forbade clergy to appeal to the pope. In 1534 he persuaded Parliament to pass the "Act of Supremacy," which declared that "the king's majesty justly and rightfully is and ought to be the supreme head of the Church of England." Now England had a national church headed by the English king, who ignored the Roman pope. Henry seized the monasteries and distributed many of their estates among his followers, whose qualms about the break with Rome were thereby quieted. In 1536 he permitted publication of an English translation of the Bible; but in 1539 Parliament passed the "Act of the Six Articles," which reaffirmed most of the basic Catholic doctrines.

Many opposed these actions. Henry executed Sir Thomas More and others who supported papal authority, and in 1536 he had to suppress a Catholic uprising in the north of England. He treated Lutherans with equal severity. On one occasion, to show that he would tolerate neither, he had three Lutherans burned and three Catholics beheaded at the same time.

In accordance with Henry's last wishes, his crown passed to his young son, Edward VI (king 1547-1553); then to his daughter by Catherine of Aragon, Mary I (queen 1553-1558); and finally to his daughter by Anne Boleyn, Elizabeth I (queen 1558-1603). Edward was a sickly and short-lived youth dominated by his mother's family, who were more Protestant than Henry VIII had been. During his reign the articles of faith of the Church of England were revised, and the *Book of Common Prayer* in English replaced the Latin missal of the Catholic Church. The clergy were allowed to marry, and some of the Catholic sacraments were no longer used.

Mary, who remained a Catholic, attempted during her short reign to restore Catholicism to England by force. She failed, and after her death the English turned gladly to her half-sister Elizabeth. Elizabeth restored the Church of England to what it had been under Edward VI, but she toler-ated most kinds of worship as long as they did not challenge her authority. Most of her people accepted this arrangement, and the English turned from religion to other matters. (Chapter 27.)

❧ OTHER PROTESTANT SECTS

Late in the sixteenth century other Protestant sects were founded. Some, such as the Anabaptists, carried the teachings of Luther and Calvin beyond anything they would have approved; others, such as the Unitarians, went so far as to deny the doctrine of the Trinity.

THE ANABAPTISTS

The Anabaptists took Luther's doctrine of the priesthood of all believers at face value. They withdrew from the world to live together in communities where everyone took part in religious services (for all were priests), and they attempted to practice their faith in all aspects of their lives. They opposed the baptism of infants, believing that this sacrament should be reserved for people old enough to consciously choose to become Christians. They therefore came to be called "Anabaptists" (from the Greek for "baptize again"), although they often called themselves simply "Baptists."

Anabaptists first appeared in Germany, where they were persecuted by both Catholics and Lutherans. Later leaders were able to organize quiet communities dedicated to peace, charity, and the simple life. One leader, Menno Simons (1496-1561), founded a sect that came to be called "Mennonites," which established communities in Poland, Hungary, Russia, and North America. In England others founded the present-day Baptist Church.

An Anabaptist preacher: a German woodcut of the sixteenth cenutry. Anabaptists, who often went about the countryside preaching their beliefs, won many followers among the peasantry.

THE UNITARIANS

Those who do not accept the doctrine of the Trinity, because to them it does not agree with the doctrine of the oneness of God, are called "Unitarians." Unitarians do not believe that Jesus was divine, but rather that he was a particularly inspired human being.

Among early Unitarians was Michael Servetus (1511-1553), a Spaniard who fled for safety to Calvin in Geneva—and was executed. Another Unitarian, the Italian Faustus Socinus (1539-1604), insisted that Luther and Calvin had not gone far enough in rejecting Catholicism and that any religious belief that did not meet the test of reason was false. He was forced to flee to Poland, where he won numerous followers. Socinus was a father of the modern school of "liberal" Christians, who believe neither in miracles nor in the divine nature of Christ, because they insist that even the tenets of religion should meet the test of reason. This liberal attitude toward Christianity now attracts even Lutherans, Calvinists, and Anglicans.

⚜ PROTESTANT AND CATHOLIC
SIMILARITIES AND DIFFERENCES

By the middle of the sixteenth century there were several important Protestant religious groups. Always excepting the Church of England, they differed from Catholics in four significant ways:

Salvation. Protestants emphasized salvation by faith; Catholics, by faith and also by works, including sacraments.

The Bible. Protestants placed special emphasis on the Bible as the source of truth; Catholics relied both on the Bible and on the traditions of the Catholic Church.

The Priesthood. Protestants believed in the "priesthood of all believers," meaning that all true Christians are equally members of the church; Catholics distinguished the clergy, who had taken holy orders, from laymen.

Service to God. Protestants denied that God could effectively be served by withdrawing from the world; Catholics accepted the special value of monasticism (life apart from the world).

Although most Protestants agreed on the above points, they had basic disagreements among themselves on five other key doctrines:

The Means of Salvation. Lutherans believed that man is saved by simple faith in Christ. Calvinists believed only those "elected" or "predestined" by God would be saved. Anglicans adopted a doctrine midway between the Lutheran and Calvinist views. Anabaptists believed men saved as a result of an emotional "conviction of sin" or "conversion." Unitarians had no final belief, because they did not believe that the problem could be solved by reason.

The Sacraments. Lutherans accepted baptism, the Lord's Supper, and confirmation. Calvinists accepted only the first two of these. Anglicans accepted all three, plus one for holy orders (and some Anglicans adopted all seven Catholic sacraments). Other Protestants rejected all sacraments, although most symbolically observed baptism and the Lord's Supper.

Transubstantiation. To Catholics, "transubstantiation" is the miracle by which bread and wine become the body and blood of Christ during the Eucharist or Mass. Most Protestants repudiated this belief. Lutherans had a compromise belief called "consubstantiation," which held that Christ is *in* the bread and wine as fire is *in* hot iron, but that it is not actually his blood and body. Calvinists rejected this doctrine, believing the sacrament to be only a symbol in remembrance of the Last Supper.

Church Organization. All Protestants rejected the authority of the pope, and most abolished the Catholic hierarchy of divinely ordained clergy. Lutherans denied the difference between clergy and laymen, but kept bishops for administrative purposes. Calvinists agreed, but abolished bishops and placed church administration under groups of elected "elders" or "presbyters" (whence the name "Presbyterian"). Anglicans kept all ranks of clergy except pope and cardinals. Most other sects had only one level of presbyter who was chosen and employed by the individual congregations (whence the name "Congregational").

Religious Ceremonies. Calvinists abolished ceremony, for they did not believe in the worship of God through physical expression. Anglicans retained most Catholic services, but in English. Lutherans steered a middle course between Anglican formality and Calvinist austerity. Other Protestents abolished everything that smacked of the worldly, even music, while others encouraged the expression of religious feeling through spontaneous prayer and song.

❧ ❧ ❧

There were great differences between Catholics and Protestants, and among the several Protestant sects as well. All groups were acting out of deep religious feeling and the sincere belief that their doctrines would secure for every believer eternal salvation in the life to come. Unfortunately, however, Christians of the sixteenth and seventeenth centuries could not agree to disagree in peace. Catholics in this era had a Reformation of their own, after which they and the Protestants rocked Europe with violent religious struggles that were among the cruelest and most destructive wars in all history.

People, Places, and Terms

Martin Luther
Frederick the Wise
Johann Tetzel
Leo X
Charles V
Huldreich Zwingli
John Calvin
Henry VIII
Catherine of Aragon
Anne Boleyn
Thomas Cranmer
Edward VI
Mary I
Elizabeth I
Menno Simons
Michael Servetus
Faustus Socinus

Wittenberg
Mainz
Saxony
Worms
Zurich
Geneva

Reformation
Fifth Lateran Council
indulgences
Ninety-five Theses
Diet of Worms
Peasants' Rebellion
Augsburg Confession
priesthood of all
    believers
Protestants

Peace of Augsburg
theocracy
The Institutes of the
    Christian Religion
the elect
Anglicanism
Defender of the Faith
Act of Supremacy
Book of Common
    Prayer
Anabaptists
Unitarians
transubstantiation
consubstantiation
presbyter
Presbyterian
Congregationalist

Getting Organized

1. In the fifteenth and early sixteenth centuries, why were people growing dissatisfied with the Catholic Church? Who were the men and groups who most criticized the Catholic Church? Why did the monarchs oppose the popes and the clergy? How did the townsmen react to this wave of criticism of the church?

2. Describe Martin Luther. Describe his early life. What important question tormented him in his early years? What solution did he find to that important question?

3. Why did Luther post the Ninety-five Theses? What was the pope's first reaction to them? How did Luther become a heretic? What happened at the Diet of Worms? What are the main beliefs of Lutheranism?

4. What people adopted Lutheranism? How did Emperor Charles V react to Lutheranism? Why? What was the Peasants' Rebellion and how did Luther react toward it? What was the basic principle of the Peace of Augsburg? What were its effects?

5. Who was Huldreich Zwingli and what did he believe? What happened to the Reformation in Switzerland?
6. Who was John Calvin? What are the main points of his belief? How was Calvinism a political religion? How did it differ from Lutheranism?
7. Why did Henry VIII break with the pope? How did he go about accomplishing his goals? What were the main points of Anglicanism when Henry was alive? How did it evolve after this death?
8. What did the Anabaptists believe? What did the Unitarians believe? Where were each established?
9. Summarize the ways in which Protestantism differed from Catholicism and the ways in which Protestants differed among themselves.

Understanding the Big Picture

1. In the sixteenth century who sought changes in the Catholic Church? For what reasons?
2. To what extent did Martin Luther's beliefs satisfy the demands of those who sought reform of the church?
3. Compare Lutheranism and Calvinism. What specific reforms was each most concerned with? How did their teachings conflict?
4. To what extent was the English Reformation a religious development? To what extent political?

Mastering the Map

Study the map of Protestant, Catholic and Orthodox regions of Europe on page 300. What countries were unaffected by the Protestant Reformation? Where was Lutheranism established? List the countries in which there were important numbers of Calvinists. From this map and from your knowledge of the European political situation in the sixteenth century, where do you predict major conflicts in the following one hundred years would be fought? Why?

For the Thoughtful

1. Do you think that a revolution was necessary to cure the problems of the Catholic Church, or could they have been solved by intelligent reform from within the structure of the Catholic Church? Support your opinion with specific evidence.
2. Do you think that the end of the unity of western European Christendom was a good thing for the future of Europe, or would Europe be better off today if all Europeans worshiped at the same church?
3. How important was Martin Luther to European history? How does he compare in importance to Muhammad? To Charlemagne?
4. Do you agree that "Erasmus laid the egg that Luther hatched"? In what ways did the doctrines of the Protestant reformers reflect the ideas of the Christian humanists?

22

the Catholic
Reformation
and the
Wars of Religion

The Protestant Reformation of the first half of the sixteenth century was paralleled by a Catholic Reformation and followed by a century of violent conflict between Catholics and Protestants. As soon as the Catholics had reformed their church and systematized its dogma, they took the offensive against the already aggressive Protestants. The conflict, which centered in France, the Netherlands, and the Holy Roman Empire, was punctuated by violence, intolerance, and bigotry on both sides.

THE CATHOLIC REFORMATION

Some historians maintain that the Catholic Reformation would have occurred even if Luther and Calvin had never left the Catholic Church. Others insist it was a "Counter Reformation" brought about by the challenge of Protestantism. There is truth in both points of view. The roots of the Catholic Reformation date from the time before the Ninety-five Theses; but the reforms were made more urgent by the need to respond to Protestant criticism. In any case, by 1550 the Catholics had made their church far stronger than it had been at the outbreak of the Protestant Reformation.

THE SOCIETY OF JESUS

Just as the Franciscans and Dominicans had been founded to meet the religious crisis of the thirteenth century (see page 121), a new religious order arose in the Age of the Reformation. Early in the sixteenth century Spain was both a center of Catholic piety and, under the Habsburgs, the strongest military power in Europe. (Chapter 25.) There, in 1522, a young soldier who had been crippled by a cannonball underwent a religious conversion similar in some ways to the one Luther had had a decade earlier. But the soldier, Ignatius of Loyola (1491-1556), did not follow Luther's course; instead, he chose to become a soldier of the Catholic Church.

Loyola went to Paris, where he studied theology and became a priest. In a book called *Spiritual Exercises,* he presented a detailed system of meditation. To put his ideas into practice, he founded the "Society of Jesus," which was approved by Pope Paul III in 1540. The "Jesuits," as members of the Society are called, were strictly organized and pledged to serve the pope unquestioningly. They became the attack forces of the Catholic Reformation. Jesuits became confessors and advisers to kings, founded schools famed for strict discipline and high scholastic standards, and won fame for their clear and simple preaching. By effective missionary work they retrieved Poland and most of southern Germany for Catholicism, risked their lives to minister to England's secret Catholics, and in the Far East and the New World made converts to Catholicism who more than outnumbered Catholic losses to Protestantism in Europe.

The Jesuits were as aggressive in Catholicism's cause as the Calvinists were for their Protestant faith. Consequently they were feared and hated by Protestants—and loved and respected by Catholics.

Ignatius of Loyola, founder of the Society of Jesus. Loyola's life was dominated by personal love of Jesus, obedience and loyalty to the pope, and great zeal for God's glory and for the salvation of souls, characteristics which made him the outstanding leader of the Catholic Reformation.

The Council of Trent in Session: detail of a French engraving of 1565. The assembled prelates are seated on the curved, rising rows of benches. Representatives of the pope are at the left; in the center are the secretary of the council and a representative of King Philip II of Spain. An expert on church doctrine, arm upraised, is addressing the council.

DOCTRINAL REFORM: THE COUNCIL OF TRENT, 1545-1563

Meanwhile a series of reforming popes led other Catholics in an effort to reorganize the church and make its doctrines clear. One of these popes, Paul III (pope 1534-1549) called hundreds of leading prelates from all over Europe to the General Council of Trent, which, in three sessions from 1545 to 1563, united Catholics for the coming religious struggle. This was not easy, for the Catholic Habsburg and Valois kings were bitter rivals, and both were eager to limit the power of the popes within their territories. In addition, some churchmen demanded reform, while others wanted no part of it; a few wanted to compromise with the Protestants, while others wanted only to stamp them out. Under these difficult circumstances, the achievement of the Council of Trent was remarkable.

In matters of belief, the council refused to compromise with Protestantism. It insisted that tradition was as much a source of truth as the Bible, and it recognized the pope and general councils as the final judges in religious doctrine and the only correct sources of Biblical interpretation. It upheld traditional Catholic beliefs about purgatory, indulgences, and the invocation of saints, and it restated that all seven sacraments were essential.

The Council of Trent strengthened the organization of the church by requiring churchmen to put religious duties ahead of secular interests. It established an improved system for the education of priests. And it did much to raise the morale of the clergy and to strengthen the church's cohesion under the direction of Rome.

THE ENFORCEMENT OF CATHOLIC DOCTRINE

Unified under papal leadership, the Catholic Church utilized the Inquisition, the Index, and concordats with Catholic kings to prevent the further spread of Protestantism.

The Inquisition, the special church court originally established in the thirteenth century to deal with the Albigensian heretics (see page 124), was revived to deal with Catholics who had strayed from the fold and Protestants who came under Catholic domination. It utilized medieval methods—torture, spying, and terror—to successfully suppress heresy in Spain and Italy and to punish Calvinists in the Netherlands. It was a fearsome device, but probably no crueler than the methods used by Protestants against Catholics.

One of the most severe of the sixteenth century popes, Paul IV (pope 1555-1559), had the "Index" (list) of prohibited books drawn up. Catholics were forbidden to read any book in the Index, and all known copies of them were destroyed—so effectively that there are no surviving copies of some books that are known to have existed at that time. Under the control of the College of Cardinals, the Index became a permanent Catholic weapon.

Papal diplomats made new concordats with the rulers of Spain, Portugal, France, Italy, and Austria in which they sacrificed some papal control over the church in return for the monarch's pledge to use his power to support Catholicism. As a result, Protestant efforts to overthrow Catholicism in countries like France and the Spanish Netherlands acquired political overtones, for an attack on the Catholic Church became an attack on the state as well. At the cost of some subservience to the monarchs, however, the Catholic Church was able to keep Protestantism out of southern Europe.

❧ THE EARLY RELIGIOUS WARS

By the middle of the sixteenth century the lines between Catholicism and Protestantism were clearly drawn. Neither would compromise with the other. Men on each side were convinced that theirs was the only road to heaven and that to allow heresy would only contribute to corruption and the damnation of souls. Hatreds hardened, and war became inevitable. With religion as an issue, civil war turned brother against brother and neighbor against neighbor, and conflicts between Catholic and Protestant states took on a new fury.

RELIGIOUS WAR IN FRANCE

The Reformation divided the French into three religious camps: (1) Calvinists, who in France were called "Huguenots"; (2) *politiques,* who were Catholics but who were more concerned with political matters than with religion; and (3) those Catholics whose first concern was that Catholicism should remain the sole religion in France. After 1560 the French government was largely controlled by Catherine de Médicis, daughter of the man to whom Machiavelli had dedicated *The Prince* (see page 239), widow of a king of France, and mother of three weakling kings who reigned in succession. Catherine was a *politique:* her first concern was maintaining the French monarchy's tradition of "one faith, one king, one law."

In 1562 Catherine tried to maintain peace by keeping Catholicism as the official religion of France but allowing Huguenots the right to worship as they pleased. This arrangement satisfied nobody, leading instead to a decade of civil and religious war. In 1572 Catherine tried to unite the country by giving her Catholic daughter in marriage to the Huguenot leader, King Henry of Navarre. At the wedding festivities another Huguenot leader was assassinated. Catherine, fearing a general Protestant uprising, thereupon authorized the "Massacre of Saint Bartholomew" (so-called because it took place on St. Bartholomew's Day, August 23). In Paris alone, 10,000 Protestants were killed. The pope struck a medal to honor an event that he thought had wiped out Protestantism in France.

But this outrage only begat more violence. After more years of bloody fighting, the Huguenot King Henry of Navarre emerged as the sole surviving heir to the French throne. In 1589 he became King Henry IV of France (the first king of the Bourbon family); and, to avoid further bloodshed, he became a Catholic. In 1598 he eased the religious struggle by issuing the "Edict of Nantes," which gave Protestants the right to worship privately, to hold public services in certain cities, and to hold certain government offices. The Edict of Nantes did for France what the Peace of Augsburg had done for Germany: it created an uneasy truce between Catholics and Protestants that lasted more than half a century.

"The Massacre of the Innocents": detail of a painting by Pieter Brueghel, the Elder. (See page 284.) The subject of the painting is the murder of the children of Bethlehem, ordered by King Herod shortly after the birth of Jesus. But Brueghel has shown Bethlehem as a Flemish village, its people as Flemish peasants—and Herod's soldiers as Spanish soldiers. By so doing, Brueghel demonstrated, in a particularly striking way, the hatred felt by the people of the Netherlands toward their Spanish overlords in the sixteenth century.

THE REVOLT OF THE NETHERLANDS

Early in the sixteenth century, the seventeen provinces that made up the Netherlands (or "Low Countries") became a part of the Habsburg empire of Charles V. At that time the term "Netherlands" referred not only to the present-day country of that name, but also to what is now Belgium. In the northern provinces, Dutch was spoken; the people of Flanders ("Flemings") spoke Flemish, a language closely related to Dutch; and in the southern provinces the people spoke French. By the middle of the sixteenth century, the Netherlands had also become religiously divided: most of the Dutch adopted Calvinism, while the majority in Flanders and the French-speaking provinces remained Catholics.

In 1555 Charles V turned over the Netherlands to his son King Philip II of Spain. (Chapter 25.) Philip's Spanish governors attempted to reduce the power of the local governing councils, to restrict all trade to the Spanish empire, to collect new taxes, and to impose Catholicism on the Calvinists.

The Protestants petitioned for religious freedom. The Spaniards scorned the petitioners as "beggars"; the name stuck, and the rebels called themselves "Beggars" from that time on. In 1566 mobs swarmed through Catholic churches, destroying their altars and defacing their statues. In response, Philip sent the duke of Alba to the Netherlands to quell the uprising. Alba established a court called the "Council of Troubles," which ordered the execution of many Protestants and seized the property of others. Thousands fled from the "Council of Blood," as they called Alba's court, and from exile their leaders plotted to overthrow the Spanish rule. After one invasion had failed, another seized the northern (Dutch) provinces in 1572, while "Sea Beggars" attacked Spanish shipping. Alba, despairing of ever putting down the revolt, returned to Spain.

Philip eventually appointed the moderate duke of Parma to restore order. Parma found that compromise could succeed where force had failed. He won the support of the Flemish Catholics, and by 1584 it seemed likely that he would win control of the northern provinces as well. At this point an English army arrived to support the Beggars and their leader, William I of Orange (called "the Silent"), forcing a stalemate that Philip tried to break by sending the Spanish Armada to win control of the English Channel. After the destruction of the Armada (Chapter 25), the Spanish remained strong enough to hold the southern Netherlands, but they could not hope to conquer the northern provinces.

Meanwhile the northern provinces had formed a union, and in 1581 they declared their independence of Spain. The union might have broken apart in the years that followed had not William the Silent been assassinated by a fanatic. William had really been more interested in politics than in religion, but in death he became a Protestant martyr the memory of whom unified the Dutch. Freed from the Spanish yoke, the Dutch grew prosperous, became rivals of the English sea power, and even built up an empire of their own. Finally in 1648 the Treaties of Westphalia (below, page 319) recognized the independence of the Protestant "Republic of the United Provinces" (also called the "Dutch Netherlands" or "Holland," and today simply "the Netherlands"). The southern provinces, or "Spanish Netherlands," remained Catholic and in the hands of the Habsburgs; later they became the "Austrian Netherlands," and later still, Belgium.

🏵 THE THIRTY YEARS WAR

During the second half of the sixteenth century, while Catholics and Protestants in France and the Netherlands struggled for control, Germany remained uneasily peaceful. But in the first half of the seventeenth century, Germany became the scene of the Thirty Years War, the last, longest, and by far the bloodiest of the wars of religion.

ORIGINS OF THE THIRTY YEARS WAR

The Peace of Augsburg of 1555 (see page 298) satisfied neither the Catholics, who could not protect their property in Protestant states, nor the non-Lutheran Protestants, who were not protected by its provisions. Among both Catholics and Protestants, leadership fell into the hands of extremists. While the Lutherans settled happily in the lands of friendly princes in the north, aggressive Calvinists forced a wedge of Protestantism into Catholic lands in the Rhine valley. Then in the first part of the seventeenth century two Holy Roman emperors, Matthias (emperor 1612-1619) and Ferdinand II (emperor 1619-1637), determined to become the real rulers of all Germany and to root out Protestantism wherever possible.

In 1600 religion remained the principal concern of most of the German people. Preachers, pamphlets, and placards aroused real and imaginary fears of heresy or suppression. Neither Catholics nor Protestants were tolerant, and a series of violent incidents created hatred on both sides. Churchmen on both sides tried to seize their opponents' property, and princes played on religious passions for their personal purposes.

Politics could not be separated from religion. The Habsburg kings of Spain and their cousins, the Habsburg Holy Roman emperors, both Catholics, were eager to join in a war with their religious and commercial rivals. The Catholic kings of France feared the Habsburgs so much that they were willing to join anyone, even a Protestant, who would oppose rising Habsburg power. The Calvinist Dutch, the Anglican English, and the Lutheran kings of Sweden and Denmark all opposed Catholic and Habsburg policies in Germany and elsewhere.

In 1608 Germans began to choose sides for the approaching conflict when Calvinist princes formed the "Protestant Union." The following year the "Catholic League" was formed. But war did not come for a decade, for neither side was unified: the Lutherans still hoped for a religious compromise, and Catholic princes feared that a war would make them tools of the Habsburg emperors.

THE COURSE OF THE THIRTY YEARS WAR

The Thirty Years War had four distinct phases: (1) the Bohemian period, 1618-1625; (2) the Danish period, 1625-1629; (3) the Swedish period, 1630-1635; and (4) the Swedish-French period, 1635-1648.

The Bohemian War, 1618-1625. The spark that set off the war was a dispute between the Bohemian nobility and the Habsburg emperors. The Habsburgs had been kings of Bohemia for almost a century. But in the 1610's Protestant Bohemian noblemen, alarmed at the prospect of soon being governed by the resolutely Catholic Ferdinand, asserted their ancient right to elect their own king. In 1618 a group of noblemen invaded the room in Prague, the Bohemian capital, where two representatives of the emperor were staying and threw them out the window to the ground some 70 feet below. The emperor's representatives landed in a manure pile and so were not seriously hurt; but the event obviously made it impossible for the emperor and the Bohemians to reach any agreement. Thus this "Defenestration of Prague" (from the Latin *de fenestra,* "out the window") started a struggle for control of Bohemia.

The Catholic armies of the Holy Roman emperor swept everything before them. In 1620 the forces of the Catholic League under the count of Tilly destroyed the power of the Bohemian Protestants. Ferdinand II, with the aid of the Jesuits and the Inquisition, set out to erase all traces of Protestantism from Bohemia and Austria. Meanwhile Tilly marched against the Calvinists in central Germany. The Protestant Union collapsed, and the imperial armies swept through western Germany. It seemed likely that Tilly would drive the Protestants out of the empire entirely.

The Danish War, 1625-1629. Another of Ferdinand's brilliant generals, Albrecht von Wallenstein, leading his own private army of mercenary soldiers, drove a Protestant force all the way to Hungary before turning north in 1625 to join Tilly in an attack on the Lutherans of northern Germany. This threat brought the Lutheran King Christian IV of Denmark into the fray; but he was driven back to his own country, and in 1629 he had to promise not to interfere in German affairs again.

Flushed with victory, the Emperor Ferdinand made two mistakes. He led the Lutherans to believe that he would govern them directly and that he intended to impose upon them his Catholic faith. And he heightened these fears by signing the "Edict of Restitution" of 1629, which restored to Catholics all the lands they had lost since 1552 and deprived all Protestants except Lutherans of their religious and political rights. At Ferdinand's order, Tilly and Wallenstein mercilessly began to enforce the edict.

The Swedish War, 1630-1635. Alarmed by Ferdinand's policies in Germany, the Lutheran king of Sweden, Gustavus II (known as "Gustavus Adolphus"; king 1611-1632) entered the war in 1630. Gustavus Adolphus was a good soldier, and he commanded what was then the best-trained army in Europe. Equally important, he had the support of the French whose leader, the Catholic Cardinal Richelieu (Chapter 26), was alarmed by the rising Habsburg power in Germany. At first Gustavus Adolphus could not find other allies who dared take on the seemingly unbeatable Catholic forces. But in 1631 Tilly captured Magdeburg, an early Protestant center; his troops, disobeying his orders, killed some 90 per cent of the inhabitants and burned the city to the ground. Outraged Protestants everywhere took up arms. The Dutch invaded the Habsburg-dominated Flanders. German princes flocked to Sweden's standards. Gustavus Adolphus won a great victory at Leipzig in 1631, and soon afterward Tilly was killed. In the following year Protestant forces fought Wallenstein's army to a stand-off in bloody battles in which many were killed, including Gustavus Adolphus. Wallenstein, against the emperor's wishes, tried to negotiate a peace, but he was assassinated at the order of another Catholic general. Ferdinand's principal generals were now dead, and the war entered its final phase.

The Swedish-French War, 1635-1648. In its last phase the war became a great international conflict. The Spanish Habsburgs allied with the Habsburg Holy Roman emperors, while the French and Dutch joined the Swedes and Protestant Germans. The French attacked the Habsburgs in Spain, the Spanish Netherlands, the Rhine valley, and Franche Comté (the part of Burgundy in the Holy Roman Empire, held at that time by the king of Spain). Philip IV of Spain had all he could do to protect himself and no longer could aid his cousin, the Holy Roman emperor.

In Germany there were alternating periods of war and truce. The Swedes invaded; but at the same time they were attacked from behind by the Danes, who probably thereby saved the emperor from complete rout. After a lull, the French invaded in 1643 and threatened to separate Habsburg Austria from vital supply bases in Italy. Five years later a combined French and Swedish thrust into southern Germany broke the emperor's will to resist further. Finally, in 1648, both sides were ready to make peace.

THE TREATIES OF WESTPHALIA

The series of treaties that ended the Thirty Years War, called the "Treaties of Westphalia," are among the most important in the history of Europe. They were immensely complicated, for, in addition to the major provisions, many details concerning the boundaries of the more than 300 German states had to be worked out. Among the major provisions were these: (1) Each German prince became, in effect, free from any kind of control by the Holy Roman emperor. (2) The United Provinces (the Dutch Netherlands) became officially independent, while the southern Netherlands remained a possession of Spain. (3) French possession of Metz, Toul, and Verdun (see page 241) was confirmed, and France in addition received much of the German-speaking province of Alsace. (4) Sweden received lands in northern Germany on the Baltic and North Sea coasts. (5) Switzerland became totally independent of the Holy Roman Empire. (6) France and Sweden won the right to interfere in German affairs, and Sweden won a voice in the diet of the Holy Roman Empire. (7) A number of German states gained or lost territory. The most notable gainer was Brandenburg, which received important lands on the North Sea and in central Germany.

The Treaties of Westphalia also made provisions regarding religion in the Holy Roman Empire. The most important of these were (1) Calvinists were to have the same privileges as Lutherans, and (2) the ruler of each state could determine its official religion, but (except in the hereditary lands of the Habsburgs) he must permit freedom of private worship and must allow his subjects to emigrate if they wished.

The long-range effects of the treaties were even more important than their provisions. First, they ended a century of religious conflict. The toleration, albeit limited, proclaimed in Germany soon became customary elsewhere. Some on each side were furious. The pope called the treaties "null, void, invalid, iniquitous, unjust, damnable, reprobate, inane, empty of meaning and effect for all time." A Protestant leader commented, "They have sacrificed us." But the war had burned out the religious enthusiasm of most Europeans, who preferred to turn their attention to other matters.

Second, the Treaties of Westphalia broke the Habsburg power, ending the possibility that they could come to dominate Europe. A balance-of-power system emerged, similar to that which had been employed by the city-states of Renaissance Italy (see page 254)— except that now the units of government were great monarchies rather than little city-states. International relations came to be characterized by shifting alliances of the great powers.

Third, the Thirty Years War had a long-lasting effect upon Germany. Most parts of the country suffered at one time or another from the widespread havoc and destruction of the war. The economy and the civilization of Germany received a setback from which they did not recover for many

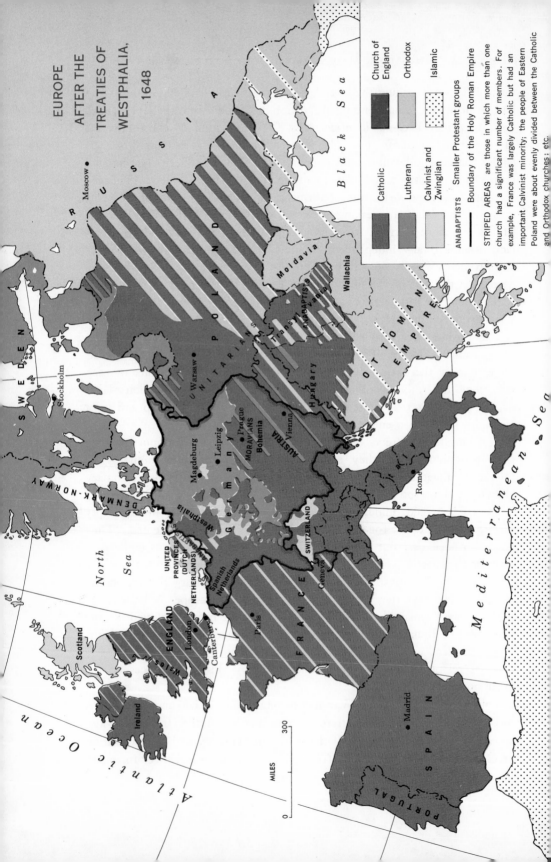

EUROPE
AFTER THE
TREATIES OF
WESTPHALIA,
1648

Catholic	Church of England	
Lutheran	Orthodox	
Calvinist and Zwinglian	Islamic	

ANABAPTISTS Smaller Protestant groups

⎯⎯⎯ Boundary of the Holy Roman Empire

STRIPED AREAS are those in which more than one church had a significant number of members. For example, France was largely Catholic but had an important Calvinist minority; the people of Eastern Poland were about evenly divided between the Catholic and Orthodox churches; etc.

RUSSIA

Black Sea

Moscow •

SWEDEN

Stockholm •

POLAND

• Warsaw

UNITARIANS

Moldavia

TRANSYLVANIA

ANABAPTISTS

Wallachia

OTTOMAN EMPIRE

DENMARK-NORWAY

Germany

Magdeburg •

• Leipzig

• Prague

MORAVIANS

Bohemia

AUSTRIA

Vienna •

Hungary

North Sea

Westphalia

UNITED PROVINCES (DUTCH NETHERLANDS)

Spanish Netherlands

ENGLAND

London •

Canterbury •

Scotland

Wales

SWITZERLAND

Geneva

Italy

Rome •

Mediterranean Sea

FRANCE

Paris •

Ireland

Atlantic Ocean

MILES

300

0

SPAIN

Madrid •

PORTUGAL

decades. And the Treaties of Westphalia, by leaving Germany divided into hundreds of independent little states, further hindered economic development and all but abolished the hope of ever establishing a strong, unified national government.

✿ ✿ ✿

After the Treaties of Westphalia, the center of political power in Europe passed from the Habsburgs to the states along Europe's Atlantic shore. Already wealthy from their rapidly expanding trade, they also profited from another development: the exploration and exploitation by Europeans of the four corners of the world.

People, Places, and Terms

Ignatius of Loyola	Netherlands	Huguenot
Paul III	United Provinces	*politique*
Catherine	Spanish Netherlands	Massacre of Saint
de Médicis	Bohemia	Bartholomew
Henry of Navarre	Prague	Edict of Nantes
Philip II	Magdeburg	Beggars
William the Silent	Alsace	Protestant Union
Matthias		Catholic League
Ferdinand II	*Spiritual Exercises*	Defenestration of
Count of Tilly	Society of Jesus	Prague
Albrecht von	Jesuits	Edict of Restitution
Wallenstein	Council of Trent	Treaties of
Gustavus Adolphus	Inquisition	Westphalia
Cardinal Richelieu	Index	

Getting Organized

1. Who was Ignatius of Loyola? What function did the Society of Jesus perform in the reformation of the Catholic Church?
2. Why was the Council of Trent assembled? What difficulties did it face? What did it accomplish?
3. How did the Catholic Church enforce its doctrine? What agreements did it make with the various monarchs of Europe, and with what important results?

4. What were the religious divisions in France after the middle of the sixteenth century? Who were the principal figures in the struggle between these forces? What did each accomplish? How was this division finally patched up?
5. Why did the Netherlands revolt from Spanish rule? Who were the principal figures in this struggle? What did each accomplish? What was the final result of this conflict? How did Spain manage to save one half of its provinces?
6. What had happened in Germany after the Peace of Augsburg? What were the major causes of the Thirty Years War? Describe each of the four phases of the war. How did the war become international? How did it finally end?
7. What were the major provisions of the Treaties of Westphalia? What were the major effects of the Thirty Years War?

Understanding the Big Picture

1. How did the Catholic Church reform itself in the sixteenth century?
2. Were France, the Netherlands, and Germany all torn by war for the same reasons? Discuss the origins and effects of each conflict.
3. Why were the Treaties of Westphalia such important treaties? What problem did they solve? What problems did they leave for the future?

Mastering the Map

1. Study the map on page 320, and compare it with the map on page 300. How effective was the Catholic Reformation in regaining lands from Protestantism? What lands returned to the Catholic Church? Which remained Protestant?
2. Compare the map on page 320 with the one on page 242. What territories changed hands between 1560 and 1648? Who were the principal gainers? Who the principal losers? What effect might these changes be expected to have on the balance of power in Europe? Demonstrate your point on the map.

For the Thoughtful

1. From what you know of the Protestant and Catholic Reformations, explain why the Catholic Church reformed itself in the sixteenth century. Why did the two groups go to war?
2. How did the Treaties of Westphalia change the course of European history? Answer the question drawing on your knowledge of Europe before and after the treaty.
3. Are wars of religion being fought today? Why? Why are wars fought today? Compare the causes of war in the sixteenth and early seventeenth centuries to its causes today.

23

EUROPE AND
the far East

At the same time that the Renaissance and Reformation were transforming the intellectual and religious life of most of Europe, navigators were putting out from the once quiet and backward ports of Portugal and Spain to explore and colonize parts of the world that medieval Europeans had not even known existed. In less than a century and a quarter after the first Portuguese seamen hesitantly investigated the western shore of Africa, the world known to Europeans increased threefold. New products and ideas brought great wealth to the lucky countries that controlled the newly discovered trade routes. Almost every aspect of European civilization was affected in important ways. The Portuguese opened up the first trade routes, which went around the southern tip of Africa to the Far East. In the Far East, especially in India and China, the Portuguese (and other Europeans who followed them) came into contact for the first time with highly developed civilizations that had been flourishing for centuries.

🌸 THE BACKGROUND OF EXPLORATION

Every educated Renaissance man knew that the earth was round. But the men of the fifteenth century had no idea how large it was, and they knew almost nothing of what lay beyond Europe. There were, to be sure, tales of places that no one had ever seen: the lost continent of Atlantis, an island called "Cipangu" (Japan), a Christian kingdom somewhere in Africa or Asia headed by one "Prester John." Sailors told of sea monsters that swal-

323

lowed ships whole, of tropical heat that made the oceans boil, and of a place in the Arctic ice where Judas spent his annual day's vacation from the fires of hell.

During the Middle Ages a few men had ventured beyond Europe. Viking sagas told of Eric the Red, who discovered and named Greenland, and of his son Leif Ericson, who was said to have established a short-lived settlement in an even more distant place called "Vinland" (and apparently did, for a Norse settlement in Newfoundland dating from about A.D. 1000 has recently been discovered). But the sagas that told of these adventures were not known in the rest of Europe. More important were the reports of a few thirteenth-century Italians, most notably Marco Polo, who traveled to China and returned with reports that China could be reached by sea.

The curiosity of men of the Renaissance was stirred both by the legends and by the reports of actual trips to far lands. Sailors became eager to go behind the horizon and see these distant places for themselves. This attitude came at the same time that technical developments were making navigation easier. Among these developments were the compass, the astrolabe (a device for determining location by sighting the stars), and improved ships that could more easily survive the ocean storms.

⚜ PORTUGUESE VOYAGES AND DISCOVERIES

The era of European exploration and discovery of the world was begun by the small kingdom of Portugal. Portugal depended upon the sea. Its soil was poor, and Spain, its neighbor to the east, cut off its land contact with the rest of Europe. Its great advantage was its location on the sea lanes from Italy to northern Europe, for its harbors became ports of call for fleets from Venice, England, and the Hanse. Portuguese sailors learned much from the foreigners who visited their country, and they became some of the best mariners in Europe.

The man most responsible for Portugal's accomplishments was Prince Henry "the Navigator" (1394-1460), a son of the king of Portugal. Henry gathered the best mapmakers he could find, gave them the finest equipment and the latest information, and sent them out on one voyage after another southward along the coast of Africa. He had several reasons for encouraging exploration. A religious man, he hoped to continue the struggle against the Muslim Moors by establishing a Christian country to their south. He also hoped to discover a new and profitable trade route around the coast of Africa to the Far East. And as a man of the Renaissance, he eagerly sought all the information about distant places that he could get.

The first Portuguese voyagers set out along the African coast during the 1420's. By 1445 they had reached Cape Verde, the westernmost point in Africa, some 1,500 miles from Portugal. There they discovered something new to trade—slaves. It was hard to persuade captains to sail beyond the profitable slave markets, and for a time exploration nearly ceased.

But later Portuguese kings took up the work that Prince Henry had begun, sending a new generation of navigators southward. One of them, Bartholomeu Dias, rounded the southernmost point of Africa in 1488. He named it the "Cape of Storms"; but his king rejoicingly renamed it the "Cape of Good Hope" and, realizing that a route to India was now a real possibility, sent out new expeditions.

In 1497 the king dispatched four vessels under Vasco da Gama "to make discoveries and go in search of spices." Da Gama followed Dias's route around the Cape of Good Hope and explored the east coast of Africa, skirmishing with hostile Africans on the way. Finally he reached the port of Malindi, in present-day Kenya. There he picked up some experienced Arab pilots who guided him across the Indian Ocean to Calicut, a spice port on the western shore of India. The sea route to the East was completed at last. Da Gama took on a cargo of pepper and cinnamon worth twenty times the cost of the expedition and returned in triumph to Portugal.

For the next century the Portuguese dominated the sea route to the Far East. They owned the Madeira and Cape Verde Islands off the west coast of Africa, a port on the Indian Ocean island of Madagascar, and numerous trading posts and way stations that dotted the African coastline from Morocco all the way around to the Gulf of Aden. Tiny Portugal had discovered the best route to the Far East. Other countries soon followed it, starting a wave of European invasions of Asia.

ASIA ON THE EVE OF WESTERN INVASION

In the sixteenth century the four most important countries of Asia—India, China, Japan, and the East Indies—had certain similarities, but each had a highly developed way of life of its own. Each, in its own way, resisted the efforts of the European intruders to make any changes.

INDIA: DIVIDED AND OTHERWORLDLY

The huge southern peninsula of Asia called India is half as large as the continental United States, and its geography is nearly as varied. Along its northern border the highest mountains in the world, the Himalayas, separate it from the rest of Asia and are subject to Arctic temperatures. In the south, less than ten degrees from the equator, the climate is tropical. Between are jungles, plateaus, arid plains, rich coastal lands, and the two river systems of the Indus and the Ganges, in whose valleys the greatest number of Indians live.

The rigid "caste" system determined the way in which each individual Indian lived. The origins of this hierarchy of social classes are obscure. Apparently it began around 1500 B.C., when tribes of white Indo-Europeans invaded India. The invaders learned to control the native inhabitants by dividing them into classes from which they could not escape, retaining for themselves the governing castes: the *Brahman* (priestly) caste and the *Kshatriya* (warrior) caste. Members of both these groups were likely to be educated and cultured, possessors of wealth and political power. Beneath them were the *Vaishya* (merchants) and the *Shudra* (laborers), who were subdivided into several thousand castes depending on their occupation. At the bottom of the social scale were the "casteless," called "untouchables," who had no social standing at all and lived in abject poverty. The system was far more rigid than medieval feudalism. Members of the upper classes were not allowed to eat food touched by the lower castes, were not allowed to speak to them, and were required to marry within their own caste.

The caste system was reinforced by Hinduism, India's principal religion. Its priests taught that the ways of the flesh were evil and that men would be judged on the kind of life they led and reincarnated accordingly. A bad man might be reborn as a dog or crawling creature, but a good man might be reborn in a higher caste. Living continued exemplary lives would lead one eventually to a reuniting with the One (*Moksha*) and release from the dreadful burden of rebirths. As time passed, however, the Brahmans became more interested in ritual than in actively practicing the moral precepts of their faith. Thus, Hinduism contributed to the caste system's gulf between the upper classes and the common people.

In the sixth century B.C., a religious reformer named Gautama Buddha, "the Enlightened," rejected the formalism of the Brahmans and taught that man can attain *Nirvana*, or final release from pain, only by recognizing that desire is the root of unhappiness. Buddhism spread to Ceylon and Southeastern Asia and, in other forms, to Tibet, China, and Japan.

Religion also complicated the political situation. The Mughal Empire, which Tamerlane had founded in 1398 (see page 199), decayed soon after his death and, even though it continued in name in the sixteenth century, India was actually divided among large numbers of little quarrelsome states. The influence of Islam was strong in the north, where the princes were Muslims. The chief potentates in the south were Hindu. Around 1525 a Mughal chief named Baber, a descendant of Tamerlane, conquered his neighbors and revived the power of the Mughal Empire. His grandson Akbar (king 1556-1605) extended Muslim rule to the south, and by wise and just administration won the loyalty of the people. Akbar attempted to take what he considered the best elements of several religions and to construct a creed that everyone could accept. Akbar's grandson built the Taj Mahal, one of the most beautiful and famous buildings in the world. His great-grandson Aurangzeb continued the conquest of southern India, driving the Portuguese from many of their colonies and weakening European influence everywhere. But after Aurangzeb's death in 1707, the Mughal Empire disintegrated, and the local rulers again became virtually independent.

CHINA: UNITED AND PROUD

The great majority of the Chinese, who were (as they still are) the world's most numerous people, lived in an area about half the size of the United States. This area, sometimes referred to as "China Proper" or, by the Chinese, as the "Middle Kingdom," contains fertile plains, low but sometimes rugged mountains, and the great river systems of the Yangtze River and the Hwang Ho (Yellow River). Its climate is favorable for agriculture, the basic crops being wheat in the north and rice in the south.

About 2,000 B.C., a civilization began to develop in the river valleys of China Proper. For almost 4,000 years it underwent a continuous development, unbroken by such drastic changes as the collapse of the Roman Empire or the rise of Islam. So far as is known, it was never affected in any important way by contacts with other civilizations.

The greatest single influence on China's development was the philosophy of Confucius (Kung Fu-tse; traditionally, 551-479 B.C.). Because Confucius was concerned with men's living in harmony with one another, his teachings were ethical (moral) rather than religious. He revered age more than youth, the past more than the present, and righteous behavior toward others more than individual freedom and self-expression. He placed great emphasis on a person's duty to his family, which was thought of as including married sons, their wives and children, and the spirits of dead ancestors. A person's successes and failures, his righteous and unrighteous actions, were thought of as reflecting not his own character, but the character and honor of his entire family. Another of Confucius's teachings was the idea of "government by goodness": the emperor should command obedience by setting an example of righteousness and by using reason, rather than force, in dealing with his subjects.

Confucianism provided the educated classes of Chinese society not only a framework for their thinking, but also a rigid code of personal behavior. As time went on, the Chinese came to believe that Confucius and other ancient sages had said all that was necessary to be said about moral living, and that it was man's duty to preserve and promote these teachings. Although the ordinary people knew little of Confucianism's intricate codes, its teachings strongly affected the attitudes of all Chinese. Chinese ideals were later influenced to some extent by Buddhism (above, page 326), and by Taoism, a philosophy that taught its believers to accept the buffets of life without complaint. But the influence of Confucius remained paramount.

Confucian ideals were the basis of China's society and government. The great majority of the Chinese were peasants. About half of them owned their own land; the rest paid rent, which was usually high. There was also a middle class of artisans and merchants in the towns. The merchants enjoyed little of the great wealth, power, or prestige that some of the

"A Gathering of Philosophers": detail of a Chinese painting, which indicates the high regard in which scholars were held in China. The emphasis given to the mountains and stream is evidence of another characteristic of Chinese civilization: the tendency to accept nature and adjust to it, rather than, as in Europe and America, to try to conquer it.

European middle class was then attaining, and their social status was considered to be lower than that of the peasants. There was no hereditary nobility in China. The top social position and the greatest social prestige were held by the "mandarins," the scholar-officials of the Chinese government. These civil servants were chosen by a grueling series of competitive examinations, which only a small percentage of the competitors passed. In theory, the examinations were open to any young man; but in practice, only the well-to-do could compete, for only they could afford the years of study required for success in the examinations. Almost all Chinese education was geared to preparing for these exams. It involved mastery of a complex written language that has more than 40,000 characters and a thorough study of the writings of Confucius and other ancient sages. Since this system discouraged originality, Chinese civilization gradually became stagnant; but for centuries the system provided China with the most effective government in the world.

At the head of the Chinese government was the emperor, who was believed to be the ruler of all mankind. He was regarded as the "son of heaven," possessing clear instructions (the "mandate of heaven") on how the world should be ruled. A corrupt emperor, however, was thought of as having lost the mandate of heaven. Thus, although the emperorship was hereditary, ruling dynasties could be overthrown. A dynasty of Chinese origin tended to be followed by a dynasty of military leaders of a foreign, less civilized people. For example, Kublai Khan, the emperor whom the Italian Marco Polo had served in the thirteenth century, was a Mongol. The Mongols ruled China for about a century before they were overthrown by the Ming, a dynasty of Chinese, who held power for almost 300 years. In 1644, the Ming were in turn ousted by the Manchus, foreigners from across the northeastern border, who survived until 1912.

China was separated from India by the Himalayas and from the civilizations of the Middle East and Europe by mountains and vast stretches of desert. Its principal contact with the outside world, therefore, was with the uncivilized nomadic tribes of northern Asia. These tribes were a constant threat to China's northern frontier: it was they who sometimes succeeded in conquering China and taking over its government, as had the Mongols and the Manchus. But each of these conquerors soon adopted the long-established traditions of Chinese civilization and became "more Chinese than the Chinese." It is not surprising, then, that the Chinese took it for granted that theirs was the only real civilization and that all other peoples —including Europeans—were "barbarians."

JAPAN: FEUDAL AND WARLIKE

The Japanese islands extend 1,200 miles along the northern coast of east Asia. There are four main islands and several hundred smaller ones. All are mountainous, so that the people are crowded into tiny valleys and narrow coastal plains. Heavy seasonal rains allow the growth of lush green vegetation and the crops of rice that are the principal food of the people.

Japan's island separation from the Asian mainland, but its nearness to it (less than 125 miles at the narrow Strait of Korea), have colored Japanese history from very early times. In the fourth century, Japanese armies seized Korea, which brought the Japanese into contact with Chinese civilization. In the next three centuries, the Japanese copied Chinese architecture, adapted Chinese writing to the Japanese language, modeled their government on that of China, and became converts to Buddhism. During the ninth century, however, the Japanese deliberately separated themselves from the mainland and began to create their own distinctive customs. Court nobles cultivated a unique Japanese literature and developed an official religion called "Shinto," which encouraged elaborate ceremonies and worship of the emperor. And the Japanese became far more aggressive, both in war and in business, than were the Chinese: early in the sixteenth century, Japanese traders were sailing to the East Indies and the Philippines, establishing trading posts as they went.

Unlike the Chinese, the Japanese developed a governmental and social system much like European feudalism. As in Europe, the nobles for centuries failed to pay more than lip service to the emperors they supposedly worshiped, and the country was torn by their destructive civil wars. In the sixteenth century, the emperor still inhabited the royal palace; but the real rulers were the feudal warlords called "daimyos," one of whom, called the "shogun," was a sort of hereditary prime minister. The rulers followed the Shinto religion for the most part, but many of the people were Buddhists.

THE EAST INDIES: WEALTHY BUT UNDEVELOPED

The East Indies lie along the equator, extending some 3,000 miles from the Indian Ocean to Australia. The ancestors of the Indonesians, as the inhabitants are called today, immigrated from Asia some 4,000 years ago. As might be expected of island dwellers who are separated from each other by the seas, they speak a variety of dialects and have a number of different beliefs, most of them imported from the Asian mainland. From India and China came the Hindu and Buddhist religions, which were later replaced by Islam in many places. The Indies were never brought under a single government; instead, there were a number of little and often short-lived kingdoms.

To outsiders, the East Indies were important principally as a source of spices. About the twelfth century, Arab merchants began trading with the Spice Islands (now called the Moluccas), the richest spice-producing area of the Indies. The Arabs carried the spices to the Levant, where eager European merchants flocked to buy them. Thus the spices of the East Indies were important in European trade long before any Europeans themselves sailed to the Indies.

🦋 THE EUROPEANS IN THE FAR EAST

Soon after the Portuguese discovery of the route to India, countries along Europe's Atlantic coast hastened to establish trading posts and colonies in the Far East. Their monarchs gave trade monopolies, direct financial aid, and naval and military protection to merchants and colonists. Merchants used this aid to establish trading posts called "factories," where they collected spices, sugar, and other local products for shipment to Europe. Out of these activities there gradually developed a new economic system called "mercantilism" (Chapter 26) under which national governments controlled and taxed trade in return for the aid and protection given to the merchants. In this way both the governments and the traders benefited from the growth of the colonies.

Both Catholics and Protestants made great efforts to carry their faiths to the colonies, and missionaries followed the explorers. The missionaries often won converts in the less well-developed areas. But they were less successful in India, China, and Japan, where most people clung to their own ancient religions.

THE PORTUGUESE EMPIRE

During the sixteenth century the Portuguese were masters of the largest European empire in the Far East, and Lisbon replaced Venice as the center of trade with the Orient. In India, Portuguese colonists played one native ruler against another and set Hindus against Muslims to win control of the Malabar coast and the ports of Calicut and Goa. They introduced European ideas of government and forbade customs they considered

The harbor of Lisbon, the capital and principal port of Portugal, as it appeared in the seventeenth century. When the Portuguese empire was at its height, ships from all Europe came to Lisbon to trade for spices, coffee, and other products of the Far East.

immoral. Portuguese missionaries converted the ancestors of many of the more than 8,000,000 Indians who are Christians today.

From India, Portuguese sailors moved west to seize control of the Persian Gulf and the profitable trade with Arabia, and east to seize the Malacca Straits, which control the sea route to the East Indies, China, and Japan. Soon they had established trading factories in Java, Borneo, and the Spice Islands and at the Chinese port of Macao. In 1542 they reached Japan. By 1580 they were not only trading profitably with the Japanese, but their missionary leader, Francis Xavier, who had been one of the co-founders of the Jesuits, and his followers had converted 150,000 to Catholicism.

But the Portuguese empire soon began to fall apart. In 1580 King Philip II of Spain seized Portugal itself. During the years that Spain controlled Portugal, the Portuguese colonies were poorly protected from native resistance and from attacks by other Europeans. The Japanese expelled all foreigners including the Portuguese. The English seized Portuguese factories in Persia and India; the Dutch invaded the China coast and the Spice Islands; and both England and the Dutch Netherlands developed rival trading posts in Africa. After regaining its independence in 1640, Portugal made a series of alliances with England and regained some of its former strength; but it could never again dominate the trade with Asia.

THE SPANISH IN THE PHILIPPINES

The Spanish concentrated their colonial efforts in the New World. (Chapter 24.) Their only colony in Asia was the Philippines, which the explorer Ferdinand Magellan discovered and claimed for Spain in 1521. In 1565 the Spanish established their first outpost and set about conquering the islands. The Filipinos, who did not have a highly developed civilization, for the most part accepted Spanish government, the Spanish language, and the Catholic Church. The Spanish established their capital at Manila, which became an important and flourishing city. The Filipinos were the only people of the Far East to be largely westernized and Christianized by their European rulers. The Philippines remained under Spanish control until they were taken over by the United States in 1898.

THE ENGLISH, FRENCH, AND DUTCH

The English, French, and Dutch were comparative latecomers in the Far East, but they managed to divide most Portuguese possessions among themselves and to add many others of their own. The Dutch and English were less interested in missionary activity than were the Catholic countries, but they were more successful in developing large-scale commerce and in establishing colonies that survived until very recent times.

All three countries vied with each other to establish East India companies —large private businesses that were given trade monopolies and were allowed to set up colonies of their own. By 1660 the Dutch had seized Portuguese possessions in India and Ceylon, and in 1674 the French took over Pondicherry on the east coast. The English were even more active: they took Surat and the Malabar coast, defeated a Mughal emperor who tried to restrict their trade, and marched north to build Calcutta near the mouth of the Ganges River. By the end of the seventeenth century the English and French were poised for a struggle to dominate India.

In China, the British and Dutch set up factories at the port of Canton to compete with the Portuguese at nearby Macao. Few if any merchants were allowed to penetrate into the Chinese interior, but a remarkable group of Catholic missionaries preached to the Chinese for almost two centuries.

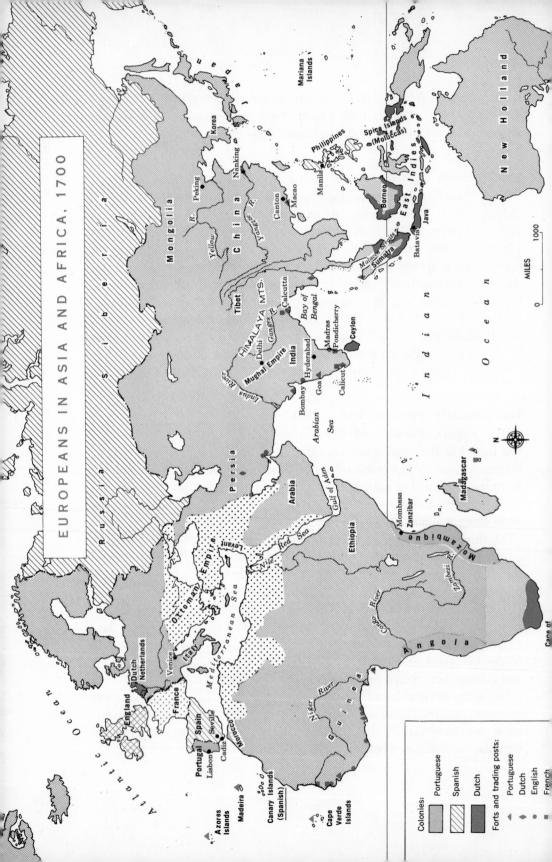

EUROPEANS IN ASIA AND AFRICA, 1700

Colonies:
- Portuguese
- Spanish
- Dutch

Forts and trading posts:
- Portuguese
- Dutch
- English
- French

MILES
0   1000

N

Atlantic Ocean

Indian Ocean

Azores Islands

Madeira

Canary Islands (Spanish)

Cape Verde Islands

England

Netherlands
Dutch

France

Portugal
Lisbon

Spain
Seville
Cadiz

Morocco

Venice
Italy

Mediterranean Sea

Ottoman Empire

Levant

Nile

Red Sea

Gulf of Aden

Arabia

Persia

Siberia

Russia

Mongolia

Tibet

HIMALAYA MTS.

China

Peking

Yellow R.

Yangtze R.

Nanking

Canton

Macao

Korea

Philippines

Manila

Mariana Islands

Spice Islands (Moluccas)

Borneo

Sumatra

Malacca Straits

Batavia

Java

East Indies

New Holland

Delhi

Mughal Empire

Indus River

Ganges R.

India

Calcutta

Bay of Bengal

Hyderabad

Bombay

Goa

Madras

Pondicherry

Calicut

Ceylon

Arabian Sea

Ethiopia

Mombasa

Zanzibar

Mozambique

Zambezi R.

Congo River

Angola

Guinea

Niger River

Madagascar

Cape of

The most outstanding of these was Matteo Ricci (1552-1610) who in twenty years worked his way from Macao to the imperial court at Peking. He and his followers wore Chinese dress, adopted Chinese names and the Chinese language, and attempted to reconcile the ethics of Confucius with the teachings of Christianity. By 1685 there were Catholic bishops in Peking, Nanking, and Macao, and a hundred churches, and Jesuit missionaries had become trusted advisers to the emperors. But in 1724 the Chinese emperor, fearing that the pope's claim to divine authority challenged his position as absolute monarch, forbade Christianity altogether, banished the missionaries, and persecuted their converts. For more than a century thereafter, contact between Europeans and Chinese was limited to the trading posts at Macao and Canton.

In the first half of the seventeenth century the Dutch whittled away at Portuguese possessions in the East Indies. They took over Java, half of Timor, many of the Spice Islands, and finally seized the Malacca Straits in 1641. They based their Dutch East India Company at the new city of Batavia on Java, ousted some English interlopers, and monopolized the profitable spice trade. They made the natives produce the products they wanted, but otherwise left them and their culture undisturbed. The Dutch dominated the East Indies for three centuries.

In Africa both British and Dutch challenged Portuguese control of the gold, ivory, and slave markets. The Dutch set up posts in the Gold and Guinea Coasts of West Africa. In 1652 they built a trading center at the Cape of Good Hope, which became the nucleus of the white colony of South Africa. Twelve years later the British established a factory at the mouth of the Gambia River in West Africa. By 1700 the coast of Africa was dotted with little forts and factories; but there were no large colonies, for none of the European countries bothered to annex much territory. Most of the interior remained unexplored, and its people were not exposed to European influence. Only in Ethiopia, where Portuguese Jesuits won a few followers, was there much missionary activity; but there the Europeans were expelled and their missions destroyed in 1633.

☸ ☸ ☸

By the end of the seventeenth century Europeans had explored most of the coasts of Africa and East Asia, establishing profitable trading posts and starting a struggle for colonial domination of the region. But most Africans and Orientals had little direct contact with the European intruders.

This was not the case in the New World that Columbus discovered in 1492. There the native population was far less civilized and was unable to resist European conquerors successfully. In the New World, first Spain and Portugal, and later the other countries along the Atlantic coast of Europe, established flourishing settlements whose numerous colonists imported the customs of their homelands to lands they called "New Spain," "New France," and "New England."

People, Places, and Terms

Eric the Red
Leif Ericson
Marco Polo
Henry the Navigator
Bartholomeu Dias
Vasco da Gama
Gautama Buddha
Baber
Akbar
Aurangzeb
Ming dynasty
Manchu dynasty
Confucius
Francis Xavier
Ferdinand Magellan
Matteo Ricci

Cape Verde
Cape of Good Hope
Indian Ocean
Malindi
Calicut

Himalayas
Ganges River
Indus River
China
Middle Kingdom
Yangtse River
Hwang Ho
Japan
Korea
East Indies
Spice Islands
Malabar Coast
Goa
Malacca Straits
Macao
Philippine Islands
Manila
Ceylon
Pondicherry
Calcutta
Canton
Peking

Java
Batavia

caste system
Brahman
Kshatriya
Vaisya
Shudra
untouchables
Hinduism
Buddhism
Nirvana
mandarin
Confucianism
Taoism
Shinto
daimyo
shogun
factory
mercantilism
East India companies

Getting Organized

1. In the sixteenth century, what did the average educated European know about the rest of the world? Had anyone explored beyond Europe before 1400? Why did exploration increase in the fifteenth century?
2. Why was Portugal a leader in the exploration of the world? Why did Henry the Navigator want to explore Africa and beyond? What were the achievements of Bartholomeu Dias and Vasco da Gama?
3. Describe the geography of India. What was the social structure of India? What did Hinduism teach? What did Buddhism teach?

4. How did sixteenth-century China differ from Europe? What was its social structure? What did Confucius teach? How important were his teachings? How was China governed?
5. How did the early Japanese copy Chinese customs? How was Japan ruled? What religion did the Japanese follow?
6. Describe the East Indies. Why were they important?
7. What were the roles of the various European national governments in exploration and discovery? What was the role of the church?
8. What areas of the Far East did Portugal control at the height of its power? What was the role of missionaries in Portugal's conquests? How and why did the Portuguese empire fall apart?
9. What part of the Far East did Spain control? What were the goals of the English, French, and Dutch in the Far East? How successful was each of these countries in achieving its goals? By 1700 how great was European influence in Asia and Africa?

Understanding the Big Picture

1. What were the causes of the great era of discovery, exploration, and colonization in the fifteenth century? Why did Portugal lead the way?
2. How different were the Asian civilizations from that of Europe? Be specific as to social structure, religion, and government.
3. What were the goals of the various European nations in the Far East? How successful was each country? Which was the most successful? Why? Which the least successful? Why?

Mastering the Map

Study the map of Europe and the Far East on page 334. Trace the routes of Dias and da Gama. How could a European ship best get from Europe to each of the Far Eastern regions? In 1700, which European nation had the largest Far Eastern empire? Which had the most valuable empire? In what areas of the Far East do you think conflicts between the European powers would be most likely to break out in the eighteenth century? Why?

For the Thoughtful

1. Explain the ways in which the urge of Europeans to explore and colonize was related to the ideas and the attitudes of the Renaissance. What effect did the Catholic Reformation have on European activities in the Far East?
2. Compare the European exploration in the fifteenth and sixteenth centuries with the twentieth-century exploration of outer space. In what ways are the two eras similar? In what ways different?

24

Europe and the New World

The islands and continents of the Western Hemisphere were literally a "New World" to the Europeans. In the Far East they had set up little forts and factories to trade with the ancient Oriental civilizations. In the New World there were vast lands whose existence had not even been suggested in medieval legend. Lightly populated but richly endowed with natural resources, these lands gave their European developers greater wealth than had been dreamed possible. Europeans flocked to settle large and prosperous colonies in which they adapted the customs of the Old World to meet the needs of the New.

In the fifteenth and sixteenth centuries the Spanish, and to a lesser extent the Portuguese, explored and colonized most of South and Central America and many of the Caribbean Islands. In the sixteenth and seventeenth centuries the countries along the northern coast of Europe—France, England, and the Dutch Netherlands—explored and colonized the Atlantic shores of North America and other islands in the Caribbean. By 1700 there were European settlements all the way from Canada to Argentina.

THE DISCOVERIES AND COLONIES OF SPAIN

The Spanish empire was the result of a mistake. Because Christopher Columbus thought the world to be much smaller than it really is, and because he gained the backing of the queen of Spain, Spain acquired the largest and richest empire of the time.

338

Christopher Columbus: portrait by Sebastiano del Piombo (1485?-1547). The greatest seaman of the Age of Discovery was described by his son as follows: "In eating and drinking, and in the adornment of his person, he was very moderate and modest. He was affable in conversation with strangers and very pleasant to members of his household, though with a certain gravity. He was so strict in matters of religion he might have been taken for a member of a religious order."

COLUMBUS DISCOVERS AMERICA

Christopher Columbus (1451-1506) was an Italian navigator and mapmaker who settled in Lisbon, the capital of Portugal. Columbus became obsessed with the idea of reaching Asia by sailing west, having convinced himself that Japan was only about 3,600 miles from Portugal (or about where the East Coast of the United States really is). He presented his plan to the king of Portugal, who rejected it. So Columbus went to Spain, whose Queen Isabella (see page 237) agreed to give him three vessels, a crew of Spanish sailors, the title "Admiral of the Ocean Sea," and permission to find what he could by sailing west.

With his little fleet Columbus headed southwest to the Canary Islands, off the coast of West Africa. From there he sailed west across the Atlantic, quieting the fears of his superstitious seamen with the assurance that they would soon sight land. After a voyage of a little more than a month he did find land, on October 12, 1492. But it was not the land he expected; it was a little island he christened San Salvador, "Holy Saviour," but which today is called Watlings Island in the Bahamas. He sailed on, discovering Cuba and Hispaniola (the island now shared by the Dominican Republic and Haiti), but not the gold or the educated Orientals he expected. Nevertheless he returned in triumph to Spain with the news that he had found a new route to the Indies.

Isabella was delighted, and sent him back the next year with 1500 men and a large fleet. This time he discovered Puerto Rico and Jamaica and founded the first permanent settlement in the New World at Santo Domingo in what is now the Dominican Republic. On a third journey he explored the north coast of South America and realized for the first time that he had discovered an entire new continent. Because of a dispute with the governor of Hispaniola, he was sent back to Spain in chains; but Isabella forgave him, and in 1502 allowed him to leave on a fourth voyage, during which he charted the coast of Central America. He returned to Spain a sick man and died soon afterward, loudly claiming the recognition that he was sure he deserved and that later generations have given him. Ironically, his discoveries were not named for him, but for a navigator named Americus Vespucius, whose letters home were so popular that people began calling the new lands "America."

LATER SPANISH EXPLORERS

Hundreds of explorers and colonists followed Columbus to the West Indies (the name "Indies" was retained even after people learned they were half the globe away from the East Indies). Some searched for gold. Others established plantations, where the natives were forced to work so hard that the Caribbean Indians soon died out. Others were monks and priests who sought to convert the Indians to Catholicism. The most renowned were the "conquistadors," warrior-adventurers who explored, conquered, plundered, and opened mines and fertile plantations whose profits made Spain for a century the most powerful country in Europe.

Vasco Nuñez de Balboa, seeking gold mines, crossed the Isthmus of Panama in 1513 and discovered the Pacific Ocean on the other side. Her-

Spaniards under Cortes attacking the Aztecs in Mexico: an illustration from an early Spanish-American book. The vastly outnumbered Spanish force was victorious largely because its cannons, muskets, and horses terrified the Aztecs.

nando Cortes, with an army of 508 soldiers, sixteen horses, and ten brass cannon, in 1519-1521 attacked and conquered the Aztec civilization in Mexico. Cortes made the Aztec capital at Mexico City a Spanish head-quarters, and in 1535 moved on to explore the region around the Gulf of California. As governor of Mexico, Cortes established a pattern that was followed by later Spanish colonizers: he did not kill off the Indians, but rather forced them to work in the mines and on the plantations owned by Spanish colonists. He also worked to convert the Indians by aiding the efforts of missionary monks and priests. Cortes was successful in almost everything he did; Mexican silver flowed into the Spanish treasury, and Mexico became as Catholic as Spain.

In the 1530's Francisco Pizarro conquered the Inca civilization of Peru with an army even smaller than that of Cortes. But Pizarro exploited both the Inca natives and his Spanish followers so viciously that his lieutenants murdered him in his palace in Lima in 1541. Pizarro's conquest was the unhappy start of two centuries of misgovernment in Peru, where harsh rulers killed many Incas and heavily taxed and cruelly overworked those who labored in the mines and fields. The Spanish skillfully extracted Peru's great riches at the cost of reducing the people to near slavery.

Other Spaniards crisscrossed the southern half of North America. In 1513 Juan Ponce de León discovered and explored Florida while searching for a "fountain of youth." Alvar Nuñez Cabeza de Vaca, who was shipwrecked west of the mouth of the Mississippi in 1528, spent eight years wandering through what is now Texas and New Mexico. Hernando de Soto con-quered Florida and in 1541 discovered the Mississippi River. Francisco Vásquez de Coronado set out in 1540 to find the legendary Seven Cities of Cibola, where the streets were supposedly paved with gold. He did not find them, but he did discover the Grand Canyon and crossed the Great Plains into what is now Kansas before returning empty-handed.

None of these men, however, proved the theory that the East Indies could be reached by sailing west. Ferdinand Magellan did that. With five ships he sailed from Spain westward to the coast of South American, south along the coast to what is now called the Strait of Magellan, and through it into the Pacific. After a long voyage, during which his men ran short of water and had so little food that they learned to consider rats a delicacy, Magellan reached the Mariana Islands. Continuing westward, Magellan dis-covered the Philippines, which he claimed for Spain (see page 333), and where in 1521 he was killed in a fight with the natives. Magellan's lieutenant, Juan Sebastian del Cano, took command and completed the voyage by sailing around Africa, reaching Spain the following year. King Charles of Spain gave him a coat of arms that included a globe surrounded by the Latin words for "You were the first to go around me."

THE SPANISH EMPIRE

By the Treaty of Tordesillas of 1494, Spain and Portugal agreed that each would not interfere with the other in exploring and exploiting the non-Christian parts of the world. In effect, they divided the world between themselves. Portugal was to have a free hand in Africa and Asia, and also in Brazil; Spain, in all the rest of the Americas. By the middle of the sixteenth century the Spanish had taken advantage of their freedom to colonize the New World, and soon they were firmly established in an empire that extended from northern California to southern Chile. Royal administrators came to govern in the name of the Spanish king, and gentlemen and adventurers flocked to make their fortunes from plantations, mines, or trade. Besides establishing European customs throughout Spanish America, these men proved to be remarkably successful governors. The king retained final authority, but he turned much of the actual administration over to the "Council of the Indies." A group of able men, the council made laws and regulations that, by the standards of the day, were enlightened and humane. They divided the empire into three "viceroyalties" (districts ruled by "viceroys," or deputies of the king) with capitals at Mexico City, Lima, and Buenos Aires. These were subdivided into provinces, which were governed by native Spaniards assisted by partly legislative and partly judicial bodies that took care of local government matters.

Jesuit and Franciscan missionaries converted most of the Indians to Catholicism and established schools and colleges to disseminate Spanish culture. The church did much to protect the natives from exploitation. There was more tolerance in the Spanish colonies than in the mother country: the Indian natives were allowed to retain many of their local religious customs, and Jews and Protestants were given considerable freedom.

Social classes in the Spanish colonies were clearly defined. At the top were the Spanish governor and his Spanish-born advisers. Next were the "Creoles," American born of Spanish blood, who owned prosperous businesses or large estates and often held government office as well. Below them were the "mestizos," of mixed Spanish and Indian ancestry, who ran small businesses or practiced skilled trades. At the bottom were the masses of native Indians and, in some places, Negro slaves. Most Indians were "peons," whose life was restricted in much the same way as that of medieval serfs.

During the first two centuries of Spanish rule, the colonies' most profitable exports were gold and silver. The mines in one mountain alone produced some $1,000,000,000 in silver. There were other minerals, too, but the Spanish were primarily interested in precious metals and left undeveloped the huge deposits of iron, copper, zinc, tin, and lead.

As they occupied the new lands during the seventeenth century, the Spanish set up great agricultural estates. These estates were usually owned by Creoles, administered by mestizos, and worked by peons or Negro slaves. Eventually the value of the crops these estates produced rivaled that of silver.

Trade with the mother country grew as the population and productivity of the colonies increased. Goods were carried overland to ports such as Vera Cruz in Mexico and Cartagena on the Caribbean, then in convoys to Havana, in Cuba. There every year a fleet assembled to make the dangerous voyage to Spain. Stately Spanish galleons protected the merchant vessels as they sailed through waters infested by pirates and privateers. Westward they carried the precious metals and agricultural products of the colonies; on the return they brought armor, leather goods, religious items, olive oil, and wine for the colonists. The voyage was so dangerous that the government regulated all trade and discouraged individual merchants from striking out on their own.

In the seventeenth century the royal government in Spain fell slowly into decay (Chapter 25), and the colonial governments consequently grew weaker. Control over trade was therefore less effective. Merchants began to engage in a profitable but illegal smuggling business with French, Dutch, and English shipmasters. The Creoles became restive under Spanish governors, and the slaves and peons, always an unstable element in the population because of their low status, occasionally rose in unsuccessful but violent rebellion. As the supply of precious metals began to give out, the colonies became more and more agricultural, for the Spanish did not develop new industries to replace the gold and silver mines.

🜊 THE PORTUGUESE IN BRAZIL

The Portuguese claimed to have discovered Brazil by accident. In 1500 a Portuguese fleet sailed for India under Pedro Cabral and, so Cabral said, got blown all the way across the Atlantic to the shores of Brazil. Cabral promptly claimed it for his country. Settlers soon followed him, establishing colonies that remained in Portugal's hands for almost 300 years.

The history of Brazil under the Portuguese paralleled that of Spanish America during the sixteenth and sevententh centuries. The government was controlled by royal officials, and the coastline was dotted with huge estates where Negro slaves and Indians raised sugar for Portuguese aristocrats. The landlords spent most of their time in their capital, Bahia.

The powers of northern Europe eyed Brazil jealously. The Dutch actually established a colony in a section of its northeast coast in 1630; but the Portuguese drove them out a quarter-century later, and there were no more intrusions. Brazil's colonists were forced to stay close to the coast because the rugged lands in the interior and the torrid Amazon valley made inland expansion difficult. In the late seventeenth century some adventurous settlers set up cattle ranches in the southern interior; others discovered gold and diamonds, which helped relieve the poverty of the Portuguese monarchs. But under the Portuguese, Brazil did not become a great center of mining or trade.

🐚 THE CARIBBEAN

In the century after Columbus, the Caribbean Sea was usually called the "Spanish Main" in recognition of Spain's great power there. Spaniards settled Cuba, Hispaniola, Jamaica, and many of the lesser islands; built ports to trade with the American mainland and with Spain; and set up plantations to raise sugar for European markets.

CHALLENGES TO SPANISH POWER

During the sixteenth century, when Spanish power was at its height, northern Europeans began to attack Spanish shipping and to look jealously on the West Indies—the lush, tropical Caribbean islands. Late in the century Sir Francis Drake and other English "Sea Dogs" preyed on Spanish merchantmen, treasure ships, and even cities. In the smaller islands that the Spanish had not bothered to fortify, they established colonies whose occupants first raised cattle and later turned to piracy. Soon the area was infested with pirates from many countries who preyed on the commerce of all nations.

In the seventeenth century northern Europeans rushed to colonize the remaining unsettled islands and turned aggressively on the Spaniards. In 1628 a Dutch force captured the Spanish treasure fleet; in 1655 the English seized Jamaica; and in 1697 the French won Haiti (the western part of

Hispaniola). As nations battled, law and order almost broke down entirely; the pirates grew bolder than ever: one even seized and looted two important towns. After 1700 the Caribbean became a battleground for European navies and a magnet for the most dangerous outlaws of the sea.

By 1700, however, the Caribbean islands had grown rich satisfying Europe's appetite for sugar and tobacco. The tropical climate and rich land supported estates so profitable that West Indian colonies became major prizes in the wars of European countries. These island possessions became centers of smuggling, which was usually far more profitable than legal trade; officials were either powerless to prevent it or willing to be bribed to ignore it. The West Indies were the lawless boom town of the seventeenth century.

THE SLAVE TRADE

Few Caribbean natives or American Indians willingly worked in the fields; many succumbed to European diseases or mistreatment, and others committed suicide rather than become laborers. Consequently, docile Negro slaves brought high prices. Dealers bought them in Africa, herded them onto specially designed ships, chained them to the decks, and hurried them across the Atlantic. Conditions on shipboard were so bad that often one third to one half of the miserable captives died during the passage; but the prices in the New World were so high that slave traders nonetheless made fabulous profits.

Most Negro slaves were sold to the sugar plantation owners in the West Indies. Others were taken to Spanish, Portuguese, or English colonies in North and South America. They were able to perform plantation labor, which required much back-breaking work in tropical heat. Their food and living conditions were so wretched that the typical slave in the Caribbean lived only seven years after his arrival. Even so, the Negroes multiplied, and much of the island population today is of African origin.

EXPLORATION IN NORTH AMERICA

The Atlantic coast of North America was explored by men of many nationalities, many of whom were seeking a "Northwest Passage" by sea to the Pacific. In 1496 King Henry VII of England commissioned a Genoese sailor named John Cabot to "seek out, discover, and find whatsoever isles, regions, or provinces of the heathen and infidels which have before this been unknown to all Christians." In two voyages, Cabot discovered New-foundland and sailed south along the coast, probably as far as what later became Virginia. In 1500 Gaspar Corte-Real, a Portuguese, reached Green-land, and in a second voyage sent back some sixty slaves captured in New-foundland before disappearing into the icy Arctic waters. Giovanni da Verrazano explored the coasts of North America and Nova Scotia for the French in 1524, and ten years later the Frenchman Jacques Cartier sailed up the Saint Lawrence River in the hope that it was the Northwest Passage.

Early in the sixteenth century fishermen charted the Grand Banks, the fishing area of the North Atlantic where they caught cod and other fish to feed Europe's growing population. Later English mariners gave their names to Frobisher Bay and Davis Strait in the bitterly cold waters off Greenland and Labrador. An Englishman, Henry Hudson, discovered Hudson Bay for the English and, in the service of the Dutch, sailed up the Hudson River as far as the site of Albany. Each time he thought that he had found the Northwest Passage; each time he was disappointed.

Few of the sixteenth-century explorers seriously considered colonizing North America. The disadvantages were all too obvious—cold winters; the Appalachian Mountains, which cut off easy access to the interior country; unfriendly and primitive Indians; forests that made farming difficult and overland travel all but impossible; few easily developed natural resources; and no gold or silver. On the other hand, the region had long-range advan-tages—a climate similar to Europe's, which would allow settlers to transfer European crops and customs reasonably intact to the New World; such natural resources as the timber and furs of the forests and the fish of the sea; and no well-organized native civilizations to be conquered.

Therefore, North America was a second choice for settlers, most of whom would have preferred the warmer climates and richer soils of the Caribbean. But, once developed in the seventeenth century, the North American settlements proved to be the richest and most profitable of all.

THE FRENCH IN NORTH AMERICA

In 1608 Samuel de Champlain set up the colony of New France in the Saint Lawrence River valley and founded its capital city of Quebec. In the fertile river valley "habitants," as French settlers were called, farmed in much the same way as in their homeland; and along the shores of the Gulf of Saint Lawrence and on the Acadian peninsula to its south, French fishermen built their tiny villages. The most important export of the colony

THE NEW WORLD
1700

Greenland (Danish)

Hudson
Bay

Labrador

Newfoundland

Sault
Ste.
Marie

Quebec

Cape Breton Island

Acadia

New England

New York

Philadelphia

Virginia

Florida

Gulf of Mexico

California

New Spain (Mexico)

Vera
Cruz

Mexico
City

Caribbean Sea

West Indies

New
Granada

New
Andalusia

Surinam
(Dutch)

Amazon   R.

New
Castile
(Peru)

Brazil

Bahia

Lima

New Estremadura (Chile)

La Plata

Buenos
Aires

Strait of
Magellan

Pacific   Ocean

Atlantic   Ocean

Louisiana

New France

Mississippi R.

Great Lakes

Spanish

Portuguese

French

English

MILES

0   400

Bahama Islands (Eng.)

Atlantic
Ocean

Havana

Cuba

Santo
Domingo

Puerto
Rico

Hispaniola

Haiti

Santo
Domingo

Jamaica

Antigua (Eng.)

Guadeloupe
(Fr.)

Dominica
(Sp.)

Martinique
(Fr.)

Caribbean   Sea

Curacao
(Dutch)

Barbados
(Eng.)

Spanish   Main

Trinidad
(Sp.)

Puerto
Bello

Cartagena

Valencia

Caracas

Panama

Panama

Pacific Ocean

Surinam
(Dutch)

MILES

0   1000

N

was furs, in pursuit of which trappers called *coureurs de bois* ("woods runners"), accompanied by Jesuit missionaries seeking souls, ranged farther and farther inland. They canoed up the Saint Lawrence to the Great Lakes, establishing trading posts with names like Detroit and Sault Sainte Marie. In 1673 Father Jacques Marquette, a Jesuit, and his companion Louis Jolliet crossed what is now Wisconsin and discovered the upper Mississippi River. Nine years later Robert Cavelier de La Salle followed the river all the way to the Gulf of Mexico and took possession of its valley in the name of King Louis XIV of France. In 1699 the French established the colony of Louisiana (named for Louis XIV) and in 1718 the city of New Orleans near the mouth of the Mississippi. Their search for furs and souls enabled the French to claim not only what is now eastern Canada, but all of the central part of North America.

Despite its great size, New France never became very strong. Because the French government believed that the colonies should exist only for the power and profit of the motherland, the king rigidly controlled the colonial government and regulated all trade. Rigid control of trade discouraged merchants and slowed economic growth. The population remained small, for few Frenchmen wished to emigrate, and many of those who might have wished to—Huguenots, for example—were not allowed in New France. The French population of New France probably never was greater than 80,000, and it was thinly spread all the way from the Gulf of Saint Lawrence to the mouth of the Mississippi. At the end of the seventeenth century New France was huge, but poor and weak.

THE ENGLISH IN NORTH AMERICA

No permanent English settlements were made in North America until the seventeenth century, when there was a sudden burst of colonization. English patriots were eager to establish colonies in the New World to rival Spain and demonstrate the power of their rising country. Companies of merchants hoped to reap the rewards of trade. Puritans, Catholics, and Quakers sought freedom to worship as they chose.

After a century and a quarter of settlement (1607-1733), the English owned thirteen colonies along the Atlantic coast from New England to Georgia. Early in the seventeenth century, Virginia and Maryland were founded by businessmen and Catholics, respectively. Farther north, in New England, Calvinists founded Massachusetts, Rhode Island, Plymouth (which later became part of Massachusetts), New Hampshire, and two colonies that later joined to become Connecticut. Political and religious turmoil in England (Chapter 27) stimulated a "Great Migration" of settlers, who quickly made their new colonies prosperous and populous. Later, in 1664, the English took over the Dutch colony of New Netherland, which they renamed New York, and the formerly Swedish colony of Delaware. In 1681 the king gave a patent to a Quaker leader named William Penn to found Pennsylvania. In the eighteenth century, areas already occupied by European settlers were organized into new colonies: parts of New York and Pennsylvania were combined to form the colony of New Jersey (1702); scattered settlements to the south of Virginia were organized (1729) into North and South Carolina; and James Oglethorpe was authorized to found Georgia as a haven for debtors and religious refugees (1733).

By 1700 the English colonies had developed several unique characteristics that set them apart from the colonies of other countries. They were far more heavily populated by Europeans than were the other colonies. They were also more self-sufficient, for they not only raised their own food but also manufactured most of the products they needed. The settlers lived

Jamestown, Virginia, the first permanent English settlement in North America, as it appeared in 1622. Jamestown was the capital of Virginia from its founding in 1607 until 1698, when the seat of government was moved to Williamsburg. Thereafter, Jamestown declined rapidly, and finally it was abandoned.

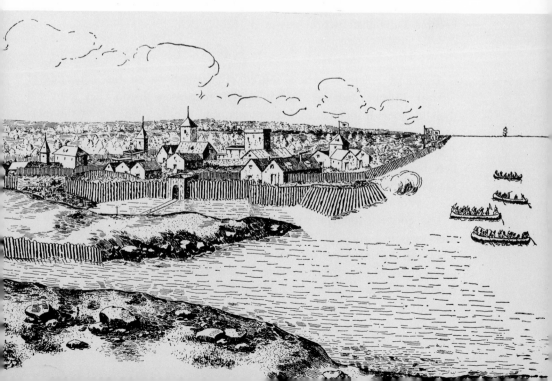

close together, relatively speaking, for the Appalachian Mountains prevented their ranging inland. Unlike other colonists, they refused either to tolerate or to enslave the native Indians, whom they drove back from their frontiers. Although there were distinct social classes, it was easier in the English colonies than anywhere else to move from one class to another.

Some of the colonies were self-governing; they elected their own governors, who paid only lip service to royal officials. Others were "proprietary," owned in theory by a "proprietor," who chose the governor. The rest were "royal" colonies, whose governors were appointed by the king. All had a notable degree of local self-government, in the form of town meetings in New England and colonial legislatures almost everywhere. These practical schools of politics trained most of the leaders of the American Revolution and from the first sought to restrict the authority of the monarchs.

The English attempted to control colonial trade. Beginning in 1651, Parliament passed a series of "Acts of Trade and Navigation," which restricted the colonists' trade with foreign settlements. The English rarely bothered to enforce them, however; so the colonial merchants smuggled extensively, ignoring rather than protesting the restrictions.

Each of the English colonies developed its own individual character. But they all had some things in common—local self-government, expanding economies, and loyalty to England tempered by a growing sense of independence. By 1700 they were already among the strongest European outposts in the New World and were a major factor in England's rise to become a dominant world power.

☙ ☙ ☙

American colonies were a source of strength to all the countries of western Europe that were lucky enough to possess them. They provided their kings with income, military power, and prestige. They gave the merchant middle class gold and silver (which increased the amount of money they could use in trade) as well as raw materials for their shops and markets for their products. They influenced writers who wrote of "noble savages," exotic places, and the accomplishments of the conquerors of the New World.

The colonies took on many characteristics of their mother countries—their religions, their political ideas, their systems of trade and commerce. They also became allies of their mother countries in war and battlegrounds in conflicts of European powers. In short, the New World became an extension of European civilization.

People, Places, and Terms

Christopher
Columbus
Isabella
Americus Vespucius
Vasco Nuñez
de Balboa
Hernando Cortes
Francisco Pizarro
Juan Ponce de León
Hernando de Soto
Francisco Vásquez
de Coronado
Ferdinand Magellan
Juan Sebastian
del Cano
Pedro Cabral
John Cabot
Gaspar Corte-Real
Giovanni da
Verrazano
Jacques Cartier
Henry Hudson
Samuel de Champlain
Jacques Marquette
Louis Jolliet
Robert Cavelier
de La Salle

William Penn
James Oglethorpe

Lisbon
San Salvador
Bahama Islands
Cuba
Hispaniola
Puerto Rico
Jamaica
Santo Domingo
Central America
West Indies
Isthmus of Panama
Mexico
Peru
Lima
Florida
Mississippi River
Strait of Magellan
Caribbean Sea
Brazil
Haiti
Greenland
Newfoundland
Saint Lawrence River
Hudson Bay

Appalachian
Mountains
Quebec
Acadia
Great Lakes
Louisiana
Virginia
New England
New Netherland

conquistador
Treaty of Tordesillas
Council of the Indies
viceroy
Creole
mestizo
peon
habitant
coureurs de bois
Great Migration
self-governing colony
proprietary colony
proprietor
royal colony
Acts of Trade
and Navigation

Getting Organized

1. Who was Christopher Columbus? What did Columbus plan to do? Who supported him? How successful was his first voyage? What did he accomplish in his later voyages?
2. What lands did the later Spanish explorers conquer for Spain? Who were the principal explorers and what did each accomplish?
3. How did the Spaniards and the Portuguese divide the world? How did the Spaniards rule their huge empire? What was the role of missionaries in the Spanish colonies?
4. What was the social class structure within the Spanish colonies? How did the Spaniards profit from their new colonies? How and why did the Spanish Empire decline?
5. How did the Portuguese claim to have discovered Brazil? How did they rule this colony? Who challenged their control of Brazil?
6. What groups and countries attempted to undermine Spanish power in

the Caribbean? How successful were they? How profitable were the Caribbean islands to those that held them? How were the fields worked, and by whom? How did the goods and raw materials and precious metals get back to Europe?

7. Who were the principal explorers of North America, and what area did each man explore? Why was North America a second choice for most settlers? What advantages did it have over other areas?

8. How did the French govern their North American colonies? What areas of North America did the French control? What government policies held back the development of the French colonies?

9. What areas of North America did the English control? Why did Englishmen settle in North America? Describe the three distinct divisions of the English colonies. What was the relation of the English colonies to the English government?

Understanding the Big Picture

1. How did the Spaniards gain such a huge empire in Central and South America? What was the relationship between Spain and its colonies? Did these colonies help Spain in the short run? In the long run?

2. What happened to the once-powerful Spanish Empire? What countries took its place as the colonial powers?

3. How did the various colonial powers treat the natives of the lands they were colonizing? What role did the church, missionaries, and religion play in these new colonies?

4. Compare the French colonies to the English colonies. Which country had the firmer grip on its colonies? Why?

Mastering the Map

Study the map of Europeans in the New World on page 347. Which European nation had the largest empire? Which nation had the most valuable? Try to predict where colonial conflicts between the European powers in the New World would be likely to break out in the eighteenth century, and give your reasons for your predictions.

For the Thoughtful

1. Compare European policies in the New World to European policies in the Far East. Were the explorers and colonizers in both parts of the world driven on by the same motives? Did the European nations handle their respective colonies of both areas in the same ways?

2. From what you know of the European expansion overseas, both in the fifteenth, sixteenth, and seventeenth centuries and in more recent times, which European nation do you think treated its colonies with the greatest wisdom? Why?

Summing up the Era of Transition

A new Europe emerged out of the economic, cultural, and religious transformations of the era of the Renaissance, the Reformation, and the discovery of new routes to Asia and America. Man's ability to produce and distribute goods began to increase rapidly. His appreciation of the world he lived in —and of his own abilities—was heightened by the artists and humanists of the Renaissance. After a period of intense religious fervor caused by the Reformation, interest in religion declined.

The Peace of Westphalia marked the end of one era and the beginning of another. It marked the end of the religious wars and the triumph of dynastic monarchies ruled by powerful kings. In the decades to come, these absolute monarchs would be able to devote themselves to their own and their countries' problems without paying major attention to religious affairs. The next century and a half would be the Age of the Absolute Monarchies in Europe.

Some Questions to Answer

1. During the years 1450-1648, how were the European monarchies strengthened? Which had emerged as the strongest by 1648? What obstacles had the monarchs overcome? How did economic, religious, and nationalistic changes affect the growing strength of the monarchies?
2. How did the church change during this period? Why did Christendom break up into separate groups? How did the religious changes of this age affect the monarchies? Art and literature?
3. In 1600 in what ways could a man make a living? How different were the choices open to him from those of the Middle Ages? What economic changes had brought about this change? How did the growth of cities affect the monarchies and feudalism? How did the various economic changes affect the arts? The wave of discovery and exploration that took place during this era?
4. Why did nations go to war during this period? How did these wars differ from those of Middle Ages? What was the influence of nationalism on warfare? On the monarchies? On the arts? On the wave of discovery?

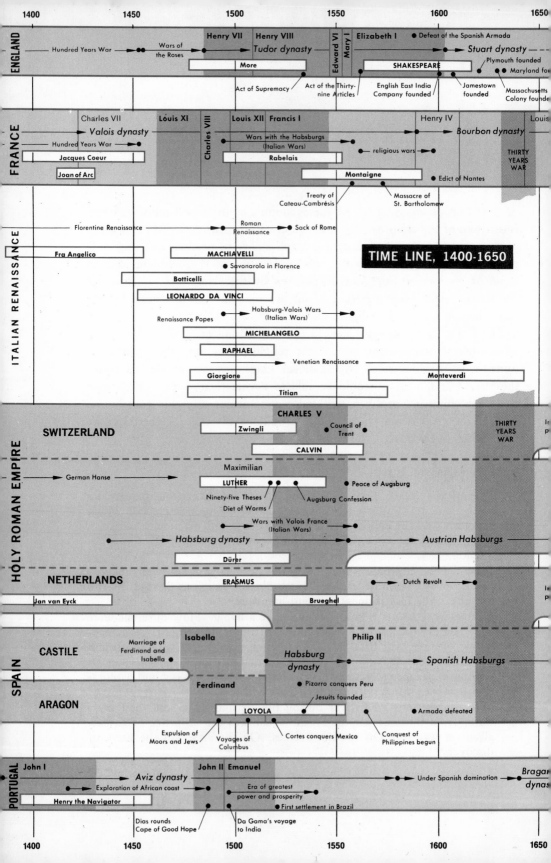

TIME LINE, 1400-1650

Scale (top and bottom): 1400 · 1450 · 1500 · 1550 · 1600 · 1650

ENGLAND
- Hundred Years War
- Wars of the Roses
- Henry VII
- Henry VIII
- *Tudor dynasty*
- Edward VI
- Mary I
- Elizabeth I
- Defeat of the Spanish Armada
- *Stuart dynasty*
- More
- SHAKESPEARE
- Act of Supremacy
- Act of the Thirty-nine Articles
- English East India Company founded
- Jamestown founded
- Plymouth founded
- Maryland fo[unded]
- Massachusetts Colony founde[d]

FRANCE
- Charles VII
- *Valois dynasty*
- Louis XI
- Charles VIII
- Louis XII
- Francis I
- Henry IV
- *Bourbon dynasty*
- Louis
- Hundred Years War
- Wars with the Habsburgs (Italian Wars)
- religious wars
- THIRTY YEARS WAR
- Jacques Coeur
- Rabelais
- Montaigne
- Joan of Arc
- Edict of Nantes
- Treaty of Cateau-Cambrésis
- Massacre of St. Bartholomew

ITALIAN RENAISSANCE
- Florentine Renaissance
- Roman Renaissance
- Sack of Rome
- Fra Angelico
- MACHIAVELLI
- Savonarola in Florence
- Botticelli
- LEONARDO DA VINCI
- Renaissance Popes
- Habsburg-Valois Wars (Italian Wars)
- MICHELANGELO
- RAPHAEL
- Venetian Renaissance
- Giorgione
- Monteverdi
- Titian

HOLY ROMAN EMPIRE

CHARLES V

SWITZERLAND
- Zwingli
- Council of Trent
- CALVIN
- THIRTY YEARS WAR

- German Hanse
- Maximilian
- LUTHER
- Ninety-five Theses
- Diet of Worms
- Augsburg Confession
- Peace of Augsburg
- Wars with Valois France (Italian Wars)
- *Habsburg dynasty*
- *Austrian Habsburgs*
- Dürer

NETHERLANDS
- ERASMUS
- Dutch Revolt
- Jan van Eyck
- Brueghel

SPAIN

CASTILE
- Marriage of Ferdinand and Isabella
- Isabella
- Philip II
- *Habsburg dynasty*
- *Spanish Habsburgs*

ARAGON
- Ferdinand
- Pizarro conquers Peru
- Jesuits founded
- LOYOLA
- Armada defeated
- Expulsion of Moors and Jews
- Voyages of Columbus
- Cortes conquers Mexico
- Conquest of Philippines begun

PORTUGAL
- John I
- *Aviz dynasty*
- John II
- Emanuel
- Under Spanish domination
- *Braga[nza] dynas[ty]*
- Exploration of African coast
- Era of greatest power and prosperity
- Henry the Navigator
- First settlement in Brazil
- Dias rounds Cape of Good Hope
- Da Gama's voyage to India

5. With what kinds of subjects did the artists and writers of the Renaissance deal? How did they feel about man? About his past accomplishments? About his future? How were the artistic changes of the period affected by religious and economic development?

Further Reading for Part Three

GENERAL ACCOUNTS

BAINTON, ROLAND H. *The Reformation of the Sixteenth Century*. Boston: Beacon, 1956 (paper). A standard work.

CLARK, GEORGE N. *Early Modern Europe from about 1450 to about 1720*. New York: Oxford University Press, 1957 (paper). A short account.

HARBISON, E. HARRIS. *The Age of Reformation*. Ithaca, N.Y.: Cornell University Press, 1955 (paper). An excellent study.

NOWELL, CHARLES E. *The Great Discoveries and the First Colonial Empires*. Ithaca, N.Y.: Cornell University Press, 1954 (paper). A useful introduction to this facet of the period.

PARRY, J. H. *Establishment of the European Hegemony, 1415-1715*. New York: Harper, 1961 (paper). Another useful survey.

PIRENNE, HENRI. *A History of Europe*. 2 vols. New York: Doubleday, 1958 (paper). A standard work that stresses the interpretation of events.

SELLERY, GEORGE C. *The Renaissance: Its Nature and Origins*. Madison: University of Wisconsin Press, 1950 (paper). A helpful introduction.

BOOKS ON SPECIFIC SUBJECTS

BAINTON, ROLAND H. *Here I Stand: A Life of Martin Luther*. Nashville: Abingdon Press, 1951 (hard cover or paper). A fine biography, with fascinating illustrations from the period.

BURCKHARDT, JACOB. *The Civilization of the Renaissance in Italy*. A classic work, outdated in some respects but still valuable. Available in several editions.

BUTTERFIELD, HERBERT. *The Origins of Modern Science, 1300-1800*. Rev. ed. New York: Macmillan; New York: Collier (paper). A readable introduction to an important aspect of modern history.

FOX, EDWARD W., Ed., *Atlas of European History*. New York: Oxford University Press, 1957.

HACKETT, FRANCIS. *Personal History of Henry the Eighth*. New York: Random House. A lively biography of this English king.

HUIZINGA, JOHAN. *Erasmus and the Age of Reformation*. New York: Harper, 1957 (paper). A study of Erasmus and his times.

MORISON, SAMUEL ELIOT. *Christopher Columbus, Mariner*. Boston: Atlantic —Little, Brown, 1955; New York: New American Library (paper). A superbly written short biography.

NEALE, JOHN E. *The Age of Catherine de Medici.* New York: Barnes & Noble, 1959; New York: Harper (paper). A survey of sixteenth-century France.

PATER, WALTER. *The Renaissance.* A group of sketches of important Renaissance figures. Available in several editions.

PENROSE, BOIES. *Travel and Discovery in the Renaissance, 1420-1620.* Cambridge, Mass.: Harvard University Press, 1952; New York: Atheneum, 1962 (paper). A good account of this aspect of the period.

PIRENNE, HENRI. *Early Democracies in the Low Countries: Urban Society and Political Conflict in the Middle Ages and the Renaissance.* New York: Harper, 1963 (paper). Valuable analysis by a great Belgian historian.

WEDGEWOOD, CICELY V. *The Thirty Years War.* New York: Doubleday (paper). A highly readable account.

SOURCE MATERIALS

BAINTON, ROLAND H. *The Age of the Reformation.* Princeton, N.J.. Van Nostrand, 1956 (paper). Contains many important documents, with notes by an expert on the Reformation.

BETTENSON, HENRY S., Ed. *Documents of the Christian Church.* 2nd ed. New York: Oxford University Press, 1963. Another valuable collection of documents.

CABEZA DE VACA, ÁLVAR NÚÑEZ. *Adventures in the Unknown Interior of America.* Ed. and trans. by CYCLONE COVEY. Gloucester, Mass.: Peter Smith. The report of a sixteenth-century Spanish explorer.

CASTIGLIONE, BALDASSARE. *The Book of the Courtier.* Trans. by CHARLES·S. SINGLETON. New York: Doubleday, 1959 (paper). The handbook of the Renaissance man.

COLUMBUS, CHRISTOPHER, *Four Voyages to the New World.* Trans. by R. H. MAJOR. New York: Citadel, 1961 (paper). Columbus's own account of his explorations.

ERASMUS, DESIDERIUS. *In Praise of Folly.* Ann Arbor: University of Michigan Press, 1958 (paper). The famous satire by the leading Christian humanist.

MACHIAVELLI, NICCOLÒ. *The Prince.* The classic work that influenced generations of monarchs and statesmen. Available in several editions.

MATTHEWS, G. T., Ed. *News and Rumor in Renaissance Europe: The Fugger Newsletters.* New York: Putnam, 1959 (paper). Reports to the fabulous Fuggers by their agents in all parts of Europe.

VINCI, LEONARDO DA *Notebooks.* Ed. by PAMELA TAYLOR. New York: New American Library, 1960 (paper). A collection that provides many insights into the mind of a Renaissance genius.

WEBER, EUGEN. *The Western Tradition.* Vol. 3, *From the Renaissance to the Atomic Age.* Boston: Heath, 1959 (paper). A useful collection of documents.

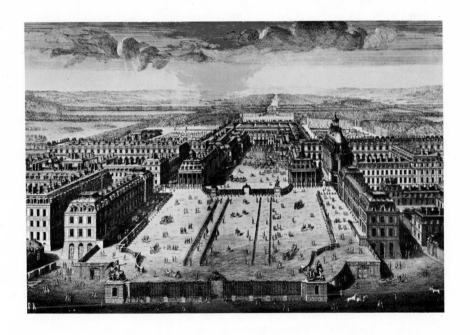

the age of absolutism

The seventeenth and eighteenth centuries were the age of the absolute monarchies. Absolutism had its beginning in the great national monarchies of the sixteenth century. The leading example was Spain, where Habsburg kings presided over a "Golden Age" made possible by their rich possessions in the New World and their dynastic lands in Europe.

The age of the absolute monarchies really dates, however, from the time of the Treaties of Westphalia of 1648, when real or would-be absolute rulers triumphed over local princes and the religious conflicts of the Reformation. The model for these almost all-powerful kings was the Bourbon monarch of France, Louis XIV, who dominated Europe in the late seventeenth century. In England, where Queen Elizabeth had won great power by earning the love of her subjects, the Stuart kings who followed her tried unsuccessfully to gain absolute power over Parliament and the common law. In Russia, Austria, and Prussia, Romanov, Habsburg, and Hohenzollern rulers governed their countries with iron hands.

These mighty monarchs were ambitious men who sought to win new lands and powers for themselves and their families. Each also sought to increase his country's economic strength at the expense of its neighbors. As a result, the age of the absolute monarchies was also an age of commercial and dynastic wars, which were fought not only in Europe but also in colonies and on oceans all over the world.

In the eighteenth century, however, the idea of absolute monarchy began to be seriously challenged. In England, Parliament triumphed over the kings. And everywhere in Europe, the philosophy of the "Enlightenment," which taught that man was essentially good and reasonable and therefore able to rule himself, challenged the concepts of the absolute monarchs— some of whom tried to be both absolute and "enlightened," without particular success.

The end of the eighteenth century was also the end of the age of absolute monarchies. In the last decade of the century an attempt to reform the Bourbon monarchy in France suddenly turned into a violent revolution —which was the first phase of the contemporary period of world history.

25

the Golden Age
of Spain

During most of its "Golden Age," the sixteenth and early seventeenth centuries, Spain was the most influential state in Europe. Governed by kings who also ruled a vast empire in Europe and the New World, and enriched by the gold and silver of the Americas, the Spanish had the most feared armies and the greatest prestige of the time. They also supported artists and writers who were worthy successors to the men of the Renaissance.

The history of Spain's Golden Age is at once glorious and tragic, for, powerful as it was, Spain tried to accomplish too much. Its Golden Age was only the prelude to a long period of decay.

SPAIN IN THE
EARLY SIXTEENTH CENTURY

During the reigns of Ferdinand and Isabella (see pages 236-237), the kingdoms of Aragon and Castile were united into a single state that included all the Iberian peninsula except Portugal. But Spain remained a poor country, and its few natural resources were largely undeveloped. The richest regions were along the Mediterranean coast, where there were lush agricultural lands; but mountains and rapidly flowing rivers made communication between one coastal area and another difficult, so that they were divided and no one became predominant. The heart of the country was an interior plateau, which was thinly populated, divided by high hills and rivers, and subject to droughts. The people of Spain also differed among themselves. They spoke several languages (one of which, Basque, is unrelated to any other on earth) and were deeply attached to their local customs and suspicious of all outsiders. There were scattered communities of Jews and Moors who had been forcibly converted to Christianity. They were distrusted by most Spaniards because they were questionably loyal to their new faith and because they dominated the skilled trades and much of the commerce of the country. The Spaniards themselves tended to look down on business; everyone who could lived like a "hidalgo" (literally "son of somebody"—a gentleman of leisure).

By the early sixteenth century the Spanish had developed a number of characteristics that set them apart from the other peoples of Europe. Their struggles with the Moors gave them a fierce pride in their country and its destiny that helps explain the sacrifices many of them made to establish a world-wide empire for their monarchs. They were so devoted to their religion that Spain was little influenced by the Protestant Reformation, remaining a stronghold of Catholicism. Convinced that as hidalgos they had special duties and privileges, they set new standards of ambition and heroism. At the same time, they refused to lower themselves by taking an active part in manufacturing and commerce. Much of Spanish history can be explained in terms of these qualities.

The monarchs of the united kingdoms of Castile and Aragon imposed a central Spanish government by limiting each local "cortes" (parliament) and by utilizing the *hermandades*, police forces organized by the cities to prevent banditry. Royal councils conducted affairs of state according to the wishes of the monarchs. Royal revenues were increased in several ways, notably by the addition of a number of sales taxes.

The Spanish army became the most feared and respected in Europe. The infantry was armed with pikes (wooden shafts with steel-pointed heads, which made medieval cavalry all but obsolete) and organized into well-drilled and disciplined units of professional soldiers who were famed for their bravery. Spain also developed a strong navy, equipped to wage successful campaigns against the Muslims in the Mediterranean and to protect the merchant vessels sailing to and from the distant colonies.

United under a single monarch and soon to be enriched by a flow of gold and silver from the New World, Spain was on the eve of its period of greatest achievement.

⚜ THE GOLDEN AGE

Charles I, grandson of Ferdinand and Isabella, led Spain into its golden age. This was the same man who, as the Holy Roman Emperor Charles V, was the opponent of the French King Francis I (see pages 241-243) and of the Protestant reformer Martin Luther in Germany. (See pages 296-298.) He was also ruler, as King Charles I, of Spain and its possessions in Italy and the New World. Charles made Spain the center from which he directed his drive to dominate Europe.

THE REIGN OF CHARLES I

Charles (king 1516-1556) was no Spaniard. Raised on his Habsburg father's estates in Flanders, he did not even speak the native tongue of his mother, a daughter of Ferdinand and Isabella. When he arrived in Spain, he brought with him Flemish advisers whose foreign ways brought on a revolt of Spanish nobles and townsmen in 1520. This uprising was soon put down; but thereafter Charles was careful to please his Spanish subjects.

Charles was a conscientious ruler who came to distrust his advisers and insisted on making all major policies himself. He listened carefully to his ministers to learn all he could about his kingdom—and then often ignored their advice. He traveled constantly so that he could take personal command wherever there was trouble in his empire.

Charles fought several wars with France and was always ready to do battle for Catholicism. Besides fighting the Protestants in Germany, he led one expedition after another against the Turkish Muslims. In the 1520's he prevented the Turks from taking control of all of Hungary, and in 1535 he led a force that captured Tunis. During his reign the mines of the New World were producing fortunes, and Charles received his "royal fifth" of all their gold and silver; but he spent his income on his wars as fast as it came in.

In fact, Spain paid the price of his ambition. As early as 1523 Charles formed the "Hacienda Council," which increased his domestic revenues two- or threefold by rigidly controlling the economy. But this income, as well as the income from the colonies, was spent in Germany, France, and Italy, so that Spanish industry failed to develop. Spain won the glory of Charles's foreign wars—and the rest of Europe reaped the profits. When Charles, worn out by four decades of ceaseless war, abdicated in 1556 and retired to die in a Spanish monastery, he left his son a country whose ambitions were greater than its strength could justify.

King Philip II of Spain: a sixteenth-century marble bust. Philip took seriously his responsibilities as king, but he was even more devoted to the cause of Catholicism than to the interests of his country. No failure could weaken his belief in his policies, which he thought of as being solely for the greater glory of God.

THE REIGN OF PHILIP II

When Charles abdicated, he divided his empire into two parts. His brother Ferdinand received Austria and the other Habsburg lands in central Europe and became Holy Roman emperor. His son mounted the Spanish throne as Philip II (king 1556-1598) and received Charles's possessions in the New World, the Philippines, the Netherlands, and Italy. Philip, unlike his father, was Spanish to the core. He spoke only Spanish, and his ambition was to become the absolute ruler of the country. He inherited Charles's determination to make all the decisions himself; but instead of traveling throughout his kingdom, he retired to the Escorial, a mammoth, austere palace he built near the capital city of Madrid. Here, far removed from the people he ruled, he worked to establish a centralized state. He asked his nobles for information but not for advice; he reduced the power of the cortes by making them represent only taxpayers (which meant that the nobles and churchmen, who were not required to pay taxes, could not participate). He ruthlessly put down a revolt in Aragon and an uprising by the persecuted Moors. He turned the administration of the government over to an immense bureaucracy (body of government officials), which he personally headed and which referred even the most minor decisions to him. Philip loved paperwork, but he hated to make decisions, leading one of his courtiers to comment, "The original sin of our court is never to decide anything in time." When Philip would not decide, no one else could either.

Philip continued his father's policy of intervening in the affairs of Europe, and the success of his armies brought Spain's military reputation to a peak. In 1559 he forced the French to sign the Treaty of Cateau-Cambrésis, which reaffirmed Spanish possessions in Italy and the Franche Comté. (See page 241.) In 1571 his navies destroyed Turkish sea power in the Mediterranean at the battle of Lepanto. His greatest success was an invasion of Portugal in 1580, which led to the annexation of that country the following year. He ruled Portugal moderately and well, keeping the Portuguese government separate from Spain's and allowing its traditions to continue.

Philip allied himself even more closely with the Catholic Church than his father had. Within the boundaries of Spain he encouraged the Inquisition (see page 236) to ferret out and repress even the slightest suspicion of discontent or heresy. But his efforts to impose similar policies in other countries led to one disaster after another. In France his support of the most conservative Catholic faction served only to drive the *politiques,* or liberal Catholics, toward the Protestants. In the Netherlands, Philip's efforts to stamp out Protestantism led only to stiffened resistance and eventually to the independence of the northern (Dutch) Netherlands. (See page 315.) In England, Philip married Mary I, the Catholic daughter of Henry VIII, and encouraged her to take repressive measures against the Protestants. (See page 303.) But her reign was brief, and her successor, the Protestant Elizabeth I, spurned Philip's offer of marriage; repressed Catholicism; and beheaded Mary, Queen of Scots, whom Philip had championed. (Chapter 27.) In response, Philip sent the "Invincible Armada," a fleet of 132 ships, against England in 1588. The English and a heavy storm combined to destroy it. Spain's losses were immense, and England became more Protestant than ever.

The fourth day of the defeat of the Spanish Armada by the English: an English engraving of the eighteenth century. At the left the galleon of the Spanish commander is being captured by Sir Francis Drake; at the right the remainder of the Armada, in the form of a half moon, is pursued by other English ships. The coat of arms is that of England.

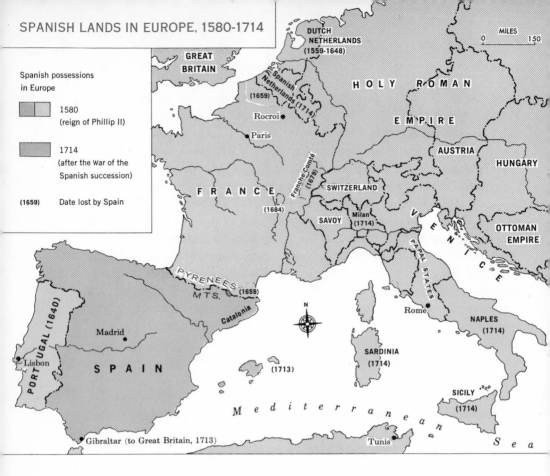

MILES

0   150

DUTCH
NETHERLANDS
(1559-1648)

GREAT
BRITAIN

HOLY   ROMAN

Spanish
Netherlands
(1714)

EMPIRE

Spanish
Netherlands
(1659)

Rocroi

Paris

AUSTRIA

HUNGARY

Spanish possessions
in Europe

1580
(reign of Phillip II)

1714
(after the War of the
Spanish succession)

(1659)   Date lost by Spain

FRANCE

Franche-Comté
(1678)

SWITZERLAND

Milan
(1714)

V
E
N
I
C
E

OTTOMAN
EMPIRE

(1684)

SAVOY

PAPAL STATES

Rome

NAPLES
(1714)

PYRENEES
MTS.   (1659)

Catalonia

N

SARDINIA
(1714)

Madrid

PORTUGAL (1640)

SPAIN

(1713)

SICILY
(1714)

Lisbon

Mediterranean   Sea

Gibraltar (to Great Britain, 1713)

Tunis

The people of Spain and the mines of America shared the costs of these unsuccessful campaigns. Rich as they were, the mines could meet only part of the expenses of the Spanish armies and navies. Philip therefore increased the taxes on his people. The most important of these was a 10 per cent sales tax, which brought in some additional income. But it also drove Spanish merchants out of business, because they could no longer compete with untaxed foreigners; and it forced the prices of goods so high that Spain entered a period of disastrous inflation. Philip also borrowed heavily from bankers in Italy and Germany; but three times he refused to pay his debts, so that it became increasingly difficult for him to obtain additional loans, even at very high rates of interest. At the end of his reign, Philip was poorer than he had been at the beginning—and so were most of his people.

Although many of Philip's policies led to disaster, few at the time realized that his kingdom was steadily weakening. The great lords, who paid no taxes, were as rich as ever. Philip still had the most feared army in Europe. His people were as convinced as ever that Spain was the greatest of European states, and they remained unswervingly loyal to the monarchy and the

Catholic Church. Even foreigners thought of Spain as the strongest state, with its huge empire in America, its central monarchy, and its mighty armies. Philip hid himself in his gloomy palace, concealed his disappointment, and worked harder than ever to restore his fortunes and impose his will on all of western Europe. He was always determined that Spain and Catholicism should predominate.

THE REIGNS OF PHILIP III AND PHILIP IV

In the reigns of Philip III (king 1598-1621) and Philip IV (king 1621-1665) it became obvious that Spain's Golden Age was fading away. These later Habsburg rulers were not interested in ruling; Philip III was a shy and religious man who cared most about the church and its numerous Spanish monasteries; his son, Philip IV, was a friendly man who was bored with politics. As a result, the real authority fell into the hands of a series of royal favorites called *privados*. Ambitious nobles fought bitterly for power, corrupted the government, and made the court a nest of intrigue. As the quality of government declined, Spain steadily fell behind the better governed nations of Europe.

The *privados* were unable to advance their country's cause. Early in the seventeenth century, the first of them was ousted from office for attempting to make peace with the English and the Dutch. A successor, the "Count-Duke" Olivares, revived the ambitious· policies of Philip II. Besides reviving the war in the Netherlands, he involved Spain in the Thirty Years War on the side of the Austrian Habsburgs and in opposition to France. To meet the demands of war, Olivares imposed additional heavy taxes and strict government controls, which led to a series of local rebellions. French troops crossed the Pyrenees to support a revolt in Catalonia, the north-eastern part of Spain. In 1643 the French decisively defeated the Spanish army in the battle of Rocroi, ending the long supremacy of the Spanish infantry. The Catalans won the liberties they fought for, although they remained under Spanish rule. Their example inspired a revolt in Portugal, which began in 1640 and continued until Spain was forced to recognize Portuguese independence in 1668.

Olivares was dismissed in 1643. His successor staved off complete defeat by signing a peace with the Dutch in 1648 that allowed Spain to retain the southern (Belgian) Netherlands. The general peace of Westphalia later that same year (see page 318) did not settle the war between France and Spain, however, and it dragged on for more than a decade before the Treaty of the Pyrenees was signed in 1659. After this treaty, Spain could no longer even pretend to be supreme in Europe. France won borderlands in the Netherlands and in the Pyrenees. Philip reluctantly sealed the agreement by promising his daughter to Louis XIV as his wife—with a dowry so large his impoverished country could not afford to pay it. The Treaty of the Pyrenees marked the end of the Golden Age of Spain.

THE GOLDEN AGE OF SPANISH LITERATURE AND ART

During the Spanish years of glory, several great writers and painters were active in Spain. Their accomplishments are the greatest legacy of Spain's Golden Age.

SPANISH LITERATURE: CERVANTES. VEGA. CALDERÓN

The greatest writer of Spain's Golden Age was Miguel de Cervantes Saavedra (1547-1616). Cervantes was a professional soldier who lost the use of his left hand fighting the Turks in the battle of Lepanto, fought with Spanish armies in Italy and Tunis, and was captured and carried off into slavery by Algerian pirates. Ransomed, he returned home to a life of poverty which he tried to relieve by writing. After a series of failures, Cervantes produced the greatest work in Spanish literature, the novel *Don Quixote*. His hero, Don Quixote, is a mad knight, inflamed by impossible ideals of chivalry. Accompanied by his earthy and worldly servant Sancho Panza, he goes off across the countryside like one of King Arthur's knights of old. But the age of chivalry has gone: Don Quixote finds no one with whom to do battle, and fights windmills instead. He strives mightily to save nonexistent damsels in distress. He starves himself pointlessly because the knights of old had gone hungry. Meanwhile his patient servant humors him along, protecting him from real danger and making the best of a bad situation. Cervantes knew that chivalry was dead, but that people still needed to believe in great ideas and impossible goals. He mocked his hero—and the impractical ideas of Spanish hidalgos—but he mocked them gently.

Only slightly less brilliant than Cervantes were Spain's two major dramatists. Lope de Vega (1562-1635) wrote more than 1,800 romances filled with love and violence. An amazing worker, he passed his time on board a ship in the Spanish Armada writing an epic poem of 11,000 lines; and in his plays he provided succeeding generations of writers with enough plots, themes, and characters to establish a whole literary tradition. Lope's disciple

"St. Jerome": a painting by El Greco. El Greco achieved remarkable effects by his techniques, quite evident here, of strongly contrasting the light and dark areas of the painting and lengthening the features of the figure. The result is that the great scholar and Bible translator appears as a man of power, intensity, and stark single-mindedness. Compare this vision of St. Jerome, which reflects the attitudes and ideals of the Catholic Reformation and the Spain of Philip II, with the Northern Renaissance outlook reflected in the St. Jerome of Albrecht Dürer on page 284.

Pedro Calderón (1600-1681) wrote fewer plays than his master, but he was a keener judge of character and a master at depicting the effects of the strong Spanish sense of individual and family honor, which often led to violence and bloodshed.

SPANISH PAINTING: EL GRECO AND VELÁZQUEZ

In the Golden Age, Spanish art, like Spanish literature, was dominated by a few geniuses who captured the characteristics of Spain in their own individualistic styles. Interestingly, the first of these artists was not a Spaniard at all, but an immigrant named Kyriakos Theotokopoulos (1541-1614), whom the Spaniards called simply "El Greco" ("The Greek"). El Greco's paintings show the influence both of Byzantine art and of the Venetian painter Titian (see page 274), with whom he had studied in Italy. After he moved to Spain, El Greco developed his own style, using bright colors, strong contrasts of light and darkness, and elongated figures. El Greco was a mystic who was more interested in expressing his faith and emotion in paint than in achieving photographic accuracy.

The last great figure of Spain's Golden Age was the painter Diego Velázquez. A court painter to King Philip IV, Velázquez was in many ways the opposite of El Greco. His paintings, many of them portraits of the king and his court, are cool and objective, simple and dignified. His greatness lies in his complete mastery of such artistic problems as space and light and, even more, in the profound respect for every individual person that is evident in all his work. The paintings of Velázquez also express the mood as well as the appearance of the court in the declining years of the Golden Age.

❧ SPAIN AFTER THE GOLDEN AGE

After the Peace of the Pyrenees of 1659, Spain was no longer able to pretend that it was a great power. Weak and inept rulers, economic stagnation, and the rise of rival powers combined to hasten the decay of a state that had once hoped to dominate both the New World and the Old.

THE REIGN OF CHARLES II

The son of Philip IV, Charles II (king 1665-1700), "the sickly king," was the last Habsburg to occupy the Spanish throne. He was only four when his father died, and nobody expected him to live long. Charles lived to be almost forty, but he remained ill, shy, and ineffective all his life.

The empire began to be whittled away. In 1667 Louis XIV successfully attacked the Spanish Netherlands, but his other enemies forced him to give back most of his conquests. In the 1670's and again in the 1690's Spain sought revenge by joining with Louis's enemies; in the first of these wars it lost Franche Comté and a province in the Netherlands, and in the second it lost Haiti.

As Charles grew older and sicker, it became obvious that he would never have a son of his own. King Louis XIV of France challenged Charles's cousins the Austrian Habsburgs for control of the Spanish throne, each hoping to name Charles's successor. Charles finally named a grandson of Louis XIV as his heir. The Dutch and English joined the Austrians to oppose this threatened union of French and Spanish forces. Almost immediately after Charles's death in 1700, the "War of the Spanish Succession" broke out, and for thirteen years the great powers fought over the far-flung Spanish possessions. (Chapter 31.) No longer able to determine the fate of Europe, the Spanish could not even determine who would be their own king. Louis's grandson, Philip of Anjou, was eventually confirmed as King Philip V of Spain, and a Bourbon dynasty replaced the Habsburgs. Once-mighty Spain had become a mere prize in the contests of greater states.

SPAIN IN THE EIGHTEENTH CENTURY

Two centuries of Habsburg monarchy (1516-1700) resulted in the political, social, and economic exhaustion of Spain. Although the fiction of strong monarchy continued during the eighteenth century, local revolts defied the efforts of the kings to win absolute power. Spain retained most of its colonies, but these, too, were able to ignore many of the efforts of the monarchy to control them.

The economic effects of two centuries of foreign wars were disastrous. Money spent on campaigns in Italy, Germany, and the Netherlands remained there, and so could not be used to finance the growth of Spanish industry. After 1700 the mines of the New World no longer provided a steady stream of gold and silver to the mother country, and the agricultural products of the colonies could not make up the loss. Efforts to make the colonies trade only with Spain and to purchase only Spanish products were unsuccessful. After the expulsion from Spain of the Jews by Ferdinand and Isabella and of the Moors by Philip III, the Spaniards who remained were more interested in living like hidalgos than in sullying themselves with trade. Therefore the goods sold to the colonies were purchased from other countries in Europe, which reaped the profits. High taxes created an inflation that wiped out most of the middle class. The population of the central plateau declined as men joined the army or emigrated to the colonies, and farms were replaced by large wool-growing estates. The Hacienda Council, which still regulated every aspect of commerce, shuffled its papers vigorously. But it could not stimulate manufacturing, and Spain became a backward agricultural country.

Eighteenth-century Spanish society was divided between the very rich and the very poor. The lords who dominated the courts and owned the sheep-raising estates knew and cared little about the masses of uneducated peasants, who barely survived on the arid plateaus. The peasants, cut off from other parts of the country by the lack of good roads, returned to their intense local loyalties and settled into a life of poverty broken by occasional glorious fiestas. Catholicism remained more influential in Spain than anywhere else in western Europe. Cervantes's Don Quixote typified the Spanish hidalgo way of life: deeply religious, idealistic, devoted to the memory of past glories, and unrealistic in his expectations of future greatness, he, like his country, was a holdover from an age that had passed, who could not adjust effectively to an era he could not understand.

⚜   ⚜   ⚜

In the sixteenth and early seventeenth centuries, Spain had its Golden Age. But two centuries of rule by absolute monarchs who forced her to pay the price of their grandiose ambitions had brought the country to its knees. After 1660 Spain was only a minor influence in the affairs of Europe. As Spain declined, France's Bourbon kings were raising their country to a peak of power. For more than seventy years in the seventeenth and early eighteenth centuries, France was ruled by the most absolute of all absolute monarchs, a man who wielded even greater power than Charles V. Louis XIV, called the "Grand Monarch" and the "Sun King," dominated not only France but much of Europe, and he gave his name to the second half of the seventeenth century.

People, Places, and Terms

Charles I	Charles II	Hacienda Council
Philip II	Louis XIV	Escorial
Philip III	Philip V	Treaty of Cateau-
Philip IV		Cambrésis
Count-Duke	Tunis	Battle of Lepanto
Olivares	Madrid	Invincible Armada
Miguel de Cervantes	Catalonia	*privados*
Saavedra		Treaty of the
Lope de Vega	hidalgo	Pyrenees
Pedro Calderón	*hermandades*	*Don Quixote*
El Greco	cortes	War of the Spanish
Diego Velázquez	royal fifth	Succession

Getting Organized

1. Describe Spain in the early sixteenth century. How different were its various regions and people? What characteristics set the Spaniards apart from the other peoples of Europe?
2. What lands did Charles I rule? What was the Spaniards' first reaction to him? What principles determined Charles's policies? What kind of ruler was he? In what ways and with what success did he serve as the champion of Catholicism? Where did he get his money?
3. How did Philip II rule? Where and with what success did Philip intervene in the affairs of Europe?
4. How were Philip's campaigns financed? Why was this a poor method? At Philip's death, what was Spain's position in Europe?

5. Who ruled Spain after Philip II? Were the *privados* good rulers of Spain? What happened when they were in power? How did the Peace of the Pyrenees mark the end of Spain's Golden Age?
6. Who was Cervantes? What does his *Don Quixote* tell us about the Spain of 1600? What was the contribution to Spain's Golden Age of Lope de Vega? Calderón? El Greco? Velázquez?
7. What happened to Spain during Charles II's reign? What was the result to Spain of the War of the Spanish Succession?
8. By 1700 what had happened to the Spanish monarchy? Could the Spanish king still control all of his nobles and colonies? What was Spain's financial status? Describe eighteenth-century Spanish society.

Understanding the Big Picture

1. Who was the more effective and successful ruler of Spain, Charles I or Philip II? Support your answer with specific evidence.
2. In what ways did the various Spanish kings finance their ambitious and international ventures? With what results?
3. What were the major principles behind the policies of the sixteenth- and seventeenth-century Spanish kings?
4. Why did Spain decline after its Golden Age? When did this decline start? What made it obvious to everyone?

Mastering the Map

1. Compare the Habsburg possessions in the time of Charles V (map, page 242) with those of Spain in 1648 (map, page 364). How do the maps show the decline of Spanish power to 1648?
2. Study the map on page 364. What lands did Spain lose to France, 1648-1715?

For the Thoughtful

1. How is Cervantes's character Don Quixote a symbol and a prediction of the decline of Spain? In what ways can a novel (or other form of art) help to illuminate political, economic, and social conditions?
2. Discuss the role of economics in the rise and decline of Spanish power. How important is economics to history? What other examples are there of economics playing a crucial role in the development of a country that you've studied?
3. How does the history of Spain in the sixteenth and seventeenth centuries help explain present-day Spain's institutions and problems?

$\approx$ 26

ΔBSOLUTISM TRIUMPHANT:
FRANCE IN THE
SEVENTEENTH CENTURY

From 1589 to 1715, France was ruled by the first three kings of the Bourbon dynasty: Henry IV, Louis XIII, and Louis XIV. During this period the Bourbons, taking over a land that had been divided and impoverished by civil and religious war, made it so strong that France became the dominant country in Europe, and the Bourbons replaced the Habsburgs as the most powerful European dynasty. The first two Bourbon kings, aided by three remarkable ministers, organized the government so effectively that Louis XIV could use it to make himself the most influential figure in an age to which he gave his name. Louis XIV came to embody the doctrine of absolutism—that the ruler was supreme within his country and the wielder of "absolute" or unlimited authority.

🌸 THE FIRST BOURBONS

In 1589 Henry of Navarre became King Henry IV of a troubled France. (See page 313). Religious wars had divided not only Protestants from Catholics but also the moderate Catholics (*politiques*) from the conservative Catholics. In the confusion the power of the kings had greatly declined. Yet Henry IV had certain advantages as he set out to rebuild the power of the monarchy. The strong kings of medieval France had done more to

372

weaken local loyalties than had the kings in, for example, Spain. France was relatively unified geographically, less divided by mountains and arid plains than was Spain. The concordats of the late Middle Ages, which had given the French kings the authority to appoint most of the bishops in France, were still in effect. In the time of the popular king Francis I, a French national literature had begun to flourish. Thus in 1589 the French people were ready to unite behind a leader who seemed able to restore peace and order.

THE REIGN OF HENRY IV

Henry IV (king 1589-1610) was just such a king. He was popular, a friendly, down-to-earth man who was able to charm his enemies into doing his will. Henry put the welfare of his country above personal or religious considerations, surrendering his Huguenot faith ("Paris is worth a Mass," he supposedly remarked) to win the support of Catholic Frenchmen.

Henry assured his country of relative peace. In his foreign policy, he attempted to avoid taking sides in the struggles going on elsewhere in Europe. In his domestic policy, he retained the loyalty of the Huguenots by granting them the "Edict of Nantes" in 1598, which guaranteed them the right to worship as they wished, some participation in the government, and the right to fortify certain cities. (See page 313.) The nobles were more difficult to deal with, for they were not yet ready to surrender their freedoms to the king; but Henry bought their allegiance with huge bribes. When someone complained that these were too large, Henry replied that they were less costly than war. Strangely, he was able to keep the loyalty he had bought, and the principal dukes supported most of his policies.

Henry could afford these expenses because he put the economic affairs of the government into the hands of the duke of Sully, a loyal and efficient minister who balanced the royal budget, reduced taxes, and even built up a surplus in the treasury. Sully believed that "the plowed field and pasture land are the two fountains of life" and encouraged the peasants to improve their methods of agriculture. Henry, like Sully, was sympathetic toward the peasants—who, he said, should be assured "a chicken in the pot every Sunday"—but his greatest interest was in improving industry and foreign trade. He founded the French silk industry, encouraged the establishment of tapestry works and glass factories, and constructed a network of roads and bridges to stimulate commerce. Even the cities benefited from his interest; in Paris, for example, he extended the royal palace at the Louvre, constructed a magnificent series of buildings, and built the beautiful *Pont Neuf* ("New Bridge") across the Seine.

Henry was still at the height of his powers when he was struck down by an assassin in 1610. His son and heir, Louis XIII, was only nine years old.

THE REIGN OF LOUIS XIII AND RICHELIEU

Having a child as king threw France into confusion once again. The confusion lasted until 1624, when young Louis XIII (king 1610-1643) made Cardinal Richelieu his chief minister. Louis, son of one great king and father of another, was afraid to exercise his authority and remained a background figure in the affairs of state. But he followed one brilliant policy: he supported Richelieu against all his many enemies. In return, Richelieu served Louis and France well. He was a Catholic churchman, but his guiding principle was the *raison d'etat*, "the good of the state." In the interests of the state and the monarchy (which to him were the same thing), Richelieu worked for the rest of his life to attain two goals: to make the monarchy absolute within France, and to make France the strongest power in Europe. He was remarkably successful in achieving both.

Cardinal Richelieu: a seventeenth-century engraving. Despite poor health, Richelieu achieved the foremost position in France by his patience, cunning, and ruthless will power. His driving ambition resulted in his becoming not only a cardinal but also a duke, and in the course of his career he amassed · a vast fortune. Yet he was devoted to France, and few men have influenced the course of their country's history as much as did Richelieu.

The nobles had reasserted their independence from royal control during the childhood of Louis XIII. Richelieu responded by abolishing major government offices that the nobles had traditionally held, thereby removing one of their bases of strength. He forbade dueling, the last holdover from the private warfare of the feudal age. And he increased the duties of the "intendants," middle-class officials who were appointed to head provincial governments that had previously been in the hands of the nobility.

Believing that the fortified cities allowed the Huguenots by the Edict of Nantes should be brought under royal control, Richelieu made efforts to restrict their independence. The Huguenots rebelled; so in 1627-1628 Richelieu personally led an eighteen-month siege of La Rochelle, the principal Huguenot stronghold. After the Huguenot armies had been destroyed, Richelieu issued the "Edict of Grace" (1629), which took away many of the Huguenots' political liberties but allowed them to continue to worship as they pleased. The Huguenots were not pleased, but most of them remained in France.

In order to achieve his other goal, making France the strongest state in Europe, Richelieu had somehow to humble the Austrian and Spanish Habsburgs. He recognized Habsburg leadership of the Catholic cause in the Thirty Years War (see page 316), and, as a Catholic prelate, he had no desire to strengthen the Protestants by attacking the Habsburgs. But when it seemed that the Habsburgs were about to gain control of all Germany, his love of country overcame his love of Catholicism. In 1625 he sent French armies to cut the supply lines in northern Italy that connected the Spanish Habsburgs with their Austrian cousins. Five years later he aided the Protestant Swedes when they invaded Germany. In 1635 he declared open war on Habsburg Spain and formally allied his country with the Protestants. Richelieu died in 1642, before the Thirty Years War ended, but his policies were continued, and France won the victories he sought. In 1643 French soldiers defeated the famed Spanish infantry at Rocroi. (See page 365.) In 1648 the Treaties of Westphalia (see pages 318-320) gave France key territories along the German boundary and the right to interfere in the affairs of the Holy Roman Empire, where the domination of the Austrian Habsburgs had been broken. In 1659 the Peace of the Pyrenees (see page 365) gave France lands in the Netherlands and demonstrated to the world that the power of the Spanish Habsburgs had ended. The ring of Habsburg lands around France had been broken; France, not Spain, had become the power to contend with in Europe.

Cardinal Richelieu's greatest failing was his inability to cut the cost of government. Wars, court expenses, and his own extravagance (he took his personal choir with him when he traveled, for example) led to heavy taxes on both the middle class and the peasantry. Many Frenchmen rejoiced when he died. Louis XIII, the monarch Richelieu had served so well, died in 1643, only six months after his minister, leaving the throne to his four-year-old son and the government to Richelieu's chosen successor, Cardinal Mazarin.

CARDINAL MAZARIN

Another child king, Louis XIV, (king 1643-1715) succeeded to the crown of France. He was destined to rule longer than any other monarch in European history and to become the most famous, wealthiest, and most powerful of all French kings. But for the first eighteen years of his reign, France was governed by another, the Italian-born Cardinal Mazarin.

Mazarin, who spent much of his time lining his own pockets, failed to end the costly war with Spain or to reduce Richelieu's high taxes. The people grew restless and the nobles rebelled, attempting to regain their former independence in a revolt called the "Fronde" (1648-1653). The Fronde took its name from the slingshots used by children of the Paris slums to throw mud at passers-by—and was not much more effective. Nobles changed sides, fought with each other, ousted Mazarin, then allowed him to return, and generally discredited themselves. By 1652 Mazarin was back in charge of Paris and the government.

Mazarin added little that was new to Richelieu's policies. But he successfully concluded the Spanish War, forcing the Spanish Habsburgs to give lands and their daughter Maria Theresa as wife to Louis XIV in the Treaty of the Pyrenees of 1659. (See page 366.) Two years later Mazarin died, leaving France with power, glory, and an almost empty treasury.

❦ THE AGE OF LOUIS XIV:
THE EARLY DECADES

To everyone's surprise, the twenty-two-year-old king did not appoint a new chief minister to succeed Mazarin. In 1661 Louis assumed personal control of his government, and from then until his death in 1715 he was the central figure in European events. His subjects called him the "Grand Monarch" and the "Sun King." This was the Age of Louis XIV.

THE PERSONALITY AND IDEAS OF LOUIS XIV

Louis looked upon himself as the real head of the government—which he was—and worked hard at what he called "the business of being king." He was aware, especially during the first thirty years of his career, that despite his great power and influence, there were practical limits to his authority. He absorbed the classical ideal of *mesure*—"too much is too much," he used to say. In his admiration for reason and moderation, he practiced rigid self-control; for example, he almost never lost his temper in public.

At the same time Louis was a religious man. He believed strongly in the seventeenth-century concept of the "divine-right monarchy," which was best expressed by one Bishop Bossuet in a book entitled *Political Ideas Derived from the Very Words of Holy Scripture.* "All power is of God," Bossuet taught, and kings "act as the ministers of God and as his lieutenants on earth." Therefore, according to Bossuet, "The royal throne is not the throne of a man, but the throne of God himself . . . the person of the king is sacred, and . . . to attack him in any way is sacrilege." Therefore the king does not have to answer to his people for his actions, but only to God. As Bossuet put it, "God will demand an account . . . Kings should tremble then as they use the power God has granted them; and let them think how horrible is the sacrilege if they use for evil a power which comes from God."

"Majesty," Bossuet concluded, "is the image of the grandeur of God in the prince. So great is this majesty that it cannot reside in the prince as its source; it is borrowed from God, who gives it to him for the good of the people."

Convinced of his destiny as the Grand Monarch, and aided by two of the greatest ministers in his country's history, Louis XIV spent the first part of his long reign strengthening his grip on France, taming the nobility, restoring the economy, and building up the army.

CAGING THE NOBILITY AND REFORMING THE GOVERNMENT

Early in the period of his personal reign, Louis directed his architects to build him a palace at Versailles, ten miles from Paris. The palace, designed to be a suitable home for the mightiest king in Europe, was almost a third of a mile long. It was filled with gilded furniture and elaborate paintings according to Louis's somewhat gaudy tastes, and was surrounded by formal gardens and 1,600 fountains. In its "Hall of Mirrors" were seventeen mirrors, each thirty feet high, that had been carried overland from Venice. It was large enough to house 10,000 people.

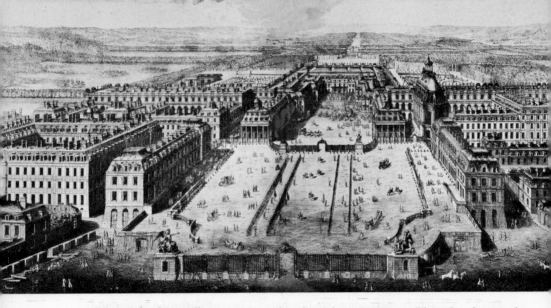

The palace of Versailles as it appeared in the eighteenth century. The palace became the royal residence and the seat of the French government in 1682, twenty-one years after construction had begun. The court that Louis XIV established here dazzled all Europe, contributing to France's prestige and to Louis's reputation as the "Grand Monarch," and its way of life soon was being imitated at almost every other court on the continent.

Versailles was not simply the residence of the king: it was an elegant cage for the French nobility. Here, like a well-bred gentleman entertaining his friends, Louis lured the aristocrats whose ancestors for centuries had jealously defended their independence. These courtiers spent their incomes and more on silk clothes and elaborate entertainments. Instead of plotting to regain their former power, they scrambled for crumbs of recognition from their royal host. Almost every important noble in France lived, or hoped to live, at Versailles, where the king made sure that their every hour would be filled with pleasures not to be found anywhere else in Europe. For this, the nobles paid a heavy price. Their expensive life consumed their incomes. In their absence their country estates fell into disrepair, their incomes were reduced, and their farms were neglected. A few years at Versailles accomplished what centuries of struggle had failed to do: they reduced the nobility to dependence on the king. The aristocrats, who once had administered the local governments of France, were now only elegant and ornamental.

Meanwhile the king made himself the head of government. His will was carried out by officials recruited from the middle class. Louis made the final decisions himself; but he surrounded himself with the best and most loyal middle-class ministers he could find, organizing them into councils where they were allowed to speak their minds fully and freely. Louis attended all their meetings and took part in their deliberations.

Louis increased the power of the middle-class intendants, whom Richelieu had found so useful, over the provincial governments. The king appointed these career government officials to rule the provinces, and he made them responsible only to him and his ministers. They then gave orders to the lesser officials in towns and villages. Because Louis's directives usually gave the intendants only a general policy to follow, they had a good deal of freedom to rule as they wished. Since most of these men were loyal and capable public servants, devoted to their king and country, France had probably the most honest and efficient government in Europe.

COLBERT AND MERCANTILISM

Louis was determined to dominate the economic as well as the political life of France, his goal being to make the economy of France an instrument of French national power. Under the direction of his great minister Jean Baptiste Colbert, the confused remnants of the medieval guild system were replaced by what has come to be called "mercantilism."

As Colbert administered it, the mercantile system was based upon three basic concepts: bullionism, a favorable balance of trade, and self-sufficient national economy. "Bullionism" was the mercantilist doctrine that the real wealth of a country consisted of the amount of gold and silver ("bullion") it possessed. A "favorable balance of trade" meant that the country exported more than it imported from other countries. Other countries would therefore have to make up the difference between what they bought and what they sold abroad by payments of gold and silver. This, of course, was "favorable," because it brought more bullion into the country. A "self-sufficient" national economy was one that could by itself provide for all the country's needs. Such an economy not only would lead to a favorable balance of trade, but also would free the country from depending on other countries in time of war. To attain national self-sufficiency, Colbert believed, the government should stimulate manufacturing, restrict imports, encourage exports, and control as many sources of raw materials as possible. Colonies, according to mercantilist doctrine, existed to help a country achieve these goals: their main purpose was to supply raw materials and to buy the manufactured products of the mother country.

From the time he became Louis's most important minister in 1661 until he died in 1683, Colbert worked tirelessly to achieve these mercantilist goals. To encourage manufacturing, he established government standards of quality for manufactured goods and lowered the taxes paid by certain key industries. To stimulate commerce within France, he built canals and a network of well-maintained roads. He ordered forest conservation to assure a steady lumber supply for France's shipbuilders who, under his direction, increased the size of the navy from twenty ships to 276. To promote a favorable balance of trade, he placed high tariffs (import taxes) on foreign manufactured goods and low tariffs on imported raw materials; encouraged government-sponsored trading companies; and worked hard to stimulate the growth of colonies.

At first these policies worked to France's benefit; its commerce grew rapidly during Colbert's time, and the government's income tripled. But in the long run mercantilism was probably harmful. One bad effect was that other countries soon adopted similar policies, with the result that competition for trade and colonies led to a series of costly wars. Another was that the government regulations on manufacturing often were more of a hindrance than a help to commerce, and many of them came to be resented by businessmen. A third was that the government aid tended to develop some areas of the French economy at the expense of other important areas. Finally, Louis did not always co-operate with Colbert, spending money so lavishly on Versailles, the army, and foreign wars that Colbert found it almost impossible to lay aside money to stimulate economic growth.

LOUVOIS AND THE REORGANIZATION OF THE FRENCH ARMY

Louis XIV made his army an instrument to extend his political and economic power throughout western Europe. As he turned over control of the economy to Colbert, he turned over the army to the marquis of Louvois, who was secretary of war from 1666 to 1691. Louvois, a hard worker and a gifted administrator, reorganized the army into Europe's most effective fighting force. He established officer training schools and organized "crack" infantry regiments to serve as models for other regiments. He introduced new weapons, including the bayonet and the hand grenade, and established a system of supply forces so that his armies were the best equipped of their day. And he increased the size of the French army so that it was far larger than any other in Europe.

Louvois was fortunate to have two brilliant subordinates: the marquis of Vauban, a military engineer, who directed sieges of fifty-three cities and the fortification of three hundred others; and the viscount of Turenne, a field general, who defeated the best generals sent against him until he himself was killed in a little skirmish in 1675.

With an army organized by Louvois, engineered by Vauban, and led by Turenne, Louis directed the most powerful fighting force in Europe.

King Louis XIV of France, as he looked in the later decades of his reign: portrait by Hyacinthe Rigaud. The elaborate costume and haughty bearing of the "Sun King" reflect his desire to give an impression of great glory and splendor.

🜲 THE AGE OF LOUIS XIV: THE LATER DECADES

Louis's career came to a turning point in the early 1680's. Throughout the first two decades of his period of personal rule, he had kept his sense of his own limitations and followed the advice of his brilliant subordinates. But Turenne was killed in 1675, and both Colbert and Queen Maria Theresa died in 1683. Now, surrounded by fawning followers and living in the unreal splendor of Versailles, Louis began to make the mistakes of an arrogant and overconfident man. He lost his sense of classical *mesure* and became an aggressive tyrant.

THE REVOCATION OF THE EDICT OF NANTES

Louis's first mistake was to revoke the Edict of Nantes, which had granted freedom of worship to the Huguenots. During the first part of his reign Louis generally had left the Protestants alone, for many were important and prosperous businessmen, and they posed no threat to his supremacy.

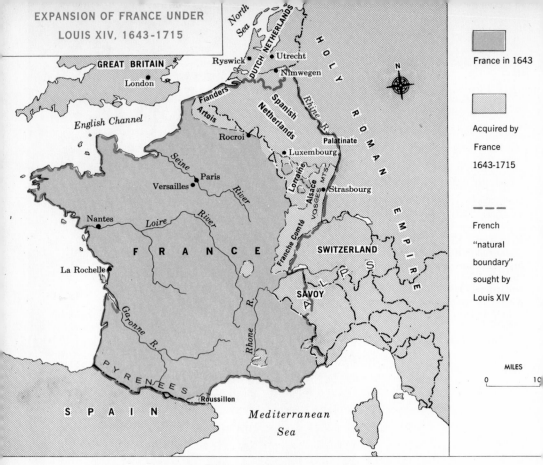

EXPANSION OF FRANCE UNDER
LOUIS XIV, 1643-1715

France in 1643

Acquired by
France
1643-1715

- - -

French
"natural
boundary"
sought by
Louis XIV

MILES

0   10

But as the years went by, he began to chip away at their freedoms, enforc-
ing Richelieu's Edict of Grace (above, page 375) to the letter. In 1681 he
ordered the quartering of troops in Huguenot households. These brutal and
insulting men terrified many Protestants into joining the Catholic Church,
in name at least, just to get rid of them. Then, after Maria Theresa's death,
Louis married the devout Madame de Maintenon, who convinced him that
there were so few remaining Huguenots that he could safely outlaw their
religion altogether.

Louis revoked the Edict of Nantes in 1685. He forbade Protestant worship, banished Protestant ministers, and closed Protestant churches. Some
200,000 Huguenots fled to England, the Dutch Netherlands, Brandenburg,
the Dutch Cape Colony in South Africa, or the English colonies in North
America. Others went to prison or were sentenced to be galley slaves in the
French navy. By revoking the Edict of Nantes, Louis drove from France
many of its most skilled and industrious citizens. The French economy
suffered, and other European countries gained at France's expense.

LOUIS'S FOREIGN WARS

Louis's second great mistake was to involve France in a series of wars. It is not surprising that Louis, convinced that he ruled by divine right, believing in the mercantilist doctrine of commercial competition for trade and markets, ambitious for himself and for France, and the master of Europe's most powerful army, went to war to attain his ends. Nor is it surprising that much of the rest of Europe rallied to check his ambitions.

Louis's foreign policy had two principal aims: to weaken or capture the Dutch Netherlands, France's strongest commercial rival; and to attain the "natural boundaries" of France, which he considered to be the coastline, the Pyrenees, the Alps, and the Rhine River. After the Treaty of the Pyrenees in 1659, France had all of these except the Rhine. Louis therefore directed his armies at the countries between France and the Rhine: the Spanish Netherlands, the Dutch Netherlands, and a number of small German states.

In his First Dutch War, or the "War of Devolution" (1667-1668), Louis sent Turenne and his armies into the Spanish Netherlands, which he claimed were part of his wife's inheritance. When the Dutch, Swedes, and English united against him, he quickly made a peace in which he settled for some border towns. But his appetite for conquest was whetted. He set out to isolate the Dutch from their allies by making treaties with Sweden and some of the German states and by buying off the English king. In 1672 Louis began his Second Dutch War by attacking the Dutch Netherlands, which, under the leadership of William III of Orange, allied with Spain, the Holy Roman emperor, and the rising German state of Brandenburg. After six years of war, Louis succeeded in dividing his enemies. In the Treaties of Nimwegen (1678), he forced Spain to surrender Franche Comté and some towns in the Spanish Netherlands; but the Dutch remained free, and nothing had been settled.

The Treaties of Nimwegen were a high point of Louis's reign, for he had matched his enemies and forced a peace. But, unsatisfied, he now laid claim to all lands in the Rhine valley that had ever been subject to any of the lands he ruled, and he managed to annex a few of them. This worried his neighbors, and Protestant Europe was further alarmed when Louis revoked the Edict of Nantes in 1685 and began to persecute Protestants. The next year the Dutch leader, William of Orange, organized Sweden, Spain, Austria, several German states, and his own Dutch Netherlands into the "League of Augsburg" to oppose Louis. Nothing daunted, Louis invaded the Rhineland in 1688, the League of Augsburg opposed him, and another war was under way. In 1689 William of Orange became king of England (Chapter 27), and England joined the league against France.

The story of the "War of the League of Augsburg" (1688-1697) belongs elsewhere. (Chapter 31.) In summary, the English greatly weakened France's naval power, and there were ten years of costly but indecisive land campaigns on five separate fronts. Louis claimed that he had written the Treaty of Ryswick, which ended the war in 1697; but his only gains were guarantees to territories that he had seized even before the fighting broke out.

Four years later another of Louis's adventures led to the most costly war of all. Louis wanted his grandson, Philip of Anjou, to succeed to the throne of Spain. The other countries of Europe felt that Bourbon kings in both France and Spain would upset the balance of power in Europe, and most of them united in support of the Habsburg candidate for the throne. The resulting "War of the Spanish Succession" (1701-1713) was fought all over the world (Chapter 31) and in battles on the continent that took as many as 20,000 lives at a time. At its conclusion, the Treaty of Utrecht (1713) put Philip on the Spanish throne, but France gained nothing in Europe and lost three important territories in America.

Louis was 75 years old at the time of the Treaty of Utrecht, and he had actively ruled his country for 52 years. People still considered him to be the Grand Monarch of France and the most powerful king of an age of absolute monarchs. But his last two great wars had cost his country dearly and brought it next to nothing. As he lay dying in 1715, the five-year-old great-grandson who was to inherit his throne was brought to his bedside. The old man turned to the child and said, "Do not imitate me in my taste for war."

🏺 🏺 🏺

Some insist that Louis was the best and greatest of absolute monarchs; and others maintain that he was the worst and most destructive. He was neither. On the positive side, his ministers Colbert and Louvois improved France's economy and army, and Louis himself tamed the nobles, improved the organization of the government, and made himself the symbol of *la gloire*, that sense of the greatness and glory of France that has moved Frenchmen ever since. He also encouraged French artists and writers. (Chapter 32.)

On the negative side, his method of rule left the people no way to express their needs and desires. Shut up in Versailles, Louis lost contact with the middle class, the peasantry, and even the capital at Paris, and he became increasingly unrealistic in his later years. Colbert's mercantilist policies were good for France in the short run; but as time passed, the defects of mercantilism came to outweigh its virtues, so that France's economic growth was hindered. By persecuting Protestants, Louis drove an important segment of the population into exile. Finally, Louis's wars cost much more than they gained; at his death, Louis owed the equivalent of sixteen years annual income.

When he died, a man who knew him well wrote that Louis was "six feet tall . . . and well-proportioned." Actually the Grand Monarch, without his high heels, was only five feet five. He just seemed a little larger than life. Even those who hated him respected him. And for more than half a century after his death, the France he created was considered the greatest power in Europe. *La gloire de France* did not easily tarnish.

People, Places, and Terms

Henry IV	Philip of Anjou	favorable balance
Duke of Sully		of trade
Louis XIII	La Rochelle	national
Cardinal Richelieu	Versailles	self-sufficiency
Cardinal Mazarin		protective tariff
Louis XIV	Gallican	natural boundaries
Maria Theresa	*raison d'état*	War of Devolution
Bishop Bossuet	intendants	Treaty of Nimwegen
Jean Baptiste Colbert	Edict of Grace	League of Augsburg
Marquis of Louvois	Fronde	Treaty of Ryswick
Marquis of Vauban	divine-right	War of the Spanish
Viscount of Turenne	monarchy	Succession
William III of	mercantile system	Treaty of Utrecht
Orange	bullionism	*la gloire*

Getting Organized

1. How strong was the French monarchy in 1589? What steps did Henry IV take to strengthen the monarchy? What was Sully's contribution to Henry's success?
2. What was the relationship of Louis XIII and Richelieu? What steps did Richelieu take to control the nobles? The Huguenots? The Habsburgs? How successful was he? What was his great failing?
3. Why did the nobles revolt against Mazarin's government? What was the effect of the Fronde? What did Mazarin accomplish?

4. Describe the character of Louis XIV. How did he feel about being king? Summarize the theory of the divine-right monarchy.
5. Describe the palace at Versailles. In what way was it a cage for the French nobles? How did Louis ensure his absolute authority in all matters of government?
6. Describe in detail Colbert's mercantile system. On what three basic concepts was it based? How successful were Colbert's mercantilist policies?
7. What steps did Louvois take to improve the French army? How successful was he? Who were his chief subordinates?
8. Why was the turning point of Louis's career in the early 1680's? Why did he revoke the Edict of Nantes? What was the effect of the revocation?
9. What were the chief aims of Louis's foreign policy? What were the origins and results of the War of Devolution? What were the origins of his war against the Dutch in 1672? Why does the Treaty of Nimwegen mark a high point of Louis's career?
10. What wars did Louis fight after the Treaty of Nimwegen in 1678? What was the effect of these wars on France?

Understanding the Big Picture

1. In your opinion, who was the most successful of the royal ministers? Who was the wisest? Who did the most good for France? Who did the most harm for France? Support your answers with specific evidence.
2. Compare the reigns of Louis XIV and Henry IV. Who was the greater king? Which did more for France?
3. Whom did Louis follow more, Colbert or Louvois? Whom should he have followed? Why? Did Louis help France?

Mastering the Map

Study carefully the map of France under Louis XIV on page 382. What new areas did Louis gain for France? Did he reach France's "natural boundaries"? Why? Describe the European balance of power in 1700.

For the Thoughtful

1. Compare the golden age of Spain under Philip II to that of France under Louis XIV. Which had the stronger monarchy? Which had the greater prestige and power in Europe?
2. Without looking ahead, try to predict what would happen to France in the eighteenth century. Explain the reasons for your prediction.
3. Do you think that absolute monarchy is a good form of government? What are its advantages and disadvantages, and which is greater? Use examples of your points from the twentieth century as well as from the history of France.

27

England under Elizabeth and the Stuarts

English history in the late sixteenth century and throughout the seventeenth century followed a pattern quite different from that of France. In the second half of the sixteenth century, when France was divided by civil war (see page 313), England was united under one of the most successful sovereigns in its history, Queen Elizabeth I. In the seventeenth century, when France was being brought under absolutism by such men as Richelieu and Louis XIV, England moved in the opposite direction. The Stuart monarchs who succeeded Elizabeth did, indeed, try to impose absolutism and to rule by "divine right." But the English Parliament, asserting its ancient rights and privileges, challenged them. The result was a struggle that lasted through the better part of the seventeenth century, culminating in the victory of Parliament over the kings. In the age when absolutism triumphed almost everywhere, England was the striking exception to the rule.

THE ELIZABETHAN AGE

Elizabeth I (queen 1558-1603) was the last of England's Tudor monarchs. In the late fifteenth and early sixteenth centuries, the Tudors had brought stable government and the Reformation to England. Henry VII (king 1485-1509) had made the monarchy strong and prosperous. (See pages

230-232.) His son, Henry VIII (king 1509-1547) had made Parliament his willing tool and had replaced Catholicism with the Church of England. (See pages 302-303.) Henry was succeeded by three of his children in succession. The first, the young boy Edward VI (king 1547-1553), was dominated by advisers who made the Church of England more Protestant than it had been. (See page 303.) The second, the unhappy Mary I (queen 1553-1558), brought unrest to her country when she married Philip II of Spain and attempted to restore Catholicism as the state religion. (See page 303.) The third was Elizabeth I, the daughter of Henry VIII and Anne Boleyn. (See page 302.)

Elizabeth, who never married and thus came to be called the "Virgin Queen," was one of England's most successful monarchs. Proud that she was "mere English," she personified her people's love for their island kingdom. She was remarkable for her ambition, her love for life, and her willingness to put what she considered the good of her country before her personal desires. With the aid of brilliant ministers and skillful diplomats, she brought her country order and prosperity at home and safety from foreign invasion. At the same time she strengthened English influence in the nearby lands of Wales, Ireland, and Scotland. In her time, English literature flourished as it never had before; hers was the era of Shakespeare. The "Elizabethan Age" was a high point in English history.

THE CHURCH OF ENGLAND UNDER ELIZABETH

When Elizabeth came to the throne, her greatest problem was to ease the religious tensions that divided her people. In 1559 Parliament re-enacted the Act of Supremacy (see page 303), which declared her supreme governor of the English church, and the Act of Uniformity, which gave her the power to enforce a uniform system of worship. Three years later Parliament passed the "Act of the Thirty-nine Articles," which restored the Protestantism of the reign of Edward VI. There were still, however, some Catholic forms of worship, and the church continued to be governed by bishops and archbishops. Archbishop Cranmer's *Book of Common Prayer* once again became the Anglican's religious guidebook.

But Elizabeth cared little for a strict interpretation of religious doctrines, so she allowed factions within the Church of England to interpret them in different ways. At one extreme were "High Churchmen," conservatives who emphasized a number of Catholic forms of worship. At the other extreme were "Puritans," Calvinists (see page 299) who wanted to purify the Church of England of any customs that were not based directly upon the Bible. Some of these Calvinists wanted the bishops to be replaced by "synods" (assemblies) of presbyters (elders or ministers), following the Presbyterianism of the Church of Scotland. Another group of stricter Calvinists refused to compromise with the Anglican Church at all and became "Separatists," leaving the Church of England entirely and forming self-governing congregations. These were the future Congregationalists.

Elizabeth allowed any form of worship that fit into the rather loose framework of ideas that Parliament had established for the Church of England. But she would accept none that conflicted with her authority as the head of that church. She therefore tolerated the Presbyterians who stayed within the church, but she would not allow any outsiders of either the Catholic or the Calvinist variety. She put down a Catholic revolt in the first years of her reign and vigorously persecuted priests. After the pope excommunicated her in 1570, she had Parliament declare that Catholicism was treason. Elizabeth persecuted Separatists as well. But the Church of England was moderate enough to satisfy the vast majority of her Protestant subjects.

ELIZABETH AND PARLIAMENT

Parliament shared Elizabeth's moderate opinions and was remarkably loyal to her. It constantly urged her to strengthen the monarchy by marrying this person or that, or to persecute the Catholics more vigorously; but she turned their pleas aside graciously. Parliament lost power during her reign. It did not meet often, as she seldom needed to ask it to levy taxes for her. When it did meet, she saw to it that its debates were directed by the trusted ministers who composed her Privy Council. In theory, however, Parliament continued to have all of the powers it had won during the Middle Ages. Elizabeth was strong because she won the respect and support of Parliament, not because she interfered with its ancient rights and privileges.

RELATIONS WITH WALES, IRELAND, AND SCOTLAND

During the Middle Ages the Celtic inhabitants of the outlying regions of the British Isles—the Irish, the Welsh, and Scots—successfully resisted, for the most part, the attempts of the English to control them. During the Tudor period, however, important steps were taken toward bringing the entire British Isles under English control.

Wales, conquered by Edward I in 1286 (see page 177), had never taken kindly to English rule until the Welshman Henry VII became king. Under the Tudors, the Welsh won representation in Parliament and adopted English forms of law and government. Their leaders even became English in speech and outlook.

Ireland's history was less happy. The Tudors never understood the Irish. After he had put down a rebellion in 1537, Henry VIII, ignoring Irish resentment, had imposed the Church of England on them. By the 1570's, early in Elizabeth's reign, the Irish were again in open rebellion. Elizabeth responded by allowing a number of English "gentlemen-adventurers" to settle in Ireland to keep order and take over great estates. Hatred of the English united the Irish and led to three and a half centuries of hostility. The Irish became the most strongly Catholic people of northern Europe, detesting the English and Protestantism. The English in return imposed foreign rule that put down all opposition with the sword.

Scotland was small, poor, divided by tribal conflict, and troubled by religious struggles between Catholics and the Protestant followers of John Knox, a disciple of Calvin. Its ancient enmity with England was lessened somewhat when a daughter of Henry VII married the Scottish king James IV. But in Elizabeth's reign, relations were complicated when the Catholic Mary, Queen of Scots, was exiled by Protestants after a series of scandals. Mary fled to England, where, because Catholics considered her the rightful queen of England, she became involved in intrigues against Elizabeth. (See below, page 391.) The Scots put her infant son on the throne as James VI and the government into the hands of a council of Protestants.

Elizabeth named James VI as her successor to the English throne. Thus in 1603, when Elizabeth died, James became King James I of England, and the two countries now had the same sovereign. Yet for more than a century their governments remained separate.

ELIZABETH'S FOREIGN POLICY

The principal goal of Elizabeth's foreign policy was to protect England and keep it at peace. Protestant though she was, she had little desire to embroil England in the religious struggles that were then raging throughout much of Europe. Instead she followed a flexible foreign policy that kept her country safe from invasion and for the most part out of war. She encouraged the growth of an effective navy of small but heavily armed vessels, which guarded England's coasts and attacked Spanish shipping in the Caribbean. She supported Protestant causes that would weaken the Catholic rulers of France and Spain so that neither would be able to mount an attack on England. At the same time, she flirted with Spanish and Austrian Habsburgs and French nobles who hoped to win England as an ally by marriage. She supported the Dutch Rebellion against Spain in 1577 (see page 315), and in 1586 she allowed Sir Francis Drake to sack Spanish colonies in the Caribbean. But she avoided open warfare as long as she could, realizing that Spain's military power might be more than England could resist.

Elizabeth's desire for peace was eventually upset by the presence in England of Mary, Queen of Scots. When Mary sought refuge in England in 1568, Elizabeth faced a dilemma. To send her back would be to send her to her death. But to keep her was dangerous, for Mary, a descendant of Henry VII, was next in line for the English throne—and Catholics, led by Philip II of Spain, insisted that she, not Elizabeth, was the rightful ruler of England. Elizabeth bought time by allowing Mary to remain in England as a royal prisoner with a miniature court of her own. But as the years passed, Mary became a center of Catholic and Spanish intrigue against Elizabeth. Finally, in 1586, Mary was accused of being involved in a plot to overthrow Elizabeth. Mary claimed that the evidence against her was forged, but she was convicted and beheaded the following year.

Mary's execution convinced Philip II that he must invade England in the name of Catholicism and Spanish power. In 1588 he sent the "Invincible Armada" of 132 galleons (large warships) sailing in stately lines to the Spanish Netherlands, where they were to pick up soldiers to attack the English coast. Little English vessels peppered them with cannon fire as they moved up the English Channel and used fire ships to drive them from the port of Calais, where they had gone to take on troops. Back in the Channel, the Spaniards lost a series of running sea battles and were driven into the North Sea, where a terrific storm finished the job the English had begun. The ungainly galleons were driven by high winds clear around the northern coasts of Scotland and Ireland, where more than half of them were wrecked. The survivors limped back to Spain in defeat.

"He blew, and they were scattered," the English exulted. The year of the Armada was the greatest of the Tudor period. After 1588 the Spanish could no longer reasonably hope to invade England, to put down the Dutch rebellion, or to determine the history of France. After 1588 it was clear that English and Dutch seaman dominated the seas.

Queen Elizabeth I addressing her troops at Tilbury, near London, in 1588. The troops were assembled to meet the threatened Spanish invasion—the invasion that never occurred, thanks to the defeat of the Spanish Armada at sea. One of the ways in which Elizabeth won the loyalty of her people was by making frequent public appearances such as this.

ELIZABETH'S ENGLAND

After the defeat of the Armada, all England swelled with pride and self-confidence. It was a time of rapid change and growth, and English commerce prospered. English mariners opened up Hudson Bay and other regions near the Arctic Circle, where they founded a profitable trade in fish and furs. They sailed northeastward to open new trade routes to Russia, and they began to compete with the Portuguese by sailing around Africa to India. Companies of "merchant adventurers" were formed to finance this trade: the East India Company, the Muscovy Company, the Virginia Company. At home the cloth trade grew, and English woolens won new markets on the continent. Cities grew, but most people still lived in villages and little towns, and even near London one could still see the trees and green fields of the countryside. A poor harvest meant a season of hunger, and the houses of the poor were little better than hovels; but in general the English people lived in greater comfort than ever before.

A peculiarly English middle class emerged during Elizabeth's reign. The middle class on the continent was usually limited to a small number of wealthy merchants and lawyers in the towns. In England there was a similar middle class in the towns, but there was also a middle class in the country-side. There the "gentry," who were landowners but were not members of the nobility, came to hold much of the power that had once been in the hands of the great lords. The gentry devoted themselves to improving their little estates and to serving their neighborhoods as justices of the peace. (See page 231). In the villages they shared power with the local Anglican clergymen, cementing an alliance of gentry and clergy that controlled England's local government well into the nineteenth century. In the towns and cities the merchant middle class also prospered. Representatives of these two middle class groups made up the House of Commons. By serving Elizabeth as justices of the peace and as members of Parliament, the middle class learned to govern England.

The "English Renaissance" (see pages 286-287) flowered during the last twenty years of Elizabeth's reign, which was also a time of political achievement. The symbol of it all was Elizabeth herself. To the end of her long life she retained the affection and respect of her people. Two years before she died she told Parliament, "Though God hath raised me high, yet this I count the glory of my throne, that I have reigned with your loves."

🪷 THE STUARTS
AND THE ENGLISH REVOLUTION

Elizabeth was succeeded on the English throne by King James VI of Scotland, who became James I (king 1603-1625) of England. Son of Mary, Queen of Scots, James was the first English king of the Stuart dynasty. He and his Stuart successors had the bad judgment to claim by divine right the power that Elizabeth had received as the gift of her countrymen. In a learned book entitled *The True Law of Free Monarchies,* James I proclaimed that "The king is the overlord of the whole land, so is he master over every person who inhabiteth the same." It was bound to be hard to put this idea across in a country that had had Parliament and the common law since the Middle Ages. The Stuart monarchs continually ran afoul of three English political traditions: the belief that government is limited by a "higher law" that neither kings nor Parliaments can violate; the concept that king and Parliament must share power; and the tradition of leaving the administration of local government to the justices of the peace. The result was a long conflict between the Stuarts and Parliament, from which Parliament emerged triumphant.

THE FIRST STUARTS: JAMES I AND CHARLES I

The first two Stuart kings, James I and his son Charles I (king 1625-1649) lacked Elizabeth's understanding of the English people. James was, as Henry IV of France remarked, a "wise fool." He knew all about the theory of government and very little about how to govern. He was undignified and awkward, and people laughed when he claimed that he ruled by divine right. His son Charles looked more like a king; but he was equally insistent on his right to absolute power, and he flew into temper tantrums when his claim was challenged. Neither man was an able ruler, and together they lost for the monarchy the popularity that Elizabeth had brought it.

Stuart foreign policy was unfortunate. In 1604 James ended the war with Spain that had dragged on since the days of the Armada, but in 1623 he made an unpopular attempt to marry his son to a Spanish Catholic princess. This scheme failed, and James then allowed himself to be maneuvered into another war with Spain. Charles finally married a Catholic sister of the French king Louis XIII, but in 1626 he went to war with France, so that England was fighting both France and Spain at the same time.

The Stuarts soon discarded Elizabeth's moderate religious policy. The Puritans at first had high hopes of James, for he had been brought up as a Scottish Calvinist. But their hopes were dashed in 1604, when James high-handedly announced that he planned to exercise rigid control of the Church of England through the system of bishops that the Puritans detested. His great religious achievement was to support a group of scholars who completed the "King James" translation of the Bible, a literary masterpiece that is still used by most English-speaking Protestants. Charles, with the aid of William Laud, archbishop of Canterbury, tried to enforce strict conformity to High Church Anglican practices and persecuted Calvinists who refused to go along. The result was a "Great Migration" of Calvinists to the New England Puritan colonies, where they established their own "Bible Commonwealth."

Growing opposition to the Stuarts centered in Parliament, where the representatives of the gentry and merchant middle class sat in the House of Commons and insisted that they had a right to share in England's rule. The Stuarts disliked Parliament, but were dependent upon it because only the House of Commons had the right to levy taxes (the "power of the purse"). Parliament often refused to impose taxes when the king advocated policies it did not like; the Stuarts insisted they had absolute authority to follow whatever policies they chose. The conflict that resulted led to a series of significant developments in English constitutional law.

The conflict between Parliament and the king came to a climax under Charles I. In 1626 Charles found himself at war with both France and Spain. War or no war, Parliament refused to grant new taxes until it had had "redress of grievances." Led by Sir John Eliot, the members of Commons finally forced Charles to sign the "Petition of Right" in 1628. This "Magna Carta of the Stuart Period" guaranteed certain rights of Parliament and of individual Englishmen against their king. It reaffirmed the power of the purse; it stated that no individual could be thrown in prison unless he was charged with a crime; and it forbade the government to billet soldiers in private homes or to impose martial law (rule by the military) in peacetime.

Although Charles signed the Petition of Right, he had no intention of honoring it. After obtaining the money he sought, he dissolved Parliament in 1629 and put eight of its members, including Eliot, in jail. Eliot died there, a martyr to the Parliamentary cause.

For the next eleven years (1629-1640) Charles tried to rule without Parliament. He raised the money that he needed by imposing long-forgotten medieval taxes. This policy threatened not only the power of the purse but also the system of common law. In 1635 it was challenged in the courts by one John Hampden, a Puritan member of Parliament. The royal judge upheld the king on the ground that the royal will was the law of the land. It was clear that the courts were coming to be controlled by the king and that the common law was in danger. In the 1630's it seemed that the king might gain the absolute control over England he sought.

THE PURITAN REVOLUTION AND THE COMMONWEALTH

Charles turned much of his government over to two favorites, Laud, who harshly persecuted Puritans and all who dissented from the High Church Anglican viewpoint, and Thomas Wentworth, earl of Strafford, whose high-handed methods antagonized the gentry.

Laud and Strafford hastened their king's downfall. In 1637 Laud attempted to impose the English system of bishops on the Church of Scotland, which had a Presbyterian form of government. The Scots resisted, raising an army that in 1639 seized Edinburgh, the capital of Scotland, from the king's troops. Charles, needing money to fight the Scots, in 1640 was forced to call Parliament back into session.

The first Parliament of 1640, the so-called "Short" Parliament, met less than a month. The king became so enraged by its demands for redress of grievances that he dissolved it. But soon after Charles was forced to call another Parliament, which came to be called the "Long" Parliament because it met off and on for twenty years (1640-1660). The leaders of the Long Parliament were Puritan squires, lawyers, and merchants who were determined to restore the common law and the power of the purse and to reform the Church of England along Calvinist lines. Its leaders had the support of the wealthier and more populous sections of England.

In 1641 the Long Parliament set out to dominate the government. It forced the king to dismiss both Laud and Strafford (and later it had both executed). More important, it passed a series of acts to make absolute monarchy impossible. One of these acts required Parliament to meet every three years, whether called by the king or not. Another forbade the king to dissolve Parliament without its own consent. Others abolished the royally dominated courts and made the Common Law once again supreme. And another required the king to appoint advisers acceptable to Parliament. Extremists even proposed, but could not enact, a bill that would have abolished bishops.

At this point Charles, his position improved by victories in Scotland, attempted to intimidate Parliament by seeking to arrest five of its key members. The maneuver failed, and early in 1642 Charles fled to the north of England and gathered his supporters to attack Parliament. Parliament, in response, began to assemble an army of its own. The English people now had to choose between a government dominated by the monarch and one dominated by Parliament. High Church Anglicans and most of the nobles and gentry flocked to the royal standard; the middle class, Puritans, the navy, and a minority of the nobles and gentry took up arms for Parliament. From 1642 to 1645 these groups fought a civil war which, despite its religious overtones and the fact that it pitted brother against brother, was surprisingly free of cruelty and destructiveness. At first the "Cavaliers," as the king's men called themselves, won the skirmishes against Puritan-Parliamentary "Roundheads," so called because they cut their hair short. But the Puritans, after reorganizing their army and making an alliance with the Scots, won the major battles of Marston Moor (1644) and Naseby (1645). After Naseby, Charles surrendered to the Scots, who sold him to the Parliamentary army in 1647.

The Parliamentary forces, victorious on the battlefield, now became divided among themselves. Moderate Presbyterians and Low Church Anglicans wanted some kind of central religious organization and a government in which Parliament and the king shared power. Others, radical

"Independents" or Congregationalists, wanted each local congregation to be independent of the others and favored weakening, or even abolishing, the monarchy. At this point the Presbyterian Scots, fearing the growing power of the Independents, switched their support to Charles and invaded England. Hopeful that he still might win the war, Charles fled from imprisonment to an island off the south coast of England, where he waited for his forces to rally. But the Independents, led by the great Roundhead general Oliver Cromwell, defeated the Scots. Soon thereafter, Charles was captured. Cromwell then purged Parliament of its moderates. The members who remained came to be called the "Rump"—the sitting part of Parliament.

Early in 1649 the Rump tried and beheaded Charles. He met death bravely, and in so doing won support for his cause, for not one Englishman in ten wanted to kill the king.

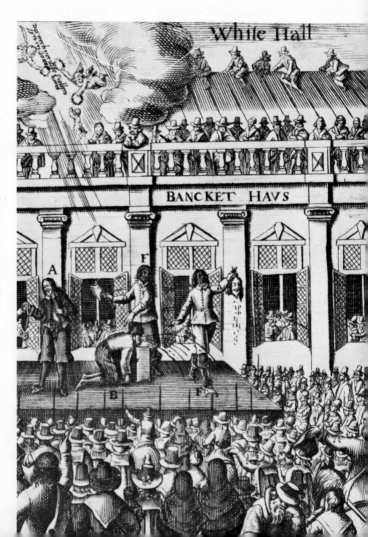

The execution of Charles I, London, January 30, 1649: a Dutch engraving of the time. The execution took place outside Charles's own palace of Whitehall which, as this engraving shows, was crowded to the rooftop with spectators. Charles, courageous and deeply sincere but sadly lacking in judgment, remains to this day a figure of tragedy and of controversy in English history.

Now that it had no king, England became a "Commonwealth" ruled in theory by the Rump but in matter of fact by Oliver Cromwell. Cromwell was an idealistic and iron-willed man who was determined to do what he considered right, whether it was popular or not. In 1649 he restored order in Ireland by massacring 2,000 rebels—an atrocity that the Irish have never forgotten. Two years later he put down a Scottish revolt led by Charles Stuart, son of the executed king. In 1653 Cromwell dismissed the Rump, which had become un-co-operative. Under a constitution called the "Instrument of Government," Cromwell became "lord protector" of England for life. He himself appointed a new Parliament, called "Barebone's Parliament" because it had a member named Praisegod Barebone; but because it did not always agree with Cromwell, this Parliament, too, was sent home. Thereafter Cromwell took full control of England, which he governed with the aid of the generals of his Roundhead army.

Cromwell's economic and foreign policies were successful. In 1651 he had the Rump enact the first "Navigation Act," which helped to revive English commerce by requiring that English cargoes be carried in English ships. In 1652-1654 he fought a successful war with the Dutch, strengthening

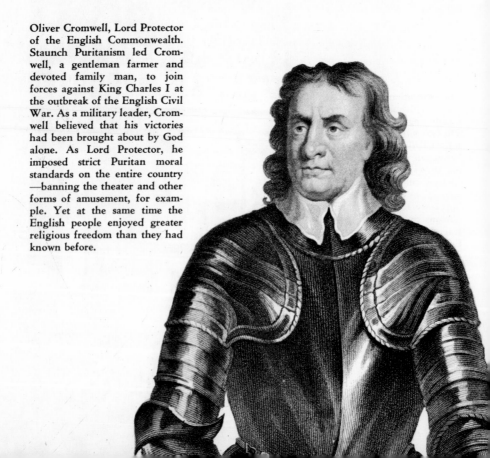

Oliver Cromwell, Lord Protector of the English Commonwealth. Staunch Puritanism led Cromwell, a gentleman farmer and devoted family man, to join forces against King Charles I at the outbreak of the English Civil War. As a military leader, Cromwell believed that his victories had been brought about by God alone. As Lord Protector, he imposed strict Puritan moral standards on the entire country —banning the theater and other forms of amusement, for example. Yet at the same time the English people enjoyed greater religious freedom than they had known before.

English commerce at Dutch expense. In 1655 his navy captured Jamaica from Spain, and later it captured a Spanish treasure fleet, seizing a fortune in silver. By encouraging Protestant refugees and Jews to come from the continent, Cromwell attracted to England men with trades and skills that the English had not known before.

Cromwell died in 1658. He was succeeded by his son Richard Cromwell, who proved a poor ruler and soon resigned. In 1660 the surviving members of the Long Parliament were called back into session to invite Charles Stuart to become King Charles II of England.

THE RESTORATION ERA

Only a few die-hard Puritans wept when Charles II (king 1660-1685) was restored to his Stuart father's throne. During the next three decades, called the "Restoration" era, he and his brother James II governed a country that underwent a gay and frivolous reaction against the austerity of the Puritan Commonwealth. The lively court became the center of social life; the theater, which the Puritans had banned, became once again the most important of English arts; and moral standards declined. John Milton spoke for only a few in his solemn religious poems, such as "Paradise Lost" and "Samson Agonistes," written during the reign of Charles II. More typical was Samuel Pepys, a social-climbing, practical civil servant who nosily noted in his famous diary everything that he saw.

Charles II realized that he could not repeat his father's autocratic high-handedness. He had learned to be patient and to get what he wanted by charm rather than by bluster. Fond of food, wine, the stage, and women, he was more likely to be found playing tennis than attending meetings of his Privy Council. But he was a successful monarch, for he restored peace and order to a country that badly needed both.

In 1661 a new Parliament, called the "Cavalier" Parliament because it was filled with royalists, met to solve the problems left by departing Puritans. It disbanded the army, pardoned most of the Puritan rebels, and restored the authority of the Church of England in a series of laws called the "Clarendon Code." The code required all clergymen and officials to conform to the Anglican *Book of Common Prayer*, and it forbade those who refused (called "nonconformists") to worship publicly, to teach their faith to others, or to attend the universities. These laws affected Catholics as much as Puritans, and Charles, who sympathized with Catholicism, approved them only reluctantly.

Charles had his problems with Parliament; but he was usually able to surmount them, and he always knew when the time had come to back down. In the mid-1660's, after the House of Commons refused to vote funds for a war with the Dutch, he decided (like his father before him) to try to rule alone. To obtain money, he made a secret treaty with Louis XIV of France in which he agreed to attack the Dutch and to ease the laws against Catholics and Puritans. Charles carried out his first promise by declaring war on the Dutch; but when his pro-Catholic "Declaration of Indulgence" (1672) aroused much resentment, Charles withdrew it. Parliament, back in session the next year, rubbed salt in his wound by passing the "Test Act," which imposed requirements for public office that Catholics could not meet.

The Dutch War ended in 1674, and the crisis between king and Parliament passed. In the years that followed, England's first political parties were formed. The earl of Shaftesbury rallied those who were anti-French and anti-Catholic into the "Country" or "Whig" party; Charles's supporters formed the "Court" or "Tory" party. In 1678 a corrupt clergyman named Titus Oates announced that he had uncovered a "Popish Plot" to murder Charles and replace him with James, his Catholic brother. Nonconformists rushed to support the Anglican Whigs, who won a great majority in the House of Commons. In 1679 the Whigs passed the "Exclusion Act" to keep James from the throne, but the act failed to pass the House of Lords. Charles patiently waited out the crisis. It later developed that Oates had lied, and Englishmen shuddered to realize how close they had been to a civil war. Whig popularity declined rapidly, and some of them became so desperate that they concocted a plot of their own to murder the king. When the plot was discovered, its leader fled into exile, and some of his aides were executed.

Charles emerged unscathed and governed peacefully during the last years of his reign. Not until he was on his deathbed did he make known his true religious preferences: twenty-four hours before he died, he called for a priest and was received into the Roman Catholic Church.

JAMES II AND THE GLORIOUS REVOLUTION

James II (king 1685-1688) encountered the same problems of Parliament, religion, and French aid that had plagued his brother. But James, unlike Charles, lacked the sense to deal wisely with them. His reign started out well when, Catholic though he was, Parliament voted him a good income. But almost immediately his lack of moderation became evident: after a minor uprising James had 300 men hanged and 900 others sent as slaves to the West Indies. He began to appoint Catholics to public office in violation of the law, and he tried to impose Catholic practices on the Anglican church. To support his actions, he stationed 30,000 troops near London.

These actions angered even the Tories, who until that time had loyally supported the king. Yet no action was taken, for it seemed that James would die soon and be succeeded by one of his daughters by his first marriage. Both daughters were Protestants, and both were married to Protestants. But in 1688 James's second wife, a Catholic, gave birth to a son, who was now heir to the throne—and who obviously would be brought up as a Catholic.

Leaders of both the Whigs and the Tories now turned to Mary, the elder of James's Protestant daughters, and to her husband, the Dutch leader William of Orange. William, who was desperately defending his country against the attacks of the powerful army of Louis XIV (see page 383), welcomed the opportunity to become king of England and so bring England into the war against France.

In November, 1688, William crossed the Channel to claim the throne. James panicked. Some of his troops deserted to William, and others refused to fight. James fled to France in December. William marched into London and announced that James, by leaving the country, had abdicated the throne. He and his wife became William III and Mary II, joint monarchs of England. Englishmen called this revolution the "Glorious Revolution," because no blood had been shed. It was to prove to be the last in their history.

THE BILL OF RIGHTS

The accession of William and Mary was the final triumph for Parliament after eighty-five years of conflict with the Stuarts. Early in 1689 it passed the "Bill of Rights," which settled all the issues between crown and Parliament in Parliament's favor. The Bill of Rights forbade the king to interfere in Parliamentary elections, debate, or sessions. It stated that only Parliament could lay taxes and maintain the army. It weakened royal control over the judges; it outlawed ecclesiastical courts and excessive bail; it guaranteed trial by jury; and it forbade punishments before conviction. The Bill of Rights made Parliament and the common law the equal partners of the king and assured that England would never follow France and Spain down the road to absolutism.

After the Glorious Revolution, England had a monarchy in which Parliament and the courts limited and shared authority with the king. But this limitation of the king's power did not mean that England had a democracy. Both houses of Parliament were aristocratic. Only bishops and the principal lords sat in the House of Lords, and only the gentry and the more well-to-do merchants voted for members of the House of Commons.

⚜ ⚜ ⚜

The Glorious Revolution of 1688 and the Bill of Rights of 1689 established Parliament once and for all as the equal partner of the king. This division of power was soon to prove itself a far more effective means of government than the absolute monarchies of the continent; and it assured that the constitutional development of England would continue.

People, Places, and Terms

Elizabeth I	Naseby	Roundheads
Mary, Queen of		Rump
Scots	Act of Supremacy	Commonwealth
Sir Francis Drake	Act of Uniformity	lord protector
James I	Act of the Thirty-	Instrument of
Charles I	Nine Articles	Government
William Laud	High Churchmen	Barebone's
Sir John Eliot	Puritans	Parliament
Earl of Strafford	Presbyterians	Cavalier Parliament
John Hampden	Congregationalists	Clarendon Code
Oliver Cromwell	Privy Council	Nonconformists
Charles II	gentry	Declaration of
Earl of Shaftesbury	*The Law of Free*	Indulgence
James II	*Monarchies*	Test Act
William of Orange	power of the purse	Whigs
Mary II	Petition of Right	Tories
	Long Parliament	Glorious Revolution
Marston Moor	Cavaliers	Bill of Rights

Getting Organized

1. Describe the character of Elizabeth. How did she ease the religious tensions that divided her people? What were the various religious groups during her reign? Which did Elizabeth tolerate? Which did she persecute? Why, in each case?
2. Describe Elizabeth's relations with Parliament. How did Parliament lose power during her reign?

3. How did the Tudors cope with the problems of Wales, Ireland and Scotland? Was English policy in all of these regions successful?
4. What was Elizabeth's foreign policy? What role did Mary, Queen of Scots, play in this policy? What happened to Mary? Why and with what result did Philip II of Spain finally decide to invade England?
5. What was the effect of the defeat of the Armada on England? Describe England in the late sixteenth century. Describe its middle class.
6. What did James I's book *The Law of Free Monarchies* proclaim? Against what ancient English traditions did the Stuarts run afoul?
7. How did the early Stuarts, James I and Charles I, antagonize Parliament? How did Parliament react to these Stuart abuses?
8. Why was the Long Parliament called and what did it accomplish? What were the causes of the Puritan Revolution? How and why did Charles lose this civil war?
9. Describe Oliver Cromwell's personality and policies. What success did he enjoy in his foreign and economic policies? What happened after his death?
10. How did Charles II establish himself on the throne of England after so many years of exile? How was the religious conflict resolved? What brought Charles and Parliament into conflict with each other?
11. How did political parties arise in England? What was the Popish Plot and what was its effect on Charles's popularity? On James's status as the future king?
12. How did James II help to bring on the Glorious Revolution? Describe this revolution. Why did the English choose William and Mary? What did the Bill of Rights establish? What did the Glorious Revolution achieve?

Understanding the Big Picture

1. How do you account for Elizabeth's great success as the queen of England? Why did she have so little trouble with Parliament?
2. How do you account for the Stuart kings' failure as kings of England? Why did they have so much difficulty with Parliament? Which of the Stuarts had the most difficulty? Which the least? Why?
3. Compare the constitutional and political power held by Elizabeth to the power held by William and Mary.

For the Thoughtful

1. After the Glorious Revolution the English government was to prove far more durable and powerful than the absolute monarchies of the continent. What factors might be expected to contribute to this strength?
2. What significance to English history did the rise of a strong middle class have? How important has the rise of the middle class been to political and constitutional history in western Europe generally?

$\mathcal{C} \mathcal{O}$ **28**

two Giants of
Eastern Europe:
the Ottoman Empire
and Russia

The Ottoman Empire and Russia were the principal powers of eastern Europe in the sixteenth and seventeenth centuries. Like Spain, France, and England in the west, they were ruled by hereditary monarchs. But they differed significantly from these western kingdoms and from each other in their forms of government, their religion, and their social customs. The Ottoman Empire was an heir of the earlier Islamic empire of the Arabs. (See pages 61-63.) Russia had adopted the Orthodox Christianity and many of the political ideas of the Byzantine Empire. (See page 207.) Both states tried to extend their boundaries into central Europe; at the same time they competed vigorously with each other for control of southeastern Europe.

🌼 THE EXPANSION AND DECLINE
OF THE OTTOMAN EMPIRE

The Ottoman Turkish leader Mehmed II had conquered Constantinople in 1453. (See page 201.) His successors conquered many regions of the Near East, Africa, and eastern Europe. By the sixteenth century the Ottoman Empire was one of the world's major states.

404

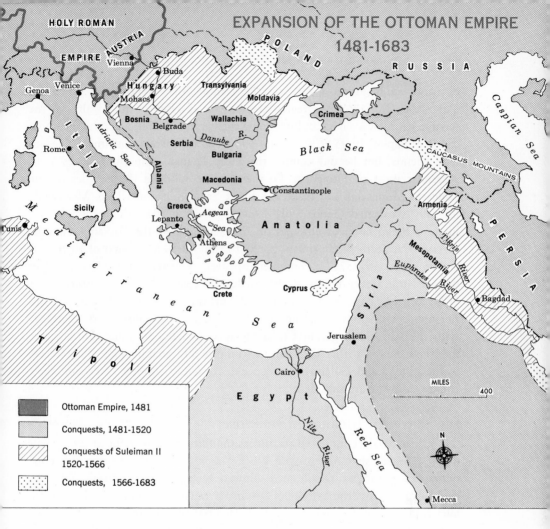

EXPANSION OF THE OTTOMAN EMPIRE
1481-1683

Legend:
- Ottoman Empire, 1481
- Conquests, 1481-1520
- Conquests of Suleiman II 1520-1566
- Conquests, 1566-1683

MILES 400

OTTOMAN TURKISH EXPANSION

For a century after the fall of Constantinople in 1453, Ottoman Turkish sultans sent their armies south and east from Turkey to conquer vast regions in the Middle East and North Africa. Sultan Selim I (sultan 1512-1520), who claimed to be the successor both of the Byzantine emperors and of the Abbasid caliphs (see page 62), extended the empire to include Syria, Egypt, and the upper valley of the Tigris and Euphrates rivers. His successors took over the Red Sea area, including Mecca, and all of the coast of North Africa as far west as Morocco.

The Ottoman Empire was at its greatest during the reign of Suleiman I "the Magnificent" (sultan 1520-1566), who turned the full force of his Islamic state against Christian Europe. The year after he assumed his throne he captured Belgrade, a city on the Danube that is now the capital of Yugoslavia. In 1526 he defeated the flower of Hungarian chivalry in the terrible battle at Mohacs and occupied the capital of Hungary, the city now called Budapest. In 1529 his armies laid siege to Vienna. Suleiman failed to take Vienna, but he did compel the Holy Roman Emperor Charles V to surrender most of Hungary. To the east, he subdued the peoples of the Caucasus Mountains and made the Black Sea an Ottoman lake. Meanwhile his navy weakened Genoa and Venice by seizing from them their islands in the Aegean Sea and colonies on the mainland of the Balkan Peninsula.

After the death of Suleiman, the Ottoman Turks lost much of their crusading spirit. In 1571 a combined Spanish, Venetian, and Genoese fleet defeated the Turkish fleet at the battle of Lepanto, off the western coast of Greece (see page 363), and checked Turkish power in the Mediterranean. Beginning with Suleiman, the sultans made treaties called "capitulations" with the Christians, giving Christians special rights to trade and manage their own affairs within the Ottoman Empire and guaranteeing them access to the Holy Land. Suleiman's successors ceased attempting to expand their empire, and warfare subsided.

THE OTTOMAN TURKISH GOVERNMENT

To their newly conquered territories the Ottomans introduced the system of government that had proved successful in governing their earlier conquests. Each subject people was allowed to retain its language, religion, and form of government. The Ottomans remained aloof and kept their own traditions, not adopting the customs of their subjects.

The Ottoman Turkish system of government was unique. Every year Ottoman soldiers seized a number of the most promising children of their Christian subjects and took them to Constantinople, where the children were brought up as Muslims. The ablest of these slaves were trained to become government officials; others became "Janissaries," members of a special army that was the terror of its opponents. The system worked well at first, but by the end of the eighteenth century it had become corrupt and inefficient.

OTTOMAN TURKISH DECLINE

After the battle of Lepanto, the Ottoman Empire went slowly into decline. At the same time there was a gradual rebirth of national feeling among the empire's European subject peoples. Christians, more heavily taxed than

Muslims and forbidden to hold central government offices, became restless and dissatisfied with their distant rulers. There began a slow revival of interest in native traditions—Greek, Romanian, Serbian, Croatian, Bulgarian.

Meanwhile European countries chipped away at the boundaries of the empire. At the end of the seventeenth century the Austrians, after initial setbacks that included a second siege of Vienna by the Turks in 1683, regained Hungary and the neighboring province of Transylvania. In the eighteenth century Russia seized a number of Turkish provinces along the northern shore of the Black Sea.

By the end of the eighteenth century, the Ottoman Empire was being called "the sick man of Europe." But whenever the heart of the empire was seriously challenged, the Ottomans revived long enough to defend themselves. Meanwhile, southeastern Europe slept fitfully under Ottoman rule, falling behind the rest of Europe in political and economic development.

✤ RUSSIA BECOMES A GREAT POWER

The Ottoman Empire's neighbor to the northeast, Russia, grew more slowly. Throughout the sixteenth and seventeenth centuries, it remained isolated on the eastern fringe of Europe. But during the eighteenth century, when the Ottoman Empire was decaying, Russia began to take a decisive part in European affairs for the first time.

THE REIGN OF IVAN THE TERRIBLE

For much of the sixteenth century, Russia was ruled by a madman. Ivan IV "the Terrible" (tsar 1533-1584) frequently behaved in ways that are generally regarded as insane. Yet so strong was the Russian tradition of autocracy (see pages 208-209) that Ivan's rule was never seriously threatened, and in some ways Russia was strengthened during his reign.

When Ivan inherited the throne in 1533, he was only three years old. When he was seventeen (1547) he had himself crowned tsar—the first Russian ruler to adopt the title officially—and set out to wrest control of the government from the boyar (noble) families who had ruled during his childhood. In 1564 the boyars rose in a revolt that Ivan put down with incredible cruelty. The following year he took over about half the estates of Russia and put them under the administration of men called *oprichniks*. Then he set the *oprichniks* against the boyars in a deliberate civil war.

Wearing black, riding black horses, and carrying the emblem of a broom and a dog's head, the *oprichniks* rode across the steppes killing boyars and seizing their lands. Ivan retired to a "monastery" where he played at being the abbot, taking part in mock religious services and indulging in fantastic orgies. By 1572, when the terror of the *oprichniks* began to wane, Russia's old boyar nobility had been permanently weakened.

Russia continued to expand. Although worsted in a long series of wars with Poland and Sweden, the Russians succeeded in conquering the southern part of the Volga valley, stretching the country's boundaries to the Caspian Sea. And at the end of Ivan's reign, the first of a series of Russian adventurers began to push eastward into Asia. Within sixty years these remarkable pioneers had reached the Pacific Ocean, some 3,500 miles east of Moscow, and brought all of northern Asia (Siberia) under Russian control. (See map, page 334.)

THE TIME OF TROUBLES

All the pent up pressures caused by Ivan's violent policies erupted after the death of Ivan's weak and ineffective son in 1598. The next tsar, Boris Godunov (tsar 1598-1605), ruled a divided people. Boyars and clergymen opposed the tsar—and each other. Peasants sought freedom. Merchants wanted orderly government and lower taxes. The Don Cossacks, bandit soldiers who lived along the Don River in southern Russia, opposed any government at all. The country was ripe for revolution.

Russia's "Time of Troubles" began in 1604 and continued for almost a decade. Boyars, Cossacks, and nobles from neighboring Poland supported their own claimants to the throne. There were years of confused intrigue, assassinations, and civil war. Finally it seemed that the tsardom would go to a Polish noble whose followers had seized Moscow.

At this point the Russians stopped fighting each other and united in opposition to having a Polish Catholic tsar in the Kremlin. A volunteer militia drove the Poles from Moscow. Control of Russia fell into the hands of the *zemsky sobor*, a council of leaders, which in 1613 elected as tsar a young native Russian named Michael Romanov. The Time of Troubles was over.

THE FIRST ROMANOVS: MICHAEL AND ALEXIS

The first two Romanovs, Michael and his son Alexis, ruled Russia from 1613 to 1676. Neither was a dynamic or a talented man, although they restored some order to their country and kept out foreign invaders. Russia continued to stagnate.

Michael and Alexis re-established the authority of the tsar in Russia. The only group that might have challenged them, the *zemsky sobor,* was only a council of advisers; it had no real power. It met continually during the first decade of Michael's reign. But its membership comprised leaders of the boyars, the clergy, and the townsmen, three groups that had so little in common that the *zemsky sobor* could agree on very little. The tsars called it into session less and less frequently, and after 1653 it met only once, in 1682. There was now no governmental body that might in any way challenge the authority of the tsars.

At the same time the boyars were constantly increasing their authority over the peasants, who attempted to resist the serfdom that was being forced upon them. A series of peasant uprisings culminated in 1669 in a violent rebellion in the Volga valley led by Stephen Razin, a picturesque bandit whose name is enshrined in Russian folk song and story. At the head of thousands he marched up the Volga toward Moscow. It took the tsar's armies two years to put down the peasants and capture and execute Razin. The peasants were suppressed but still rebellious.

There were even revolts in the church. In 1656 the patriarch Nikon attempted to make the Russian Orthodox Church more like its parent Greek Orthodox Church. The educated upper clergy welcomed what seemed like mild reforms, such as revising the Orthodox prayer books to correct spelling mistakes; but parish priests and their faithful followers were horrified at the idea of changing the church. Calling themselves "Old Believers," they resisted every effort to make them change their ways. As a result of the controversy, the influence of the Orthodox Church declined further.

The tsars and the men who surrounded them began to take an interest in European ways during the seventeenth century. European doctors, engineers, merchants, and technicians began to appear in Russian cities, but most of the inhabitants suspected and avoided them. Then, as the seventeenth century drew to a close, the most outstanding of all the tsars set out to drag Russia into Europe by brute force.

THE REIGN OF PETER THE GREAT

After a period of confusion following the death of Alexis in 1676, his son Peter mounted the throne as Peter I (tsar 1682-1725). Peter became sole effective ruler of Russia in 1689. He was a giant of a man, nearly seven feet tall, with strength and vigor to match. He had been brought up in a Moscow suburb near the part of the city where foreigners lived, and as a child had avidly learned all that these outsiders could teach him. A Scottish soldier of fortune taught him the art of war and helped him to organize a regiment of young aristocrats, who played at battle so earnestly that both Peter and his tutor were wounded. The young tsar (he was only seventeen when he assumed the throne) had a practical turn of mind. He later boasted that he had studied fifteen trades, including dentistry; and he was not afraid of physical work, which he preferred to book learning. His drinking bouts were notorious, and he loved practical jokes, women, and rough company. But above all Peter was ambitious: he devoted his life to gaining as much power as possible for himself and for his country.

Peter's Reforms. All of Peter's policies were planned to make Russia strong in war. He realized that much could be learned in this regard from the powerful countries of western Europe. In 1697 he led a group of Russians on a trip to the Dutch Netherlands, where he worked in a shipyard and recruited skilled workers for his factories, and to England, where he studied Parliament, which he respected though he neither liked nor understood it. When reports reached him of a revolt in Moscow, he hurried home to supervise the torture and execution of the revolutionaries. Then he set out to make Russia more like the west.

As a symbol of his determination to end old Tatar and Byzantine customs, Peter supplied his customs houses with scissors to cut off the beards of conservative Russians. He required the members of his court to wear western clothing. More important, he invited foreigners to Russia, assuring them of religious and legal independence, and he sent hundreds of young Russians to western Europe to study shipbuilding, industry and crafts, medicine, and the arts of war. Inside Russia he established schools and even an Academy of Sciences modeled on those he had seen in the west.

Peter left few aspects of Russian life unchanged. He encouraged industry, ordered construction of canals, and built military roads between the principal cities. His political reforms were equally ambitious. After a series of experiments, he appointed twelve-man "colleges," each of which had responsibility for a specific department of the government. He set up a civil-service system through which able administrators could advance to the power and status of the nobility. He brought the church directly under his control by replacing the patriarch of Moscow with a group of bishops called the "Holy Synod," headed by a layman appointed by the tsar.

At the same time he revitalized Russia's army. His childhood regiment became a model for new regiments of palace guards. He founded the Russian navy. And he required his nobles to serve as officers and drafted peasants to serve as soldiers under strict discipline and training.

All these reforms were expensive, and made financial reforms necessary. Peter taxed his nobles, but the heaviest burden fell upon the peasantry, each of whom was required to pay a "soul" or head tax. Thousands were conscripted to work on Peter's industrial projects, roads, and canals.

Peter's Wars. Peter used his army and navy to win what he called a "window on the west"—that is, an outlet on the Baltic Sea, which at the time was still under Swedish control. In 1700 he attacked Sweden, beginning a twenty-one year conflict called the "Great Northern War." At first Peter's poorly trained army was no match for the Swedes. But in 1709 it scored a major victory at the battle of Poltava, which sent the Swedish forces flying and their king as a fugitive to the Ottoman Empire. During the next decade the Swedish empire in the Baltic began to dissolve. The Russians had already seized the southern shores of the Gulf of Finland, where they began to build the city of St. Petersburg in 1703. They now conquered Finland itself and occupied islands close to the Swedish shore. Finally, in 1721, Sweden acknowledged defeat. By the Treaty of Nystad, Sweden surrendered all its possessions south of the Gulf of Finland in return for the restoration to them of Finland and a sum of money. Peter had won his window on the west.

The foundation of St. Petersburg: an eighteenth-century print. Peter the Great is shown examining the plans for part of the city, while construction proceeds on all sides. Work began in 1703. After ten years, during which hundreds of laborers at the marshy site died of disease or exposure, St. Petersburg became the capital of Russia. The city, now called Leningrad, has long been considered one of the most beautiful in the world.

Still unsatisfied, Peter turned southward, and the following year attacked Persia's provinces on the landlocked Caspian Sea. He was planning expeditions to the frontiers of India and China when, in 1725, he died.

Peter's Legacy. His Russian senate gave Peter the title *Pater Patriae, Imperator, Maximus*—"Father of his Country, Emperor, Great." He deserved it. In many ways his capital at St. Petersburg, the city he fought to found as an outlet to the Baltic, was a symbol of his accomplishments. It was built at great expense by peasant labor on piles driven into a marsh in what had recently been foreign soil. It was magnificent, but it was not typical of Russia. Just as his laws about beards and his clothing reforms influenced only a few people at the top of the social scale, so his economic, political, and cultural reforms affected only a few. Industrial growth took place in only a few regions and in a few industries. The government remained in the hands of the aristocrats, even though they were subject to the tsar's authority. The rulers of the church changed, but the priests worshiped as before. And the costs fell most heavily on the peasants, who therefore slid even further down the road to a serfdom that approached slavery.

Thus Peter's attempts to remake his country in the image of the west did not radically change the basic lines along which Russia was developing. It remained an autocracy rooted in peasant serfdom and a backward system of agriculture. But Peter did make Russia strong enough to compete with the powers of western Europe, and he crystalized policies that Russian rulers have followed ever since: the drive into eastern Europe; the domination of the military forces; and the willingness to impose change by force upon a reluctant people.

Peter's Successors. In the thirty-seven years after Peter's death (1725-1762) there were six rulers of Russia. Three of the six were women, who were often influenced by foreign favorites. The three men were weaklings.

Despite some resulting confusion in the government, Russia's military strength continued. The rulers allied with Austria and Britain in order to further reduce the power of Sweden and to contain expanding Prussia (Chapter 29) in the Baltic. They won territory from the Swedes in Finland and almost destroyed Prussia. It was clear that a strong ruler could lead Russia to a position of the first rank in European affairs.

THE REIGN OF CATHERINE THE GREAT

The strong ruler who appeared was a woman and a foreigner. Catherine was the daughter of a minor German noble. She had married the heir to the tsardom, an unpredictable eccentric named Peter III. Soon after

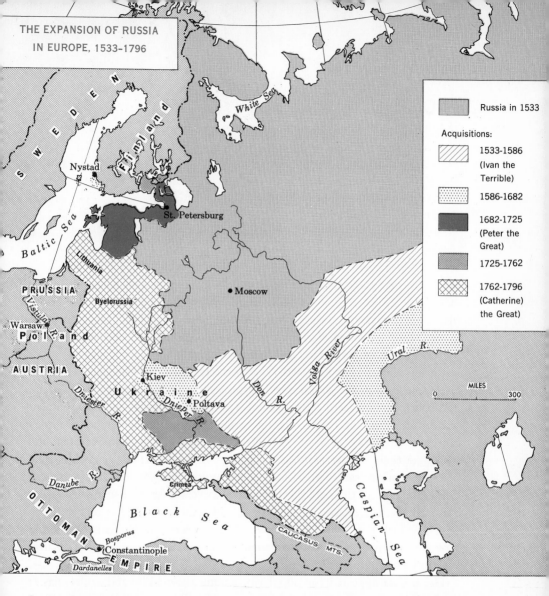

White Sea

SWEDEN

Finland

Nystad

St. Petersburg

Baltic Sea

Lithuania

PRUSSIA

Byelorussia

Moscow

Warsaw

Poland

Vistula R.

AUSTRIA

Kiev

Ukraine

Dniester R.

Dnieper R.

Poltava

Don R.

Volga River

Ural R.

Danube R.

Crimea

OTTOMAN

Black   Sea

Bosporus

Constantinople

Dardanelles

EMPIRE

CAUCASUS MTS.

Caspian Sea

MILES

0   300

Russia in 1533

Acquisitions:

1533-1586
(Ivan the
Terrible)

1586-1682

1682-1725
(Peter the
Great)

1725-1762

1762-1796
(Catherine)
the Great)

mounting the throne in 1762, Peter called off a successful Russian campaign
against the Prussians because he liked the Prussian king; he emancipated
the nobility from their obligation to serve the state; and at the same time
he made enemies of everyone by his arrogance. After six months on the
throne, a group of nobles deposed him and turned to his wife, who gladly
accepted the throne, saw that her husband was quietly killed, and ruled for
the next thirty-four years as Catherine II.

Catherine (tsarina 1762-1796) loved flattery, pleasure, and fine clothes.
She surrounded herself with men whom she made her lovers and the
servants of Russia; but she never allowed her intrigues to interfere with

THE PARTITIONS
OF POLAND

her authority as tsarina. She read the liberal writers of western Europe (Chapter 32), corresponded with them, and paid lip service to their liberal ideas; but she never allowed any real liberalism in Russia. Like Peter the Great, she introduced such western ideas as pleased her, at the same time increasing Russian autocracy and military power.

As an ambitious ruler with a shaky claim to her throne, Catherine attempted to win the support of the nobles and at the same time to extend her control over them. She created government offices which she filled with grateful minor nobles. At the same time she made her court into a glittering Russian version of Versailles. To it she attracted the great nobles who, like their counterparts in the France of Louis XIV, spent their time plotting against each other instead of uniting to oppose their tsarina. Catherine gave all the nobles ever greater powers over their serfs, who were confined to their estates, heavily taxed, and sometimes bought and sold like slaves. When the serfs of southwest Russia rose up in arms, Catherine repressed them severely and had their leader carried to Moscow in an iron cage to be cut in quarters.

The tsarina appealed for popularity among the middle and upper classes by issuing a vaguely worded "Instruction" calling for a legislative commission to rewrite the laws of Russia. The commission met in 1767, and for a year and a half its members debated. Finally Catherine dismissed the commission, having made her nod in the direction of reform without having had to reform anything.

Catherine took advantage of the growing weakness of the Turks and Poles to continue Russia's westward expansion. In 1763, the year after she assumed power, she was able to install a former lover, Stanislas Poniatowski, on the Polish throne. Her subsequent meddling in Polish affairs began to alarm Poland's allies, France and Austria, who drew Turkey into a war

with Russia to distract Catherine from Poland. Catherine acted rapidly; she sent her Baltic fleet all the way around Europe and through the Mediterranean to the Black Sea, where it destroyed a Turkish squadron. The Russians were also remarkably successful against the Turks in land battles in the Crimea and the Danube valley—so much so that Austria, fearful for its own possessions in the Balkan Peninsula, seemed on the verge of joining the Turks against Catherine. To prevent such a war, Frederick the Great of Prussia (Chapter 29) drew their attention back to Poland by suggesting that Russia, Austria, and Prussia help themselves to large areas of Poland. In the resulting "First Partition of Poland" (1772), Poland lost about one fourth of its land and one third of its population. (See map, page 414.) Two years later, Catherine successfully concluded the Turkish war. The Ottoman Empire gave up the Crimea and other lands along the north coast of the Black Sea. It also agreed not to interfere with the Black Sea and to allow Russian commerce to pass through the straits of the Bosporus and the Dardanelles. In 1787-1792 Catherine strengthened Russia in the Black Sea area in a second war against the Turks.

In the final years of her reign, Catherine took part in two further partitions of Poland. (See maps above.) After the first partition, the Poles had decided to strengthen their central government for self-protection. Catherine, thinking this was a threat to her influence in Poland, joined Prussia in the Second Partition of Poland in 1793. The Poles in what was left of their kingdom fought to regain their lands under the leadership of Tadeusz Kościuszko, who had been a hero of the American Revolution. But they were quickly overwhelmed. In 1795 Russia, Prussia, and Austria partitioned Poland for the third time, and Poland ceased to exist as an independent state. By the partitions of Poland, Catherine moved Russia's frontiers some 200 miles westward and aquired Byelorussia, Lithuania, and all the Ukraine.

415

RUSSIA IN 1796

By Catherine's death in 1796, Russia had acquired much of the vast territory it now holds. Powerful Prussia and Austria blocked further expansion into Europe; but the quiet settlement of the thinly populated Siberia was continuing rapidly. Expanding boundaries brought additional foreign influences into Russia, both from western Europe and from the many nationalities whose lands the Russians had conquered.

The court, the leading nobles, and a small group of scholars responded to western influence, but 95 per cent of the population remained serfs on the country estates. There they lived in their isolated villages, scratching the earth with their crude wooden plows, making almost everything they needed, and giving their lords between three and six days service a week. In some areas they also paid cash rents, and everywhere they were heavily taxed. Their subjugation was complete: they had no rights in the law courts, and their landlords could sell them or exile them to Siberia.

The separation of the ruling class and the common people was complete. Peasant rebellions were frequent, but they were always put down. Russian rulers might, like Peter and Catherine, pay lip service to western liberal ideals, but in practice they governed with the whip and the sword.

♠ ♠ ♠

At the end of the eighteenth century Russia had become an important military and political force in the affairs of Europe, but it was still a backward, feudal country, far removed from the main stream of European political and economic development.

People, Places, and Terms

Selim I	Belgrade	boyar
Suleiman the Magnificent	Siberia	*oprichnik*
Ivan IV	St. Petersburg	Time of Troubles
Boris Godunov	Finland	*zemsky sobor*
Michael Romanov	Crimea	Holy Synod
Alexis	Bosporus	Window on the West
Peter I	Dardanelles	Great Northern War
Peter III	caliph	Battle of Poltava
Catherine II	Battle of Mohacs	Treaty of Nystad
Stanislas Poniatowski	Battle of Lepanto	Partitions of Poland
Tadeusz Kościuzko	capitulations	
	Janissaries	

Getting Organized

1. What new areas did the Turks conquer after 1453? How far into Europe did Suleiman threaten? What happened after his death?
2. How did the Ottomans treat the peoples and areas that they conquered? Why did this empire decline after 1571?
3. How was Russia strengthened during the reign of Ivan the Terrible? What problems faced Russia in the early seventeenth century? What was the Time of Troubles? How and why did it end?
4. How successful were the early Romanov tsars? What happened to the *zemsky sobor?* What revolts were there against the early Romanovs?
5. Describe Peter the Great. Why did he travel to western Europe? What reforms did he try to bring about and how successful were they? How did he finance these reforms?
6. What were the objects of Peter's wars? How successful was he? What legacy did Peter leave to Russia? What happened after his death?
7. What kind of a ruler was Catherine? How did she treat the nobles? How did she treat the serfs? Was she a "liberal"?
8. What new areas did Catherine win for Russia? Describe Russia at the end of the eighteenth century.

Understanding the Big Picture

1. Why did the Turkish Empire become so powerful in the sixteenth century? Why did it decline?
2. Was Peter a wise ruler? Did Russia really need his westernizing reforms? Why did the Russian people react to these reforms as they did?
3. Who was the wiser and more effective monarch, Peter or Catherine? Whose was the more effective foreign policy? Who acted more in the interests of the Russian people?

Mastering the Map

1. Study carefully the map of the Ottoman Empire on page 405. How serious a threat to Christian Europe did the Turks pose?
2. Study carefully the map of the expansion of Russia in Europe on page 413. Did Peter or Catherine gain more territories for Russia? Why did Russia seek the lands that it did?

For the Thoughtful

1. Compare the threats posed to Christian Europe by Suleiman, Saladin, and Muhammad's followers. Which was the most dangerous threat?
2. In what ways did the policies of Peter and Catherine foreshadow the Soviet Union of today? In what very basic ways has it always differed from the western European nations?
3. Were Peter and Catherine wise rulers? Did they act in the interests of their people or of themselves? Compare them to Louis XIV.

29

PRUSSIA, AUSTRIA, and the STRUGGLE for GERMANY

Even after the catastrophic Thirty Years War had ended, Germany remained a giant—a wounded giant, but nevertheless a giant. In the eighteenth century it became the prize in a bitter struggle for power between Habsburg Austria and the rising state of Prussia.

🌼 GERMANY AFTER THE TREATIES OF WESTPHALIA

The Treaties of Westphalia, which ended the Thirty Years War in 1648 (see page 318), left the Holy Roman Empire intact in theory but divided in fact. The emperors, who were supposedly supreme, had lost most of what had remained of their authority over the German princes.

The Thirty Years War had given France and Sweden an excuse to interfere in Germany's affairs, and later Louis XIV had seized Alsace and neighboring areas for his growing French monarchy. Within Germany, the real authority fell increasingly into the hands of the princes of the more than 300 states, few of whom had any desire to become part of a united Germany. Many of them imitated Louis XIV, establishing courts patterned on Versailles and trying, like Colbert, to make their countries self sufficient—often with

418

the financial support of France, which wanted a divided Germany. Each of the major states was primarily concerned with its own problems.

At the end of the Thirty Years War, much of Germany had been in ruins. (See page 319.) Generations of hard-working German people gradually repaired the damages of war, and before the middle of the eighteenth century their country had largely recovered. But Germany still lagged far behind the more rapid development of France and Britain. The mercantilists of France and Britain discriminated against German products, and none of the little German states had the political or economic strength to participate in the race for colonies in the seventeenth century. The little states hampered the growth of trade by adopting such mercantilist practices as imposing customs duties and tolls on each other's products, which discouraged large-scale manufacturing and commerce. Some of the German princes were able to make their states prosperous; but their prosperity, like their governments, was on a small scale. As a result, Germany remained even more agricultural than either France or Britain.

The flourishing German civilization that had produced Dürer and Holbein and encouraged Erasmus had been all but destroyed. For the remainder of the seventeenth century and much of the eighteenth century, Germans copied foreign ways. In the princes' courts the manners, ideas, and even the language of France were adopted. Artists and builders imitated Italian or French styles—often with brilliant results, as the lovely churches of southern Germany testify. Some princes patronized artists and scholars, but others imprisoned anyone who criticized them. Late in the eighteenth century Germany finally developed a native group of philosophers and poets, but this was more than a century after the Treaties of Westphalia.

Without a strong central government, the German lands of the once mighty Holy Roman Empire could not hope to regain their former power. There were only two states that might someday prove capable of uniting them. In the south was Catholic Austria, ruled by the Habsburg dynasty; and in the north was Protestant Brandenburg, governed by a series of exceptional rulers of the Hohenzollern family and soon to become important as the kingdom of Prussia.

THE RISE OF BRANDENBURG-PRUSSIA

Of all the hundreds of dynasties in the Holy Roman Empire, it was the Hohenzollern that, by a combination of luck, fortunate marriages, intelligence, energy, and ambition, rose to challenge the Habsburgs. Until

1415 the Hohenzollerns had been an old but undistinguished German family. In that year the Holy Roman emperor gave them the northeastern German territory of Brandenburg, centered on the little city of Berlin. This became the basis for their rise to power.

THE GROWTH OF BRANDENBURG

Brandenburg was a march (frontier territory) on the boundary of the Holy Roman Empire, next to the kingdom of Poland. Its ruler was one of the seven electors who chose the Holy Roman emperor. (See page 155.) The Hohenzollerns, using Brandenburg as a base, created a typical German patchwork state: by inheritance they gained Cleves (in the valley of the lower Rhine) and East Prussia, a duchy on the Baltic Sea that owed allegiance to the king of Poland. By skillful diplomacy during the Thirty Years War, they won eastern Pomerania, on the Baltic coast, and lands in central Germany that had formerly been ruled by Catholic bishops.

The real founder of the Hohenzollern family fortunes, and therefore of the fortunes of Brandenburg as well, was Frederick William "the Great Elector" (elector 1640-1688), who modeled his government on the strong French and Swedish monarchies. The Great Elector saw himself as the servant of his people, but he did not hesitate to use force and violence to make himself as absolute a ruler in Brandenburg as his contemporary, Louis XIV, was in France. He made himself unchallenged ruler by unifying the separate assemblies, armies, and government administrations of the different provinces so that he could control them more easily. Then he increased taxes, using the proceeds to encourage industry, to drain swamps, and to build a canal connecting the Oder and the Elbe rivers. When Louis XIV revoked the Edict of Nantes in 1685 (see page 381), Frederick William encouraged some 20,000 Huguenot refugees to settle in his territories, to which they brought skills and knowledge that his native Germans lacked.

Like later Hohenzollerns, the Great Elector was most interested in military affairs and in increasing his possessions. He increased his army to some 50,000 men, but used it sparingly to take advantage of the rivalry of his two larger neighbors, Sweden and Poland. By siding first with one and then with the other, he won concessions from both. The king of Poland surrendered his claim to East Prussia, in which Frederick William now held supreme authority for the first time, and the Swedes came to consider him their principal rival for the domination of the Baltic. Before he died Frederick William made Brandenburg the most powerful as well as the most prosperous of the north-German states.

THE ESTABLISHMENT OF THE PRUSSIAN KINGDOM

The Great Elector's son, Frederick I, spent most of his time trying to make his court into a little Versailles. But he made an important contribution to history by assuming the title "king in Prussia" in 1701. From that time onward, the Hohenzollern possessions collectively were called "Prussia."

The man who made Prussia into a strong kingdom was Frederick's son, Frederick William I (king 1713-1740). He believed that an absolute monarchy was the only proper form of government and that as the king he was the only man who knew what was best for his people. Frederick William sincerely believed that he was obligated to provide his people with honest and efficient government and that he was justified in using extreme methods to do this. He was perfectly willing to beat a loafer in the streets with his cane—both for the good of the man and for the good of Prussia. He built up his army, enforced rigid military discipline on his people, and brought most aspects of his country's life under control of the state. As a result, the German writer Goethe called Prussia "the most slavish country in Europe," and an Italian was even more to the point when he described it as a "great barracks." After the reign of Frederick William, the adjective "Prussian" became a synonym for warlike and harsh in discipline.

Frederick William I, like the Great Elector, encouraged manufacturing by restricting the outdated guilds and allowing craftsmen to move freely from job to job. He welcomed middle-class officials because he knew they would serve him well, but at the same time he gave Prussia one of the most rigid systems of social classes of any country in Europe. The ruling class of the Prussian state was the *Junker* aristocracy. The *Junkers* personally managed their own estates, and they were the only class allowed to become officers in the army. As soldiers the *Junker* officers accepted rigid discipline for themselves, obeying without question the commands of those above them; and they imposed equally rigid discipline on the peasant-born common soldiers. The same pattern was repeated in the countryside, where in return for service to the monarchs the *Junkers* were allowed to retain the restrictions that made their peasants serfs. Thus in both the army and the countryside, the peasants served the nobles and the nobles served the king. It would have been like the tsarist regime in Russia except for one thing: the Hohenzollerns won and kept the unfaltering loyalty and obedience of the nobles. They learned to enforce Prussian discipline on all their people and to inspire them with a faith in their kings and the destiny of their country. Fiercely, the kings of Prussia drove their kingdom, as they drove themselves, to greatness.

Frederick William was the founder of the highly centralized governmental bureaucracy for which Prussia became famous. He created the "General Superior Directory for Finance, War, and Domains," which supervised almost every aspect of government with rigid emphasis on economy. The "sergeant king," as he was called, was interested above all else in the army, which he increased to 81,000—one of the largest in Europe at the time. He was content to drill his troops, however, and never used them to attack any other country.

FREDERICK THE GREAT, THE "ENLIGHTENED DESPOT"

Frederick II "the Great" (king 1740-1786) was an almost perfect example of the benevolent or "enlightened" despot. The enlightened despot was what many *philosophes*, French writers of the time, thought the ideal king should be. The *philosophes* (Chapter 32) believed that human beings should be governed by reason and by the "laws of nature," which their reason could discover. Emphasizing scientific more than religious truth, they demanded reforms in government, church, society, and education, in order to clear aside the outdated laws that held back progress. Although a few of the *philosophes* advocated limited monarchies or even republics, most felt that progress could come faster if the government were directed by a reasonable, benevolent, "enlightened" despot, who would make his state's welfare his highest aim. Frederick the Great was just such a man; he used his father's Prussian methods to attain "enlightened" goals.

Frederick put many of the reformers' concepts into practice. He was much influenced by the *philosophes'* idea that the king was the servant of his people. He even wrote a book, the *Anti-Machiavel*, in which he insisted that "the monarch is not the absolute master, but only the first servant of the state." His ideal was to "see, think, and act for the whole community," and he worked hard at his job.

He was no bigot by the standards of his time. He scandalized many of his Protestant subjects by welcoming Catholic immigrants. He did persecute the Jews, but not so much as most other rulers of the time, and if he found them useful, Frederick gave them special privileges.

All his life, Frederick enthusiastically supported the intellectual life of his country. As a boy he preferred playing the flute to playing soldier, and as a man he played his flute while he plotted the downfall of his enemies. He wrote learned essays, poetry, and music; talked literature with learned friends; and even invited the leading literary light of the time, Voltaire, to teach him to write elegant French. He founded elementary schools for

Frederick the Great reviewing troops of the Prussian army: an eighteenth-century engraving. The goal of all Frederick's policies was to make Prussia strong: "A well-conducted government," he wrote, "must have a system as closely knit as any system of philosophy. All the measures must be well thought out . . . [with] the same objective in view, the consolidation of the authority of the state and the increase of its power."

peasants and high schools for future technicians and officials, and he helped make the Berlin Academy of Sciences an important center of learning.

In the first decades of his reign, Frederick fought two major wars (below, pages 428-430), which left his country exhausted; but once they had ended, he worked hard to repair the damage they had done. In the single decade after 1763 he brought some 300,000 colonists into Prussia, repaired damaged villages, built 900 new ones, and restored war-damaged workshops. He urged his nobles to adopt more efficient methods of agriculture, to plant new crops, to drain marshes, and to treat their peasant serfs more decently. The costs of war and reconstruction forced him to increase taxes, but he spent the money frugally and well. Much concerned with the administration of justice, he reformed the courts, codified and published the laws, and abolished torture in criminal cases.

All of these were "enlightened" policies. Yet Frederick was equally a despot: having little respect for his subjects or faith in human nature, he kept everything firmly under his own control. *Junker* aristocrats remained supreme on their estates, and commoners, even wealthy middle-class merchants, were excluded from high government positions. Frederick was unwilling to change the rigid class structure of Prussian life. He always thought of Prussia in much the same terms he did of its army—a body of peasant soldiers officered by *Junker* gentlemen and headed by himself, "the first servant of the state."

Under Frederick, Prussia became strong enough to challenge by force Austria's traditionally dominant position in Germany.

✿ HABSBURG AUSTRIA

The Thirty Years War weakened but did not destroy the power of the Austrian Habsburgs. They continued to be regularly elected Holy Roman emperors, which gave them great prestige, and they remained by far the most powerful of the German princes. In the middle of the seventeenth century they retained a huge and motley assortment of dynastic possessions, including most of the southeastern part of the Holy Roman Empire (Austria, Silesia, and Bohemia) and, in southern Germany, the Tyrol. They also were kings of Hungary, which had become theirs in 1526, just before much of it was overrun by the Turks.

THE REVIVAL OF HABSBURG FORTUNES

Habsburg fortunes were nevertheless at a low point after the Treaties of Westphalia of 1648, for they had suffered major losses to the Protestants in Germany and to the Turks in Hungary. Consequently they turned their attention to their hereditary archduchy of Austria and their capital of Vienna, which was the base of their power, and consolidated their government. Then they became the leaders of the Christian defense against a renewed Ottoman onslaught up the Danube. In 1683 Ottoman forces laid siege to Vienna itself, and the Austrians were hard put to it to defend the city. But Poland, which feared Turkish expansion to the north, rushed an army to their aid, which helped raise the siege and drive back the invaders. The popes then called for a last crusade against the infidel. The Poles and Venetians responded, and Peter the Great of Russia helped by attacking the Turks in the Black Sea region. The combined forces were able to push the Turks back: the Habsburgs and their allies took Budapest in 1686, and the following year they won a major battle at Mohacs (scene of the great

Turkish victory a century and a half before; see page 406). The war continued to 1699; when it ended, the Austrian Habsburgs were for the first time undisputed rulers of all Hungary.

Thus, as the eighteenth century began, the Habsburgs were monarchs of a large empire. But their various possesions had little in common with each other. Austria was peopled by German-speaking Catholics. In Bohemia most of the nobles and many townspeople were German; but the majority of the people were Czechs who resented German rule, and many were Protestants. In Hungary, the Magyar aristocracy lorded it over the peasant Slavs. Each of these three major Habsburg territories had its own laws, courts, and customs. Each had its own feudal diet, or parliament. Each resented any attempt to unite it closely with the others. Bohemia and Austria were part of the Holy Roman Empire; Hungary was not and never had been.

Nevertheless, the strength of these states added together was great and, as the eighteenth century began, the Habsburgs were ready to resume the offensive in western Europe. When their childless Habsburg cousin Charles II of Spain died (see page 368), the Austrians contested for his throne with Louis XIV in the War of the Spanish Succession (1701-1713). Louis won Spain for his grandson; but as consolation the Austrians won the former Spanish Netherlands and important territories in Italy. The Emperor Charles VI (1711-1740), satisfied with these gains, devoted much of his long reign to the internal problems of his lands, trying unsuccessfully to reduce the hostility among the various parts of his empire. But he was not a particularly effective ruler, and he left behind a disorganized state, an empty treasury, and an ineffective army.

MARIA THERESA AND JOSEPH II

Charles's successors, Maria Theresa and Joseph II, attempted to reform and strengthen Austria's government. Maria Theresa (ruled 1740-1780) was Charles's daughter, in 1740 a young, pretty woman seemingly quite mild and placid. But she soon demonstrated that she had a strong mind and will of her own. She fought her arch rival Frederick the Great of Prussia to a standstill. Although she was a devout Catholic, she showed that at times she preferred her own judgment to that of the pope. She subscribed to many of the liberal ideas of the eighteenth-century *philosophes;* and, like the "enlightened despots," she was willing to use force to compel her people to accept reform.

Maria Theresa made herself strong by adopting some ideas of the *philosophes* and some of the succesful policies of her hated Prussian rivals. In the liberal eighteenth-century tradition, she tried to improve the condition of her serfs by releasing them from their labor services, and she encouraged her nobles to do the same. (They refused.) Even though she was a devout Catholic, she curtailed the traditional privileges of the priests; and she suppressed the Jesuits, who, she thought, had become too powerful. She attempted to establish a Prussian type of strong central government by suspending the provincial parliaments and forcing German officials and the German language on all of her possessions. She even resorted to feminine wiles; for example, she once appeared before her reluctant Hungarian nobles with her child in her arms to appeal for their support in a war with Frederick the Great. At a time when they were being attacked by their western rivals, she made the Habsburg lands stronger and more unified than they had ever been before.

Maria Theresa, her husband the Emperor Francis I, and their children. Maria Theresa bore sixteen children, of whom ten reached adulthood. All but one were forced by their mother to make marriages that would promote the interests of the Habsburg dynasty. Among them were the future Emperor Joseph II (standing nearest the center) and the future Queen Marie Antoinette of France (at the left of the group of younger children in the background).

When Maria Theresa's husband died in 1765, her son became Holy Roman emperor as Joseph II (emperor 1765-1790). For fifteen years he was also co-ruler with his mother of the Habsburg lands, and after her death in 1780 he ruled them by himself. Joseph attempted to carry further the enlightened policies that his mother had introduced; he was perhaps the most dedicated of all the enlightened despots. But he was also the least successful, for he tried to impose his liberal ideas on his people whether they liked them or not. Not surprisingly, he met such strong resistance that most of his reforms came to nothing.

When his nobles proved reluctant to improve the lot of the peasantry, Joseph abolished serfdom throughout the Habsburg lands, appointed state officials to defend the peasants in the manor courts against their masters, and regulated their taxes and labor services. He required the lords to pay the same taxes as the commoners, planning to use some of the money to provide free education for everyone and to encourage the growth of industry. But the peasants, misunderstanding their ruler's goals, rebelled against enforced military service, and the nobles violently opposed the ending of their feudal authority. Even the middle class resented Joseph's well-intentioned interference in its business affairs.

Not satisfied with his mother's restrictions on the clergy, Joseph determined to make the state supreme and to force the priests to accept the principles of French religious reformers. He gave toleration to Protestants, forbade the clergy to communicate with Rome except through his officials in Vienna, and required the bishops to swear allegiance to the crown. The Catholic majorities in the Habsburg lands resentfully opposed this sudden attack on old customs.

To centralize the government even further, Joseph abolished the ancient diet (parliament) of Hungary, and he replaced the traditional local governments with a bureaucratic system controlled from Vienna. The Hungarians revolted, refusing to send him tax money or military supplies for his armies. The Austrian Netherlands also rose in revolt, as did the Tyrol, and even the Austrians fought bitterly to retain their local governments. No simple orders from a king could erase traditions built up over centuries.

Maria Theresa's program of gradual reform led to real progress before she died. Joseph's reforms, by contrast, were too ambitious; after his death in 1790, his successor abandoned almost all of Joseph's reforming policies. Shortly before he died, Joseph wrote his own accurate epitaph: "Here lies a prince whose intentions were pure, but who had the misfortune to see all his endeavors fail."

♨ PRUSSIA VS. AUSTRIA

Both Frederick the Great of Prussia and Maria Theresa of Austria mounted their thrones in 1740, and for the next four decades their rivalry dominated German history. Their fierce struggle for the position of greatest strength in the Holy Roman Empire resulted in two major wars that came to involve most of the great powers of Europe. The larger story of these wars belongs in Chapter 31; here we shall concern ourselves only with their effects upon Germany proper.

Tradition dictated that a woman could not succeed to the throne of the Holy Roman Empire. But Emperor Charles VI, who had no sons, was determined that his daughter Maria Theresa should inherit all the Habsburg lands, even though she could not be empress. He therefore persuaded the major powers of Europe to agree to so-called "Pragmatic Sanctions," which declared that the Habsburg lands could not be divided and that Maria Theresa would inherit them.

"No one, I think, will contradict me," Maria Theresa wrote later, "when I claim that it would be difficult to find another example in history in which a crowned head came to power under more difficult and unfortunate circumstances." For in addition to the internal problems of the Habsburg

The battle of Leuthen, Silesia, in 1757, the second year of the Seven Years War. The Austrians here suffered a disastrous defeat by Prussian forces under Frederick the Great. The war continued until 1763; but Leuthen assured that Silesia, which Prussia had seized from Austria fifteen years earlier, would remain under Prussian control.

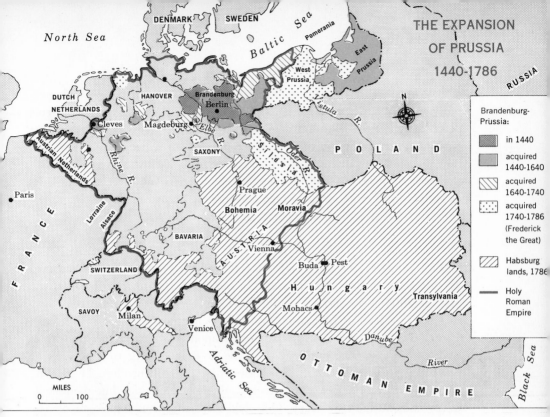

North Sea

DENMARK   SWEDEN

Baltic Sea

Pomerania

RUSSIA

DUTCH
NETHERLANDS

HANOVER

East
Prussia

West
Prussia

Brandenburg
Berlin

Cleves

Magdeburg

Elbe R.

Vistula R.

P O L A N D

SAXONY

Silesia

Oder R.

Austrian Netherlands

Rhine R.

Paris

F R A N C E

Lorraine

Alsace

Prague

Bohemia   Moravia

BAVARIA

A U S T R I A

Vienna

SWITZERLAND

SAVOY

Milan

Venice

Buda   Pest

H u n g a r y

Transylvania

Mohacs

Danube River

Adriatic Sea

O T T O M A N   E M P I R E

Black Sea

MILES
0   100

Brandenburg-
Prussia:

in 1440

acquired
1440-1640

acquired
1640-1740

acquired
1740-1786
(Frederick
the Great)

Habsburg
lands, 1786

Holy
Roman
Empire

lands, she had to cope with the invasions of rival rulers who ignored the Pragmatic Sanctions in their greed to help themselves to her possessions. In 1740 Frederick the Great of Prussia led the attack by invading Silesia, a large and wealthy Austrian province southeast of Berlin. He expected Maria Theresa to surrender it without a fight, but he was disappointed. For even though his armies quickly drove the Austrians out of Silesia, and France, Spain, Saxony, and Bavaria joined him in what became known as the "War of the Austrian Succession" (1740-1748), Maria Theresa stubbornly refused to quit. With the support of her Hungarian subjects and of England, which was anxious to maintain the balance of power, she fought the aggressors to a standstill in southern Germany. Finally, in 1748 Maria Theresa agreed to give up Silesia in return for Frederick's promise to support her husband's election as Holy Roman emperor.

During the eight years of uneasy peace that followed, the diplomats scurried to make new alliances for a second war for the domination of Germany. Maria Theresa, who never faltered in her desire to win back Silesia, put together an alliance with France and rising Russia against Prussia. Frederick, seeing himself surrounded, decided to attack before his enemies were organized. In 1756 he invaded Saxony, starting what came to be called the "Seven Years War" (1756-1763.) With the help of English money he planned brilliant campaigns in which he used daring and ingenuity to win battles with his war-weakened armies. Yet he was saved from defeat only by the withdrawal of Russia from the war in 1762. With the Russians neutral, the Austrians could not hope for a decisive victory, and the exhausted combatants finally made peace in the following year on almost the same terms as in 1748. Frederick kept Silesia. And after two decades of struggle and large losses of men and money, he had made Prussia almost as powerful as Austria in German affairs.

♛ ♛ ♛

During the century and a half that followed the Peace of Westphalia, two developments profoundly affected the history of Germany. One was the gradual shift of the interest of the Habsburg rulers in Vienna from their role as Holy Roman Emperors, primarily concerned with German affairs, to their role as heads of a dynasty based upon Austria and the Hungarian lands to the east. The other was the rise of Brandenburg to a position of power as the kingdom of Prussia, headed by its Hohenzollern kings. The monarchs of both states sought to be enlightened despots, but their lands were fundamentally different. One day Germany would have to choose between them if it hoped to become united once more.

People, Places, and Terms

Hohenzollerns	Saxony	Tyrol
Frederick William,	Hanover	Milan
"the Great Elector"	Brandenburg	Vienna
Frederick I	Berlin	
Frederick William I	Cleves	*Junker*
Frederick II	East Prussia	enlightened despot
"the Great"	Magdeburg	*Anti-Machiavel*
Voltaire	Pomerania	Treaty of Utrecht
Charles VI	Oder River	Pragmatic Sanctions
Maria Theresa	Elbe River	War of the Austrian
Joseph II	Silesia	Succession
	Bohemia	Seven Years War
Bavaria	Austria	

Getting Organized

1. Describe the condition of Germany after the Thirty Years War. Who held the political power within the Holy Roman Empire?

2. Trace the rise of Brandenburg. By 1640 what areas did it control? How did the Great Elector strengthen Brandenburg, both internally and in its foreign relations?

3. What did Frederick I contribute to the rising power of his country? How did Frederick William I strengthen Prussia? How did he control all of the people in his country?

4. What is an enlightened despot? In what ways was Frederick the Great enlightened? In what way was he a despot?

5. At the beginning of the eighteenth century, how much power did the Austrian Habsburgs hold? What areas of Europe did they control? What problems did they have?

6. How did Maria Theresa better the position of the Habsburgs? How enlightened were her policies? How enlightened were the policies of Joseph II? How successful was he?

7. Trace the Prussian-Austrian conflict of the eighteenth century. Who were its principal figures? What were its results?

Understanding the Big Picture

1. How did Prussia become so powerful in such a short period of time? What were the main factors in this rapid progress?

2. What is an enlightened despot? Which of the Prussian and Austrian rulers was the most enlightened? Which was the least?

3. How strong was Austria's position in the Holy Roman Empire? Was it as strong as always? Explain fully.

4. Make a chronological chart showing the principal events in the developments of both Austria and Prussia.

Mastering the Map

Study carefully the map of Central Europe on page 429. Note the Prussian territories and the possessions of the Habsburgs. Judging by the map, how might the rise of Prussia to great-power status be expected to alter the European balance of power? Explain fully.

For the Thoughtful

1. Was the enlightenment of its rulers or its armies the more important factor in the rising power of Prussia? How are these two factors related to each other? Which usually is the more important cause of a nation's strength?

2. How do the aims and achievements of Frederick the Great compare with those of Louis XIV? Be specific.

3. From what you know of eighteenth-century German history, what seems to you the most likely course of events in Germany in the nineteenth century? Give your reasons for your prediction.

30

Britain and France in the Eighteenth Century

At the time that Russia and Prussia were rising in eastern Europe, two long-established monarchies of western Europe underwent less drastic change. Britain and France were the two richest and most powerful countries of the age. Both had large empires, strong military and naval forces, prosperous cities with a growing middle class, and relative peace and order within their boundaries. Both were undergoing slow but significant commercial and agricultural "revolutions." But they were traditional enemies and a study in contrasts; for Britain was the only fully developed "constitutional" monarchy of its day, governed by an alliance of aristocrats and great merchants; while France under the "Old Regime" was an absolute monarchy, ruled by descendants of Louis XIV and the model for lesser monarchies all over Europe.

BRITAIN UNDER THE FIRST THREE GEORGES

The successors to those would-be absolute monarchs, the Stuart kings of England, took to heart the lesson of the Glorious Revolution of 1689 (see pages 400-402) and made no attempt to rule by divine right. William III (king 1689-1702) and his wife Mary II (queen 1689-1694) realized that they had been put on the throne by Parliament, not God. Their successor,

432

Mary's sister Anne (queen 1702-1714), also left most matters in the hands of Parliament. The principal event of Anne's reign was the "Act of Union" of 1707, which united England and Scotland. Parliament henceforth included Scottish representatives. The crosses of Saint George and Saint Andrew, patron saints of England and Scotland, were superimposed on each other in a new "Union Jack" as a symbol that the two countries were now one—the "United Kingdom of Great Britain."

After Anne's death, the British throne passed to the Hanoverian dynasty (so-called because its members were also the electors of the German state of Hanover), whose first two members, George I (king 1714-1727) and George II (king 1727-1760) were more German than British. They preferred Hanover, where they were absolute monarchs, to Britain with its foreign ways and unruly Parliaments. They seldom interfered in the affairs of Britain, so that control passed more and more to Parliament.

A STABLE AND PROSPEROUS SOCIETY

Life never seemed more stable and secure than in England under the Hanoverian kings. Safe from invasion, prosperous, and conservative, many Englishmen came to feel that at last they had found the solution to all their problems. However, gradual changes were preparing the way for the Industrial Revolution of the early nineteenth century, which would remake England into a land of factories and cities.

On the surface all remained as before. Most Englishmen lived in quiet villages surrounded by open farmlands. Industry was conducted in little shops by master craftsmen, their journeymen, and their "jolly apprentices." Sturdy yeomen worked the farms, and the parson and the squire ruled the countryside with firm but sympathetic hands. But beneath the calm surface an important change was taking place. The larger landholders were buying out the smaller and enclosing the "common" lands of the villages, where the yeomen had once been able to keep their farm animals, with hedges behind which the lords now kept their sheep. This "enclosing" had been going on since Elizabeth's time, but in the eighteenth century it gained momentum. Over 1,400 "enclosure acts" were passed by Parliament during the century, depriving the yeomen of their traditional rights to common land. Dispossessed, they flocked to the growing cities, where they often could not find work or were at the mercy of factory owners. As a result, the proportion of yeomen in the population decreased; poverty and unemployment increased in the cities, as did vice and crime; and highwaymen robbed the unwary country traveler.

"Laughing Audience": an engraving by William Hogarth (Chapter 32). Hogarth caught much of the spirit of eighteenth-century England in his works, although he frequently, as here, made merciless fun of the self-satisfied Londoners of his time.

But most Englishmen prospered with the aristocracy. Mercantilist laws passed by a friendly Parliament gave the great merchants high protective tariffs and assured them markets for their goods in the colonies. Bankers prospered by financing new ventures. Members of the wealthy middle class intermarried with the aristocrats and bought country estates to become aristocrats themselves.

Meanwhile the population grew from some 5,000,000 at the time of the Glorious Revolution to more than 9,000,000 at the end of the eighteenth century. Wages for the most part rose while prices remained about the same, and the standard of living of all but the very poor rose measureably.

The aristocrats who controlled the government set the tone of every major aspect of England's life. Like aristocrats everywhere, they admired the French, even though they hated France's religion and politics; and they modeled their behavior and their dress on the fashions of Versailles. Young aristocrats went on the "grand tour" of France and Italy to learn manners, with the result that they grew more refined, dueled less, and acquired continental tastes. The country houses of the aristocrats were the centers of English culture, where the squires collected paintings and fine furniture, read the classics and the eighteenth-century liberal French writers, and devoted themselves to the good life.

GOVERNMENT BY PARLIAMENT

During much of the eighteenth century, Britain was governed by an alliance of the aristocrats and country gentlemen with the merchants and lawyers in the towns. These men controlled Parliament. They made it an all-powerful instrument of government that not only wrote but also administered the laws. Britain was no democracy, for the common people had little political influence; yet it was the most liberal and freedom-loving country of the eighteenth century.

The Aristocrats in Parliament. In the House of Lords sat the heads of the great noble families and the bishops of the Church of England. The House of Commons was almost as aristocratic. Members were either "knights of the shire," representing the squires in the rural counties, or "burgesses," representing certain towns. Only those who had property producing 40 shillings rent a year were eligible to vote, and many of these sold their ballots to the highest bidder. The distribution of seats was out of date and unfair. Many of the growing industrial towns had no representation at all, while many "rotten boroughs" that had drastically declined in population continued to be represented in Parliament. For example, Old Sarum, a hillside populated only by grazing sheep, was represented in Parliament, while the expanding cities of Manchester, Birmingham, and Leeds had no representation.

During the reigns of George I and George II, national policy was made by the "Whig Oligarchy," a clique of some seventy aristocratic families who controlled both houses of Parliament. They favored the interests of the great landholders and, by voting mercantilist measures, continued to support commercial and industrial growth. Their Tory opponents remained a minority. The Tories were aristocrats themselves, who found it hard to unite to oppose Whig policies that were similar to their own.

The Cabinet and Prime Minister. Because neither George I nor George II was interested in the day-to-day matters of government, Parliament gradually developed a system for administering the government itself. It became customary for the king to ask the leader of the majority party in Parliament to become "prime minister," or the executive head of state. The prime minister in turn selected, with the royal approval, ministers to head the various departments of the government. The ministers as a group were his "cabinet," the principal policy-making body of the British government. The prime minister and the members of his cabinet retained their seats in Parliament, to which they were responsible; they remained in office as long as they retained Parliament's approval. If the prime minister lost a "vote of confidence," however, he and his cabinet were expected to resign and to either hold new elections for Parliament or be replaced by members of the opposition party. The fiction of royal rule remained—it was still "His Majesty's government" and even "His Majesty's loyal opposition." But the fact was that during the eighteenth century Parliament came to control every aspect of the English government. It not only made laws but, through the prime minister and his cabinet, it enforced them as well.

The English Constitution. The authority of Parliament has never been defined in a written constitution like that of the United States. The English "constitution" instead is based upon tradition built up over the centuries. In the eighteenth century, Parliamentary government became a part of this tradition, supplementing the common law, which had emerged triumphant from the turmoil of the seventeenth century. The common law, originating in the Middle Ages and forged in centuries of battles between Parliaments and ambitious kings, interpreted by lawyers and judges, was never seriously challenged after the seventeenth century. It protected the rights of all Englishmen to freedom of speech and assembly, and it guaranteed speedy and impartial justice to all who sought it. English judges were appointed for life or "good behavior," which freed them from dependence on the king. They continued to develop the common law slowly and carefully, gradually modifying it to meet changing needs. In Parliament the minority party opposed any change that might affect its rights, and the people were quick to protest if they felt their traditional liberties were being challenged. But at the same time the "London fog" that surrounded the constitution, making it next to impossible to define its limits exactly, allowed a gradual evolution of the powers of government, which prevented any piling up of grievances that would lead to a violent revolution. The "Glorious Revolution" of 1689 was the last revolution in England's history.

THE REIGNS OF GEORGE I AND GEORGE II

The first two Hanoverian kings turned the administration of the government over to the leaders of Parliament. George I (king 1714-1727) was an "honest blockhead" who never learned to speak English properly, and his son, George II (king 1727-1760) is best remembered as the last British king to lead troops into battle.

The Hanoverians were made cautious by a Scottish uprising in 1715. The revolt was led by James Stuart, called the "Old Pretender," the Catholic son of the deposed King James II. (See page 401.) James's uprising was a dismal failure, but it influenced George I to turn the government over to Robert Walpole, a Whig country squire, who was Britain's first prime minister. Walpole held office from 1721 to 1742. He kept down the taxes and avoided foreign wars, reporting proudly on one occasion that "There are 50,000 men slain this year in Europe, and not an Englishman."

But war eventually brought Walpole's downfall. In 1739 Parliament, against Walpole's wishes, declared war on Spain (the "War of Jenkins's Ear"). This war led to British participation in the War of the Austrian Succession (Chapter 31) the following year. Walpole continued to oppose these wars; so in 1742 he was forced from office by more warlike leaders, and British troops went off to fight in Europe, India, and North America. This encouraged the Old Pretender's son, Charles Stuart (called the "Young Pretender" or "Bonnie Prince Charlie") to start a revolt in Scotland in 1745. Charles was soon sent back into exile; but the British had to call their troops home from Europe to defeat him. So Britain gained little from all its fighting. Britain subsided into peace, and Parliament sank into corruption under lesser men than Walpole.

In the 1750's the French struck at British colonies in America and India. Britain would have lost the resulting Seven Years War (Chapter 31) had not a new statesman, William Pitt, arisen in Parliament to lead his country to victory. With his high spirits and a rare gift for winning support, Pitt dominated Parliament. His policies led to British victories; and at the war's end in 1763, Britain's prestige and power were higher than ever before.

THE REIGN OF GEORGE III

In 1760 George III (king 1760-1820) became king of Great Britain. Unlike the first two Georges, George III was determined to "be king"; in other words, to direct the British government himself. By various means —notably by paying large bribes—he won the support of a majority in Parliament. Parliament came to be dominated by a clique of Tories, called the "king's friends" and led by Lord North (prime minister 1770-1782).

George and his "friends" attempted to increase the king's power, but succeeded only in reducing it. Three times they excluded from the House of Commons one John Wilkes, who had criticized the king in print. Three times the voters, outraged by this attack on the freedom of the press, re-elected Wilkes. In reaction, Parliament established the principle of freedom of election to the Commons. Later, in 1782, the Commons, angered by North's inefficiency, nearly passed a motion "that the House could no longer repose confidence in the present ministers." Rather than have it proposed again, North resigned, thus setting the precedent that a prime minister should remain in office only as long as he has the "confidence" of Parliament.

After the Seven Years War (Chapter 31), George and his ministers attempted to impose a system of taxes and controls on the colonies, with the double object of raising money and bringing the colonies more directly under the British authority. But it was too late to make such an attempt in North America, where from the time of their establishment the colonies had enjoyed much freedom in the control of their own affairs. (See page 350.) After the British conquest of Canada in the Seven Years War, the colonists could see no need for royal troops in their cities, nor for taxes to support them. They also resented British attempts to control their trade, and they were insulted by arrogant royal officials. Riots against George's Stamp Tax in 1765 were followed by a decade of protests that culminated in an attack on British troops at Lexington, Massachusetts, in 1775. The next year, by the Declaration of Independence, the colonies announced their separation from Britain. In 1778 France came to America's aid, and Spain and the Dutch Netherlands attacked the British at Gibraltar, in the Caribbean, and at sea. Britain once again found itself in a major war.

George and his friends could not run a war. After four years of disaster, Parliament finally in 1780 declared "that the influence of the crown has increased, is increasing, and ought to be diminished." But it had acted too late to save the North American colonies. In 1781 a large British force surrendered to George Washington at Yorktown, Virginia; and the British had no choice but to recognize, in the Treaty of Paris (1783), that the thirteen American colonies had become the independent United States of America.

In London a revived Tory party under William Pitt, the Younger, came into power and set out to restore government by Parliament through the cabinet and prime minister. Further reforms of the British government were planned. But in 1789 the French Revolution broke out, and the reforms were put aside as Britain found itself being drawn into another war with France.

Even so, in 1789 Great Britain was governed by a larger portion of its population than was any other country in Europe, and it protected the rights of its people more jealously. The men who started the French Revolution would gladly have settled for such a system of government.

✤ THE OLD REGIME OF FRANCE

Louis XIV outlived both his son and his grandson and was succeeded by his five-year-old great-grandson, who for almost six decades reigned as Louis XV (king 1715-1774). Throughout his long reign, Louis XV basked in the reflected glory of the Sun King, content to continue the system of government he inherited. Louis sat at the council tables, where he "opened his mouth, said little, and thought not at all." The control of the governments passed into the hand of corrupt or ineffective advisers and pretty but light-headed mistresses. Yet in the eighteenth century France was still the most powerful and stable of the autocratic monarchies. The "Old Regime," as its government and way of life later came to be called, was admired and copied by other countries, who hoped to win for themselves some of the glory they felt was France's.

THE FRENCH PEOPLE IN THE EIGHTEENTH CENTURY

The population of France continued to be divided into the three "estates" represented in the now nearly forgotten Estates-General: the First Estate, or clergymen; the Second Estate, or nobles; and the Third Estate, or commoners. The churchmen, some 130,000 of them, were themselves divided. At the top of the hierarchy were the bishops and archbishops, often closely related to the nobility and now seldom distinguished for piety or devotion

"The Lover Crowned": a painting by Jean Honoré Fragonard (1732-1806; Chapter 32). This painting, one of a series entitled "The Progress of Love," is the kind that was fashionable at the frivolous courts of Louis XV and Louis XVI: delicate, lighthearted—and completely out of touch with real life.

to duty. The church owned approximately one fifth of all the land in France; the control of these estates provided some of the higher clergy with huge incomes. The parish clergymen, by contrast, lived among their poverty-stricken flocks practicing the Christianity they preached.

The nobility of the Second Estate owned another fifth of the country. But the land was unevenly divided among them, so that a minority of the 150,000 titled aristocrats were far richer than the rest. Those who could afford it flocked to Versailles, as they had in Louis XIV's time, to spend their lives and their fortunes twittering in that gilded cage. The rest, too poor to live with the king, either served as government, army, or church officials, or remained on their estates trying to squeeze enough money from their peasants to enable them to travel to the capital. Unlike the English gentry, the French nobles saw little advantage in making their estates their principal interest; and, cut off from the right to rule, they less and less fulfilled their functions of feudal times.

The great mass of the French population, nearly 25,000,000 persons, were members of the Third Estate, or commoners. Nine tenths of these were peasants who lived on the rural estates of the nobles, the church, or the king, cultivating the fields in much the same way as had their ancestors centuries before. Their primitive methods of farming and the heavy taxes meant that the poorer of them lived on the verge of famine in good times or starved in bad. Only rarely did the peasant farmer get a glimpse of the glory and wealth for which his country was famed.

But some 2,000,000 commoners lived in the growing cities. Paris was the largest, with nearly 600,000 people, and there were seventy-eight others with populations of 10,000 or more. The influence of the cities was on the increase. The large majority of the urban population were day laborers; but there was also a lower middle class of tradesmen and skilled workers, who were increasingly important as commerce grew. At the top of the middle class were the government officials, property owners, merchants, and professional men, who were in many ways the real leaders of France.

This "bourgeoisie" (middle class) was held in contempt by the nobles, but its members were an able and ambitious class of men who imitated the nobles' manners and dress while envying and resenting their privileges. They were eager, on the one hand, to reform the evils of the Old Regime and, on the other, to improve their status within it. They were educated and intelligent enough to see the faults in the world around them, and they were energetic and aggressive enough to try to do something about it.

THE GOVERNMENT OF THE OLD REGIME

The system of government established by Louis XIV continued without important changes during the eighteenth century. France was divided into thirty-two "intendancies," each administered by an "intendant" appointed by the king. The intendants supervised the world of local officials and reported to the capital. (See page 375.) This system would have been fairly simple, were it not that several older administrative systems continued to exist side by side with it. There were separate religious districts; separate educational districts, each with its own university; separate judicial districts, each with its own high court or *parlement;* and separate tax districts. To add to the confusion, there were no national standards for coining money nor for setting weights and measures, and taxes were levied at different rates in different parts of the country.

The finances of France were as confused as the government. Taxes were collected by "farmers-general," middle-class merchants who paid for the privilege and kept as a commission a considerable part of what they took in. There was no royal budget. The personal income of the king was never separated from the general funds of the kingdom, and royal officials could not control the king's expenses.

The Third Estate bore the burden of taxation. The clergy were exempt (although they made good-sized annual "contributions"), and the nobles were not required to pay direct taxes; the commoners had to pay for all. The peasant paid rents and a variety of special local taxes to his lord, to whom he often owed labor service as well. He paid a "tithe," which amounted to between six and eight per cent of his income, to the church. To the crown he paid a *taille,* a land tax based upon the value of his property; a poll tax; and a *gabelle,* a tax on salt that he had to buy whether he wanted it or not. By the time he had finished with these, he had few funds left with which to improve his farm.

Versailles continued to be the center of French government, the home of the king and his family, and the focus of the nobles' interests. The power of the crown was unlimited. For example, by signing a *lettre de cachet* (a "sealed letter"), the king could order anyone sent to jail without charges and without a trial. At Versailles sat his Council of State with its six ministers: the chancellor, the controller of the finances, and the secretaries of war, the navy, foreign affairs, and the royal household. The English cabinet represented Parliament and could defy the king; the Council of State was appointed by the king and could be dismissed by a wave of his hand.

THE REIGN OF LOUIS XV

While Louis was a child, the French government fell into the hands of a corrupt duke. But in 1726 he was succeeded by the king's able tutor, André Cardinal Fleury, who for seventeen years worked to maintain peace and prosperity. Fleury adopted mercantilist policies (see page 379), which more than doubled France's colonial trade. He cut spending and reduced the national debt. But he could not keep Louis from involving France in wars, first in the War of the Polish Succession in the 1730's and then in the War of the Austrian Succession in the 1740's. (Chapter 31.) Fleury died despairing, and in 1743 Louis became his own prime minister.

Louis XV tried to be a king like Louis XIV, but he was not the man for it. Proud and on occasion arrogant, he was also lazy, bored by the details of governing, unable to grasp the larger problems that he faced, and unwilling to allow others to make firm policy for him. His mistress, Jeanne de Pompadour, became one of the most influential persons in France.

Louis's first two wars ended indecisively, and the Seven Years War (1756-1763) was a disaster for his country. (Chapter 31.) The people, feeling that victories had been thrown away, came to resent governmental inefficiency and "petticoat rule." Members of the middle class attempted to restrict the rulers and make a start toward reform by using the *parlements* (courts of law) as a means of protest. Louis reacted by dismissing the *Parlement* of Paris, his principal critic; then he allowed it to return; and finally he abolished it altogether. After twenty years of struggle with the *parlements*, Louis was on the verge of victory when, in 1774, he died.

Louis XV had been called "the Well Beloved" when he was young; but in his later years he was detested, and he knew it. In one of his rare moments of wisdom, he is said to have prophesied, "After us, the deluge."

THE REIGN OF LOUIS XVI

Louis XV was succeeded by his nineteen-year-old grandson, Louis XVI (king 1774-1792). "The young king of France will need strength and genius," Frederick the Great remarked—and Louis XVI had neither. He was well-intentioned in a small way, eager to make people happy but fearful of criticism. He was dominated by his greedy relatives and was much influenced by his beautiful wife, Marie Antoinette, a daughter of Maria Theresa of Austria. Marie Antoinette had inherited none of the good sense of her mother nor the reforming instincts of her brother, Joseph II. (See page 427.) Thinking of France only as a source of wealth that was hers to enjoy, she resisted any change that might interfere with her pleasures; and she willingly served her mother's interests as a sort of highly placed Austrian spy in the court of France. The people hated her as a foreigner.

The problems that Louis inherited were great, but they were not insoluble. Although the court grew poorer year by year, the country was growing more prosperous and was capable of supporting even Versailles. Resistance to the crown increased, but in 1774 the prestige of the Bourbons was still immense, the habit of obedience to the crown still firm. But the problems of government could not be solved without reform. Louis XVI had inherited all the powers of an absolute ruler, and he could have enforced reforms if he had chosen to do so. But Louis, weakling that he was, had an unfortunate tendency to back down in the face of opposition.

Louis XVI nevertheless made a good beginning. To placate the middle classes, he restored the *Parlement* of Paris that his grandfather had abolished —and it promptly began to criticize him anew. He appointed A.R.J. Turgot, a man devoted to the principle of an enlightened monarchy, as controller general, and assigned him the task of reforming the royal finances. Turgot reduced the profits of the farmers-general and took them for the crown, but he ran into strong opposition when he proposed to revise the tax system. The nobles and clergy fought his attempt to impose even light taxes upon them. The middle classes objected when he tried to abolish the guilds. Marie Antoinette led the hue and cry against Turgot, and Louis meekly dismissed him in 1776. Turgot was succeeded by an able banker, Jacques Necker, who staved off financial disaster by floating loans. But when Necker published an accounting of government expenses to satisfy his critics and creditors, the nobles took offense because it showed the extravagance and waste at the court. So Necker was dismissed in 1781, and France's finances returned to their normal, desperate state.

When the Americans declared their independence in 1776, they sent Benjamin Franklin to Paris to win support. Louis's advisers were eager to help the Americans, partly because some of them were influenced by Franklin and the liberalism that he represented, but mostly because it seemed a chance to weaken Great Britain. In 1778 France came to America's aid, turned the tide of the war, and helped the United States to become free. The French, cautiously and wisely, refused to make the American war a general European struggle as well. But the result of their caution was that they gained little for themselves, and the costs of the war intensified the financial crisis of the French government.

In the decade of the 1780's events turned even more against the French monarchy. Crop failures brought the peasants to the edge of starvation.

An unfortunate treaty with Britain allowed English imports to compete with French products, which resulted in an economic depression. People became restless, bandits infested the highways, and mobs formed in the cities. The need for reform of the government grew ever greater. The success of the Americans in forming a constitutional government helped undermine Louis's government by demonstrating that an absolute monarchy might not be a necessity. In 1787 Louis admitted that he could not cope with France's problems by calling an assembly of notables to discuss the problems of the nation; but it could accomplish nothing.

The monarchy lacked both money and ideas to solve the greatest crisis of its history. Yet in 1787 the concept of the Old Regime still had a strong hold on the minds of the French people; most wanted reform, but few gave even a thought to revolution or violence.

❧ THE ECONOMIC REVOLUTIONS

Economic changes were to influence the future history of Europe every bit as much as political restlessness. Spurred by rapid economic growth, merchants, farmers, and manufacturers adopted new and larger forms of business organization and new method of production. Slowly at first, then increasingly rapidly, these changes revolutionized the economic life of Britain and France in the seventeenth and eighteenth centuries, and later influenced the rest of Europe as well.

THE COMMERCIAL REVOLUTION

Improvements in banking and in large-scale production during the Renaissance period (see pages 249-250) did not meet the needs of the colonial powers of western Europe in the eighteenth century. It took a huge capital investment to equip fleets sent to trade with the Americas and the Indies— far more than any individual investor could provide. Therefore groups of investors joined to finance such British and French trading monopolies as the East India companies. These "joint-stock" companies were chartered by the governments and were authorized to sell shares (or "stock") on the open market. The shareholders elected officers to administer the companies, and shared the profits according to the amount of their investment. These joint-stock companies, the ancestors of modern corporations, were far larger than any previous business enterprises had been.

An auction sale at the London headquarters of the British East India Company, held in the room also used for meetings of the company's directors and shareholders. London merchants are bidding for the goods imported by the company. The director of the sale is seated beneath the clock; at either side of him are two company officials noting the bids; and beneath them a group of clerks record the transactions and draw up contracts. Sometimes these sales became so noisy that passers-by feared that a riot had broken out.

The joint-stock companies led to the development of stock exchanges, where shares were bought and sold. The development of exchanges led in turn to speculation that created the first "booms" and "busts." In the early eighteenth century the French government gave a Scottish banker named John Law the right to set up a "Mississippi Company" to monopolize trade with Louisiana. Law predicted great profits for his company, and investors competed so fiercely for shares in it that they forced the price of its stock to forty times its original value. In 1719 the speculative "bubble" burst, a wave of selling forced the prices of stock down, and thousands of investors were ruined. A similar speculation in shares of a "South Sea Company" in England led to a stock market crash there in 1720, which ruined the reputations as well as the fortunes of many prominent persons. This "South

Sea Bubble" helped cause a crisis in the government that brought Robert Walpole to power in 1721. (Above, page 437.)

Throughout the eighteenth century, the growth of large businesses was held back by local restrictions on trade, medieval guild restrictions, and inadequate systems of currency, weights, and measures. Such obstacles were more numerous in central Europe than in western Europe. One of the reasons that commerce developed most rapidly in France and England was that in these countries the governments eliminated many of these outdated restrictions.

THE AGRICULTURAL REVOLUTION

In Britain in the eighteenth century, farming on a large scale began to replace medieval agricultural practices. As money became more important, landowners became more interested in profit than they had been before. In Elizabethan and Stuart times, many had found that they could increase their profits by ousting their tenants, "enclosing" their fields with fences and hedges, and raising sheep to provide wool for the textile industry. This movement toward enclosure gained momentum in the eighteenth century. (Above, page 433.)

In the eighteenth century a number of British country gentlemen became interested in increasing the outputs of their farms by scientific methods of agriculture. Their experiments led to improved methods of farming, which increased not only the size of crops but also the variety of crops. Jethro Tull (1674-1741) invented horse-drawn seed planters and cultivators, which enabled one man to do the work that many had done before. His contemporary, Viscount Charles "Turnip" Townshend (1674-1738) discovered that clover improved the fertility of the soil, and that turnips could be raised as winter feed for livestock. (Previously many livestock had been slaughtered in the fall because there was no way of feeding them during the winter.) Late in the century Robert Bakewell (1725-1795) learned to improve the quality of his livestock by "selective" breeding. A publicist named Arthur Young (1741-1820) spread the word of the new agricultural improvements so effectively that they soon were adopted throughout the country. Thanks to such men, England became a country of large and productive farms, efficiently operated by far fewer men than had been needed in the past. The surplus population of the countryside moved to the industrial towns and provided the needed manpower for the factories.

THE BEGINNINGS OF THE INDUSTRIAL REVOLUTION

In the nineteenth century the "Industrial Revolution" was to change European ways of life drastically. Its roots lay in the scientific and technical discoveries of the seventeenth and eighteenth centuries, when practical men learned to apply the scientific discoveries of their time (Chapter 32) to industry. In 1640 a French physicist Denis Papin (1647-1712) built the first crude steam engine. Thomas Newcomen (1663-1729), an English blacksmith, developed an improved steam engine that could be used to pump water out of mines. But the steam engine did not become really practical until the last third of the eighteenth century, when the Scottish engineer James Watt (1736-1819) built engines that could power large industrial machinery. Shortly thereafter a new era—the "Factory Age"—began.

Most large shops of Renaissance times had merely assembled large numbers of people in one place to work with old-fashioned tools. Only in the eighteenth century were genuinely new machines developed. The textile industry was revolutionized by the invention of the "flying shuttle," which doubled the amount of cloth a man could weave in a day. Other inventions quickly followed: the "spinning jenny," which could spin eight threads at a time; the "spinning mule," which increased this number several times over; and, in 1785, Edmund Cartwright's steam-powered loom. To meet the rapidly rising demand for cotton that these machines created, an American named Eli Whitney in 1792 developed the cotton "gin" to separate seeds from raw cotton.

New industries created ever greater demands for iron and coal. British output of iron increased from 10,000 tons in 1700 to 50,000 in 1770. At first British iron was smelted by charcoal; but after the forests had been cut down, a new fuel was needed. Coal was unsatisfactory because it left undesirable chemicals in the iron that made it brittle. But in mid-century a method for removing these chemicals (resulting in a product called "coke") was developed. Britain, which had large deposits of both coal and iron, was on the road to becoming the workshop of the world.

At the end of the eighteenth century the groundwork of the Industrial Revolution was well established in Britain. Belgium and France lagged about three decades behind Britain, and the rest of Europe followed more slowly. In the nineteenth century the Industrial Revolution, more than any other single force, would change the face of Europe.

& & &

On the surface the eighteenth century was a placid age in Britain and France. Both countries were stable and prosperous, the most powerful states of western Europe and the world. But they were also bitter enemies, and their rivalries played a dominant role in the commercial and dynastic struggles of the age.

People and Terms

Anne	A. R. J. Turgot	prime minister
George I	Jacques Necker	cabinet
George II	Jethro Tull	vote of confidence
Robert Walpole	Viscount	Treaty of Paris
Bonnie Prince Charlie	Townshend	First Estate
William Pitt	Arthur Young	Second Estate
George III	Robert Bakewell	Third Estate
Lord North	James Watt	bourgeoisie
John Wilkes	Edmund Cartwright	intendancies
William Pitt	Eli Whitney	*parlement*
the Younger		farmers-general
Louis XV	Act of Union	tithe
Cardinal Fleury	Union Jack	*taille*
Jeanne de	Hanoverians	*gabelle*
Pompadour	enclosure acts	*lettre de cachet*
Louis XVI	rotten borough	joint-stock company
Marie Antoinette	Whig Oligarchy	

Getting Organized

1. What did Queen Anne accomplish? Who succeeded her? Describe the English people in the eighteenth century. What was happening to the yeomen? Was this a prosperous age for Great Britain?
2. In what way was Great Britain governed by an aristocracy? Who was in Parliament? Who could vote? What was a rotten borough? Who were the Whigs and the Tories? How did they differ?
3. What was Parliament's new system for administering the government? What was the relationship of the prime minister and the cabinet to the king? Could they be removed? How and by whom? What was the place in the English government of the Common Law? The minority party? The justices of the peace?
4. Describe the reign of George II. Who was Robert Walpole and why was he forced to resign? What wars and revolts did the British have to face during the reign of George II? How was each resolved?

5. How and with what success did George III attempt to win absolute power from Parliament? What was the importance of the John Wilkes case? of Lord North's resignation? Why did the American colonies revolt? What was the political situation in Great Britain after 1783?

6. What were the three estates in France? Describe each. In the eighteenth century how were the French systems of government and finance confused? What taxes did the government levy, and on whom?

7. What kind of a king was Louis XV? Who was Cardinal Fleury and how successful was he? How successful was Louis XV in war? What groups were critical of his rule?

8. How was Louis XVI influenced by his wife? What problems did he face and how did he attempt to deal with them? Why did France aid the American colonies? Describe France in the 1780's.

9. What important changes were taking place in commerce, business, agriculture, and industry? Who were the principal figures in this economic revolution?

Understanding the Big Picture

1. Continuing the trend so apparent in the Glorious Revolution, how did Parliament in the eighteenth century further extend its authority over the king? By 1800 how much power did the king hold?

2. Compare the government of England in the eighteenth century to that of France. Which was the more efficient? Which had more popular participation? Which was more popular?

3. What effect did the economic changes of the eighteenth century have on government? On social structure?

For the Thoughtful

1. What was the role of the aristocracy in Great Britain? In France? How important was this class in each country? Explain the significance of the differences between the British and French aristocracies. What should the role of an aristocracy be?

2. Clearly the governments of Great Britain and France were quite different from each other by 1780. By comparing the histories of the two countries through the seventeenth and eighteenth centuries, explain how the differences came to be.

3. How does the history of England in the eighteenth century help explain why the Glorious Revolution was the last revolution that Britain ever had? In answering this question, compare Britain and France in the eighteenth century.

31

Commercial and Dynastic Wars

Most monarchs in the eighteenth century were practical and ambitious men who were trying to reach two goals at once. On the one hand, they sought to strengthen their countries. On the other hand, they were the heads of dynasties (ruling families) whose power and possessions they sought to increase.

To achieve these goals, the monarchs involved their countries in a series of wars. These wars sometimes were competitions for trade: the monarchs hoped to strengthen their countries by gaining new colonies, markets, and raw materials. At other times they went to war in hopes of seizing new provinces to add to their dynastic landholdings. The most important wars were fought to achieve both commercial and dynastic goals. There were five of these commercial and dynastic wars between 1688 and 1763. When they were over, Europe was a far different place from what it had been when the wars began.

THE BACKGROUND OF THE WARS

By 1688 the national monarchies of western Europe were already well developed, and the states of central and eastern Europe had begun to follow their examples. The countries along the Atlantic coast had acquired colonies in many parts of the world and were gradually gaining in wealth as they developed new commerce.

DEVELOPMENTS WITHIN THE NATIONAL MONARCHIES

Inside each of the principal national monarchies of Europe, three gradual changes were taking place: (1) the authority of the central government was increasing; (2) national loyalties were becoming stronger; and (3) trade and manufacturing were growing.

Increased Power of Central Governments. In most states the power of the central governments was steadily increased by tax reforms, which brought in more income; by mercantilistic controls over commerce and industry; by more effective governmental organization; by larger armies and navies; and by revised systems of law. At the same time, the authority of the kings over the governments was increasing, often at the expense of the nobles and clergy, continuing a trend that had begun in the Middle Ages. Great Britain was the only important exception to this rule. Most monarchs copied the model for absolute monarchs, Louis XIV of France, and worked hard to assure their dynastic succession.

Increased National Loyalties. Improved roads and better communications continued to break down local loyalties. Europeans increasingly thought of themselves as Frenchmen, Spaniards, or Russians, rather than as Parisians, Castilians, or Muscovites. At the same time, each nationality was becoming ever more aware of the language and cultural differences that set it off from other nationalities. The kings came to symbolize these growing national loyalties and won the support of the great masses of their people. Peasants were loyal for personal and emotional reasons; the middle class because it was to their economic interest; and the nobles and clergy because they had no choice. Thus each state could command the support of its people in its more and more aggressive efforts to win new markets for its merchants and lands for its king.

Changes in International Relations. After the religious enthusiasm of the Reformation had died down, monarchs paid little heed to moral considerations. The "state system" came to determine international relations. This was a cynical system based upon pure power politics, which put each country on its own to fend for itself in the scramble for wealth and domination. Smaller countries formed defensive alliances to discourage their larger neighbors from attacking them and taking them apart. These alliances shifted with bewildering speed as countries cast off one ally in favor of another more helpful.

Since the state often had reason to resort to military power, armies of professional soldiers were better organized and equipped. Fighting navies grew, and they were supplemented by armed merchant ships and by "privateers"—ships that made a private business of war and raiding. In peacetime, professional diplomats scurried from capital to capital advancing their country's interests by making new treaties and alliances. Each nation was judged by its military and economic power, and any that showed signs of weakness was in danger of attack by stronger, greedy neighbors.

Increased Commerce and Manufacturing. Commerce grew most rapidly in western Europe, but it was increasing everywhere. The result was that the middle class became increasingly influential as its size and wealth increased. Urged on by this middle class, monarchs adopted mercantilism (see page 379), which provided protective tariffs for "infant" industries, favored the acquisition of new lands in Europe or overseas, and hoped to establish a "favorable" balance of trade. Governments sometimes subsidized key industries and at other times gave commercial monopolies (as in the East India companies of England, France, and the Dutch Netherlands). The kings felt that they, too, profited from mercantilism, which assured them a loyal and prosperous middle class and a country that was rich and self-sufficient.

EUROPE IN 1688

In 1688, on the eve of the eighteenth century and of the series of dynastic and commercial wars, there were in western Europe three major countries, France, England, and Spain, and two lesser but still important states, Portugal and the Dutch Netherlands. France was the dominant land power in Europe, ruled by Louis XIV, who was just beginning his drive to include western Germany and the Low Countries within his "natural boundaries" (see page 383) and simultaneously beginning to encourage the growth of his colonies in North America, the West Indies, and India. England was on the eve of the Glorious Revolution, which placed the Dutchman William of Orange and his Stuart wife Mary on the throne as William III and Mary II. (See page 401.) England was blessed with a Parliamentary government and owned a prosperous string of colonies in North America and trading posts in India and the West Indies. Spain, still ruled by the Spanish Habsburgs, suffered from internal decay and a weak king. But it was the proud possessor of the largest colonial empire, which included colonies in South and Central America, Mexico, Florida, the West Indies, and the Philippines. Smaller, but still to be reckoned with, were Portugal, which owned Brazil and trading posts in Africa and India; and the Dutch Netherlands, with its prosperous cities, a huge merchant fleet, and colonies in the East Indies, the West Indies, and South Africa. All these states along the Atlantic coast were colonial as well as European powers.

The countries of eastern Europe were less well developed at this time, and their interests were confined to the continent. The most powerful was Habsburg Austria, a state of many nationalities whose rulers were also emperors of the Holy Roman Empire in Germany. To the southeast was the Ottoman Empire, still powerful but content to remain isolated from European affairs. To the north was little Brandenburg, just started on its way to nationhood by Frederick William, the Great Elector, and about to become the kingdom of Prussia. To the east was Russia, whose aggressive Tsar Peter the Great was about to begin his attempt to westernize his country and to win it an outlet on the Baltic. Between Austria, Prussia, and Russia lay Poland, without an effective government and dominated by unruly nobles. In the north was Sweden, whose control of the Baltic Sea would soon be challenged by Russia and Prussia.

The issues that divided these many countries were complex and led inevitably to war. (1) The great powers of western Europe all sought to increase their empires at the expense of others. For example, England and France struggled to dominate North America; England, France, the Dutch Netherlands, and Spain all had rival colonies in the Caribbean; in the Far East, France and England were rivals in India, and both competed with the Dutch in the East Indies. (2) Louis XIV dreamed of making the continent a Bourbon empire. This made him the rival of the Habsburgs in Germany and Spain; of the Dutch; and of the English, who favored a "balance of power" in Europe and were determined not to allow the Netherlands to fall into the hands of a strong enemy. (3) There were three weak areas which, since they lacked strong governments, became "power vacuums" that attracted their stronger neighbors. These were Italy, where France, Spain, and Austria all had interests; Germany, where France and Austria had influence that would soon be challenged by rising Prussia and by Britain under the Hanoverian kings; and Poland, with its three aggressive neighbors, Prussia, Austria, and Russia.

Europe needed only a spark to set off a series of struggles among the great powers. Five major wars took place in a period of only seventy-five years (1689-1763). All but one were world wars fought in the colonies as well as in Europe. Before they were finished, these wars had profoundly affected the states that participated in them and had determined much of the history that was to follow.

🌸 THE WAR OF
THE LEAGUE OF AUGSBURG

Louis XIV's persecution of Protestants and his desire to win the "natural boundaries" of France (that is, the Rhineland and the Spanish Netherlands) won him the enmity of most of his neighbors. In 1686 the kings of Sweden and Spain, the Holy Roman emperor, and a number of German princes signed a defensive alliance against France called the "League of Augsburg." In 1687 Louis invaded the Rhineland. In 1689, William III of England and the Dutch Netherlands brought his two countries into a "Grand Alliance" with the league, and the "War of the League of Augsburg" began.

The English justly feared that if Louis conquered the Netherlands and their magnificent ports, he would challenge English control of the sea. The English had already experienced Louis's meddling in their internal affairs when he supported the Stuart kings and the Catholic cause in England during the Restoration period. In the War of the League of Augsburg, they were able to defeat the French, and they put down a French-backed revolt in Ireland so mercilessly that the Irish never forgave them. In the Battle of La Hogue in 1692, English and Dutch ships all but destroyed French naval power, and English control of the seas was assured. In America, where the campaigns were called "King William's War," the French were able to damage some frontier settlements, but nothing more. On the continent Louis's superb armies found themselves outnumbered, and the war became a contest of endurance.

The Treaty of Ryswick (1697) ended the nine-year conflict. Each side surrendered its conquests, and all the fighting seemed to have been for nothing. But not quite, for Louis's drive for his natural boundaries had failed, the allies remained free, and the balance of power in Europe was unchanged. And, especially important, the English dominated the seas.

🌸 THE WAR OF
THE SPANISH SUCCESSION

Stymied in the Netherlands, Louis turned his attention to Spain, where his ambassadors convinced the weak and feeble-minded Habsburg king Charles II to make Louis's grandson, Philip of Anjou, his heir. Charles died in 1700, and the Bourbon Philip of Anjou became King Philip V of Spain. Assured of Spanish support, Louis turned again to attack in the Rhine valley and, in 1701, the "War of the Spanish Succession" began.

William III formed a new Grand Alliance of countries that supported the claims of an Austrian Habsburg to the Spanish throne. William's death in 1702 almost broke up the alliance, but two brilliant generals, the English duke of Marlborough and the Austrian Prince Eugene of Savoy, proved more than a match for the aggressive French. They drove back a French invasion of Austria at the battle of Blenheim (1704). With the support of the Portuguese, British troops invaded Spain. Louis had to sue for peace in 1709, but the terms imposed were so harsh that he rallied France and continued the war until 1713. The war was fought everywhere. There were naval battles in the West Indies and the Mediterranean, and a series of campaigns in America called "Queen Anne's War," which the British usually won. But the Allies did not remain united, and the outcome was another stalemate.

The Peace of Utrecht of 1713-1714 preserved the balance of power. The allies recognized the Bourbon Philip V as king of Spain, with the condition that Spain and France would never be united under one ruler. In return France surrendered its claims to Newfoundland, Nova Scotia, and the Hudson Bay region to the British. From Spain the British won Gibraltar, at the western entrance of the Mediterranean, and Minorca, an island

The taking of Gibraltar by English and Dutch naval forces, 1704. The huge rock, which rises more than 1,400 feet, dominates the western entrance to the Mediterranean Sea at the southern tip of Spain. Heavily fortified by Britain, it was after 1704 a key to the British navy's control of the Mediterranean. Spain has more than once tried to recover it —notably in a three-year siege during the American Revolution—but without success.

in the western Mediterranean. At the same time the "Asiento" treaty gave the British the right to sell slaves in Spanish America. The Austrians were given the former Spanish possessions in Italy (Naples, Sardinia, and Milan) and the former Spanish Netherlands, which for the rest of the century were called the Austrian Netherlands. A new kingdom, Savoy, was created in Italy. Frederick I was confirmed as king in Prussia. The Dutch Netherlands' territory remained intact, and the Dutch won trading privileges in the Austrian Netherlands.

But the terms of the peace tell only part of the story. The exhausted Dutch Netherlands fell behind its larger rivals and became a minor power. British sea power in the Atlantic and the Mediterranean was stronger than ever. Britain was the real victor, for the Netherlands remained in friendly hands and the British, less affected by the war than had been other countries, were able to recover more quickly and to enter a period of unprecedented prosperity. The attempt of France to dominate western Europe had failed again. Two major problems remained unsolved: the commercial rivalry between England and France continued; and Italy had become a bone of contention between the Austrians and the Spanish, who were not willing to surrender their Italian possessions without another fight. To add to these problems, the Hohenzollerns in Prussia were now preparing to challenge the Austrian Habsburgs for control of Germany, and rising Russia was becoming more aggressive.

⚜ THE WAR OF THE POLISH SUCCESSION

In 1733, the ambitions of rival dynasties ended two decades of peace. Louis XV tried to have his father-in-law elected king of Poland so that that country would aid France in its opposition to the Austrian Habsburgs. This scheme distressed the Russians almost as much as the Habsburgs, for neither country wanted a French ally in eastern Europe. So Russia and Austria combined to oust the French candidate and to replace him with a candidate of their own. Louis took revenge by invading the Austrian Netherlands. The Spanish Bourbons seized the opportunity to attack Austrian lands in Italy, aided by the king of Sardinia. (The kingdom of Savoy, in northern Italy, had acquired the island of Sardinia in 1720 and changed its name to "kingdom of Sardinia.") Thus the so-called "War of the Polish Succession" was fought principally in Italy and the Netherlands.

After two years of conflict (1733-1735) the contestants signed a treaty that reunited the kingdom of the Two Sicilies (the kingdoms of Naples and Sicily) under a Bourbon cousin of the king of Spain; gave Sardinia a part of the Habsburg duchy of Milan; and confirmed the Austrian candidate for the Polish crown. Another dynastic struggle between the Habsburgs and the Bourbons had ended in a virtual stalemate. But it had served to whet the appetites of several rulers for possessions of the Habsburgs, and thus paved the way for a larger war that followed almost immediately.

🐚 THE WAR OF THE AUSTRIAN SUCCESSION

Two outbreaks, one commercial and the other dynastic, merged to form the War of the Austrian Succession. When the British abused the rights they had won in the Peace of Utrecht to trade with Spanish America, the Spanish were none too careful to protect the legitimate privileges of the British. In 1739 a war broke out between Britain and Spain, called the "War of Jenkins's Ear" because earlier the Spanish had captured and cut off the ear of a British smuggler named Robert Jenkins. The following year, 1740, the death of the Habsburg monarch, Charles VI, left his daughter Maria Theresa on the Austrian throne, at almost the same moment that Frederick the Great became king of Prussia. Maria Theresa had the paper protection of the Pragmatic Sanctions (see page 428), but few of her neighbors intended to respect their promise to preserve her throne and empire.

Frederick the Great had little difficulty persuading France, Spain, and Saxony to join him in an attempt to dismember the Habsburg lands. To weaken the Habsburgs further, the allies supported the ruler of Bavaria over Maria Theresa's husband for the Holy Roman emperorship. Britain, already at war with Spain, entered the conflict as Austria's ally in order to preserve the balance of power and to protect the German lands of its Hanoverian kings. Thus, the "War of the Austrian Succession" became a struggle of Britain and Austria against France, Spain, Prussia, Bavaria, and Saxony in Europe, and of Britain against France and Spain in the colonies.

There were many lulls in the fighting, for each nation would fight only for its own interests. Frederick the Great overran Silesia. (See page 429.) The French Bourbons conquered the Austrian Netherlands, but the Spanish Bourbons suffered losses in Italy. Maria Theresa survived because Austria could fight its enemies one at a time. Finally Russia joined Austria, and Frederick decided to quit. "King George's War", as it was called in America, was not fought hard, and there were minor campaigns in India.

The fighting ended in 1745, but it was three years before the Treaty of Aix-la-Chapelle was signed in 1748. Maria Theresa had to surrender Silesia to Frederick the Great, Parma (in northern Italy) to Spain, and part of Lombardy to Sardinia. Otherwise everybody returned his conquests, and on the map it seemed that almost everything was as before. But the war had made significant changes. Frederick the Great had challenged Austrian domination of Germany, and the Holy Roman Empire had become more meaningless than ever. Austria, rebuffed in Germany, became more eastern in its interests. France had again failed to dominate the continent. The British were more determined than ever to defend and expand their colonies. The important rivalry between Britain and France remained unresolved.

🕮 THE SEVEN YEARS WAR, 1756-1763

The struggle of Britain and France for control of North America, and the maneuvers of the Austrians seeking new alliances, led to the most important and most destructive of the commercial and dynastic wars.

THE BACKGROUND OF THE WAR

In the eight years of uneasy peace that followed the Treaty of Aix-la-Chapelle, the rivalries of the great powers continued in the colonies. In Europe, diplomats continued the struggle that the generals had not been able to resolve.

The Struggle for the Ohio Valley. The Seven Years War began in North America, where it was called the "French and Indian War." The British had colonies along the coast, while the French were expanding into the interior. (See pages 346-350.) Most British colonists lived close to the Atlantic, where they were content to fish and to farm. The French had colonies that controlled the mouths of the St. Lawrence and Mississippi Rivers. The French also had fur-trading posts along the banks of these rivers and in the Great Lakes region, which impeded British advance across the Appalachian Mountains into the interior. By 1754 the French were moving into the Ohio River valley, where they built Fort Duquesne at the site of modern Pittsburgh.

At the same time, enterprising British colonists were becoming interested in the fertile Ohio valley. Some of them obtained from the British government a grant of 500,000 acres of land in the area of modern Cincinnati, down the river from Fort Duquesne and in territory claimed by the French. But the French fort on the upper river made this grant worthless. Therefore, in 1754, young Colonel George Washington made an unsuccessful attempt to take Fort Duquesne. In the following year a more ambitious expedition led by the British General Edward Braddock was ambushed and all but destroyed by the French as it marched against the fort. It was clear that Britain and France were beginning another colonial war.

The Diplomatic Revolution. Meanwhile the Austrian foreign minister, Count Wenzel von Kaunitz, set out to offset the growing power of Frederick the Great by forming an alliance against him. Kaunitz's goal was to bring about a "diplomatic revolution" by making an alliance with France, which had been Austria's enemy for centuries. The French were at first reluctant to enter into such an alliance. But in 1756 Great Britain, France's enemy, signed a treaty with Prussia, Austria's enemy, agreeing to defend each other's possessions in Germany. Now that Britain and Prussia were allies, the French had no one to turn to but Austria, and Louis XV agreed to Kaunitz's proposed alliance.

This completed the "diplomatic revolution." After centuries of enmity, Habsburg Austria and Bourbon France were allies for the first time. Russia, also an enemy of Frederick the Great, joined the alliance, which set about preparing to attack Prussia. Great Britain and Prussia, enemies in the War of the Austrian Succession, were now partners. The line-up for the greatest of the commercial and dynastic wars was complete.

THE COURSE OF THE WAR

At the beginning of the war, Frederick the Great led his well-trained armies to a series of victories. In 1756 he invaded Saxony; the following year he routed first the Austrians, then the French, and then the Austrians again. But his victories were costly: they reduced his armies, which he had to fill up with raw recruits. At first the British failed to give him their promised support; but in 1759 the great wartime leader William Pitt persuaded Parliament to send an army to Germany and to subsidize Frederick, in the hope that this would divert the French from the wars in the colonies. With British aid, Frederick was just able to hold his own against great odds.

The British, as Pitt had promised, won startling successes in the colonies. In 1759 James Wolfe led a successful British attack on Quebec, the capital of New France. The following year the last of the French armies in North America surrendered, leaving the British in sole possession of all of North America east of the Mississippi. The British were equally successful in India, where Robert Clive combined diplomacy and generalship to win native allies and defeat French troops. By 1761 the French had been ousted from all of their Indian possessions except a few trading posts.

British victories in North America and India almost cost Frederick the Great the war. George III came to power in 1760 (see page 437), and the following year Pitt fell from office. George had little interest in aiding Frederick now that Britain's goals had been achieved. The British subsidies to Frederick ceased. Prussia's enemies pressed their attacks. But fortune smiled on Frederick. In 1762 Peter III became tsar of Russia. (See page 412.) Peter, an admirer of Frederick, called back his armies and returned his conquests. Without Russian aid the Austrians were not strong enough to continue the war.

Thus, early in 1763 the Seven Years War came to an end. By the Treaty of Paris, France surrendered to Britain all Canada (except two tiny islands

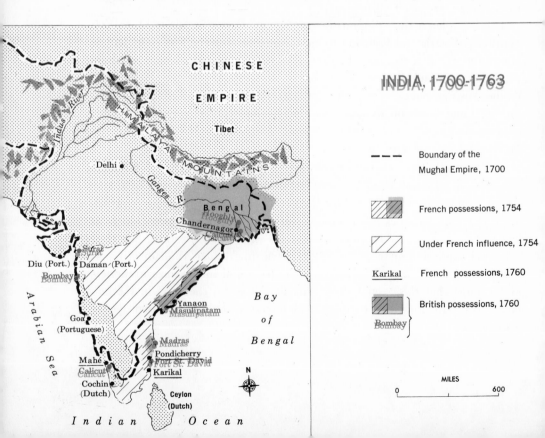

INDIA, 1700-1763

- - - Boundary of the Mughal Empire, 1700

French possessions, 1754

Under French influence, 1754

Karikal   French possessions, 1760

British possessions, 1760

MILES
0   600

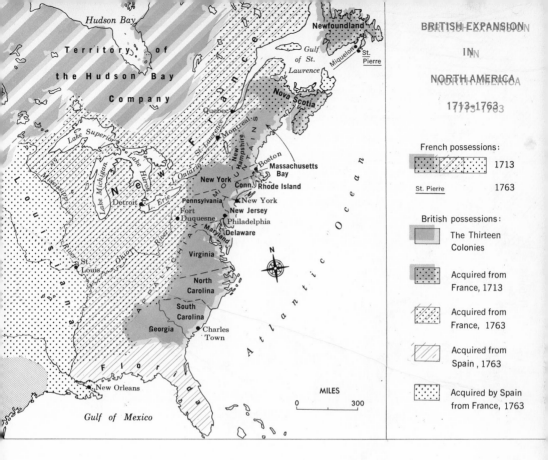

French possessions:

| | | | 1713 |

St. Pierre | 1763

British possessions:

The Thirteen Colonies

Acquired from France, 1713

Acquired from France, 1763

Acquired from Spain, 1763

Acquired by Spain from France, 1763

off the coast of Newfoundland), her claims to North America east of the Mississippi, an island in the West Indies, and some African outposts. France kept a few towns in India, but her prestige there was shattered, and the British won the lion's share of the lucrative Indian trade. Spain surrendered Florida to Great Britain and as compensation received French claims to Louisiana, west of the Mississippi. By the Treaty of Hubertusburg, Maria Theresa ceded Silesia once and for all to Frederick the Great, who promised in return to support the future Joseph II, Maria Theresa's son, as Holy Roman emperor. In Europe the map remained unchanged: "a million men had perished, and yet not a hamlet had changed its ruler."

THE EUROPEAN POWERS IN 1763

The Seven Years War was the last great commercial and dynastic war. They had been limited wars, fought for limited goals, and so were far less devastating than modern total wars in which the combatants try to erase their enemies from the face of the earth. But they nonetheless had far-

EUROPE
1763

ATLANTIC

OCEAN

North
Sea

Scotland

GREAT
BRITAIN
England
Wales

Ireland

London

DUTCH
NETHERLANDS

Paris

Versailles

F R A N C E

Avignon
(to Papal
States)

Marseilles

SPAIN

Madrid

PORTUGAL

Lisbon

Gibraltar (British)

Norway
(to Denmark)

D E N M A R K

SWEDEN

Stockholm

Finland
(to Sweden)

St. Petersburg

Baltic Sea

P R U S S I A

P O L A N D

Brandenburg

Berlin

Silesia

Saxony

Bohemia

Bavaria

Hanover

Rhine

Austrian
Netherlands

Switzerland

Savoy

Milan

Venice

KINGDOM OF SARDINIA

Sardinia

A U S T R I A

Vienna

Hungary

Adriatic Sea

PAPAL STATES

Rome

NAPLES

KINGDOM
OF THE
TWO SICILIES

SICILY

Mediterranean Sea

R U S S I A

Moscow

Danube River

Black Sea

Bosporus

O T T O M A N   E M P I R E

Constantinople

Dardanelles

Athens

Lands of major
European dynasties:

Habsburg

Bourbon (French)

Bourbon (Spanish)

Romanov

Hanover

Hohenzollern

Holy
Roman
Empire

The battle of Quebec, September 13, 1759: an English print of the time. The daring plan of the British General James Wolfe was to steal at night up the steep, heavily wooded —and poorly guarded—cliff, which is actually much higher than it appears here. The plan succeeded: by dawn a large British force was gathered on the Plains of Abraham (left) above Quebec, the only point from which the well-fortified city could be attacked. In the ensuing battle the French were defeated, and the British takeover of New France was assured.

reaching results, many of which had not been expected. Wars rarely have the results that those who fight them expect them to have.

Europe in 1763 was a far different place from what it had been when the War of the League of Augsburg broke out in 1689. There were now only two major powers in western Europe, Great Britain and France; for the wars had proved the basic weakness of Spain. France had not come to dominate the continent, as Louis XIV had hoped it would; it had lost most of its colonies; and in 1763 its government was bankrupt. But it had prosperous industries and a growing population. It also was infected with the liberalism of "enlightened" philosophers and with a restlessness arising from heavy taxation. Great Britain was the real victor of the commercial wars. Under the arrogant George III it was still to undergo one last attempt to impose royal absolutism, which would cost it thirteen of its American colonies. Yet even after this setback it remained the strongest nation in Europe, unchallenged on the seas, possessing Canada, and dominating the trade with India. The smaller countries, Portugal and the Dutch Netherlands, had become less influential than ever in European affairs.

The most startling changes were in eastern Europe. Habsburg Austria was now increasingly interested in eastern affairs after it had lost influence in Germany. Little Brandenburg had become the kingdom of Prussia and emerged as dynastic victor of the struggles; and Frederick the Great was about to start his program of economic reform to make Prussia as strong as it was influential. Russia had emerged from the background to take part in the last three of the wars. Under Catherine the Great, it would soon assume its place among the great powers of Europe.

🜲 🜲 🜲

Three more decades of comparative peace followed the treaties of Hubertusburg and Paris, during which the scientific, political, and cultural ideas of the "Enlightenment" and demands for political reform affected Europeans as much as the wars and diplomacy of their rulers.

Peoples, Places, and Terms

Duke of
  Marlborough
Eugene of Savoy
George Washington
Edward Braddock
Wenzel von Kaunitz
James Wolfe
Robert Clive

Savoy
Sardinia
Bavaria
Silesia
Parma

Ohio River
Fort Duquesne
Quebec

power vacuum
War of the League
  of Augsburg
Treaty of Ryswick
War of the Spanish
  Succession
Peace of Utrecht
Asiento Treaty
War of the Polish
  Succession

War of Jenkins's Ear
War of the Austrian
  Succession
Treaty of
  Aix-la-Chapelle
diplomatic revolution
natural
  boundaries
French and
  Indian War
Treaty of Paris
Treaty of
  Hubertusburg

Getting Organized

1. In the eighteenth century, how was the power of the central governments being increased? How were the kings controlling these central governments? How did increased national loyalties aid this trend?

2. Why was national loyalty increasing? What effects did this increase have? What motivated nations to act as they did? What were the results of increased commerce and manufacturing?

3. Describe the European balance of power in 1688. Which were the strongest nations and which were the weakest? Where were the areas. of greatest tension?

4. What were the causes of the War of the League of Augsburg? Who were the major participants in this war? What were the results of the Treaty of Ryswick?

5. What were the causes of the War of the Spanish Succession? Who were the major participants? What were the results of the Treaty of Utrecht? What great problems remained?
6. What were the causes of the War of the Polish Succession? Who were the major participants in this war? What were the results of the war?
7. What were the causes of the War of Jenkins's Ear and of the War of the Austrian Succession? Who were the major participants in these two wars? What were the results of the Treaty of Aix-la-Chapelle? What changes had taken place during the war? What problems remained?
8. What were the causes of the renewed Anglo-Franco conflict in North America? What was the "diplomatic revolution" and what brought it about? What were the results of the wars and of the two treaties, Paris and Hubertusburg?
9. How different was the Europe of 1763 from the Europe of 1688? Which powers had gained? Which had declined? Which were now the strongest?

Understanding the Big Picture

1. Trace the workings of the balance of power from 1688 until 1763. Did this principle work well during this period?
2. What were the major goals of the foreign policies of each of the European combatants in the wars of the eighteenth century?
3. In terms of military and naval power, why had France declined while Great Britain gained?

Mastering the Map

Study carefully the map of Europe in 1763 (page 462) and compare it with the map on page 320. What areas had changed hands? With what effect on the balance of power?

For the Thoughtful

1. How would you predict the course of European diplomatic relations after 1763? Where would be the biggest trouble spots? Which would be the strongest nations? Give reasons for your answers.
2. What were the goals of wars in the eighteenth century? Compare the causes of these wars to those of both the sixteenth and seventeenth centuries and to those of the twentieth century.
3. What should be the guiding principles of a nation's foreign policy? Explain your answer by using examples from the eighteenth and twentieth centuries.

Scientific thought and the Age of Enlightenment

32

In the fifteenth and sixteenth centuries, a few men had begun to question the concepts of their classical and medieval forebears, preferring to draw conclusions by observing themselves and the world around them. In the seventeenth and eighteenth centuries, this scientific attitude came to dominate the thinking of educated men, who laid the foundations of modern science. The scientific approach in turn led to new and revolutionary philosophies of government, which insisted that men could rule themselves.

REACTION AGAINST THE AGE OF REFORMATION

In 1648 the Thirty Years War ended (see page 318); twelve years later the Puritans lost control of the British government. (See page 399.) By the end of these conflicts, most Europeans had had their fill of religious controversies. Many tended to moderate their faiths or to turn to secular activities, and the influence of the churches declined.

Many Christians became "pietists," who believed that it was more important to lead a simple, Christlike life than to insist on any specific dogma. Among them were George Fox and his followers, the "Society of Friends" or "Quakers," who taught that Christianity is a matter of personal experience, plain living, and high thinking, and that it has nothing to do with government, clergy, or ceremony. In the eighteenth century, John Wesley (1703-1791) founded a reform movement within the Church of England whose members later broke away to form their own church, the "Methodist." An important Catholic pietist group, the "Jansenists," was declared heretical; but some of its members persisted in France and the Netherlands.

Meanwhile others subjected Christianity to the same careful observation that scientists were then applying to nature. They insisted that such traditional beliefs as the virgin birth, Christ's divinity, and the divine origin of the Bible were "unreasonable"; but they did continue to believe in God, and so are called "Deists" (from the Latin *Deus*, God). To the Deists, God was a "God of Nature" who had created the universe and set it to running according to an unchanging set of "natural laws," which man could discover for himself by using his powers of observation and reason. The most famous Deist was the French author Voltaire. Other Deists were leaders of an organization called the "Freemasons," which included George Washington and Benjamin Franklin among its members.

Because both pietists and Deists insisted that religion was a personal affair, both favored religious toleration. Other Christians also became more tolerant. In 1773 the pope suppressed the Jesuit order, which had been organized to fight aggressively for Catholicism. Governments also tended to adopt more tolerant policies than had previously been the rule.

Jews and Christians also became more tolerant of each other than they had been. For centuries, Jews had been forced to move from one part of Europe to another, to live in restricted areas called "ghettos," and to wear clothing that set them off from Christians. But the Deists and others introduced a new spirit of toleration among Christians; and many Jews, influenced by the liberal leader Moses Mendelssohn (1729-1786), made efforts to know and better understand the Christians among whom they lived.

🐌 THE BEGINNINGS OF MODERN SCIENCE

In the seventeenth century, men came increasingly to rely on conclusions drawn from direct observation of nature, rather than on conclusions drawn from the teachings of the classical writers. By so doing, they created a "new science," which is the basis of modern scientific thought.

Classical teachings were challenged first by Copernicus (see page 288), who insisted that the sun, not the earth, was the center of the universe.

Few believed him, however, until Johannes Kepler (1571-1630) supported his concept by telescopic observations and mathematical proof. But when Galileo Galilei (1564-1642) wrote a book supporting the Copernican theory, he was forced to retire into obscurity because he seemingly was challenging the teachings of the Catholic Church. The limits of scientific knowledge were also extended by the Englishmen William Gilbert (1544-1603), who showed that the earth is a huge magnet, and William Harvey (1578-1657), who discovered that blood circulates through the body.

At the same time three men made significant contributions to the developments of the philosophy of science. Francis Bacon (1561-1626) distinguished between the "deductive" ways of thinking of the Middle Ages and the "inductive" method of science. Whereas the deductive method tried to fit observed facts into an already accepted pattern, the inductive method accumulated the facts first and then attempted to draw conclusions from them, forming new patterns if necessary. The true "scientific method," Bacon insisted, was inductive. René Descartes (1596-1650), the inventor of analytic geometry, which combines algebra and geometry, said there are two "worlds," the world of mind and the world of physical being. He said that religious truths are the truths of the world of mind, and that scientific truths are the truths of the world of physical being. He thus was able to remain a devout Roman Catholic and at the same time to accept Bacon's insistence on using the inductive method to determine scientific truth. Blaise Pascal (1623-1662) was a practical man who experimented with barometers and built a calculating machine. But he was also a religious man who could not accept Descartes's separation of religious truth from the physical world. Science could not give him the faith he needed. In a remarkable book called the *Pensées* ("Thoughts"), Pascal concluded that there probably is a God, and therefore one must "wager" that He exists and act accordingly. Pascal contended that the entire universe is infused with meaning—and most modern scientists agree.

All scientists found that mathematics was one of their essential tools. The introduction of Arabic numerals and algebra to Europe in the Middle Ages led to a flood of later discoveries. In 1585 a Dutch engineer, Simon Stevin, explained how to use the decimal system. In 1614 a Scotsman, John Napier, published his *Marvelous Rule of Logarithms*, which simplified many mathematical calculations and made the slide rule possible. Descartes introduced analytical geometry, and Pascal worked on the law of probabilities. And then came Newton.

Sir Isaac Newton: an engraving based on a portrait by Sir Godfrey Kneller. Although many of Newton's theories have been disproved in the twentieth century by Albert Einstein and other scientists, his work remains as probably the greatest single contribution in the history of science. To Newton, in the words of Einstein, "nature was an open book whose letters he could read without effort. . . . He stands before us, strong, certain, and alone."

SIR ISAAC NEWTON

Sir Isaac Newton (1642-1727) had the genius and insight to combine the ideas of earlier scientists with mathematical discoveries of his own to create an entirely new concept of the universe. When he was twenty-four, tradition has it, he was inspired by the sight of an apple dropping from a tree to think about gravity. He decided that gravity might apply to the moon and planets as well as the earth and thus explain Kepler's concept of the movement of the solar system. Newton concluded, for example, that the reason that the moon does not fly off into space is that the pull of the earth's gravity constantly pulls it back and keeps it in its orbit. In 1687 he published his theory under the title *Mathematical Principles of Natural Philosophy* (usually called the *Principia*). With mathematical evidence, Newton explained the "law of gravitation"—that every particle of matter in the universe attracts every other particle. He had explained the workings of the heavens in terms of the same laws that govern earthly objects.

Newton taught at Cambridge, became a member of Parliament, and ended his career as master of the mint, but he continued his scientific investigations. He explained why planets travel in ellipses rather than in circles, discovered that white light is really made up of all the colors of the spectrum, and learned how to make the first reflecting telescope. He also investigated the motion of waves; made up tables showing the future position of the stars, which made more accurate navigation possible; and took a guess on the nature of light that has proved to be remarkably accurate.

Great as Newton's scientific discoveries were, his greatest impact on the world was to stimulate the development of a scientific state of mind. With magnificent simplicity, the law of gravity explained why the apple dropped from the tree and why the moon and the planets revolve in their orbits. It showed a universe that operated according to unchanging laws, and it encouraged men to seek new knowledge and other laws that would extend their understanding of their world. Science for the scientists became a religion in itself, and the world became a source of infinite interest.

OTHER SCIENTIFIC DISCOVERIES

Following Newton's discoveries, later astronomers charted the skies. William Herschel (1738-1822) improved the telescope; charted sunspots, the mountains on the moon, and polar snow on Mars; and discovered the planet Uranus in 1781. Robert Boyle (1627-1691), a contemporary of Newton, discovered "Boyle's Law" that the volume of gases varies inversely with the pressure. In the eighteenth century other Englishmen discovered carbon dioxide, hydrogen, and oxygen. The Frenchman Antoine Lavoisier (1743-1794) systematized these discoveries and founded modern chemistry by proving that although matter may alter its state through chemical changes, its quantity remains the same.

Geology owes much to an Englishman, James Hutton, who in 1785 explained that the surface of the earth assumed its present form over a long period of time. Biology benefited from the Dutch lens grinder Anton von Leeuwenhoek (1632-1723), whose improved microscopes enabled him to discover protozoa and microscopic bacteria. Medical men began experimenting with animals, proving Harvey's theory that blood circulates and developing pathology (the branch of medicine that deals with the nature of disease). Robert Hooke (1635-1703) discovered the plant cell and gave it its name. The Anglican clergyman John Ray (1627-1705) classified and compared different plants and animals. The Swedish botanist Carl von Linné (or Linnaeus; 1707-1778) improved Ray's methods, developing the system of naming plants that is still in use. The French Count Georges de Buffon (1707-1788) classified (in forty-four volumes) all animals then known.

These men were for the most part descriptive scientists, studying and classifying the world around them. They developed and used new tools, such as the telescope, the microscope, mathematical analysis, and scientific detachment. Their findings were revolutionary, challenging some of the most deeply held teachings of church and schoolroom. No wonder that at the same time other men began to subject society and government to the same rigorous observation—and to draw new revolutionary conclusions about the nature of man and the way he should be governed.

⚜ SCIENCE AND THE ENLIGHTENMENT

Newton's *Principia* was one of those rare books that few people can read or understand, but that many discuss and interpret in ways far different from what the author had intended. Newton himself had little expectation that revolutionary ideas would be based on his discoveries. Certain that God had created the universe, Newton wrote that He "endures forever and is everywhere present." But at the same time, he was certain that he could trust his own powers of reason. The Deists, who based their ideas (above, page 467) on Newton, pointed out that if Newton's assumption that the heavens are governed by one set of laws was correct, then many traditional Christian beliefs were mistaken. And the concept of medieval Catholics and of Protestant reformers that man is basically evil ran counter to Newton's trust in human reason.

Newton's *Principia* inspired a whole new way of looking at the world. He and the scientists who followed him insisted that ideas meet the tests of reason and of observation. Other men soon began applying these same yardsticks to other aspects of the world—to government, literature, art, and music, for example. The result was an intellectual movement called the "Enlightenment," which gave the eighteenth century the name "Age of Reason." The movement centered in France, where the writers who expounded the enlightened ideas came to be called *philosophes*.

The Enlightenment was based upon the Newtonian ideas (1) that man has the power of reason and (2) that the universe is governed by certain universal "natural laws." The men of the Enlightenment were sure that they could discover the laws of nature by observing the world. They further believed that they could assure the progress of mankind by applying these laws of nature to government and society.

🏛 POLITICAL PHILOSOPHY
OF THE ENLIGHTENMENT

In the eighteenth century, political philosophers expressed the ideals of the Enlightenment in their purest form. In so doing, many came to advocate new and revolutionary theories of government.

VOLTAIRE AND ENLIGHTENED DESPOTISM

There were some seventeenth and eighteenth century thinkers who defended the absolute monarchy, the form of government most common at the time. An Englishman, Thomas Hobbes (1588-1679), defended monarchy on the ground that people are utterly selfish and short-sighted and if left to themselves will only create anarchy. In his *Leviathan*, Hobbes maintained that the only solution was for the people to surrender voluntarily all authority to an all-powerful state. This state—Hobbes's "Leviathan"—would be governed by a monarch who would have to maintain order to protect his own safety. The blessing of order, Hobbes said, would justify any tyranny that might result.

In the eighteenth century, Voltaire (François Marie Arouet, 1694-1778), the most famous spokesman of the Enlightenment, wrote in favor of monarchy. Voltaire was in most ways the leading liberal of Europe; he argued in all his writings for freedom of thought and particularly for

Voltaire, the leading poet, historian, playwright, and pamphleteer of the Enlightenment: from an eighteenth-century engraving. The talented and immensely clever son of a wealthy middleclass family, Voltaire early in life came to resent the haughty arrogance toward him of the French aristocrats. He therefore devoted his life to protesting the injustices in the government and society of his day. The biting wit of his writing won him a large audience, with the result that his ideas had a lasting effect.

tolerance in matters of religion. But he believed that for their own good the people must be governed by an "enlightened despot." It was the enlightened despot's duty to govern in a liberal and enlightened way, if necessary *forcing* enlightened policies on his people. Voltaire's idea had some influence: we have seen that Catherine the Great (page 414), Frederick the Great (page 422), and Joseph II (page 427) considered themselves to be enlightened despots, with varying results.

JOHN LOCKE AND THE NATURAL RIGHTS OF MAN

The first theory that the powers of government lay in the hands of the people originated in England, where Parliament had existed for hundreds of years and twice in the seventeenth century had driven kings from their thrones. (See pages 395, 401.) Believers in divine-right monarchy maintained that the Englishmen who supported the Glorious Revolution were rebels against God, and Hobbes said revolution could only lead to anarchy. John Locke (1632-1704) insisted the rebels were only exercising their "natural right" to overthrow tyranny.

Locke, a contemporary of Newton, was a physician who was as much interested in his patients' minds as he was in their bodies. He studied people in much the same way as Newton studied the planets and stars. His *Essay Concerning Human Understanding*, which maintains that all men know is derived from their experience, is a landmark in the history of psychology.

In two *Treatises on Government*, published in 1689 (just after the Glorious Revolution), Locke applied similar methods to the study of the origin of political power. He assumed that all men are born with "natural rights" to life, liberty, and such property as they can accumulate by their own efforts. He also assumed that they have the power of reason, which enables them to use their natural rights to their own good advantage. To protect their natural rights, he continued, they had joined together in a "social compact," or contract with their rulers. Like any other contract, each party has an obligation to the other: the people agree to obey their rulers, and the rulers agree to protect the natural rights of their people. If either party breaks the compact, he is no longer protected by it. Thus an individual who breaks the law may have his natural rights to his liberty, his property, or even his life taken away. But on the other hand, if a ruler breaks the compact by failing to protect the rights of the people, he, too, may be punished—by having his right to rule taken away. This idea of the "right of revolution" made Locke's theory revolutionary indeed.

Locke's natural rights theories were far different from the prevailing ideas of the seventeenth century. (1) He emphasized that *all* the people, not just a few, had natural rights. (2) He emphasized that since *all* the people have the power of reason, they must be allowed to think for themselves. If they are to do so, freedom of speech, of the press, and of religion are necessary. (3) He maintained that political power originated from the people, not from God. And (4) he emphasized that the government is the servant of the people, not their master.

In the seventeenth century Locke used this theory to justify the Glorious Revolution. In the eighteenth century others would use it to justify the American Revolution and the French Revolution which, in the last decade of the century, was to overthrow the Old Regime. One of Locke's most ardent admirers was Thomas Jefferson, who summarized the natural-rights philosophy magnificently in the United States Declaration of Independence.

MONTESQUIEU AND "THE SPIRIT OF THE LAWS"

In the eighteenth century the British government actually protected most of the natural rights that John Locke had claimed for the people. By contrast, the French monarchy in the eighteenth century failed to give liberty to its people, to win its wars, to dominate the continent, to collect its taxes fairly, or to make any serious effort to reform. As a result, it was subjected to a barrage of criticism by liberal writers, who proposed one system of reform after another.

One of the most prominent reformers was the Baron Charles de Montesquieu (1689-1755). Montesquieu was much impressed by the British government and by Locke's philosophy. After spending two years in London, he published *The Spirit of the Laws,* in which he attempted to explain how the British kept their freedoms.

Montesquieu completely misunderstood the British government. In the eighteenth century, Parliament was supreme. (See page 435.) It made the laws, chose one of its own members as prime minister, and was the highest court of appeal. Montesquieu thought—wrongly—that in England there was a "separation of powers" in the government. He thought that there was a legislative branch, which passed the laws; an executive branch, which enforced them; and a judicial branch, which interpreted them. He assumed that since these branches were jealous of each other, none of them would agree to allow another to become supreme. By a system of "checks and balances," they would restrain one another, thus preventing tyranny and assuring the liberty of the people.

The British were pleased that Montesquieu admired their government, but they never adopted his ideas. Parliament remained supreme in Great Britain. But the authors of the United States Constitution took his ideas to heart. Thanks to Montesquieu, the United States government has three separate branches—the executive, the legislative, and the judicial—and is limited by a "separation of powers" and a system of checks and balances.

JEAN JACQUES ROUSSEAU AND THE SOCIAL CONTRACT

Montesquieu indirectly attacked the French monarchy by proposing a different system. Another Frenchman, Jean Jacques Rousseau (1712-1778) not only assailed the French monarchy but also attacked the very foundations of French society. Rousseau, a warped and twisted man but a brilliant writer, could criticize French society from the point of view of an underdog because he was one. He spent most of his life wandering unhappily from place to place, preferring to beg rather than to work. But Rousseau was undoubtedly talented, and he was taken up by Paris intellectuals.

In 1749, thirty-seven years old and a failure, he dashed off an essay called *A Discourse on the Moral Effects of the Arts and Sciences,* which made him a famous and influential man. In this and other essays he attacked the roots of the society in which he could not succeed, and he even attacked civilization itself. Reports from the colonies led him to believe that "noble savages" lived in the wilderness in a "state of nature," where they were all free and equal, noble, brave, and virtuous. This was the way man should live, Rousseau insisted. But instead man had been corrupted by civilization.

Jean Jacques Rousseau, the most radical writer of the Enlightenment: an eighteenth-century engraving. The underlying idea of all Rousseau's writing is that man is basically good; evil comes only as a result of the unnatural ways of civilization. He proposed drastic changes in many areas of life, so that all men would be free to develop the natural goodness that they are born with.

The civilized man was filled with jealousy, suspicion, and hatred of others. Worse, there was no longer equality among men. Rousseau admitted that there were natural inequalities in such personal characteristics as intelligence. But he believed that civilization fostered unnatural inequalities based upon social, political, and economic privileges. This led the privileged classes to support war and tyranny, and the underprivileged to resort to thievery, vice, and rioting. To Rousseau, government was an organized effort by the rich and strong to impose unnatural inequality on the poor and weak. Civilization leads only to problems it cannot solve; disorder leads to despotism. Back to nature!

Rousseau proposed an alternative in an essay entitled *The Social Contract*, in which he wrote:

> Man is born free; and everywhere he is in chains. One thinks himself the master of others; and still remains a greater slave than they. How did this change come about? I do not know. What can make it legitimate? That question I think I can answer.

Rousseau's answer was vague and somewhat contradictory, for he was dealing with the question of how man can be ruled and still be free. He agreed with Locke that men made a social compact to form a government that would protect their natural rights. But Locke thought the only function of a government was to protect the rights of its people. Rousseau went further: once formed, he insisted, the community had interests of its own, which were decided by the citizens meeting democratically to determine the "general will." Once a man joined a community, he surrendered himself, "together with all his rights, to the whole community." Rousseau was certain that the will of the community, if determined democratically, was far more important that the will of any individual, and far more likely to be right. True freedom to Rousseau lay in serving the best interests of the community. And if an individual did not want to do this, the community had the right to *force* him to be free.

Rousseau's ideas were printed and discussed everywhere. He inspired a back-to-nature movement: Queen Marie Antoinette of France, for example, built herself a country cottage in the "wilds" of Versailles, where she pretended she was a simple milkmaid. When Benjamin Franklin went to Paris as the representative of the rebelling American colonies, aristocrats took him up as a sort of living example of a noble savage—and Franklin played the role to the hilt. Rousseau's political ideas were equally popular: he was the first to propose a reform that would assure that government would be *good* as well as limited. His trust in the people's ability to make their own decisions, and in the willingness of the individual to make the interests of the community his own interests, offered a hope for a better government than monarchy could ever provide.

🐚 THE LIBERAL REFORMERS

Men who believed in reason and in natural law came also to believe that no one should be prevented from speaking or acting according to his reason. Thinking men, they said, should be liberated from such restrictions. They therefore evolved a program of "liberal" reform that proposed major changes in eighteenth century education, law, and economic policy.

The liberals were appalled by the laws of the European monarchies that enabled rulers to put men like Voltaire in prison or to punish minor crimes with the death penalty. In 1764 the Italian Marquis di Beccaria, in *An Essay on Crimes and Punishments*, recommended a system of law that applied equally to all classes, and proposed far milder punishments than were then customary. Beccaria insisted that the strict enforcement of reasonable laws would prevent crime far more effectively than would severe laws that could not easily be enforced.

The liberals were almost equally appalled by the traditional system of education, which emphasized the classics, theology, and rote learning, and which favored rigid discipline of students. Reformers believed that the schools should emphasize practical subjects, such as history, modern languages, and science, which would help students to understand the world around them. They also believed that discipline should be relaxed so that the student would be encouraged to use his own good sense and reason. The most famous of the liberal educational treatises was Rousseau's novel *Émile*, in which he described the ideal education. The pupil was exposed to practical situations and allowed to discover his own solutions. Much modern education is based upon Rousseau's educational philosophy.

A school of "liberal" economists attacked the premises of mercantilism (see page 379) and proposed a radically different way of increasing the world's wealth. A group of economists called "physiocrats" maintained that land, not gold and silver, was the source of real wealth. The physiocrats insisted that the best way to increase the output of land was to allow each individual to produce as much as he could and to trade without government interference. François Quesnay (1694-1774), a spokesman for the physiocrats, argued that if each individual were to put his mind to bettering his production, the total output of a country would increase far faster than it would under any system of state control.

In 1776 a Scotsman, Adam Smith (1723-1790) published his *Inquiry into the Nature and Causes of the Wealth of Nations*. Smith's book was both a further attack on mercantilism and a classic statement of the beliefs of the "liberal" school of economics. Smith believed that labor, not land, is the source of wealth. He argued that the best way to improve output is to let each person and each region produce those things that they can produce most efficiently. It follows, therefore, that mercantilistic control of international trade is wrong, because it interferes with efficient production; and, according to Smith, government controls on the economy within a country are equally bad. Smith argued that the only duties of government were to maintain order, to administer justice, and to undertake public projects that would benefit the country as a whole rather than any specific individual. *Laissez faire, laissez passer*—let each individual do what he does best, and, by natural development, progress will be sure to come.

None of these practical reforms was adopted by any major eighteenth century power in Europe, for they were too far in advance of the accepted customs of the day. But in the nineteenth century they were to become widely accepted, and many are still in effect today.

❧ THE FINE ARTS

The fine arts of the seventeenth and eighteenth centuries were less affected than science and political thought by the emphasis on reason and natural law. Most artists, architects, and musicians were employed by aristocrats or churchmen who were disinterested in or rejected the teachings of the *philosophes*. And because the fine arts are more personal and emotional than science and philosophy, the artists themselves were more concerned with expressing their own ideas and feelings than in following any set system of ideas. Yet during this period there were many outstanding artistic achievements that testified to the *philosophes'* faith in the power of the individual.

ARCHITECTURE: BAROQUE AND ROCOCO

Most major buildings in the seventeenth and eighteenth century were designed in the "baroque" style, which originated in Italy in the sixteenth

The chapel of the Benedictine monastery at Melk, Austria, on the Danube River near Vienna. Completed in 1736, the monastery is considered the finest example of the light, graceful, highly decorated baroque style of Austria and southern Germany.

century. The style is based on Renaissance classicism, but it hides the outlines of buildings behind masses of elaborate ornamentation that give a feeling of rich, emotional splendor.

The first major baroque architect was Giovanni Bernini (1598-1680), an Italian whose masterpiece is the huge colonnade and square in front of St. Peter's Basilica in Rome. The baroque style was made popular by the Jesuits, who believed that it demonstrated the revived enthusiasm and piety of the Catholic Reformation. Soon it spread to most parts of western Europe, where many cities are still filled with monumental baroque buildings. Louis XIV, who in his day dominated the artistic life of France as well as its government, ordered his palace at Versailles built in a somewhat simplified baroque style. Peter the Great, Frederick the Great, and Catherine the Great filled their capitals with baroque structures.

Eighteenth-century French architects modified the baroque into a lighter, more graceful style called "rococo," which emphasized gentle, graceful curves. Artists decorated the palaces of Louis XV with rococo designs and puffing fat little angels, and filled them with furniture with curved legs in what is now called the "Louis XV" style. In the 1760's there was a reaction against both baroque and rococo, and in the reign of Louis XVI there was a return to the classical style of the Renaissance. Most other countries copied these same changing French styles, so that there are eighteenth-century rococo and classical structures all over Europe.

Baroque and rococo were less popular in Protestant England, where a simpler classicism dominated architecture. After a great fire destroyed most of the center of London in 1666, Sir Christopher Wren (1632-1723) designed fifty-two new churches, the magnificent St. Paul's Cathedral, and a number of other buildings. Wren's style used much wood and brick and emphasized simple, elegant lines. He put a gracefully pointed spire on top of the square belfry of one of his churches, with such success that the style was copied in hundreds of churches throughout England and New England. Wren's influence dominated English architecture throughout the eighteenth century, and in America was adapted in what is now called the "colonial" style.

PAINTING IN THE SEVENTEENTH AND EIGHTEENTH CENTURIES

In the seventeenth and eighteenth centuries, most painting followed baroque, rococo, or classical styles. In addition, a unique style of *genre* art —warm, accurate depictions of everyday scenes—developed in the Dutch Netherlands.

The Seventeenth Century. The seventeenth century was the great age of Dutch painting. A Protestant country, it was less influenced by Italian baroque art than were the Catholic countries. Its artists instead developed a realistic style, in accord with the tastes of the country's prosperous merchants. The greatest of the *genre* painters was Jan Vermeer (1632-1675), who is known for his quiet, pleasant, sun-filled everyday scenes. Frans Hals (1580-1666) painted portraits and landscapes with quick brush strokes and rare technical perfection. Other *genre* painters—Pieter de Hooch (1629-1677), Jan Steen (1626-1679), and Jacob van Ruisdael (1628-1680)— were almost equally good. But one Dutch painter stands out above all others. Rembrandt van Rijn (1606-1669) painted the life around him, but he was also a deeply religious man and painted many Biblical subjects. Rembrandt probed deeply into the characters of his subjects, using deep shadows and golden light to illuminate the sorrow and the faith of his people. His brooding and melancholy pictures did not appeal to the prosperous Dutch burghers, however, and he went bankrupt. Only later did people recognize that he was one of the great painters of all time.

Rembrandt van Rijn: a self-portrait. More than any other artist of his time, Rembrandt thought of painting as a way of expressing his own moods and thoughts. In this connection, he did a large number of self-portraits (of which this is one of the later ones) that show an unusual degree of observation and analysis of himself. Rembrandt is famous for his subtle yet dramatic use of light and shadow, characteristic of all his paintings.

In the seventeenth century most French artists, supported by Louis XIV, devoted themselves to glorifying Louis and his courtiers. But there were two notable artists with the courage to go their own ways: Nicolas Poussin (1594-1665), "the father of French classicism," noted for his powerful landscapes and mythological scenes; and Claude Lorraine (1600-1682), whose country scenes glowed with warm colors.

The greatest of the baroque painters, the Flemish artist Peter Paul Rubens (1577-1640), painted fleshy nudes, portraits, and religious scenes with all the vitality and extravagance of the finest baroque buildings. He was so much in demand that he set up what might be called a "painting factory," in which students filled in backgrounds and mixed paints while Rubens himself concentrated on the main features of his works. Rubens had many imitators but no equals; probably the best was the celebrated Anthony Van Dyck (1599-1641), court painter to England's Charles I.

The seventeenth century was also the age of the great Diego Velázquez in Spain. (See page 367.)

The Eighteenth Century. Artistic life in the eighteenth century centered in France and Britain and reflected the differences between these two countries. French painters tossed off polished but trivial rococo paintings that mirrored the elegance and satisfied the pride of the courtiers who bought them. Jean Antoine Watteau (1684-1721) set the style with paintings in idealized surroundings. Later François Boucher (1703-1770) and Jean Honoré Fragonard (1732-1806) followed along with paintings of plump nudes and effeminate shepherds and gentlemen set against backgrounds of feathery trees and dramatic clouds. The paintings often had classical titles, but the subjects were French courtiers, no matter what they were called. The only first-class painter outside the rococo school was Jean Baptiste Chardin (1699-1779), who did *genre* paintings of the tradesmen and simple people among whom he lived.

The eighteenth century was the great age of English painting. English painting, like English attitudes toward life, was more realistic than the French. The great Joshua Reynolds (1723-1792) portrayed the gentry in the classical style, while Thomas Gainsborough (1727-1788) pictured them in somewhat more romantic settings. William Hogarth (1697-1764) stimulated English reformers by publishing several series of vigorous satirical etchings with such titles as *Marriage à la Mode* and *The Rake's Progress*.

NATIONAL LITERATURES

National literatures continued to develop during the seventeenth and eighteenth centuries. Most of the major countries of western Europe supported a number of major authors, who contributed to their growing literary traditions. In France the *philosophes*—the writers of the Enlightenment—wrote graceful and polished prose, and in both England and France there were playwrights, novelists, and poets of the first rank.

France. Seventeenth-century French literature matched the glory of Louis XIV. The French language was the most widely used in Europe and was an effective tool for some of the greatest prose writers of all time. Blaise Pascal (above, page 468) was as good a writer as he was a philosopher and mathematician. His *Provincial Letters*, an attack on the Jesuits, were as effective for their style as for their content. This was also the time of the three great masters of the French drama. Pierre Corneille (1606-1684) and Jean Racine (1639-1699) wrote lofty poetic tragedies, while Molière (Jean Baptiste Poquelin, 1622-1673) wrote satirical comedies that are both psychologically sound and screamingly funny.

The *philosophes* of the eighteenth century developed a clear style of their own, which they used in hundreds of essays, articles, and treatises. Jean Jacques Rousseau (above, page 475) wrote one of the first important French novels, *La Nouvelle Heloise*, a highly emotional work that influenced the "romantic" literature of the nineteenth century.

England. The last phase of the English Renaissance (see page 286) ended with the Puritan Revolution. The Puritans distrusted literature written solely to entertain, but they produced in John Milton (1608-1674) one of the giants of English literature. Milton, who had been an important official in Cromwell's government, expressed his deep religious feeling in such poems as *Paradise Lost*. His poems are hard to read today because of their many classical references and their involved style. John Dryden (1631-1700), the best poet and playwright of the Restoration period, wrote in a simpler and more direct style. Influenced by the French, he was brief, polished, and to the point. Other important English writers of the time were John Bunyan (1628-1688), author of *A Pilgrim's Progress*, and Daniel Defoe (1659-1731), whose novel *Robinson Crusoe*, about the triumph of civilized man over untamed nature, has become a children's classic.

Eighteenth-century novelists wrote to please the large and growing English middle-class audience. Samuel Richardson (1689-1761) wrote *Clarissa Harlowe* and *Pamela: or Virtue Rewarded*, long, sentimental novels about the trials of young heroines. Henry Fielding (1707-1754) wrote more robust books, such as *Joseph Andrews* and *Tom Jones*, which satirized the country gentry, London low life, and Samuel Richardson. In this Age of Reason other writers developed a spare and disciplined style that displayed their love of logic. Samuel Johnson (1709-1784) wrote a dictionary which he hoped would set a standard for English usage. James Boswell immortalized Dr. Johnson in his classic biography, *The Life of Samuel Johnson*. Edward Gibbon (1737-1794) wrote a brilliant, multi-volume history, *The Decline and Fall of the Roman Empire*, in which he tried to prove that Christianity had been the cause of Rome's collapse. In this reasonable age there were few good poets. One of the few, the Deist Alexander Pope (1688-1744), summed up the attitude of the age:

> Know then thyself, presume not God to scan;
> The proper study of mankind is man.

The Beginnings of Romanticism. Most eighteenth-century French and English writers were classical realists. But there were a few "romantics," who ignored classical traditions and turned for inspiration to nature, to primitive life, or to their own emotions. Among them were the Englishmen Thomas Gray (1716-1771) and William Blake (1757-1827) and the Scotsman Robert Burns (1759-1796). Such poets forshadowed the "Romantic Movement," which was to dominate literature and the arts in the nineteenth century. The Romantic Movement also began to develop in Germany, where Johann Gottfried Herder (1744-1803), an admirer of Rousseau, collected folklore and customs of an earlier and presumably happier and simpler day. He in turn influenced two younger men, Johann Wolfgang von Goethe (1749-1832) and Friedrich Schiller (1759-1805), whose romantic plays and poems set the tone of German literature in the next century.

BAROQUE AND CLASSICAL MUSIC

Baroque music, like baroque architecture, originated in Italy, where seventeenth-century composers developed musical forms that were as elaborate as the churches and theaters in which they were played. The most important of the early baroque composers was Claudio Monteverdi (1567-1643). Monteverdi raised a newly invented art form called "opera," a combination of music and drama, to its first peak of greatness. Other Italian composers developed another musical-dramatic form called "oratorio," which, unlike opera, was presented without stage action, costumes, or scenery. Still others developed new forms of instrumental music.

The vogue of the baroque spread rapidly. Louis XIV employed Jean-Baptiste Lully (1632-1687) to write pieces to be played at Versailles, and Marc-Antoine Charpentier (1634-1704) to write music for his private chapel. Henry Purcell (1659-1695), an Englishman whom many consider the greatest composer his country ever produced, wrote music for Charles II and James II and founded an opera house in London.

Germany produced Europe's finest musicians in the eighteenth century. In the first half of the century George Frederick Handel (1685-1759), a German who spent most of his life in England, wrote more than forty operas, numerous oratorios, and many pieces in such new musical forms as the sonata and the concerto. Handel's oratorio *Messiah* is to this day the most popular choral work in the English-speaking countries. Handel's contemporary Johann Sebastian Bach (1685-1750), possibly the greatest composer of all time, wrote largely for the Lutheran church services in Leipzig. Bach perfected the fugue, a composition in which the theme is repeated and elaborately developed in different ways. His *Brandenburg Concertos* for small orchestra, written for the margrave of Brandenburg, are technical

The orchestra and organist of a cantata performance in Leipzig, Germany, in 1732. The cantata—a sung composition in several parts, usually about a half hour long—was a popular form of music in the baroque period. The first cantatas, written in Italy, were for a solo singer with one accompanying instrument. Later more elaborate cantatas, employing several solo singers, a chorus, a small orchestra, and an organ, were written in Germany for use in Lutheran church services. Many of these feature the brilliant trumpet parts that are one of the most appealing characteristics of baroque music. The outstanding composer of cantatas was Johann Sebastian Bach, who wrote more than 300.

masterpieces. And in his major church works, such as the *Mass in B Minor* and *The Passion According to St. Matthew*, Bach achieved an intensity of religious feeling that has never been equaled.

Later in the century Joseph Haydn (1732-1809) and Wolfgang Amadeus Mozart (1756-1791) continued to develop orchestral music with a lighter touch than their predecessors. The style that they developed is now called "classical." Haydn standardized the four-movement string quartet and the four-movement symphony. Mozart wrote majestic Masses, operas, symphonies, concertos—everything—and had completed more than 600 works before he died at the age of thirty-five. Mozart's compositions, which combine technical perfection and lightness of touch with deep emotion and penetrating insight, were perfect expressions of the spirit of his age.

⚜ ⚜ ⚜

The distinguishing characteristics of the Age of Reason were rationalism and empiricism. By asking two questions—Is it reasonable? Does it fit the observable facts?—scientists made important new discoveries about man, nature, and the universe. The same tests applied to governments led to devastating criticism of the absolute monarchies and then to proposals for reform of government, law, education, and the economic system. The enlightened philosophy of the *philosophes* of the Age of Reason had won thousands of followers by the middle of the eighteenth century. It was not surprising that it would lead eventually to a political Age of Revolution and to the downfall of old regimes in many parts of Europe.

People and Terms

George Fox
John Wesley
Moses Mendelssohn
Johann Kepler
Galileo Galilei
William Gilbert
William Harvey
Francis Bacon
René Descartes
Blaise Pascal
Isaac Newton
Robert Boyle
Antoine Lavoisier
Anton Leeuwenhoek
Robert Hooke
Linnaeus
Georges de Buffon
Voltaire
John Locke
Charles de
   Montesquieu
Jean Jacques
   Rousseau
Adam Smith
Giovanni Bernini
Christopher Wren
Jan Vermeer
Frans Hals
Rembrandt van Rijn
Peter Paul Rubens
Anthony Van Dyck

Jean Honoré
   Fragonard
Jean Baptiste Chardin
Joshua Reynolds
Thomas
   Gainsborough
William Hogarth
Pierre Corneille
Jean Racine
Molière
John Milton
John Dryden
John Bunyan
Daniel Defoe
Samuel Richardson
Henry Fielding
Samuel Johnson
James Boswell
Edward Gibbon
Alexander Pope
Thomas Gray
William Blake
Robert Burns
Johann Wolfgang
   von Goethe
Friedrich Schiller
Claudio Monteverdi
Jean-Baptiste Lully
Marc-Antoine
   Charpentier
Henry Purcell

George Frederick
   Handel
Johann Sebastian
   Bach
Joseph Haydn
Wolfgang Amadeus
   Mozart

pietists
Quakers
Methodists
Jansenists
Deists
Principia
Leviathan
*Treatises on
   Government*
natural rights
*The Spirit of the
   Laws*
separation of powers
checks and balances
Social Contract
physiocrats
Wealth of Nations
laissez faire
baroque
rococo
genre art
opera
oratorio

Getting Organized

1. Why did Europeans generally moderate their views in the eighteenth century? Who were the pietists and what did they believe? Who were the Quietists and what did they believe? Who were the Deists and what did they believe? What factors encouraged religious toleration.
2. Describe the scientific method. Who were the most important of the scientists in the seventeenth and eighteenth centuries? What did each discover?
3. What was the importance of Newton's laws? How did his *Principia* inspire a whole new way of looking at the world? What were the most important conclusions based on Newton?
4. What men defended the institution of monarchy? How did John Locke apply Newton's principles to society? What conclusions did he reach? What was the main idea of Montesqueu's writing? Of Rousseau's writing?
5. Who were the liberal reformers and what was the basis of their thinking? With what subjects did they deal? Who were the most important of these reformers, and what did each recommend?
6. Why did the fine arts not change as rapidly as other areas of thought and expression? Describe baroque. Describe rococo.
7. Who were the most important architects of the period? Who were the most important painters? Who were the major writers? Who were the major composers? What were the most important accomplishments of each?

Understanding the Big Picture

1. Why did religion become less a matter of controversy than it had been in the sixteenth and early seventeenth centuries?
2. What was the overall contribution of the various scientific discoveries to man's thought? How were scientific principles applied to other fields of inquiry?
3. How revolutionary were the thoughts of the political philosophers during this period? How did their writings help prepare for a revolutionary period at the end of the eighteenth century?
4. How did baroque art differ from what had gone before? What is classical art? What is rococo art? Give examples of each of these styles.

For the Thoughtful

1. Can social, political, and religious questions be answered by approaching them scientifically? Explain the reason behind your opinion.
2. What does the constitutional and political structure of the United States owe to the *philosophes* of the Enlightenment?

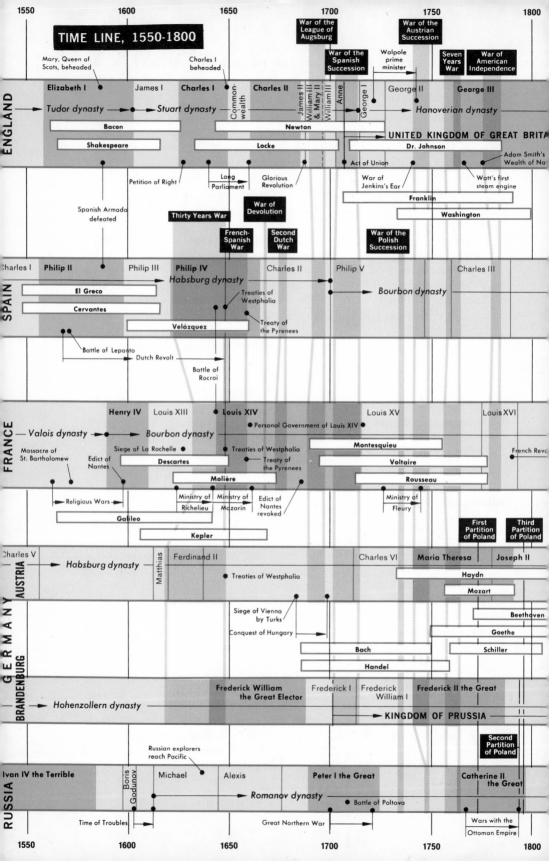

TIME LINE, 1550-1800

Summing up the Age of Absolutism

The absolute monarchs of the seventeenth and eighteenth centuries were the most powerful rulers in European history up to that time. Many of them were power-hungry men who paid more attention to their dynastic interests than they did to the welfare of their subjects. As a result, they involved Europe—and the world—in a century of major wars.

At the same time they presided over an era of rapid change and growing prosperity. They continued the centuries-old trend of increasing the strength of national governments at the expense of local ones. In their efforts to strengthen themselves, they adopted the mercantile system, which stimulated economic growth and encouraged the growth of overseas colonies. Some of them made genuine efforts to improve social and economic conditions in their countries.

The age of the absolute monarchs was also the age of the Enlightenment, when scientists, writers, and philosophers greatly increased not only man's knowledge of the world but also his faith in his ability to think logically and to govern himself. The men who wrote the American Declaration of Independence and the Constitution put many of the ideas of the Enlightenment into practice.

The ideas of the Enlightenment proved to be contagious. They led Europeans to call for reform. When the absolute monarchs refused to reform, the same ideas led to revolutions that established republican governments to rule in place of the monarchs.

But that is part of later history, beyond the province of this book. It is important to remember, however, that almost all of the highest ideals and greatest achievements of our own time—and most of our greatest problems, too—are rooted deep in the history of the past. Without the heritage of the past, we cannot fully understand the present.

🐝 🐝 🐝

Some Questions to Answer

1. Why did absolute monarchies flourish in the seventeenth and eighteenth centuries? Explain how their rise affected or was affected by the nobles, the middle class, the peasantry, and the church.

2. How did England's development differ from that of other European nations? What explains its difference?

3. What were the basic foreign policies of each major European country in the seventeenth and eighteenth centuries? Discuss the importance in each country's policies of each of the following influences: balance of power, *raison d'état*, desire for glory, dynastic interests, religion, and economic matters. Which country had the most successful foreign policy in this period?

4. What were the basic economic policies of the major countries? In each country, how did these policies affect the power of the monarchy? The lives of the ordinary people of the country? The prosperity and power of the country? The prosperity and power of other countries?

5. Summarize the progress during this period in science, in agriculture, and in manufacturing. How did this progress affect European life?

6. What was the influence of the political philosophers of the Enlightenment? In particular, how did they affect the enlightened despots? The attitude of the middle class toward the monarchies?

7. What were the most important developments during this period in architecture? In painting? In literature? In music? In what ways did these developments reflect the religious, scientific, economic, and political trends of the time?

Further Reading for Part Four

GENERAL ACCOUNTS

CLARK, GEORGE N. *The Seventeenth Century*. 2d Ed. New York: Oxford University Press, 1947 (paper). An excellent analysis, with emphasis on cultural developments.

OGG, DAVID. *Europe in the Seventeenth Century*. 8th Ed. New York: Macmillan, 1960; New York: Collier (paper). A fine survey of the century's politics.

LANGER, WILLIAM L., Ed. *The Rise of Modern Europe*. New York: Harper (hard covers and paper). A well-written and most useful series, of which the following apply to this period:

    FRIEDRICH, CARL J. *The Age of the Baroque: 1610-1660*. 1952.

    NUSSBAUM, F. L. *The Triumph of Science and Reason: 1660-1685*. 1953.

    WOLF, JOHN B. *The Emergence of the Great Powers: 1685-1715*. 1951.

    ROBERTS, PENFIELD. *The Quest for Security: 1715-1740*. 1947.

    DORN, WALTER L. *Competition for Empire: 1740-1763*. 1940.

    GERSHOY, LEO. *From Despotism to Revolution: 1763-1789*. 1944.

BOOKS ON SPECIFIC SUBJECTS

ASHLEY, MAURICE. *England in the Seventeenth Century*. Baltimore: Penguin (paper). A fine introduction to the era of the Stuarts and Cromwell.

ASHLEY, MAURICE. *Louis XIV and the Greatness of France*. New York: Macmillan, 1948; New York: Collier (paper). A good biography.

BECKER, CARL. *The Heavenly City of the Eigheenth Century Philosophers*. New Haven: Yale University Press, 1932; 1959 (paper). A delightful and very readable essay by a great historian.

BINDOFF, S. T. *Tudor England*. Baltimore: Penguin, 1950 (paper). A useful handbook of the Tudor period.

BRINTON, CRANE. *The Shaping of Modern Thought*. Englewood Cliffs, N.J.: Prentice-Hall (paper). A fine survey of intellectual history from the Renaissance to modern times. Hard going at times, but worth the effort.

BUTTERFIELD, HERBERT. *The Origins of Modern Science, 1300-1800*. Rev. ed. New York: Macmillan, 1957; 1963 (paper). A readable introduction to this tremendously important aspect of the modern period.

COBBAN, ALFRED. *A History of Modern France*. Vol. 1: *1715-1799*. Rev. ed. Baltimore: Penguin, 1961. A survey of France's critical century.

DAVIES, R. TREVOR. *The Golden Century of Spain, 1501-1621*. Rev. ed. New York: St. Martin's, 1954. A survey of Spain's great era.

MATTINGLY, GARRETT. *The Armada*. Boston: Houghton Mifflin, 1959; 1962 (paper). A fascinating, exciting account, superbly written.

NEALE, JOHN E. *Queen Elizabeth I*. New York: St. Martin's, 1959; New York: Doubleday, 1957 (paper). Probably the best biography of the great English queen.

PLUMB, J. H. *England in the Eighteenth Century*. Baltimore: Penguin, 1950. A good survey of the period.

THOMSON, GLADYS S. *Catherine the Great and the Expansion of Russia*. New York: Macmillan, 1947 (hard covers and paper). A thorough introduction.

WEDGWOOD, C. V. *Richelieu and the French Monarchy*. New York: Macmillan, 1950; New York: Collier (paper). A short, useful introduction.

WILLEY, BASIL. *The Seventeenth Century Background*. New York: Columbia University Press, 1942; New York: Doubleday, 1953 (paper). Excellent essays on several of the leading figures of the time.

SOURCE MATERIALS

BRINTON, CRANE, Ed. *The Portable Age of Reason Reader*. New York: Viking, 1956 (hard covers or paper). A good collection of representative writings of the Enlightenment.

LOCKE, JOHN. *Locke on Politics, Religion, and Education*. New York: Collier, 1965 (paper). A good introduction to the writings of a man who influenced many later thinkers.

PEPYS, SAMUEL. *Diary*. Ed. by J. P. KENYON. New York: Macmillan, 1963 (hard covers and paper). Fascinating gossip of Restoration London.

ROUSSEAU, JEAN JACQUES. *The Social Contract*. Ed. by CHARLES FRANKEL. New York: Hafner, 1954 (paper). Interesting and readable.

Glossary

ABBOT, the head of a monastery.

ARISTOCRACY, aristocrats (noblemen) taken as a group.

AUTOCRACY, government by a ruler, usually a hereditary monarch, who has absolute power, not limited by any other person or group of persons.

BALANCE OF POWER, distribution of power among nations in a way that prevents any one nation from becoming too strong or dangerous to the others.

BARBARIAN, having to do with a nation or tribe regarded by others as being uncivilized or backward.

BARON, a high-ranking nobleman of the Middle Ages.

BARTER, the direct exchange of goods, without the use of money.

BASILICA, (1) in architecture, a rectangular church or other building with a broad nave flanked by columns and aisles and ending in an apse; (2) a Catholic church or cathedral with certain special privileges.

BOURGEOISIE, town dwellers; the middle class.

BOYAR, in pre-eighteenth-century Russia, a high-ranking nobleman.

BUREAUCRACY, the body of appointed officials who carry out the instructions of an autocrat or of an elected government.

BURGHER, a medieval town dweller.

CANON LAW, the body of laws governing the Catholic Church.

CAPITALISM, an economic system based on privately owned property, the desire for profits, hired labor, and consumer demand.

CHIVALRY, an elaborate code of behavior for medieval knights.

CHRISTENDOM, (1) all Christians, taken as a group; (2) the parts of the world where the majority of the people are Christians.

CLERGY, those who have been ordained for religious services (priests, ministers, etc.), taken as a group.

CLERICAL, having to do with the clergy.

COMMON LAW, the system of law developed in England, based on custom and the decisions of law courts rather than on statutes.

CONCORDAT, an agreement on church matters between a government and the pope.

DESPOTISM, autocracy; absolute monarchy.

DIOCESE, the district under the jurisdiction of a bishop.

DIVINE RIGHT, the supposedly God-given right of kings to rule.

DYNASTY, a series of rulers from the same family.

ECONOMY, the total of all activities by which people earn their livings.

ENLIGHTENED DESPOT, an eighteenth-century absolute monarch who attempted to govern according to the more advanced ideas of the time.

ESTATES, the social classes represented in medieval parliaments, usually including the clergy (first estate), the noblemen (second estate), and well-to-do commoners (third estate).

EXCOMMUNICATE, to cut off from communion with the church.

FACTORY, from the fifteenth to the nineteenth century, a trading center maintained by the agents of a merchant or of a trading company.

FEALTY, the loyalty and duty owed by a vassal to his feudal lord.

FEUDALISM, government and economic life based on personal loyalties and the holding of land.

FIEF, in feudalism, land held from a lord in return for service.

GENTRY, a class of landholders just below the status of noblemen.

GUILD, a union of merchants from the same town (*guild merchant*) or of persons in the same craft or trade (*craft guild*) to uphold standards, provide protection, and promote other common interests of the members.

HERESY, a religious belief opposed to official church doctrines.

HERETIC, a person who professes a heresy.

HIERARCHY, a system of government by graded ranks of officials.

HOMAGE, in feudalism, a vassal's formal acknowledgment that he was his lord's faithful follower.

HUMANISM, (1) any set of beliefs or attitudes that emphasizes the interests and ideals of people, rather than the natural world or religion; (2) in the Renaissance, an intellectual and cultural movement of this kind that placed great emphasis on the study of ancient Greek and Latin writers.

INFIDEL, a term of contempt applied to a person who does not accept some particular religion.

INVESTITURE, the formal installing of a person in office or the granting to him of certain power or authority.

KNIGHT, in the Middle Ages, (1) a nobleman who possessed armor and had been trained in its use; (2) the lowest rank of those who held land from a feudal overlord in return for military service.

LORD, in feudalism, a king or any nobleman to whom other noblemen owed homage as vassals.

MANOR, an estate over which a feudal lord held authority.

MARCH, a region on the border of a country, especially one disputed between countries or that needs to be strongly defended.

MERCANTILISM, an economic theory which held that a nation should achieve self-sufficiency—provide as many as possible of its needs itself, and acquire others from colonies—by strict government regulation of commerce.

MERCENARY, a soldier serving in a foreign army for pay.

MIDDLE CLASS, a social class of town dwellers, with a status between that of the aristocracy and the peasantry.

MONARCHY, a state or government headed by a king or emperor (or, sometimes, by a queen or empress). In an *absolute* monarchy the ruler's power is not limited by any other person or group of persons; in a *constitutional* monarchy, the ruler shares his power with others.

MONASTERY, a place where monks live under the rule of a religious order.

MONK, a man who takes vows of poverty, chastity, and obedience and lives away from the world under the rule of a religious order.

MYSTICISM, the doctrine that each person is capable of having a direct and personal relationship with God.

NATIONALISM, an intense pride in and loyalty to one's own country, coupled with jealousy and distrust of other countries.

NOBLEMAN, in medieval Europe and later, a member—usually by hereditary right—of the ruling class.

PARLIAMENT, a lawmaking body, usually elected; a legislature.

PEASANT, in Europe, an agricultural worker.

POLITICAL, having to do with government.

PRELATE, a high church official, as a bishop or an abbot.

PRIME MINISTER, the highest appointed official of a government.

PRIMOGENITURE, the right of the eldest son to inherit all his father's estate.

REPUBLIC, a government without a hereditary monarch, usually headed instead by elected officials.

REVOLUTION, (1) any thorough change, especially (2) the overthrow of an established government.

SACRAMENT, in Christianity, a ceremonial observance or procedure believed to have been ordained by Jesus. The Catholic and Orthodox churches recognize seven sacraments; most Protestant churches, only two.

SECULAR, (1) of or belonging to the world, as opposed to church and religious matters; (2) having to do with clergy living in the outside world, as opposed to *regular* clergy (monks and others bound by monastic vows or rules).

SERF, in feudalism, a peasant bound to a manor, transferred with the manor to a new landholder.

STATUTE, a law established by a monarch or a legislature (as opposed to *common law*).

TEMPORAL, (1) temporary, not lasting; (2) of this world, as distinguished from *spiritual*.

TITHE, a tax, frequently one tenth of a person's income or of the produce of his land, paid to support the church or the clergy.

VASSAL, a noble holding a fief from another noble of a higher rank.

VERNACULAR, the everyday language of the ordinary people.

VILLAGE, in the Middle Ages, a group of houses where peasants lived, from which they walked out to their fields; different from a town in that townsmen made their living by handicrafts to be sold for money, which they exchanged for food that they did not themselves raise.

Index

Figures in *italics* are references to maps or pictures.

Key to Pronunciation (based on pronunciation key in *Webster's New World Dictionary of the American Language, College Edition,* © 1959 by The World Publishing Company): a = fat; ā = ape; â = bare; ä = car; e = ten; ē = even; ê = here; ē = over; i = is; ī = bite; o = lot; ō = go; ô = horn; o͞o = tool; oo = look; oi = oil; ou = out; u = up; ū = use; û = fur; g = get; j = joy; y = yet; ch = chin; sh = she; th = thin; th = then; zh = leisure; ŋ = ring; ə = ago, comply; ' = able (ā'b'l); à = French bal (intermediate between [a] and [ä]); ë = French coeur (round the lips for [ô] and say [e]); ö = French feu, German König (round the lips for [ō] and say [ā]); n = French mon (vowel just before is pronounced through the nose); ỗ = French coq, German doch (between [ō] and [ô]); ü = French duc, German grün (round the lips for [o͞o] and say [ē]); kh = German doch, Scottish loch (a guttural sound produced by arranging the speech organs as for [k] and allowing the breath to escape in a continuous stream, as in [h]); н = German ich (intermediate between [kh] and English [h]).

Abelard (ab'ə-lärd'), Peter, 135-138
Abbasid caliphate (ə-bas'id), 62-63, 197, *198*, 405
Acadia, 346, *347*
Adrianople, battle of, 9
Africa, 325, *334*, 335
Agincourt (aj'in-kôrt'), battle of, 218, *219*
Aix-la-Chapelle (āks'lä-sha-pel'), 72, *72*, 76, *77*; Treaty of, 458
Akbar (Mughal Empire), 327
Alamanni (al'ə-man'ī), 8, 20
Alba, duke of, 315
Albertus Magnus, 136
Albigensian Crusade, 123-124, 163, 192
Alcuin of York (al'kwin), 75
Aldine Press (ôl'dīn), 278
Alexander III (pope), 153
Alexander VI (pope), 240, 271
Alexis (Russia), 408, 409
Alexius I (Byzantine Empire), 184, 186
Alfred the Great, 21-24, *21*, 79, 171
Alhambra, 65, *65*
Al-Khwarizmi, 64
Al-Kindi, 64
Al-Masudi, 63
Alsace (al-sās'), 319, *382*, *429*
American Revolution, 415, 438, 443, 474
Ambrose, 34, 35, 38, 118
Anabaptists, *300*, 304, 320
Angles, 20, 21, *21*; *see also* Anglo-Saxons
Anglicanism, *see* England, Church of
Anglo-Saxons, 14, 21-23, 37, 79
Anglo-Saxon Chronicle, 23
Anjou (an'jo͞o), *152*, 162, 172
Anne (Great Britain), 433
Antioch, Principality of, 186, *187*
Apprenticeship system, 112-113
Aquinas (ə-kwī'nas), Thomas, 136-138, *137*, 139

Aquitaine, *72*, *77*, *152*, 159, 162, 172, *219*
Arabs, 47, 58; *see also* Islam
Aragon, *152*, 235, 236, 359, 362; *see also* Spain
Architecture, baroque and rococo, 478-480; early Christian, 39-41; Gothic, 132, 139-142, *141*, 159, 179; Renaissance, 262; Romanesque, 132, 138-139
Arian heresy, 11, 13, 14
Aristotle (ar'is-tot''l), 268
Armada, Spanish, 315, 363, 391
Arras (ar'əs), 105, 109, *246*, 248, 251
Artevelde (är'tə-vel'də), Jacob van, 217
Arthur, 99, 100
Asiento treaty, 456
Asser, 23
Attila (at''l-ə), 9, 197
Augsburg Confession, 298
Augsburg, League of, 383, 384, 454
Augsburg, Peace of, 298, 316
Augustine (ô'gəs-tēn), 35-36, 38, 121
Augustinian order, 35, 121
Aurangzeb (ôr'əŋ-zeb'), (Mughal Empire), 327
Austria, and Charles V, 237, 241, *242*; in eighteenth-century wars, 368, 407, 429-430, 453, 455-461, *462*; under Maria Theresa, *413*, 424-430, *429*, *462*; in Middle Ages, *152*, 154; Partitions of Poland, *414-415*, 415; Reformation Era, *300*, 312, *320*; *see also* Germany, Habsburg dynasty, Holy Roman Empire
Austrian Succession, War of the, 429, 437, 442, 457-458
Avars, 46, 71, *72*
Avignon papacy (à-vē-nyôn'), 130, 166, 211-213, *219*, 271
Aviz dynasty (a'vēsh), (Portugal), 234
Aztecs, 341
Baber (bä'bēr), (Mughal Empire), 327
Babylonian Captivity, *see* Avignon papacy

Bach (bäkh), Johann Sebastian, 484-485
Bacon, Francis, 468
Bacon, Roger, 287
Bagdad, *62*, 63, 64, 66, *198*, *405*
Bakewell, Robert, 446
Balance of power, 254
Balboa (bal-bō'ə), Vasco Nuñez de, 340
Baldwin of Lorraine, 186
Banking, development of, 249-250
Baptists, 304
Barbarossa (bär'bə-rôs'ə), Frederick, *see* Frederick I (Holy Roman Empire)
Barebone's Parliament, 398
Barebone, Praisegod, 398
Baroque (bə-rōk'), architecture, 478-479, *479*; painting, 481; music, 484-485, *485*
Basel (bä'z'l), Council of, 213
Bavaria, *77*, 80, *152*, *242*, 429, *429*, 457, *462*
Beccaria (bāk'kä-rē'ä), marquis di, 477
Becket (bek'it), Thomas à, 173-174, *173*
Bede (bēd), 23
Beggars, 315
Belgium, 315, 447; *see also* Flanders; Netherlands; Netherlands, Austrian; Netherlands, Spanish
Belisarius (bel'ə-sâr'-i-əs), 25
Bellini (bel-lē'nē), Gentile and Giovanni, *253*, 274
Benedict, 13, 80
Benedictine order, 13, 14, 121
Benedictine rule, 13, 121
Benevolences, 230
Bernard of Clairvaux (klâr-vō'), 99, 121, 128, 135-138, 161, 187, 214, 266
Bernini (ber-nē'nē), Giovanni, 479
Bill of Rights (England), 400
Black Death, 216, 220
Blanche of Castile, 164
Blake, William, 484
Blenheim (blen'əm), battle of, 455
Blood, Council of, 315
Boccaccio (bô-kät'chô), Giovanni, 267, 268
Boethius (bō-ē'thi-əs), 19, 38
Bohemia, 81, 82, *82*, *152*, 155, 241, *242*, *300*, 317, 425, *429*
Boleslav II (Bohemia), 81
Boleyn (bool'in), Anne, 302, 303, 388
Boniface (bon'ə-fās'), St., 14
Boniface VIII (pope), 129-130, 165-166, 211
Bonnie Prince Charlie, 437
Borgia (bôr'jä), Cesare, 271
Bosch, Hieronymus, 283
Bossuet (bô-swe'), Bishop, 377
Boswell, James, 483
Bosworth, battle of, 230, *242*
Botticelli (bot'i-chel'i), Sandro, 269
Boucher (bōo-shā'), François, 482
Bourbon dynasty, *462*; in France, 313, 372-385; in Spain, 368, 454, 456-457; *see also* France, Spain
Bouvines (bōo-vēn'), battle of, 162, 175
Boyle, Robert, 470
Braddock, Edward, 459
Brandenburg, *152*, 155, *242*, 319, 382, 383, 420, *429*, 453, 484; *see also* Prussia
Brazil, 235, 342-344, *347*, 452
Britain, 37; *see also* England, Great Britain, Scotland, Wales

Brueghel (broo'g'l), Pieter, the Elder, 284, *314*
Bruges (brōōzh), 109, 159, *246*, 248, 251
Brunelleschi (brōō'ne-les'kē), Filippo, 270
Buddhism, 326, 328, 330
Buffon (bü-fôn'), Georges de, 470
Bulgaria, 7, 46, *47*, *82*, *198*, *200*, *405*, 407
Bunyan, John, 483
Burgundy, 9, 23, *72*, *77*, *82*, *152*, 159, *219*, 221, 234, 238, 241; *see also* Franche Comté
Burns, Robert, 484
Byzantine Empire (bi-zan'tin), 45-55, *47*, *62*, 74, 78, *198*, 263, 404; art, 53-54; church, 49-51, *82*, 125 (*see also* Orthodox Church); crusades, 182-184, 186, *187*, 188-190, 192; end of, 199-202; government, 48-49; invasions, 46-48, 62; way of life, 51-54; *see also* Eastern Roman Empire
Cabeza de Vaca (kä-be'tha *the* vä'kä), Álvar Nuñez, 341
Cabot, John, 345-346
Cabral (kə-bräl), Pedro, 343
Calderón (käl'de-rôn), Pedro, 367
Calvin, John, 299-301, *301*, 305
Calvinism, 299-301, *300*, 305-306, 312-315, 319, *320*, 348, 388-389; *see also* Huguenots, Protestantism, Puritans
Cambrai (kän-bre'), Treaty of, 241
Canada, 348, 438, 460
Cano, Juan Sebastian del, 341
Canon law, 81
Canossa, 127, 150, 151, *152*
Capetian dynasty (France), 158-166
Capitalism, 249
Cardinals, college of, 125, 126
Caribbean Sea, 344-345, *347*
Carolingian Renaissance, 75-76
Carthusian order, 121
Cartwright, Edmund, 447
Cassiodorus, 19, 38
Caste system (India), 326
Castiglione (käs'tē-lyō'ne), Baldassare, 263
Castile (kas-tēl'), *82*, *152*, 191, 235, 236, 359; *see also* Spain
Castles, medieval, 104-106, *105*
Catalonia, *364*, 365
Cateau-Cambrésis (kà-tō' kän-brä-sē'), treaty of, 241, 362
Catherine of Aragon, 231, 237, 302, 303
Catherine of Siena, 212
Catherine II the Great (Russia), 412-415, *413*, 464, 473, 479
Catholic Church, in the Americas, 340-342, 348; Avignon papacy, 130, 166, 211-213; canon law, 119-120; and Charlemagne, 73-74; in China, 333-335; Cluniac reforms, 161; Conciliar movement, 213; crusades, 182-194; early history, 10-14, 39-43; and Dutch Rebellion, 314-315; and feudalism, 94-95; and French religious wars, 313; Great Schism, 212-213; and heretics, 11, 123-124, 214-215; Inquisition, 124, 236, 312, 317, 363; in Ireland, 390; hierarchy, 11-12; Jansenism, 467; and medieval education, 132-135; and medieval French kings, 160-161, 163, 165-166, 211-213; in medieval Germany, 146; in Middle Ages, 108, 111, 116-130; missionary activity, 331; and Orthodox Church, 49-51, 74, 82, 201; in Protestant England,

Catholic Church (continued)
389-391, 399-401; and Protestantism, 243, 291-296, 298-303, *300*, 305-307, 309-321, *320*; Reformation, 309-312, 479; Renaissance popes, 271; ritual, 118; sacraments, 117-118; in Spain, 236, 360, 363, 365, 369; spread into western Europe, 81; and Thirty Years War, 316-321

Catholic League, 316

Catholic Reformation, 309-312, 479

Cavaliers, 396

Celts, 7

Cervantes (sẽr-van'tẽz) Saavedra, Miguel de, 366, 369

Champagne, 109, 110, *152*, 159

Champlain, Samuel de, 346

Chansons de geste (shän-sōn' də zhest'), 100, 167

Chardin (shár-dan'), Jean Baptiste, 482

Charlemagne (shär'lə-mān'), 71-79, *72*, *73*, 144, 145, 148, 158, 160, 182

Charles I (England), 394-397, *397*, 481

Charles II (England), 399-400, 484

Charles V (France), 233

Charles VI (France), 218

Charles VII (France), 219-221, 233, 254

Charles VIII (France), 240

Charles V (Holy Roman Empire), 236, 240-241, *240*, *242*, 256, 272, 274, 296, 298, 302, 314, 342, 361, 406

Charles VI (Holy Roman Empire), 425, 428, 457

Charles I (Spain), 361; *see also* Charles V (Holy Roman Empire)

Charles II (Spain), 368, 425, 454

Charles Martel, 62, 70-71, *72*, 219

Charles the Bald, 76, 77, 158

Charles the Fat, 76, 79

Charles the Simple, 76, 79

Charpentier (shár-pän-tyā), Marc-Antoine, 484

Charter of Liberties, 171

Chartres (shár'tr'), Cathedral of, *141*, 261

Chaucer (chô'sẽr), Geoffrey, 174, 285, 286

China, 66, 194, 197, *198*, 235, 278, 324, 326-330, 333-335, *334*

Chivalry, 96-101

Chrétien de Troyes (krā-tyan' də trwä'), 100

Christian IV (Denmark), 317

Cid, the, 191

Cistercian order, 121, 123, 135

Civil War, English, 396-397

Clarendon, Assize of, 172

Clarendon Code, 399

Clericis laicos, 129, 166

Clement V (pope), 129, 166

Clement VII (pope), 302

Clermont, Council of, 183

Clive, Robert, 460

Clovis, 19-21, *20*, 24, 33, 39, 69, 70, *72*, 144, 182

Cluny, monastery at, 120, 123, 136, 139, *152*, 161

Coeur (kūr), Jacques, 141, 233, 254

Colbert (kôl-bár'), Jean Baptiste, 379-381, 384, 385

Colet (kol'et), John, 282

Columbus, Christopher, 236, 338-340, *339*

Comitatus, 8, 18, 70

Common law, 172-173, 393

Common Prayer, Book of, 286, 303, 388, 399

Commonwealth (England), 398

Conciliar movement, 291

Condottieri (kŏn'dŏt-tye'rẽ), 114, 238

Confucius, 327-329, 335

Congregationalism, 389, 397; *see also* Calvinism, Puritans

Conquistadores, 340-341

Conrad III (Holy Roman Empire), 187

Constance, Council of, 213

Constantine I (Roman Empire), 9, 10, 202

Constantine XI (Byzantine Empire), 201, 202

Constantinople, becomes Roman capital, 9; as capital of Byzantine Empire, 51-53; fall of (1453), 201-202, *201*

Copernicus, Nicolaus, 288, 467

Corneille, Pierre, 482

Coronado, Francisco Vásquez de, 341

Corpus Juris Civilis, 27, 28

Corte-Real, Gaspar, 346

Cortes, Hernando, 341

Corvée (kôr-vā'), 108

Cossacks, 408

Counter Reformation, *see* Reformation, Catholic

Courtly love, 99-101

Cranach (krä'näkh), Lucas, 285, *294*

Cranmer, Thomas, 286, 302, 388

Crécy (kres'i), battle of, 217, *219*

Cromwell, Oliver, 397-399, *398*, 483

Cromwell, Richard, 399

Crusades, 99, 128, 182-194, *185*, *190*; background, 182-184; First, 185-186; Second, 187-188; Third, 153, 188; Fourth, 189-190, 253; crusader states, 186-187, *187*; Louis IX, 165, 191; decline, 190-191; in Spain, 191-192; effects, 109, 192-194

Cuba, 339, 343, 344, *347*

Cyril, 81

Cyrillic alphabet, 82

Danelaw, *21*, 22

Danes, 20, 22, 78; *see also* Denmark, Vikings

Dante (dän'te), 154, 266-268

Declaration of Independence, American, 438, 474

Declaration of Indulgence, 400

Defenestration of Prague, 317

Defoe, Daniel, 483

Deism, 467, 471

Denmark, 79, 81, *82*, *152*, 153, 298, *300*, 316-318, *320*, *429*, *462*

Descartes (dā-kärt), René, 468

De Soto, Hernando, 341

Devolution, War of, 383

Dias (dē'əs), Bartholomeu, 325

Divine-right monarchy, 377

Domesday Book, 171

Dominic, 121-124, 128

Dominican order, 122-124

Donatello, 270

Donation of Pepin, 71

Drake, Sir Francis, 344, 381

Dryden, John, 483

Dürer (dü'rẽr), Albrecht, 284, *284*, 419

East India Companies, 333, 392, 444-445, *445*, 452

East Indies, 235, 330-331, *334*, 453

Eastern Roman Empire, *20*, 24-28, *26*, 45; *see also* Roman Empire, Byzantine Empire

Eckhart, Meister, 214, 292

Edessa, county of, 186, 187, *187*

Edward I (England), 95, 177-178, *178*, 390

Edward III (England), 217-218, 229
Edward IV (England), 230
Edward VI (England), 303, 388
Edward the Black Prince, 217-218
Edward the Confessor, 169
Egypt, 46, 47, 61, 62, 165, 188, 197, 405
Eleanor of Aquitaine, 100, 172
Eliot, Sir John, 395
Elizabeth I (England), 286, 303, 363, 387-393, 392
England, 234, 240, 241, 242, 247, 248, 250, 282;
  Act of Union, 433; American colonies, 344, 347,
  348-350, 382; Anglo-Saxons, 21-23, 21, 82; Civil
  War, 396-397; and Dutch Netherlands, 398-400;
  Elizabeth I, 387-393; Glorious Revolution, 401-
  402, 473, 474; Henry VII, 230-232; Hundred
  Years War, 216-221, 219, 229; and India, 332,
  333, 334; Magna Carta, 175-176; and medieval
  church, 128, 173, 175, 212; in Middle Ages, 92,
  103, 108, 109, 152, 169-179; Norman Conquest,
  79, 162, 169-171, 170; Parliament, 176-178, 178,
  220, 230-232, 381, 393-402; Restoration Era, 399-
  400; and Spain, 231, 363, 390-391, 394; Wars of
  the Roses, 230; wars with Louis XIV, 368, 384,
  452, 454; see also Great Britain
England, Church of, 282, 286, 300, 302-303, 320,
  388-389, 394, 399, 467
Enclosure acts, 258, 433, 446
Enlightenment, 471, 482
Erasmus, Desiderius, 278-282, 281, 285, 292, 295
Eric the Red, 324
Ericson, Leif, 78, 79, 324
Estates-General, 166, 220
Ethiopia, 58, 62, 334, 335
Eugene of Savoy, 455
Eusebius, 38
Eyck (īk), Hubert and Jan van, 283
Fabliaux (fá-bli-ō'), 100, 167
Fatimid caliphate (fat'i-mid), 66, 82, 187
Ferdinand II (Holy Roman Empire), 316, 362
Ferdinand (Spain), 236, 238, 240, 241, 359, 361, 369
Feudalism, 91-96, 145; decline, 215-216
Fielding, Henry, 483
Finland, 207, 242, 411, 413, 462
Flanders, 109, 152, 159, 217, 231, 246, 247-248,
  251, 283-284, 318, 382; see also Netherlands
Fleury (flü-rē'), André Cardinal, 442
Florence, 146, 238, 246, 248, 252, 253, 257, 266,
  268-271; Council of, 201
Fontenoy (fôn̄t-nwá'), battle of, 77, 77
Fox, George, 466
Fra Angelico, 269
Fragonard (frà-gō̄-nàr'), Jean Honoré, 439, 482
France, 79, 246, 247, 248, 250, 272, 282, 418, 447;
  American colonies, 344, 347, 347-348, 454-455,
  458-461, 461; American Revolution, 438, 443;
  Catholic Reformation, 312; under Henry IV, 372-
  374; Hundred Years War, 216-221, 219; and
  India, 333, 334, 460; under Louis XI, 232-234;
  under Louis XIV, 376-385, 382, 452, 454-456;
  and medieval popes, 128, 165-166, 211-213; in
  Middle Ages, 92, 103, 140, 141, 152, 159-166;
  Old Regime, 429, 439-444, 456-458; Protestant-
  ism, 243, 300, 320 (see also Huguenots); Religious
  Wars, 313; under Richelieu, 374-376; Seven

France (continued)
  Years War, 429, 437, 442, 458-461, 462; and
  Spain, 362, 363, 364, 365-366, 368, 375, 376;
  Thirty Years War, 316, 318-319, 320; see also
  Frankish Empire, Franks, Gaul
Franche Comté (fränsh kō̄n-tä'), 159, 238, 241, 318,
  362, 364, 368, 382, 383
Francis I (France), 241, 361, 373
Francis of Assisi, 121-122, 122, 128
Franciscan order, 122, 123, 342
Franks, 8, 9, 14, 19-21, 20, 26, 39, 62
Frankish empire, 49, 62, 69-80, 72, 77, 94
Franklin, Benjamin, 443, 467, 476
Frederick I Barbarossa (Holy Roman Empire), 150-
  154, 151, 162, 188
Frederick II (Holy Roman Empire), 154, 162, 190
Frederick I (Prussia), 421, 456
Frederick II the Great (Prussia), 422-426, 423, 428-
  430, 429, 457-461, 473, 479
Frederick III the Wise (Saxony), 294
Frederick William, the Great Elector (Brandenburg),
  420, 453
Frederick William I (Prussia), 421
Freemasons, 467
Free Spirit, Brethren of the, 214
French and Indian War, 458-461
Froben, Johann, 278, 279
Fronde, 376
Fugger (foog'ēr), Jacob, 254
Gabelle (gȧ-bel'), 233, 441
Gainsborough, Thomas, 482
Galahad, 99
Galileo (gal'ȧ-lē'ō), 468
Gama, Vasco da, 325
Gaul, 9, 19-21, 70; see also France, Franks, Frankish
  Empire
Genghis Khan, 197, 198, 205
George I (Great Britain), 433, 435, 436-437
George II (Great Britain), 433, 435, 436-437
George III (Great Britain), 437-438, 460, 463
Germanic peoples, 7-10, 8, 14, 18, 20, 33, 38, 45, 73
Germany, 77, 82, 238-239, 246, 247, 254, 310, 383,
  452, 453; in Middle Ages, 92, 103, 145-156;
  Protestantism in, 241, 243, 293-298, 300, 304;
  Renaissance, 282-285; Thirty Years War, 316-321,
  375, 418-419; see also Austria, Holy Roman Em-
  pire, Prussia
Ghent, 109, 159, 246, 248, 251
Ghiberti (gē-ber'tē), Lorenzo, 270
Gibbon, Edward, 483
Gibraltar (ji-brôl'tēr), 62, 79, 364, 438, 455, 455, 462
Gilbert, William, 468
Giorgione (jôr-jō'ne), 274
Giotto (jôt'tō), 268-269, 270
Glorious Revolution, 401, 402, 432, 436, 473, 474
Godfrey of Bouillon, 186
Godunov (gō̄-doo-nôf'), Boris, 408
Goethe (gö'te), Johann Wolfgang von, 421, 484
Golden Bull (1356), 155, 237
Golden Horde, 197-198, 198, 205-206, 207
Gothic architecture, 132, 139-141, 141, 159, 179
Gothic War, 25-26, 28, 36
Goths, 8; see also Ostrogoths, Visigoths
Gottfried von Strassburg, 100

Grace, Edict of, 475
Grand Assize, 172
Gratian (grā'shi-ən), 119, 136
Gray, Thomas, 484
Great Britain, eighteenth-century life, 433-438, 446-447; eighteenth-century wars, 429, 437, 438, 454-461, *455, 460, 461, 462*; in North America, 437, 438, 454, 455, 458-461, *461*; Parliamentary government 435-436, 474-475; *see also* England, Scotland, Wales
Great Migration, 349, 394
Great Northern War, 411
Great Schism, 271
Greco, El, 367, *367*
Greece, *405*, 407; *see also* Byzantine Empire
Greenland, 78, 324, 346
Gregory I the Great (pope), 36-38, *37*, 42
Gregory VII (pope), 125-128, 149-150, 184
Gregory XI (pope), 212
Gregory of Tours, 39
Guilds, 112-113
Gustavus II Adolphus (Sweden), 318
Gutenberg (gōō't'n-bĕrg), Johann, 278
Habsburg dynasty, 154, 155, 237, 239-243, *242*, 316-319, 361-362, 368-369, 375, 419, 424-427, 429, 452-453, 456-457, 462; *see also* Austria, Holy Roman Empire, Spain
Hacienda Council, 361, 369
Hagia Sophia (hä'gi-ä sō-fē'ä), 28, *29*, 42, 52, 65, 189, 207
Haiti, 339, 344, *347*, 368
Hals, Frans, 480
Hampden, John, 395
Handel, George Frederick, 484
Hanoverian dynasty, 433
Hanse, German, 110, *246*, 251, 257
Harold (England), 170
Harun al-Rashid (hä-rōōn' är'rə-shēd'), 63
Harvey, William, 468, 470
Hastings, battle of, 170, *170*
Haydn (hī'd'n), Joseph, 485
Henry I (England), 171-172
Henry II (England), 162, 172-174
Henry III (England), 176-177, 179
Henry V (England), 218
Henry VI (England), 218, 229-230
Henry VII (England), 230-232, 237, 345, 387, 390
Henry VIII (England), 237, 241, 282, 285, 302-303, 363, 388, 390
Henry IV (France), 313, 372-374, 394
Henry II (Holy Roman Empire), 125, 148
Henry III (Holy Roman Empire), 149
Henry IV (Holy Roman Empire), 126-128, *127*, 149-150
Henry V (Holy Roman Empire), 150
Henry the Fowler (Germany), 146
Henry the Lion, 153
Henry the Navigator, 234, 324-325
Heraclius (Byzantine Empire), 46
Herder, Johann Gottfried, 484
Herschel, William, 470
Hinduism, 326, 328, 330
Hispaniola, 339, 340, 344, *347*
Hobbes, Thomas, 472, 473

Hogarth, William, *434*, 482
Hohenstaufen (hō'ən-shtou'fən) dynasty, 150-151
Hohenzollern (hō'ən-tsōl'ĕrn) dynasty, 155, 419, *462*; *see also* Brandenburg, Prussia
Holbein (hōl'bīn), Hans, the Younger, *280, 281*, 285, 419
Holy Leagues, 240
Holy Roman Empire, under Charles V, 241, 278, 361, 362 (*see also* Charles V); in eighteenth century, 429, 453, *462*; in fifteenth century, 237-238, 248; medieval decline, 154-156, 162-163; and medieval papacy, 125-128, 149-150; in Middle Ages, *82*, 144-156, *152*; Thirty Years War, 317-321, *320*, 375, 418; *see also* Germany, Italy
Hooke, Robert, 470
Hospitalers, 99, 187
Hubertusburg, Treaty of, 461
Hudson, Henry, 346
Huguenots (hū'gə-not'), 313, 348, 373-375, 381-382
Humanism, 265-267, 279-283
Hundred Years War, 216-221, *219*, 229, 232, 233, 251
Hungary, *152*, 153, 155, 256, 427; early history, 80-82, *82*; and Habsburgs, 241, 407, 424-425, *462*; and Mongols, 198, *198*; and Ottoman Empire, 202, *242*, *405*, 406; Protestantism, *300*, 301, 304; Thirty Years War, 317, *320*; *see also* Magyars
Huns, 7, 9
Huss, John, 214-215, *214*, 292, 295
Hutton, James, 470
Île de France (ēl də fräns), *152*, 160, 166
Iceland, 78
Iconoclastic Controversy, 49-50, 54
Incas, 341
Index of Prohibited Books, 312
India, *198*, 325-327, *334*; and Great Britain, 333, 452, 453, 458, 460, *460*, 461; and France, 333, 452, 453, 458, 460, *460*, 461; Mughal Empire, 199, 327; and Portugal, 235, 331-332
Indians, American, 340-342, 345-346, 350
Indulgences, 292, 294-295, 312
Industrial Revolution, 433, 447
Innocent III (pope), 100, 128-129, 142, 144, 154, 163, 174, 175, 189
Inquisition, 124, 236, 312, 317, 363
Instrument of Government, 398
Ireland, 14, 79, *82*, *242*, *300*, *320*, 388, 390, 391, 398, 454
Isabella (Spain) 236, *237*, 238, 241, 339, 359, 361, 369
Isidore of Seville, 39
Islam (is-läm'), 47, 57-67, 79-80, 182-183, 196-198, 263, 327; *see also* Ottoman Empire
Italy, early Middle Ages, 9, 19, 25-26, 28, 79-80, *82*; eighteenth century, 453, 456-457; high Middle Ages, 109, 113-114, 146, 148, 150, 153-155; Reformation era, *300*, 312, *320*, 362; Renaissance era, 238-242, *246*, 247-248, 252-254, *252*, 261-274; *see also* Holy Roman Empire
Ivan I (Russia), 206
Ivan III (Russia), 206-208
Ivan IV the Terrible (Russia), 407-408, *413*
Jacquerie (zhȧk-rē'), 220
Jamaica, 339, 344, *347*, 399

James I (England), 390, 393-394
James II (England), 399-401, 437, 484
James IV (Scotland), 390
Jansenists, 467
Japan, 198, 235, 324, 326, 330, 334
Java, 332, 334
Jefferson, Thomas, 474
Jenkins's Ear, War of, 437, 457
Jerome, 5, 9, 34-35, 38, 75, 284, 367
Jerusalem, Latin Kingdom of, 186-189, 187
Jesuits (jezh′-ōō-it), 310, 317, 335, 342, 348, 426, 467, 479
Jews, 58, 236, 249, 360, 369, 399, 422, 467
Jiménez (hē-mā′nāth), Francisco Cardinal, 282
Joan of Arc, 218-221
John VIII (Byzantine Empire), 201
John (England), 162, 163, 174-176, 212
John I (Portugal), 234
John II (Portugal), 235
John Chrysostom, 38
John of Salisbury, 98, 136
Johnson, Samuel, 483
Joint-stock companies, 445
Jolliet (jō′-li-et′), Louis, 348
Jonson, Ben, 286
Joseph II (Holy Roman Empire), 425, 426, 427, 442, 461, 473
Julius II (pope), 240, 271-272
Junkers (yooŋ′kĕrz), 421, 423-424
Justinian, 24-28, 26, 29, 36, 45, 46
Jutes, 20, 21, 22; see also Anglo-Saxons
Kaunitz, Wenzel von, 459
Kepler, Johannes, 468, 469
Kiev (kē-ev′), 78, 82, 198, 203-205, 207
King George's War, 458
King James Bible, 394
King William's War, 454
Knights, in feudalism, 96-101
Knights of Saint John in Jerusalem, 99
Knights Templars, 99, 121, 126, 128, 179, 187
Knox, John, 390
Koran, 60
Korea, 197, 198, 330
Kościuszko (kôsh-chōōsh′kô), Tadeusz, 415
Kossovo, battle of, 200, 200
Kublai Khan, 198, 198, 329
Kyd, Thomas, 286
La Hogue, battle of, 454
Lancastrians, 230
Langton, Stephen, 175
La Rochelle, siege of, 375, 382
La Salle, Robert Cavelier de, 318
Lateran Council, Fourth, 128; Fifth, 291
Latvia, 82, 251
Laud, William, 394-396
Lavoisier (là-vwà-zyā′), Antoine, 470
Law, Anglo-Saxon, 23; common (England), 172-173, 393; Roman, 24, 27, 215; Salic, 21
Law, John, 445
League of Augsburg, War of the, 383-384, 454
Lechfeld, battle of the, 80, 82, 147
Leeuwenhoek (lā′vǝn-hōōk′), Anton van, 470
Lefèvre d'Étaples (lĕ-fâ′vr′ dā-ta′pl′), Jacques, 282
Legnano (lā-nya′-nô), battle of, 152, 153
Leipzig (līp′sig), battle of, 318

Leo III (Byzantine Empire), 49
Leo III (pope), 74
Leo IX (pope), 125, 149
Leo X (pope), 241, 264, 271, 272, 279, 292, 294-296, 302
Lepanto, battle of, 242, 363, 366, 406
Lexington, battle of, 438
Linnaeus (li-nē′ǝs), 470
Lippi, Fra Filippo, 269
Lithuania, 82, 206, 207, 209, 242, 300, 413
Locke, John, 473-474, 476
Lollards, 215, 218
Lombard League, 153
Lombards, 20, 37, 71, 72
Long Parliament, 396
Lorraine, 77, 152, 429
Lorraine, Claude, 481
Lothair, 77, 146
Lotharingia, 77, 77
Louis VI (France), 160-161
Louis VII (France), 161, 172, 187
Louis IX (France), 158, 164-166, 164, 176, 191
Louis XI (France), 232-234, 232
Louis XII (France), 240
Louis XIII (France), 374-376
Louis XIV (France), 348, 366, 368, 376-385, 381, 418; as patron of the arts, 479, 481, 482, 484; wars, 382, 383-385, 400, 401, 425, 451-456
Louis XV (France), 439, 442, 456, 459, 479
Louis XVI (France), 442-444, 480
Louis the Pious, 76, 77, 79, 94
Louisiana, 347, 461, 461
Loyola (loi-ō′lǝ), Ignatius of, 310, 310
Lully (lü-lē′), Jean Baptiste, 484
Luther, Martin, 241, 279, 281, 293-298, 294, 297, 299, 361
Lutheranism, 293-298, 300, 301, 302, 305-306, 316-319, 320; see also Protestantism
Macao, 332, 334
Macchiavelli (mä′kyä-vel′lē), Niccolò, 239, 266, 271, 313
Magellan, Ferdinand, 333, 341
Magna Carta, 175-176
Magyars, 7, 80, 145, 147, 184; see also Hungary
Maintenon (mant-nōn′), Madame de, 382
Manorial system, 103-108
Manutius (mǝ-nū′shi-ǝs), Aldus, 278-280
Manzikert, battle of, 183, 187
Maria Theresa (Austria), 425-429, 426, 442, 457, 458, 461
Marie Antoinette (France), 426, 442, 443, 476
Marignano, battle of, 240
Marlborough, duke of, 455
Marlowe, Christopher, 286
Marquette, Jacques, 348
Marsilius of Padua, 212
Marston Moor, battle of, 396
Mary I (England), 302, 303, 363, 388
Mary II (England), 401, 432, 452
Mary, Queen of Scots, 363, 390, 391, 393
Masaccio (mä-zät′chô), 269
Matthias (Holy Roman Empire), 316
Maximilian I (Holy Roman Empire), 236, 238, 240, 241, 256
Mazarin (maz′ǝ-rin), Cardinal, 376

Mecca, 58, 59, *62*, 405
Medici (med'ə-chē'), Cosimo de, 257, 269
Medici, Lorenzo de, 264, 269-271
Medici, Salvestro dei, 257
Médicis (mā-dē-sēs'), Catherine de, 313
Mehmed II (Ottoman Empire), 200-202, 404
Mendelssohn, Moses, 467
Mercantilism, 331, 379-380, 419, 452
Merovingian dynasty, 70, *72*
Methodism, 467
Methodius, 81
Mesopotamia, *62*, 183-184, 188, 197, 199, *200*, *405*
Mexico, 341, *347*, 452
Michael III (Byzantine Empire), 50
Michael (Russia), 408-409
Michelangelo (mī'k'l-an'jə-lō'), *262*, 271-272, *273*
Middle class, 254-258, 392-393, 440
Milan (mi-lan'), 34-35, 110, 146, 238, 240-241, 252, *252*, *364*, *429*, 457
Milton, John, 399, 483
Minorca, 455
Missi dominici, 72, 160
Mississippi Bubble, 445
Mohacs (mō'häch), battles of, *405*, 406, 424, *429*
Molière (mō-lyâr'), 482
Mongols, 7, 196-199, *198*, 205-206, 329
Montaigne (mōn-ten'y'), Michel de, 285, 286
Montesquieu (mōn-tes-kyö'), Charles de, 474-475
Monteverdi (mōn'te-vâr'dē), Claudio, 484
Montfort (mont'fērt), Simon de, 177
Moors, 182, 191-192, 234-236, 360, 362, 369
Moravian Church, *214*, *300*, *320*
More, Sir Thomas, *280*, 282, 285, 286, 303
Morocco, 234, 325
Mosaics, 40-42, *41*, *53*, 54
Moscow, rise of, 206-208, *207*
Mozart (mō'tsärt), Wolfgang Amadeus, 485
Mughal Empire (mōōg'häl), 327, 333, *334*, *460*
Muhammad (moo-ham'mad), 47, 59-61, 66
Nantes, Edict of, 313, 373, 375; revocation of, 381-383, 420
Napier, John, 468
Naseby, battle of, 396
Navas de Tolosa, Las, battle of, *152*, 192
Necker, Jacques, 443
Negroes, 342-345
Netherlands, 103, *152*, 247-248, 375; Habsburg possession, 238, 241, *242*; Rebellion, 314-315, *314*, 362, 391; Reformation era, *300*, 312; *see also* Netherlands, Austrian; Netherlands, Dutch; Netherlands, Spanish
Netherlands, Austrian, 425, 427, *429*, 456-457, *462*
Netherlands, Dutch, 363, *364*, 438, 480; colonies, 332-335, *334*, 344, *347*, 349; Thirty Years War, 316, 318-319, *320*; wars with England, 398-400; wars with Louis XIV, 368, *382*, 383-384, 452-454, *455*, 456
Netherlands, Spanish, 319, *320*, *364*, 365, 368, *382*, 383, 391, 425, 454, 456
Newcomen, Thomas, 447
New England, *347*, 348, 350, 394
Newfoundland, 79, 324, 346, *347*, 455, *461*
New France, *347*, 348, *461*
New Netherland, 349
Newton, Sir Isaac, 469-470, *470*, 471, 473

Nicaea (nī-sē'ə), Council of, 11, 14
Nicholas II (pope), 125
Nicholas V (pope), 271
Nimwegen (nim'vä'gən), Treaties of, *382*, 383
Norbert of Xanten, 121
Normandy, 79, *82*, *152*, 159, 162, 172
Normans, 78, 79, 109, 149, 153, 162, 169-171, *170*; *see also* Vikings
North, Lord, 437-438
Northwest Passage, 345, 346
Norway, 81, *82*, *242*, 298, *300*, *320*, *462*
Nova Scotia, 346, 455, *461*
Novgorod, 78, *82*, 203-204, 206, *207*
Nystad, Treaty of, 411, *413*
Oates, Titus, 400
Odo of Bayeux, 99
Odovacar, 10, 19
Oglethorpe, James, 349
Old Believers, 409
Olivares (ō'lē'vä'räs), Count-Duke, 365
Ommiad Caliphate, *62*, *82*, 166
Oprichniks, 407-408
Ordeal, trial by, 23, 73
Orthodox Church, 81-82, 182, 202, *300*, *320*; and Catholic Church, 49-51, 74, 82, 201; in Russia, 54, 82, 204-208, 404, 409-410
Osman, 199
Ostrogoths, 8, 18-19, *20*, 25, 38
Otto I the Great (Holy Roman Empire), 80, 146-148, *147*, 156
Otto II (Holy Roman Empire), 148
Otto III (Holy Roman Empire), 148
Otto IV (Holy Roman Empire), 162, 175
Ottoman Empire, *242*, *320*, 453, *462*; decline, 406-407; expansion, 199-202, *200*, 241, 404-406, *405*; and Russia, *413*, 415
Papal States, *152*, 238, 240, *252*, *364*, *462*
Papin, (på-pan'), Denis, 447
Paris, Treaty of (1763), 460-461; Treaty of (1783), 438; University of, 133
Parliament (pär'lə-mənt), 176-178, *178*, 220, 230-232, 381, 393-402, 435-438, 474-475
Parma, duke of, 315
Pascal (pås-kål'), Blaise, 468, 482
Patrick, 14
Patrimony of St. Peter, 37, *72*
Patristic writers, 34-39
Paul III (pope), 310, 311
Pavia, battle of, 241, *242*
Peace of God, 94-95
Peasantry, medieval, 106-108, *106*
Penn, William, 349
Pepin III (pep'in), the Short, 71, *72*
Persia, 46-47, 61-62, *62*, 183-184, 194, 197, 199, *334*, *405*, 412
Peru, 341, *347*
Peter I the Great (Russia), 409-412, *411*, *413*, 424, 453, 479
Peter III (Russia), 412-413, 460
Peter the Hermit, 186
Petition of Right, 395
Petrarch (pē'trärk), 252, 268
Petrine succession (pē'trīn), 12
Philip II Augustus (France), 153, 158, 162-163, 174-175, 188

Philip IV the Fair (France), 129, 159, 165-166, 211, 232, 233
Philip VI (France), 217
Philip II (Spain), 314-315, 332, 362-365, *362*, *364*, 388, 391
Philip III (Spain), 365, 369
Philip IV (Spain), 318, 365-368
Philip V (Spain), 368, 384, 454-455
Philippines, 333, *334*, 341, 362, 452
Philosophes (fē-lō-sôf'), 422, 425-426, 478, 482, 483
Physiocrats, 477
Pico della Mirandola (pē'kŏ del'lä mē-rän'dô-lä), Giovanni, 263-264
Pietists, 466-467
Pisa, Council of, 213
Pitt, William, 437, 459-460
Pitt, William, the Younger, 438
Pizarro (pi-zä'rō), Francisco, 341
Poland, *242*, 408, 420, 453, *462*; conversion, 80-82, *82*; in Middle Ages, *152*, 153, 155, 198, 206, 209; Partitions, *414-415*, 415; in Reformation era, *300*, 304, 305, 310, *320*; War of the Polish Succession, 456-457
Polish Succession, War of the, 442, 456-457
Politiques (pō-lē-tēk'), 313
Polo, Marco, 194, 198, 324, 329
Poltava, battle of, 411, *413*
Pompadour (pom'pɔ-dôr'), Jeanne de, 442
Ponce de León (pons dɔ lē'ɔn), Juan, 341
Poniatowski (pô'nyä-tôf'skē), Stanislas, 414
Pope, Alexander, 483
Portugal, *242*, 312, 452, *462*; and Brazil, 342-344, *347*; and Far East, 324-325, 327, 331-333, *334*, 342; in Middle Ages, *152*, 191-192; rise and decline, 234-235; and Spain, 235, 332, 363, *364*, 365
Poussin (pōō-san'), Nicolas, 481
Popish Plot, 400
Praemonstratensian order, 121, 128
Pragmatic Sanctions, 428, 429, 457
Preachers, Order of, 122
Presbyterianism, 389, 395-397; *see also* Calvinism
Prester John, 324
Primogeniture, 94, 145
Printing, invention of, 277-279
Protestantism, 241, 290-307, 313-321, 331; *see also* Baptists; Calvinism; England, Church of; Huguenots; Lutheranism; Methodism; Puritans; Quakers
Protestant Union, 316-317
Prussia, *82*, *242*; to 1740, 420-422, *429*; reign of Frederick II, 412-413, 422-424, 428-430, *429*, 457-461, *462*; Partitions of Poland, *414-415*, 415
Public Weal, League of, 234
Purcell (pûr's'l), Henry, 484
Puritans, 348, 388-399, 483; *see also* Calvinism
Putting-out system, 249, 251
Pyrenees, Treaty of the, 365, 366, 375, 376, 383
Quakers, 348-349, 467
Quebec, 346; battle of, 460, *461*, *463*
Queen Anne's War, 455
Quesnay (ke-nä'), François, 477
Rabelais (rab'ɔ-lā'), François, 285-286
Racine (rà-sēn'), Jean, 482
Raphael (raf'i-ɔl), 272, *273*
Ray, John, 470
Razin, Stephen, 409

Reason, Age of, 471-486
Reformation, Catholic, 309-312
Reformation, Protestant, 290-307; *see also* Protestantism
Regular clergy, 12-13
Rembrandt, 480, *481*
Renaissance (ren'ɔ-säns'), Italian, 261-274; Northern, 277-288
Restitution, Edict of, 317
Reuchlin (roiH'lēn), Johann, 282
Reynard the Fox, 100
Reynolds, Joshua, 482
Ricci (rēt'chē), Matteo, 335
Richard I (England), 153, 162, 174, 188
Richard III (England), 230-231
Richard, duke of York, 230
Richardson, Samuel, 483
Richelieu (rē'shɔ-lyö'), Cardinal, 318, 374-376, *374*, 379
Rienzi (ryen'tsē), Cola di, 212
Rococo (rɔ-kō'kō), architecture, 479-480; painting, 482
Rocroi, battle of, *364*, 365, 375, *382*
Rois Fainéants (rwȧ fe-nā-än'), 70
Rollo (Normandy), 79, 159
Roman de la Rose (rô-man' dɔ lȧ rôz), 100
Roman Empire, decline and collapse, 5-10, 17, 33; and Christianity, 10; revival under Charlemagne, 74; *see also* Byzantine Empire, Eastern Roman Empire, Holy Roman Empire
Romanesque architecture, 132, 138-139
Roses, Wars of the, 229-230
Roundheads, 396
Rousseau (rōō-sō'), Jean Jacques, 475-477, *475*, 482, 484
Rubens, Peter Paul, 481
Rudolph of Habsburg, 154
Rump, 397, 398
Rurik, 203
Russia, 304, 392, 407; early history, 54, 78, 82, *82*, 198, 202-209; eighteenth century, 409-415, *413*, 429-430, *453*, 456, 458-460, *462*; under Ivan the Terrible, 407-408; Partitions of Poland, *414-415*, 415; serfdom, 208, 414, 416
Ryswick (riz'wik), Treaty of, *382*, 384, 454
Sacraments, in Catholicism, 117-118, 312; in Protestantism, 305-306
St. Bartholomew, Massacre of, 313
St. Peter, Basilica of, *40*, 80, 261-262, *262*, 271, 292, 294, 479
St. Petersburg, 411, *411*, 412
Saladin, 188
Salisbury Oath, 170
Saracens, *see* Islam
Sardinia, 109, *252*, 456-457
Sassanid Empire, 46-47, 61, *62*
Savonarola (sä'vō-nä-rō'lä), Girolamo, 270-271
Savoy, *252*, *364*, *382*, 456, *462*
Saxons, 8, *20*, 21, *22*; *see also* Anglo-Saxons
Saxony, *72*, 77, 80, *152*, 155, *242*, 429, *429*, 457, 459, *462*
Scandinavia, 78; *see also* Denmark, Norway, Sweden, Vikings
Schiller, Friedrich, 484
Scholasticism, 132, 135

Science, 287, 467-471
Scotland, 21, 82, 152, 177, 218, 231, 242, 300, 301, 320, 388, 390, 391, 395, 397-398, 433, 437; see also Great Britain
Scotland, Church of, 300, 301, 320, 389, 395
Secular clergy, 12
Selim I (Ottoman Empire), 405
Seljuk Turks, 182-183, 186, 187, 188, 197-199
Separatists, 389
Serbia, 47, 82, 200, 405, 407
Serfdom, medieval, 107; Russian, 208, 414, 416
Servetus, Michael, 305
Seven Years War, 429-430, 437, 442, 458-461, 460-462
Shakespeare, William, 286-287, 388
Shinto, 330
Siberia, 334, 408, 415
Sicily, 80, 109, 146, 149, 152, 236, 238, 253, 364, 462
Silesia, 429, 429, 430, 457, 462
Simons, Menno, 304
Sistine Chapel, 271, 272, 273
Six Articles, Act of the, 303
Sixtus IV (pope), 271
Slavery, medieval, 107; Negro, 342-345
Slavs, 7, 46, 82-83, 203
Sluys (slois), battle of, 217, 219
Smith, Adam, 478
Society of Jesus, 310
Socinus, Faustus, 305
Song of Roland, 97, 100, 167
South Sea Bubble, 445-446
Spain, crusades in, 152, 191-192; colonies, 333, 334, 338-344, 347, 361, 364, 369, 452, 453; Dutch Revolt, 314-315, 314; early Middle Ages, 9, 23, 37, 39, 62, 65, 66, 71; eighteenth-century wars, 368, 384, 425, 429, 437-438, 452, 454-457, 455, 461, 462; and England, 231, 315, 363, 390-391, 394; under Ferdinand and Isabella, 235-237; Golden Age, 242, 359-370, 364; and Italy, 238, 240, 272; and Louis XIV, 375, 376, 383; Reformation era, 300, 310, 312, 320
Spanish Main, 344, 347
Spanish March, 71, 72
Spanish Succession, War of the, 364, 384, 425, 454-456, 455
Spenser, Edmund, 286
Spice Islands, 331, 332, 334
Spurs, battle of the, 240, 242
Stamp Act, 438
Star Chamber, Court of, 231
Stephen (Hungary), 80
Stevin, Simon, 468
Strafford, earl of, 395-396
Stuart dynasty, 393-402
Stuart, Charles, the Young Pretender, 437
Stuart, James, the Old Pretender, 436-437
Sueves, 8, 9
Suger (sü-zhâr'), Abbot, 160-161
Suleiman I (sü'lä-män'), (Ottoman Empire), 405-406
Sully, duke of, 373
Supremacy, Act of, 303, 388
Sweden, 81, 82, 207, 242, 298, 300, 349, 383, 408, 411-412, 413, 418, 420, 453-454, 462; Thirty Years War, 316, 318-319, 320, 375

Switzerland, 155, 238, 299, 300, 320, 382
Sylvester II (pope), 148
Syria, 61, 62, 62, 183, 200, 405
Taille (tá'y'), 165, 233, 441
Tamerlane, 198, 199-200, 327
Taoism, 328
Tatars, 197, 198, 205-206
Tauler, Johannes, 214
Teutonic Knights, 99
Test Act, 400
Tetzel, Johann, 295
Tewkesbury, battle of, 230, 242
Theodora (thē'ə-dôr'ə), 25
Theodoric (thē-od'ēr-ik), 19, 24, 33, 38, 40
Theodosius, 10
Thirty-nine Articles, Act of the, 388
Thirty Years War, 316-321, 320, 365, 375, 418, 419
Thousand and One Nights, 63
Three-field system, 107
Tilly, count of, 317, 318
Tintoretto (tēn'tô-ret'tô), 274
Tithes, 108
Titian (tish'ən), 274, 367
Tordesillas, treaty of, 342
Tories, 400, 435, 437
Totila, 25
Tournament, medieval, 98
Tours, battle of, 62, 62, 71
Townshend, Charles "Turnip," 446
Transylvania, 300, 320, 405, 407, 429
Trent, Council of, 311-312, 311
Tripoli, county of, 186, 187
Troubadours, 99-100, 159, 285
Troubles, Council of, 315
Truce of God, 94-95
Tudor dynasty, 221, 230, 232, 387
Tull, Jethro, 446
Turenne (tü-ren'), viscount of, 380, 381, 383
Turgot (tür-gō'), A.R.J., 443
Tyler, Wat, 220
Ukraine, 203, 206, 207, 413, 415
Ulfila (ul'fi-lə), 13
Unam sanctam, 129, 166, 291
Uniformity, Act of, 388
Union, Act of, 433
Unitarianism, 300, 305, 320
United Provinces, Republic of the, 315, 319; see also Netherlands, Dutch
United States of America, 333, 415, 436, 438, 443, 444, 474
Universities, medieval, 133-135
Urban II (pope), 183-185
Utrecht (ū'trekt), Treaty of, 382, 384, 455, 457
Valens (Roman Empire), 9
Valois (vàl-wä'), dynasty, 232, 239-243
Vandals, 9, 10, 20, 23, 25, 33
Van Dyck (van dīk'), Anthony, 381
Vassalage, 92
Vassi dominici, 71, 72
Vauban (vō-bän'), marquis of, 380
Vega (ve'gä), Lope de
Velázquez (ve-läth'keth), Diego, 367-368, 481
Venice (ven'is), 109, 110, 146, 189-190, 193, 238, 240, 242, 246, 248, 252, 252-253, 253, 274
Verdun (vâr-dun'), Treaty of, 77, 77, 145

Vermeer (vĕr-mêr′) Jan, 480
Veronese (ver′ə-nēz′), Paolo, 274
Verrazano (ver′rä-tsä′nỗ), Giovanni da, 346
Versailles (vĕr-sī′), palace of, 377-378, *378*, *382*, 440-441, 443, 479
Vespucius, Americus, 340
Vikings, 22, 78-79, 203-204, 324
Vinci (vin′chi), Leonardo da, 264-265, *265*, 268, 269, 287
Vinland, 78-79, 324
Virginia, 346, *347*, 348, *349*, 392, *461*
Visigoths, 8, 9, 13, *20*, 23, 26, *26*, 36-37, 39, 62
Vladimir I of Kiev, 82, 204
Voltaire (vol-târ′), 422, 467, 472-473, *472*, 477
Vulgate Bible, 35, 75
Waldensian heresy, 123, *300*
Waldo, Peter, 123
Wales, *21*, *82*, *152*, 177, 218, *242*, *300*, *320*, 388, 390
Wallenstein, Albrecht von, 317, 318
Walpole, Robert, 437, 446
Walter the Penniless, 186
Washington, George, 438, 459, 467
Watt, James, 447
Watteau (wä-tō′), Jean Antoine, 482
Wenceslas, Good King, 81
Wergild, 23, 73
Wesley, John, 467

West Indies, 340, 344-345, 452-453
Westphalia, Treaties of, 315, 318-321, *320*, 365, 375, 418, 424
Whigs, 400, 435
Whitney, Eli, 447
Wilkes, John, 437
William I the Conqueror (England), 79, 99, 108, 162, 169-171
William II (England), 171
William III (England and Dutch Netherlands), 383, 401, 432, 452, 454, 455
William I the Silent (Netherlands), 315
William of Ockham, 213
Witan (wit′ən), 8, 18
Welf dynasty, 150, 151, 153
Wolfe, James, 460, *463*
Worms (vôrmz), Concordat of, 148, 151
Worms, Diet of, 296
Wren, Sir Christopher, 480
Wycliffe (wik′lif), John, 214-215, 292, 295
Xavier (zā′vi-ēr), Francis, 332
Yaroslav (yu-ru-släf′) the Wise, 203
Yorkists, 230-231
Yorktown, Surrender at, 438
Young, Arthur, 446
Zemsky sobor (zem′skē sō-bôr′), 408, 409
Zwingli (tsviŋ′lē), Huldreich, 299